Microsoft® SharePoint® 2010 Developer Reference

Paolo Pialorsi

Acquisitions and Development Editor: Russell Jones
Production Editor: Kristen Borg
Production Services: Octal Publishing, Inc.
Technical Reviewer: Giuseppe Marchi
Indexing: Potomac Indexing, LLC
Cover: Karen Montgomery
Illustrator: Robert Romano

978-0-735-63903-4

To my family: Paola, Andrea, and Marta.
Thanks, my loves!

Contents at a Glance

Part I **Getting Started**
  1   **Introducing Microsoft SharePoint 2010** 3
  2   **Data Foundation** 31

Part II **Programming Microsoft SharePoint 2010**
  3   **Server Object Model** 55
  4   **LINQ to SharePoint** 101
  5   **Client-Side Technologies** 137

Part III **Developing Web Parts**
  6   **Web Part Basics** 183
  7   **Advanced Web Parts** 209

Part IV **Extending Microsoft SharePoint 2010**
  8   **SharePoint Features and Solutions** 241
  9   **Extending the User Interface** 265
  10   **Data Provisioning** 315
  11   **Developing Custom Fields** 345
  12   **Event Receivers** 385
  13   **Document Management** 401
  14   **Site Templates** 423
  15   **Developing Service Applications** 445

Part V **Developing Workflows**
  16   **SharePoint Workflows Architecture** 479
  17   **Workflows with SharePoint Designer 2010** 495
  18   **Workflows with Visual Studio 2010** 515
  19   **Workflow Forms** 535
  20   **Advanced Workflows** 555

Part VI **Security Infrastructure**

   21 **Authentication and Authorization Infrastructure**.........589

   22 **Claims-Based Authentication and Federated Identities**....607

   23 **Code Access Security and Sandboxed Solutions**..........629

Part VII **Enterprise Features**

   24 **Programming the Search Engine** 659

   25 **Business Connectivity Services** 689

Table of Contents

Introduction xvii

Conventions and Features in This Book xx

Errata & Book Support xxiii

Acknowledgments xxiv

Part I   Getting Started

1   Introducing Microsoft SharePoint 2010 3

What Is SharePoint? 3

Main Capabilities 4

Sites 5

Communities 5

Content 5

Search 6

Insights 6

Composites 6

SharePoint Basic Concepts 7

SharePoint Central Administration 7

Site Collections and Websites 8

Lists, Libraries, Items, and Documents 10

Web Parts and Web Part Pages 12

Architectural Overview 12

Logical and Physical Architecture 14

Service Applications 16

The Role of Databases 17

SharePoint Editions 18

SharePoint Foundation 18

SharePoint Server Standard 19

SharePoint Server Enterprise 19

SharePoint for Internet Sites 20

SharePoint Online 20

SharePoint for Developers 20

ASP.NET Integration 21

Server-Side Technologies 21

Client-Side Technologies 22

Web Parts and UI. 22

Data Provisioning. 22

Event Receivers and Workflows. 23

Security Infrastructure. 23

Business Connectivity Services 23

Windows PowerShell Support 24

Developer Tools 24

Microsoft SharePoint Designer 2010 24

Microsoft Visual Studio 2010. 26

SharePoint Server Explorer. 28

Solution Explorer and Feature Designer 29

Summary 29

2   Data Foundation 31

Lists of Items and Contents 31

Site Columns 46

Content Types. 47

Websites. 50

Summary 51

Part II   **Programming Microsoft SharePoint 2010**

3   Server Object Model 55

Startup Environment 56

Objects Hierarchy. 56

SPFarm, SPServer, SPService, and *SPWebApplication* 57

SPSite and *SPWeb.* 59

SPList and *SPListItem* 65

SPDocumentLibrary and *SPFile* 68

SPGroup, SPUser, and Other Security Types 69

SPControl and *SPContext* 71

Common and Best Practices. 72

Disposing Resources 73

Handling Exceptions 76

Transactions 78

AllowUnsafeUpdates and *FormDigest*. 78

Real-Life Examples 80
    Creating a New Site Collection 80
    Creating a New Website 82
    Lists and Items 83
    Document Libraries and Files 92
    Groups and Users 97
Summary 100

4   LINQ to SharePoint 101
LINQ Overview 101
    The Goal of LINQ 102
    LINQ Under the Covers 104
Introducing LINQ to SharePoint 106
Modeling with SPMetal.EXE 107
Querying Data 117
Managing Data 122
    Inserting a New Item 124
    Deleting or Recycling an Existing Item 125
Advanced Topics 126
    Handling Concurrency Conflicts 126
    Identity Management and Refresh 130
    Disconnected Entities 132
    Model Extensions and Versioning 134
Summary 136

5   Client-Side Technologies 137
Architectural Overview 137
SharePoint Client Object Model 138
    Managed Client Object Model 139
    Silverlight Client Object Model 147
    ECMAScript Client Object Model 152
Client Object Model by Examples 158
    Lists and Items 159
    Document Libraries and Files 165
SOAP Services 168
The REST API 171
    Querying for Data with .NET and LINQ 173
    Managing Data 177
Summary 180

Part III **Developing Web Parts**

6   Web Part Basics 183

Web Part Architecture 183

A "Hello World" Web Part 184

Web Part Deployment 188

Real Web Parts 192

Classic Web Parts 192

Visual Web Parts 195

Configurable Web Parts 197

Configurable Parameters 198

Editor Parts 200

Handling Display Modes 204

Custom Web Part Verbs 205

The SharePoint-Specific *WebPart* class 207

Summary 208

7   Advanced Web Parts 209

Connectable Web Parts 209

Supporting AJAX 215

Connectable Web Parts with AJAX 217

Silverlight and External Applications 220

Asynchronous Programming 223

XSLT Rendering 226

Deployment, Security, and Versioning 233

Deployment and Versioning 233

SafeControls and Cross-Site-Scripting SafeGuard 236

Summary 238

Part IV **Extending Microsoft SharePoint 2010**

8   SharePoint Features and Solutions 241

Features and Solutions 241

Feature Element Types 246

Features and Solutions Deployment 248

Packaging with Visual Studio 2010 254

Upgrading Solutions and Features 256

Feature Receivers 259

Handling *FeatureUpgrading* Events 262

Summary 264

9   Extending the User Interface **265**

Custom Actions...265

The *CustomAction* Element 265

The *CustomActionGroup* Element............................273

The *HideCustomAction* Element 275

Server-Side Custom Actions.................................276

Ribbons 279

Ribbon Command 279

Delegate Controls 291

Custom Contents 295

Images and Generic Content................................295

Application Pages 297

Content Pages, Web Part Pages, and Galleries..................299

Status Bar and Notification Area...............................305

Dialog Framework 309

Summary 313

10   Data Provisioning **315**

Site Columns..315

Content Types...320

Content Type IDs 323

More about Content Types 326

Document Content Types..................................328

List Definitions 329

List Schema File 329

Defining a Custom View...................................339

Summary 343

11   Developing Custom Fields. **345**

Fields Type Basics..345

The SPField Class 347

Developing Custom Field Types 349

A Basic E-Mail Field Type 349

A Multicolumn Field Type..................................354

Field Rendering Control 358

Field Rendering Templates.................................361

Field Rendering Using CAML...............................365

Field Rendering Using XSLT 367

Supporting Mobile Devices 369

Field Rendering Mobile Templates 374

Custom Field Editor 376

Custom Properties Persistence 381

Summary 384

12   Event Receivers 385

Types of Receivers 385

Item-Level Event Receivers. 386

List-Level Event Receivers. 391

Web-Level Event Receivers. 393

Workflow Event Receivers 394

E-Mail Event Receivers. 395

Avoiding Event Loops 396

Event Deployment and Binding. 397

Event Synchronization. 398

Event Security 400

Summary 400

13   Document Management 401

Document Sets. 401

Provisioning Document Sets 403

Handling Document Sets by Code 410

Document ID. 411

Custom Document ID Provider 414

File Conversion Services 417

Word Automation Services 417

Summary 422

14   Site Templates 423

Native Site Definitions. 424

Site Definitions 428

Site Definitions with Visual Studio. 431

Custom Web Templates 439

Site Definitions versus Web Templates. 444

Summary 444

15   Developing Service Applications **445**

Service Application Architecture....................................445

Service Application Framework.................................449

Creating a Service Application...................................449

Custom Protocol Service Application...........................450

Solution Outline..453

Service Application 454

Service Application Database 456

Service..458

Service Instance 465

Administrative Pages..466

Service Application Deployment...............................467

Service Application Proxy....................................469

Service Application Consumer.................................473

Service Application Proxy Deployment 473

Final Thoughts 474

Summary 475

Part V   Developing Workflows

16   SharePoint Workflows Architecture...................... **479**

Workflow Foundation Overview 479

Workflow Foundation Architecture 479

Workflow Types 483

Workflows Definition.......................................484

Custom Activities 486

Workflow Execution Model 489

Workflows in SharePoint...489

Workflow Targets and Association 491

SharePoint 2010 Custom Activities............................492

Summary 494

17   Workflows with SharePoint Designer 2010................. **495**

SharePoint Designer 2010 Workflows...............................495

Workflow Designer 496

Conditions and Actions......................................498

Structure of a Published Workflow.............................502

Designing a Workflow. 502
    Workflow Outline Definition 503
    Workflow Settings 507
    Workflow User Experience 508
Visio 2010 Integration 510
Summary 513

18   Workflows with Visual Studio 2010 515
Workflow Modeling. 515
    Creating the Workflow Project 515
    Workflow Outline. 519
Correlation Tokens. 533
Site Workflows 534
Summary 534

19   Workflow Forms 535
Management Forms. 535
    Association Form 537
    Initiation Form 544
    Modification Form. 547
Task Forms. 547
    Workflow Tasks. 547
Forms Deployment 553
Summary 554

20   Advanced Workflows 555
Custom Actions and Conditions 555
    Dependency Properties 555
    Custom Actions for SharePoint Designer 2010. 557
    Custom Conditions for SharePoint Designer 2010. 563
Workflow Event Receivers. 565
Workflow Services 566
    Implementing the Service 568
    Workflow Service Deployment 573
    Communication Activities. 575
Workflow Management by Code 576
    Workflow Server Object Model. 576
    Workflow Web Service 579

SPTimer Service and Workflows 585

Summary 586

Part VI Security Infrastructure

21 Authentication and Authorization Infrastructure. 589

Authentication Infrastructure. 589

    Classic Mode Authentication 590

Claims-Authentication Types 592

Configuring FBA with SQL Membership Provider 597

    Configuring the SQL Server Database 597

Authorization Infrastructure. 603

Summary 606

22 Claims-Based Authentication and Federated Identities 607

Claims-Based Authentication and WS-Federation 607

Implementing an STS with Windows Identity Foundation 611

    Building a Security Token Service 611

    Building a Relying Party 617

SharePoint Trusted Identity Providers 621

    Trusting the IP/STS. 622

    Configuring the Target Web Application. 625

Summary 627

23 Code Access Security and Sandboxed Solutions 629

Code Access Security. 629

    Partially Trusted ASP.NET Code 631

Sandboxed Solutions Overview. 639

    Sandboxed Solutions Architecture 640

Creating a Sandboxed Solution 645

Implementing a Solution Validator 647

Full-Trust Proxies 650

    Implementing a Full-Trust Proxy 651

    Registering the Full-Trust Proxy. 652

    Consuming the Full-Trust Proxy 654

Sandboxed Solutions and Office 365 655

Summary 656

Part VII **Enterprise Features**

24   Programming the Search Engine **659**

Search Engine Overview for Developers 659

Customizing and Extending the User Interface 662

Customizing the Output via XSLT 664

Developing Custom Web Parts 668

Federation Framework 670

Implementing a Custom Federation Provider. 674

Using the Search Engine by Code. 678

Federated Search Object Model 678

Query Object Model 681

Query Web Service 684

Summary 687

25   Business Connectivity Services **689**

Overview of Business Connectivity Services 689

Accessing a Database 691

BDC Model File. 700

Offline Capabilities. 703

Accessing a WCF/SOAP Service 705

.NET Custom Model. 710

Developing a Custom Model from Scratch. 712

Associating Entities 719

Programming with BCS Object Model 721

Summary 723

Index 725

What do you think of this book? We want to hear from you!

Microsoft is interested in hearing your feedback so we can continually improve our books and learning resources for you. To participate in a brief online survey, please visit:

www.microsoft.com/learning/booksurvey/

Introduction

Microsoft SharePoint is one of the biggest productivity frameworks released during the last ten years. Microsoft SharePoint 2010 is just the last step of a fabulous journey (that began in 2001) in the world of business productivity, collaboration, knowledge sharing, search technologies, and social networking.

From a developer's perspective, SharePoint is simply a rich set of tools, classes, libraries, controls, and so on that are useful for building custom solutions focused on making business collaboration possible.

Microsoft SharePoint 2010 Developer Reference is an organized reference that provides the support that you need as you develop real and concrete SharePoint solutions, taking advantage of the main libraries and tools offered by the product. This book covers the key topics in the fields of developing SharePoint solutions, targeting both junior and intermediate programmers who want to improve their knowledge of SharePoint.

Beyond the explanatory content, each chapter includes clear examples and downloadable sample projects that you can explore for yourself.

Who Should Read This Book

This book exists to help existing .NET developers understand the architecture and the core topics of SharePoint 2010 while building Internet, intranet, and extranet sites, as well as developing custom solutions and extensions of the basic platform provided by Microsoft.

Although most readers likely will have no prior experience with SharePoint 2010, the book is also useful for those familiar with earlier versions of SharePoint, and who are interested in getting up to date on the newest features.

Who Should Not Read This Book

This book does not target IT Professionals who are seeking information on how to deploy, configure, and maintain a SharePoint farm. Similarly, it does not cover marketing topics concerning site branding or public-facing Internet sites.

Assumptions

This book expects that you have at least a minimal understanding of .NET development and object-oriented programming concepts. Moreover, to develop SharePoint solutions you need to have a solid knowledge of ASP.NET and related technologies such as SOAP and Web Services. Although you can extend and customize SharePoint with most, if not all, .NET language platforms, this book includes examples in C# only. If you are not familiar with this language, you might consider reading John Sharp's book, *Microsoft Visual C# 2010 Step by Step* (Microsoft Press, 2010).

With a heavy focus on web development and server-side technologies, this book assumes that you have a basic understanding of web platforms, application servers, and scalable software architectures. Some of the topics covered in this book require a robust knowledge of .NET Framework 3.x, and specifically, Windows Communication Foundation.

Organization of This Book

This book is divided into seven sections, each of which focuses on a different aspect or technology within SharePoint 2010.

Part I, "Getting Started," provides a quick overview of SharePoint 2010 and its data foundations, with a focus on using the technology as shipped, but not yet extending it with custom code.

Part II, "Programming Microsoft SharePoint 2010," focuses on the core libraries for developing solutions both on the server side, using the SharePoint Server Object Model or the new LINQ to SharePoint provider, or on the client side, using the various flavors of the new SharePoint Client Object Model, the REST API, and SOAP services. This section is full of examples and code excerpts, and you can use it as a concrete reference for everyday solutions.

Part III, "Developing Web Parts," covers how to develop Web Parts, starting from basic scenarios and moving gradually toward more complex and real-world solutions.

Part IV, "Extending Microsoft SharePoint 2010," provides deep coverage of the various techniques and extensibility points available for customizing and extending the native SharePoint environment. Eight chapters full of realistic examples will help you master SharePoint as a business productivity framework.

Part V, "Developing Workflows," delves into workflow development. It starts with a brief introduction of Windows Workflow Foundation and the workflow architecture in SharePoint, moving to workflows designed with Microsoft SharePoint Designer 2010 or developed with Microsoft Visual Studio 2010. This part ends with more advanced topics, such as workflow forms, custom activities, and workflow communication.

Part VI, "Security Infrastructure," examines the security infrastructure of SharePoint, both from an architectural viewpoint, covering topics like authentication, authorization, and the new claims-based approach, and delving into Code Access Security and the new Sandboxed Solutions deployment option.

Part VII, "Enterprise Features," covers a couple of useful capabilities offered by the SharePoint 2010 environment when developing enterprise-level solutions. In particular, it covers programming the Search Engine and consuming external data to make use of the new Business Connectivity Services.

Finding Your Best Starting Point in This Book

The different sections of *Microsoft SharePoint 2010 Developer Reference* cover a wide range of technologies associated with SharePoint. Depending on your needs and your existing understanding of the SharePoint platform, you might wish to focus on specific areas of the book. Use the following table to determine how best to proceed.

If you are	Follow these steps
New to SharePoint development, or an ASP. NET developer	Focus on Parts I, II, III, and IV, or read through the entire book in written order.
Familiar with earlier releases of SharePoint	Briefly skim Part I, Chapter 3 of Part II, and Part III if you need a refresher on the core concepts. Then, read about the new client-side technologies in Part II, and be sure to read from Part IV to Part VII.
Interested primarily in developing workflows	Read Part II and Part V.

Most of the book's chapters include hands-on samples that let you try out the concepts just learned. No matter which sections you choose to focus on, be sure to download and install the sample applications on your system.

Conventions and Features in This Book

This book presents information using conventions designed to make the information readable and easy to follow.

- The book has downloadable samples available for C# programmers. Be aware that the text of the chapters often uses only code excerpts, not full code samples. Thus, to have the best experience with the samples, I highly recommended that you start from the downloadable, full-code sample files, rather than copying code excerpts from the book text.

- Boxed elements with labels such as "Note" provide additional information or alternative methods for completing a step successfully.

- Variables, types, keywords and code syntax in general (apart from code blocks) appear in italic.

- A vertical line between two or more menu items (for example. File | Open), means that you should select the first menu or menu item, then the next, and so on.

System Requirements

You will need the following hardware and software to run the code samples in this book:

- Operating system: Windows 7, Windows Server 2008 with Service Pack 2, or Windows Server 2008 R2

- Visual Studio 2010 Professional Edition or higher

- Microsoft SQL Server 2008 Express Edition, 64-bit or higher (2008 or R2 release), with SQL Server Management Studio 2008 Express or higher (included with Visual Studio, Express Editions require separate download)

- A computer that has a 64-bit four cores processor

- At least 4 GB (64-bit) of RAM (6 GB are suggested if running multiple services on the same server)

- An additional 2 GB of RAM if running in a virtual machine

- 80 GB of available hard disk space

- 5400 RPM hard disk drive

- DVD-ROM drive (if installing Visual Studio from DVD)

- Internet connection to download software or chapter examples

Depending on your Windows configuration, you might require Local Administrator rights to install or configure Visual Studio 2010 and SQL Server 2008 products.

Before executing the code samples available with the book, you need to install a SharePoint 2010 farm, creating a web application and a default Site Collection. Most of the code samples target either Microsoft SharePoint Foundation 2010 or Microsoft SharePoint Server 2010. However, there are topics that are suitable only for the Server edition of the product. In such cases, the book text explicitly alerts you to the restriction.

Code Samples

Most of the chapters in this book include exercises that let you interactively try out new material learned in the main text. All sample projects are available for download from the book's page on the website for Microsoft's publishing partner, O'Reilly Media:

http://oreilly.com/catalog/9780735639034/

Click the Examples link on that page. When a list of files appears, locate and download the SP2010-Developer-Reference.zip file.

> **Note** In addition to the code samples, you should have Visual Studio 2010, SQL Server 2008 R2, and SharePoint 2010 installed on your computer. The instructions below use Microsoft SQL Server Management Studio 2008 to set up the sample database used with the practice examples. If available, install the latest service packs for each product.

Installing the Code Samples

Follow these steps to install the code samples on your computer so that you can use them with the exercises in this book.

1. Unzip the SP2010-Developer-Reference.zip file that you downloaded from the book's website (name a specific directory along with directions to create it, if necessary).

2. If prompted, review the displayed end user license agreement. If you accept the terms, select the accept option, and then click Next.

> **Note** If the license agreement doesn't appear, you can access it from the same webpage from which you downloaded the SP2010-Developer-Reference.ZIP file.

Using the Code Samples

The SP2010-Developer-Reference.zip file contains another ZIP file for every chapter that has related code samples. You should unzip each chapter file on the root of your hard disk or under a folder with a short name, to avoid having file paths that are too long. In fact, you could experience issues with the packaging and deployment tools of Visual Studio 2010 if your file paths are longer than 255 characters.

Code samples of Chapter 25, "Business Connectivity Services," include a sample database of Microsoft SQL Server 2008 R2. You should restore that database from the file SampleCRM.bak available in the Ch-25-BCS.zip file included in the SP2010-Developer-Reference.zip file.

For further details and samples about SharePoint 2010 development you can browse to the author's site (*http://www.sharepoint-reference.com/*), where you will find a blog dedicated to SharePoint 2010 and Microsoft Office 365.

Errata & Book Support

We've made every effort to ensure the accuracy of this book and its companion content. If you do find an error, please report it on our Microsoft Press site at oreilly.com:

1. Go to *http://microsoftpress.oreilly.com*.

2. In the Search box, enter the book's ISBN or title.

3. Select your book from the search results .

4. On your book's catalog page, under the cover image, you'll see a list of links.

5. Click View/Submit Errata.

You'll find additional information and services for your book on its catalog page. If you need additional support, please e-mail Microsoft Press Book Support at mspinput@microsoft.com.

Please note that product support for Microsoft software is not offered through the addresses above.

We Want to Hear from You

At Microsoft Press, your satisfaction is our top priority, and your feedback our most valuable asset. Please tell us what you think of this book at:

http://www.microsoft.com/learning/booksurvey

The survey is short, and we read every one of your comments and ideas. Thanks in advance for your input!

Stay in Touch

Let's keep the conversation going! We're on Twitter: *http://twitter.com/MicrosoftPress*

Acknowledgments

This book has been a large, long-term goal for me. I have worked toward and followed this dream for many years. However, a book is the result of the work of many people. Unfortunately, only the author has his name on the cover. This section is only partial compensation for other individuals who helped out.

First, I would like to thank Microsoft Press, O'Reilly, and all the publishing people who contributed to this book project. Mainly, I'd like to thank Ben Ryan and Russell Jones, who—one more time—trusted in me and gave me the opportunity to realize an idea in which I have believed for a long time. Russell has influenced this book from the beginning, for more than a year; he helped me to stay on track, answered all my questions, motivated me when I was late on the schedule, and improved all of my drafts.

In addition, I would like to thank all the people from Microsoft who helped me to study and discover SharePoint during the last years: Roberto D'Angelo, Luca Bandinelli, Carmelo Ferrara, Antonio Gazzeri, and Davide Colombo.

I would also like to thank Giuseppe Marchi for his accurate review and for his big effort in tech reviewing the entire book so fast. Giuseppe, you did a great job, thank you!

My colleagues at DevLeap deserve a special thanks, because during the last year I've been very busy writing this book, and I know that the time spent was taken from my contribution to them.

I wrote this book about SharePoint 2010 because—about nine years ago—starting with the early versions, I began using and developing with SharePoint. However, my great passion for the product started seven years ago, when one of my customers gave me the opportunity to write a deep customization of the native environment. During that project I learned a great deal about SharePoint. Thus, I would like to thank Mauro Oliani for that opportunity.

There is one person who is a reliable and solid lighthouse in my life: Giovanni Librando. One more time Giovanni helped me to make the right choices at the right time. Giovanni, I'm honored to have you as a friend and as a mentor.

I'd like to thank my parents and my original family for their support and presence during the last year and for having trusted me during my entire professional career.

Lastly, but most importantly, I want to thank my wife, Paola, my son, Andrea, and my upcoming daughter, Marta, for their support, patience, and understanding during the last year. It has been a difficult and very busy year. You have supported me greatly, and my thanks for that support will never end!

PART I

Getting Started

Chapter 1
Introducing Microsoft SharePoint 2010

This chapter explores what Microsoft SharePoint 2010 is and what it offers to developers who are creating real-world business solutions. To begin, you will focus on the architecture of SharePoint, as well as on the rich set of capabilities provided by the platform. Next, you will get an overview of the various SharePoint editions. Finally, you will explore the available developer tools. If you already know or work with SharePoint 2010, you can probably skip this chapter; however, if you haven't yet acquired SharePoint at all, or if you are working on SharePoint 2007, you should continue on from here.

What Is SharePoint?

Microsoft often defines SharePoint as a business collaboration platform, but I prefer to define it as a rich framework for developing business collaboration solutions. In fact, from a developer's perspective, SharePoint is simply a rich set of tools, classes, libraries, controls, and so on that are useful for building custom solutions that are focused on making business collaboration possible.

Many people think about SharePoint as a platform that's "ready-to-use" for building websites—usually for intranet or extranet scenarios. That's true, but it's just half the story! Certainly, SharePoint *is* a platform for building websites, and of course, it can target intranet and extranet sites. But it is more than just that; you can use it to build any kind of web solution, including Internet publishing sites, by taking advantage of a well-defined and ready-to-use set of tools, based on a secure, scalable, and maintainable architecture. You can think of SharePoint as a superset of ASP.NET, with a broad set of services that can speed up the development of collaboration solutions.

You should use SharePoint as a shared connection point between users, customers, or whoever uses your website, and the applications they utilize. In fact, the basic idea of SharePoint is to share contents, applications, and data to improve collaboration and provide a unique user experience.

SharePoint itself is primarily a container of lists. Each list is made up of items. A list can consist of simple items with custom metadata properties called "fields." Lists can also be libraries of documents, which are a particular kind of item that corresponds to document files. Each time you develop a SharePoint solution, you manage lists and items. In Chapter 2, "Data Foundation," you will learn more about the architecture of data management in SharePoint 2010.

Main Capabilities

Microsoft grouped the features and services in SharePoint 2010 into six main categories: Sites, Communities, Content, Search, Insights, and Composites. Figure 1-1 shows these capabilities along with their main characteristics.

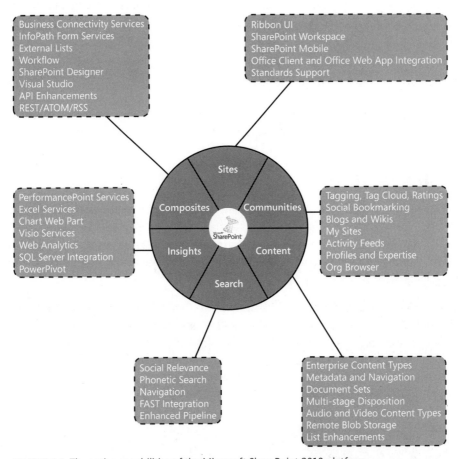

FIGURE 1-1 The native capabilities of the Microsoft SharePoint 2010 platform.

The sections that follow provide a brief description of the six main categories and their functions.

Sites

The Sites category corresponds to the main and most visible features of SharePoint, including the basic engine for building websites, the site editing features, and the theming and branding capabilities. This group also contains the user interface elements of SharePoint 2010, which is composed of Ribbons, dialogs, Web Parts, Silverlight support, and so on—all available with cross-browser support for maximum user inclusiveness and wide platform adoption. At the same level, you'll find the accessibility compliance (for WCAG 2.0) that SharePoint 2010 offers.

Another great feature of the SharePoint 2010 Sites category is Microsoft SharePoint Workspace 2010 and the capability to manage offline content with Microsoft Office.

Finally, this category includes SharePoint's collaboration features, which help you create intranet, extranet and Internet solutions. web features such as the CMS features and capabilities fit here as well.

Communities

The Communities category contains features such as social networking, information sharing, content tagging and rating, and user feedback collection capabilities. In addition, you'll find the blogging engine, feeds, alerts, Wiki pages, and other features that support sharing of informal knowledge.

User profiling features and knowledge sharing across enterprise networks are also a part of this category. To achieve the goal of sharing knowledge, SharePoint offers established online/offline support, as well as support for mobile devices and integration with existing social applications and networks.

Content

For content management, SharePoint 2010 offers an engine that stores lists of items and provides rich integration with the Microsoft Office platform. The engine's ability to store items that have custom metadata and built-in tagging and rating support makes it possible to rapidly search and access list contents.

For the enterprise market, SharePoint 2010 offers records management features, legal holds, taxonomies and folksonomies, and document sets, as well as the ability to share policies and rules for content shared across different server farms.

SharePoint 2010 also offers support for multimedia content, including audio, video, and streams. That means you can now use SharePoint to develop enterprise-level multimedia solutions.

Search

Since it was first introduced, one of standout features of SharePoint has been its search engine. This is why the search feature in SharePoint 2010 warrants its own category. With the latest release of the product, Microsoft has introduced an improved and more accurate relevance engine that's based on usage and history.

This updated search engine provides better support for multilanguage content, and phonetic support for enterprise scenarios. The social relevance features gives you the ability to use community features synergistically. And SharePoint's new deployment architecture supports large scenarios with high volumes of content and searches.

Given all these capabilities, you can consider SharePoint 2010 as a solid platform for building search-driven applications.

Insights

In accordance with the basic philosophy of the product, SharePoint 2010 offers native integration and support for other Microsoft products and services, such as Performance Point Services, Excel Services, Access Services, Visio Services, PowerPivot, Microsoft SQL Server Reporting Services, and so on.

SharePoint 2010 is the right technology to use for sharing content and applications, allowing end users to employ and experience a unique client interface to access many different content types and applications. The idea behind all of this is to give you the tools to create a unique set of company portals that expose the information and services that are useful for everyday jobs and information sharing.

Composites

Finally, SharePoint includes a category that contains features related to building custom solutions, external software integration, external data connectivity, and solution deployment.

Here, you'll find features such as Business Connectivity Services, which is useful for consuming external data from ERPs, DBMS, SOAP services, and so forth, using the standard SharePoint's UI. Another feature of the Composites category is the open workflow engine, which is suitable for any custom process management and document approval solution. Additionally, this category defines the server and client APIs for developing software solutions that integrate with SharePoint 2010, as well as SharePoint's native integration with development tools such as SharePoint Designer 2010 and Microsoft Visual Studio 2010.

This last group of capabilities will be the main focus of this book, because these are the features a SharePoint developer will draw upon to build custom SharePoint solutions.

SharePoint Basic Concepts

To better understand what SharePoint is and how to best use its features, this section takes a brief tour through the product and provides introductions to a few of its most useful features and capabilities.

SharePoint Central Administration

The target audience for this book is SharePoint developers and not IT Pros. Therefore, it does not cover administrative tasks, and it does not provide instructions on how to set up SharePoint from scratch. Nevertheless, as soon as you install a SharePoint server farm, you are presented with an administrative console called SharePoint Central Administration (SPCA) with which you manage the entire farm.

> **More Information** To learn how to deploy and administer a SharePoint farm, read *Microsoft SharePoint 2010 Administrator's Companion*, by Bill English, Brian Alderman, and Mark Ferraz (Microsoft Press, 2010. ISBN: 978-0-7356-2720-8).

The SPCA is a website based on SharePoint's engine that is designed to administer and monitor a SharePoint server farm. When you deploy a new farm, one server takes the role of SPCA host. Using the SPCA, you can configure servers and servers' roles, define farm topology, and create new web applications and Site Collections.

Because the SPCA is an actual SharePoint site, you can use everything you will learn in this book to customize this site. Thus, you can build solutions to extend the SharePoint administrative interface.

The main areas of the SPCA are:

- **Application Management**   Here, you can manage existing web applications, as well as create new web applications, Site Collections, and Content Databases. You will learn more about these topics later in this chapter and in Chapter 2.

- **Monitoring**   From this area, you have access to a set of tools for monitoring the farm, checking for issues, and solving problems.

- **Security**   Here you can manage administrative accounts and services' account of the farm.

- **General Application Settings**   This is the area where you manage general settings, such as site directory, search engine, content deployment features, InfoPath form services, etc.

- **System Settings**   From this area, you can manage servers in the farm, the farm topology, services on servers, and farm customization features.

- **Backup and Restore**   This area provides access to all the tools for managing and handling disaster recovery tasks.

- **Upgrade and Migration**   Here, you can manage upgrade and patching tasks.

- **Configuration Wizards**   This area provides a wizard to configure the farm from scratch.

Figure 1-2 shows the SPCA home page.

FIGURE 1-2 The SharePoint Central Administration home page.

Note the status bar at the top of the screen, which in this illustration highlights some issues about the current configuration of the farm that was detected by the SharePoint Health Analyzer service. The SharePoint Health Analyzer is a very useful tool that monitors the status of the farm, helping to maintain it at the optimum service level.

Site Collections and Websites

One fundamental concept embodied by SharePoint is that of a Site Collection. A Site Collection is a logical container that holds a set of websites, hosted in a web application.

Whenever you work in SharePoint and you want to publish a site, regardless of whether it's an Internet, intranet, or extranet solution, you will have at least one web application, with one Site Collection, made of one website. The idea of grouping websites in Site Collections allows those sites to share contents, administrative settings, security rules, and optionally, users and groups.

To create a new Site Collection you need a parent web application, which you can create by selecting the Manage Web Applications menu item from the SPCA home page. After you have a web application, you can create a new Site Collection by selecting the Create Site Collection menu item on the SPCA home page. A dialog box will appear, asking you for a Title, a Description, and a URL relative to the parent web application.

Every Site Collection is administered by a Site Collection Administrator—a user authorized to administer an entire Site Collection, including the websites it contains. Every Site Collection must have at least one Site Collection Administrator, but it can have more than one. Thus, when creating a new Site Collection you need to designate a primary Site Collection Administrator, and optionally, a secondary one. A Site Collection Administrator has the right to create, update, or delete any website contained in a Site Collection. The administrator also has full rights to administer content within those websites.

When you create a Site Collection, you should also choose a template from which to start. If you need, you select from a number of predefined templates that are shipped with SharePoint. By default, the template will create a new Site Collection with at least one web-site at the root of the Site Collection. Templates are divided into functional groups; the following presents the main groups in SharePoint Server 2010 Enterprise plus Microsoft Office Web Applications:

- **Collaboration**   These are sites whose structure has been designed to facilitate collaboration. Collaboration includes the following templates: Team Site, Blank Site, Document Workspace, Blog, Group Work Site, and Visio Process Repository.

- **Meetings**   These are templates for sites related to meetings and meeting organization. The possible templates are: Basic Meeting Workspace, Blank Meeting Workspace, Decision Meeting Workspace, Social Meeting Workspace, and Multipage Meeting Workspace.

- **Enterprise**   These templates target enterprise-level needs in the areas of document management, policies, and so on. They include Document Center, Records Center, PowerPoint Broadcast Site, Business Intelligence Center, Enterprise Search Center, My Site Host, Basic Search Center, and FAST Search Center.

- **Publishing**   This group corresponds to sites intended for web publishing purposes. The possible templates are Publishing Portal and Enterprise Wiki.

- **Custom**   This is where you can develop your own site templates. Also in this group is a list of all the available custom templates, if any exist.

Figure 1-3 shows the home page of a Site Collection created by using the Team Site template.

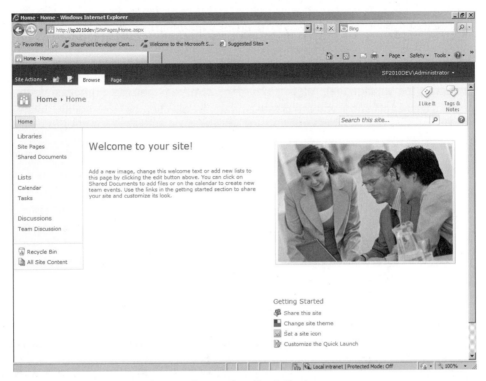

FIGURE 1-3 The home page of a Team Site template Site Collection.

Lists, Libraries, Items, and Documents

Every SharePoint website is composed of lists of items. When the items are simple items—that is, they don't correspond to documents or files, but are simply made of custom metadata properties—they're simply termed lists and list items. When the items correspond to files, they're called document libraries, or just libraries.

Every site template includes some predefined lists that are created when you construct a site using that template. For example, a Team Site provides a list of Shared Documents, a list of Site Pages, a list of events named Calendar, a list of Tasks, and a Discussion area.

You can browse for contents of these lists or, if you have the proper permissions, you can create new lists of contents or upload new files (for libraries). Figure 1-4 shows the user interface of SharePoint 2010 while browsing the contents of a document library.

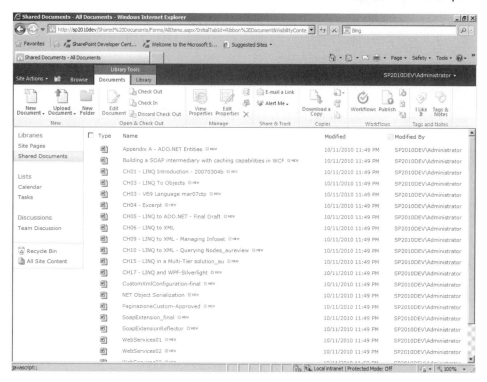

FIGURE 1-4 The default user interface of SharePoint while browsing the contents of a document library.

Note also that Figure 1-4 shows the Ribbon menu, which is a new feature of SharePoint 2010, introduced to better support end users through an Office-like user interface.

When you want to create a new list, you simply click Site Actions, located in the upper-left corner of the screen, and then select More Options. As shown in Figure 1-5, you'll see a prompt that asks you to select the type of content that you would like to create.

Note The prompt that SharePoint presents is determined by the browser that you are using. If your browser supports Silverlight, the prompt will be based on a Silverlight control, like the one shown in Figure 1-5, or it will be based on standard HTML when Silverlight is unavailable.,

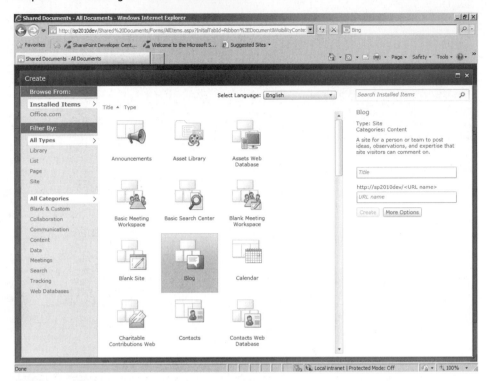

FIGURE 1-5 The Silverlight user interface for creating a new list in a SharePoint site.

Web Parts and Web Part Pages

Web Parts are one of the most notable features of SharePoint. In fact, in SharePoint you can define pages made of configurable building blocks that can be enabled, moved, or hidden by end users. The goal of this feature is to allow users to define their own pages, selecting content from a set of available Web Parts, with full personalization. Every page made of Web Parts is called a Web Part Page.

A typical SharePoint solution contains some custom lists and document libraries, along with some Web Parts configured in custom Web Part Pages that show and manage the data stored in those lists.

Architectural Overview

In this section you'll take a look at SharePoint architecture from a developer's perspective. Figure 1-6 shows the architecture of SharePoint, starting from the foundation elements, up to the main enterprise level features.

Search	InfoPath Service	Visio Service
Business Connectivity	Word Conv. Serv.	Access Service
Excel Service	PowerPoint Broadcast Service	Managed Metadata
User Profiles	Web Analytics Service	PerformancePoint

SharePoint Server 2010

Alerts	External Data	Files/Docs	Mobile Support	Queries/Views	Web/Site Coll.
Colums/Fields	Event Handling	Health Rules	Pages,UI& Ribbon	Solutions	Workflows
Content Types	Features	Lists/Doc Libs	Perf. Monitoring	Web Parts	Admin/Manag.

SharePoint Foundation 2010

.NET Framework 3.5 and ASP.NET 3.5 SP1

Internet Information Services 7.x

Windows Server 2008/R2 (64 bit only) Windows 7 or Vista SP1/SP2 (64 bit only)	SQL Server 2005 SP3 (64 bit only) SQL Server 2008/R2 (64 bit only)

FIGURE 1-6 The architecture of Microsoft SharePoint 2010.

At the very base of SharePoint 2010 sits the operating system. Starting with SharePoint 2010, the minimum requirement for a production environment is Microsoft Windows Server 2008 or Microsoft Windows Server 2008 R2. You can also install the SharePoint platform on a machine running Microsoft Windows 7 or Microsoft Windows Vista SP1/SP2, but solely for development purposes. Because SharePoint 2010 is available only in 64-bit versions, the minimum requirement for a deployment environment is a 64-bit operating system.

More Information For further details about the software and hardware requirements of SharePoint 2010 read the document "Hardware and Software Requirements (SharePoint Server 2010)" on MSDN Online at *http://technet.microsoft.com/en-us/library/cc262485.aspx*.

In addition to the operating system, SharePoint 2010 also requires a database server based on Microsoft SQL Server 2005 SP3 or Microsoft SQL Server 2008, optionally R2. Regardless of which edition of SQL Server you plan to use, you must be running a 64-bit version of the product. SharePoint uses the SQL Server database to store the configuration of SharePoint server farms as well as the contents of deployed websites.

On top of the operating system and database, there is an application server, provided by Internet Information Services 7.x (IIS 7). IIS 7 is mandatory, both because it hosts the web applications and because it publishes endpoints for SharePoint's infrastructure services, making use of the Windows Process Activation Service (WAS) feature of IIS 7.

> **More Information** You can find more details about WAS on the "Hosting in Windows Process Activation Service" page, on MSDN Online at *http://msdn.microsoft.com/en-us/library/ms734677. aspx.*

Because SharePoint 2010 is based on Microsoft .NET Framework 3.5 and extends Microsoft ASP.NET 3.5 SP1, the .NET Framework 3.5 SP1 is another infrastructure requirement. At the time of this writing (February 2011) SharePoint 2010 does not provide support for Microsoft .NET Framework 4.0.

On top of this foundation sits the basic portion of SharePoint, called Microsoft SharePoint Foundation 2010. This is a free platform for building basic SharePoint solutions. Nevertheless, as shown in Figure 1-2, SharePoint Foundation contains a great deal of functionality that developers can use to meet the needs of basic portal scenarios.

At the top of the architecture is the Microsoft SharePoint Server 2010 platform, together with its high-level and enterprise-level services, such as Excel Service, Word Conversion Service, the Search engine, and so forth.

Logical and Physical Architecture

Whenever you deploy a SharePoint environment, in reality, you're deploying a logical architecture called "SharePoint farm." A SharePoint farm is a set of servers that have different roles and offer various services that together make up a server farm suitable for hosting a full SharePoint deployment. Here are the common server roles in a SharePoint farm:

- **Front-end web servers**   These servers publish websites, often called web applications.
- **Application servers**   These servers host back-end services, such as the search index service, the crawler service, and so forth.
- **Database servers**   These servers store configuration and content data for the entire SharePoint farm.

The smallest farm you can build is based on a single server; this type is often called a "single-tier deployment." However, it is highly recommended that you avoid such a scenario, except for testing or development.

In fact, for the sake of scalability and business continuity, you should deploy a minimum of two front-end web servers and a back-end database server. This topology is commonly termed a "two-tier deployment." If you need to scale out and support a wider range of users and sites, you can deploy a three-tier farm by introducing some dedicated application servers.

Regardless of the deployment topology you choose, as the previous section illustrated, SharePoint uses a Microsoft SQL Server database for storing farm configurations and content. Specifically, it creates a main and fundamental farm configuration database as soon as you deploy a new farm. Usually this database is called *SharePoint_Config* or *SharePoint_Config_<UniqueId>*. If you use the automated setup process, this database is created for you when you deploy the farm for the first time. Furthermore, the SharePoint Deployment And Configuration Wizard creates a set of satellite database files for the main services deployed. For example, it creates a database that stores the contents of the SharePoint Central Administration administrative site.

From a hierarchical perspective, each SharePoint farm is composed of services, which include all the infrastructure services that make up the SharePoint environment. The most important kinds of services are web application services, which correspond to the entry point for web-published solutions. Each web application is made up of at least of one Site Collection and one Content Database. However, you can deploy multiple Site Collections within a single web application, and you can deploy multiple Content Databases for a single web application. A Content Database is a database file that stores content for one or more Site Collections. As it relates to SharePoint, content can be items, documents, documents versions, pages, images, and so on. Thus, the database behind a Site Collection can grow very fast.

With SharePoint 2010, the server roles and the configurable services have been improved to better support scale-out scenarios. In fact, you can now distribute different roles to dedicated servers, eventually with hardware redundancy.

Figure 1-7 shows a graphical representation of a SharePoint farm with a couple of front-end web servers, both of which publish the same web applications with network load balancing. The first web application (Web Application #1) is made of two Site Collections (Site Collection #1 and #2), both of which share a common content database (Content #1). The second web application (Web Application #2) is made up of a third Site Collection (Site Collection #3) and stores its contents in a dedicated content database (Content #2). All the Site Collections contain one or more websites.

On the back-end, there are four application servers, hosting the SharePoint Central Administration, the Search Services, the Excel Service, and a user-defined custom service.

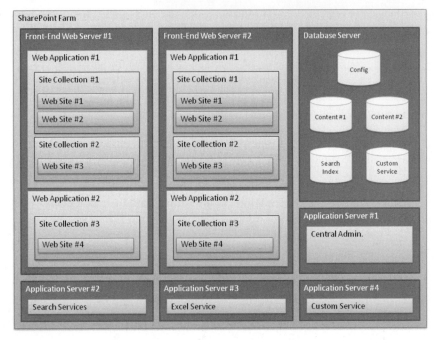

FIGURE 1-7 A simplified schema of a sample SharePoint farm with a three-tier topology.

All the data are persisted in a back-end database server that stores various database files for different purposes.

> **Note** For simplicity, the schema in Figure 1-7 does not necessarily correspond to a real scenario and lacks many details.

Service Applications

A Service Application is a software service that runs in a SharePoint farm. Service Applications are intended for sharing resources and capabilities across multiple sites and servers in the same farm, or even cross-farm. The idea of Service Applications represents a great new feature in SharePoint Foundation 2010 that was missing in previous versions of the product. Microsoft Office SharePoint 2007 included the concept of Shared Service Providers (SSPs), but an SSP wasn't extensible and scalable as Service Applications are.

To clarify the idea of a Service Application, consider a couple of examples. The search engine in SharePoint 2010 is based on a Service Application. This means that you can share the same search engine across different servers in the same farm, which is not surprising, but you can also share the same search service across multiple farms. For example, in very large scenarios, you could deploy a search-dedicated farm, without any front-end web server, and that exposes only a wide set of Query and Index servers. You could then use this farm to serve many other SharePoint 2010 farms, taking advantage of that shared search service.

Another example might be Excel Services. In fact, if you have a farm that uses Excel Services extensively to make calculations and to create reports on external data, you could decide to deploy the Excel Service on two or more dedicated servers in the farm, using them from all the other servers.

These configurations are possible because the architecture of Service Applications has been designed with scalability in mind. Thus, every Service Application that runs on a server in the farm can be developed to support scalability, and can be installed on two or more servers. At the same time, a farm uses a proxy to consume a Service Application published locally or by a third-party farm. However, while a front-end web server consumes a Service Application, it ignores the real location of the service and simply concentrates on consuming it. This is possible because each SharePoint Foundation 2010 farm has a native Service Application, called the Application Discovery and Load Balancer Service, that coordinates service discovery and load balancing for services deployed on more than one application server.

Under the covers, by default, each Service Application proxy communicates with the back-end Service Application by using a secure channel based on Windows Communication Foundation (WCF). In Chapter 15, "Developing Service Applications," you will learn how to develop your own Service Applications.

The Role of Databases

Every SharePoint farm includes one or more back-end database servers. In fact, as was pointed out earlier in this chapter, the back-end SQL Server stores the entire configuration of the farm as well as contents of every Site Collection and the data for many Service Applications. For example, the Search Service stores crawled content, properties for crawled data, and configuration properties in separate dedicated database files. The Word Conversion Service has another dedicated database file. This list could be longer.

> **Important** Even though you can open a SharePoint database in Microsoft SQL Server Management Studio and inspect the databases of a SharePoint farm, you should avoid doing that. In addition, you should not base your software solutions on the data structure of SharePoint databases. Thus, you should avoid querying and writing the content of these databases directly. If you do need to read or write their content, take advantage of the various libraries and object models discussed later in this book.

Now let's concentrate on pages and content. Recall that each time you create a new Site Collection using the SPCA, you have the opportunity to choose a starting site template . The site template is a set of configuration, layout, and content files that define a site model. You can build your own site templates (you will learn how to do that in Chapter 14, "Site

Templates"), or you can select one of the existing site templates that are packaged with SharePoint. Whichever site template you choose, under the covers, SharePoint starts from a set of files stored in the file system of all front-end web servers, and then creates some records in the content database that will host the Site Collection that you are creating. After the Site Collection has been created, when you browse to a page using a web browser, the SharePoint engine determines whether the page you have requested resides entirely on the file system, or whether it needs to retrieve some personalized content from the content database and merge that with the page model from the file system, or even whether the page content is completely stored in the content database.

Having a back-end content database available gives you the option to deploy multiple front-end web servers that can share the same content, improving horizontal scalability when necessary. At the same time, maintaining basic page models in the file system improves performance, because loading a page from the file system, unless it has been personalized, is generally faster than retrieving it from an external database server. In the section "SharePoint for Developers," on page 20, you'll see how SharePoint differentiates between file system and database content sources.

SharePoint Editions

SharePoint 2010 is offered in several different editions. Even though this book is for developers (as opposed to sales or marketing personnel), it is useful to know the main differences between each edition of the product. The goal of this section is to give you the base knowledge required to choose the appropriate SharePoint edition for each of your projects.

More Information For a full comparison of the SharePoint editions, see the page "Editions Comparison" at *http://sharepoint.microsoft.com/en-us/buy/Pages/Editions-Comparison.aspx.*

SharePoint Foundation

Microsoft SharePoint Foundation 2010 is the most basic edition of the product. It is free—providing that you run it on a licensed copy of Microsoft Windows Server 2008—and it offers the fundamental features for building simple document storage and collaboration solutions. Figure 1-6 demonstrated that you can use this version to build custom solutions, using Microsoft Visual Studio 2010 and SharePoint Designer 2010. By default, this edition's main capabilities are: accessibility, cross-browser support, basic search features, out-of-the-box Web Parts, Silverlight support, new UI features based on dialogs and ribbons, blogs and wikis, and the workflow engine.

The Foundation edition also supports the basic infrastructure of Business Connectivity Services, although without any client-side/Office capability. Of course, you'll also find the

SharePoint Central Administration functionality and all the farm management tools and services such as SharePoint Health Analyzer. In fact, if wanted to, you could deploy a multi-tier farm using just SharePoint Foundation.

Another fundamental feature of SharePoint Foundation is its ability to upgrade from previous versions of Microsoft SharePoint.

Finally, SharePoint Foundation offers all the features supporting custom development, including the Web Parts programming model, the Server Object Model, the Client Object Model, Event Receivers, Claims-Based security, and so on.

You should use this edition of SharePoint whenever you want to develop custom solutions that do not require any high-level features, such as the document management tools, user profiles, and so on. When you simply need to use SharePoint as a web-based "sharing point" to store content, such as documents, contacts, tasks, etc., this is the edition that best meets those needs.

SharePoint Server Standard

The Microsoft SharePoint Server 2010 Standard edition is built on top of SharePoint Foundation and adds some features useful for building business-level solutions. This edition provides legal compliance capabilities, including records management, legal holds, and document policies. It also offers support for Document Sets, which gives you the ability to manage related contents as if they were a single entity. This edition supports Document IDs, which assign a unique protocol number to SharePoint site content. Using this edition you can target content based on audiences, which are profile-based groups of targets.

This is the right choice when you need to create a Content Management System solution that provides features, such as content publishing, content approval, page layouts, web standards (XHTML, WCAG 2.0, etc.) support, and so forth.

This edition also supports tags and metadata-driven search refinement, people search, and some other social features. As a business-level tool, it also provides features for managing people, profiles, and personal sites.

You should implement this edition of the product when developing business-level solutions that use the features and capabilities you have seen in this section, not just those hosted in SharePoint.

SharePoint Server Enterprise

Microsoft SharePoint Server 2010 Enterprise edition targets large business solutions and enterprise-level organizations. It extends the capabilities of SharePoint Server Standard by offering support for dashboards, key performance indicators (KPIs), and business intelligence features. It improves search capabilities by offering contextual search, deep search query refinement, extreme scale-out search capabilities, rich web indexing, and so on. It also provides support for Excel Services, Visio Services, InfoPath Forms Services, and Access Services.

When you need to develop business analysis solutions, or complex search-based solutions, you should choose this edition of the product.

SharePoint for Internet Sites

Beginning with SharePoint 2010, the product family has been expanded with two new editions: Microsoft SharePoint Server 2010 for Internet Sites Standard and Enterprise editions.

These editions target web publishing sites. They were created to support public Internet scenarios with an unpredictable number of users coming from the Internet, whether the users are anonymous or authenticated. The features available in the Standard edition and in the Enterprise edition are the same for the Internet Sites as those of the corresponding classic editions.

The Standard Edition for Internet Sites is licensed for publishing a single domain website, while the Enterprise Edition for Internet Sites can publish multiple domains.

SharePoint Online

Microsoft SharePoint Online is the cloud-based SharePoint offering, based on the Software as a Service (SaaS) paradigm included in Microsoft Office 365. With this edition, you can build SharePoint solutions without building a SharePoint farm on premises. Instead, by having your farm in the cloud, you can enjoy an externalized and management cost-free solution. As a developer, you need to focus only on data, processes, ideas, and the content that you want to share.

At the time of this writing (February 2011), the official SharePoint Online offering is based on Microsoft Office SharePoint Server 2007. However, an upgrade to SharePoint 2010 is planned for when Microsoft Office 365 is released.

SharePoint for Developers

SharePoint offers developers numerous features and capabilities for building custom web solutions. This section provides an overview of those features and services, so you can better understand the topics that you will be exploring in the rest of this book.

ASP.NET Integration

As a developer, you might be wondering how SharePoint 2010 integrates with ASP. NET to service requests and provide its high-level features on top of the ASP.NET native infrastructure.

In IIS 7, application pools can run in one of two modes: integrated mode or classic mode. Classic mode works like older versions of IIS (IIS 6), taking advantage of the ISAPI Filter Aspnet_isapi.dll. Integrated mode provides a unified request-processing pipeline for requests that target both managed (.NET) and unmanaged (non .NET) resources. Every request is served by a module registered in the application configuration.

SharePoint 2010 provides a *Microsoft.SharePoint.ApplicationRuntime* namespace in the Microsoft.SharePoint.dll assembly. This namespace contains a set of classes that integrate and/or override the default behavior of ASP.NET while in IIS 7 integrated mode. The primary class that handles SharePoint requests is called *SPRequestModule*. It is configured in the web.config of every SharePoint site, in the system.webServer/modules section. This class registers a number of application events that handle requests, authentication, errors, and so on. One fundamental task of this module is to register the virtual path provider (*SPVirtualPathProvider*), which resolves requests by determining whether the requested content should be retrieved from the content database or from the file system. In fact, a virtual path provider is a class that provides contents to the ASP.NET pipeline by retrieving them from a virtual file system.

Server-Side Technologies

SharePoint offers developers a rich set of server-side tools. First, you can use the SharePoint Server Object Model, which allows you to interact with SharePoint through a large set of libraries and classes. Using these classes, you can read, manage, and administer data stored in SharePoint. More generally, you can use the Server Object Model to do everything that SharePoint itself can do, because SharePoint itself uses that same object model. You can only use the Server Object Model on a SharePoint server because it has some dependencies that are satisfied only on a SharePoint server. You will learn more about this tool in Chapter 3, "Server Object Model."

On the server side, beginning with SharePoint 2010, you can also use the LINQ programming model, exploiting the LINQ to SharePoint provider, by which you can query and manage SharePoint data using a fully typed programming model, much as you would when managing data stored in Microsoft SQL Server using LINQ to SQL. Chapter 4, "LINQ to SharePoint," discusses this new LINQ query provider in more detail.

Client-Side Technologies

When you need to develop a client solution that interacts with SharePoint 2010, you can exploit some client-side technologies offered specifically for this purpose. For example, the SharePoint Client Object Model lets you interact with SharePoint from a client using a set of classes that are similar to the Server Object Model, but work on any client that supports .NET, Silverlight, or ECMAScript. In fact, the Client Object Model is available in three different flavors: .NET managed, Silverlight, and ECMAScript. The Client Object Model versions are almost functionally identical on all three platforms. You can also use SOAP services published by SharePoint. Finally, you can use the REST API to access and manage SharePoint data by using a new protocol for querying and updating data via an HTTP/XML communication channel, called OData, which is documented at *www.odata.org*.

All of these client-side technologies are discussed in Chapter 5, "Client-Side Technologies."

Web Parts and UI

Another area of interest for developers is customizing the user interface (UI). Many SharePoint developers spend their time developing Web Parts, Web Part Pages, and UI customizations. SharePoint 2010 not only provides a rich object model for building custom Web Parts, but it also offers a set of UI customization tools that simplify working with AJAX, dialogs, the Ribbon, and so on. You will see how to develop Web Parts in Chapter 6, "Web Part Basics," and Chapter 7, "Advanced Web Parts," while in Chapter 8, "SharePoint Features and Solutions," and Chapter 9," Extending the User Interface," you will learn how to customize the UI.

Data Provisioning

As soon as you begin working with SharePoint, you will face the need to define packages for automatically deploying data structures. In fact, working with SharePoint generally involves designing new lists and new content types, which are reusable typed definitions of metadata models. However, if you define your models using the web browser you won't have a high-level modeling approach; everything you do must be migrated and/or executed again in the production environment.

Fortunately, there are tools and techniques that allow you to model a data structure—optionally based on custom contents and fields—and deploy that model to customers' sites. These tools also provide support for deploying updated versions of the solution in the future. You'll see more on this subject later in this chapter, in the section "Features, Solutions Deployment, and Sandboxing," on page 23. You will learn how to define custom data models for automated provisioning in Chapter 10, "Data Provisioning."

Event Receivers and Workflows

With SharePoint, you can use some Event Receivers to intercept users' actions and/or events and subsequently execute some light weight code. This is a useful feature for implementing simple process handling solutions. Chapter 12, "Event Receivers," dives into this subject.

Similarly, when you need to define complex and long-running business processes that respond to events from the UI and interact with end users, you can define Workflows. This functionality deserves a thorough exploration, so this book discusses it in five dedicated chapters, in Part V, "Developing Workflows."

Features, Solutions Deployment, and Sandboxing

SharePoint 2010, as a complete development platform, provides deployment services and capabilities by which you can deploy and upgrade solutions during a project's life-time. Specifically, SharePoint offers the opportunity to create deployment packages, called Windows SharePoint Services Solution Packages (WSP). You can use these packages to auto-mate setup and maintenance tasks across an entire server farm. In addition, you can deploy these solutions in a sandboxed environment. The packages consist of Features, which are atomic sets of extensions that you can develop, install, activate, and manage with a specific set of administrative tools. In Chapter 8 you will learn how to create and deploy standard packages, while Chapter 23, "Code Access Security and Sandboxed Solutions," shows you how to make use of sandboxed solutions.

Security Infrastructure

SharePoint's security infrastructure is another topic that affects both software development and the architecture of solutions. In fact, to develop robust and solid solutions, a developer should have a high degree of confidence in, and knowledge about SharePoint's authentica-tion and authorization policies. As it relates to SharePoint 2010, the key aspect of security is its claim-based approach. The section, "Security Infrastructure," contains three chapters that are fully dedicated to security matters.

Business Connectivity Services

Business Connectivity Services is another feature that is generally useful when developing solutions. Recall from the earlier discussion on the Composites capability that this feature supports consuming external data within SharePoint. In Chapter 25, "Business Connectivity Services," you will see how to utilize this new engine.

Windows PowerShell Support

One last interesting capability for developers is administering and automating administrative tasks of SharePoint 2010 by using the new Microsoft Windows PowerShell. Windows PowerShell is a new task-based command-line shell and scripting language designed especially for system administration and developers. It can execute commands and scripts authored by developers or system administrators, as long as they have some minimal development expertise. What makes Windows PowerShell a powerful tool is its extensibility model, together with the capability to execute custom code. For example, SharePoint 2010 installs a set of libraries that extend the standard commands of Windows PowerShell, providing some new statements that are useful when administering a SharePoint farm. From the Windows PowerShell console you can create Site Collections, configure features, install packages, and do everything a SharePoint system administrator can do using the standard web-based administrative interface of the SPCA—and more.

> **More Information** To learn more about Windows PowerShell, read the document, "Windows PowerShell," which is available on MSDN Online at *http://msdn.microsoft.com/en-us/library/dd835506.aspx*.

Developer Tools

SharePoint developers can take advantage of some Microsoft-supplied tools to support their work and reduce the effort involved in developing custom solutions. This section lists these tools and identifies when they might be useful.

Microsoft SharePoint Designer 2010

SharePoint Designer 2010 is a free tool that you can download from Microsoft's website at *http://sharepoint.microsoft.com/en-us/product/related-technologies/pages/sharepoint-designer.aspx*. SharePoint Designer 2010 is a Rapid Application Development (RAD) tool for developing SharePoint no-code solutions. It targets advanced users, who can use it to design and compose solutions without writing any code.

Using SharePoint Designer 2010, you can

- Personalize pages, page layouts, Web Parts, Web Part Pages, layouts and themes.
- Create and manage lists and document libraries.
- Design simple workflows or import workflows designed using Microsoft Visio 2010.
- Manage content-types and site columns, to model typed lists of contents.

- Model and register external data sources using the Business Data Connectivity engine.

- Create pages with lists data bound to external data sources.

- Manage users and groups.

- Manage files and assets of the target site.

Figure 1-8 shows the main page of SharePoint Designer 2010 when connected to a SharePoint site. As you can see, it provides a user-friendly interface, consistent with the Microsoft Office 2010 user experience.

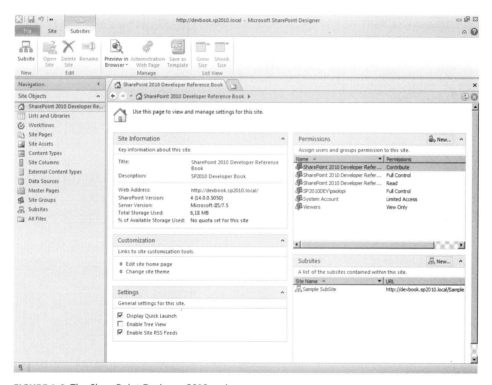

FIGURE 1-8 The SharePoint Designer 2010 main page.

As a developer, you will primarily use this tool to prototype solutions, to design Business Data Connectivity models (as you will see in Chapter 25), and to customize layouts, working with themes, master pages, XSLTs, and Web Part Pages.

This book will not cover SharePoint Designer 2010 in depth, because this book is aimed at developers who are willing to develop SharePoint solutions by writing custom code. For deep coverage of SharePoint Designer 2010, read *Microsoft SharePoint Designer 2010 Step by Step*, by Penelope Coventry (Microsoft Press; 2010, ISBN: 978-0-7356-2733-8).

Microsoft Visual Studio 2010

Visual Studio 2010 natively offers a set of extensions for developing code-based SharePoint 2010 solutions. In fact, when you install Visual Studio 2010, you have the opportunity to activate the Microsoft Visual Studio 2010 SharePoint Developer Tools option, which installs a set of project and item templates, ready-to-use in your own SharePoint solutions. It also installs some deployment tools, which are useful for packaging, releasing, and upgrading a SharePoint solution. Chapter 8 provides more details about how you can take advantage of these deployment tools.

> **Note**   To use Visual Studio 2010 for developing SharePoint 2010 solutions, you need to run it under an administrative account. This is because you need some high-level permissions to manage the SharePoint server while deploying solutions, and because you need to attach to the IIS worker process while debugging code. I suggest that you run your desktop as a standard user, but run Visual Studio 2010 with a "Run As" command to impersonate an administrative user.

Figure 1-9 shows the Add New Project form of Visual Studio 2010, showing the project templates installed by the SharePoint extensions.

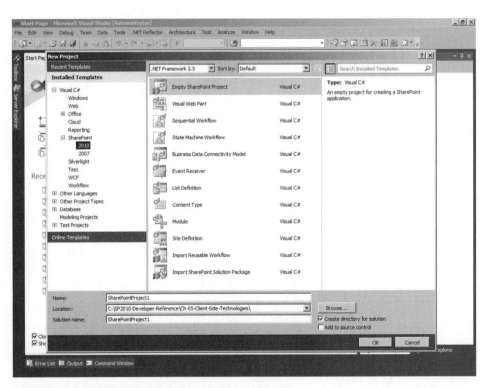

FIGURE 1-9 The Add New Project form in Visual Studio 2010.

You can create the following types of projects:

- **Empty SharePoint Project**   This is an empty project, ready to start a new SharePoint implementation. It provides a set of references to only the most useful libraries of Share-Point, and it provides support for automatic deployment.

- **Visual Web Part**   This is a project intended for developing a Web Part with a graphical UI. You will see more about Visual Web Parts in Chapter 6.

- **Sequential Workflow**   This project type is suitable for developing a sequential work-flow. The available workflow models will be explained in detail in Chapter 16, "Share-Point Workflows Architecture."

- **State Machine Workflow**   This project type is suitable for developing a state machine workflow. It will be explained in detail in Chapter 16.

- **Business Data Connectivity Model**   With this project template, you can develop cus-tom entity models for connecting SharePoint with custom external data sources.

- **Event Receiver**   This is a project template for adding an event receiver.

- **List Definition**   This is a project type that is intended for deploying a new list definition.

- **Content Type**   This template creates a project to deploy a new content type.

- **Module**   With this project template, you can deploy content, such as images, pages, Web Parts, and so on into a SharePoint site.

- **Site Definition**   This is a project intended for defining an entire site template, from which you might later create many site instances.

- **Import Reusable Workflow**   This project template is useful for importing workflows designed with SharePoint Designer 2010 that need to be extended and/or improved with Visual Studio 2010.

- **Import SharePoint Solution Package**   Imports an old or third-party solution package (WSP).

Regardless of which project template you start from, you can develop any of these extension types, because these models simply prepare a pre-configured environment. In fact, it's quite common to start with an Empty SharePoint Project, and then add items as you need them.

The Microsoft Visual Studio 2010 SharePoint Developer Tools also provide a rich set of item templates that are useful for creating various types of content. Here is a list of some of the available items:

- **Visual Web Part**   Defines a custom Web Part with a graphical UI

- **Web Part**   Defines a code-only custom Web Part

- **Sequential Workflow**   Declares a sequential workflow

- **State Machine**   Declares a state machine workflow

- **Business Data Connectivity Model**   Defines a model for connecting SharePoint to custom external data sources

- **Application Page**   Creates a custom administrative webpage

- Event Receiver   Defines an event receiver to handle events related to sites, lists, items, or workflows

- **Module**   Supports deploying any kind of item (image, file, page, whatever) using a deployment package (WSP)

- **Content Type**   Allows the definition of a new content type

- **List Definition**   Defines a list definition from scratch

- **List Definition From Content Type**   Useful for creating a custom list definition based on a custom content type

- **List Instance**   Creates an instance of a specific list definition. In general you use this in conjunction with a list definition item

- **Empty Element**   Supports deploying any kind of feature using a deployment package (WSP)

- **User Control**   Installs a custom user control that defines UI elements based on an .ascx file

SharePoint Server Explorer

Another interesting feature offered by Visual Studio 2010 is SharePoint Server Explorer, a new extension for the Server Explorer in Visual Studio 2010 that targets SharePoint servers. Through this extension, you can register as many SharePoint servers as you need and browse their topology and configuration using the classic treeview approach, such as in Visual Studio Server Explorer windows.

As shown in Figure 1-10, the SharePoint Server Explorer interface lets you browse and manage:

- Sites and Sub-Sites

- Content Types

- Features

- List Templates

- List and Document Libraries

- Workflows

In addition, because SharePoint Server Explorer is based on an extensible object model, you can extend it to provide new functionality, using Visual Studio 2010 to develop such solutions. You can already find many custom extensions that can be downloaded for free.

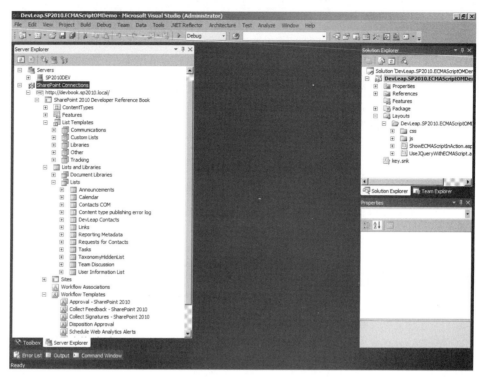

FIGURE 1-10 The SharePoint Server Explorer user interface in Visual Studio 2010.

Solution Explorer and Feature Designer

One last set of tools available in Visual Studio 2010 is the Solution Explorer and the Feature Designer. These are tools for graphically designing and managing SharePoint packages (WSP) and features. They are particularly useful for automating deployment of SharePoint solutions. You will see more about these tools in Chapter 8.

Summary

This chapter explained what SharePoint is, what its main capabilities are, and how to use those capabilities from the perspective of a developer. You saw the product architecture and a quick comparison of the various SharePoint editions so that you can choose the one that best fits your needs. Lastly, you discovered the main tools available for developing SharePoint solutions.

Chapter 2
Data Foundation

Beginning with this chapter, you will be performing hands-on work with Microsoft SharePoint 2010 and its fundamental capabilities: the data management features. Chapter 1, "Introducing Microsoft SharePoint 2010," showed that SharePoint's main focus is managing lists of items using a rich set of ancillary features. This chapter explores the different kinds of data and functionality that SharePoint offers as support for creating SharePoint solutions. While this chapter concentrates on topics about standard features, future chapters will show you how to extend and customize the native environment. If you already know about SharePoint data management features and capabilities, you can probably skip this introductory chapter; however, if you want to learn more about lists, libraries, columns, Content Types, and so on, keep on reading.

Lists of Items and Contents

This section concentrates on general management tasks involved in managing lists and content. You need to have a new Site Collection to use as the target for the examples in this chapter. Chapter 1 illustrated how to create a new Site Collection; however, each SharePoint Farm installed with the standalone configuration has a default web application, published on the Internet Information Service (IIS) default site. This default web application hosts the default Site Collection, as well. This means that you already have a target site to use to experiment with the procedures you will see in the following pages.

Depending on the site template you chose while creating the first site, you should have some more or less predefined list instances and content. In the next section you'll see how to create a list that's independent of the site template you started with. Nevertheless, before creating a new list instance, you need to log on to the SharePoint portal as a user with sufficient rights to create lists.

A SharePoint site has at least four levels of preconfigured rights, corresponding to four different user groups, which are:

- **Viewers**   Users who have "View Only" permission for the contents of the site.
- **Site Visitors**   Users belonging to this group can "Read" the contents of the site.
- **Site Members**   Users in this group can (by default) "Contribute" (add, update, delete) the contents of the site and items in the lists. However, they cannot change the overall structure of the site, so they cannot create new list instances or change the definition of existing lists.

- **Site Owners**   Users registered in this group have "Full Control" of both site content and structure, so they can change items, create new lists, or update the definition of existing lists.

Finally, as Chapter 1 showed you, there are also users in the Site Collection Administrators group who are responsible for administering the entire Site Collection. The permissions described in the previous bulleted list arise from the following definitions:

- **View Only**   The user can view pages, list items, and documents. Document types with server-side file handlers can be viewed in the browser but not downloaded.
- **Limited Access**   The user can view specific lists, document libraries, list items, folders, or documents when given permissions. It cannot be assigned directly by an end user.
- **Read**   The user can view pages and list items and download documents.
- **Contribute**   The user can view, add, update, and delete list items and documents.
- **Design**   The user can view, add, update, delete, approve, and customize.
- **Full Control**   The user has full control.

Part VI of this book, "Security Infrastructure," contains an in-depth discussion of the security and permissions logic in SharePoint 2010.

Creating a New List

If you are logged into the site as a user with sufficient rights, you can create new list instances. In Chapter 1, you learned that to create a new list, you just need to go to the Site Actions menu of the current site, and then select More Options. A Silverlight control appears, from which you to choose the list type that you want to use as the model for your new list.

 Note   There is also a down-level HTML-only user experience offered for those users who do not have a Silverlight-enabled web browser.

For example, suppose that you want to create a list of contacts. As shown in Figure 2-1, there is a standard template for creating a contacts list.

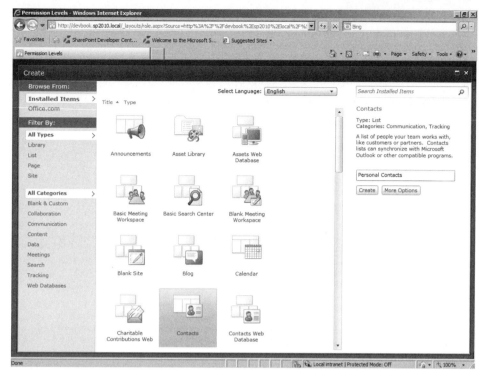

FIGURE 2-1 The Silverlight user interface for creating a new list instance.

The result will be the creation of a new list with a set of predefined columns (metadata) for each contact item.

After you have created a list instance, you can leverage the full set of features and capabilities that the data foundation of SharePoint 2010 provides. Some of the main features and capabilities of a list instance are:

- **Columns**   You can define a set of custom columns describing the metadata of each item of the list.

- **Folders**   Like file system folders, they can be used to partition data in subfolders. Through folders, you can also define custom permissions and partition data visibility.

- **Content Types**   These are models of data that can be used to store different kind of items within a unique list instance. For example, you could have contacts of various types, such as customers, suppliers, employees, and so on. They could share some common columns, and have some specific columns, too. Content Types will be covered in detail in Chapter 10, "Data Provisioning."

- **Views**   Every list can render with various views. A view can be used to group items by a specific field value or Content Type, to filter and/or order items, page the results, and so forth.

- **Permissions**   Each list can have its own set of permissions, which can be different from the default permissions applied to the site.

- **Versioning**   The list can keep track of changes and versions of items.

- **Workflows**   These are business processes that execute when an item is created or modified.

- **Content Approval**   This is a content approval engine that you can use to enrich content provisioning, adding approval rules and processes.

- **Alerts**   An alerting infrastructure that you can employ to alert people about new, updated or deleted contents.

- **RSS Feeds**   This provides the capability to subscribe to and monitor a feed from any kind of feed aggregator.

- **Offline capabilities**   You candata elect to keep data offline using tools such as Outlook or SharePoint Workspace.

- **Office Integration**   This provides the ability to integrate list contents with Excel, Access, and other Office applications.

- **E-mail–enabled libraries**   You can configure a document library to automatically receive e-mails, storing the messages, and optionally any attachment, as a document in the target library.

In fact, you can benefit from these features without having to write any code.

Standard List Templates

The richest edition of SharePoint 2010 offers nearly 50 list templates out of the box. Table 2-1 presents some of the more common list templates.

TABLE 2-1 Some of the Main List Templates Available in SharePoint

Template Name	Description
Announcements	A list for publishing news items and information.
Asset Library	A list for sharing rich media assets, including images, audio, and video files.
Calendar	A calendar that lets users schedule meetings and events and set deadlines. You can synchronize a Calendar list with Microsoft Outlook.
Contacts	A list of people, including their addresses. You can synchronize a Contacts list with Microsoft Outlook.
Custom List	This uses a "blank" list model, meaning that you can create whatever type of list that you like by defining custom columns and views.
Data Connection Library	A list for sharing connections to external data sources, such as databases, web services, OLAP cubes, and so on.

Template Name	Description
Document Library	A list for sharing documents and files.
External List	A list that supports reading and managing data from external data sources via Business Connectivity Services. You'll see more about this in Chapter 25, "Business Connectivity Services."
Form Library	A list for sharing XML-based business forms, such as those produced with Microsoft InfoPath.
Links	A list that stores hyperlinks to sites and resources.
Picture Library	A list for sharing pictures. This list type includes upload, preview, slideshow, and thumbnail functionalities.
Slide Library	A list to share slideshows built with Microsoft PowerPoint that includes slide management functionality.
Survey	A list to create surveys, polls, or lists of questions. This type provides features for viewing a graphical summary of the responses.
Tasks	A list of tasks to execute, with deadlines, notes, and completion status.

Table 2-1 shows that you can create a variety of lists. You can also customize any list that so that it meets your specific needs.

Custom List Templates

If none of the predefined list templates suit your needs, you can create a Custom List instance and define its columns and views manually. Of course, whenever you create any list, you can define custom views and columns, but when working with Custom List instances, (which are blank lists with the minimal set of fields required by SharePoint), you always need to customize the columns to add your own fields.

By default, a Custom List has only three public and visible fields, which are:

- **Title**   This is a mandatory field that defines a title for each item in the list. It is useful for rendering list items and for accessing the contextual menu that SharePoint provides for each individual item in a list.

- **Created By**   This is an auto-calculated field that stores information about the user who created the current item.

- **Modified By**   Another auto-calculated field that stores information about the user who last modified the current item.

The set of fields you have just seen belongs to the base *Item*, from which every SharePoint list item inherits.

Imagine that you want to create a list of Products. If you create a custom list for this purpose, you will need to add some custom columns. For example, you could have columns such as *ProductID*, *Description*, *Price*, and so on.

To set this up, just after creating the list instance, browse to the List Settings page by clicking the List Settings command on the List Ribbon tab, as shown in Figure 2-2.

FIGURE 2-2 The List Ribbon menu of a list with the List Settings command (highlighted).

The List Settings command takes you to a page specifically designed for configuring the settings of the current list. For example, from this page you can customize appearance information such as the title and description of the current list, enable and configure settings about versioning of items, define validation rules, manage workflows, configure advanced settings, and so forth. In particular, on the advanced settings page you can configure the following parameters:

- **Content Types**   Specifies whether to allow management of Content Types in the list. You can use Content Types to define data-item template models. By default, a list hosts items with a specific Content Type with a default set of fields, depending on the model of list you are configuring. For example, a Tasks list is made up of items of type Task, while a Calendar is made up of items of type Event, and so on. However, as you will see later in this chapter, you can define more specific Content Types to better define and manage the metadata. As an example, you can define such concepts as Customer, Employee, Order, and so on, each with its specific fields.

- **Item-Level Permissions**   Specifies which items users are authorized to read, create, and edit. It is a setting specific for a list of items and not available in document libraries.

- **Attachments**   Specifies whether list items can have file attachments or not. It is another setting specific for list of items and not available in document libraries.

- **Folders**   Defines whether the New Folder command is available on the Ribbon.

- **Search**   Controls whether items in the list should appear in search results. Users who do not have permission to see the items of the list will not see them in search results, no matter what this setting is.

- **Offline Client Availability**   Specifies whether the items in the list can be downloaded to offline clients.

- **Datasheet**   Enables datasheet view for bulk-editing data in the list.

- **Dialogs**   Controls whether the new, edit, and display forms of items are displayed in a dialog or in place.

Just after the list of available configuration parameters and commands you'll see a list of Columns, where you can manage the columns of the current list (see Figure 2-3).

On this page, you can create new custom columns from scratch or add an existing site column (which will be discussed later in the section, "Site Columns," on page 46).

Another option on this page allows you to alter the ordinal position of columns. This helps when you have many columns, and you want to re-organize their positions. Finally, you can define custom indexes on this page, which is useful whenever you need to search the contents of a list using indexed columns as the search criteria.

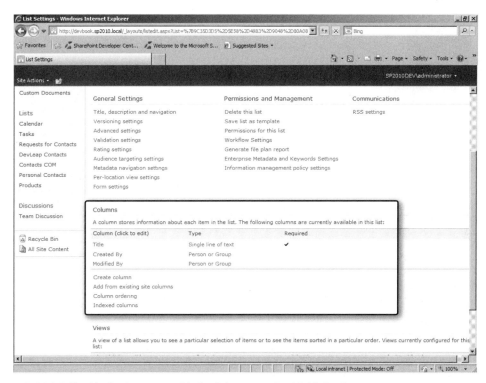

FIGURE 2-3 The List Settings page with the Columns section highlighted.

When you select Create Column, a specific SharePoint administrative page appears, requesting information about the type of column that you want to create. Figure 2-4 shows the Create Column page.

Here, you can define the name of the new custom column, the field type, enter a brief description, and supply other validation rules and constraints. For example, you can define whether the new column is required or optional, whether it should have a default value, whether it should contain a value that's unique across the whole list instance, and so on.

As Figure 2-4 shows, you can choose from a variety of data types when creating a new column.

FIGURE 2-4 The Create Column page for a new column of a list.

By default the available field types are:

- **Single Line Of Text**   Corresponds to a single line of text.
- **Multiple Lines Of Text**   Corresponds to a text area with multiple columns and rows.
- **Choice (Menu To Choose From)**   This is a field with a predefined set of values. You can configure it to accept single or multiple values, and whether it should render as a drop-down menu, a radio button list, or a list of check boxes.

- **Number (1, 1.0, 100)** Defines a numeric column that can have decimals and minimum and maximum value.

- **Currency ($, ¥, €)** Corresponds to a money field, which behaves almost like a Number field type. You can choose the currency format that you prefer.

- **Date And Time** Defines a Date and Time field that you can configure to handle date-only fields or date and time fields.

- **Lookup (Information Already On This Site)** Retrieves its values from an external list within the same website.

- **Yes/No (Check Box)** Defines a *Boolean* column.

- **Person Or Group** This is a particular type of lookup field that searches for a user or group defined in the current site.

- **Hyperlink Or Picture** This column type holds an external URL, which can be either a page URL or an image URL. In the latter case, you can configure this field type to render the image available at that URL.

- **Calculated (Calculation Based On Other Columns)** Defines a formula that can be calculated based on other fields defined in the current list, and then renders the result.

- **External Data** A specific field type that looks up values via Business Connectivity Services. You'll see more on this topic in Chapter 25.

- **Managed Metadata** This field is related to the managed metadata service.

If these options don't meet your needs, you can define field types of your own. You will see how to do this in Chapter 11, "Developing Custom Fields."

Views

In addition to lists and columns, you can create one or more custom views for a list. In fact, every list has at least one default view that renders the fields of each item, using predefined ordering and filtering criteria. Any user with the proper permissions can create personal views of a list, and those with sufficient permissions can create a new shared view for the target list. As an example, imagine that the Products list discussed in the preceding section is ready to use, containing custom fields such as *ProductID*, *Description*, and *Price*. Figure 2-5 shows the default view for this list.

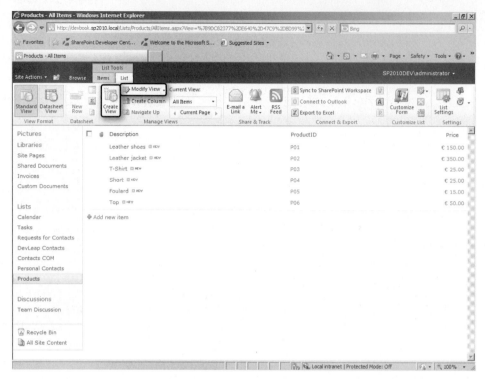

FIGURE 2-5 The Default View provided by SharePoint for the custom list of Products.

You can use the Modify View command (highlighted on the Ribbon in Figure 2-5), to change the current view. Alternatively, by clicking the Create View command (also highlighted in Figure 2-5), you can create a completely new view. If you choose to create a new view, a page appears that asks you to choose a view format, based on a set of six predefined formats:

- **Standard View** This is the classic view style. You can choose fields, sorting and filtering rules, grouping, paging, and so on. The result will be a webpage.

- **Calendar View** This view shows data in a calendar format (daily, weekly, or monthly). You would likely use this only when you have data related to dates.

- **Access View** This view launches Microsoft Access so users can create forms and reports based on the list's data.

- **Datasheet View** This view renders data in an editable spreadsheet format (such as Excel), which is convenient for bulk editing.

- **Gantt View** This option creates a view that renders data in a Gantt chart. It is useful primarily when rendering the tasks of a project.

- **Custom View In SharePoint Designer** This option launches Microsoft SharePoint Designer 2010, in which you can design a new view by taking advantage of the full set of capabilities provided by SharePoint Designer 2010.

For the sake of simplicity, select a Standard View template. You will be prompted with a configuration page, on which you will define the rendering criteria for the new view, as shown in Figure 2-6.

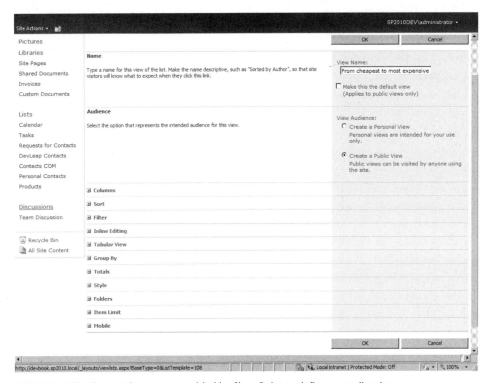

FIGURE 2-6 The Create View page provided by SharePoint to define a new list view.

You have the opportunity to configure many aspects of the view, such as:

- **Columns**   Here, you can choose the columns to render in the view and their ordinal position in the display.

- **Sort**   Use this to define up to two columns for use when sorting data.

- **Filter**   Use this to filter the output items. It is suggested to use indexed columns for better performances in filtering.

- **Inline Editing**   Use this to specify whether an edit button is provided on each row for inline editing of items.

- **Tabular View**   You can specify whether a multiple selection check box should be rendered adjacent to each row.

- **Group By**   You can define up to two columns to use for grouping data.

- **Totals**   Use this to establish total rows selectively on each visible column.

- **Style**   Select a graphical rendering style for the list view.

- **Folders**   You can choose whether to view items by browsing through folders, or all at once with a folder flat view.

- **Item Limit**   Use this to define a limit to the amount of data to return. This is useful when working with very large lists.

- **Mobile**   This allows you to configure settings to better render the view on a mobile device.

In the example list of Products, you could plan to order products based on their price, listed from least to most expensive. Figure 2-7 shows the custom view output.

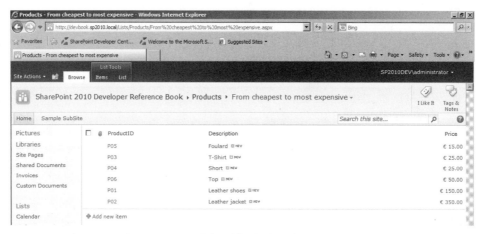

FIGURE 2-7 The output of a custom view defined for the list of Products.

Custom views are useful for browsing and managing data stored in large custom lists of items.

Creating a Document Library

A Document Library is a particular kind of list that is designed to host files (for instance, documents) instead of generic items. Each file corresponds to a single list item, which can also have a rich set of metadata fields to make it more meaningful. To create a Document Library, simply select the Document Library list template on the Create page, as shown in Figure 2-1. (There is also a shortcut available in the Site Actions menu.)

Suppose that you want to create a list of "Offers," which includes some custom metadata for each offer file, such as Protocol Number, Target Customer, and Offer Date Time. Begin by selecting the Site Actions menu for creating the library. You will be prompted with a Silverlight control such as that illustrated in Figure 2-8.

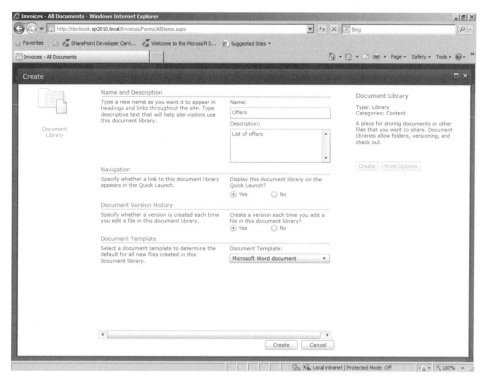

FIGURE 2-8 The Silverlight control that assists you when creating a new Document Library.

Using this control, you specify the title of the library, its description, whether you want to display a shortcut to the library in the SharePoint's Quick Launch menu (which is commonly located on the left side of the page), if you want to support versioning of files, and finally, which document template to use for each new document created in the library.

After you have created the library, you can access it through a user interface that is basically the same as the one you used to manage lists of simple items. However, a document library has some additional features and commands. For example, rather than an Items Ribbon, there is a Documents Ribbon, with commands specifically tailored for managing files and documents. Instead of a List Ribbon to manage the list, there's a Library Ribbon. Figure 2-9 shows the commands available in this new Ribbon.

FIGURE 2-9 The Documents Ribbon menu of a document library.

Some of the most important commands available on this Ribbon are:

- **New Document**   Use this command to create a new document, starting from a document template.

- **Upload Document**   Use this command to upload a single document or a set of documents.

- **New Folder**   This command creates a new folder for organizing and navigating documents.

- **Edit Document**   Use this command to open a selected document using its corresponding editing program. For example, if you have selected a .doc/.docx file, this command opens the file in Microsoft Word.

- **Check Out**   This locks others out of the document so that you can have exclusive access to the file in read and write mode.

- **Check In**   Releases the exclusive lock on the file, confirming any changes and creating a new version of the file (if file versioning is enabled).

- **Discard Check Out**   Releases the exclusive lock on the file, discarding any changes.

- **View Properties**   Use this to see the metadata properties of a selected file.

- **Edit Properties**   Edits the metadata properties of a selected file.

- **Delete Document**   Deletes one or more selected files.

- **Download a Copy**   Downloads a copy of a selected file.

- **Send To**   Sends the selected file to a specific destination.

Just like a standard list, when working with a document library, you can configure settings and create custom columns and custom views. However, in a document library you can also configure a document template used when creating any new documents. To configure this feature, select the Library Settings command on the Library Ribbon. The Document Library Settings page appears. Select the Advanced Settings menu item to open a page on which you can configure a number of interesting parameters (see Figure 2-10).

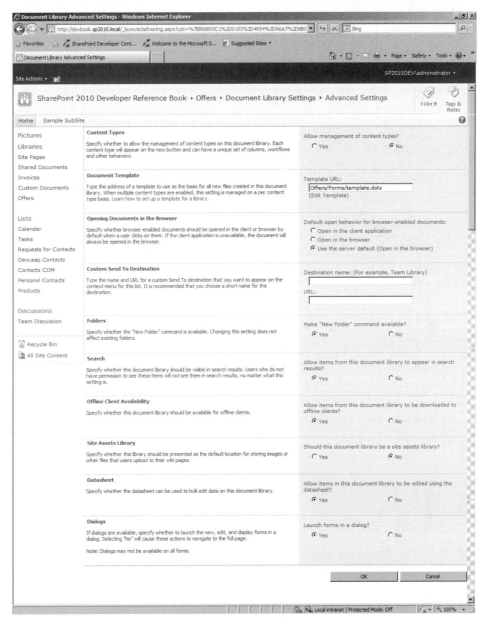

FIGURE 2-10 The Document Library Settings page for a document library.

Some of these parameters are the same as with the common lists, others are specific for Document Libraries. Following is a list of the Document Libraries' specific advanced settings:

- **Document Template**   With this you can specify the relative URL of a document that will be used as the template for all new files created in the Document Library.

- **Opening Documents In The Browser**   Here, you can define how SharePoint behaves when opening browser-enabled documents—that is, documents that can be opened within the browser. You can choose between Open In The Client Application, to open the file on the client side, within the specific client application; Open In The Browser, to open the file in the browser; and Use The Server Default, which is set by the Farm administrator.

- **Custom Send to Destination**   Use this to add a custom target to the Send To menu.

- **Site Assets Library**   This determines if this library will be the default "Assets Library" for storing images, videos, and other files when users upload contents to their blogs or wiki pages.

Site Columns

In the previous sections, you defined custom lists and columns by simply configuring them at the list level. However, there are situations in which you need to define the same column type in multiple list instances. For example, consider a hypothetical "protocol number" that you might want to share across many document libraries. It would be great to have the capability to define the concept of a "protocol number" column once, and then use it in many libraries. In addition, having a unique concept for describing metadata simplifies defining search queries and improves the quality of search results. As an example, you could define a query to retrieve all documents that have a protocol number field containing a value within a specified range, regardless of the library in which they are stored. A list of similar examples could be very long.

SharePoint provides the concept of a "site column" to satisfy the need to share a metadata definition across multiple lists and libraries. A Site Column is the formal definition of a field type (a metadata type) shared at the website level. Site Column definitions are hierarchical. In fact, you can define a site column in the root website of a Site Collection and use it in all the websites of the collection.

To define a new site column, browse to the Site Settings page through the Site Actions menu (see Figure 2-11). Under the Galleries group you will find a menu item named Site Columns, which brings you to the page on which you manage existing site columns or create new ones.

The Site Columns page enumerates all the existing site columns, divided into groups. By clicking the Create button at the top of the page, you can create a new site column definition. The page for creating a new site column is similar to the one you used earlier (see Figure 2-4) to create a list-level column; however, the site column definition page contains settings that control grouping of columns, to make it easier to retrieve them on the Gallery page.

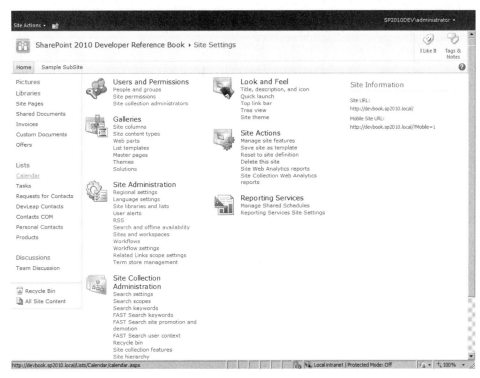

FIGURE 2-11 The Site Settings page for a Site Collection.

After you have defined a site column, you can reference it in any list or library by selecting the Add From Existing Site Columns command (see Figure 2-3) on the List Settings page. You can also use a site column to define a custom Content Type, as you will see in the next section.

Content Types

A Content Type is a formal definition of a data template or item template. Each time you create a new item in a list or a new document in a library, you are creating an instance of a Content Type. In fact, every list or library uses the idea of "content type" as the model for the data you store in it. By default, every list or library has one default Content Type under the cover. For example, if you create a list of type Contacts, and you add a new item, this item will be made of a set of columns that are defined in the *Contact* Content Type, which is a default Content Type provided by SharePoint. If you create a list of type Document Library, as you did in the previous section, by default the library will host items with a Content Type of *Document*.

A Content Type is based on a set of Site Column references, together with some other optional information related to forms, rendering templates, a specific document template (for document items only), and custom XML configuration.

As you will see in more detail in Chapter 10, "Data Provisioning," Content Types are hierarchical and exploit an inheritance pattern. At the root, there is a "System" Content Type, which is essentially a low-level base class for every other Content Type. Figure 2-12 depicts the hierarchical inheritance tree for native Content Types.

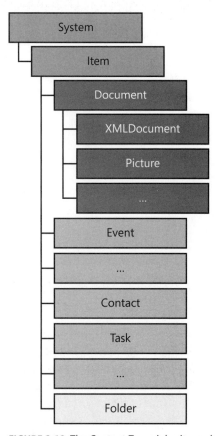

FIGURE 2-12 The Content Types inheritance hierarchy in SharePoint.

Figure 2-12 illustrates that the *System* Content Type is inherited by the *Item* Content Type, which acts as the base class, either directly or indirectly, for every other Content Type. For example, the *Contact* Content Type you used in the list of contacts inherits from *Item*, as does the *Document* Content Type. The *Picture* Content Type, which is the default Content Type for a "Picture Library," inherits from the *Document* Content Type.

You can manage existing Content Types or define custom Content Types by clicking the Site Content Types command on the Site Settings page, under the Galleries group. To create a new Content Type, click the Create button at the top of the page. A page appears, asking you to supply a few settings, such as the name, description, logical group, and parent Content Type of your new Content Type. Immediately after creating the new Content Type, you will be redirected to the page for Content Type management, shown in Figure 2-13.

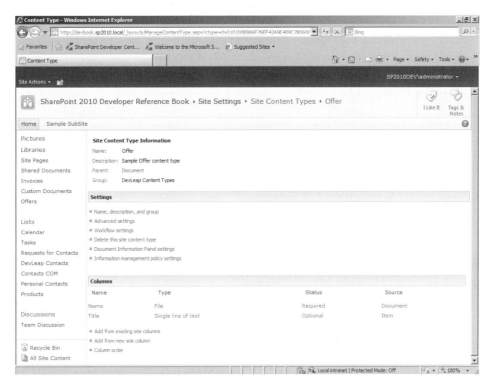

FIGURE 2-13 The page for managing a Content Type configuration.

On this page, you can configure all the Content Type settings, including general information about the Content Type, specifying a custom document template (in the event of a Content Type inheriting from Document), managing workflows, user interface elements for editing in the Office client (also known as document information panel, again available only in case you are working with a document), and information management policies. You can also configure a Content Type that uses a specific set of site columns. Doing this lets you share the same field types across multiple Content Types.

After defining one or more custom Content Types, you can map them to lists or libraries using the list or library advanced settings page. Thus, the process of designing content in a SharePoint site is to first define the site columns, create the Content Types that will use those columns, and then finally, create the lists or libraries that leverage the Content Types. By working in that sequence, you will end up with a common set of data items (Content Types) that share a common set of data fields (site columns), stored in custom data repositories (lists and libraries).

Websites

One last kind of data repository that you can define is websites. Generally, you can use a website as a place to hold collections of lists and libraries that are shared by the same target audience or that share the same functional meaning. For example, you could have a website for each department of your company (Sales, Human Resources, Information Technology, and so on). websites are stored in Site Collections, so before you can create a new website, you first need to have a Site Collection.

After you have a Site Collection, you will have one root website, too. To create another website, you just need to invoke the New Site command on the Site Actions menu. You will be prompted to choose from a wide list of website templates, of which these are the most interesting:

- **Team Site**   A site that targets a team of people who want to share documents, a calendar, announcements, and tasks.

- **Blank Site**   A blank site ready for customization.

- **Document Workspace**   A site for a team working on a document. It provides a document library for storing the output document, attachments, and any related files. It also provides a list of tasks, and a list of useful links.

- **Basic Meeting Workspace**   A site for managing a meeting. It provides lists for handling agenda, attendees, and documents.

- **Blank Meeting Workspace**   A blank site for managing a meeting, ready for customization.

- **Decision Meeting Workspace**   A site specifically defined to track decisions made during a meeting. It provides lists for handling agenda, attendees, documents, and meeting decisions.

- **Social Meeting Workspace**   A site for managing a social event. It provides lists for storing attendees, directions, pictures, and other social contents.

- **Blog**   A site for publishing a blog.

- **Group Work Site**   A site for groups that supports sharing ideas, documents, tasks, links, phone call memos, and so on.

- **Document Center**   A site to centrally manage documents in an enterprise-level company.

- **Records Center**   A site to manage records of documents in an enterprise level company. It provides configurable routing tables to direct files to specific locations based on custom company rules.

- **Enterprise Search Center**   A site that supports searching for documents or people in an enterprise-level company.

- **Basic Search Center**   A site that delivers a basic search experience.

Although these are the most common website templates, you might see others, depending on which SharePoint edition you have installed.

Summary

This chapter discussed the fundamental parts of SharePoint Data Foundation. You saw how to create lists of items, site columns, Content Types, and sites or workspaces. By capitalizing on the information discussed in this chapter, you will be able to create simple data management solutions using SharePoint 2010 as your data repository. However, as you read further in this book, you will see why you should not use SharePoint as a database management system (DBMS) surrogate; instead, SharePoint is an appropriate *companion* for a relational database. In Chapter 10, you will learn how to provision data structures using code, rather than simply designing them through the web browser interface as you did in this chapter.

PART II

Programming Microsoft SharePoint 2010

Chapter 3
Server Object Model

As you learned in Chapter 1, "Microsoft SharePoint 2010 Architecture," Microsoft SharePoint 2010 is a product that is based directly on Microsoft .NET and Microsoft ASP.NET. Thus, one of the main tools that you will use to develop solutions interacting with the SharePoint engine is the .NET object model offered by the SharePoint infrastructure. This Server Object Model comprises a set of namespaces and classes, divided into several .NET assemblies, which you can reference and use in any kind of .NET solution running on a SharePoint server.

The solution must run on a SharePoint server because this is the only server on which the Server Object Model runs; it has some dependencies that are satisfied only on servers in a SharePoint farm.

If you are writing a software solution that interacts with SharePoint, but does not run on a SharePoint server, you can leverage the Client Object Model or SharePoint SOAP Services, discussed in Chapter 5, "Client-Side Technologies."

The key point of the Server Object Model is that you can use it to do in code everything (and more) that you can do with SharePoint's user interface, whether through the browser, using the command line tools, or with Windows PowerShell.

This chapter shows you how to use the major classes of the Server Object Model by examining their main members. You won't find a full and complete reference for the entire object model here, because it contains thousands of types—an encyclopedia would probably not be sufficient.

 More Information If you are looking for a complete reference of all the types in the SharePoint Server Object Model, see MSDN Online at *http://msdn.microsoft.com/en-us/library/ff462061.aspx.*

Because the user interface is not a goal of this chapter, the code samples shown herein will mainly use a console application. However, you can see the Server Object Model in action within SharePoint Web Parts in Chapter 6, "Web Part Basics," and Chapter 7, "Advanced Web Parts," as well as in many other chapters.

Startup Environment

To test the code samples in this chapter, you need to create a new Console project in Microsoft Visual Studio 2010. Then, if you use the default Visual Studio configuration, you should change the Target Framework setting in the Application configuration tab of the project from ".NET Framework 4.0 Client Profile" to ".NET Framework 3.5." You should also change the Platform Target setting in the Build configuration tab of the project from "x86" to "x64" or to "Any CPU," because Microsoft SharePoint 2010 works on 64-bit machines only; the "x86" configuration is not supported.

> **More Information** For further details about setting up your SharePoint development environ-
> ment, read the MSDN Online article, "How to: Set the Correct Target Framework and CPU," at
> *http://msdn.microsoft.com/en-us/library/ff407621.aspx.*

Lastly, you need to reference some of the SharePoint Server Object Model assemblies. You will definitely need to reference Microsoft.SharePoint.dll, which is the main Server Object Model assembly. You can find it, along with many of the other assemblies, in the SharePoint14_Root\ISAPI folder.

> **Note** SharePoint14_Root represents the SharePoint root folder, which is usually located in C:\
> Program Files\Common Files\Microsoft Shared\Web Server Extensions\14.

Objects Hierarchy

All the main types of the Server Object Model are defined in namespaces that end with *Microsoft.SharePoint.** or *Microsoft.Office.**, and in general, have a name that begins with *SP*, which stands for SharePoint. For example, the type that represents a user is named *SPUser* and belongs to the namespace *Microsoft.SharePoint*. The type that represents a website, also defined in that namespace, is named *SPWeb*. Figure 3-1 shows the main classes and their hierarchical organization in the Server Object Model.

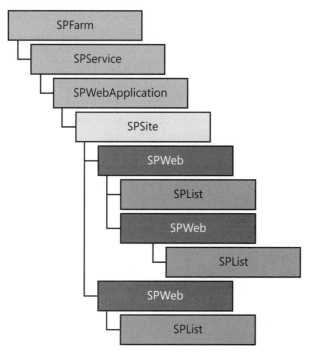

FIGURE 3-1 A graphical representation of the SharePoint Server Object Model hierarchy.

This section explores the main types of the Server Object Model, briefly discussing their main members and showing some quick code samples. In later sections you will learn how to take advantage of these types in everyday solutions by working through some examples.

SPFarm, *SPServer*, *SPService*, and *SPWebApplication*

The first and main object of the Server Object Model is the *SPFarm* class, which represents a reference to an entire SharePoint Server Farm. This class belongs to the *Microsoft.SharePoint. Administration* namespace. You can use it to create a fresh new Farm from scratch, or you can connect to an existing Farm. To create a new Farm, you need to invoke one of the many overloads of the public static *Create* factory method. To connect to an existing Farm (the most common scenario), you provide a SQL Server connection string and the Farm's secret passphrase to the public static *Open* method, which has the following signature:

```
public static SPFarm Open(SqlConnectionStringBuilder connectionString, SecureString
passphrase)
```

The connection string corresponds to the Farm configuration database that is defined while configuring the Farm using the SharePoint 2010 Products Configuration Wizard. It can also be found in the system registry at *HKLM\Software\Microsoft\Shared Tools\Web Server Extensions\14.0\Secure\ConfigDB\dsn*. Alternatively, you can connect directly to a local Farm, using the static property *SPFarm.Local*.

> **Important** By default, the SharePoint Server Object Model impersonates the current user. Thus, whenever you create an instance of an SP* type, without providing any specific set of user credentials, your code is impersonating the user running the process or the web request when you invoke the Server Object Model from a webpage.

After obtaining an instance of *SPFarm*, you can browse and manage servers and services that belong to that Farm. For example, you can browse the collection of *Servers* to enumerate all the physical servers that belong to the Farm as objects of type *SPServer*. You can browse the *Services* property, which has the type *SPServiceCollection* and contains different kinds of services—all sharing a common base class of type *SPService*. You can examine all the Windows Services, which are objects of type *SPWindowsService*, or you can access the Web Services, which are of type *SPWebService*. Every Web Service is composed of one or more web applications, each with the type *SPWebApplication*. Listing 3-1 shows a code example that browses for all these kinds of objects in the local Farm.

LISTING 3-1 A code excerpt that browses objects in the local Farm.

```
SPFarm farm = SPFarm.Local;

Console.WriteLine("Here are the servers of the Farm");
foreach (SPServer server in farm.Servers) {
    Console.WriteLine("Server Name: {0}", server.Name);
    Console.WriteLine("Server Address: {0}", server.Address);
    Console.WriteLine("Server Role: {0}", server.Role);
}

foreach (SPService service in farm.Services) {




    Console.WriteLine("-------------------------------------");

    if (service is SPWindowsService) {
        Console.WriteLine("Windows Service: {0}", service.DisplayName);
        Console.WriteLine("Type: {0}", service.TypeName);
        Console.WriteLine("Instances: {0}", service.Instances.Count);
    }
    else if (service is SPWebService) {
        Console.WriteLine("Web Service: {0}", service.DisplayName);
        Console.WriteLine("Type: {0}", service.TypeName);
        Console.WriteLine("Instances: {0}", service.Instances.Count);
```

```
                SPWebService webService = service as SPWebService;

                if (webService != null) {
                    foreach (SPWebApplication webApplication in webService.WebApplications) {
                        Console.WriteLine("Web Application: {0}",
                            webApplication.DisplayName);

                        Console.WriteLine("Content Databases");
                        foreach (SPContentDatabase db in webApplication.ContentDatabases) {
                            Console.WriteLine("Content Database: {0}", db.Name);
                            Console.WriteLine("Connection String: {0}",
                                db.DatabaseConnectionString);
                        }
                    }
                }
            }
            else {
                Console.WriteLine("Generic Service Name: {0}", service.DisplayName);
                Console.WriteLine("Type Name: {0}", service.TypeName);
                Console.WriteLine("Instances: {0}", service.Instances.Count);
            }
        }
    }
```

The bold code in Listing 3-1 highlights the most interesting types and properties. In real life, you do not need to edit a Farm's configuration on a daily basis; however, it is important to know that the Server Object Model allows you to do that. Moreover, sometimes it's useful to begin browsing your Farm topology from the root node (the *SPFarm*) so you can explore the Site Collections and websites in greater detail.

SPSite and *SPWeb*

SPSite and *SPWeb* are fundamental types in the Server Object Model. They represent a site collection and a website, respectively. As you will see later in this chapter, these classes are the basis for many typical operations in your solutions. Every time you need to access the content of a SharePoint website, you will need to reference its parent *SPSite*, and then open the corresponding *SPWeb* instance. To access an *SPSite* instance, you can create it using one of the available constructors, or you can obtain a reference to it through its parent *SPWebApplication* instance. Here are the constructors provided for building an *SPSite*:

```
public SPSite(Guid id);
public SPSite(string requestUrl);
public SPSite(Guid id, SPUrlZone zone);
public SPSite(Guid id, SPUserToken userToken);
public SPSite(string requestUrl, SPUserToken userToken);
public SPSite(Guid id, SPUrlZone zone, SPUserToken userToken);
```

Using the appropriate constructor, you can reference a site collection by its unique ID, which is a GUID, or with a URL that corresponds to a resource published by the site collection. Some

of these six overloads of the constructor let you access the site by using a specific zone, from
the *SPUrlZone* enumeration, the definition of which is shown in the following:

```
public enum SPUrlZone {
    Default,
    Intranet,
    Internet,
    Custom,
    Extranet
}
```

These values correspond to the zones that you can create using SharePoint's administrative
tools. Other *SPSite* constructors accept an *SPUserToken* instance. The *SPUserToken* class represents a token for a valid SharePoint user. When you create an *SPSite* instance using such a
token, you can impersonate the user who owns that token rather than the current user. You
can import an *SPUserToken* instance from a previously exported array of bytes, or you can
create one from a generic *System.Security.Principal.IIdentity*. You would, for example, take
advantage of these constructor overloads to execute code on behalf of another user, probably one with elevated privileges.

> **More Information** In the SharePoint Server Object Model, starting from *SPSite* and moving
> down to the *SPWeb*, *SPList*, *SPListItem* (refer to Figure 3-1), almost every object instance has a
> unique and identifying *ID* property, which can be a GUID or an *Integer*. You should become ac-
> customed to the idea of having an *ID* to uniquely reference each of these types. In general, you
> can also use URLs or titles to reference items, but using the unique *ID* helps to prevent errors.

Listing 3-2 shows a code excerpt that browses all the *SPSite* and *SPWeb* instances in a set of
SPWebApplication objects.

LISTING 3-2 Browsing for *SPSite* and *SPWeb* objects of an *SPWebApplication*.

```
foreach (SPWebApplication webApplication in webService.WebApplications) {
    Console.WriteLine("Web Application: {0}", webApplication.DisplayName);

    foreach (SPSite site in webApplication.Sites) {
        using (site) {
            Console.WriteLine("Site Collection: {0}", site.Url);

            foreach (SPWeb web in site.AllWebs) {
                using (web) {
                    Console.WriteLine("Web Site: {0}", web.Title);
                }
            }
        }
    }
}
```

The example in Listing 3-3 shows how to obtain a reference to an *SPSite* using its public URL.

LISTING 3-3 Getting a reference to an *SPSite* using its public URL.

```
using (SPSite site = new SPSite("http://devbook.sp2010.local/")) {
    Console.WriteLine("Current Site URL: {0}", site.Url);

    SPWeb web = site.RootWeb;
    Console.WriteLine("Current Site RootWeb Title: {0}", web.Title);
}
```

After you have a reference to an *SPSite* instance, you can browse for the websites contained in the collection, or you can change the configuration of the Site Collection itself. Table 3-1 lists the main members of the *SPSite* type, along with a brief description of each member.

TABLE 3-1 Some of the Members of the *SPSite* type

Member Name	Description
AllowUnsafeUpdates	Property to get or set whether to accept updates via HTTP GET or without validating POSTed data security. Setting this property to a value of *true* reduces the security of the website. For further details on this, read the "Common and Best Practices" section, on page 72.
AllWebs	Collection property that holds references to all the websites contained in the current Site Collection.
CheckForPermissions	This method checks the permissions for a given set of rights and throws an exception if the check fails.
Delete	This method (along with some overloads), deletes the current Site Collection from the parent web application.
DoesUserHavePermissions	Almost the same as *CheckForPermissions*, but returns a *Boolean* result rather than throwing an exception when the check fails.
EventReceivers	Collection property that contains references to the event receivers configured for the current Site Collection. For further details about event receivers, refer to Chapter 12, "Event Receivers."
Features	Collection property that you can use to enumerate the features associated with the current Site Collection. For more information about features, refer to Chapter 8, "SharePoint Features and Solutions."
GetCustomListTemplates	This method returns the list of custom list templates for a specific website in the current Site Collection.
GetCustomWebTemplates	This method returns the list of custom website templates available in the current Site Collection, based on a specific Locale ID.
GetEffectiveRightsForAcl	This method returns the effective rights of the current user for a specified target Access Control List (ACL).
GetRecycleBinItems	Lets you query the current contents of the Recycle Bin.
GetRecycleBinStatistics	Lets you obtain the size and the number of items in the Recycle Bin.

Member Name	Description
ID	Read-only property that represents the ID of the current Site Collection.
IISAllowsAnonymous	Read-only *Boolean* property that indicates whether anonymous access is configured in IIS for the web application containing the current Site Collection.
Impersonating	Read-only *Boolean* property that returns *true* when the current instance of *SPSite* has been created by impersonating a third-party identity using an *SPUserToken*.
OpenWeb	This method (and its overloads) returns an *SPWeb* instance corresponding to a specific website, contained in the current Site Collection.
ReadLocked	Property to get or set the *ReadLocked* status of the current Site Collection. When *true*, the site will not be accessible via the Object Model or RPC, and will return an HTTP 403 (FORBIDDEN) status code to any web browser request. To set this value, you need global administrative rights. For example, you can use this property to suspend service for a customer with a payment overdue. In that scenario, you should set the *LockIssue* property before setting the *ReadLocked* property to *true*.
ReadOnly	Property to get or set the read-only status for the contents of the current Site Collection. Setting this property to *true* also sets the *WriteLocked* property to *true*.
RecycleBin	Collection property by which you can enumerate the items currently contained in the Recycle Bin of the current Site Collection.
RootWeb	Property that returns a reference to the root website of the current Site Collection.
Solutions	Collection property that supports enumerating the sandboxed solutions associated with the current Site Collection. For further details about sandboxed solutions, see Chapter 23, "Code Access Security and Sandboxed Solutions."
Url	Read-only property that returns the full URL to the root website of the current Site Collection.
WorkflowManager	Read-only property that gives you access to the object managing workflow templates and instances in the current Site Collection. For further details about workflows, go to Part 5, "Developing Workflows."
WriteLocked	A *Boolean* property similar to *ReadLocked*, but that affects write access only.
Zone	Returns the *Zone* used to construct the current *SPSite* instance.

An *SPSite* object is required to obtain access to an *SPWeb* instance. In fact, the *SPWeb* class does not have a public constructor. The only way to obtain a reference to a website is through its parent *SPSite*, although you can get access to the current website using the *SPControl* and *SPContext* types that you will see later in this section. The *SPSite* class provides the *OpenWeb* method (see Table 3-1) for this purpose. Listing 3-4 shows an example of accessing a specific website by using its parent Site Collection.

LISTING 3-4 Getting a reference to an *SPWeb* through its parent *SPSite*.

```
using (SPSite site = new SPSite("http://devbook.sp2010.local/")) {
    Console.WriteLine("Current Site URL: {0}", site.Url);

    using (SPWeb web = site.OpenWeb("SampleSubSite")) {
        Console.WriteLine(web.Title);
    }
}
```

Listing 3-4 uses the *SPSite.OpenWeb* method, which has the following overloads:

```
public SPWeb OpenWeb();
public SPWeb OpenWeb(Guid gWebId);
public SPWeb OpenWeb(string strUrl);
public SPWeb OpenWeb(string strUrl, bool requireExactUrl);
```

The first overload opens the lowest-level website, as defined by the URL provided to the constructor of the current Site Collection. For example, if you created the *SPSite* instance using the root site URL, you will get a reference to the root website. In contrast, if you created the *SPSite* instance using a child website URL, you will get a reference to that website. The second overload opens the website using its unique ID. The two last overloads accept the relative URL of the website, which must be exact for the last overload if the *requireExactUrl* argument is *true*.

You can use an *SPWeb* reference to navigate the contents of the website, or simply to read or change its configuration. You will learn how to manage website contents later in this chapter. Table 3-2 lists some of the main members of the *SPWeb* type.

TABLE 3-2 Some of the Members of the *SPWeb* Type

Member Name	Description
AllowUnsafeUpdates	Property to get or set whether to accept updates via HTTP GET or without validating POSTed data security. Setting this property to a value of *true* reduces the security of the website. For further details on this, read the "Common and Best Practices" section, on page 72.
AllUsers	Collection property that holds references to all the users who are members of the website, or who have browsed to the site as authenticated members of a domain group in the site. For further details about users and groups, see Chapter 21, "Authentication and Authorization Infrastructure."
CheckPermissions	Checks whether the current user has a specific set of permissions. Throws an exception in case of failure.
ContentTypes	Collection property for enumerating all the content types in the website.
Delete	This method deletes the current website.

Member Name	Description
EventReceivers	Collection property that holds references to all the event receivers of the website. For more information, refer to Chapter 12 "Event Receivers."
Features	Collection property by which you can enumerate the features associated with the current website. For more information, see Chapter 8.
Fields	Collection property by which you can enumerate all the site columns of the website.
Files	Collection property that holds references to all the files in the root directory of the website.
Folders	Collection property that holds references to all the first-level folders of the website.
GetFile	This method returns a file, based on its GUID or URL.
GetFolder	This method returns a folder, based on its GUID or URL.
GetRecycleBinItems	This is a method that allows querying the current content of the Recycle Bin.
GetSiteData	A method to query for list items across multiple lists and multiple *SPWeb* instances within a Site Collection. It returns a *System.Data. DataTable* of ADO.NET.
GetUserEffectivePermissions	This method returns the effective permissions for a specified username.
Groups	Collection property by which you can enumerate all the groups of the website. For more information about users and groups, see Chapter 21.
ID	Read-only property that represents the ID of the current website.
Lists	Collection property by which you can enumerate all the lists of the website.
RecycleBin	Collection property by which you can enumerate the items currently in the Recycle Bin of the current website.
Site	Property for referencing the parent Site Collection.
SiteUsers	Collection property that holds references to all the users of the current Site Collection. For more information about users and groups, see Chapter 21.
Title	Property to get or set the title of the website.
Update	This method saves any changes applied to the website to the database.
Users	Collection property containing references to all the users with explicitly assigned permissions in the current website. For more information about users and groups, see Chapter 21.

One of the most interesting members of this type is the *Update* method. While working with the Server Object Model, you are reading and changing an in-memory representation of the current object. Thus, any changes you make will not be applied to the database unless you explicitly request the object to persist its state using the *Update* method. Of course, if you change an in-memory *SPWeb* instance and do not invoke the *Update* method, your changes will be lost. This behavior is common for many types in the Server Object Model.

Listing 3-5 shows an example that modifies the *Title* property of the current website, and then invokes the *Update* method to confirm the action.

LISTING 3-5 Modifying the *Title* of an *SPWeb*.

```
using (SPSite site = new SPSite("http://devbook.sp2010.local/")) {
    Console.WriteLine("Current Site URL: {0}", site.Url);

    using (SPWeb web = site.OpenWeb("SampleSubSite")) {
        web.Title = web.Title + " - Changed by code!";
        web.Update();
    }
}
```

SPList and *SPListItem*

Quite often you open an *SPSite* and one of its child *SPWeb* instances to gain access to the contents of one or more lists. The Server Object Model offers a two types that target the concept of SharePoint lists and list items: *SPList* and *SPListItem*. *SPList* corresponds to a single list instance, whether that is a list of items or a document library. *SPListItem* defines a reference to a specific item of a list. In general, you open the list to extract one or more items, and then work with those items. Listing 3-6 shows an example that obtains a reference to a list and then browses its items.

LISTING 3-6 Browsing the items contained in an *SPList* of an *SPWeb*.

```
using (SPSite site = new SPSite("http://devbook.sp2010.local/")) {
    Console.WriteLine("Current Site URL: {0}", site.Url);

    using (SPWeb web = site.OpenWeb()) {
        SPList list = web.Lists["DevLeap Customers"];

        foreach (SPListItem item in list.Items) {
            Console.WriteLine(item.Title);
        }
    }
}
```

Listing 3-6 extracts an *SPList* object by using the *Lists* indexer of the current *SPWeb* instance, which uses the list *Title* as a key. Then it enumerates the contents of the *Items* collection property of the list instance. The *SPList* type offers a rich set of members. In Table 3-3, you can see an excerpt of those members.

TABLE 3-3 **Some of the Members of the *SPList* Type**

Member Name	Description
AddItem	This method creates a new item in the current list.
BreakRoleInheritance	Method that breaks inheritance of role assignments for the current list and eventually copies role assignments from the parent website.
CheckPermissions	Checks whether the current user has a specific set of permissions. Throws an exception if the call fails.
ContentTypes	Collection property containing all the content types in the list.
Delete	Deletes the current list.
DoesUserHavePermissions	Checks whether the current user has a specific permission. Returns a *Boolean* value.
EventReceivers	Collection property containing all the event receivers of the website. For further details about event receivers, see Chapter 12.
Fields	Collection property containing all the fields and/or site columns in the current list.
Folders	Collection property containing all the folders, if any, in the current list.
GetItemById	Method to get an item by using its unique numeric *ID*.
GetItems	Method with multiple overloads, used to get a subset of items. You will see more about this in the next section, "Lists and Items."
Hidden	Property that hides or shows the current list.
ID	Read-only property that represents the *ID* of the current list.
ItemCount	Read-only *Int32* property that returns the number of items contained in the current list, including folders.
Items	Collection property containing the items in the current list.
RootFolder	Read-only property that returns the root folder of the list.
SchemaXml	Read-only *String* property that describes the list schema in XML, using CAMLcode (see the Note following this table), of the currently selected list.
Title	Property to get or set the list title.
Update	Saves any pending list changes to the database.

> **Note** CAML stands for "Collaborative Application Markup Language." This is an XML-based querying language that is useful for defining filtering, sorting, and grouping on SharePoint data. The CAML language reference is available on MSDN at *http://msdn.microsoft.com/en-us/library/ ms467521(office.14).aspx*

Just as with the *SPWeb* type, the *SPList* class also provides an *Update* method that saves any changes applied in-memory. Using the Server Object Model, you can browse the contents of existing lists, or you can create new lists from scratch and populate them with fresh new items. Whether you create new items or browse for existing ones, you must manage them as *SPListItem* instances. Table 3-4 shows some of the main members of the *SPListItem* type.

TABLE 3-4 **Some of the Members of the *SPListItem* Type**

Member Name	Description
Attachments	Collection property containing the attachments, if any, of the current item.
BreakRoleInheritance	Method that breaks inheritance of role assignments for the current item and eventually copies role assignments from the parent list.
CheckPermissions	Checks whether the current user has a specific set of permissions. Throws an exception if the call fails.
ContentType	Read-only property that returns a reference to the content type associated with the current item.
ContentTypeId	Read-only property that returns the ID of the content type associated with the current item.
Copy	Static method to copy an item from one location to another, within the same server. The method has a couple of overloads.
CopyFrom	Overwrites the current item with a source item provided as a URL from the same server.
CopyTo	Overwrites the target item, provided as a URL on the same server, with the current item.
Delete	Deletes the current item.
DoesUserHavePermissions	Checks whether the current user has a specific permission. Returns a *Boolean* value.
File	Read-only property that returns a reference to the file that corresponds to the current item, when the item resides in a Document Library.
Folder	Read-only property that returns a reference to the folder associated with the current item, when the item is a folder item.
ID	Read-only property that represents the *ID* of the current item.
Recycle	Deletes the current item, putting it into the Recycle Bin.
SystemUpdate	Saves any changes applied to the current item without affecting the Modified and the Modified By fields, and optionally the item version.
Title	Gets the item title.
Update	Saves any pending changes applied to the current item.
UpdateOverwriteVersion	Saves any changes applied to the current item without creating a new version of the item.
Url	Read-only property that returns the site-relative URL of the current item.
Versions	Collection property containing the version history for the current item.
Workflows	Collection property containing the workflows running on the current item.
Xml	Read-only property that returns the current item as an XML fragment, using an XMLDATA (*<z:row />*) format.

Later in this chapter, the section "Lists and Items" on page 83 shows how you can leverage some of these members in realistic scenarios.

SPDocumentLibrary and *SPFile*

Whenever you use an *SPList* instance, which corresponds to a document library, you can cast that instance to an *SPDocumentLibrary* type. This type represents a document library, which is almost the same as the base *SPList*, but has a small set of more specific members related to file handling. As an example, an *SPDocumentLibrary* object provides a collection property through which you can enumerate all the currently checked-out files. When you need to enumerate the files contained in a document library, you can browse the *SPListItem* elements of the list, accessing their *File* property, which is of type *SPFile*. Listing 3-7 shows some sample code that browses the files of a document library and displays their name and size in bytes.

LISTING 3-7 Browsing the files contained in an *SPDocumentLibrary* of an *SPWeb*.

```
using (SPSite site = new SPSite("http://devbook.sp2010.local/")) {

    Console.WriteLine("Current Site URL: {0}", site.Url);

    using (SPWeb web = site.OpenWeb()) {
        SPDocumentLibrary docLibrary = web.Lists["Shared Documents"] as
          SPDocumentLibrary;

        foreach (SPListItem item in docLibrary.Items) {
            Console.WriteLine("{0} - {1}",
                item.File.Name,
                item.File.Length);
        }
    }
}
```

The *SPFile* class offers a rich set of members, as shown in Table 3-5.

TABLE 3-5 Some of the Members of the *SPFile* Type

Member Name	Description
Approve	Approves a file submitted for content approval.
CheckedOutByUser	Read-only property that returns a reference to the *SPUser* for the user who checked out the file.
CheckIn	Checks in the current file.
CheckOut	Checks out the current file.
CheckOutType	Read-only property that returns the check-out status type for the current file. The possible values are defined in the *SPCheckOutType* enumeration: *Online*, *Offline*, and *None*.

Member Name	Description
CopyTo	Copies the current file to a specified destination URL within the same site, overwriting the target, if it exists. There are two overloads.
Delete	Deletes the current file.
Deny	Deny approval for a file submitted for content approval.
Length	Read-only property that returns the size in bytes (*long*) of the current file. When the file is a page, the property excludes the size of any Web Parts used in the page.
Lock	Applies a lock on the current file, preventing other users from modifying it.
LockedByUser	Read-only property that returns a reference to the *SPUser* for the user who locked the file.
MoveTo	Moves the current file to a specified destination URL within the same site, overwriting the target, if it exists. There are four overloads.
Name	Read-only property that returns the file name.
OpenBinary	Reads the file's content into a *Byte* array. There are two overloads.
OpenBinaryStream	Reads the file's content as a *Stream*. There are three overloads.
Publish	Submits the file for content approval.
Recycle	Deletes the current file, putting it into the Recycle Bin.
SaveBinary	Saves the contents of the current file, using a *Stream* or a *Byte* array. There are seven overloads.
Title	Gets or sets the file title.
UndoCheckOut	Undo the current check-out process for a file.
Update	Saves any changes applied to the current file.
Url	Read-only property that returns the site-relative URL of the current item.
Versions	Collection property containing the version history for the current item.

In the section, "Document Libraries and Files," on page 92, you will see how to use some of these members to manage files stored in SharePoint.

SPGroup, *SPUser*, and Other Security Types

Another set of useful types for developing real solutions are the *SPGroup* and *SPUser* classes. These correspond to a group and a SharePoint user, respectively, and both inherit from *SPPrincipal*. This last type ultimately inherits from *SPMember*. From a security point of view, a set of permissions is assigned to an *SPPrincipal* using an *SPRoleAssignment* class. Thus, you can configure permissions equivalently for a user or for a group, using the same classes and syntax. An *SPRoleAssignment* maps an *SPPrincipal* to an *SPRoleDefinition*. The *SPRoleDefinition* is the type that defines a SharePoint permission level. In Part VI of this book, "Security Infrastructure," you will explore how SharePoint security works internally; for now all you need is a high-level overview of these types. For example, Listing 3-8 shows how to enumerate role assignments and role definitions.

LISTING 3-8 Browse role assignments and definitions for an *SPWeb*.

```
using (SPSite site = new SPSite("http://devbook.sp2010.local/")) {
    Console.WriteLine("Current Site URL: {0}", site.Url);

    using (SPWeb web = site.OpenWeb()) {
        foreach (SPRoleAssignment ra in web.RoleAssignments) {
            Console.WriteLine("=> Member Name: {0}", ra.Member.Name);

            foreach (SPRoleDefinition rd in ra.RoleDefinitionBindings) {
                Console.WriteLine("Permissions: {0}", rd.BasePermissions);
            }
        }
    }
}
```

When you target an *SPUser* object with a custom *SPRoleAssignment*, you will probably find the list of the main members of the *SPUser* type useful. You can see the most important members in Table 3-6.

TABLE 3-6 Some of the Members of the *SPUser* Type

Member Name	Description
Alerts	Collection property containing any alerts configured by the user.
Email	Gets or sets the user's e-mail address.
Groups	Collection property containing the groups to which the user belongs.
ID	Read-only property that returns the user member ID (inherited from *SPMember*, through *SPPrincipal*).
IsSiteAdmin	Read-only property that returns *true* if the current user is a Site Collection Administrator.
LoginName	Read-only property that returns the login name of the user.
Name	Property to get or set the display name of the user.
RawSid	Read-only property to get the raw binary Security ID (SID) of the user, in case he is a Windows's user.
Sid	Read-only property to get the Security ID (SID) of the user, in case he is a Windows's user.
Update	Method to save any changes applied to the current user.
UserToken	Read-only property to get a reference to the *SPUserToken* of the current authentication process. It can be used to create an *SPSite* instance in order to impersonate the user, as you have already seen at the beginning of this chapter.
Xml	Read-only property to get the current user as an XML fragment.

If you are targeting an *SPGroup* instance, you can find its main members explained in Table-3-7.

TABLE 3-7 **Some of the Members of the *SPGroup* Type**

Member Name	Description
AddUser	Method to add an *SPUser* to the current *SPGroup*.
Description	Property to get or set the description of the group.
ID	Read-only property to get the group member ID (inherited from *SPMember*, through *SPPrincipal*).
Name	Property to get or set the display name of the group.
RemoveUser	Method to remove an *SPUser* from the current *SPGroup*.
Update	Method to save any changes applied to the current group.
Users	Property that allows enumerating the users belonging to the current group.
Xml	Read-only property to get the current group as an XML fragment.

These classes can be used to make authorization checks by code, or for users and groups management automation. For example, you can add a user to a group inside a custom workflow activity written using these classes. In the section, "Groups and Users," on page 97, you will see how to write this code.

SPControl and *SPContext*

One last group of types provided by the Server Object Model of SharePoint consists of some infrastructural classes such as *SPControl* and *SPContext*. The *SPControl* type is defined in the *Microsoft.SharePoint.WebControls* namespace. It is the base class for many SharePoint server controls, and it helps when developing web controls or Web Parts. You will see it in action in Chapter 6 and Chapter 7. Aside from its base class role, *SPControl* provides a small set of static methods, the most useful of which let you retrieve a reference to the current *SPSite*, *SPWeb*, or *SPWebApplication*. Here are the signatures of these methods:

```
public static SPModule GetContextModule(HttpContext context);
public static SPSite GetContextSite(HttpContext context);
public static SPWeb GetContextWeb(HttpContext context);
public static SPWebApplication GetContextWebApplication(HttpContext context);
```

All of these methods require an *HttpContext* object instance as their sole input argument.

Another way of obtaining a reference to the current *SPSite* and *SPWeb* is to use the *SPContext* class, which provides a static property named *Current* that references the current SharePoint context. The current *SPContext* gives you direct access to all the most useful information about the current request. Table 3-8 shows the main members offered.

TABLE 3-8 **Some of the Members of the *SPContext* Type**

Member Name	Description
ContextPageInfo	Read-only property that contains information about the current list item (permissions, list ID and list item ID, and so on) for the current request.
File	Read-only property that returns a reference to the *SPFile*, if any, corresponding to the *SPListItem* served by the current request.
IsDesignTime	Read-only *Boolean* property to check whether the current request is running at design-time.
IsPopUI	Read-only *Boolean* property to check whether the current request is for a pop-up dialog.
Item	Read-only property that returns either a reference to the *SPListItem* determined by the specified list and item ID, or to the *SPItem* object set when the context is created.
ItemId	Read-only property to get the ID (*Int32*) of the list item associated with the current context.
List	Read-only property that returns a reference to the *SPList* associated with the current context.
ListId	Read-only property that returns the ID (GUID) of the list associated with the current context.
ListItem	Read-only property that returns a reference to the *SPListItem* associated with the current context.
RegionalSettings	Read-only property that returns the regional settings of the current request context.
ResetItem	Method that forces a refresh of the current item. Internally, the method reloads the in-memory cached item from the content database.
Site	Read-only property that returns a reference to the *SPSite* object corresponding to the Site Collection of the current request context.
Web	Read-only property that returns a reference to the *SPWeb* object corresponding to the website of the current request context.

Common and Best Practices

You will utilize the types discussed in the previous section, together with many others, throughout this book and in your real-world SharePoint solutions. However, it is very important to use them correctly. The goal of this section is to share some thoughts and provide some best practices so that you can profitably use the Server Object Model.

Disposing Resources

The first and most important hint you need to know is how to correctly release resources while working with objects of the Server Object Model. In fact, .NET framework has a concept concerning "non deterministic" release of allocated managed objects, based on the Garbage Collector, provided by the Common Language Runtime. Whenever you create an instance of a managed type, when it is no longer used, the Garbage Collector will automatically release the memory allocated. However, the Garbage Collector will release that memory at a non deterministic (unpredictable) point in time. When the managed object holds references to unmanaged resources—such as window handles, files, streams, database connections, sockets, and so forth—these unmanaged resources will be released only when the Garbage Collector collects memory. When such unmanaged resources are scarce, critical, happen to lock physical resources, or use a large amount of unmanaged memory, it's better to release them as soon as possible rather than waiting for the .NET Garbage Collector. To accomplish this goal, the .NET Framework infrastructure provides the *IDisposable* interface, which exposes a *Dispose* method that you should call to explicitly release these unmanaged resources. Here's the definition of the *IDisposable* interface:

```
public interface IDisposable {
    void Dispose();
}
```

There are many patterns for implementing *IDisposable*; however, it is beyond the scope of this book to give you full coverage of this topic.

> **More Information** To dig deeper into the Common Language Runtime and Garbage Collector internals, I recommend that you read Jeffrey Richter's book, *CLR via C#* (Microsoft Press, 2010; ISBN: 978-0-7356-2704-8), available at *http://oreilly.com/catalog/9780735627048/*.

For now, suffice it to know that, whenever a .NET type implements the *IDisposable* interface, you should invoke the *Dispose* method as soon as you no longer need the object. Calling *Dispose* lets you release unmanaged resources in a deterministic manner, decoupling the non-deterministic managed memory release performed by the Garbage Collector from the explicit manual release of unmanaged resources.

To invoke *Dispose*, you should adopt a standard technique, such as one of the following: use the *using* keyword; use a *try/finally* code block; or explicitly invoke the *Dispose* method. Listing 3-9 shows a code excerpt that takes advantage of the *using* keyword.

LISTING 3-9 Employing the *using* keyword while working with an *SPSite* instance to ensure timely disposal of unmanaged resources.

```
using (SPSite site = new SPSite("http://devbook.sp2010.local/")) {
    // Work with the SPSite object
}
```

The compiler converts the *using* keyword into a *try/finally* code block, such as the one in Listing 3-10.

LISTING 3-10 Using the *try/finally* block while working with an *SPSite* instance to ensure timely disposal of unmanaged resources.

```
SPSite site = null;
try {
    site = new SPSite("http://devbook.sp2010.local/");

    // Work with the SPSite object
}
finally {
    if (site != null)
        site.Dispose();
}
```

If you need to catch exceptions that might occur while working with disposable objects, wrap the *using* block or the *try/finally* block with an external *try/catch* block, as shown in Listing 3-11.

LISTING 3-11 Wrapping the *using* block in an external *try/catch* block while working with an *SPSite* instance so it can handle any exceptions.

```
try {
    using (SPSite site = new SPSite("http://devbook.sp2010.local/")) {
        // Work with the SPSite object
    }
}
catch (SPException ex) {
    // Handle exception
}
```

Writing code this way ensures that any unmanaged resources will be released as soon as they are no longer needed. It also ensures that exceptions can be handled without overloading the environment.

You should apply this technique even when using objects from the SharePoint Server Object Model. For example, the *SPSite* and *SPWeb* types both implement the *IDisposable* interface, and both allocate unmanaged memory. If you do not correctly release *SPSite* and *SPWeb* instances, you will probably experience memory leaks, crashes, and frequent application pool recycles because of extra (and unnecessary) memory consumption.

However, you must also be careful, because you should dispose these types only when you have created them. For example Listing 3-12 illustrates a situation in which you *should not* dispose of an *SPSite* instance.

LISTING 3-12 *Incorrect* object disposal through the *using* keyword.

```
try {
    using (SPSite site = SPControl.GetContextSite(HttpContext.Current)) {
        // Work with the SPSite object
    }
}
catch (SPException ex) {
    // Handle exception
}
```

In Listing 3-12, the *SPSite* instance is retrieved from the request context through the *SPControl* type; thus, you didn't create it—it's created by the internal SharePoint Foundation code. This means you are not responsible for disposing of it. The same logic applies to *SPSite* or *SPWeb* references retrieved from the current *SPContext*. In contrast, Listing 3-13 shows you the correct way to write the code.

LISTING 3-13 The correct way to handle objects that do not need to be disposed explicitly.

```
try {
    SPSite site = SPControl.GetContextSite(HttpContext.Current);
    // Work with the SPSite object
}
catch (SPException ex) {
    // Handle exception
}
```

For situations in which you create both *SPSite* and *SPWeb* instances within the same code excerpt, you should employ nested *using* keywords, as you will see in many examples in this chapter (for example, see Listing 3-8).

Keep in mind that if you are browsing a collection of *SPWeb* items—for example, enumerating the *AllWebs* property of an *SPSite* object—you are responsible for releasing each single *SPWeb* instance, as exemplified in Listing 3-14.

LISTING 3-14 Object disposal while iterating collections.

```
try {
    using (SPSite site = new SPSite("http://devbook.sp2010.local/")) {
        // Work with the SPSite object
        foreach (SPWeb web in site.AllWebs) {
            using (web) {
                // Work with the SPWeb object
            }
        }
    }
}
catch (SPException ex) {
    // Handle exception
}
```

Furthermore, there are types that internally create instances of *SPSite* or *SPWeb* that you'll need to dispose of explicitly. For example, the *SPWebPartManager* and the *SPLimitedWebPartManager* classes internally use an *SPWeb* instance that must be disposed. These types all implement *IDisposable,* so you should handle them almost the same way as you do the *SPSite* and *SPWeb* types.

Finally, to check whether your code has been implemented correctly against these coding rules, you can use the free downloadable SharePoint Dispose Checker Tool (available at *http://code.msdn.microsoft.com/SPDisposeCheck*).

Handling Exceptions

A perennially interesting area when developing software solutions is that of exception handling, to intercept code failures. The SharePoint Server Object Model provides a base class named *SPException*, which is the default exception thrown by the SharePoint Server Object Model and is also the type from which almost every specific SharePoint exception inherits.

While handling exceptions consider these suggestions. First, catch and handle only those exceptions that you anticipate and can manage. In other words, you should avoid simply catching all exceptions using a *catch all* block, or an empty *catch* block. That way, when an exception that you don't anticipate occurs, it will bubble up to higher-level code that is able to handle it, if any exists. If the exception is unexpected through the entire stack of the current request, it's best to let the software crash—of course, you would inform the end user and possibly automatically alert technical support. That is exactly what SharePoint does by default for unhandled exceptions. Figure 3-2 shows the default error message that SharePoint pops up when an unexpected error occurs.

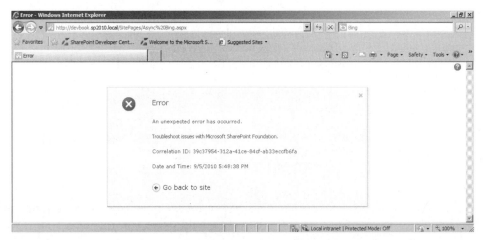

FIGURE 3-2 The default message box that SharePoint 2010 displays when an unexpected error occurs.

The Correlation ID (GUID) shown in the message box refers to the current request context, which you can use to search for the exception in the SharePoint log.

> **More Information** The default location for the Microsoft SharePoint 2010 log is in the SharePoint14_Root\LOGS folder. You can search the log manually using any basic text editor. Alternatively, the log is compatible with the free ULS Viewer, which you can download from *http://code.msdn.microsoft.com/Project/Download/FileDownload.aspx?ProjectName=ULSViewer& DownloadId=7482*.

You want to search for a row of type *Unexpected* that contains the Correlation ID from the error dialog at the end of the row. That's where you can find the unhandled exception details and stack trace.

If you do decide that you want to avoid the default message box and catch unexpected exceptions with code of your own, you will probably still want to log/trace the exception by yourself. To do that read the SharePoint Guidance document, "Developing Applications for SharePoint 2010," which is available on MSDN at *http://msdn.microsoft.com/en-us/library/ ff650022.aspx*. The SharePoint 2010 Guidance provides a set of documents and classes useful for writing enterprise-level solutions based on SharePoint 2010. One group of types provides exception-logging features, using a Service Locator Pattern to resolve the location of the logging engine, through a dependency injection pattern. Listing 3-15 shows how to manage an unexpected exception by utilizing this library.

LISTING 3-15 Using the logging types provided by the SharePoint 2010 Guidance.

```
try {
    using (SPSite site = new SPSite("http://devbook.sp2010.local/")) {
        // Work with the SPSite object
        foreach (SPWeb web in site.AllWebs) {
            using (web) {
                // Work with the SPWeb object
            }
        }
    }
}
catch (SPException ex) {
    // Handle exception
    ILogger logger = SharePointServiceLocator.Current.GetInstance<ILogger>();
    logger.LogToOperations(ex);
}
```

Listing 3-15 illustrates that the *SharePointServiceLocator* type resolves the currently configured logger engine, which implements the *and*, and returns it to you, ready to log the exception using the *LogToOperations* method.

Transactions

Working within a transactional environment when manipulating data is a common application need. However, the SharePoint data engine and the SharePoint Server Object Model are not transactional, so you cannot rely on them to build a transactional system. In fact, SharePoint is *not a DBMS*! Data you store in SharePoint lists should not be critical, and should not require a transactional environment. If you do need to store information in SharePoint using a kind of transactional behavior, you need something like a compensatable system. For example, you can use a Windows Workflow Foundation 3.x workflow that makes use of a *CompensatableSequence* activity. Let's see what that means in concrete terms.

> **More Information** For further details about Windows Workflow Foundation, read the chapters dedicated to Workflows in Part V of this book, "Developing Workflows."

Whenever you invoke the *Update* method for a Server Object Model object (such as an *SPListItem*), SharePoint will update the corresponding data in the Content Database. If you change two or more items and you want to update either all or none of them, you will need to keep track of such changes yourself (in case you need to revert back to the original values if the process fails) because SharePoint doesn't provide support for this.. The same is true when you need to update some data on SharePoint and some other data using an external resource manager, such as a DBMS. If you update the SharePoint Content Database first, and then the DBMS update fails, you will need to manually restore the original content values on the SharePoint side, using some custom code.

You might see this behavior as a serious issue. However, if you must have transactional support while managing data stored in SharePoint, you should probably ask yourself whether SharePoint is truly the appropriate place to store that data. And of course, the answer would be "no." In such critical cases, you need a transactional DBMS instead. However, you can still use SharePoint to present such data to end users by taking advantage of Business Connectivity Services and External Lists for this purpose.

> **More Information** For further details about Business Connectivity Services, see Chapter 25, "Business Connectivity Services."

AllowUnsafeUpdates and *FormDigest*

Another topic of which you should be aware is this: to avoid cross-site scripting issues, SharePoint applies a security check whenever you change data through the Server Object Model during HTTP requests. In fact, by default, SharePoint web forms use a form digest control to enforce security. The form digest is a hidden field *POST*ed by SharePoint web forms and checked by the security infrastructure on the server. When you make changes to objects by using the Server Object Model during an HTTP *GET* request, this input field will be missing, so by default SharePoint will throw an exception that looks like this excerpt:

```
Microsoft.SharePoint.SPException: The security validation for this page is invalid.
```

Similarly, if you send an HTTP *POST* request with a missing or invalid form digest value, you will receive the same error. This behavior applies only during HTTP requests. Therefore, when you reference the Server Object Model in a class library or a batch tool that runs outside of the ASP.NET pipeline, the security check will not occur. In fact, the check process looks for the *HttpContext.Current* variable; if it is *null* the digest validation will not occur.

With that in mind, if you are developing a webpage that will respond to HTTP *GET* requests, or a custom web form page that doesn't inherit from the *WebPartPage* type and doesn't use the Form Digest control, you will need to instruct SharePoint to skip the digest validation; otherwise, your code will not work.

To instruct SharePoint to skip the validation, set the *Boolean AllowUnsafeUpdates* property of the current *SPSite* or *SPWeb* to *true*. Listing 3-16 shows an example.

LISTING 3-16 Using the *AllowUnsafeUpdates* property of the *SPWeb* type to skip a security check.

```
SPWeb web = SPContext.Current.Web
SPList list = web.Lists["DevLeap Customers"];

try {
    web.AllowUnsafeUpdates = true;

    list.Title = list.Title + " - Changed!";
    list.Update();
}
finally {
    web.AllowUnsafeUpdates = false;
}
```

The code in Listing 3-16 works with an *SPWeb* instance provided by the current *SPContext*. It sets the *AllowUnsafeUpdates* property to *true* before changing an *SPList* instance property and then resets the property to *false* (its default value) just after invoking the *SPList.Update* method. To ensure that the *AllowUnsafeUpdates* property always reverts to its original value, the code uses a *try/finally* code block.

Conversely, when you develop a custom ASPX page, and you *want* to exploit the security environment provided by SharePoint, you have a couple of choices: you can inherit from *WebPartPage*, or manually include a *FormDigest* control in your page. In the first case you simply need to inherit from the *Microsoft.SharePoint.WebPartPages.WebPartPage* base class, which internally renders a *FormDigest* control. Then, in your code, you call the utility method *SPUtility.ValidateFormDigest()* to check the digest when you *POST* the page back to the server. In the latter case you need to include the *Microsoft.SharePoint. WebControls.FormDigest* control in your page(s), and you still need to invoke the *SPUtility. ValidateFormDigest()* method to check the digest.

Of course, in a custom ASPX page, you could also invalidate the security check by setting the *AllowUnsafeUpdates* property to *true*. However, that would be both an unsecure behavior and a poor practice.

Real-Life Examples

The purpose of this section is to give you some concrete examples from real-life solutions that illustrate how to work with SharePoint Server Object Model types. The examples are divided into groups, based on the target object and target goal. You should consider this section as an everyday reference for developing SharePoint solutions.

Creating a New Site Collection

This first example shows how to create a new Site Collection in code (see Listing 3-17).

LISTING 3-17 Creating a new Site Collection.

```
using (SPSite rootSite = new SPSite("http://devbook.sp2010.local/")) {
    SPWebApplication webApplication = rootSite.WebApplication;

    using (SPSite newSiteCollection = webApplication.Sites.Add(
        "sites/CreatedByCode", // Site URL
        "Created by Code", // Site Collection Title
        "Sample Site Collection Created by Code", // Site Collection Description
        1033, // LCID
        "STS#0", // Web Site Template
        "SP2010DEV\\PaoloPi", // Owner Login
        "Paolo Pialorsi", // Owner DisplayName
        "paolo@devleap.com", // Owner EMail
        "SP2010DEV\\MarcoR", // Secondary Contact Login
        "Marco Russo", // Secondary Contact DisplayName
        "marco@devleap.com", // Secondary Contact EMail
        "SP2010DEV\\SHAREPOINT", // Database Server Name for Content Database
        "WSS_Content_CreatedByCode", // Content Database Name
        null, // Database Login Name
        null // Database Login Password
        )) {
            Console.WriteLine("Created Site Collection: {0}",
                newSiteCollection.Url);
    }
}
```

Listing 3-17 utilizes the method of the *SPSiteCollection* type, to which you can get a reference from the *SPWebApplication.Sites* property. The method has many different overloads; the code excerpt uses one of the most complete signatures, which is as follows:

```
public SPSite Add(
    string siteUrl,
    string title,
    string description,
    uint nLCID,
    string webTemplate,
    string ownerLogin,
    string ownerName,
    string ownerEmail,
    string secondaryContactLogin,
    string secondaryContactName,
    string secondaryContactEmail,
    string databaseServer,
    string databaseName,
    string userName,
    string password
)
```

This example shows that you can define each and every detail of the Site Collection configuration, including the website Template name to use, and even assigning a dedicated Content Database. Table 3-9 lists some of the most common Web Site Template values.

TABLE 3-9 Some of the Most Common Web Site Template Names Available in SharePoint for Creating a New Site Collection

Site Template Name	Description
STS#0	Team Site
STS#1	Blank Site
STS#2	Document Workspace
MPS#0	Basic Meeting Workspace
MPS#1	Blank Meeting Workspace
MPS#2	Decision Meeting Workspace
MPS#3	Social Meeting Workspace
MPS#4	Multipage Meeting Workspace

Listing 3-17 assumes that the Site Collection (*http://devbook.sp2010.local/*) will allow you to create another Site Collection under the *"sites"* managed path of the parent web application. However, if you need to create a root Site Collection from scratch, you should retrieve a reference to the *SPWebApplication* through an *SPFarm* object.

Creating a New Website

After you have a Site Collection, at some point, you will probably need to create one or more websites in it. Listing 3-18 contains a code excerpt that leverages the *SPWebCollection.Add* method. The method also has many overloads. The following is the overload signature used in Listing 3-18.

```
public SPWeb Add(
    string strWebUrl,
    string strTitle,
    string strDescription,
    uint nLCID,
    string strWebTemplate,
    bool useUniquePermissions,
    bool bConvertIfThere
)
```

LISTING 3-18 Creating a new website.

```
using (SPSite site = new SPSite("http://devbook.sp2010.local/sites/CreatedByCode/")) {
    using (SPWeb newWeb = site.AllWebs.Add(
        "MyBlog", // Web Site Url
        "Blog Created By Code", // Web Site Title
        "Blogging Site Created By Code", // Web Site Description
        1033, // LCID
        "BLOG#0", // Web Site Template Name
        true,  // Use Unique Permissions
        false // Convert an existing folder
        )) {
            Console.WriteLine("New Web Site URL: {0}", newWeb.Url);
    }
}
```

While creating a website you can specify a Web Site Template name. Some of the available values for this argument are illustrated in Table 3-10.

TABLE 3-10 Some of the Web Site Template Names Available in SharePoint for Creating a New Website

Site Template Name	Description
STS#0	Team Site
STS#1	Blank Site
STS#2	Document Workspace
MPS#0	Basic Meeting Workspace
MPS#1	Blank Meeting Workspace
MPS#2	Decision Meeting Workspace

Site Template Name	Description
MPS#3	Social Meeting Workspace
MPS#4	Multipage Meeting Workspace
WIKI#0	Wiki
BLOG#0	Blog

Note the *Boolean useUniquePermissions* argument that's used in Listing 3-18. This is useful for specifying whether to inherit permissions from the parent Site Collection or whether the new site should have unique permissions. The *bConvertIfThere* argument is also interesting; when *true*, it instructs SharePoint to convert an existing folder into the child website; when *false*, it causes SharePoint to throw an exception if a folder already exists with the URL requested for the new website.

Of course, to be able to create a new website inside an existing Site Collection at all, you need to access the Server Object Model with a user account that has sufficient permissions.

Lists and Items

This section includes several examples related to managing lists and list items.

Creating a New List

To create a new List of items, you'd write code such as that in Listing 3-19, which creates a new list of Contacts.

LISTING 3-19 Creating a new List of Contacts in a website, and configuring the List properties.

```
using (SPSite site = new SPSite("http://devbook.sp2010.local/sites/CreatedByCode/")) {
    using (SPWeb web = site.OpenWeb()) {
        Guid newListId = web.Lists.Add(
            "Contacts", // List Title
            "Company's Contacts", // List Description
            SPListTemplateType.Contacts // List Template Type
            );

        SPList newList = web.Lists[newListId];
        newList.OnQuickLaunch = true;
        newList.ReadSecurity = 1; // All users have Read access to all items
        newList.WriteSecurity = 2; // Users can modify only items that they created
        newList.Update();

        Console.WriteLine("Created list: {0}", newList.Title);
    }
}
```

Listing 3-19 exploits the *SPListCollection.Add* method, using one specific overload that specifies the list template using an enumeration value. Here's the signature of the specific *Add* method used:

```
public virtual Guid Add(
    string title,
    string description,
    SPListTemplateType templateType
)
```

The *SPListTemplateType* enumeration defines more than fifty templates that cover the most common list scenarios. If you wish to create a list using a custom template, you can browse the *ListTemplates* property of the current *SPWeb* instance, selecting the corresponding *SPListTemplate* instance and using the following overload of the *SPListCollection.Add* method instead:

```
public virtual Guid Add(
    string title,
    string description,
    SPListTemplate template
)
```

All the overloads of the *SPListCollection.Add* method return a *Guid* value that corresponds to the *ID* of the just-created list. To configure the list you just created, you need to retrieve a reference to it using that *ID*. Listing 3-19 uses the *SPList* object to configure the list so that it will appear on the Quick Launch menu. It configures the default Item-Level permissions to let all users read every item but change only items that they created. You can see the result of this Item-Level Permissions configuration made through code in Figure 3-3.

Remember, as soon as you have finished configuring any object from the Server Object Model, you must invoke the *Update* method to confirm the changes.

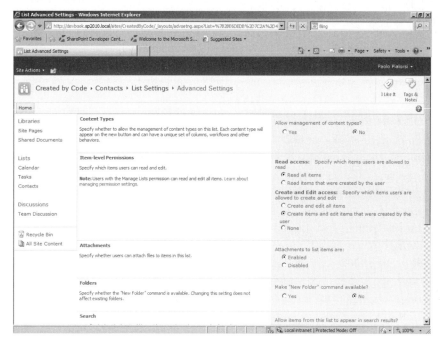

FIGURE 3-3 Item-Level Permissions resulting from the code in Listing 3-19.

Creating a New List Item

After creating a list, you will probably want to populate it with new items. The code in Listing 3-20 adds a new Contact item to the list created in Listing 3-19.

LISTING 3-20 Populating a List with new items.

```
using (SPSite site = new SPSite("http://devbook.sp2010.local/sites/CreatedByCode/")) {
    using (SPWeb web = site.OpenWeb()) {
        try {
            SPList list = web.Lists["Contacts"];

            try {
                SPListItem newItem = list.Items.Add();
                newItem["Last Name"] = "Pialorsi";
                newItem["First Name"] = "Paolo";
                newItem["E-mail Address"] = "paolo@devleap.it";
                newItem.Update();
            }
            catch (ArgumentException) {
                Console.WriteLine("Invalid Field Name!");
            }
```

```
        }
        catch (ArgumentException) {
            Console.WriteLine("Invalid List Title!");
        }
    }
}
```

Again, you need to invoke an *Add* method for the corresponding collection—in this case, an *SPListItemCollection*. The method returns a new *SPListItem* instance ready to be configured and updated against the Content Database. To be accurate, the *Add* method simply creates a new item configured according to the target list in terms of fields, content-type, and so on. However, despite its name, the *Add* method does not really add the item to the list; in fact, the new *SPListItem* instance has an *ID* with a value of zero (*0*). Only after you invoke the *Update* method of the item for the first time will it be inserted into the list and have a unique *ID* assigned. The code in Listing 3-20 configures three fields of the target item. The syntax you use to assign values to the fields uses each field's *DisplayName*; however, the indexer of an *SPListItem* lets you provide the *DisplayName*, the *Name*, the *StaticName* of the field, the unique *ID* of the field, which is useful when you are working with provisioned Site Columns, or the ordinal position (index) of the field within the *Fields* collection of the current item.

> **More Information** To better understand topics such as Site Columns, *DisplayName*, *Name*, *StaticName*, and so on, see Chapter 2, "Data Foundation," and Chapter 10, "Data Provisioning."

For completeness, the example code catches exceptions of type *ArgumentException*, just in case you provide an invalid list title or field name. In general, you should avoid writing list titles or field names in source code; instead, you should work with provisioned contents and their corresponding *IDs*. Using the *IDs* essentially eliminates the possibility of an invalid value at runtime (unless you make a typing mistake while writing the code)—but those types of issues should become apparent during testing, before the application ever reaches a production environment.

Modifying an Existing List Item

Another common task is modifying the metadata of an existing item. The procedure is similar to creating a new list item; the only difference is that you need to query the list to get a reference to the item that you want to update. The example in Listing 3-21 retrieves the item to update using its unique *ID*, via the *SPList.GetItemById* method.

LISTING 3-21 Modifying an existing item of a List.

```
using (SPSite site = new SPSite("http://devbook.sp2010.local/sites/CreatedByCode/")) {
    using (SPWeb web = site.OpenWeb()) {
        try {
            SPList list = web.Lists["Contacts"];
            SPListItem itemToChange = list.GetItemById(1);

            itemToChange["Last Name"] += " - Changed!";
            itemToChange.Update();
        }
        catch (ArgumentException) {
            Console.WriteLine("Invalid List Title or invalid List Item ID!");
        }
    }
}
```

Note that the *SPList.GetItemById* method retrieves the full item, with all its columns of meta-data. When you need to change just a few columns, it's best to retrieve only those specific columns. To do that, use the *SPList.GetItemByIdSelectedFields* method, which retrieves only the columns you specify. In this case, the line from which the example retrieves the item to change could be:

```
SPListItem itemToChange = list.GetItemByIdSelectedFields(1, "Last Name");
```

But the *SPList.GetItemByIdSelectedFields* method also accepts a list of fields to retrieve from the Content Database as a *params* array of *String*.

When you don't know the *ID* of the item that you want to update, you can use the SharePoint 2010 query engine—a topic we'll cover later in this chapter.

Concurrency Conflicts

Any server-side code has the potential to serve an unpredictable number of users, so changing data in a back-end DBMS carries the possibility of a concurrency conflict. Concurrency issues can also happen when working with data stored in SharePoint. Thus, due to the nature of SharePoint, which is a web-based product with (hopefully) a large number of concurrent users, it is highly probable that concurrency conflicts *will* arise while managing SharePoint's items. Fortunately, the SharePoint team provided a standard pattern for catching concurrency conflicts. Consider the example in Listing 3-22, which changes an *SPListItem* with two different concurrent sessions.

LISTING 3-22 A code excerpt showing how to catch concurrency in *SPListItem* management.

```
using (SPSite site = new SPSite("http://devbook.sp2010.local/sites/CreatedByCode/")) {
    using (SPWeb web = site.OpenWeb()) {
        try {
            SPList list = web.Lists["Contacts"];
            SPListItem itemToChange = list.GetItemById(1);

            itemToChange["Last Name"] += " - Changed!";

            // Before Update, simulate a concurrent change
            ChangeListItemConcurrently();

            itemToChange.Update();
        }
        catch (SPException ex) {
            Console.WriteLine(ex.Message);
        }
    }
}
```

When the code in Listing 3-22 invokes the *Update* method to save changes, a concurrency conflict exception will be raised because the *ChangeListItemConcurrently* procedure has already changed that item. The exception will be a *Microsoft.SharePoint.SPException* with this error message:

```
Save Conflict. Your changes conflict with those made concurrently by another user. If you
want your changes to be applied, click Back in your Web browser, refresh the page, and
resubmit your changes.
```

The error message is tightly tied to a web scenario ("... click Back in your Web browser ..."). However, the exception itself can be caught within any kind of software solution—even running on a SharePoint server. In order to solve this exception you must reload the *SPListItem* from the Content Database and then apply your changes again, just as a web user would do using his web browser.

Deleting an Existing List Item

Deleting an *SPListItem* is a common task, similar to inserting or updating items. The program flow for deleting an item is both simple and quick, as you can see in Listing 3-23.

LISTING 3-23 Deleting an *SPListItem* instance.

```
using (SPSite site = new SPSite("http://devbook.sp2010.local/sites/CreatedByCode/")) {
    using (SPWeb web = site.OpenWeb()) {
        SPList list = web.Lists["Contacts"];
        SPListItem itemToDelete = list.GetItemById(1);

        itemToDelete.Delete();
    }
}
```

You simply need to retrieve the *SPListItem* instance that corresponds to the item that you want to delete, and then invoke the *Delete* method (to permanently delete the item) or the *Recycle* method (to move the item into the Recycle Bin).

Querying for List Items

As previously discussed, retrieving an *SPListItem* by *ID* is an uncommon task, unless you have a custom ASPX page that receives the *ListID* and the *ListItemID* as *QueryString* parameters. More generally, you need to retrieve items from lists using a query that is based on the metadata of the items you want to extract. For example, considering the list of Contacts used in the previous examples, you might need to extract all Contacts whose e-mail address contains "@devleap.com." The Server Object Model provides a class named *SPQuery*, through which you can execute a CAML query against an *SPList* instance, to retrieve items corresponding to the query. Listing 3-24 shows an example.

> **Tip** If you don't like writing CAML queries, here's a free tool by U2U that you can download from *http://www.u2u.net/res/Tools/CamlQueryBuilder.aspx*. The tool targets SharePoint 2003 and was ported to SharePoint 2007. However, it also works correctly with SharePoint 2010.

LISTING 3-24 Querying an *SPList* using an *SPQuery* object.

```
using (SPSite site = new SPSite("http://devbook.sp2010.local/sites/CreatedByCode/")) {
    using (SPWeb web = site.OpenWeb()) {
        SPList list = web.Lists["Contacts"];

        SPQuery query = new SPQuery();

        // Define columns to retrieve
        query.ViewFields = "<FieldRef Name=\"Title\" />
            <FieldRef Name=\"FirstName\" /><FieldRef Name=\"Email\" />";

        // Force retrieving only the selected columns
        query.ViewFieldsOnly = true;

        // Define the query
        query.Query = "<Where><Contains><FieldRef Name=\"Email\" />
        <Value Type=\"Text\">@devleap.com</Value></Contains></Where>";

        // Define the maximum number of results for each page (like a SELECT TOP)
        query.RowLimit = 10;
```

```
        // Query for items
        SPListItemCollection items = list.GetItems(query);
        foreach (SPListItem item in items) {
            Console.WriteLine("{0} {1} - {2}",
                item["First Name"],
                item["Last Name"],
                item["E-mail Address"]);
        }
    }
}
```

Listing 3-24 configures some of the properties of the *SPQuery* type, the most important of which is the *Query* argument, which contains the CAML code. However, there are other properties that are even more fundamental for performance, such as the *ViewFields* property, which returns only specifically referenced columns, and thus avoids forcing the server to retrieve useless columns. The previous example marks the *ViewFieldsOnly* property as *true*. There is also the *RowLimit* property that supports partitioning of data results, such as for paging results. Listing 3-25 shows how to take advantage of the *RowLimit* property together with the *SPQuery.ListItemCollectionPosition* property to page results in blocks of five items for each page.

LISTING 3-25 Querying an *SPList* using an *SPQuery* with paging.

```
using (SPSite site = new SPSite("http://devbook.sp2010.local/sites/CreatedByCode/")) {
    using (SPWeb web = site.OpenWeb()) {
        SPList list = web.Lists["Contacts"];

        SPQuery query = new SPQuery();

        // Define columns to retrieve
        query.ViewFields = "<FieldRef Name=\"Title\" />
            <FieldRef Name=\"FirstName\" /><FieldRef Name=\"Email\" />";

        // Force retrieving only the selected columns
        query.ViewFieldsOnly = true;

        // Define the query
        query.Query = "<Where><Contains><FieldRef Name=\"Email\" />
        <Value Type=\"Text\">@domain.com</Value></Contains></Where>";

        // Define the maximum number of results for each page (like a SELECT TOP)
        query.RowLimit = 5;

        Int32 pageIndex = 1;
        Int32 itemIndex = 1;
```

```
      do {
          Console.WriteLine("Current Page: {0}", pageIndex);

          // Query for items
          SPListItemCollection items = list.GetItems(query);

          foreach (SPListItem item in items) {
              Console.WriteLine("{0} - {1} {2} - {3}",
                  itemIndex,
                  item["First Name"],
                  item["Last Name"],
                  item["E-mail Address"]);
              itemIndex++;
          }

          // Set current position to make SPQuery able
          // to set the start item of the next page
          query.ListItemCollectionPosition =
              items.ListItemCollectionPosition;
          pageIndex++;
      } while (query.ListItemCollectionPosition != null);
  }
}
```

When you execute the code in Listing 3-25 against a list of Contacts with a fictitious set of items, you will see the following *Console* output:

```
Current Page: 1
1 - First Name 001 Last Name 001 - email_001@domain.com
2 - First Name 002 Last Name 002 - email_002@domain.com
3 - First Name 003 Last Name 003 - email_003@domain.com
4 - First Name 004 Last Name 004 - email_004@domain.com
5 - First Name 005 Last Name 005 - email_005@domain.com
Current Page: 2
6 - First Name 006 Last Name 006 - email_006@domain.com
7 - First Name 007 Last Name 007 - email_007@domain.com
[etc. ]
```

The *ListItemCollectionPosition* property is of type *SPListItemCollectionPosition*. It offers a *PagingInfo* property of type *String*, which contains the following data:

```
Paged=TRUE&p_ID=8
```

The *_ID* is the unique identifier of the last item retrieved so that SharePoint can know the starting position of the next page.

The *SPQuery* type offers many other properties; however, what you have seen here will generally suffice for everyday tasks.

Document Libraries and Files

Document Libraries and Files are critical areas for many real-world SharePoint solutions. In this section you will learn how to create document libraries, and how to upload, download, update, and manage documents.

Creating a New Document Library

To create a new Document Library you just need to write code using an *SPListTemplateType* value of *DocumentLibrary*, such as that shown previously in Listing 3-19. However, quite often, when creating a Document Library, you also need to provide a document template to use for new documents. The code in Listing 3-26 creates a library of "Invoices," with an Excel spreadsheet document template.

LISTING 3-26 Creating a new *SPDocumentLibrary* with a document template.

```
using (SPSite site = new SPSite("http://devbook.sp2010.local/sites/CreatedByCode/")) {
    using (SPWeb web = site.OpenWeb()) {
        SPListTemplate listTemplate = web.ListTemplates["Document Library"];
        SPDocTemplate docTemplate =
            (from SPDocTemplate dt in web.DocTemplates
                where dt.Type == 122
                select dt).FirstOrDefault();

        Guid newListId = web.Lists.Add(
            "Invoices", // List Title
            "Excel Invoices", // List Description
            listTemplate, // List Template
            docTemplate // Document Template (i.e. Excel)
            );

        SPDocumentLibrary newLibrary = web.Lists[newListId] as SPDocumentLibrary;
        newLibrary.OnQuickLaunch = true;
        newLibrary.EnableVersioning = true;
        newLibrary.Update();
    }
}
```

When you run the code in Listing 3-26, it will create a new Document Library that you can reference as an instance of the *SPDocumentLibrary* type. Notice the LINQ to Objects query that is used to determine the *SPDocTemplate* item that corresponds to an Excel spreadsheet. Table 3-11 lists all the available document templates along with their *DocTemplateID* identifiers.

TABLE 3-11 **The Document Templates Available in SharePoint**

DocTemplate ID	Description
100	The document library will not use templates.
101	A blank Microsoft Word 97-2003 document.
103	A blank Microsoft Excel 97-2003 document.
104	A blank Microsoft PowerPoint 97-2003 document.
121	A blank Microsoft Word document.
122	A blank Microsoft Excel document.
123	A blank Microsoft PowerPoint document.
111	A basic Microsoft OneNote 2010 Notebook.
102	A blank Microsoft SharePoint Designer HTML document.
105	A blank Microsoft basic page ASPX document.
106	A blank Microsoft Web Part Page ASPX document.
1000	An empty Microsoft InfoPath form, ready for design.

Uploading a New Document

After you have created a library, uploading new content to it is simple. Recall that Table 3-3 showed that each *SPList* instance has a *RootFolder* property and a *Folders* collection property. You can reference any *SPFolder* to browse for its contents or to upload new content using the *Add* method of the *Files* property, which is of type *SPFileCollection*. The code excerpt in Listing 3-27 uploads a dummy Excel invoice file to the root folder of the library that was created in Listing 3-26.

LISTING 3-27 Uploading a new document to a *SPDocumentLibrary*.

```
using (SPSite site = new SPSite("http://devbook.sp2010.local/sites/CreatedByCode/")) {
    using (SPWeb web = site.OpenWeb()) {
        SPDocumentLibrary library = web.Lists["Invoices"] as SPDocumentLibrary;

        using (FileStream fs = new FileStream(@"..\..\DemoInvoice.xlsx",
            FileMode.Open, FileAccess.Read, FileShare.Read)) {
            SPFile fileUploaded = library.RootFolder.Files.Add(
                "DemoInvoice.xlsx", fs, true);
            Console.WriteLine("Uploaded file: {0}", fileUploaded.Url);
        }
    }
}
```

The *Add* method has twenty different overloads. The preceding code used the one that accepts the destination URL of the file, an argument of type *System.IO.Stream*, for the content of the file to upload, and a Boolean value that, when *true*, instructs SharePoint to overwrite any previously existing file. Listing all of these overloads is beyond the scope of this book; however, it is interesting to group them on a functional basis. All the overloads accept the destination URL of the file as their first argument. But one group of overloads accepts the file as a *System.IO.Stream*, and another group takes a *System.Byte[]* array as input. Additionally, there is a group that accepts a *HashTable*, which is a property bag for a file's metadata. This family of methods is useful whenever you need to upload a file along with its metadata in a unique transaction. Lastly, there are a couple of overloads that accept an argument of type *SPFileCollectionAddParameters*, which lets you specify some options about how to handle virus check, check-in, etc.

Downloading a Document

For document libraries, downloading is of course a frequent task. Every *SPListItem* in a Document Library has a *File* property of type *SPFile*. Through that property, you can access the file's content as either a *System.IO.Stream* or as an array of bytes (*System.Byte[]*).Listing 3-28 presents an example that downloads the file that was uploaded in the previous example.

LISTING 3-28 Downloading a document from a *SPDocumentLibrary*.

```
using (SPSite site = new SPSite("http://devbook.sp2010.local/sites/CreatedByCode/")) {
    using (SPWeb web = site.OpenWeb()) {
        SPDocumentLibrary library = web.Lists["Invoices"] as SPDocumentLibrary;

        SPFile fileToDownload = web.GetFile(library.RootFolder.Url +
            "/DemoInvoice.xlsx");

        Int32 bufferLength = 4096;
        Int32 readLength = bufferLength;
        Byte[] buffer = new Byte[bufferLength];


        Stream inStream = fileToDownload.OpenBinaryStream();

        using (FileStream outStream = new FileStream(
            @"..\..\DemoInvoiceDownload.xlsx",
            FileMode.OpenOrCreate, FileAccess.Write, FileShare.None)) {
            while (readLength == buffer.Length) {
                readLength = inStream.Read(buffer, 0, bufferLength);
                outStream.Write(buffer, 0, readLength);
                if (readLength < bufferLength) break;
            }
        }
    }
}
```

The key points in Listing 3-28 are the *SPWeb.GetFile* method, which is a shortcut to retrieve an *SPFile* instance for a specified file URL, and the *OpenBinaryStream* method of the *SPFile* class. The remaining code is plumbing to manage streams and save bytes on the hard disk.

Document Check-In and Check-Out

Another common task while managing documents is working with check-out and check-in features. As shown in Table 3-5, the *SPFile* class provides some specific methods to handle these tasks. Listing 3-29 shows a code excerpt that checks out a file, and then checks it back in again, adding a comment.

LISTING 3-29 Document check-out/check-in example.

```
using (SPSite site = new SPSite("http://devbook.sp2010.local/sites/CreatedByCode/")) {
    using (SPWeb web = site.OpenWeb()) {
        SPDocumentLibrary library = web.Lists["Invoices"] as SPDocumentLibrary;

        SPFile file = web.GetFile(library.RootFolder.Url + "/DemoInvoice.xlsx");

        if (file.CheckOutType == SPFile.SPCheckOutType.None) {
            // If the file is not already checked out ... check it out
            file.CheckOut();
        }
        else {
            // Otherwise check it in leaving a comment
            file.CheckIn("File Checked-In for demo purposes",
                SPCheckinType.MajorCheckIn);
        }
    }
}
```

When checking out a document, you should first evaluate the *CheckOutType* property, which is of type *SPFile.SPCheckOutType*—an enumeration of the following values:

- *None* The file is not checked out
- *Offline* The file is checked out for editing on the client side
- *Online* The file is checked out for editing on the server side

When the *CheckOutType* value is *None*, you can invoke the *CheckOut* method, optionally specifying the type (*Offline* or *Online*) of check-out that you want to occur. Otherwise, you can check the file in, using the *CheckIn* method, providing a comment, and optionally an argument of type *SPCheckinType*, which can assume the following values:

- *MajorCheckIn* The check-in increments a major version of the file
- *MinorCheckIn* The check-in increments a minor version of the file
- *OverwriteCheckIn* The check-in overwrites the current file version

One last option you have is the *UndoCheckOut* method, which releases a check-out without modifying the existing stored copy of the file.

Copying and Moving Files

Quite often in workflows and event receivers, you need to copy a file from one folder to another or move a file from one library to another.

> **More Information**   For further details about SharePoint workflows, see Part V of this book, "Developing Workflows." For further details about event receivers, see Chapter 12, "Event Receivers."

These actions are fully supported by the SharePoint Server Object Model. The example in Listing 3-30 copies or moves a file, based on a provided argument.

LISTING 3-30 Copying and moving a document from one location to another.

```
using (SPSite site = new SPSite("http://devbook.sp2010.local/sites/CreatedByCode/")) {
    using (SPWeb web = site.OpenWeb()) {
        SPDocumentLibrary sourceLibrary =
            web.Lists["Invoices"] as SPDocumentLibrary;
        SPDocumentLibrary destinationLibrary =
            web.Lists["Invoices History"] as SPDocumentLibrary;

        SPFile file = web.GetFile(sourceLibrary.RootFolder.Url +
            "/DemoInvoice.xlsx");

        if (move) {
            // It is a file moving action
            file.MoveTo(destinationLibrary.RootFolder.Url +
                "/DemoInvoice_Moved.xlsx", true);
        }
        else {
            // It is a file copy action
            file.CopyTo(destinationLibrary.RootFolder.Url +
                "/DemoInvoice_Copied.xlsx", true);
        }
    }
}
```

Listing 3-30 assumes that you have an "Invoices" library and another "Invoices History" library, and that you are copying or moving files between these two libraries. Whether you move or copy the file, both the methods receive a *Boolean* argument to force overwriting of any previously existing file in the target folder. Note that both of these methods work only within the same site.

Managing Versions of Documents

While working with files, you often need to manage versioning, to keep track of changes during a file's lifecycle, and to retrieve older versions of a document. Listing 3-31 shows an example that extracts the next-to-last version of a document.

LISTING 3-31 How to manage file versions.

```
using (SPSite site = new SPSite("http://devbook.sp2010.local/sites/CreatedByCode/")) {
    using (SPWeb web = site.OpenWeb()) {
        SPDocumentLibrary library = web.Lists["Invoices"] as SPDocumentLibrary;

        SPFile file = web.GetFile(library.RootFolder.Url + "/DemoInvoice.xlsx");

        Console.WriteLine("Available versions:");
        foreach (SPFileVersion v in file.Versions) {
            Console.WriteLine("Version: {0} - URL: {1}", v.VersionLabel, v.Url);
        }

        SPFile fileOfSecondLastVersion =
            file.Versions[file.Versions.Count - 1].File;

        Console.WriteLine(fileOfSecondLastVersion.Name);
    }
}
```

Listing 3-31 demonstrates that SharePoint makes such tasks simple. For each and every available version of the document, you have access to an *SPFile* instance that you can manage exactly as you would the current version of the document.

Groups and Users

This group of tasks is dedicated to managing users and groups. In this section you will learn how to create and manage a user, how to control users' membership against groups, and how to define custom permission levels to assign specific permissions to users or groups.

Creating a New User

As usual, the first step in the sequence of common tasks is to be able to create a new item. Remember that a user in SharePoint is an *SPUser* instance. Each *SPWeb* instance offers a set of user collections (*AllUsers*, *SiteUsers*, *Users*) which were listed in Table 3-2. Listing 3-32 shows how to add a new user, taken from Active Directory, into the list of *SiteUsers* for a website.

LISTING 3-32 Adding a new user to the *SiteUsers* collection of a website.

```
using (SPSite site = new SPSite("http://devbook.sp2010.local/")) {
    using (SPWeb web = site.OpenWeb()) {
        web.SiteUsers.Add("SP2010DEV\\TestUser", "test@devleap.com",
            "Test User", null);

        SPUser userAdded = web.SiteUsers["SP2010DEV\\TestUser"];
        Console.WriteLine(userAdded.Xml);
    }
}
```

The *SPUserCollection.Add* method accepts the logon name of the user, the e-mail address, the display name, and an optional argument with textual notes about the *SPUser*. When adding an previously existing user, the infrastructure ignores any duplicate insertion. However, if you simply want to get a valid *SPUser* instance that corresponds to a logon name—and you don't want to worry about whether that user exists—you can invoke the *SPWeb.EnsureUser* method. This method adds the user if that user is not already defined in the site, or uses the existing user, if there is one. Listing 3-33 shows a revised example.

LISTING 3-33 Revised code showing how to add a new user to the users of a website.

```
using (SPSite site = new SPSite("http://devbook.sp2010.local/")) {
    using (SPWeb web = site.OpenWeb()) {
        SPUser userAdded = web.EnsureUser("SP2010DEV\\AnotherTestUser");
        Console.WriteLine(userAdded.Xml);    }
}
```

This time, the *EnsureUser* method directly returns the *SPUser* that you're probably expecting.

Managing Groups Membership

Deleting a user or managing user properties are trivial tasks, so this chapter will not cover them. But it is interesting to know how to add a user to a specific SharePoint group. There are many techniques to accomplish this; however, here you'll see how to do that by working with the *Groups* collection of the current *SPWeb* instance.

LISTING 3-34 Adding a user to a website group.

```
using (SPSite site = new SPSite("http://devbook.sp2010.local/")) {
    using (SPWeb web = site.OpenWeb()) {
        SPUser user = web.EnsureUser("SP2010DEV\\AnotherTestUser");

        web.Groups[web.Title + " Members"].AddUser(user);
    }
}
```

The example is clear; the last line invokes the *AddUser* method of an *SPGroup* object retrieved by group name. Using the *SPWeb.Groups* collection, you can also add, update, or delete existing SharePoint groups; however, you should be very careful when performing such actions in code.

Managing Users and Groups Permissions

In the section "SPGroup, SPUser and Other Security Types," on page 69, both users and groups internally inherit from *SPPrincipal*, which is a fundamental type for assigning permissions. In SharePoint 2010 permissions are based on permission levels. A permission level consists of a set of low-level permissions such as "Browse Directory," "View Pages," "View Items," "Add Items," and so forth. For a full and detailed list of all the available permissions and native permission levels, see Chapter 21, "Authentication and Authorization Infrastructure." For now, you just need to know that you can define custom permission levels using either the browser UI or the Server Object Model. Additionally, you can assign a permission level to an *SPPrincipal* (an *SPUser* or *SPGroup*). Listing 3-35 shows a code excerpt that creates a new permission level (composed of the following permissions: "View Pages," "Browse Directories," and "Update Personal Web Parts") and assigns it to a specific *SPUser*.

LISTING 3-35 Creating a new permission level and assigning it to a user.

```
using (SPSite site = new SPSite("http://devbook.sp2010.local/")) {
    using (SPWeb web = site.OpenWeb()) {
        SPUser user = web.EnsureUser("SP2010DEV\\AnotherTestUser");

        SPRoleDefinition newRoleDefinition = new SPRoleDefinition();
        newRoleDefinition.Name = "Custom Permission Level";
        newRoleDefinition.Description = "View Pages, Browse Directories, " +
            "Update Personal Web Parts";
        newRoleDefinition.BasePermissions = SPBasePermissions.ViewPages |
            SPBasePermissions.BrowseDirectories |
            SPBasePermissions.UpdatePersonalWebParts;
        web.RoleDefinitions.Add(newRoleDefinition);

        SPPrincipal principal = user;
        SPRoleAssignment newRoleAssignment = new SPRoleAssignment(principal);
        newRoleAssignment.RoleDefinitionBindings.Add(
            web.RoleDefinitions["Custom Permission Level"]);
        web.RoleAssignments.Add(newRoleAssignment);
    }
}
```

The code in Listing 3-35 first retrieves a reference to an *SPUser, and* then it creates a new permission level—a new instance of *SPRoleDefinition*—and assigns a set of selected permissions to it using a bit mask of permissions. Finally, it adds a binding between the *SPPrincipal* representing the user and the permission level, using a new *SPRoleAssignment* instance.

Summary

This chapter provided an overview of the SharePoint Server Object Model, starting with the main SharePoint object hierarchy. It then provided a description of the main types. The last part of the chapter illustrated basic types of everyday tasks, their problems, and solutions. You also saw some suggestions and best practices for writing better and more efficient code. Many of the following chapters will use and expand this knowledge.

Chapter 4
LINQ to SharePoint

One of the most significant new features of Microsoft SharePoint 2010 is the support for LINQ on the server side. This is a satisfying alternative to the classic object model that you saw in Chapter 3, "Server Object Model." This chapter will begin with a quick overview of LINQ, just in case you're not familiar with it, and then show you how to work with it. Next, you'll learn about LINQ to SharePoint as a LINQ query provider implementation, which is useful for querying and managing items in SharePoint lists using the LINQ data access model. If you already know about LINQ, you can skip the next section and move directly to the section titled "Introducing LINQ to SharePoint," on page 106.

 More Information To learn more about LINQ, read *Programming Microsoft LINQ in .NET 4.0*, by Paolo Pialorsi and Marco Russo (Microsoft Press, 2010; ISBN: 978-0-7356-4057-3). Remember that SharePoint works on top of Microsoft .NET Framework 3.5, not .NET 4.0. Nevertheless, the contents of the book are suitable for understanding LINQ to SharePoint, too.

LINQ Overview

LINQ stands for Language Integrated Query, which is a programming model that introduces queries as a first-class concept into any Microsoft .NET language. Complete support for LINQ, however, requires some extensions in the language that you are using. These extensions boost developer productivity, thereby providing a shorter, more meaningful, and expressive syntax with which to manipulate data.

LINQ provides a methodology that simplifies and unifies the implementation of any kind of data access. LINQ does not force you to use a specific architecture; it facilitates the implementation of several existing architectures for accessing data, such as the following:

- RAD/prototype
- Client/server
- N-tier
- Smart client

The architecture of LINQ is based on the idea of having a set of LINQ providers, each of which can target a different kind of data source. Figure 4-1 shows a schema of the main LINQ providers available in .NET Framework 3.5/4.0. Out of the box, with .NET Framework 3.5/4.0 and Visual Studio 2010, LINQ includes many providers suitable for accessing several different types of data sources, including:

- **LINQ to Objects**   This is used to query in-memory data and object graphs.

- **LINQ to SQL**   This was specifically designed to query and manage data stored in a Microsoft SQL Server database, using a lightweight, simplified Object-Relational Mapper (O/RM) that maps entities to tables with a one-to-one relationship.

- **LINQ to Entities**   The first class O/RM offered by Microsoft to design solutions based on the domain model, with a real abstraction from the underlying persistence storage.

- **LINQ to DataSet**   This is a LINQ implementation targeting old-style ADO.NET *DataSet* and *DataTable* types. It is mainly offered for backward compatibility reasons.

- **LINQ to XML**   This is a LINQ implementation targeting XML contents, useful to query, manage and navigate across XML nodes.

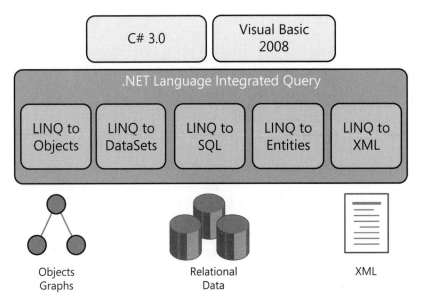

FIGURE 4-1 A graphical representation of the main LINQ providers available in .NET Framework 4.0.

LINQ is likely to have an impact on the way applications are coded. It would be incorrect to think that LINQ will change application architectures, because its goal is to provide a set of tools that improve code implementation by adapting to several different architectures.

The Goal of LINQ

Today, data managed by a program can originate from many and varied data sources, such as an array, an object graph, an XML document, a database, a text file, a registry key, an e-mail message, Simple Object Access Protocol (SOAP) message content, a Microsoft Office Excel file, and so forth. The list is extensive.

Each data source has its own specific data access model. When you need to query a database, you typically use SQL. You navigate XML data by using the Document Object Model (DOM) or XPath/XQuery. You iterate an array and build algorithms to navigate an object graph. You use specific application programming interfaces (APIs) to access other data sources, such as an Excel file, an e-mail message, or the Windows registry. Put briefly, you use different programming models to access different data sources.

The unification of data access techniques into a single comprehensive model has been attempted in many ways. For example, Open Database Connectivity (ODBC) providers allow you to query an Excel file as you would a Windows Management Instrumentation (WMI) repository. With ODBC, you use an SQL-like language to access data represented through a relational model.

Sometimes, however, data is represented more effectively in a hierarchical or network model instead of a relational one. Moreover, if a data model is not tied to a specific language, you probably need to manage different type systems. All these differences create an "impedance mismatch" between data and code.

LINQ addresses these issues by offering a uniform method to access and manage data without forcing the adoption of a "one size fits all" model. LINQ makes use of common capabilities in the operations in different data models instead of flattening the different structures between them. In other words, by using LINQ you keep existing heterogeneous data structures, such as classes or tables, but you gain a uniform syntax to query all these data types, regardless of their physical representation. Think about the differences between a graph of in-memory objects and relational tables with proper relationships. With LINQ you can use the same query syntax over both models.

Here is a simple LINQ query for a typical software solution that returns the names of customers in Italy.

```
var query =
    from   c in Customers
    where  c.Country == "Italy"
    select c.CompanyName;
```

The result of this query is a list of strings. You can enumerate these values with a *foreach* loop in C#:

```
foreach ( string name in query ) {
    Console.WriteLine( name );
}
```

Both the query definition and the *foreach* loop are regular C# 3.0 statements, but what is *Customers*? At this point, you might be wondering what it is we are querying. Is this query a new form of Embedded SQL? Not at all. You can apply the same query (and the *foreach* loop) to an SQL database using LINQ to SQL; to a third-party DBMS using LINQ to Entities; to a *DataSet* object using LINQ to DataSet; to an array of objects in memory using LINQ to Objects; to a remote service; or to many other kinds of data using their specific LINQ provider.

Customers could be a collection of objects, such as in the following example:

```
Customer[] Customers;
```

Customers could be an entity class that describes a physical table in a relational database:

```
DataContext db = new DataContext( ConnectionString );
Table<Customer> Customers = db.GetTable<Customer>();
```

Or, *Customers* could be an entity class that describes a conceptual model mapped to a relational database, as shown here:

```
NorthwindModel dataModel = new NorthwindModel();
ObjectSet<Customer> Customers = dataModel.Customers;
```

And in SharePoint 2010, *Customers* could be an entity class that describes a collection of *SPListItem* types retrieved from an *SPList* of customers stored in SharePoint:

```
MySiteContext sp = new MySiteContext ( siteUri );
EntityList<Customer> Customers = sp.GetList<Customer>("Customers");
```

These examples highlight that the main goal of LINQ is to provide a unified querying and programming model, fully integrated with programming languages, that abstracts code from the underlying infrastructure.

LINQ Under the Covers

The examples in the previous section demonstrated that a LINQ query can target any kind of data source supported by a LINQ provider. Now, you might be wondering how LINQ works, under the covers.

Suppose you write the following code that uses LINQ:

```
Customer[] Customers = GetCustomers();
var query =
    from   c in Customers
    where  c.Country == "Italy"
    select c;
```

From that query, the compiler generates this code:

```
Customer[] Customers = GetCustomers();
IEnumerable<Customer> query =
        Customers
        .Where( c => c.Country == "Italy" );
```

When the query becomes more complex, as you can see in the following code (from now on, I'll skip the *Customers* declaration for the sake of brevity):

```
var query =
    from    c in Customers
    where   c.Country == "Italy"
    orderby c.Name
    select  new { c.Name, c.City };
```

The generated code is more complex too:

```
var query =
        Customers
        .Where( c => c.Country == "Italy" )
        .OrderBy( c => c.Name )
        .Select( c => new { c.Name, c.City } );
```

The code calls instance members on the object returned from the previous call; It calls *Where* on *Customers*, *OrderBy* on the object returned by *Where*, and finally *Select* on the object returned by *OrderBy*. This behavior is regulated by what are known as extension methods in the host language (C# in this case). The implementation of the *Where*, *OrderBy*, and *Select* methods—called by the sample query—depends on the type of *Customers* and on namespaces specified in relevant *using* statements. Extension methods are a fundamental syntax feature used by LINQ so it can maintain the same syntax across different data sources.

The basic concept behind LINQ is that queries target objects that implement either the *IEnumerable<T>* interface for in-memory data, or the *IQueryable<T>* interface for data retrieved from an external store. Here's the definition of the *IEnumerable<T>* interface:

```
public interface IEnumerable<T> : IEnumerable {
    IEnumerator<T> GetEnumerator();
}
```

And here's the definition of the *IQueryable<T>* interface, together with its base interface, *IQueryable*:

```
public interface IQueryable<T> : IEnumerable<T>, IQueryable, IEnumerable {
}
public interface IQueryable : IEnumerable {
    Type ElementType { get; }
    Expression Expression { get; }
    IQueryProvider Provider { get; }
}
```

Whenever you browse for (enumerate) the results of a query, for example by using a *foreach* statement, the compiler invokes the *GetEnumerator* method of the *IEnumerable<T>* interface, and at that point the query is effectively executed.

When the target object of your query implements only the *IEnumerable<T>* interface, the extension methods targeting that type will work against in-memory objects. For example, LINQ to Objects and LINQ to XML both work in this way.

However, when the query target object implements *IQueryable<T>*, the extension methods construct an expression tree, which describes the query from a provider-independent point of view. The expression tree is then processed by the *IQueryable* implementation of the query target object, invoking the *IQueryProvider* object published by the *IQueryable.Provider* property. The query provider visits the expression tree, using an expression visitor, and produces a query syntax that targets the concrete persistence storage. For example, for a LINQ to SQL query engine, the query provider will generate a T-SQL query that corresponds to the LINQ query you defined in your .NET code. Similarly, when using LINQ to SharePoint, the query provider generates a CAML query that will be executed against the target *SPList* using the standard Server Object Model querying syntax.

> **Note** CAML stands for Collaborative Application Markup Language, which is an XML-based querying language that is useful for defining filtering, sorting, and grouping operations on SharePoint data.

Introducing LINQ to SharePoint

Now that you have seen what LINQ is and generally how it works, you can dive into LINQ to SharePoint, which is just another LINQ query provider that targets SharePoint data. Figure 4-2 shows the Data Access Model Architecture of SharePoint 2010, illustrating the role of LINQ to SharePoint compared to other data access technologies available in SharePoint 2010.

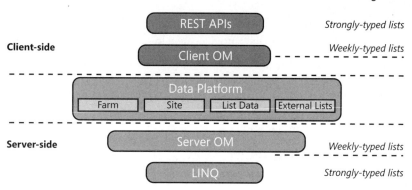

FIGURE 4-2 The SharePoint 2010 Data Access Model Architecture and the role of LINQ to SharePoint.

The key feature of LINQ to SharePoint is that it can query SharePoint data with a fully-typed approach, using a common querying language (LINQ), and retrieving typed entities.

Modeling with SPMetal.EXE

The first and main task when developing solutions that make use of LINQ to SharePoint is to model the typed entities. You can define these manually, but it is general more useful to use a specific tool, named SPMetal.EXE, which can automatically generate entities for you. You can find the SPMetal.EXE utility in the SharePoint14_Root\BIN folder. SPMetal.EXE is a command-line tool that accepts a wide range of arguments, listed in Table 4-1.

TABLE 4-1 Arguments That You Can Provide to SPMetal.EXE

Argument	Description
/web:<url>	Specifies the absolute URL of the target website. Host address can be local, in which case, the tool uses the Server Object Model to connect to the server.
/useremoteapi	Specifies that the website URL is remote. You might not use this option if any of the lists on the website contain lookup fields. Secondary lookups are not supported by the Client Object Model.
/user:<name>	Specifies the logon username (or domain).
/password:<password>	Specifies the logon password.
/parameters:<file>	Specifies an XML file with code generation parameters.

Argument	Description
/code:<file>	Specifies the output location for generated code (default: console).
/language:<language>	Specifies the source code language. Valid options are *csharp* and *vb* (default: inferred from source code file name extension).
/namespace:<namespace>	Specifies a namespace used for auto-generated code (default: no namespace).
/serialization:<type>	Specifies a serialization type. Valid options are *none* and *unidirectional* (default: *none*). The entities serialization topic will be discussed in the "Disconnected Entities" section.

Note that the default behavior of SPMetal.EXE is to output auto-generated code to the console. That's not terribly useful except for testing, so you should generally provide a */code* argument to instruct the tool to generate a code file, instead. Next, you need to provide the target website URL by using the */web* argument, and then instruct the tool to use the client object model (*/useremoteapi*), if the site is remote. It's common to also provide a namespace by using the */namespace* argument. Here's a typical command-line invocation of the tool:

```
SPMETAL.EXE /web:http://devbook.sp2010.local/ /code:devbook.cs
/namespace:DevLeap.SP2010.Linq2SP
```

As you will see when you execute SPMetal.EXE, by default it creates a full model for the target site, defining a class for almost every supported content type, and a list for every list instance, except for hidden lists. The tool will also create a class named *[WebSiteName]DataContext*, where *[WebSiteName]* is the name of the target website without spaces, in case the site name has spaces in its content. This class represents the entry point for using LINQ to SharePoint, and it inherits from the *Microsoft.SharePoint.Linq.DataContext* base class. Quite often, you do not really need to model each and every content type and list instance of the target site. Usually, you need to model only some custom data structures that you plan to query and manage with LINQ to SharePoint. The */parameters* command line argument is provided for this purpose. In fact, using this argument you can provide SPMetal.EXE with an XML file that instructs the tool about what to skip and what to include in the auto-generated model. Listing 4-1 shows a sample XML parameters file that excludes all the common "Team Site" default contents, while it includes all other content-types and lists.

LISTING 4-1 A sample XML parameters file suitable for SPMetal.EXE.

```xml
<?xml version="1.0" encoding="utf-8"?>
<Web AccessModifier="Internal"
xmlns="http://schemas.microsoft.com/SharePoint/2009/spmetal">
  <ExcludeList Name="Announcements"/>
  <ExcludeList Name="Calendar"/>
  <ExcludeList Name="Customized Reports"/>
  <ExcludeList Name="Form Templates"/>
  <ExcludeList Name="Links"/>
```

```
    <ExcludeList Name="Shared Documents"/>
    <ExcludeList Name="Site Assets"/>
    <ExcludeList Name="Site Pages"/>
    <ExcludeList Name="Style Library"/>
    <ExcludeList Name="Tasks"/>
    <ExcludeList Name="Team Discussion"/>
</Web>
```

Listing 4-1 shows that the XML file is based on a custom XML namespace. Table 4-2 describes the supported elements that you can use to define such a file.

TABLE 4-2 The Elements Available for Defining an XML Parameters File

Element Name	Description and Purpose
Web	The root element of the schema. This tag defines the name of the *DataContext* generated class, configuring the *class* attribute. It also defines the access modifier used for auto-generated types. By default SPMetal.EXE uses a *public* access modifier.
List	Instructs SPMetal.EXE to include a specified list definition. It is useful for including hidden lists. It also allows you to override the name of the list in the auto-generated code. The tag requires a *Name* attribute whose value is the list name.
ExcludeList	Excludes the generation of the specified target list from the auto-generated code. This tag requires a *Name* attribute whose value is the list name.
ExcludeOtherLists	Instructs SPMetal.EXE to avoid generating any list definition except those that you explicitly define using a *List* element.
-IncludeHiddenLists	Requests that SPMetal.EXE generates list definitions for hidden lists. You cannot use this element together with the *ExcludeOtherLists* element.
ContentType	Forces SPMetal.EXE to generate the code for a specific content-type, referenced by *Name*, using a specific attribute. You can use this tag, for example, to include a hidden content type. This element can be a child of the *Web* or *List* elements.
Column	Instructs SPMetal.EXE to output a property representing a field (site column) that it would not model by default. For example you can use this element to include a hidden field. It requires a *Name* attribute, whose value is the name of the field to include.
ExcludeColumn	Excludes a field from code generation. This element requires a *Name* attribute, whose value is the name of the field to include.
ExcludeOtherColumns	Configures the tool to block code generation for columns that are not explicitly referenced by a *Column* element.
IncludeHiddenColumns	Causes SPMetal.EXE to generate code for hidden column. This element cannot be used together with the *ExcludeOtherColumns* element.

Element Name	Description and Purpose
ExcludeContentType	Blocks code generation for the content type specified by the value of a *Name* attribute. This element can be a child of *Web* or *List* elements.
ExcludeOtherContentTypes	Configures SPMetal.EXE to block code generation for content types not explicitly referenced by a *ContentType* element.
IncludeHiddenContentTypes	Requests that SPMetal.EXE also generates code for any hidden content type. This element cannot be used together with the *ExcludeOtherContentTypes* element.

Now suppose that you have a website with a couple of custom lists: a standard document library named Invoices, and a list of items named DevLeap Contacts, in which each item can be a DevLeap Customer or a DevLeap Supplier. Both types share a base Content Type called DevLeap Contact.

> **Note** To provision these content types and lists, see the code samples in Chapter 10, "Data Provisioning."

Listing 4-2 shows another XML parameters file that includes these custom content types and lists, and excludes all other content types and lists.

LISTING 4-2 Sample XML parameters file for SPMetal.EXE.

```xml
<?xml version="1.0" encoding="utf-8"?>
<Web AccessModifier="Internal" xmlns="http://schemas.microsoft.com/SharePoint/2009/
spmetal">
  <List Name="DevLeap Contacts">
    <ContentType Name="DevLeapContact" Class="DevLeapContact" />
    <ContentType Name="DevLeapCustomer" Class="DevLeapCustomer" />
    <ContentType Name="DevLeapSupplier" Class="DevLeapSupplier" />
  </List>
  <List Name="Invoices" />
  <ExcludeOtherLists />
</Web>
```

Assume you've executed this with SPMetal.EXE; now you'll examine the resulting auto-generated code. First, you have a *DevbookDataContext* class that provides entry points to access the content lists of the target site. Listing 4-3 shows the definition of this *DataContext* inherited class.

LISTING 4-3 The *DevbookDataContext* class, auto-generated using the XML parameters file from Listing 4-2.

```
internal partial class DevbookDataContext : Microsoft.SharePoint.Linq.DataContext {

    #region Extensibility Method Definitions
    partial void OnCreated();
    #endregion

    public DevbookDataContext(string requestUrl) :
            base(requestUrl) {
        this.OnCreated();
    }

    [Microsoft.SharePoint.Linq.ListAttribute(Name="DevLeap Contacts")]
    public Microsoft.SharePoint.Linq.EntityList<DevLeapContact> DevLeapContacts {
        get {
            return this.GetList<DevLeapContact>("DevLeap Contacts");
        }
    }

    [Microsoft.SharePoint.Linq.ListAttribute(Name="Invoices")]
    public Microsoft.SharePoint.Linq.EntityList<Document> Invoices {
        get {
            return this.GetList<Document>("Invoices");
        }
    }
}
```

The class has a constructor that accepts the URL of the target website as its only argument. Internally, it invokes a partial method (*OnCreated*), which you can use to customize the context initialization. Next, there are a couple of public properties that correspond to the two modeled lists (Invoices and DevLeap Contacts). It is interesting to see that both of these properties are decorated with the *ListAttribute* attribute, stating the name of the underlying SharePoint list. Also, both of these properties are of type *EntityList<T>*, which is the type LINQ to SharePoint uses to represent a collection of typed items.

Internally these properties invoke the *DataContext.GetList<T>* method. If you have any experience with LINQ to SQL, you will find many similarities between LINQ to SharePoint and LINQ to SQL. The *Invoices* list is made up of a set of *Document* instances, where *Document* is the typed entity auto-generated by SPMetal.EXE that describes a SharePoint document from a conceptual viewpoint. The *DevLeapContacts* list is composed of items of type *DevLeapContact*, which is the typed entity corresponding to the base content type *DevLeapContact*.

One last thing to consider about the *DataContext* type is that it implements *IDisposable*, because internally it uses some types that exploit unmanaged resources such as the *SPSite* and *SPWeb* types. Therefore, you should always call *Dispose* whenever you create an instance.

> **More Information** See the "Disposing Resources" section on page 73 in Chapter 3 to better understand the reasons for disposing of unmanaged resources.

Figure 4-3 shows the class diagram of the generated types.

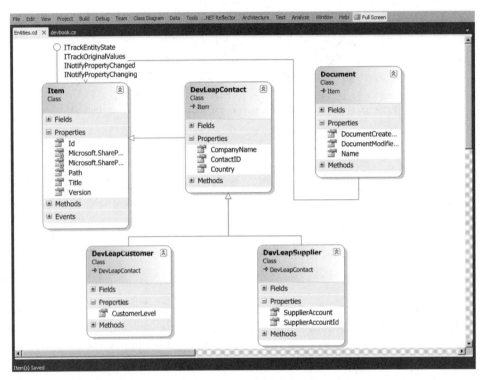

FIGURE 4-3 Class diagram of typed entities generated by SPMetal.EXE.

Figure 4-3 illustrates that the tool generated an *Item* base class, which internally implements some infrastructural interfaces for data management tracking (*ITrackEntityState*, *ITrackOriginalValues*) and for data binding (*INotifyPropertyChanged*, *INotifyPropertyChanging*), as well as some properties that correspond to the common data of every SharePoint list item (*Id*, *Path*, *Title*, and *Version*).

Then there is a *Document* entity, which inherits from *Item* and adds some document-specific properties (*DocumentCreatedBy*, *DocumentModifiedBy*, and *Name*). The most interesting part of the model is how it defines entities that map to custom content types. In fact, SPMetal.EXE modeled a *DevLeapContact* class, which inherits from *Item*, and is the base class for the types *DevLeapCustomer* and *DevLeapSupplier*. This is challenging behavior; SPMetal.EXE modeled the content types and lists of SharePoint, mapping them to an object-oriented model of entities, with full inheritance support.

> **Important** Because of the need for a set of typed entities that model the content types de-
> fined in the target SharePoint site, it is good practice to use LINQ to SharePoint only against sites
> that have a well-defined and stable structure. To learn how to correctly provision data structures
> in SharePoint, see Chapter 10. Similarly, it is not as useful to use LINQ to SharePoint on sites that
> frequently change their structure, because you would need to refresh the typed model frequent-
> ly as well. Instead, you should access and query sites with a high change frequency using the
> standard Server Object Model and the untyped approach.

Listing 4-4 shows a portion of the code corresponding to the base *Item* type.

LISTING 4-4 The *Item* type auto-generated code.

```
/// <summary>
/// Create a new list item.
/// </summary>
[Microsoft.SharePoint.Linq.ContentTypeAttribute(Name="Item", Id="0x01")]
[Microsoft.SharePoint.Linq.DerivedEntityClassAttribute(Type=typeof(DevLeapContact))]
[Microsoft.SharePoint.Linq.DerivedEntityClassAttribute(Type=typeof(Document))]
internal partial class Item : Microsoft.SharePoint.Linq.ITrackEntityState,
Microsoft.SharePoint.Linq.ITrackOriginalValues,
System.ComponentModel.INotifyPropertyChanged,
System.ComponentModel.INotifyPropertyChanging {

    // Code omitted for the sake of brevity ...

    #region Extensibility Method Definition
    partial void OnLoaded();
    partial void OnValidate();
    partial void OnCreated();
    #endregion

    Microsoft.SharePoint.Linq.EntityState
    Microsoft.SharePoint.Linq.ITrackEntityState.EntityState {
        get {
                return this._entityState;
        }
        set {
                if ((value != this._entityState)) {
                        this._entityState = value;
                }
        }
    }

    System.Collections.Generic.IDictionary<string, object>
    Microsoft.SharePoint.Linq.ITrackOriginalValues.OriginalValues {
```

```
        get {
                if ((null == this._originalValues)) {
                        this._originalValues = new
                            System.Collections.Generic.Dictionary<string,
                            object>();
                }
                return this._originalValues;
        }
}

public Item() {
        this.OnCreated();
}

[Microsoft.SharePoint.Linq.ColumnAttribute(Name="ID", Storage="_id",
    ReadOnly=true, FieldType="Counter")]
public System.Nullable<int> Id {
        get {
                return this._id;
        }
        set {
                if ((value != this._id)) {
                        this.OnPropertyChanging("Id", this._id);
                        this._id = value;
                        this.OnPropertyChanged("Id");
                }
        }
}

// Code omitted for the sake of brevity ...

[Microsoft.SharePoint.Linq.ColumnAttribute(Name="Title", Storage="_title",
    Required=true, FieldType="Text")]
public virtual string Title {
        get {
                return this._title;
        }
        set {
                if ((value != this._title)) {
                        this.OnPropertyChanging("Title", this._title);
                        this._title = value;
                        this.OnPropertyChanged("Title");
                }
        }
}

// Code omitted for the sake of brevity ...

}
```

It is interesting to see the class attribute decorations, which are specific for LINQ to SharePoint, that instruct the engine about the content-type ID (*ID=0x01*) behind the *Item* class, as well as about the types that inherit from this base class. You can see that the base

Item, and thus every typed entity in the model, provides an *EntityState* property related to the *ITrackEntityState* interface implementation, and an *OriginalValues* property of type *Dictionary*, related to the *ITrackOriginalValues* interface implementation. You'll see these properties used for tracking entities' states and changes in the section "Managing Data" on page 122. In addition, the entity offers two public properties useful for accessing the current item *ID* and *Title*. These properties are marked with the *ColumnAttribute* attribute, which defines the underlying storage field and the corresponding SharePoint column. Lastly, the class provides three partial methods that you can implement to add custom behaviors to the type when loading (*OnLoaded*), validating (*OnValidate*), and creating (*OnCreated*) a type instance.

Starting from this base type, the tool inherited all the specialized entities corresponding to the content-types. Listing 4-5 contains an excerpt of the *DevLeapContact*, *DevLeapCustomer*, and *DevLeapSupplier* types.

LISTING 4-5 The custom *DevLeap** custom types auto-generated code.

```
[Microsoft.SharePoint.Linq.ContentTypeAttribute(Name="DevLeapContact",
    Id="0x0100A60F69C4B1304FBDA6C4B4A25939979F")]
[Microsoft.SharePoint.Linq.DerivedEntityClassAttribute(
    Type=typeof(DevLeapCustomer))]
[Microsoft.SharePoint.Linq.DerivedEntityClassAttribute(
    Type=typeof(DevLeapSupplier))]
internal partial class DevLeapContact : Item {
    private string _contactID;
    private string _companyName;
    private System.Nullable<Country> _country;

    #region Extensibility Method Definitions
    partial void OnLoaded();
    partial void OnValidate();
    partial void OnCreated();
    #endregion

    public DevLeapContact() {
            this.OnCreated();
    }

    [Microsoft.SharePoint.Linq.ColumnAttribute(Name="DevLeapContactID",
        Storage="_contactID", Required=true, FieldType="Text")]
    public string ContactID {
        // Code omitted for the sake of brevity ...
    }

    [Microsoft.SharePoint.Linq.ColumnAttribute(Name="DevLeapCompanyName",
        Storage="_companyName", FieldType="Text")]
    public string CompanyName {
        // Code omitted for the sake of brevity ...
    }
```

```
    [Microsoft.SharePoint.Linq.ColumnAttribute(Name="DevLeapCountry",
      Storage="_country", FieldType="Choice")]
    public System.Nullable<Country> Country {
        // Code omitted for the sake of brevity ...
    }
}

[Microsoft.SharePoint.Linq.ContentTypeAttribute(Name="DevLeapCustomer",
  Id="0x0100A60F69C4B1304FBDA6C4B4A25939979F01")]
internal partial class DevLeapCustomer : DevLeapContact {
    private System.Nullable<CustomerLevel> _customerLevel;

    #region Extensibility Method Definitions
    partial void OnLoaded();
    partial void OnValidate();
    partial void OnCreated();
    #endregion

    public DevLeapCustomer() {
            this.OnCreated();
    }

    [Microsoft.SharePoint.Linq.ColumnAttribute(Name="DevLeapCustomerLevel",
      Storage="_customerLevel", Required=true, FieldType="Choice")]
    public System.Nullable<CustomerLevel> CustomerLevel {
        // Code omitted for the sake of brevity ...
    }
}

[Microsoft.SharePoint.Linq.ContentTypeAttribute(Name="DevLeapSupplier",
  Id="0x0100A60F69C4B1304FBDA6C4B4A25939979F02")]
internal partial class DevLeapSupplier : DevLeapContact {
    // Code omitted for the sake of brevity ...
}

internal enum Country : int {
    None = 0,
    Invalid = 1,
    [Microsoft.SharePoint.Linq.ChoiceAttribute(Value="Italy")]
    Italy = 2,
    [Microsoft.SharePoint.Linq.ChoiceAttribute(Value="USA")]
    USA = 4,
    [Microsoft.SharePoint.Linq.ChoiceAttribute(Value="Germany")]
    Germany = 8,
    [Microsoft.SharePoint.Linq.ChoiceAttribute(Value="France")]
    France = 16,
}
```

```
internal enum CustomerLevel : int {
    None = 0,
    Invalid = 1,
    [Microsoft.SharePoint.Linq.ChoiceAttribute(Value="Level A")]
    LevelA = 2,
    [Microsoft.SharePoint.Linq.ChoiceAttribute(Value="Level B")]
    LevelB = 4,
    [Microsoft.SharePoint.Linq.ChoiceAttribute(Value="Level C")]
    LevelC = 8,
}
```

Listing 4-5 shows that the classes are fully connected with the original SharePoint types, because each class refers to its corresponding content type using its ID, just as the *Item* base type did in Listing 4-4. Additionally, when you have a *Choice* field on the SharePoint side (for example *DevLeapContact.Country* and *DevLeapCustomer.CustomerLevel*), the tool generates an *enum* type, giving you strongly typed access to the choice values.

Of course, you could write all this code manually and get the same results, but that's not recommended.

Querying Data

Now that you have seen how to model your data with SPMetal.EXE, and what the model is, you can start querying the site for content. The key feature of this new query provider lies in its ability to query SharePoint contents using LINQ queries. As an example, Listing 4-6 contains a query that fetches the titles of documents in the "Invoices" list created by a specific user.

> **Note** To execute the custom code illustrated in this section and in those that follow, you need to reference the Microsoft.SharePoint.Linq.dll assembly, which is available in the SharePoint14_ Root\ISAPI folder of every SharePoint server. In addition, you should declare in your code a couple of *using* statements for the namespaces *Microsoft.SharePoint.Linq* and *System.Linq*.

LISTING 4-6 A LINQ to SharePoint query to find documents in the Invoices list created by a specific user.

```
using (DevbookDataContext spContext = new
    DevbookDataContext("http://devbook.sp2010.local/")) {
    var query = from i in spContext.Invoices
                where i.DocumentCreatedBy == @"SP2010DEV\PaoloPi"
                select i.Title;

    foreach (var i in query) {
        Console.WriteLine(i);
    }
}
```

Listing 4-6 creates a new instance of the *DataContext* class, passing in the URL of the target site, which can be the URL of any SharePoint site with a data structure compatible with the site from which you generated the model, and employing the *using* keyword to dispose of unmanaged resources expediently. Then, it simply queries the collection of *Invoices* provided by the current context, just as you would do with any other LINQ query. Under the covers, the query engine creates a CAML query and sends it to the Invoices list using an *SPQuery* instance, invoking the *SPList.GetItems* method. If you want to see the auto-generated CAML query, you can set the *Log* property of the *DataContext* instance to a *TextWriter* object, for example *Console.Out* if you are working with a Console application. Here's the syntax:

```
spContext.Log = Console.Out;
```

And here's the CAML code generated for the query in Listing 4-6:

```
<View>
  <Query>
    <Where>
      <And>
        <BeginsWith><FieldRef Name="ContentTypeId" />
          <Value Type="ContentTypeId">0x0101</Value>
        </BeginsWith>
        <Eq>
          <FieldRef Name="Created_x0020_By" /><Value Type="Text">SP2010DEV\PaoloPi</Value>
        </Eq>
      </And>
    </Where>
  </Query>
  <ViewFields>
    <FieldRef Name="Title" />
  </ViewFields>
  <RowLimit Paged="TRUE">2147483647</RowLimit>
</View>
```

The LINQ to SharePoint query engine allows you to define many kinds of queries, with partitioning (*where*), projection (*select*), and under some circumstances, with relationships (*join*). Imagine that the "Invoices" list of documents has a lookup field that accepts a *DevLeapContact* from the "DevLeap Contacts" custom list. If you refresh the model (via SPMetal.EXE), after adding such a lookup field in the Invoices list, you will see that the class mapped to the *Invoices* property of the *DataContext* has become a custom *InvoicesDocument*, that inherits from the original *Document* type as shown in Listing 4-7.

LISTING 4-7 The definition of the *InvoicesDocument* type.

```
[Microsoft.SharePoint.Linq.ContentTypeAttribute(
    Name="Document", Id="0x0101", List="Invoices")]
internal partial class InvoicesDocument : Document {
    private Microsoft.SharePoint.Linq.EntityRef<DevLeapContact> _devLeapContact;

    // Code omitted for the sake of brevity ...
```

```
public InvoicesDocument() {
        this._devLeapContact = new
            Microsoft.SharePoint.Linq.EntityRef<DevLeapContact>();
        this._devLeapContact.OnSync += new System.EventHandler
         <Microsoft.SharePoint.Linq.AssociationChangedEventArgs
            <DevLeapContact>> (this.OnDevLeapContactSync);
        this._devLeapContact.OnChanged += new System.EventHandler(
            this.OnDevLeapContactChanged);
        this._devLeapContact.OnChanging += new System.EventHandler(
            this.OnDevLeapContactChanging);
        this.OnCreated();
}

[Microsoft.SharePoint.Linq.AssociationAttribute(
    Name="DevLeap_x0020_Contact", Storage="_devLeapContact",
    MultivalueType=Microsoft.SharePoint.Linq.AssociationType.Single,
    List="DevLeap Contacts")]
public DevLeapContact DevLeapContact {
        get {
                return this._devLeapContact.GetEntity();
        }
        set {
                this._devLeapContact.SetEntity(value);
        }
}

private void OnDevLeapContactChanging(object sender, System.EventArgs e) {
        this.OnPropertyChanging("DevLeapContact", this._devLeapContact.Clone());
}

private void OnDevLeapContactChanged(object sender, System.EventArgs e) {
        this.OnPropertyChanged("DevLeapContact");
}

private void OnDevLeapContactSync(object sender,
    Microsoft.SharePoint.Linq.AssociationChangedEventArgs<DevLeapContact> e) {
        if ((Microsoft.SharePoint.Linq.AssociationChangedState.Added ==
            e.State)) {
                e.Item.InvoicesDocument.Add(this);
        }
        else {
                e.Item.InvoicesDocument.Remove(this);
        }
    }
}
```

This new type has a property named *DevLeapContact*, of type *DevLeapContact*, which internally works with a private storage field of type *EntityRef<DevLeapContact>*. In addition, the type constructor automatically creates an instance of that field and registers some event handlers to manage the synchronization of the association between the *InvoicesDocument* and its corresponding *DevLeapContact*.

On the other side, the *DevLeapContact* type has been changed, too. In fact, now it supports a public property of type *Microsoft.SharePoint.Linq.EntitySet<InvoicesDocument>*, which represents a reference to all the invoices for the current contact.

Now comes the nice part of the story: you can define a LINQ query that joins these entities. In addition, you can use deferred loading of entities when dynamically browsing related items. Listing 4-8 shows a sample query with a *join* syntax.

LISTING 4-8 A LINQ to SharePoint query that uses a *join* between contacts and invoices.

```
using (DevbookDataContext spContext = new
    DevbookDataContext("http://devbook.sp2010.local/")) {

    var query = from c in spContext.DevLeapContacts
                join i in spContext.Invoices on c.Id equals i.DevLeapContact.Id
                select new { c.ContactID, c.Title, InvoiceTitle = i.Title };

    // Use the query results ...
}
```

The output of this query will be a set of new anonymous types that expose the *ContactID*, contact *Title*, and Invoice *Title*. The CAML query sent to the SharePoint is as follows:

```
<View>
  <Query>
    <Where>
      <And>
        <BeginsWith>
          <FieldRef Name="ContentTypeId" />
          <Value Type="ContentTypeId">0x010100</Value>
        </BeginsWith>
        <BeginsWith>
          <FieldRef Name="DevLeap_x0020_ContactContentTypeId" />
          <Value Type="Lookup">0x0100A60F69C4B1304FBDA6C4B4A25939979F</Value>
        </BeginsWith>
      </And>
    </Where>
    <OrderBy Override="TRUE" />
  </Query>
  <ViewFields>
    <FieldRef Name="DevLeap_x0020_ContactDevLeapContactID" />
    <FieldRef Name="DevLeap_x0020_ContactTitle" />
    <FieldRef Name="Title" />
  </ViewFields>
  <ProjectedFields>
    <Field Name="DevLeap_x0020_ContactDevLeapContactID" Type="Lookup"
        List="DevLeap_x0020_Contact" ShowField="DevLeapContactID" />
    <Field Name="DevLeap_x0020_ContactTitle" Type="Lookup"
        List="DevLeap_x0020_Contact" ShowField="Title" />
    <Field Name="DevLeap_x0020_ContactContentTypeId" Type="Lookup"
        List="DevLeap_x0020_Contact" ShowField="ContentTypeId" />
  </ProjectedFields>
```

```xml
<Joins>
  <Join Type="INNER" ListAlias="DevLeap_x0020_Contact">
    <!--List Name: DevLeap Contacts-->
    <Eq>
      <FieldRef Name="DevLeap_x0020_Contact" RefType="ID" />
      <FieldRef List="DevLeap_x0020_Contact" Name="ID" />
    </Eq>
  </Join>
</Joins>
<RowLimit Paged="TRUE">2147483647</RowLimit>
</View>
```

Notice the elements *ProjectedFields* and *Joins* in the CAML code. Listing 4-9 illustrates deferred loading in action.

LISTING 4-9 A LINQ to SharePoint query using deferred loading.

```csharp
using (DevbookDataContext spContext = new
    DevbookDataContext("http://devbook.sp2010.local/")) {

    var query = from c in spContext.DevLeapContacts
                select c;

    foreach (var c in query) {
        Console.WriteLine(c.Title);
        foreach (var i in c.InvoicesDocument) {
            Console.WriteLine(i.Title);
        }
    }
}
```

In Listing 4-9, the first LINQ query is converted into CAML and executed against SharePoint within the first and external *foreach* block. Then, when the inner *foreach* block browses for the collection of *InvoicesDocument* of the current contact, the LINQ to SharePoint engine will automatically execute a CAML query to retrieve the invoices belonging to the current contact. This is a default behavior, which you can change by setting the *DeferredLoadingEnabled* property of the *DataContext* to *false*, as shown in the following:

```csharp
spContext.DeferredLoadingEnabled = false;
```

If you're familiar with LINQ, you probably use hierarchical grouped queries, making use of the *join into* (also known as "group join") clause, which avoids the need to execute a separate query to retrieve the invoices for every single contact. However, the LINQ to SharePoint query provider has some limitations, due to its use of CAML queries under the covers. For example, with CAML, you cannot query more than one list at a time, so you can't use a group join. Listing 4-10 presents a code excerpt that declares an unsupported group join query.

LISTING 4-10 An unsupported LINQ to SharePoint query syntax.

```
using (DevbookDataContext spContext = new
    DevbookDataContext("http://devbook.sp2010.local/")) {

    var query = from c in spContext.DevLeapContacts
                join i in spContext.Invoices on c.Id equals i.DevLeapContact.Id
                into invoices
                select new { c.Id, c.Title, Invoiced = invoices };
}
```

When you try to execute a query like this, the LINQ to SharePoint query provider throws an exception similar to this:

```
Unhandled Exception: System.InvalidOperationException: The query uses unsupported elements,
such as references to more than one list, or the projection of a complete entity by using
EntityRef/EntitySet.
```

Moreover, LINQ to SharePoint does not support multi-fetch queries that query across multiple lists, or join clauses on fields other than *Lookup* fields. Also, you cannot define queries across multiple websites or that query different *DataContext* instances. Finally, you cannot use mathematical functions, because CAML does not support them. Overall, LINQ to SharePoint does not support queries that cannot be translated into CAML syntax.

 More Information For a complete list of unsupported syntax and commands, please refer to MSDN Online at *http://msdn.microsoft.com/en-us/library/ee536585.aspx*.

Managing Data

The previous section showed that LINQ to SharePoint provides a convenient syntax for executing CAML queries with a fully-typed approach. Even if this might be sufficient for your needs, the story becomes more interesting when you consider that LINQ to SharePoint gives you access to data using a kind of SharePoint-specific O/RM, meaning you can also manage (insert, update, delete) data using LINQ to SharePoint and its fully-typed approach.

Here's a quick initial example. The code in Listing 4-11 queries for a specific contact in the list of DevLeap Contacts, using a LINQ to SharePoint query, and then changes the *Country* property of the retrieved item.

LISTING 4-11 Using LINQ to SharePoint to change an entity.

```
using (DevbookDataContext spContext = new DevbookDataContext(
    "http://devbook.sp2010.local/")) {

    var contact = (from c in spContext.DevLeapContacts
                   where c.ContactID == "PP001"
                   select c).FirstOrDefault();

    // Let's see if we found the target contact
    if (contact != null) {
        contact.Country = Country.USA;
        spContext.SubmitChanges();
    }
}
```

As Listing 4-11 demonstrates, the process is both simple and intuitive. You just need to retrieve the object, change its properties, and then confirm the changes by invoking the *SubmitChanges* method of the *DataContext*. You should consider *SubmitChanges* as the counterpart of the *Update* method in the standard Server Object Model. In fact, just as with the Server Object Model, whenever you change an instance of an entity that models an item in a SharePoint list, you are changing the in-memory copy of that data, not the SharePoint content database. Behind the scenes, the LINQ to SharePoint engine tracks this change, so you can apply it on the real content database when you invoke the *DataContext. SubmitChanges* method.

Internally, the *DataContext* base class provides an object tracker (an internal *EntityTracker* class) that tracks any changes you make to in-memory copies of typed entities. Furthermore, as you have already seen in the previous section, the base *Item* class that every LINQ to SharePoint entity inherits implements the *ITrackEntityState* interface, which provides an *EntityState* property that can assume one of the following values:

- *Unchanged*   The entity has not been changed.

- *ToBeInserted*   The entity is new, and will be inserted into its parent list when you call *SubmitChanges*.

- *ToBeUpdated*   The entity has been changed and will be updated in the content database when you call *SubmitChanges*.

- *ToBeDeleted*   The entity has been deleted and will be permanently removed from the content database when you call *SubmitChanges*.

- *ToBeRecycled*   The entity has been deleted and will be moved to the Recycle Bin when you call *SubmitChanges*.

- *Deleted*   The entity has been deleted or recycled.

For example, if you test the *EntityState* property of the contact in Listing 4-11, you will see that the entity is in the *Unchanged* state just after retrieval. As soon as you change the *Country* property, its state becomes *ToBeUpdated,*. Finally, just after you invoke the *SubmitChanges* method, the state returns to *Unchanged*, because the entity has been synchronized with the content database.

This tracking behavior is provided transparently by default whenever you create a *DataContext* instance and retrieve modeled entities. Note that tracking does not work on anonymous types that you get through LINQ queries that use custom projection. However, this behavior has an impact on performance and resource consumption. Therefore, if you don't need to manage data (such as when you need to query and render contents in a read-only fashion), you can disable the entity tracking service by setting the *ObjectTrackingEnabled* property of the *DataContext* class to *false*:

```
spContext.ObjectTrackingEnabled = false;
```

In the next few pages, you will see how to manage data, taking advantage of the LINQ to SharePoint tracking engine through some concrete examples. You've already seen an example of updating an item in Listing 4-11, so I won't repeat that operation.

Inserting a New Item

To insert a new item into a list, you first create the item instance, just as you would with any .NET object. Next, you need to configure its properties, and finally, you need to add the new item to its parent list and submit changes to the content database. The code in Listing 4-12 illustrates this process.

LISTING 4-12 Inserting a new item in a list using LINQ to SharePoint.

```
using (DevbookDataContext spContext = new
    DevbookDataContext("http://devbook.sp2010.local/")) {
    DevLeapCustomer newCustomer = new DevLeapCustomer {
        Title = "Andrea Pialorsi",
        ContactID = "AP001",
        CompanyName = "DevLeap",
        Country = Country.Italy,
        CustomerLevel = CustomerLevel.LevelA,
    };

    spContext.DevLeapContacts.InsertOnSubmit(newCustomer);
    spContext.SubmitChanges();
}
```

The key point of this example, aside from the *SubmitChanges* method invocation that you have already seen, is the call to the *InsertOnSubmit* method of the *EntityList<T>* class that lies behind the *DevLeapContacts* property of the *DataContext*. The *InsertOnSubmit* method accepts an item to be inserted into the target list as soon as you invoke *SubmitChanges*. The entity passed to the method will acquire a state of *ToBeInserted*. Note that the *InsertOnSubmit* method is fully typed according to the generic type *T* of the *EntityList<T>* class. Thus, in Listing 4-12 you can invoke this method by providing a class of type *DevLeapContact* or any type inherited from *DevLeapContact*, such as *DevLeapCustomer* or *DevLeapSupplier*.

The *EntityList<T>* class also provides an *InsertAllOnSubmit* method, which lets you insert a group of entities, instead of a single entity. This last method requires an argument of type *IEnumerable<T>*, representing the collection of items to insert.

Deleting or Recycling an Existing Item

Deleting an item is much like inserting a new item. The *EntityList<T>* class provides a *DeleteOnSubmit* method, as well as a *DeleteAllOnSubmit* method, similar to the methods presented in the preceding section. The former accepts a single item to delete, while the latter accepts a collection of type *IEnumerable<T>* representing the items to delete. Both of these methods permanently delete the target items from the content database when you confirm the action by invoking *SubmitChanges*. SharePoint provides a recycle bin feature, so the *EntityList<T>* class also provides a couple of methods specifically intended to move items into the recycle bin, instead of permanently deleting them. These methods are *RecycleOnSubmit* and *RecycleAllOnSubmit*. Listing 4-13 shows a code excerpt that illustrates how to delete or recycle an item.

LISTING 4-13 Deleting or recycling an item from a list using LINQ to SharePoint.

```
using (DevbookDataContext spContext = new DevbookDataContext(
    "http://devbook.sp2010.local/")) {
    var contact = (from c in spContext.DevLeapContacts
                   where c.ContactID == "AP001"
                   select c).FirstOrDefault();

    // Let's see if we found the target contact
    if (contact != null) {
        if (recycle) {
            spContext.DevLeapContacts.RecycleOnSubmit(contact);
        }
        else {
            spContext.DevLeapContacts.DeleteOnSubmit(contact);
        }
        spContext.SubmitChanges();
    }
}
```

Advanced Topics

In this section, you'll see some more advanced topics about using LINQ to SharePoint. These topics include managing concurrency conflicts, working with the identity management services, handling disconnected entities, supporting versioning, and extending the entity model.

Handling Concurrency Conflicts

Whenever you have a data management infrastructure that works when disconnected from the source repository, you will inevitably face concurrency conflicts. In fact, every single time you insert, update, or delete any data, you are working with an in-memory copy of the contents; therefore, you have no guarantee that your changes will be effectively confirmed by the back-end store when you invoke *SubmitChanges*. For example, when you retrieve an item from a list to change its properties, someone else might change that same item concurrently. Thus, when you try to apply your changes to the back-end repository, it would throw a concurrency conflict exception.

Fortunately, LINQ to SharePoint has established and complete support for concurrency conflicts. In fact, the *SubmitChanges* method has three overloads:

```
public void SubmitChanges();
public void SubmitChanges(ConflictMode failureMode);
public void SubmitChanges(ConflictMode failureMode, bool systemUpdate);
```

At this point, the first overload should be familiar (you have seen it in many of the previous code listings). Both the second and the third overloads accept an argument of type *ConflictMode*, which is an *enum* defined in the following excerpt:

```
public enum ConflictMode {
    ContinueOnConflict,
    FailOnFirstConflict
}
```

The names of the available values reveal their purposes:

- *ContinueOnConflict*   When any concurrency conflict occurs, the *DataContext* will skip the conflicting items, but it will continue to submit changes for all non-conflicting items. When the *SubmitChanges* method completes with conflicts it throws a *ChangeConflictException*, so you will have the opportunity to evaluate conflicts and decide what to do.

- *FailOnFirstConflict*   Stop processing the *SubmitChanges* method as soon as any concurrency conflict occurs. This overload also throws a *ChangeConflictException* so that you can evaluate the conflict and decide what to do. Any modifications submitted before the first conflict will be persisted to the content database.

Note The third overload also accepts a *Boolean* argument with name *systemUpdate*, which is not directly related to handling concurrency conflicts, but simply allows you to update the content database without incrementing the version number of the changed items. By default, the *SubmitChanges* overload without arguments uses a *ConflictMode* with a value of *FailOnFirstConflict*, and a *systemUpdate* with a value of *false*.

When you submit changes to the content database, and a change conflict occurs, you can catch a *ChangeConflictException*, which contains a description tightly bound to SharePoint's typical web scenario. As an example, here's the *Message* property for a concurrency conflict exception:

```
Your changes conflict with those made concurrently by another user. If you want your changes
to be applied, click Back in your Web browser, refresh the page, and resubmit your changes.
```

To solve conflicts, you can browse the *ChangeConflicts* property of the *DataContext* class instance. This property is a collection of objects of type *ObjectChangeConflict*, which you can enumerate to inspect all conflicting items. Every *ObjectChangeConflict* instance exposes a property named *Object*, of type *System.Object* that references the current conflicting item. You can cast that property to the real target entity instance. In addition, you can inspect the conflicting members of the current conflicting item by enumerating the *MemberConflicts* property of every *ObjectChangeConflict* instance. Finally, each element of the *MemberConflicts* collection is of type *MemberChangeConflict* and provides you with some detailed information about the member conflict. For example, you can see the member name and type; the original value of the member when you retrieved the entity from the SharePoint content database; the current value in memory; and the actual value in the content database.

With that information, to solve concurrency issues, you need to invoke the *Resolve* method, which has several overloads for both *ObjectChangeConflict* and *MemberChangeConflict* values. In essence, the *Resolve* method let you determine which values win—those of the current user or those in the content database (the other concurrent user).

Here are the overloads for the *Resolve* method of the *ObjectChangeConflict* class:

```
public void Resolve();
public void Resolve(RefreshMode refreshMode);
public void Resolve(RefreshMode refreshMode, bool autoResolveDeletes);
```

The *RefreshMode* argument is the most interesting part of these method overloads, because this is how you determine how to resolve conflicts. *RefreshMode* is an *enum* type, defined as follows:

```
public enum RefreshMode {
    KeepChanges,
    KeepCurrentValues,
    OverwriteCurrentValues
}
```

The *ObjectChangeConflict.Resolve* method changes its behavior depending on the *RefreshMode* value you provide:

- *KeepChanges*   Accepts the current user's changes, if any; otherwise, it reloads values from the content database. This acts like a synchronizer with the content database, without losing the user's changes.

- *KeepCurrentValues*   Causes the current user's values to win over the current database values.

- *OverwriteCurrentValues*   Makes all values match the latest values in the content database (the other concurrent user's values win).

The first overload of *ObjectChangeConflict.Resolve* internally assumes a value of *KeepChanges* for its *RefreshMode*. The third overload accepts a *Boolean* argument named *autoResolveDeletes*, which when *false* instructs the entity tracking engine to throw an *InvalidOperationException* if a target item has been deleted.

Table 4-3 contains a matrix of possible values, which helps to understand the behavior of the *ObjectChangeConflict.Resolve* method.

TABLE 4-3 **Schema of the Behavior of the *ObjectChangeConflict.Resolve* Method**

RefreshMode	Original Values	Current Values	Database Values	Final Values
KeepChanges	Country = Italy Company = A	Country = USA Company = A	Country = Germany Company = B	Country = USA Company = B
KeepCurrentValues	Country = Italy Company = A	Country = USA Company = A	Country = Germany Company = B	Country = USA Company = A
OverwriteCurrentValues	Country = Italy Company = A	Country = USA Company = A	Country = Germany Company = B	Country = Germany Company = B

The *MemberChangeConflict.Resolve* method works almost the same as the one provided by the *ObjectChangeConflict* class. However, it affects only one member at time, instead of the whole entity. It also has a couple of overloads:

```
public void Resolve(RefreshMode refreshMode);
public void Resolve(object value);
```

The first overload works exactly the same as the *ObjectChangeConflict* method, but affects only the current member. The second overload lets you provide a custom value to force onto the content database. Thus, in this last case, you can completely change the final value of the member, providing a new value that's different from the current, original, or database values.

Lastly, there is also a *ResolveAll* method provided by the *ChangeConflictCollection* class. It is useful when you want to solve all conflicts in one shot by applying the same conflict resolution logic to all the conflicts.

Listing 4-14 shows a complete code example of managing concurrency conflicts in LINQ to SharePoint.

LISTING 4-14 Concurrency conflict management using LINQ to SharePoint.

```
using (DevbookDataContext spContext = new
    DevbookDataContext("http://devbook.sp2010.local/")) {
    var contacts = from c in spContext.DevLeapContacts
                   where c.Country == Country.Italy
                   select c;

    String conflictingItemID = contacts.FirstOrDefault().ContactID;

    foreach (var item in contacts) {
        item.CompanyName += String.Format(" - Changed on {0}", DateTime.Now);
    }

    // Before submitting changes, the code simulate concurrency
    // changing one of the items from another DataContext
    using (DevbookDataContext spContextOther =
        new DevbookDataContext("http://devbook.sp2010.local/")) {
        var conflictingItem = (from c in spContextOther.DevLeapContacts
                               where c.ContactID == conflictingItemID
                               select c).FirstOrDefault();

        conflictingItem.Country = Country.USA;
        spContextOther.SubmitChanges();
    }
    try {
        spContext.SubmitChanges(ConflictMode.ContinueOnConflict)
    }
    catch (ChangeConflictException ex) {
        Console.WriteLine(ex.Message);

        // Browse for conflicting items
        foreach (var conflict in spContext.ChangeConflicts) {
            // Check if the item has been deleted by
            // someone else
            if (conflict.IsDeleted) {
                Console.WriteLine("Unfortunately the item has been deleted, " +
                    "so your changes cannot be submitted!");
            }
            else {
                // Retrieve a typed reference to the conflicting item
                DevLeapContact contact = conflict.Object as DevLeapContact;

                // If the item is a DevLeapContact
                if (contact != null) {
                    Console.WriteLine("Contact with ID {0} is in conflict!",
                        contact.ContactID);
```

```
                        // Browse for conflicting members
                        foreach (var member in conflict.MemberConflicts) {
                            Console.WriteLine("Member {0} is in conflict.\n\t" +
                            "Current Value: {1}\n\tOriginal Value: " +
                            "{2}\n\tDatabase Value: {3}",
                                member.Member.Name,
                                member.CurrentValue,
                                member.OriginalValue,
                                member.DatabaseValue);
                        }
                        Console.WriteLine("Make your choice: Override Database " +
                          "Value (Y) or Skip your Current Values (N)?");
                        String choice = Console.ReadLine().ToLower();

                        switch (choice) {
                            case "y":
                            case "yes":
                                conflict.Resolve(RefreshMode.KeepChanges, true);
                                break;
                            case "n":
                            case "no":
                                conflict.Resolve(RefreshMode.OverwriteCurrentValues,
                                    true);
                                break;
                            default:
                                break;
                        }
                    }
                }
            }
        spContext.SubmitChanges();
    }
}
```

Listing 4-14 uses a couple of *DataContext* instances to simulate a concurrency conflict. It asks the end user, via a Console-based user interface, how to solve the generated conflict. It also demonstrates that LINQ to SharePoint provides a rich set of capabilities for resolving concurrency conflicts, making it a mature technology suitable for real-world business solutions.

Identity Management and Refresh

At the base of every O/RM framework, there is an engine—generally called identity management service—that avoids having duplicate in-memory instances of the same entity. LINQ to SharePoint also provides such a service. Consider the sample code in Listing 4-15.

LISTING 4-15 Code excerpt that illustrates identity management service behavior.

```
using (DevbookDataContext spContext = new DevbookDataContext(
    "http://devbook.sp2010.local/")) {

    var contacts = from c in spContext.DevLeapContacts
                   where c.CompanyName.Contains("DevLeap")
                   select c;

    // Change the Country property of the first contact
    contacts.FirstOrDefault().Country = Country.USA;

    // Show all the retrieved contacts
    foreach (var c in contacts) {
        Console.WriteLine("Customer with ID {0} has a Country value of {1}",
            c.ContactID, c.Country);
    }

    Console.WriteLine("------------------");

    // Retrieve the same contacts with another LINQ query
    var otherContacts = from c in spContext.DevLeapContacts
                        where c.CompanyName.Contains("DevLeap")
                        select c;

    // Show all the newly retrieved contacts
    foreach (var c in otherContacts) {
        Console.WriteLine("Customer with ID {0} has a Country value of {1}",
            c.ContactID, c.Country);
    }

    // Check if the two first contacts instances are the same contact
    Console.WriteLine("Do the contacts have the same HashCode? {0}",
        contacts.FirstOrDefault().GetHashCode() ==
            otherContacts.FirstOrDefault().GetHashCode());
}
```

The code retrieves the contacts whose *CompanyName* contains "DevLeap" from the list of DevLeap Contacts, and changes the *Country* property of the first contact to "USA." A second LINQ query retrieves the same list of contacts to check whether the result comes from the content database or from existing in-memory instances. To determine which, the code writes the *Country* value of every retrieved contact and compares the *HashCode* values of the first two instances of the retrieved contacts.

The following code is the output generated by Listing 4-15 at the Console window:

```
Customer with ID PP001 has a Country value of USA
Customer with ID AP001 has a Country value of Italy
------------------
Customer with ID PP001 has a Country value of USA
Customer with ID AP001 has a Country value of Italy
Do the contacts have the same HashCode? True
```

Not surprisingly, the entities are the same; in other words, the modified contact instance takes precedence over the instance retrieved from the content database. In fact, under the cover LINQ to SharePoint queries the content database twice, the first time executing the former query, and the second time for the latter. However, because the entities requested by the second query are already in-memory, the identity management service skips the data from the content database and uses the data of the existing in-memory instances instead. You might be wondering why it still executes the database query rather than using the in-memory data directly without stressing the database. The reason is that the engine *merges* the results retrieved from the database with any existing in-memory entities. If there are more items in the database than in memory, the engine will merge the new ones from the database and the rest that are already in memory. This is good behavior because it avoids duplication of data and instances. However, it's also good to be aware of it.

Given this behavior, you're probably wondering how you can refresh an entity from the content database, skipping any existing in-memory instance. To do that, you can use a different *DataContext*, unless you have to use the same *DataContext* instance. In that case, you can call the *DataContext* class's *Refresh* method, which has these overloads:

```
public void Refresh(RefreshMode mode, IEnumerable entities);
public void Refresh(RefreshMode mode, params object[] entities);
public void Refresh(RefreshMode mode, object entity);
```

All of these overloads accept an argument of type *RefreshMode*, which you have already seen in the previous section, "Handling Concurrency Conflicts." Depending on the value you choose for the *RefreshMode* argument, the *Refresh* method will forcibly reload data from the content database (*OverwriteCurrentValues*), or it will merge your changed values with those in the content database (*KeepChanges*). Generally, the value of *KeepCurrentValues* is not very useful when provided to the *Refresh* method, because it simply forces the entities to use the values already in-memory.

Disconnected Entities

In software solutions with a distributed architecture, you sometimes need to serialize an entity, transfer it across the wire to a remote site or consumer, and eventually get it back later to update the persistent storage. When your data is stored in SharePoint, LINQ to SharePoint becomes an interesting solution for working in a disconnected manner. In fact, when you generate the entity model with SPMetal.EXE and provide it with the */serialization:unidirectional* command line argument, the tool will mark all the generated entities with the *DataContract* attribute of the .NET 3.x Runtime serialization engine. Consequently, your entities will be serializable and can be used as the content of a Windows Communication Foundation message.

More Information If you would like to learn more about Windows Communication Foundation, consider reading *Windows Communication Foundation 4 Step by Step*, by John Sharp (Microsoft Press, 2010; ISBN: 978-0-7356-2336-1).

Listing 4-16 shows a code excerpt that serializes a LINQ to SharePoint entity.

LISTING 4-16 Serializing a LINQ to SharePoint *DevLeapContact* entity.

```
using (DevbookDataContext spContext = new DevbookDataContext(
    "http://devbook.sp2010.local/")) {

    spContext.DeferredLoadingEnabled = false;

    var contact = (from c in spContext.DevLeapContacts
                    where c.ContactID == "PP001"
                    select c).FirstOrDefault();

    // Let's see if we found the target contact
    if (contact != null) {
        // Prepare a DataContractSerializer instance
        DataContractSerializer dcs = new
            DataContractSerializer(typeof(DevLeapContact),
            new Type[] { typeof(DevLeapCustomer), typeof(DevLeapSupplier) });

        // Serialize the object graph
        using (XmlWriter xw = XmlWriter.Create(Console.Out)) {
            dcs.WriteObject(xw, contact);
            xw.Flush();
        }
    }
}
```

Note the line that disables *DeferredLoadingEnabled*. This is done to avoid circular references during entity serialization. Listing 4-17 shows the XML produced by the *DataContractSerializer* engine.

LISTING 4-17 The XML produced to serialize a *DevLeapContact* entity with *DataContractSerializer*.

```
<?xml version="1.0"?>
<DevLeapContact xmlns:i="http://www.w3.org/2001/XMLSchema-instance"
  i:type="DevLeapCustomer"
  xmlns="http://schemas.datacontract.org/2004/07/DevLeap.SP2010.Linq2SP">
    <_entityState>Unchanged</_entityState>
    <_id>1</_id>
    <_originalValues xmlns:d2p1=
      "http://schemas.microsoft.com/2003/10/Serialization/Arrays" i:nil="true" />
    <_path>/Lists/DevLeap Contacts</_path>
    <_title>Paolo Pialorsi</_title>
```

```
    <_version>19</_version>
    <_companyName>DevLeap</_companyName>
    <_contactID>PP001</_contactID>
    <_country>Italy</_country>
    <_invoicesDocument xmlns:d2p1=
      "http://schemas.datacontract.org/2004/07/Microsoft.SharePoint.Linq">
        <d2p1:Loaded>true</d2p1:Loaded>
        <d2p1:entities />
    </_invoicesDocument>
    <_customerLevel>LevelB</_customerLevel>
 </DevLeapContact>
```

The XML stream contains the basic private fields of the entity, its original values, and the entity state. Thus, the XML produced is not an ideal solution for an interoperable cross-platform solution, but can be used to connect WCF consumers with WCF services (from .NET to .NET).

When the consumer makes changes to the received serialized entities and sends them back to the server, you can use the *Attach* method of the *EntityList<T>* class on the service side to re-attach the entity to the *DataContext* and update the content database. Here's the signature of this method:

```
public void Attach(TEntity entity);
```

This method simply accepts the entity to attach back to the *DataContext* tracking engine.

> **Note** Even if this serialization behavior seems to be a great opportunity for defining enterprise solutions that use SharePoint as their back-end storage, it is important to understand that when you have many thousands of items corresponding to data records, it is bad practice to use SharePoint as the persistence storage. It would absolutely be better to have an external DBMS with a specific and well-designed schema, with indexes and stored procedures. Instead, when you need to render your external content as a standard SharePoint list, you can leverage Business Connectivity Services, covered in Chapter 25, "Business Connectivity Services." In software with a distributed architecture, you should create a persistence-ignorant data access layer that ignores how, where, and what the persistence is.

Model Extensions and Versioning

A final topic to cover here relates to managing model extensions and entity versioning. I'll start with a couple of examples. Imagine that you have a well-defined LINQ to SharePoint model, such as the one created at the beginning of this chapter. At some point in time a power user changes the data schema you provisioned, adding a custom column—such as a new *Address* column—to the *DevLeapCustomer* content type. To be able to see this new property, you should refresh the model via SPMetal.EXE, which will then update the entity definition. However, it is not always possible to update the entity model and refresh all deployed assemblies.

Now consider a different situation in which you have a content type that leverages a custom field type, and you want to use that content-type with LINQ to SharePoint. Unfortunately SPMetal.EXE does not support custom field types. Thus, you need to autonomously manage the code for reading and writing the custom field type.

> **More Information**   Chapter 11, "Developing Custom Fields," discusses developing and using custom field types in detail.

To manage these situations but still use LINQ to SharePoint, you can implement the *ICustomMapping* interface for entities that you want to extend or update. This interface was specifically designed to support you when extending LINQ to SharePoint entities. Here's its definition:

```
public interface ICustomMapping {
    void MapFrom(object listItem);
    void MapTo(object listItem);
    void Resolve(RefreshMode mode, object originalListItem, object databaseListItem);
}
```

The *MapFrom* and *MapTo* methods both receive an argument of type *Object*, which inter-nally is an *SPListItem* instance that corresponds to the native SharePoint item behind the current entity. Using the *MapFrom* method, you can read untyped values from the low-level *SPListItem* instance and use them to configure a property—or whatever you want—in the entity, while the *MapTo* method writes these properties back to the underlying *SPListItem*. The *Resolve* method is a conflict resolution method similar to the *ObjectChangeConflict* and *MemberChangeConflict* methods you've already seen; however, in this case, it is up to the project developer to define the concurrency conflict behavior. Listing 4-18 shows a custom entity type created using SPMetal.EXE and extended using the *ICustomMapping* interface.

LISTING 4-18 Implementing the *ICustomMapping* interface.

```
internal partial class DevLeapCustomer : ICustomMapping {

    private String _address;
    public String Address {
        get { return (this._ address); }
        set { this._ address = value; }
    }

    [CustomMapping(Columns = new String[] { "*" })]
    public void MapFrom(object listItem) {
        SPListItem item = listItem as SPListItem;
        if (item != null) {
            this.Address = item["address"].ToString();
        }
    }
```

```
        public void MapTo(object listItem) {
            SPListItem item = listItem as SPListItem;
            if (item != null) {
                item["address "] = this.Address;
            }
        }

        public void Resolve(RefreshMode mode, object originalListItem,
            object databaseListItem) {
            // Code omitted for the sake of brevity
        }
    }
```

Note the *CustomMapping* attribute applied on top of the *MapFrom* method. This is an attribute that identifies new columns mapped with the *MapFrom* method. It requires an array of *InternalName* values of supported columns. In this example, the *CustomMapping* attribute accepts any kind of new column ("*") in order to be useful in case of versioning.

Summary

In this chapter, you have seen how to implement LINQ to SharePoint to model SharePoint data as a set of typed entities, how to query that entity model, and how to manage data retrieved from LINQ queries. Lastly, you read about some advanced topics, such as managing concurrency conflicts, identity management, serialization, and versioning of entities.

Chapter 5
Client-Side Technologies

Another powerful new feature of Microsoft SharePoint 2010 is the rich set of libraries and tools it offers to support development of client-side solutions. Before SharePoint 2010, the only out-of-the-box method to communicate between SharePoint and a consumer application was to use WebDAV or SharePoint ASMX Web Services. However, both of these communication techniques were restrictive and not terribly easy to use. With the advent of Web 2.0 and the emerging need for a dynamic web user interface, the urge to go beyond that old-style paradigm has become a necessity. In this chapter, you will see how to take advantage of the new client-side technologies offered by SharePoint 2010 to implement Web 2.0 solutions as well as client-side solutions that consume SharePoint 2010 data.

Architectural Overview

I'll start with an architectural overview of the available technologies. Figure 5-1 shows a schema that illustrates the new data access model architecture of SharePoint 2010, which you previously saw in Chapter 4, "LINQ to SharePoint."

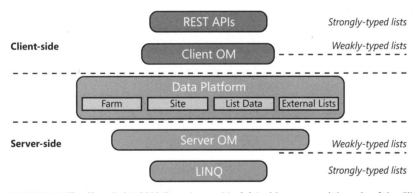

FIGURE 5-1 The SharePoint 2010 Data Access Model Architecture and the role of the Client Object Model.

When you need to access SharePoint's data in a strongly-typed manner, you can use the REST API interface, making use of the so-called "Open Data Protocol" (also known as OData). Similarly, when you simply need to access data through weakly-typed entities you can use the SharePoint Client Object Model.

> **More Information** To learn more about the Open Data Protocol, go to the official website for the protocol at *http://www.odata.org/.*

Whether you prefer a strongly-typed or weakly-typed approach, behind the scenes you'll find the same data foundation elements that already support the Server Object Model and LINQ to SharePoint.

SharePoint Client Object Model

The SharePoint Client Object Model is a set of libraries and classes with which you can consume SharePoint data through a specific object model, which can be considered a subset of the SharePoint Server Object Model.

> **Note** The Client Object Model can be downloaded as a redistributable package, targeting either x86 or x64 platforms. The package is available on the Microsoft website at *http://www. microsoft.com/downloads/en/details.aspx?FamilyID=b4579045-b183-4ed4-bf61-dc2f0deabe47.*

Figure 5-2 shows the overall architecture of the Client Object Model.

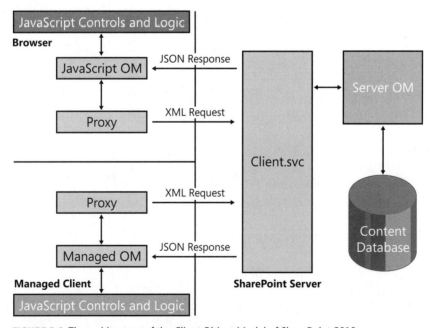

FIGURE 5-2 The architecture of the Client Object Model of SharePoint 2010.

The key advantage of the Client Object Model is that it supports multiple platforms. In fact, you can use it in any .NET managed application—even in a Silverlight solution, or in any solution that can run ECMAScript code. Under the covers, all these platforms will consume a new WCF service named *Client.svc*, published under the *_vti_bin/* folder of the current site. The service will accept XML requests and respond with JavaScript Object Notation (JSON) responses. In the following sections, you will see these different flavors of the Client Object Model.

Managed Client Object Model

The Managed Client Object Model is based on a set of .NET managed assemblies, which can be found in and referenced from the SharePoint14_Root\ISAPI folder. These assemblies are Microsoft.SharePoint.Client.dll and Microsoft.SharePoint.Client.Runtime.dll. They can be referenced by any 32-bit or 64-bit .NET 3.5 project.

Once you have referenced these assemblies, you first need to create an instance of the *ClientContext* class, defined in the *Microsoft.SharePoint.Client* namespace. This class represents the client context in which you are acting. It is also the proxy to the SharePoint server that you are targeting. The *ClientContext* class can be thought as the client-side version of the *SPContext* class. It has a couple of constructors based on the URL of the target site, provided as a *String* or as *System.Uri* type. As soon as you have a valid reference to the *ClientContext* you can browse its *Site* and *Web* properties, which are references to the Site Collection and the website that you are targeting. In Listing 5-1, you can see a code excerpt that queries the contents of a list of Contacts in the current website.

> **Note** To provision these content types and lists, refer to the code samples in Chapter 10, "Data Provisioning."

LISTING 5-1 Querying the contents of a list of contacts.

```
// Open the current ClientContext
ClientContext ctx = new ClientContext("http://devbook.sp2010.local/");

// Prepare a reference to the current Site Collection
Site site = ctx.Site;
ctx.Load(site);

// Prepare a reference to the current Web Site
Web web = site.RootWeb;
ctx.Load(web);

// Prepare a reference to the list of "DevLeap Contacts"
List list = web.Lists.GetByTitle("DevLeap Contacts");
ctx.Load(list);
```

```
// Execute the prepared commands against the target ClientContext
ctx.ExecuteQuery();

// Show the title of the list just retrieved
Console.WriteLine(list.Title);

// Prepare a query for all items in the list
CamlQuery query = new CamlQuery();
query.ViewXml = "<View/>";
ListItemCollection allContacts = list.GetItems(query);
ctx.Load(allContacts);

// Execute the prepared command against the target ClientContext
ctx.ExecuteQuery();

// Browse the result
Console.WriteLine("\nContacts");
foreach (ListItem listItem in allContacts) {
    Console.WriteLine("Id: {0} - Fullname: {1} - Company: {2} - Country: {3}",
        listItem["DevLeapContactID"],
        listItem["Title"],
        listItem["DevLeapCompanyName"],
        listItem["DevLeapCountry"]
        );
}
```

Each time you want to access an object, you first need to add a request for that object by invoking the *Load<T>* method of the *ClientContext*. You can load as many objects as you like. Many of the client-side objects have a type name that is the same as that of the Server Object Model counterpart, except that on the client side the SP prefix is missing. For example, *SPWeb* or *SPSite* on the server side, becomes *Web* or *Site* on the client side. Once you are ready to effectively query SharePoint, you must invoke the *ExecuteQuery* method of the *ClientContext* instance. It is particularly interesting to notice the syntax used in Listing 5-1 to query the items contained in the target list. The sample uses an instance of the *CamlQuery* class, which is passed to the *GetItems* method of the *List* instance variable representing the list on the client.

Although the Client Object Model provides you with a subset of the classes and methods from the Server Object Model, the object model is wide and comprises a rich set of types. Therefore, you will not see a reference of all of them here. Instead, this section will discuss more practical matters; later in the chapter, there will be some concrete examples, taken from everyday life.

Note If you would like to browse the entire set of types and members available in the Managed Client Object Model, go to the MSDN Online page at *http://msdn.microsoft.com/en-us/library/ee536622.aspx*.

One important thing to know is how to authenticate against a SharePoint server. By default, the Client Object Model uses the Windows integrated authentication. However, there may be circumstance in which you have a Forms-Based Authentication (FBA) or a custom authentication mechanism. The *ClientContext* class, through its *ClientRuntimeContext* base class, provides an *AuthenticationMode* property and a *FormsAuthenticationLoginInfo* property, which are useful to configure a set of FBA credentials. In the following code example, you can see how you should change the startup code of Listing 5-1:

```
ClientContext ctx = new ClientContext("http://devbook.sp2010.local/");
ctx.AuthenticationMode = ClientAuthenticationMode.FormsAuthentication;
FormsAuthenticationLoginInfo loginInfo = new FormsAuthenticationLoginInfo {
    LoginName = "UserLoginName",
    Password = "HereYourPassword",
};
ctx.FormsAuthenticationLoginInfo = loginInfo;
```

Note The SharePoint Client Object Model behavior could change if you use it within a public website with an anonymous user session. In fact, there are methods (for example, *List.GetItems*) that by default cannot be called by an anonymous user. Of course, you can change default permissions to enable anonymous users to call such methods.

Another important thing to know is that by default, to improve performance and reduce network traffic, the data retrieval engine of the Client Object Model does not retrieve all of the properties of the items you load. For example, when you query the items of a list, as in Listing 5-1, and you try to access the *DisplayName* property of an item, a *PropertyOrFieldNotInitializedException* exception is thrown, with the following description:

```
Unhandled Exception: Microsoft.SharePoint.Client.PropertyOrFieldNotInitializedException: The
property or field has not been initialized. It has not been requested or the request has not
been executed. It may need to be explicitly requested.
```

Table 5-1 presents the list of properties that are not automatically retrieved, unless you explicitly request them for the main client-side types.

Note For further details about data retrieval policies, go to MSDN Online at *http://msdn.microsoft.com/en-us/library/ee539350.aspx*.

TABLE 5-1 Properties That Are Not Automatically Retrieved Through the Client Object Model

Type	Properties Not Available by Default
Folder	ContentTypeOrder, UniqueContentTypeOrder
List	BrowserFileHandling, DataSource, EffectiveBasePermissions, HasUniqueRoleAssignments, IsSiteAssetsLibrary, OnQuickLaunch, RoleAssignments, SchemaXml, ValidationFormula, ValidationMessage
ListItem	DisplayName, EffectiveBasePermissions, HasUniqueRoleAssignments, RoleAssignments
SecurableObject	HasUniqueRoleAssignments, RoleAssignments
Site	Usage
Web	EffectiveBasePermissions, HasUniqueRoleAssignments, RoleAssignments

Listing 5-2 shows how to instruct the *ClientContext* to retrieve the *DisplayName* and the *RoleAssignments* properties for each *ListItem* instance.

LISTING 5-2 Querying the contents of a list of contacts, including some extra properties.

```
// Browse the result
foreach (ListItem listItem in allContacts) {
    ctx.Load(listItem,
        item => item.DisplayName,
        item => item.RoleAssignments);

    ctx.ExecuteQuery();

    Console.WriteLine("Id: {0} - Fullname: {1} - Company: {2} - Country: {3}",
        listItem["DevLeapContactID"],
        listItem["Title"],
        listItem["DevLeapCompanyName"],
        listItem["DevLeapCountry"]
        );

    Console.WriteLine(listItem.DisplayName);
}
```

The code sample uses the *ClientContext.Load<T>* method, which accepts a parameter array of expressions of type *Expression<Func<T, Object>>*. Here is the method signature:

```
public void Load<T>(
    T clientObject,
    params Expression<Func<T, Object>>[] retrievals)
where T : ClientObject
```

The expressions define the properties to retrieve from the server. In Listing 5-2, they are defined using lambda expressions. However, the code excerpt of Listing 5-2 is a little bit stressing for the server. In fact, each item in the list of contacts queries the server for its own extra properties. It would have been better to instruct the *ClientContext* to retrieve all the properties at one time. Luckily, the Client Object Model also provides an extension method, called *IncludeWithDefaultProperties* and defined in type *ClientObjectQueryableExtension*, that instructs the *ClientContext* about the properties to retrieve by default when querying a target list of objects. Listing 5-3 shows a revised version of the code of Listing 5-2.

LISTING 5-3 Querying the contents of a list of contacts, including some extra properties into the default list of properties.

```
// Prepare a query for all items in the list
CamlQuery query = CamlQuery.CreateAllItemsQuery();
ListItemCollection allContacts = list.GetItems(query);
ctx.Load(allContacts);

// Define the extra properties to include in default properties
ctx.Load(allContacts,
    items => items.IncludeWithDefaultProperties(
        item => item.DisplayName,
        item => item.RoleAssignments));

// Execute the prepared command against the target ClientContext
ctx.ExecuteQuery();
```

If you would like to selectively define the fields to retrieve from the target list, you can use the CAML query definition to specify the *ViewFields* to retrieve. Listing 5-4 shows the syntax.

LISTING 5-4 Querying the contents of a list of contacts, projecting fields in the output.

```
// Prepare a query for all items in the list
CamlQuery query = new CamlQuery();
query.ViewXml = "<View><ViewFields><FieldRef Name='DevLeapContactID'/>" +
"<FieldRef Name='Title'/><FieldRef Name='DevLeapCountry'/></ViewFields></View>";
ListItemCollection allContacts = list.GetItems(query);
ctx.Load(allContacts);

// Execute the prepared command against the target ClientContext
ctx.ExecuteQuery();
```

Of course, if you try to access a field that is not explicitly declared in the query, you will get a *PropertyOrFieldNotInitializedException* exception, as with the previous examples.

Another technique to project a subset of fields for a query is to use the *Include* extension method, still defined in type *ClientObjectQueryableExtension*. Listing 5-5 presents the syntax, which produces a result equivalent to Listing 5-4, but without involving CAML.

LISTING 5-5 Querying the contents of a list of contacts, projecting fields in the output without using CAML.

```
// Prepare a query for all items in the list
CamlQuery query = CamlQuery.CreateAllItemsQuery();
ListItemCollection allContacts = list.GetItems(query);

// Define the columns to include in the output
ctx.Load(allContacts,
    items => items.Include(
        item => item["DevLeapContactID"],
        item => item["Title"],
        item => item["DevLeapCountry"]
        ));

// Execute the prepared command against the target ClientContext
ctx.ExecuteQuery();
```

The signature of the *Include* method accepts an array of *Expression<Func<TSource, object>>* arguments, which define a set of inclusion rules. In Listing 5-5, these expressions are defined using some lambda expressions.

As with custom projection rules, you can also use CAML to define custom filters (for instance, data partitioning) on data to retrieve. For example, you could select only the contacts with a value of "Italy" in the *DevLeapCountry* field by using a *<Where />* CAML clause. However, one great feature of the Client Object Model is the support for LINQ queries. In fact, when you work with the Client Object Model you can provide LINQ queries to a *LoadQuery<T>* specific method, which will convert these queries into requests for the SharePoint server.

> **Important** Be aware that when you define LINQ queries with the Client Object Model, you are using LINQ to Objects, and not the custom LINQ to SharePoint query provider discussed in Chapter 4. This implies that you do not have all the infrastructural services provided by the LINQ to SharePoint query provider.

Listing 5-6 presents a code excerpt that uses LINQ to Objects and the Client Object Model to query for the Italian contacts.

LISTING 5-6 Querying the contents of a list of contacts using a LINQ query.

```
// Prepare a query for all items in the list
CamlQuery query = CamlQuery.CreateAllItemsQuery();
ListItemCollection allContacts = list.GetItems(query);

var linqQuery =
    from c in allContacts
    where (String)c["DevLeapCountry"] == "Italy"
    select c;
```

```
ctx.LoadQuery(linqQuery);

// Execute the prepared command against the target ClientContext
ctx.ExecuteQuery();
```

The key point of Listing 5-6 is the invocation of method *LoadQuery<T>*, which provides the following pair of overloads:

```
public IEnumerable<T> LoadQuery<T>(ClientObjectCollection<T> clientObjects)
    where T : ClientObject;
public IEnumerable<T> LoadQuery<T>(IQueryable<T> clientObjects)
    where T : ClientObject;
```

Similar to the *Load<T>* method, the *LoadQuery<T>* method works only with a result inheriting from *ClientObject*. As a consequence of this behavior, you cannot use the *LoadQuery<T>* method to retrieve custom anonymous types, projecting only a subset of the available fields of an item. The main difference between *Load<T>* and *LoadQuery<T>* is that the former loads data into the client objects retrieved from the SharePoint server; the latter returns an *IEnumerable<T>* that represents an independent collection of items. This behavior implies that the object instances allocated by *Load<T>* will be released by the Garbage Collector when the *ClientContext* goes out of scope, while object instances returned by *LoadQuery<T>* can be collected independently from the *ClientContext*.

The *ClientObject* type is the base abstract class defined in the Client Object Model to describe any object retrieved on a remote client. The Client Object Model also provides a base abstract *ClientValueObject* class, which represents a client-side version of a server-side property value. For example, a *ListItem* is a class inherited from *ClientObject*, while the *ContentTypeId* property of a *ListItem* is a class inherited from *ClientValueObject*. For the sake of thoroughness, a property like the *Title* property of a *List* instance is a scalar value, and behaves like any classic .NET type.

The main difference between an object inherited from the *ClientObject* class and another one inherited from *ClientValueObject* lies in their behavior when using them within a query or a method call. In fact, you cannot use a *ClientValueObject* inherited object as the argument of a method or inside a query, unless you have not retrieved it from the server. However, you can reference a *ClientObject* inherited object in another method call or query definition, even if you did not already retrieve it from the server, because it will be correctly resolved by the Client Object Model.

Listing 5-7 illustrates a query based on objects inherited from *ClientObject*, such as the *Web* and the *List* properties.

LISTING 5-7 Using a *ClientObject* inherited object in direct method call.

```
// Open the current ClientContext
ClientContext ctx = new ClientContext("http://devbook.sp2010.local/");

// Prepare a reference to the target list, we can directly reference
// the property ctx.Web.Lists because both Web and Lists are of types
// inherited from ClientObject
List list = ctx.Web.Lists.GetByTitle("DevLeap Contacts");

// Retrieve the title of the list
ctx.Load(list,
    l => l.Title);

// Execute the query
ctx.ExecuteQuery();

// Show the result
Console.WriteLine(list.Title);
```

The code sample works correctly because the *ClientObject* inherited properties will be handled by the Client Object Model. However, if you try to access some of the properties of the *Web* instance of the current *ClientContext*, you will get an exception. For example, the following instruction would fail, unless you do not explicitly load the *Title* property of the current website:

```
Console.WriteLine(ctx.Web.Title);
```

Listing 5-8 presents a code excerpt that illustrates the incorrect use of a *ClientValueObject* inherited object.

LISTING 5-8 Incorrect use of a *ClientValueObject* inherited object before loading its value.

```
// Open the current ClientContext
ClientContext ctx = new ClientContext("http://devbook.sp2010.local/");

// Prepare a reference to the target list
// Here you will get a PropertyOrFieldNotInitializedException
// when accessing the Title property of the current website
List list = ctx.Web.Lists.GetByTitle(ctx.Web.Title);

// Retrieve the title of the list
ctx.Load(list,
    l => l.Title);

// Execute the query
ctx.ExecuteQuery();

// Show the result
Console.WriteLine(list.Title);
```

Here, the code fails, throwing a *PropertyOrFieldNotInitializedException* exception, because you need to explicitly load the *ClientValueObject* inherited object representing the *Web* instance before using it. Listing 5-9 shows the working code example.

LISTING 5-9 Using a *ClientValueObject* inherited object properly by loading its value before referencing it.

```
// Open the current ClientContext
ClientContext ctx = new ClientContext("http://devbook.sp2010.local/");

// Retrieve the title of the website
Web web = ctx.Web;
ctx.Load(web,
    w => w.Title);

// Execute the first query
ctx.ExecuteQuery();

// Prepare a reference to the target list
List list = ctx.Web.Lists.GetByTitle(web.Title);

// Retrieve the title of the list
ctx.Load(list,
    l => l.Title);

// Execute the second query
ctx.ExecuteQuery();

// Show the result
Console.WriteLine(list.Title);
```

Listing 5-9 correctly loads the *Title* property of the current *Web* before using it in the subsequent *GetByTitle* method call.

You can also use the method *IsPropertyAvailable*, inherited from *ClientObject*, to test the presence of a specific scalar property in a current *ClientObject* instance.

> **Warning** If the property you are looking for exists in the item schema, but it is missing on the client side, you can use the *Retrieve* method to explicitly retrieve all the scalar properties of a *ClientObject* instance, or just a set of specific scalar properties. However, the *Retrieve* method is documented on MSDN Online as "reserved for internal use only," so you use it at your own risk.

Silverlight Client Object Model

The Silverlight Client Object Model behaves almost the same as the Managed Client Object Model. You can find it in the SharePoint14_Root\TEMPLATE\LAYOUTS\ClientBin folder, and you can use it in any Silverlight 3.0 or higher solution by referencing the assemblies Microsoft.SharePoint.Client.Silverlight.dll and Microsoft.SharePoint.Client.Silverlight.Runtime.dll.

Note If you would like to learn more about developing with Microsoft Silverlight, read *Microsoft Silverlight 4 Step by Step*, by Laurence Moroney (Microsoft Press, 2010; ISBN: 978-0-7356-3887-7).

The Silverlight Client Object Model is useful whenever you need to develop a Silverlight solution that needs to interact with data stored in a SharePoint site. For example, you can use it to build a custom data entry user interface or a custom visualization of data, ready for hosting with the Silverlight Web Part.

 Note You can read more about the Silverlight Web Part in Chapter 6, "Web Part Basics," and Chapter 7, "Advanced Web Parts."

Imagine that you want to show the contacts of the sample list of contacts from the previous examples by using a custom Silverlight control. First, you can start creating a Silverlight Application. Just after creating the software solution, you need to make a reference to the Silverlight Client Object Model assemblies. Now assume that you want to render the contacts with a *ListBox* control, using a custom *ItemTemplate* for rendering. In Listing 5-10, you can see the XAML code of the *Main* control of the sample application.

LISTING 5-10 The XAML code of the Main control of the sample Silverlight application.

```xml
<UserControl x:Class="DevLeap.SilverlightClientOMDemo.MainPage"
    xmlns="http://schemas.microsoft.com/winfx/2006/xaml/presentation"
    xmlns:x="http://schemas.microsoft.com/winfx/2006/xaml"
    xmlns:d="http://schemas.microsoft.com/expression/blend/2008"
    xmlns:mc="http://schemas.openxmlformats.org/markup-compatibility/2006"
    xmlns:custom="clr-namespace:DevLeap.SilverlightClientOMDemo"
    mc:Ignorable="d"
    d:DesignHeight="300" d:DesignWidth="600">
    <UserControl.Resources>
        <custom:ListItemFieldConverter x:Key="ListItemFieldConverter" />
    </UserControl.Resources>

    <Grid x:Name="LayoutRoot" Background="LightGreen">
        <ListBox x:Name="AllContactsList">
            <ListBox.ItemTemplate>
                <DataTemplate>
                    <StackPanel Orientation="Vertical">
                        <TextBlock Text="{Binding Converter=
                            {StaticResource ListItemFieldConverter},
                            ConverterParameter='DevLeapContactID', Mode=OneWay}" />
                        <TextBlock Text="{Binding Converter=
                            {StaticResource ListItemFieldConverter},
                            ConverterParameter='Title', Mode=OneWay}" />
                        <TextBlock Text="{Binding Converter=
                            {StaticResource ListItemFieldConverter},
                            ConverterParameter='DevLeapCountry', Mode=OneWay}" />
                        <TextBlock Text="{Binding Converter=
```

```
                {StaticResource ListItemFieldConverter},
                ConverterParameter='DevLeapCompanyName', Mode=OneWay}" />
            </StackPanel>
        </DataTemplate>
    </ListBox.ItemTemplate>
</ListBox>
    </Grid>

</UserControl>
```

In Listing 5-10, the XAML code by itself is not particularly exciting, it just defines a *Grid* control, with a *ListBox* inside and a *DataTemplate* for rendering each item of the contacts list. The code behind the user control is more interesting; it makes use of the Silverlight Client Object Model. Listing 5-11 gives you a look at the code behind the user control.

LISTING 5-11 The code behind the XAML user control of the sample Silverlight application.

```
using System;
using System.Collections.Generic;
using System.Linq;
using System.Net;
using System.Windows;
using System.Windows.Controls;
using System.Windows.Documents;
using System.Windows.Input;
using System.Windows.Media;
using System.Windows.Media.Animation;
using System.Windows.Shapes;
using Microsoft.SharePoint.Client;

namespace DevLeap.SilverlightClientOMDemo {
    public partial class MainPage : UserControl {
        public MainPage() {
            InitializeComponent();
            loadDevLeapContacts();
        }

        private ListItemCollection allContacts;

        private void loadDevLeapContacts() {
            // Open the current ClientContext
            ClientContext ctx = ClientContext.Current;

            // Prepare a reference to the list of "DevLeap Contacts"
            List list = ctx.Web.Lists.GetByTitle("DevLeap Contacts");

            // Prepare a query for all items in the list
            CamlQuery query = CamlQuery.CreateAllItemsQuery();
            allContacts = list.GetItems(query);
            ctx.Load(allContacts);

            // Execute the prepared command against the target ClientContext
```

```
            ctx.ExecuteQueryAsync(onQuerySucceeded, onQueryFailed);
        }

        private void onQuerySucceeded(object sender,
            ClientRequestSucceededEventArgs args) {
            this.Dispatcher.BeginInvoke(new updateUI(refreshGrid));
        }

        private void onQueryFailed(object sender,
            ClientRequestFailedEventArgs args) {
            this.Dispatcher.BeginInvoke(new showExceptionUI(
                showException), args.Exception);
        }

        private delegate void updateUI();

        private void refreshGrid() {
            this.AllContactsList.ItemsSource = allContacts;
        }

        private delegate void showExceptionUI(Exception ex);

        private void showException(Exception ex) {
            MessageBox.Show(String.Format("Exception occurred: {0}", ex.Message));
        }
    }
}
```

The syntax is almost the same as that used with the Managed Client Object Model. However, a small but significant difference is the way the code retrieves a reference to the *ClientContext*. Due to the need of hosting the Silverlight control within a website, the Silverlight version of *ClientContext* can be constructed by using the default constructor, which requires the *System.Uri* of the target website, but you can also take advantage of a shortcut to the current website context by using the *ClientContext.Current* static entry point. This is a constructive shortcut, because many times the Silverlight control will be hosted exactly in the same website that it will target. Furthermore, consider that the *ClientContext. Current* property internally uses a custom Silverlight init parameter, with the name *MS.SP.url* and the value of the current context URL, provided to the Silverlight environment at startup. If you host your control using the Silverlight Web Part, then this init parameter, together with a few others, will be automatically provided to the control. However, if you directly insert the control inside a page, without using a Silverlight Web Part, the *ClientContext.Current* property will be *null*, unless you do not provide the *MS.SP.url* init parameter by yourself.

 Note The *init* parameters automatically provided by the Silverlight Web Part are: *MS.SP.url, MS.SP.formDigest, MS.SP.formDigestTimeoutSeconds, MS.SP.requestToken,* and *MS.SP.viaUrl.*

Another fundamental difference between this sample and the one based on the Managed Client Object Model is the use of an asynchronous programming model. This is not a kind of virtuosity but a real need, because in Silverlight you have to work within the confines of the asynchronous programming pattern. In fact, while working with Silverlight, if you try to execute some blocking code from the main UI thread, you will get an exception of type *InvalidOperationException* with the following message:

```
The method or property that is called may block the UI thread and is not allowed. Please use
a background thread to invoke the method or property, for example, using System.Threading.
ThreadPool.QueueUserWorkItem method to invoke the method or property.
```

The Silverlight Client Object Model also provides a synchronous pattern based on the *ExecuteQuery* method that you have already seen in the Managed Client Object Model. However, you can call this method only from threads that do not modify the UI.

Listing 5-11 shows that the sample directly binds the *ListItemCollection* retrieved from the server to the *ListBox* control. However, as you probably know, every *ListItem* of SharePoint has its fields stored in a named collection and the XAML binding syntax does not support named collections. Nevertheless, the code of Listing 5-10 binds the fields using markup. This is possible because the XAML references a custom converter registered as a resource of the user control. In XAML (for instance, Silverlight and WPF), a converter is a type that converts one input bound to a control into another output, rendering the output of the conversion. In the XAML sample code in Listing 5-10, the converter converts the name of a field of a *ListItem* into the corresponding field value. Listing 5-12 displays the source code of the custom converter. If you do not like to use a custom converter, you can wrap *ListItem* instances with a custom type of your own.

LISTING 5-12 A custom converter, converting from a named field to its value.

```
namespace DevLeap.SilverlightClientOMDemo {
    public class ListItemFieldConverter : IValueConverter {
        public object Convert(object value, Type targetType, object parameter,
            System.Globalization.CultureInfo culture) {

            // In case the source item is NULL, just stop
            if (value == null)
                return value;

            // In case the fieldName is empty or NULL, just stop
            String fieldName = parameter as String;
            if (String.IsNullOrEmpty(fieldName))
                return null;

            // Cast the source item to ListItem
            ListItem item = value as ListItem;
```

```
            if (item != null) {
                // Return the field
                return (item[fieldName]);
            }
            else
                return (null);
        }

        public object ConvertBack(object value, Type targetType, object parameter,
    System.Globalization.CultureInfo culture) {
            // We do not support two-way conversion
            throw new NotImplementedException();
        }
    }
}
```

In a real solution, the converter could be more complete and accurate, but for the sake of simplicity, Listing 5-12 uses a concise implementation.

Aside from binding rules and asynchronous programming tasks, the Silverlight Client Object Model has the same potential, capabilities and recommended procedures of the Managed Client Object Model.

ECMAScript Client Object Model

The third kind of Client Object Model offered by SharePoint targets the ECMAScript world. It comprises a set of .js files built for ECMAScript-enabled (JavaScript, JScript) platforms. The main .js files that are available are:

- SP.js
- SP.Core.js
- SP.Ribbon.js
- SP.Runtime.js

These files are deployed in the SharePoint14_Root\TEMPLATE\LAYOUTS directory and are automatically downloaded to the client (Web browser) when a user browses to a SharePoint page. In fact, the default master pages of SharePoint define a *ScriptManager* control, which automatically includes references to these .js files. However, you could also reference them by yourself, within a custom ASPX page. Every file is also available with a "debug-enabled" version, where the file name ends with .debug.js instead of .js. For example, the SP.js file is also available in a debug version, named SP.debug.js. The browsers supported by the scripts include Microsoft Internet Explorer 7 and higher; Firefox 3.5 and higher; and Safari 4.0 and higher.

> **Important** For security reasons, you cannot use the ECMAScript Client Object Model in a page unless that page contains a form digest. SharePoint native pages, of course, include the *SharePoint:FormDigest* control. If you use the Client Object Model within a custom ASPX page, you will need to include the *FormDigest* control by yourself.

In everyday life, you will probably use the ECMAScript Client Object Model in a custom SharePoint page. Thus, you will need to create a new SharePoint empty project, and for example, add an Application Page item. In order to reference the scripts, you can use the *SharePoint:ScriptLink* control, which accepts a set of arguments, some of which are described here:

- *LoadAfterUI*   Loads the script after the code of the UI

- *Localizable*   Indicates if the current page can be localized

- *Name*   Defines the relative path of the .js file to include in the page

Then, you need to define a script block that utilizes the Object Model. While the Managed Client Object Model and the Silverlight Client Object Model share almost the same syntax, the ECMAScript Client Object Model is not exactly the same, and it does not share exactly the same syntax. The data types used do not completely correspond on both platforms, and the members' names differ. For example, to access the *Title* property of an item, you need to invoke the *get_title()* method. In addition, some arguments are case-sensitive, and there are other differences. Listing 5-13 shows an example of an application page that uses the ECMAScript Client Object Model to retrieve a *List* instance and show its *Title* property.

LISTING 5-13 A SharePoint application page using the ECMAScript Client Object Model.

```
<%@ Assembly Name="$SharePoint.Project.AssemblyFullName$" %>
<%@ Import Namespace="Microsoft.SharePoint.ApplicationPages" %>
<%@ Register Tagprefix="SharePoint" Namespace="Microsoft.SharePoint.WebControls"
  Assembly="Microsoft.SharePoint, Version=14.0.0.0, Culture=neutral,
  PublicKeyToken=71e9bce111e9429c" %>
<%@ Register Tagprefix="Utilities" Namespace="Microsoft.SharePoint.Utilities"
  Assembly="Microsoft.SharePoint, Version=14.0.0.0, Culture=neutral,
  PublicKeyToken=71e9bce111e9429c" %>
<%@ Register Tagprefix="asp" Namespace="System.Web.UI"
  Assembly="System.Web.Extensions, Version=3.5.0.0, Culture=neutral,
  PublicKeyToken=31bf3856ad364e35" %>
<%@ Import Namespace="Microsoft.SharePoint" %>
<%@ Assembly Name="Microsoft.Web.CommandUI, Version=14.0.0.0, Culture=neutral,
  PublicKeyToken=71e9bce111e9429c" %>
<%@ Page Language="C#" AutoEventWireup="true"
  CodeBehind="ShowECMAScriptInAction.aspx.cs" Inherits=
  "DevLeap.SP2010.ECMAScriptOMDemo.Layouts.DevLeap.SP2010.ECMAScriptOMDemo.
  ShowECMAScriptInAction" DynamicMasterPageFile="~masterurl/default.master" %>
```

```
<asp:Content ID="PageHead" ContentPlaceHolderID="PlaceHolderAdditionalPageHead"
  runat="server">
<SharePoint:ScriptLink ID="SPScriptLink" runat="server" LoadAfterUI="true"
  Localizable="false" Name="SP.js" />
<script language="javascript" type="text/javascript">

    var clientContext;
    var web;
    var oContactsList;

    function onQuerySucceeded(sender, args) {
        alert('Title of the List: ' + this.oContactsList.get_title());
    }

    function onQueryFailed(sender, args) {
        alert('Request failed ' + args.get_message() + '\n' + args.get_stackTrace());
    }

    function retrieveContacts() {
        this.clientContext = new SP.ClientContext.get_current();
        this.web = this.clientContext.get_web();
        this.oContactsList = this.web.get_lists().getByTitle("DevLeap Contacts");
        this.clientContext.load(this.oContactsList);
        this.clientContext.executeQueryAsync(
            Function.createDelegate(this, this.onQuerySucceeded),
            Function.createDelegate(this, this.onQueryFailed));
    }
</script>
</asp:Content>

<asp:Content ID="Main" ContentPlaceHolderID="PlaceHolderMain" runat="server">
<input type="button" onclick="retrieveContacts()"
  value="Click me to get the list!" />
</asp:Content>

<asp:Content ID="PageTitle" ContentPlaceHolderID="PlaceHolderPageTitle"
  runat="server">
ECMAScript Object Model Demo Page
</asp:Content>

<asp:Content ID="PageTitleInTitleArea"
  ContentPlaceHolderID="PlaceHolderPageTitleInTitleArea" runat="server" >
  ECMAScript Object Model Demo Page
</asp:Content>
```

The core of Listing 5-13 is in the method *retrieveContacts*, where you can see that the syntax is not so different from previous versions of the Client Object Model. You can get a reference to a *SP.ClientContext* instance either by using the *get_current()* method from Listing 5-13 or by using a constructor that accepts the server-relative URL of the target site. The latter syntax is useful when you need to work with data from a target site that differs from the site at your location. The only fundamental difference is syntactical and involves using the *get_* and *set_* prefixes for every property accessor, as well as using the asynchronous pattern when executing the query against the SharePoint server. However, the example you have just seen is not terribly exciting. Listing 5-14 is much more interesting and powerful; it uses jQuery together with the ECMAScript Client Object Model.

LISTING 5-14 A SharePoint application page using jQuery together with the ECMAScript Client Object Model.

```
<%@ Assembly Name="$SharePoint.Project.AssemblyFullName$" %>
<%@ Import Namespace="Microsoft.SharePoint.ApplicationPages" %>
<%@ Register TagPrefix="SharePoint" Namespace="Microsoft.SharePoint.WebControls"
Assembly="Microsoft.SharePoint, Version=14.0.0.0, Culture=neutral, PublicKeyToken=71e9
bce111e9429c" %>
<%@ Register TagPrefix="Utilities" Namespace="Microsoft.SharePoint.Utilities"
Assembly="Microsoft.SharePoint, Version=14.0.0.0, Culture=neutral, PublicKeyToken=71e9
bce111e9429c" %>
<%@ Register TagPrefix="asp" Namespace="System.Web.UI" Assembly="System.Web.
Extensions, Version=3.5.0.0, Culture=neutral, PublicKeyToken=31bf3856ad364e35" %>
<%@ Import Namespace="Microsoft.SharePoint" %>
<%@ Assembly Name="Microsoft.Web.CommandUI, Version=14.0.0.0, Culture=neutral, PublicK
eyToken=71e9bce111e9429c" %>
<%@ Page Language="C#" AutoEventWireup="true" CodeBehind="UseJQueryWithECMAScr
ipt.aspx.cs" Inherits="DevLeap.SP2010.ECMAScriptOMDemo.Layouts.DevLeap.SP2010.
ECMAScriptOMDemo.UseJQueryWithECMAScript" DynamicMasterPageFile="~masterurl/default.
master" %>

<asp:Content ID="PageHead" ContentPlaceHolderID="PlaceHolderAdditionalPageHead"
runat="server">
    <SharePoint:ScriptLink ID="SPScriptLink" runat="server" LoadAfterUI="true"
Localizable="false" Name="SP.js" />
    <script type="text/javascript" src="/_layouts/DevLeap.SP2010.ECMAScriptOMDemo/js/
jquery-1.5.min.js"></script>
    <script type="text/javascript" src="/_layouts/DevLeap.SP2010.ECMAScriptOMDemo/js/
jquery-ui-1.8.5.custom.min.js"></script>
    <link href="/_layouts/DevLeap.SP2010.ECMAScriptOMDemo/css/redmond/jquery-ui-
1.8.5.custom.css" rel="Stylesheet" type="text/css" />
<style type="text/css">
        #listOfContacts .ui-selecting {
            background: #FECA40;
        }
        #listOfContacts .ui-selected {
            background: #F39814;
            color: white;
        }
        #listOfContacts {
            list-style-type: none;
            margin: 0;
            padding: 0;
            width: 60%;
        }
```

```
        #listOfContacts li {
            margin: 3px;
            padding: 0.4em;
            font-size: 1em;
            height: 15px;
            width: 600px;
        }
</style>
<script language="javascript" type="text/javascript">

    var clientContext;
    var web;
    var oContactsList;
    var listItems;

    _spBodyOnLoadFunctionNames.push("InitData");

    function onQuerySucceeded(sender, args) {
        dataBindList();
    }

    function onQueryFailed(sender, args) {
        alert('Request failed ' + args.get_message() + '\n' +
            args.get_stackTrace());
    }

    function InitData() {
        this.clientContext = new SP.ClientContext.get_current();
        this.web = this.clientContext.get_web();
        this.oContactsList = this.web.get_lists().getByTitle("DevLeap Contacts");

        var camlQuery = new SP.CamlQuery();
        var q = '<View><RowLimit>100</RowLimit></View>';
        camlQuery.set_viewXml(q);
        this.listItems = this.oContactsList.getItems(camlQuery);
        this.clientContext.load(this.listItems);

        this.clientContext.executeQueryAsync(
            Function.createDelegate(this, this.onQuerySucceeded),
            Function.createDelegate(this, this.onQueryFailed));
    }

    function dataBindList() {
        var listItemsEnumerator = this.listItems.getEnumerator();

        //iterate though all of the items
        while (listItemsEnumerator.moveNext()) {
            var item = listItemsEnumerator.get_current();
```

```
                    var id = item.get_id();
                    var title = item.get_item("Title");
                    var contactId = item.get_item("DevLeapContactID");
                    var companyName = item.get_item("DevLeapCompanyName");
                    var country = item.get_item("DevLeapCountry");

                    $("#listOfContacts").append('<li class="ui-widget-content"
                      id="item_' + id + '">Title: ' + title +  ' - Contact ID: ' +
                      contactId + ' - Company Name: ' + companyName + ' - Country: ' +
                      country + '</li>');
                }

                $("#listOfContacts").selectable();
            }
        </script>
    </asp:Content>
    <asp:Content ID="Main" ContentPlaceHolderID="PlaceHolderMain" runat="server">
        <div id="listOfContactsContainer">
            <ol id="listOfContacts"></ol>
        </div>
    </asp:Content>
    <asp:Content ID="PageTitle" ContentPlaceHolderID="PlaceHolderPageTitle"
      runat="server">
        jQuery and ECMAScript Object Model Demo Page
    </asp:Content>



    <asp:Content ID="PageTitleInTitleArea"
      ContentPlaceHolderID="PlaceHolderPageTitleInTitleArea" runat="server">
        jQuery and ECMAScript Object Model Demo Page
    </asp:Content>
```

The sample uses jQuery version 1.5, which was the most current version at the time of this writing (February, 2011). It also uses a custom jQuery User Interface (named Redmond). For the sake of simplicity, the sample project includes the .js file of the jQuery world, and it also includes the CSS and images of the UI Theme. In a real scenario, you should retrieve them from a public Content Delivery Network (CDN) or publish them in the site root. Additionally, the sample page of Listing 5-14 loads the well-known list of contacts and renders them using a custom selectable order list. The core methods are *InitData*, to configure and start downloading data, and *dataBindList*, which renders the items retrieved.

The first thing you should notice in the code sample is the invocation of a method to execute the *InitData* function as soon as the page loads, which uses this syntax:

```
_spBodyOnLoadFunctionNames.push("InitData");
```

This method is provided by the ECMAScript infrastructure of SharePoint and can be implemented in any page. Then the *InitData* function prepares and loads the queries, executing them asynchronously to keep the UI fluent, even when downloading data. The syntax used here is not really different from before. As soon as data is available, the *dataBindList* method does the real job, using jQuery and enumerating the list items, binding them to HTML dynamic content. Figure 5-3 depicts the output of the application page implemented with jQuery and ECMAScript.

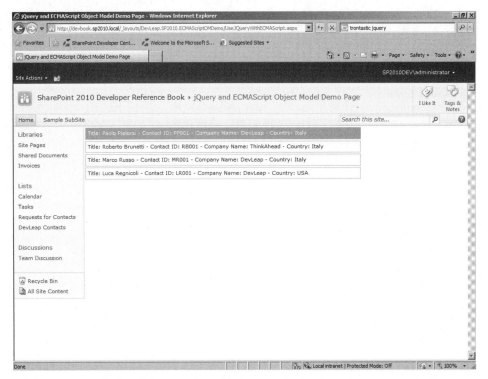

FIGURE 5-3 A sample SharePoint page that uses jQuery and ECMAScript Client Object Model.

More generally, you can consider using the ECMAScript Client Object Model whenever you need to dynamically load or even change SharePoint data from a JavaScript-enabled environment, eventually in conjunction with jQuery, or while developing custom Ribbons. You will learn about this in Chapter 9, "Extending the User Interface."

Client Object Model by Examples

In this section, you will see a set of basic examples that use the Client Object Model with the Managed version, and eventually with the Silverlight version.

Lists and Items

The sections that follow contain many examples related to managing lists and list items.

Creating a New List

Creating new contents using the Client Object Model involves using some types specifically provided for this purpose. In fact, from the client viewpoint, the creation of a new *List*—or a new *ListItem*, or whatever else—implies the need to request that the server execute that action. Thus, for creating a new list there is a class named *ListCreationInformation*, which describes the request to create a new list instance. In Listing 5-15, you can see a code excerpt that uses this type to create a new list of Contacts.

LISTING 5-15 Creating a new list instance using the Client Object Model.

```
ClientContext ctx = new ClientContext("http://devbook.sp2010.local/");

ListCreationInformation lci = new ListCreationInformation();
lci.Title = "Contacts COM";
lci.Description = "Contacts Created by Client Object Model";
lci.TemplateType = (Int32)ListTemplateType.Contacts;
lci.QuickLaunchOption = QuickLaunchOptions.On;

List newList = ctx.Web.Lists.Add(lci);
ctx.ExecuteQuery();
```

Listing 5-15 demonstrates how the *ListCreationInformation* instance defines the main properties of the list to be created like *Title*, *Description*, and *QuickLaunchOption*. Above all, the object also defines the *TemplateType*, which defines the base model to use for creating the list instance. If you want to create a new list instance based on a custom list definition, you can use the property *ListCreationInformation.TemplateFeatureId* to reference the GUID of the feature provisioning the list definition.

> **More Information** For further details about data provisioning, refer to Chapter 10.

If you try to create a list that already exists with that *Title*, you will get an exception of type *Microsoft.SharePoint.Client.ServerException*, with the following error message:

```
Unhandled Exception: Microsoft.SharePoint.Client.ServerException: A list, survey, discussion
board, or document library with the specified title already exists in this Web site.  Please
choose another title.
```

One last thing to consider is just after *ExecuteQuery* method invocation, the *List* instance you get back from the *Add* method of the *Lists* property is a fully functional instance that you can use to add items, configure properties, and so on.

Creating and Updating a List Item

When you create a list instance, you need to add new items to the list. Listing 5-16 demonstrates how to add a contact to the newly-created list of contacts.

LISTING 5-16 Creating a new list item using the Client Object Model.

```
ClientContext ctx = new ClientContext("http://devbook.sp2010.local/");

List contactsList = ctx.Web.Lists.GetByTitle("Contacts COM");

ListItem item = contactsList.AddItem(new ListItemCreationInformation());
item["Title"] = "Paolo Pialorsi";
item["Email"] = "paolo@devleap.com";
item["Company"] = "DevLeap";
item.Update();

ctx.ExecuteQuery();
```

Listing 5-16 shows the *ListItem* being added to the *List* using a *ListItemCreationInformation* type, which simply defines a creation task for a new *ListItem*. The result of the *AddItem* method is a *ListItem* instance that can be used to configure fields of the item, and then finally allows the *Update* method to be invoked to confirm the fields' values. However, as usual with the Client Object Model, you need to inform the server about what you want to do. Thus, you need to call the *ExecuteQuery* method on the *ClientContext* instance.

Updating a *ListItem* is similar to creating a new item. The only difference is that you need to retrieve the item from the store. You can do this by enumerating the items returned from a *CamlQuery*, as shown previously in Listing 5-14, or you can retrieve a specific item by *ID* using the *GetItemById* method of the *List* type. Listing 5-17 presents an example of updating the item created in Listing 5-16.

LISTING 5-17 Updating a list item by using the Client Object Model.

```
ClientContext ctx = new ClientContext("http://devbook.sp2010.local/");

List contactsList = ctx.Web.Lists.GetByTitle("Contacts COM");
ListItem itemToUpdate = contactsList.GetItemById(1);

itemToUpdate["Company"] = "DevLeap - Changed!";
itemToUpdate.Update();

ctx.ExecuteQuery();
```

Concurrency Conflicts and Exception Handling

If the item you are updating has been changed by someone else while you are working on it, when you invoke *ExecuteQuery* to update the server, the Client Object Model throws a server exception, with the following message:

```
Unhandled Exception: Microsoft.SharePoint.Client.ServerException: Version conflict.
```

You can decide whether to refresh the item and force your update on the new instance, or simply to skip your changes. However, if you update an item within a unique *ExecuteQuery* invocation, such as that in Listing 5-17, you will unlikely have a concurrency exception.

Another situation that could arise while working with lists and items is that the item you are looking for does not exist at all. Due to the architecture of the Client Object Model, to determine that the item you are looking for does not exist, you need to query the server, for example using a *try ... catch* code block, to trap the exception related to the missing item. In this case, the exception would be a *ServerException*, with the following error message:

```
Unhandled Exception: Microsoft.SharePoint.Client.ServerException: Item does not exist. It
may have been deleted by another user.
```

If you would like to follow a backup path to avoid issues on the client-side, you could create the missing item from scratch, or you could try to retrieve another item. The same problem would happen if you look for a list that does not exist. In that circumstance, you should manage the following exception:

```
Unhandled Exception: Microsoft.SharePoint.Client.ServerException: List 'Contacts COM' does
not exist at site with URL 'http://devbook.sp2010.local'.
```

Whatever you plan to do, to handle the exception, you will probably need to query the server for new data or to create the missing list. Consider the code shown in Listing 5-18, which illustrates a possible scenario like the one just described, in case of a missing list.

LISTING 5-18 Code excerpt showing how to retrieve or create a list in the event that it is missing, and then add an item to it.

```
ClientContext ctx = new ClientContext("http://devbook.sp2010.local/");
List contactsList = null;

try {
    contactsList = ctx.Web.Lists.GetByTitle("Contacts COM");
    ctx.Load(contactsList);
    ctx.ExecuteQuery();
}
```

```
catch (ServerException) {
    ListCreationInformation lci = new ListCreationInformation();
    lci.Title = "Contacts COM";
    lci.Description = "Contacts Created by Client Object Model";
    lci.TemplateType = (Int32)ListTemplateType.Contacts;
    lci.QuickLaunchOption = QuickLaunchOptions.On;

    contactsList = ctx.Web.Lists.Add(lci);
    ctx.ExecuteQuery();
}
finally {
    ListItem item = contactsList.AddItem(new ListItemCreationInformation());
    item["Title"] = "Paolo Pialorsi";
    item["Email"] = "paolo@devleap.com";
    item["Company"] = "DevLeap";
    item.Update();

    ctx.ExecuteQuery();
}
```

The bold highlighted code in Listing 5-18 shows the three calls to the *ExecuteQuery* method. In the worst situation, this code could execute all the *try ... catch ... finally* blocks, invoking the server via *ExecuteQuery* three times. This could lead to performance degradation as well as to a huge stress on the server side. Luckily the Client Object Model provides a class named *ExceptionHandlingScope* that is specifically defined to support such situations and avoid executing multiple queries against the server.

Listing 5-19 displays the prototype of the usage of *ExceptionHandlingScope* type.

LISTING 5-19 The prototype of the usage of *ExceptionHandlingScope* type.

```
ClientContext ctx = new ClientContext("http://devbook.sp2010.local/");

ExceptionHandlingScope scope = new ExceptionHandlingScope(ctx);

using (scope.StartScope()) {
    using (scope.StartTry()) {
        // Try to do something on the server-side
    }
    using (scope.StartCatch()) {
        // Do something else in case of failure on the server-side
    }
    using (scope.StartFinally()) {
        // Execute this code, whatever is the result of previous code blocks
    }
}

// Now invoke the server, just one time
ctx.ExecuteQuery();
```

Under the cover, the *ExceptionHandlingScope* instance collects activities (internally called *ClientAction*) to execute on the server side for all the three situations (*try, catch, finally*). The server will begin executing the code inside the *StartTry* block, and then in case of failure, it will execute the code in the *StartCatch*. Whether or not exceptions occurred in the *StartTry* block, it will finally execute the code in the *StartFinally* block. However, the request sent to the server is just one, as well as the response. Listing 5-20 presents a complete example.

LISTING 5-20 The complete code to retrieve or create a list in the event that it is missing, and then add an item to it.

```
ClientContext ctx = new ClientContext("http://devbook.sp2010.local/");
ExceptionHandlingScope scope = new ExceptionHandlingScope(ctx);
List contactsList;

using (scope.StartScope()) {
    using (scope.StartTry()) {
        // Try to reference the target list
        contactsList = ctx.Web.Lists.GetByTitle("Contacts COM");
    }
    using (scope.StartCatch()) {
        // Create the list, in case it doesn't exist
        ListCreationInformation lci = new ListCreationInformation();
        lci.Title = "Contacts COM";
        lci.Description = "Contacts Created by Client Object Model";
        lci.TemplateType = (Int32)ListTemplateType.Contacts;
        lci.QuickLaunchOption = QuickLaunchOptions.On;

        contactsList = ctx.Web.Lists.Add(lci);
    }
    using (scope.StartFinally()) {
        // Add the ListItem, whether the list has just been created
        // or was already existing
        contactsList = ctx.Web.Lists.GetByTitle("Contacts COM");

        ListItem item = contactsList.AddItem(new ListItemCreationInformation());
        item["Title"] = "Paolo Pialorsi";
        item["Email"] = "paolo@devleap.com";
        item["Company"] = "DevLeap";
        item.Update();
    }
}

// Now invoke the server, just one time
ctx.ExecuteQuery();
```

Deleting an Existing List Item

Another useful scenario to examine is how to delete an item from a list. Listing 5-21 shows an excerpt of code illustrating how to do this.

LISTING 5-21 Deleting a *ListItem* instance.

```
ClientContext ctx = new ClientContext("http://devbook.sp2010.local/");

List contactsList = ctx.Web.Lists.GetByTitle("Contacts COM");
ListItem itemToDelete = contactsList.GetItemById(1);

itemToDelete.DeleteObject();

ctx.ExecuteQuery();
```

This is very similar to the syntax used to update an item. The only difference is the invocation of the *DeleteObject* method.

Paging Queries of List Items

A very common task in real solutions is querying items in a list. Beginning with Listing 5-1, I have presented many ways of querying a list. However a well done solution has to consider that a list could contain thousands of items. Thus, it is not realistic to query these items with a unique query batch. For such situations, you should take advantage of the paging capabilities of the SharePoint querying engine. Listing 5-22 shows a code excerpt that demonstrates how to efficiently paginate query results.

LISTING 5-22 How to efficiently paginate query results.

```
ClientContext ctx = new ClientContext("http://devbook.sp2010.local/");

List contactsList = ctx.Web.Lists.GetByTitle("Contacts COM");
ListItemCollectionPosition itemPosition = null;
Int32 currentPage = 0;

do {
    CamlQuery query = new CamlQuery();
    query.ListItemCollectionPosition = itemPosition;
    query.ViewXml = "<View><RowLimit>10</RowLimit></View>";
    ListItemCollection pageOfContacts = contactsList.GetItems(query);
    ctx.Load(pageOfContacts);
    ctx.ExecuteQuery();

    itemPosition = pageOfContacts.ListItemCollectionPosition;
    currentPage++;
    Console.WriteLine("Page #: {0}", currentPage);

    foreach (ListItem item in pageOfContacts) {
        Console.WriteLine("Contact: {0}", item["Title"]);
    }
    Console.WriteLine();
} while (itemPosition != null);
```

First, to paginate data, you need to instruct the CAML query about the page size by using a *<RowLimit/>* element. In this example, the page size is 10 items per page. Next, you need to declare a variable of type *ListItemCollectionPosition*, which defines a paging context for the running *CamlQuery*. Each time you execute the query, which invokes the *GetItems* method of the *List* instance, you need to set the property *ListItemCollectionPosition* of the query in order to instruct SharePoint about the page that you want to retrieve. You can get back the value to provide for each page from the *ListItemCollectionPosition* property of the class *ListItemCollection.*. If you retrieved the last page, this property will be *null* and you will know that you've consumed the whole set of data.

Document Libraries and Files

Another useful context to explore is managing document libraries and files. In this section, you will see some very common scenarios and examples.

Creating a New Document Library

In addition to creating a standard list, at times you will need to create a custom document library. Listing 5-23 lays out a code excerpt that show how to do that.

LISTING 5-23 Creating a custom document library.

```
ClientContext ctx = new ClientContext("http://devbook.sp2010.local/");

ListCreationInformation lci = new ListCreationInformation();
lci.Title = "Custom Documents";
lci.Description = "Custom Documents Created by Client Object Model";
lci.TemplateType = (Int32)ListTemplateType.DocumentLibrary;
lci.QuickLaunchOption = QuickLaunchOptions.On;
List newList = ctx.Web.Lists.Add(lci);

ctx.ExecuteQuery();
```

The only difference between Listing 5-23 and Listing 5-15 is the value of *ListTemplateType* used. For a document library, you could also define a *DocumentTemplateType* property to specify a custom document template.

Uploading a New Document

Once you have a document library, you will likely need to upload a file into it. Listing 5-24 shows how you can do this.

LISTING 5-24 Uploading a file into a document library.

```
ClientContext ctx = new ClientContext("http://devbook.sp2010.local/");

List targetList= ctx.Web.Lists.GetByTitle("Custom Documents");

FileCreationInformation fci = new FileCreationInformation();
fci.Content = System.IO.File.ReadAllBytes(@"..\..\SampleFile.txt");
fci.Url = "SampleFile.txt";
fci.Overwrite = true;

File fileToUpload = newList.RootFolder.Files.Add(fci);
ctx.Load(fileToUpload);

ctx.ExecuteQuery();
```

The key point Listing 5-24 is the creation of an instance of *FileCreationInformation* type. The other thing to notice is that the *FileCreationInformation* instance accepts a relative value for the *Url* property of the file to upload, and then collects the file in the right folder, based on the folder where the *FileCreationInformation* instance will be added. To upload a file you can use the *SaveBinaryDirect* static method provided by the *File* class.

To avoid problems while uploading files, be careful to check the maximum upload file size. If neccessary, you have the option to increase the maximum upload file size.

Downloading a Document

Downloading a file is one of the simplest tasks that you can undertake. Listing 5-25 shows how to do it.

LISTING 5-25 Downloading a file from a document library.

```
ClientContext ctx = new ClientContext("http://devbook.sp2010.local/");

List targetList = ctx.Web.Lists.GetByTitle("Custom Documents");
ctx.Load(targetList, lst => lst.RootFolder);
ctx.ExecuteQuery();

String fileToDownload = (targetList.RootFolder.ServerRelativeUrl + "/SampleFile.txt");
FileInformation fileInfo = File.OpenBinaryDirect(ctx, fileToDownload);

using (System.IO.StreamReader sr = new System.IO.StreamReader(fileInfo.Stream)) {
    String content = sr.ReadToEnd();
    Console.WriteLine(content);
}
```

The most interesting part of Listing 5-25 is where it retrieves a *Stream* from the *FileInformation* object to manage the file at a low level. Additionally, the *FileInformation* instance can be retrieved invoking the *OpenBinaryDirect* static method of the *File* class.

Check-In and Check-Out of Documents

As with downloading and uploading a file, to check a document in and out, you need to use the corresponding methods *File.CheckIn* and *File.CheckOut*. It's a good habit to check the *CheckOutType* property of the current *File* instance to argue if the file has to be checked-in or checked-out. Listing 5-26 shows an example.

LISTING 5-26 Check-in and check-out of a file in a document library.

```
ClientContext ctx = new ClientContext("http://devbook.sp2010.local/");

List targetList = ctx.Web.Lists.GetByTitle("Custom Documents");
ctx.Load(targetList, lst => lst.RootFolder);
ctx.ExecuteQuery();

String fileToRetrieve = (targetList.RootFolder.ServerRelativeUrl + "/SampleFile.txt");
File file = ctx.Web.GetFileByServerRelativeUrl(fileToRetrieve);
ctx.Load(file);
ctx.ExecuteQuery();

if (file.CheckOutType == CheckOutType.None) {
    file.CheckOut();
}
else {
    file.CheckIn("Finished check-out!", CheckinType.MajorCheckIn);
}

ctx.ExecuteQuery();
```

Just as on the Server Object Model, the *CheckIn* method allows you specify the revision (minor, major, overwrite) of the document that you want to check-in.

Copying and Moving Files

The last item to look at with regard to document libraries is how to copy and move a file. As in the previous examples, you first need to retrieve a reference to the target *File* instance. Once you have the reference, you can invoke the *MoveTo* method or the *CopyTo* method, depending on whether you want to move the file or copy it. Listing 5-27 demonstrates how to do this.

LISTING 5-27 Copying or moving a file between document libraries.

```
ClientContext ctx = new ClientContext("http://devbook.sp2010.local/");

List targetList = ctx.Web.Lists.GetByTitle("Custom Documents");
ctx.Load(targetList, lst => lst.RootFolder);
ctx.ExecuteQuery();

String fileToRetrieve = (targetList.RootFolder.ServerRelativeUrl + "/SampleFile.txt");
File file = ctx.Web.GetFileByServerRelativeUrl(fileToRetrieve);

file.CopyTo("Shared Documents/SampleFileCopy.txt", true);
file.MoveTo("Shared Documents/SampleFileMoved.txt", MoveOperations.Overwrite);

ctx.ExecuteQuery();
```

Both of these methods accept some parameters beyond the destination file relative URL. The *CopyTo* method accepts a *Boolean* argument that determines if the file should overwrite any existing destination item, and the *MoveTo* method uses an enumeration for almost the same purpose. Note that both methods copy or move not only the binary content of the file, but also its field values (metadata), as well.

SOAP Services

In the previous section, you learned how to make use of the SharePoint Client Object Model while developing with .NET 3.5 or higher, Silverlight 3.0 or higher, and ECMAScript. But if you need to integrate SharePoint with a third-party solution, perhaps developed using an earlier version of .NET Framework or any other technology, such as Java, PHP, or Python, you cannot use the Client Object Model. Fortunately, SharePoint offers a set of SOAP services that can be invoked by third-party applications.

These services are built using mainly the Web Services engine of ASP.NET, and are based on a set of .ASMX files, even if in SharePoint 2010 there are also a few WCF services available for external consumers. They are published under the */_vti_bin/* virtual directory of every website that maps the SharePoint14_Root\ISAPI folder. There are about 25 services available in SharePoint Foundation 2010, and 5 more services in SharePoint Server 2010. Table 5-2 lists some of the main services.

TABLE 5-2 Some of the Main SOAP Services Published by SharePoint 2010

Service Name	Description
Alerts.asmx	Allows listing and deleting alerts subscriptions for users.
Authentication.asmx	Provides an operation for logging on to a SharePoint site that uses FBA. The *Login* operation returns a cookie that should be used in all subsequent calls to other services.
Lists.asmx	Provides operations to work with lists, content-types, list items, and files. For example, this service offers operations to check-in and check-out a file in a document library, or to query list data using CAML queries.
SiteData.asmx	Allows reading sites, webs, lists, and items. *SiteData.asmx* targets external search engines willing to crawl contents of a SharePoint site.
Sites.asmx	Allows creating, deleting, reading, exporting, and importing of SharePoint websites.
Webs.asmx	Provides operations to manage content-types, site columns, and features of a SharePoint website
Search.asmx	A service that allows querying the search engine of SharePoint Server.

To use these services, you simply need to define a reference to them, using their Web Service Definition Language (WSDL) contract definition. While working in .NET with Visual Studio, you can reference a service through its WSDL file in a couple of ways. You could create a new "Service Reference" in a project; in this case, you will use the WCF client stack to invoke the service. Alternatively, you could also define a "Web Reference," which will use the ASP.NET ASMX Web Service client stack to invoke the service.

Using the first method, simply right-click the project that you want to use to consume the service, and then click Add Service Reference from the contextual menu that appears. Using the second method, if you want to consume the service using the ASP.NET ASMX Web Service client stack, you still need to start from the Add Service Reference menu item; however, in the Advanced Configuration panel, select the Add Web Reference button to add an old-style service reference.

Listing 5-28 presents a code excerpt that uses these services to browse the contents of the list of DevLeap Contacts.

LISTING 5-28 Browsing the contents of a site using the *Lists.ASMX* service.

```
String targetListName = "DevLeap Contacts";
String baseUrl = "http://devbook.sp2010.local/_vti_bin/";

Lists wsLists = new Lists();
wsLists.Url = baseUrl + "Lists.asmx";
wsLists.Credentials = System.Net.CredentialCache.DefaultCredentials;
```

```
XElement listMetadata = XElement.Load(new XmlNodeReader(wsLists.
GetList(targetListName)));

Guid targetListId = new Guid(listMetadata.Attribute("ID").Value);

XmlNode listItemsXmlNode = wsLists.GetListItems(
    targetListId.ToString(), // ID of the target list
    String.Empty, // ID of the view or String.Empty for default view
    null, // CAML query or null
    null, // ViewFields or null
    "200", // RowLimit as a string
    null, // Query options
    null // ID of the web site or null for root website
    );

XElement listItemsXml = XElement.Load(new XmlNodeReader(listItemsXmlNode));

var xmlItems = from x in listItemsXml.Descendants("{#RowsetSchema}row")
               select x;

foreach (XElement xmlItem in xmlItems) {
        Console.WriteLine("{0} - {1}",
            xmlItem.Attribute("ows_ID").Value,
            xmlItem.Attribute("ows_Title").Value);
}
```

This example uses the *GetList* operation of the *Lists.asmx* service to retrieve the configuration of the target list to query. It then loads the items of the list by using the *GetListItems* operation, providing a default query over the default view of the list.

As shown in the example, you can target the services to the correct SharePoint website by setting the *Url* property of the proxy object. In fact, if you target the *Lists.asmx* service with a *Url* value of *http://devbook.sp2010.local/_vti_bin/Lists.asmx*, then the SOAP service will return lists of the site with URL http://devbook.sp2010.local/. If you use a value of *http://devbook.sp2010.local/SubSite/_vti_bin/Lists.asmx*, then the SOAP service will give you access to the lists of the subsite with URL http://devbook.sp2010.local/SubSite/.

Finally, you can see that both of the operations we invoked (*Lists.GetList* and *SiteData. GetListItems*) return a result in the form of XML; in fact, we use classes of LINQ to XML to read and parse them. While working with SharePoint SOAP services, you will need to be accustomed to managing different kinds of results, because it is common for XML results to be presented in various ways (*XmlNode*, *String*, arrays of custom types, and so on).

I could present a countless number of examples that demonstrate how to use all the various SOAP services offered by SharePoint. However, beginning with SharePoint 2010, the Client Object Model has become one of the favored communication technologies for SharePoint 2010, so I will not spend any further time detailing the SOAP services.

The REST API

The last client-side API that you will see in this chapter is the REST API, which is another new feature of SharePoint 2010.

Note REST stands for Representational State Transfer. It embodies the idea of accessing data across the Internet network, referencing resources using a clear and unique syntax. For example, when you open a browser and navigate to the URL *http://www.microsoft.com/*, you identify Microsoft's website using its identifying URL, and a Web server at Microsoft returns the content you requested. When you browse to *http://www.w3.org/*, you use a different URL that identifies a different resource—which that content, instead. A REST API is an API that represents commands and instructions using a similar paradigm.

As you will see in this section, you will have the opportunity to reference a resource published by a SharePoint website by using a unique URL, which is a representation of that item. For further details about REST, refer to the document that first introduced the concept of REST in 2000, which is available at *http://www.ics.uci.edu/~fielding/pubs/dissertation/rest_arch_style.htm*.

SharePoint 2010 publishes a WCF service which can provide data using a REST protocol. This service listens at the virtual URL */_vti_bin/ListData.svc* of every SharePoint website and can be used by any third-party willing to read and eventually change data stored in SharePoint. To offer and take advantage of this service, you need to install ADO.NET Data Services Update for .NET Framework 3.5 SP1 on top of your SharePoint front-end Web servers' setup.

If you open your browser and navigate to the URL of the REST service, you will get back an XML list of all the available contents of the target SharePoint website. Figure 5-4 shows an example of what the browser returns when you query the REST service for the sample site of this book (*http://devbook.sp2010.local/_vti_bin/ListData.svc*).

More Information For further detail about setting up a SharePoint 2010 developer machine, read the article on MSDN Online at *http://msdn.microsoft.com/en-us/library/ee554869.aspx.us/library/ee554869.aspx*.

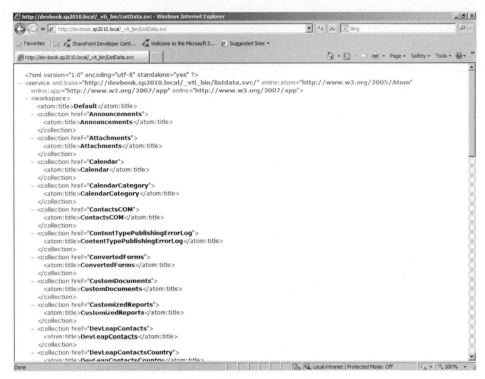

FIGURE 5-4 The result gained requesting the *ListData.svc* on this book's sample site.

> **Note**   To read the representation of the list's contents as XML Internet Explorer you first need to turn off the "Feed reading view" feature. To do so, go to Tools | Internet Options | Content | Feeds And Web Slices | Settings, and then clear the check box adjacent to Turn On Feed Reading View.

As Figure 5-4 illustrates, the result is a collection items, each with its own relative URL (*href* attribute) corresponding to the lists contained in the current site. If you try to access the REST service URL, appending one of these relative URLs to the service URL, you will gain access to the content of the corresponding list. For example, suppose you request the following URL:

```
http://devbook.sp2010.local/_vti_bin/ListData.svc/DevLeapContacts
```

By default, the browser will show you a list of items in the form of syndication feed, because the output XML is built using the Atom Syndication format (*http://www.w3.org/2005/Atom*). If you request a URL, such as the following:

```
http://devbook.sp2010.local/_vti_bin/ListData.svc/DevLeapContacts(1)
```

The REST service will return the XML representation of the contact with an ID value of 1. If you need to retrieve the value of the field *CompanyName* of the item with an ID value of 1, you can request the following URL:

```
http://devbook.sp2010.local/_vti_bin/ListData.svc/DevLeapContacts(1)/CompanyName
```

Still, the result of this last query will be wrapped in an XML element. However, if you are interested in retrieving only the bare value, you can append to the URL the command */$value* and the REST service will return only the text value of the *CompanyName* field.

```
http://devbook.sp2010.local/_vti_bin/ListData.svc/DevLeapContacts(1)/CompanyName/$value
```

In general, the URI mapping access rule is like the following:

```
http://siteurl/_vti_bin/ListData.svc/{EntityName}[({Identifier})]/[{Property}]/[{$command}]
```

This is a very useful interface for querying data by using a URL-based syntax that can be consumed by any device able to access HTTP and to read XML (which today means almost any device at all). You can use the same URL syntax to write queries to partition (filter), to order, to query paged data, and so on. The following list presents the main keywords available as query string parameters:

- *$filter={predicate}*   Filter the data
- *$expand={Entity}*   Include related objects
- *$orderby={property}*   Order results
- *$skip=n*   Skip the first *n* results (useful for paging)
- *$top=n*   Retrieve the first *n* results (also useful for paging)
- *$metadata*   Get metadata describing the published entities

The syntax that I am using is based on an open standard, as proposed by Microsoft, under the "Microsoft Open Specification Promise,", and called "Open Data Protocol" (also known as OData).

> **More Information** For further details about the Microsoft Open Specification Promise (OSP), go to *http://www.microsoft.com/interop/osp/default.mspx*. To find out find more about Open Data Protocol, go to *http://www.odata.org/*.

Querying for Data with .NET and LINQ

The previous section showed you how to consume the SharePoint REST API using any HTTP client, such as the *WebClient* class of *System.Net*. However, it wouldn't be very comfortable to manually compose all the URLs corresponding to every kind of query and then manually parse the responses in XML (Atom) format. Fortunately, Microsoft Visual Studio and Microsoft .NET provides established support for services compliant with the OData specification. In fact, if you add a Service Reference to the *ListData.svc* service within a Microsoft Visual Studio

2010 .NET project, the environment will recognize the service as an OData service and will provide you with a high-level interface to access the published resources.

Every OData service can provide a set of metadata, which is available by invoking the URL *$metadata*, and the "Add Service Reference" tool can read this metadata to create a set of typed classes representing each published resource. Figure 5-5 shows the Add Service Reference dialog box interface while a reference to an OData compliant service is being added. Remember that you must refresh the reference each time you change or update the schema of your data in SharePoint.

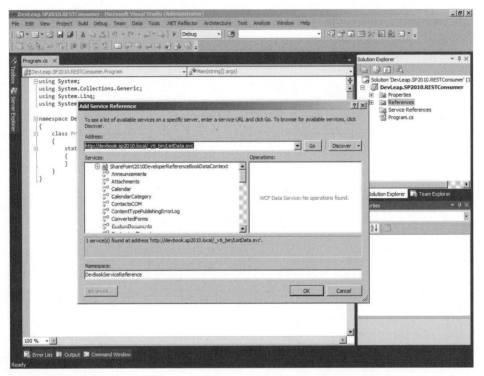

FIGURE 5-5 The Add Service Reference dialog box interface, shown while adding a reference to an OData compliant service.

Once you have created a service reference to an OData service, you will be able to create an instance of an object called *[ServiceName]DataContext* that represents the proxy to the service and inherits from *System.Data.Services.Client.DataServiceContext*. If you're using a SharePoint REST service, the proxy class will have a name like *[SiteTitle]DataContext*, where *SiteTitle* represents the title of the target site without spaces. In the example of this book, the site's title is "SharePoint 2010 Developer Reference Book," so the class will have a long but clear and self-explanatory name: *SharePoint2010DeveloperReferenceBookDataContext*.

Through instances of this class, you will be able to access and query the list items of the site as if they were collections of typed entities. In fact, every list corresponds to a collection property of the proxy class. Every content-type corresponds to an entity type. For instance, for the sample site of this book, the "DevLeap Contacts" list of SharePoint will correspond to a *DevLeapContacts* collection property of the proxy class. This collection will host typed instances of contact items. Listing 5-29 displays an example of querying the contacts using the REST proxy.

LISTING 5-29 Querying contacts using the REST proxy.

```
SharePoint2010DeveloperReferenceBookDataContext dc =
    new SharePoint2010DeveloperReferenceBookDataContext(
        new Uri("http://devbook.sp2010.local/_vti_bin/ListData.svc"));
dc.Credentials = System.Net.CredentialCache.DefaultCredentials;

foreach (var item in dc.DevLeapContacts) {
    Console.WriteLine(item);
}
```

Listing 5-29 shows that the *DataContext* class provides a constructor that requires an argument of type *System.Uri* that corresponds to the URL of the *ListData.svc*. If you need to authenticate this against the remote service, you can use the *Credentials* property of the *DataContext* class. This property accepts a type implementing *System.Net.ICredential*, like the *System.Net.CredentialCache.DefaultCredentials* that corresponds to the system credentials of the current application. Then, you only need to query (enumerate) the content of the collections in which you are interested to access the corresponding items.

One interesting thing to know is that the auto-generated code supports LINQ queries, too. Thus, you can write a query targeting the collections of items published by the *DataContext* class, as is shown in Listing 5-30. Furthermore, the LINQ query is not a LINQ to Objects query working in memory, rather a query managed by a query provider that will translate the LINQ query into a REST (OData style) query.

More Information For further details about LINQ, read the book, *Programming Microsoft LINQ in .NET 4.0*, by Paolo Pialorsi and Marco Russo (Microsoft Press, 2010; ISBN: 978-0-7356-4057-3).

LISTING 5-30 Querying contacts by using a LINQ query.

```
SharePoint2010DeveloperReferenceBookDataContext dc =
    new SharePoint2010DeveloperReferenceBookDataContext(
        new Uri("http://devbook.sp2010.local/_vti_bin/ListData.svc"));
dc.Credentials = System.Net.CredentialCache.DefaultCredentials;

var query = from c in dc.DevLeapContacts
            where c.ContentType == "DevLeapCustomer"
```

```
            select new {
                c.ContactID,
                c.Title,
                c.CompanyName,
                c.CustomerLevelValue
            };

foreach (var item in query) {
    Console.WriteLine(item);
}
```

If you take a look at the *DevLeapContacts* property of the *DataContext* class, you will see that it is of type *System.Data.Services.Client.DataServiceQuery<DevLeapContactsItem>*. The *DataServiceQuery<T>* class implements the *IQueryable<T>* interface of the LINQ infrastructure and represents the proxy to the OData LINQ query provider, also known as WCF Data Services Client Library.

> **More Information** If you would like to go deeper into WCF Data Services, go to MSDN Online at *http://msdn.microsoft.com/en-us/library/cc668792.aspx*.

If you step into the code and add a watch on the *query* variable, you will see that the variable internally represents the query as a REST request, as with the following:

```
http://devbook.sp2010.local/_vti_bin/ListData.svc/DevLeapContacts()?$filter=ContentType
    eq 'DevLeapCustomer'&$select=ContactID,Title,CompanyName,CustomerLevelValue
```

If you try to copy this URL and paste it into the browser address bar, you will get back exactly the results of the query, represented in XML format.

If you like to query data of a SharePoint site while ignoring that it is a SharePoint site, the REST way is your way, because you have a typed collection of items, even queryable with LINQ, that abstracts from the underlying repository. Of course there are some limitations with this approach. For instance, you cannot write any kind of query, and there are some keywords and operators (*join*, *average*, *First*, *FirstOrDefault*, and so on) that by now are not supported by the WCF Data Service Client Library. If you try to invoke an unsupported query command, you will get back an exception like the following one:

```
Unhandled Exception: System.NotSupportedException: The method 'Join' is not supported.
```

> **Note** The full list of unsupported keywords and methods can be found on MSDN Online at *http://msdn.microsoft.com/en-us/library/ee622463.aspx*.

Listing 5-31 displays a code excerpt of an unsupported query syntax.

LISTING 5-31 An unsupported query syntax.

```
// This query does not work, because join is not supported
var query = from c in dc.DevLeapContacts
            where c.ContentType == "DevLeapCustomer"
            join i in dc.Invoices on c.Id equals i.InvoiceCustomerLookupId
            select new { c.ContactID, c.Title, c.CompanyName, i.Name };
```

However, there are already a lot of useful commands and keywords that are supported. For example, you can do paging by using *Skip* and *Take*, or you can do ordering, and more. Listing 5-32 demonstrates how to implement paging across a list of items.

LISTING 5-32 Paging in a LINQ query.

```
// Get the second page, with a page size of 10
var query = (from c in dc.ContactsCOM
             select c).Skip(10).Take(10);
```

The URL request corresponding to the query in Listing 5-32 is the following:

```
http://devbook.sp2010.local/_vti_bin/ListData.svc/ContactsCOM()?$skip=10&$top=10
```

You can see the *$skip* and *$top* parameters illustrated in the previous section.

Managing Data

The ability to query SharePoint data using the REST API is very interesting and by itself is probably sufficient to boost the enthusiasm level for this new API. But this is just half of the story. With the REST API, from the perspective of the OData specification, you can also manage (insert, update, delete) data using a fully-typed approach, even if you are working on the client side.

The *DataContext* class provides an identity management service, which allows working with retrieved entities as though they were entities of a typical O/RM, such as LINQ to SQL, LINQ to Entities, or LINQ to SharePoint.

Whenever you retrieve an entity, not a custom anonymous type based on a custom projection, you can manage its properties and inform the source SharePoint server about your changes, applying them with a batch job. Listing 5-33 shows a code excerpt that updates the property of an existing item.

LISTING 5-33 Updating a previously existing item.

```
SharePoint2010DeveloperReferenceBookDataContext dc =
    new SharePoint2010DeveloperReferenceBookDataContext(
        new Uri("http://devbook.sp2010.local/_vti_bin/ListData.svc"));
dc.Credentials = System.Net.CredentialCache.DefaultCredentials;

DevLeapContactsItem item = (from c in dc.DevLeapContacts
                            where c.ID == 1
                            select c).First();

item.CompanyName += " - Changed!";
dc.UpdateObject(item);

dc.SaveChanges();
```

As the code sample shows, just after updating the entity you need to manually invoke the *UpdateObject* method of the *DataContext* class in order to instruct it about the change you have done. This is a requirement because internally the *DataContext* proxy class does not automatically track changes to objects. You can change many entities at the same time, and when you have finished you simply need to invoke the *SaveChanges* method of the *DataContext* in order to send your changes back to the server.

If you need to add a new item to a target list, you can use the general purpose *AddObject* method provided by the *DataContext* class. In the following snippet, you can see the signature of this method:

```
public void AddObject(string entitySetName, object entity);
```

You can also use a fully-typed method called *AddTo[ListName]*, which is a wrapper around the *AddObject* untyped method, and is automatically generated by the tools that generate the Service Reference. For the sake of clarity, the following shows the definition of the method *AddToDevLeapContacts*:

```
public void AddToDevLeapContacts(DevLeapContactsItem devLeapContactsItem) {
    base.AddObject("DevLeapContacts", devLeapContactsItem);
}
```

Listing 5-34 presents a code excerpt that adds an item to the sample list of contacts:

LISTING 5-34 Adding a new item to a list.

```
SharePoint2010DeveloperReferenceBookDataContext dc =
    new SharePoint2010DeveloperReferenceBookDataContext(
        new Uri("http://devbook.sp2010.local/_vti_bin/ListData.svc"));
dc.Credentials = System.Net.CredentialCache.DefaultCredentials;
```

```
DevLeapContactsItem item = new DevLeapContactsItem {
    Title = "Sample Customer",
    ContactID = "CC001",
    ContentType = "DevLeapCustomer",
    CompanyName = "Sample Company",
    CountryValue = "Germany",
    CustomerLevelValue = "Level A"
};

dc.AddToDevLeapContacts(item);

dc.SaveChanges();
```

The sample code creates a new instance of an object with a type compliant with the target list. Then it sets the properties of the item (for instance, the fields) and adds it to the target list using the *AddTo[ListName]* method. Lastly, it invokes the *SaveChanges* method of the *DataContext* to confirm the changes on the server side. Notice that the target list accepts two kinds of content-types, so the sample also configures the *ContentType* property of the item in order to instruct SharePoint about the right content-type to use on the server side.

The last common task in managing data is deleting entities. The *DataContext* class offers a *DeleteObject* method, which accepts an entity that will be marked to be deleted at the next *SaveChanges* invocation. Thus, to delete an item, you simply need to invoke *SaveChanges*. Listing 5-35 demonstrates this in action.

LISTING 5-35 Deleting an item from a list.

```
SharePoint2010DeveloperReferenceBookDataContext dc =
    new SharePoint2010DeveloperReferenceBookDataContext(
        new Uri("http://devbook.sp2010.local/_vti_bin/ListData.svc"));
dc.Credentials = System.Net.CredentialCache.DefaultCredentials;

DevLeapContactsItem item = (from c in dc.DevLeapContacts
                            where c.ContactID == "CC001"
                            select c).First();

dc.DeleteObject(item);

dc.SaveChanges();
```

The WCF Data Service Client Library also provides full support for handling concurrency issues while managing data. However, it is beyond the scope of this chapter (and this book) to give you the proper coverage of the WCF Data Service Client Library, so I will not go deeper into this matter. However, it is important to understand the potential of this API while managing SharePoint data and external data in general, whenever you have an OData provider available.

Summary

In this chapter, you learned about the client-side technologies offered by SharePoint 2010 with which you can query and manage data from a remote consumer. In particular, you have seen how to use the Client Object Model, together with its different flavors, such as the Managed Client Object Model, the Silverlight Client Object Model, and the ECMAScript Client Object Model. You have also seen that there are also some SOAP services, mainly based on the ASP.NET ASMX Web Services engine, that are useful for accessing and somehow managing data of a SharePoint site from any third-party consumer that can make a SOAP call. Lastly, you have learned what the REST API is and how to use it to query data—even with LINQ queries—and how to manage data. Now you are ready to develop SharePoint client solutions, armed with a solid understanding of the available tools and technologies.

PART III
Developing Web Parts

Chapter 6
Web Part Basics

If you ask a Microsoft SharePoint 2010 developer to name one of its key features, she will probably answer, "Web Parts, of course." But what are Web Parts? They are simply user-customizable regions hosted by a SharePoint webpage. Web Parts were first introduced many years ago in Microsoft SharePoint Team Services 2001. Through subsequent versions of the product, the idea of Web Parts have been consolidated and widely adopted by the market. With Microsoft .NET 2.0, the infrastructure for Web Parts moved from SharePoint to the official ASP.NET web development platform, thus making the use of Web Parts broadly adopted in many kind of ASP.NET application. From the point of view of the end user, a Web Part is simply a piece of a webpage that can be customized by the user himself, using the web browser interface. From a developer's perspective, a Web Part is a class that defines some code for rendering its content in the browser, for handling custom configuration, layout, positioning, and so on, within the SharePoint and/or ASP.NET environment. Web Parts can be added and removed from pages (often called Web Part Pages) autonomously by the end user by choosing Web Parts from a server gallery or from an online public gallery.

More important—again from the developer's point of view—Web Parts can be reused in many different pages and sites, simplifying custom solutions development, deployment, and maintenance. In fact, many SharePoint solutions are based on a set of custom Web Parts that are referenced in Web Part Pages.

This chapter explains how Web Parts work and how to develop custom Web Parts. The discussion continues in Chapter 7, "Advanced Web Parts," which covers more advanced topics about Web Parts development.

Web Part Architecture

A Web Part is an ASP.NET custom control that inherits from the base class *WebPart* from the *System.Web.UI.WebControls.WebParts* namespace. To be able to fully utilize a Web Part in a page, you need to define a *WebPartZone* control, which is a container for a set of Web Parts. The *WebPartZone* control provides a common rendering pattern to all its constituent Web Parts. Another fundamental control in the Web Parts architecture is the *WebPartManager*, which handles all the tasks related to Web Parts lifetime management, such as loading/unloading and serializing/deserializing their state within the current page, and connecting Web Parts into Web Part Zones. SharePoint has its own kind of *WebPartZone* controls that give you the ability to define a set of SharePoint specific rendering zones. Some examples of these are: the *WebPartZone* class for standard Web Parts rendering; the *EditorZone* class to render parts responsible for editing other Web Parts (we will cover Editor Parts later in this chapter). Also, the *WebPartManager* control has been redefined in SharePoint into a custom implementation called *SPWebPartManager*, which handles some specific activities exclusively available in SharePoint. In order to leverage these controls, SharePoint also provides a custom page type called *WebPartPage* (available in the *Microsoft.SharePoint.WebPartPages* namespace) that includes a preconfigured and unique instance of a *SPWebPartManager* control and the main Web Part Zones, which are useful for rendering a page made of Web Parts. Figure 6-1 exhibits the overall architectural schema of such a page.

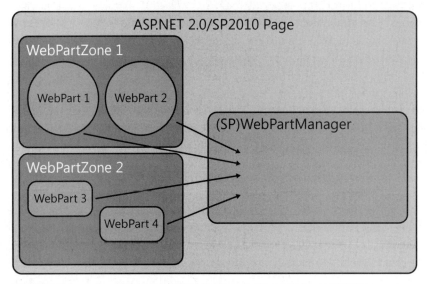

FIGURE 6-1 Overall architecture of a *WebPartPage* in SharePoint and ASP.NET.

In everyday solutions, we will work mainly with Web Parts, and rarely will we have to directly interact with Web Part Zones and the *WebPartManager*.

A "Hello World" Web Part

It's time to start developing your first Web Part. Microsoft Visual Studio 2010 provides some project templates and utilities that can help you to rapidly develop custom Web Parts. Suppose that you need to develop a "Hello World Web Part" that simply welcomes the current user, writing his name and the current *DateTime* value in the browser. You will begin creating a new project of type "SharePoint | 2010 | Empty SharePoint Project." This project template simply starts with a set of assembly references, useful for developing any kind of

SharePoint solution, and with a predefined deployment configuration. When you create a new SharePoint project, Visual Studio asks you for the URL of the website where it will deploy the solution. It also asks you what kind of deployment you want to build (Farm Solution or Sandboxed solution). For this example, choose Farm Solution deployment. You will see more about deployment later in this chapter beginning on page 188, and more deeply in Chapter 8, "SharePoint Features and Solutions." For now, you need to concentrate on the Web Part itself.

To develop your sample Web Part, you need to add to the project a new file item of type Web Part. Name the new item **HelloWorldWebPart**. A new class file is added, together with a set of configuration files that I will discuss later. Figure 6-2 shows the project layout, after you have added the Web Part item.

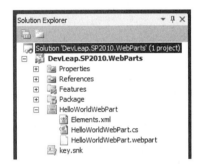

FIGURE 6-2 The project layout of the sample Web Part solution

Listing 6-1 displays the content of the HelloWorldWebPart.cs file, just after you add the Web Part item to the project.

LISTING 6-1 The startup class file for the Hello World Web Part.

```csharp
using System;
using System.ComponentModel;
using System.Web;
using System.Web.UI;
using System.Web.UI.WebControls;
using System.Web.UI.WebControls.WebParts;
using Microsoft.SharePoint;
using Microsoft.SharePoint.WebControls;

namespace DevLeap.SP2010.WebParts.HelloWorldWebPart {
    [ToolboxItemAttribute(false)]
    public class HelloWorldWebPart : WebPart {
        protected override void CreateChildControls()
        {
        }
    }
}
```

Looking at this code, the first thing you notice is that the class inherits from the base class *WebPart*, as mentioned in the previous section. However, the key point of this sample code is the override of the *CreateChildControls* method where, as with any other ASP.NET custom control, you should create the web control's tree that defines the rendering of the Web Part. Listing 6-2 adds a couple of instances of *LiteralControl* to display the welcome message text inside an H1 tag, and the current date time in a DIV element.

LISTING 6-2 The code for the sample Hello World Web Part.

```csharp
using System;
using System.ComponentModel;
using System.Web;
using System.Web.UI;
using System.Web.UI.WebControls;
using System.Web.UI.WebControls.WebParts;
using Microsoft.SharePoint;
using Microsoft.SharePoint.WebControls;

namespace DevLeap.SP2010.WebParts.HelloWorldWebPart {
    [ToolboxItemAttribute(false)]
    public class HelloWorldWebPart : WebPart {
        protected override void CreateChildControls()
        {
            SPWeb currentWeb = SPControl.GetContextWeb(HttpContext.Current);
            String currentUserName = currentWeb.CurrentUser.LoginName;

            this.Controls.Add(new LiteralControl(String.Format(
                "<h1>Welcome {0}!</h1>", currentUserName)));
            this.Controls.Add(new LiteralControl(String.Format(
                "<div>Current DateTime: {0}</div>", DateTime.Now)));
        }
    }
}
```

At the beginning of the *CreateChildControls* method implementation, the code also requests the current *SPWeb* instance from the *SPControl* class, through the current *HttpContext*, so it can get the current user *LoginName*.

> **More Information** For further details about the *SPWeb* and *SPControl* classes, refer to Chapter 3, "Server Object Model."

As you can see from this introductory example, to be a good Web Part developer, you first need to be a good ASP.NET developer. At the same time, every ASP.NET developer will be very comfortable developing Web Parts.

Figure 6-3 presents the output of the Hello World Web Part, inserted into the Home Page of a web application with claims-based authentication.

> **More Information** For more details about claims-based authentication, refer to Chapter 22, "Claims-Based Authentication and Federated Identities."

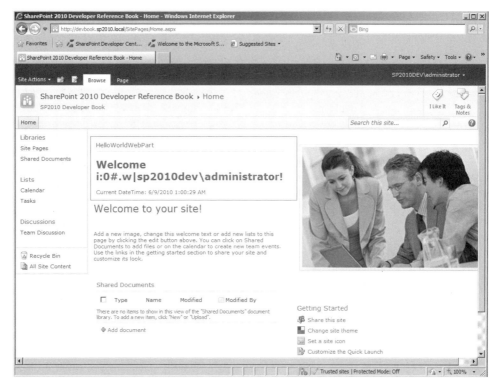

FIGURE 6-3 The output of the *HelloWorldWebPart* within a SharePoint 2010 site with claims-based authentication.

> **Note** Another way of implementing a Web Part is to inherit from the class *WebPart* of namespace *Microsoft.SharePoint.WebPartPages*; however, this class internally inherits from the ASP.NET *WebPart* base class and is primarily provided for backward compatibility with older versions of Microsoft SharePoint. If you decide to inherit your Web Parts from the SharePoint *WebPart* base class, these Web Parts will target only SharePoint sites; it will not be possible to use them in standard ASP.NET websites. By using the SharePoint custom base class, you can take advantage of some additional functionalities that are not available in standard Web Part infrastructure, but in our experience these additional capabilities are not really useful. Nevertheless, at the very end of this chapter we will discuss the few benefits of this kind of Web Parts at the end of this chapter.

Web Part Deployment

To deploy our sample Web Part, as well as any other Web Part implementation, we need to complete the following steps:

- Build the class into a .NET assembly of type DLL.

- Make the assembly available to the web application (putting it into the GAC, or into the web application local bin folder, or into the Solution Gallery of the current Site Collection).

 Note GAC stands for Globally Assembly Cache, which is the centralized and shared repository of trusted and digitally-signed .NET assemblies. For further details about .NET development and deployment we suggest reading the book, *Applied Microsoft .NET Framework Programming*, by Jeffrey Richter (Microsoft Press, 2002; ISBN: 978-0-7356-1422-2).

- Authorize the Web Part to execute within the current SharePoint environment.

- Load the Web Part into the Web Parts Gallery of the current site so that it is available to the end user.

Visual Studio 2010 makes it easy to complete all these deployment steps. Simply select the Build | Deploy Solution to automatically deploy the Web Part on the website that you configured while creating the project.

Take a look at these steps from a practical perspective. Building the .NET assembly is trivial, so I will not take care of it here; however, consider that if you ever want to put it into the GAC, you need to give it a strong name (Name, Version, Culture, and PublicKeyToken). Fortunately, Visual Studio 2010 does it for you, automatically adding a set of signing keys to the project. Putting the assembly into the GAC or web application bin folder is also trivial for any .NET developer. Conversely, installing the assembly into the Solution Gallery of the current Site Collection requires you to know about Sandboxed solutions, thus I will cover this matter later, in Chapter 8.

To authorize the Web Part to execute within the SharePoint environment, you need to add a specific configuration item into the web.config file of the current web application, declaring the Web Part as a "SafeControl." At the end of Chapter 7, you can find more details about *SafeControls*. Listing 6-3 presents an excerpt of the custom configuration that you need to apply.

LISTING 6-3 The custom configuration needed to make the Hello World Web Part safe for SharePoint.

```xml
<?xml version="1.0" encoding="UTF-8" standalone="yes"?>
<configuration>
  <SharePoint>
    <!-- Removed for the sake of simplicity -->
    <SafeControls>
      <!-- Here there are many other SafeControls -->
      <SafeControl Assembly="DevLeap.SP2010.WebParts, Version=1.0.0.0,
      Culture=neutral, PublicKeyToken=cba640f292988abf"
      Namespace="DevLeap.SP2010.WebParts.HelloWorldWebPart" TypeName="*" Safe="True"
      SafeAgainstScript="False" />
    </SafeControls>
    <!-- Removed for the sake of simplicity -->
</configuration>
```

Making the Web Part available in the Web Part Gallery requires that you add the Web Part definition to the current Site Collection. This definition is a .webpart file that Visual Studio 2010 automatically generates when we add a Web Part item to a project. Listing 6-4 illustrates the default content of this file in our example.

LISTING 6-4 The .webpart file to deploy the Hello World Web Part.

```xml
<?xml version="1.0" encoding="utf-8"?>
<webParts>
  <webPart xmlns="http://schemas.microsoft.com/WebPart/v3">
    <metaData>
      <type name="DevLeap.SP2010.WebParts.HelloWorldWebPart.HelloWorldWebPart,
        $SharePoint.Project.AssemblyFullName$" />
      <importErrorMessage>$Resources:core,ImportErrorMessage;</importErrorMessage>
    </metaData>
    <data>
      <properties>
        <property name="Title" type="string">HelloWorldWebPart</property>
        <property name="Description" type="string">My WebPart</property>
      </properties>
    </data>
  </webPart>
</webParts>
```

The key aspect of the .webpart file is the declaration of the type (a .NET type) corresponding to the current Web Part. Notice that a .webpart file can declare many Web Parts, even if by default Visual Studio 2010 creates a .webpart file for each Web Part definition. The type name of our Hello World Web Part is declared as a full name (namespace + class name), together with the containing assembly name. In this code example, the assembly name is defined using an alias *($SharePoint.Project.AssemblyFullName$)*, which will be automatically replaced by Visual Studio 2010 with the real assembly name during the deployment process.

In addition, the .webpart file declares the default values for some of the properties of our Web Part. For instance, you can see that the *Title* and *Description* properties of the Web Part are defined as custom *property* elements, within a *properties* wrapper element.

You can change the values of these properties as well as defining some other properties by simply editing the .webpart file in Visual Studio. Table 6-1 provides a list of the most useful properties that you can define.

TABLE 6-1 Some of the Main Configurable Properties of a .webpart File

Property Name	Description
Title	Defines the title of the Web Part. The title will be shown to the end user in the Web Parts Gallery as well as when inserting a Web Part in a page, and it will be the default title of a newly-inserted Web Part.
Description	Describes the current Web Part. This will be shown to the end user in the Web Parts Gallery and when inserting a Web Part in a page..
TitleIconImageUrl	Specifies the URL to an image used to represent the Web Part in its title bar. The default value is an empty string ("").
CatalogIconImageUrl	Specifies the URL to an image used to represent the Web Part in the Web Parts Catalog. The default value is an empty string ("").
ChromeType	Defines the type of border that frames the Web Part. It can assume the following values (the default value is *Default*): ■ *Default* inherits its behavior from the containing Web Part Zone; ■ *TitleAndBorder* a title bar with a border; ■ *None* no border and no title bar; ■ *TitleOnly* a title bar, without a border; ■ *BorderOnly* a border, without a title bar.
ChromeState	Determines whether the Web Part will appear *Minimized* or *Normal*.
AllowClose	Defines whether the Web Part can be closed by an end user.
AllowConnect	Defines whether the Web Part can be connected to another by an end user.
AllowEdit	Defines whether the Web Part can be edited by an end user.
AllowHide	Defines whether the Web Part can be hidden by an end user.
AllowMinimize	Defines whether the Web Part can be minimized by an end user.
AllowZoneChange	Defines whether the Web Part can be moved between different Web Part Zones by an end user.
ExportMode	Allows defining if the current Web Part configuration can be exported for reuse on another website.

Listing 6-5 demonstrates how I customized the .webpart file for the "Hello World Web Part" sample.

LISTING 6-5 The .webpart file to deploy the configured "Hello World Web Part."

```xml
<?xml version="1.0" encoding="utf-8"?>
<webParts>
  <webPart xmlns="http://schemas.microsoft.com/WebPart/v3">
    <metaData>
      <type name="DevLeap.SP2010.WebParts.HelloWorldWebPart.HelloWorldWebPart,
          $SharePoint.Project.AssemblyFullName$" />
      <importErrorMessage>$Resources:core,ImportErrorMessage;</importErrorMessage>
    </metaData>
    <data>
      <properties>
        <property name="Title" type="string">HelloWorldWebPart</property>
        <property name="Description" type="string">
          Custom WebPart to welcome end user</property>
        <property name="CatalogIconImageUrl"
            type="string">/_layouts/images/ICTXT.GIF</property>
        <property name="AllowEdit" type="bool">true</property>
        <property name="ChromeType" type="chrometype">TitleAndBorder</property>
      </properties>
    </data>
  </webPart>
</webParts>
```

Figure 6-4 illustrates the output of the customized "Hello World Web Part." Notice the custom category, the custom icon in the Web Parts Catalog, the customized description, and the customized *Chrome* (*TitleAndBorder*).

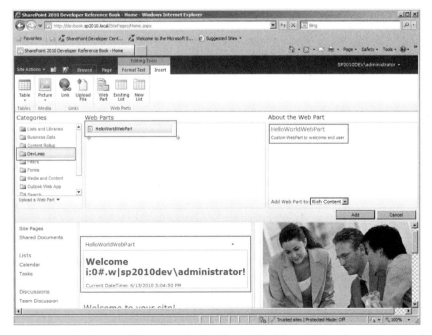

FIGURE 6-4 The output of the customized *HelloWorldWebPart* within a SharePoint 2010 site.

As you will see in the section "Configurable Web Parts" on page 197, Web Parts can also have custom properties defined by developers that are customizable by site owners or site members with the appropriate permissions. Such properties will be configurable with default values, while deploying Web Parts, exactly the same way as standard Web Part properties you've just seen.

Real Web Parts

By now, you have seen how to define and deploy a very simple and explanatory Web Part like the first Hello World Web Part. Of course, real Web Parts are a little bit more complex and are equipped with a richer set of controls and behaviors. In this section, you will explore two kinds of Web Parts: classic Web Parts made of custom code, and Visual Web Parts designed using the graphical designer of Visual Studio 2010.

Classic Web Parts

A standard classic Web Part is a control that is made up of a set of ASP.NET controls. It interacts with the end user through events and controls behavior. In this section, you will build a data entry Web Part that will collect data from the end user and insert them into a target SharePoint list. The core engine of this Web Part will use the SharePoint Server Object Model as the means to insert items into the target list. The user interface will be built using ASP.NET server controls.

Imagine that you have a target list of "Requests for Contacts" available in your SharePoint site, and you want to collect users' requests using your custom Web Part implementation. Figure 6-5 shows the final output of this Web Part.

Name the Web Part *InsertRequestForContactWebPart* and create a SharePoint project in Visual Studio 2010 to host it. Next, choose a "Farm solution" project type. The Web Part provides a small set of fields (reason of the request for contact, requesting user full name and e-mail) to describe the request. These fields correspond to a target list "Requests for Contacts" that you manually defined in the current website.

> **Note** In Chapter 10, "Data Provisioning," you will learn how to programmatically define and provision data structures of lists like "Requests for Contacts." In an actual professional solution, you will probably need to define the list, as well as the Web Parts working on it, in a common SharePoint solution that you will be able to deploy "at once."

Internally, the Web Part will have a set of ASP.NET controls that correspond to the input fields, and will use the SharePoint Server Object Model (see Chapter 3 for further details) to insert the new item into the list. Listing 6-6 displays the whole implementation of the Web Part.

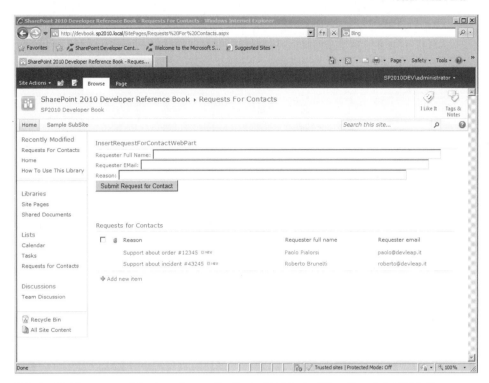

FIGURE 6-5 The output of the *InsertRequestForContactWebPart* within a SharePoint 2010 site.

LISTING 6-6 The whole implementation of the *InsertRequestForContactWebPart* Web Part.

```
namespace DevLeap.SP2010.WebParts.InsertRequestForContactWebPart {
    [ToolboxItemAttribute(false)]
    public class InsertRequestForContactWebPart : WebPart {
        protected TextBox RequesterFullName;
        protected TextBox RequesterEMail;
        protected TextBox Reason;
        protected Button SubmitRequestForContact;
        protected Label ErrorMessage;

        protected override void CreateChildControls() {
            this.RequesterFullName = new TextBox();
            this.RequesterFullName.Columns = 100;
            this.RequesterFullName.MaxLength = 255;
            this.Controls.Add(new LiteralControl("<div>Requester Full Name: "));
            this.Controls.Add(this.RequesterFullName);
            this.Controls.Add(new LiteralControl("</div>"));

            this.RequesterEMail = new TextBox();
            this.RequesterEMail.Columns = 100;
            this.RequesterEMail.MaxLength = 100;
            this.Controls.Add(new LiteralControl("<div>Requester EMail: "));
            this.Controls.Add(this.RequesterEMail);
            this.Controls.Add(new LiteralControl("</div>"));
```

```
        this.Reason = new TextBox();
        this.Reason.Columns = 100;
        this.Reason.MaxLength = 255;
        this.Controls.Add(new LiteralControl("<div>Reason: "));
        this.Controls.Add(this.Reason);
        this.Controls.Add(new LiteralControl("</div>"));

        this.SubmitRequestForContact = new Button();
        this.SubmitRequestForContact.Text = "Submit Request for Contact";
        this.Controls.Add(new LiteralControl("<div>"));
        this.Controls.Add(this.SubmitRequestForContact);
        this.SubmitRequestForContact.Click +=
            new EventHandler(SubmitRequestForContact_Click);
        this.Controls.Add(new LiteralControl("</div>"));

        this.ErrorMessage = new Label();
        this.ErrorMessage.ForeColor = System.Drawing.Color.Red;
        this.Controls.Add(new LiteralControl("<div>"));
        this.Controls.Add(this.ErrorMessage);
        this.Controls.Add(new LiteralControl("</div>"));
    }

    void SubmitRequestForContact_Click(object sender, EventArgs e) {
        SPWeb web = SPControl.GetContextWeb(HttpContext.Current);

        try {
            SPList targetList = web.Lists["Requests for Contacts"];
            SPListItem newItem = targetList.Items.Add();
            newItem["Reason"] = this.Reason .Text;
            newItem["Requester full name"] = this.RequesterFullName.Text;
            newItem["Requester email"] = this.RequesterEMail.Text;
            newItem.Update();
        }
        catch (IndexOutOfRangeException) {
            this.ErrorMessage.Text =
                "Cannot find list \"Requests for Contacts\"";
        }
    }
  }
}
```

In Listing 6-6, the code highlighted in bold declares the *protected* variables that hold the ASP.NET server controls. You can also see the code, inside the *CreateChildControls* method override, instantiating these controls. In particular, you can notice the binding between the *Click* server-side event of the button with name *SubmitRequestForContact* and the *SubmitRequestForContact_Click* method. Within this last event handling method, you create a new instance of a *SPListItem* representing a single "Request for Contact," compile its fields, and then feed the *SPList* instance with this new item.

Starting from this second example, it's easy to imagine that you can build whatever you need, using some ASP.NET code and custom controls, together with some .NET code. For instance, you can develop a Web Part that allows the end user to interact with a back-end database, or you can define a Web Part that talks with an external SOAP service provided by a third-party, and on, and on. However, keep in mind that SharePoint is a strong and secure environment, thus every kind of customization or solution must be approved and authorized if it is to do its job. In Chapter 7, in the section "Deployment, Security, and Versioning" on page 233, I will cover all of the security aspects of developing and deploying custom SharePoint Web Parts that comply with the security infrastructure of SharePoint.

Visual Web Parts

In Listing 6-6, I defined all the ASP.NET server controls that made up the Web Part using a lot of custom .NET code. However, it is not always comfortable to design a Web Part by code, because in some scenarios you need to declare UI attributes, such as CSS styles, controls positioning and alignment, and so on. In addition, there are situations for which you need to create a lot of controls inside a Web Part; writing and maintaining all that code is a hard task. One possible solution—applied before SharePoint 2010—was to define a custom ASCX control and load it dynamically into a Web Part using the *LoadControl* method of the ASP.NET infrastructure.

But begining with SharePoint 2010 and Visual Studio 2010, we now have an out-of-the-box solution for this problem. In fact, in Visual Studio 2010, we have an item template called "Visual Web Part" that defines exactly a Web Part that loads a custom ASCX control. This kind of Web Part does exactly what we would have done in earlier versions of SharePoint: a dynamic *LoadControl* of an external ASCX. Listing 6-7 shows the core implementation of a Visual Web Part that we called *VisualInsertRequestForContactWebPart*.

LISTING 6-7 The basic implementation of the *VisualInsertRequestForContactWebPart* Web Part.

```
namespace DevLeap.SP2010.WebParts.VisualInsertRequestForContactWebPart {
    [ToolboxItemAttribute(false)]
    public class VisualInsertRequestForContactWebPart : WebPart {
        // Visual Studio might automatically update this path
        // when you change the Visual Web Part project item.
        private const string _ascxPath =
            @"~/_CONTROLTEMPLATES/DevLeap.SP2010.WebParts/
            VisualInsertRequestForContactWebPart/
            VisualInsertRequestForContactWebPartUserControl.ascx";

        protected override void CreateChildControls() {
            Control control = Page.LoadControl(_ascxPath);
            Controls.Add(control);
        }
    }
}
```

In the Web Part source code, aside from the highlighted code related to the dynamic loading of the ASCX, you will place event handlers and custom procedures, leaving all the other stuff about the controls' tree in the ASCX file that you can see in Listing 6-8.

LISTING 6-8   The ASCX file for *VisualInsertRequestForContactWebPart* Web Part.

```
<%@ Assembly Name="$SharePoint.Project.AssemblyFullName$" %>
<%@ Assembly Name="Microsoft.Web.CommandUI, Version=14.0.0.0, Culture=neutral,
  PublicKeyToken=71e9bce111e9429c" %>
<%@ Register Tagprefix="SharePoint" Namespace="Microsoft.SharePoint.WebControls"
  Assembly="Microsoft.SharePoint, Version=14.0.0.0, Culture=neutral,
  PublicKeyToken=71e9bce111e9429c" %>
<%@ Register Tagprefix="Utilities" Namespace="Microsoft.SharePoint.Utilities"
  Assembly="Microsoft.SharePoint, Version=14.0.0.0, Culture=neutral,
  PublicKeyToken=71e9bce111e9429c" %>
<%@ Register Tagprefix="asp" Namespace="System.Web.UI"
  Assembly="System.Web.Extensions, Version=3.5.0.0, Culture=neutral,
  PublicKeyToken=31bf3856ad364e35" %>
<%@ Import Namespace="Microsoft.SharePoint" %>
<%@ Register Tagprefix="WebPartPages" Namespace="Microsoft.SharePoint.WebPartPages"
  Assembly="Microsoft.SharePoint, Version=14.0.0.0, Culture=neutral,
  PublicKeyToken=71e9bce111e9429c" %>
<%@ Control Language="C#" AutoEventWireup="true"
  CodeBehind="VisualInsertRequestForContactWebPartUserControl.ascx.cs"
  Inherits="DevLeap.SP2010.WebParts.VisualInsertRequestForContactWebPart.
    VisualInsertRequestForContactWebPartUserControl" %>
<p>
    Requester full name:
    <asp:TextBox ID="RequesterFullName" runat="server" Columns="100"
        MaxLength="255"></asp:TextBox>
</p>
<p>
    Requester email:
    <asp:TextBox ID="RequesterEMail" runat="server" Columns="100"
        MaxLength="100"></asp:TextBox>
</p>
<p>
    Reason:
    <asp:TextBox ID="Reason" runat="server" Columns="100"
        MaxLength="255"></asp:TextBox>
</p>
<asp:Button ID="SubmitRequestForContact" runat="server"
    onclick="SubmitRequestForContact_Click" Text="Submit Request for Contact" />
<br /><br />
<asp:Label ID="ErrorMessage" runat="server" ForeColor="Red" Visible="False" />
```

Of course, the benefit of having an ASCX file instead of standard .NET code is that an ASCX can be defined using the Visual Studio 2010 designer, as shown in Figure 6-6.

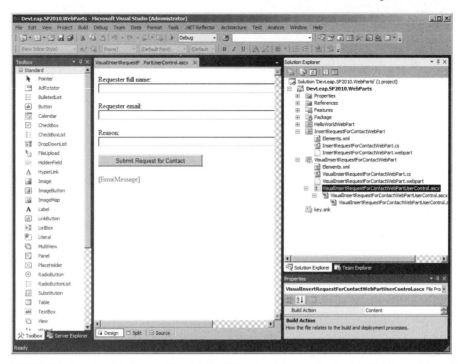

FIGURE 6-6 The visual designer of the ASCX of *VisualInsertRequestForContactWebPart* in Visual Studio 2010.

At first sight, Visual Web Parts could be seen as a better and easy solution, particularly if compared to standard Web Parts. However, there are some side effects and limitations of using a Visual Web Part. For instance, a Visual Web Part cannot be deployed as a sandboxed solution (see Chapter 7 for more details on this), thus making the solution potentially less secure than needed. Additionally, a Visual Web Part requires deploying the ASCX file into the SharePoint14_Root\TEMPLATE\CONTROLTEMPLATES shared folder, so the layout elements are shared across all the sites of a farm. In some cases it is more versatile to have an XSLT to manage and personalize the layout of a Web Part, on a single site/customer basis. In Chapter 7, I will discuss this matter in the section "XSLT Rendering" on page 226.

Note SharePoint14_Root refers to the SharePoint root folder, which is typically located at C:\ Program Files\Common Files\Microsoft Shared\Web Server Extensions\14.

Configurable Web Parts

In the previous examples, you used a predefined target list for inserting items. In real-world SharePoint solutions, however, Web Parts can be configured by authorized users. In this section, you will see how to develop configurable Web Parts and how to present a user-friendly interface for Web Parts configuration.

Configurable Parameters

The first step in creating configurable Web Parts is to define the properties that can be altered. To do that, you simply need to declare a public property in the Web Part class definition, tagging the property with the *WebBrowsableAttribute* attribute, and optionally with the *PersonalizableAttribute* attribute. Listing 6-9 shows a Web Part that declares a configurable property.

LISTING 6-9 A Web Part that provides a configurable property.

```
namespace DevLeap.SP2010.WebParts.ConfigurableInsertRequestForContactWebPart {
    [ToolboxItemAttribute(false)]
    public class ConfigurableInsertRequestForContactWebPart : WebPart {

        [WebBrowsable(true)]
        [Personalizable(PersonalizationScope.Shared)]
        public String TargetListTitle { get; set; }

        //
        // CreateChildControls code omitted ...
        //

        void SubmitRequestForContact_Click(object sender, EventArgs e) {
            SPWeb web = SPControl.GetContextWeb(HttpContext.Current);

            try {
                SPList targetList = web.Lists[this.TargetListTitle];

                SPListItem newItem = targetList.Items.Add();
                newItem["Reason"] = this.Reason.Text;
                newItem["Requester full name"] = this.RequesterFullName.Text;
                newItem["Requester email"] = this.RequesterEMail.Text;
                newItem.Update();
            }
            catch (IndexOutOfRangeException) {
                this.ErrorMessage.Text =
                    "Cannot find list \"Requests for Contacts\"";
            }
        }
    }
}
```

The *WebBrowsableAttribute* class instructs the Web Parts infrastructure that the property has to be made available in the Web Part's configuration panel. This attribute accepts a *boolean* parameter named *Browsable* that is assigned a value of *true* when declaring the attribute through its default constructor. The *PersonalizableAttribute* declares that the property can be personalized and defines the scope of the personalization. It accepts a scope of type *User*, which means that the property can be personalized on a per-user basis, or a scope of type *Shared*, which means that the property personalization will be shared between all users.

There are some other useful attributes with which you can better define the configurable property, improving the end user experience. For instance, you can define a custom category for the property by tagging it with the *CategoryAttribute* attribute. you can change the caption of the property by tagging it with the *WebDisplayAttribute*, or you can change the tooltip shown to the end user by tagging the property with the *WebDescriptionAttribute*. You can provide a default value for the property via the *DefaultValueAttribute*. Listing 6-10 displays a complete definition for the *TargetListTitle* property.

LISTING 6-10 A Web Part that provides a configurable property, with all the useful attributes.

```
[WebBrowsable(true)]
[Personalizable(PersonalizationScope.Shared)]
[WebDescription("Title of the Target list")]
[WebDisplayName("Target list")]
[Category("Data Foundation")]
public String TargetListTitle { get; set; }
```

Figure 6-7 illustrates the user interface presented to the user by a configurable property.

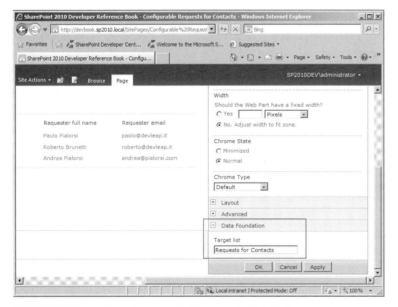

FIGURE 6-7 The configuration panel of the sample Web Part.

The Web Part editor area in Figure 6-7 is provided by SharePoint's infrastructure and is based on a set of SharePoint specific classes, called Tool Parts, which can be customized by user code. By default, SharePoint provides a *WebPartToolPart* class that provides the user interface for editing the Web Parts' standard properties (Title, Chrome Type, Size, and so on), and the *CustomPropertyToolPart* class, which automatically allows editing custom properties.

Table 6-2 covers how the *CustomPropertyToolPart* class usually behaves when rendering custom properties.

TABLE 6-2 The Standard Behavior of the *CustomPropertyToolPart* Class While Rendering Custom Properties

Custom Property Type	Behavior
Boolean	Renders a check box
Enum	Renders a drop-down list
Integer	Renders a text box
String	Renders a text box
DateTime	Renders a text box

It is possible to implement custom Tool Part classes by simply inheriting from the *ToolPart* base abstract class provided by the *Microsoft.SharePoint.WebPartPages* namespace. However, to make a custom Tool Part available to SharePoint, you need to inherit the Web Part class from the *Microsoft.SharePoint.WebPartPages.WebPart* base abstract class provided by SharePoint, instead of using the common *System.Web.UI.WebControls.WebParts.WebPart* base abstract class provided by ASP.NET. To do so, you need to override the *GetToolParts* method, returning a custom collection of Tool Parts. This kind of customization works only in SharePoint, due to the dependency on the Microsoft.SharePoint.dll assembly. But developing a Web Part that inherits from *Microsoft.SharePoint.WebPartPages.WebPart* is not considered a best practice. You should always implement ASP.NET Web Parts, which inherit from *System.Web.UI.WebControls.WebParts.WebPart*, unless you really need any of the few features available only in SharePoint Web Parts; this will be the focus of discussion at the end of this chapter in the section "SharePoint-Specific WebPart Class."

Editor Parts

Listing 6-10 defined a property that requires the end user to configure the Web Part manually, typing the target list name autonomously. You made use of the standard behavior of SharePoint and the out-of-the-box *CustomPropertyToolPart*. However, even if it were absolutely possible to publish such a Web Part, you would probably agree that this is not a user-friendly and error-free approach. The right solution would probably be to provide a drop-down list with all the lists available in the current website, thereby avoiding typo errors and the consequent time consuming debugging tasks. To customize the Web Parts' configuration user interface you can create custom classes called Editor Parts, provided by the Web Part infrastructure of ASP.NET. Editor Parts are controls hosted in a specific *WebPartZone* called *EditorZone*. They are nearly the same as a standard Web Part, except that they inherit from the base class *EditorPart* instead of inheriting from the *WebPart* class. This specific base class provides the link between the Editor Part itself and the currently editing Web Part. To provide a Web Part with a custom Editor Part, you need to override the implementation of the *IWebEditable* interface, which is implemented by the Web Part base class. Listing 6-11 shows you the definition of this interface.

LISTING 6-11 The *IWebEditable* interface definition.

```
public interface IWebEditable {
    EditorPartCollection CreateEditorParts();
    object WebBrowsableObject { get; }
}
```

The interface declares a method with name *CreateEditorParts* that should return a collection of Editor Parts that support Web Parts with a wide set of Editor Parts. The interface also defines a public read-only property to get a reference to the configurable object that the Editor Parts will target. Usually the *WebBrowsableObject* property returns the current Web Part instance (*this*). Listing 6-12 displays the new implementation of the custom Web Part.

LISTING 6-12 The new custom Web Part, implementing the *IWebEditable* interface.

```
namespace DevLeap.SP2010.WebParts.EditorInsertRequestForContactWebPart {
    [ToolboxItemAttribute(false)]
    public class EditorInsertRequestForContactWebPart : WebPart {

        [WebBrowsable(false)]
        [Personalizable(PersonalizationScope.Shared)]
        public Guid TargetListID { get; set; }

        //
        // CreateChildControls code omitted ...
        //

        void SubmitRequestForContact_Click(object sender, EventArgs e) {
            SPWeb web = SPControl.GetContextWeb(HttpContext.Current);

            try {
                SPList targetList = web.Lists[this.TargetListID];
                SPListItem newItem = targetList.Items.Add();
                newItem["Reason"] = this.Reason.Text;
                newItem["Requester full name"] = this.RequesterFullName.Text;
                newItem["Requester email"] = this.RequesterEMail.Text;
                newItem.Update();
            }
            catch (IndexOutOfRangeException) {
                this.ErrorMessage.Text =
                    "Cannot find list \"Requests for Contacts\"";
            }
        }

        public override EditorPartCollection CreateEditorParts() {
            RequestForContactEditorPart editorPart =
                new RequestForContactEditorPart();
            editorPart.ID = this.ID + "_RequestForContactEditorPart";
```

```
        EditorPartCollection editorParts =
          new EditorPartCollection(base.CreateEditorParts(),
          new EditorPart[] { editorPart });
        return editorParts;
    }

    public override object WebBrowsableObject {
        get { return(this); }
    }
  }
}
```

In Listing 6-12, I changed the property *TargetListTitle* of type *String* into a property *TargetListID* of type *Guid* so that it can store the unique ID of the target list, and I used that ID to lookup for the list instance in the *SubmitRequestForContact_Click* event handler. I also turned off the *WebBrowsable* attribute on the property to hide it from the standard property grid of the Web Part editor. This property will be managed using the custom Editor Part.

Note If you do not turn off the *WebBrowsable* attribute of a property that is also configurable through a custom Editor Part, your end user will have both the custom Editor Part and the standard property grid for editing that property, provided by the *CustomPropertyToolPart* of SharePoint. This is, of course, confusing for the end user and should be avoided.

Next, I override the *CreateEditorParts* method to invoke the base class method implementation and to add a custom Editor Part, named *RequestForContactEditorPart*, to the collection of available Editor Parts of the current Web Part. Notice also that I defined a custom ID for the Editor Part instance, based on the uniqueness of the current Web Part ID, to make the Editor Part ID unique as well.

The *EditorPart* is a base abstract class that provides some virtual or abstract methods and properties that are useful for managing the editing of the target Web Part. For instance, every class inherited from *EditorPart* has a property *WebPartToEdit* which references the Web Part instance that the Editor Part is currently editing. There are also a couple of abstract methods called *ApplyChanges* and *SyncChanges* that can be used to save any changes to the currently-edited Web Part, or to load the current configuration from it, respectively.

Listing 6-13 gives you an opportunity to evaluate the implementation of the *RequestForContactEditorPart* class.

LISTING 6-13 The *RequestForContactEditorPart* class implementation.

```
public class RequestForContactEditorPart : EditorPart {
    protected DropDownList targetLists;

    protected override void CreateChildControls() {
        this.targetLists = new DropDownList();

        SPWeb web = SPControl.GetContextWeb(HttpContext.Current);
        foreach (SPList list in web.Lists) {
            this.targetLists.Items.Add(new ListItem(list.Title, list.ID.ToString()));
        }

        this.Title = "Request for Contact EditorPart";
        this.Controls.Add(new LiteralControl("Select the target List:<br>"));
        this.Controls.Add(this.targetLists);
        this.Controls.Add(new LiteralControl("<br> <br>"));
    }

    public override bool ApplyChanges() {
        EnsureChildControls();

        EditorInsertRequestForContactWebPart wp =
            this.WebPartToEdit as EditorInsertRequestForContactWebPart;
        if (wp != null) {
            wp.TargetListID = new Guid(this.targetLists.SelectedValue);
        }
        return (true);
    }

    public override void SyncChanges() {
        EnsureChildControls();

        EditorInsertRequestForContactWebPart wp =
            this.WebPartToEdit as EditorInsertRequestForContactWebPart;
        if (wp != null) {
            ListItem selectedItem =
                this.targetLists.Items.FindByValue(wp.TargetListID.ToString());
            if (selectedItem != null) {
                this.targetLists.ClearSelection();
                selectedItem.Selected = true;
            }
        }
    }
}
```

As with any other Web Part, an Editor Part must create its controls graph to render its content. In Listing 6-13, I created a drop-down list in the *CreateChildControls* method override and bound it to the collection of lists of the current website.

Then, in the *ApplyChanges* method override, I save the currently selected list ID into the *TargetListID* property of the current Web Part instance. Similarly, in the *SyncChanges* method override, I auto-select the list with ID equal to the current *TargetListID* property value in the drop-down list. Figure 6-8 depicts the output of the custom Editor Part.

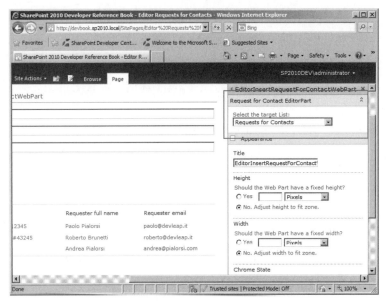

FIGURE 6-8 The configuration panel of the sample Web Part, with the Editor Part in place.

An actual SharePoint solution probably will have all of its Web Parts providing a rich and complete set of configuration parameters, configurable and customizable through custom Editor Parts.

Handling Display Modes

During the course of developing real-world Web Parts, sooner or later you will probably face the need to change your custom Web Parts' rendering, based on the status of the page that hosts them. A page hosting one or more Web Parts can be rendered in Display mode, when the end user is browsing the site; in Design mode, when the user can design the page layout; or in Edit mode, when the end user is configuring/customizing the page and/or its controls.

To query the page display mode and render a Web Part accordingly, you need to query the *DisplayMode* property of the *WebPartManager* (*SPWebPartManager* in SharePoint). Listing 6-14 shows you a sample Web Part that adapts its rendering, based on the current *DisplayMode*.

LISTING 6-14 A Web Part rendering its content relative to the current page *DisplayMode*.

```
protected override void CreateChildControls() {
    if (this.WebPartManager.DisplayMode == WebPartManager.BrowseDisplayMode) {
        // Page Display mode
        // Render standard content
    }
    else if (this.WebPartManager.DisplayMode == WebPartManager.DesignDisplayMode) {
        // Page Design mode
        this.Controls.Add(new LiteralControl("<div>
            Please move to Display mode to use this Web Part.</div>"));
    }
    else if (this.WebPartManager.DisplayMode == WebPartManager.EditDisplayMode) {
        // Page Edit mode
        this.Controls.Add(new LiteralControl("<div>
            Please move to Display mode to use this Web Part or configure its
            properties, since you are in Edit mode.</div>"));
    }
}
```

Any class inheriting from *WebPart* has a shortcut property referencing the current *WebPartManager* instance. Through this property, we can check the *DisplayMode* and many other context properties. You can also use the *WebPartManager* to subscribe to events related to *DisplayMode* changes. For instance, there are the *DisplayModeChanging* and the *DisplayModeChanged* events, with which you can monitor the *DisplayMode* status.

Custom Web Part Verbs

Another useful Web Part customization capability is the definition of custom Web Part Verbs. Web Part Verbs are menu items that are displayed in the Web Part context menu, as shown in Figure 6-9.

To configure custom verbs we need to override the read-only property *Verbs* provided by the base *WebPart* class. This property returns a *WebPartVerbCollection* and can be used to completely redefine the context menu of a Web Part. Verbs are objects of type *WebPartVerb* and can be of three different kinds:

- **Server-side** Verbs that require a POST-back to carry out their job; they work on the server side.

- **Client-side** Verbs that simply use JavaScript syntax to do their job; they work on the client side.

- **Client and server-side** Verbs that first execute some client-side JavaScript, and then can execute some server-side code, unless the client-side code cancels the request.

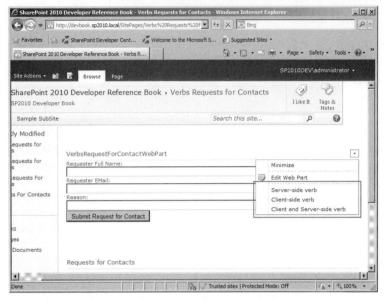

FIGURE 6-9 Sample custom verbs rendered in a custom Web Part.

Listing 6-15 presents an excerpt of the sample Web Part, which supports all three kinds of custom verbs.

LISTING 6-15 A custom Web Part with custom verbs.

```
public override WebPartVerbCollection Verbs {
    get {
        WebPartVerb serverSideVerb = new WebPartVerb("serverSiteVerbId",
            handleServerSideVerb);
        serverSideVerb.Text = "Server-side verb";
        WebPartVerb clientSideVerb = new WebPartVerb("clientSideVerbId",
            "javascript:alert('Client-side Verb selected');");
        clientSideVerb.Text = "Client-side verb";

        WebPartVerb clientAndServerSideVerb = new
            WebPartVerb("clientAndServerSideVerbId",
            handleServerSideVerb, "javascript:alert('Client-side Verb selected');");
        clientAndServerSideVerb.Text = "Client and Server-side verb";

        WebPartVerbCollection newVerbs = new WebPartVerbCollection(
            new WebPartVerb[] {
                serverSideVerb, clientSideVerb, clientAndServerSideVerb,
            }
            );
        return (new WebPartVerbCollection(base.Verbs, newVerbs));
    }
```

```
    }

    protected void handleServerSideVerb(Object source, WebPartEventArgs args) {
        EnsureChildControls();

        this.GenericMessage.Text = "You raised a server-side event!";
    }
```

The interesting aspect of this sample code is the implementation of the *Verbs* property, where we manually define and configure verbs, then add them to the resulting collection of Web Part Verbs.

Usually, custom Verbs are defined in Intranet/Extranet solutions, to provide support for custom functionalities, such as refreshing content, opening custom pop-up windows, and so forth. In general, they are not used in CMS/Publishing solutions, because the context menu is usually disabled in these.

The SharePoint-Specific *WebPart* class

As you learned at the beginning of this chapter, in SharePoint we have the capability to inherit Web Parts from a SharePoint specific base class, instead of using the standard class provided by ASP.NET. The resulting Web Parts are still fully integrated with the ASP.NET Web Parts infrastructure, because the SharePoint's *WebPart* class internally inherits from that of ASP.NET. These Web Parts can be used only in SharePoint; however, there are a few additional functionalities that in very specific conditions that make implementing SharePoint specific Web Parts a beneficial choice. These additional functionalities are:

- **Support for SharePoint Tool Parts**   You have already seen what a Tool Part is and what can be done with it.

- **Path/Code replacement tokens**   You can use these to inject tokens in the output HTML code of a SharePoint Web Part, and then have the SharePoint infrastructure replace them with their corresponding values. There are tokens for the current username, the current LCID of the website, and so on.

- **Cross page connections and connection between Web Parts that are outside of a Web Part zone**   Web Parts can be connected to each other to build master-detail solutions (for further details, read Chapter 7). SharePoint-specific Web Parts support cross-page connections, while standard ASP.NET Web Parts only support intra-page connections. SharePoint Web Parts can also be connected even if they are outside a Web Part zone.

- **Client-side connections**   These are connections between SharePoint-specific Web Parts, based on client-side (JavaScript) code.

- **Data caching**   There is a data caching infrastructure, which allows caching of Web Parts data into the content database.

Summary

In this chapter, you saw what Web Parts are, what their underlying architecture is, and how to develop and deploy them from scratch, providing custom appearance and behavior. In particular, you saw how to create configurable and customizable Web Parts, providing the end user with custom Editor Parts, Tool Parts, and custom Verbs. In Chapter 7, you will look at advanced arguments, such as Web Parts connections, supporting AJAX and Silverlight, asynchronous programming, XSLT rendering, and Web Parts security, deployment, and versioning.

Chapter 7
Advanced Web Parts

In Chapter 6, "Web Part Basics," you learned what a Web Part is and how to develop simple Web Part solutions. This chapter digs deeper into Web Part development. At its conclusion, you will be able to create powerful real-world projects.

Connectable Web Parts

A Web Part is defined as connectable when it can be connected with another Web Part in a provider/consumer relationship. These kinds of Web Parts are useful for creating filters and master-detail pages, where one Web Part—the provider—typically renders a selectable list of items or a single master item, and other Web Parts—the consumers—render filtered contents based on the provider's current item. What happens under the covers is that the provider and the consumer share some data, based on a shared communication contract. As a concrete example, you will see how to develop a provider Web Part that offers a selectable list of product categories, and a consumer Web Part that shows the products belonging to the currently selected category.

 Note There are two kinds of connectable Web Parts: those based on the Microsoft ASP.NET environment only, and those based on Microsoft SharePoint Web Parts. As you saw in Chapter 6, developing SharePoint Web Parts instead of ASP.NET Web Parts gives you access to a few more features; however, it also makes the controls strictly dependent on SharePoint. This section covers only the ASP.NET Web Parts because I consider SharePoint Web Parts as available only for backward compatibility and for some specific scenarios.

First, to develop the sample connectable Web Parts solution, you need to define a data source. For the sake of simplicity, this example uses an XML data source file, containing both categories and products, so you don't need to have access to a DBMS to build the example. Listing 7-1 shows the sample XML data source file.

LISTING 7-1 The XML data source file for the connectable Web Parts sample.

```xml
<?xml version="1.0" encoding="utf-8" ?>
<store>
  <categories>
    <category id="FOOD" description="Food" />
    <category id="BEV" description="Beverages" />
    <category id="APPAREL" description="Shoes and Dresses" />
    <category id="UTILS" description="Utilities and Tools" />
  </categories>
```

```
<products>
  <product code="P01" description="Meat" categoryId="FOOD" price="15.00" />
  <product code="P02" description="Filet" categoryId="FOOD" price="18.00" />
  <product code="P03" description="Biscuits" categoryId="FOOD" price="4.00" />
  <product code="P04" description="Olive Oil" categoryId="FOOD" price="35.00" />
  <product code="P05" description="Chips" categoryId="FOOD" price="3.00" />
  <product code="P06" description="Water" categoryId="BEV" price="0.50" />
  <product code="P07" description="Red Wine" categoryId="BEV" price="7.00" />
  <product code="P08" description="White Wine" categoryId="BEV" price="9.00" />
  <product code="P09" description="Beer" categoryId="BEV" price="3.50" />
  <product code="P10" description="Weiss Bier" categoryId="BEV" price="4.00" />
  <product code="P11" description="Cap" categoryId="APPAREL" price="45.00" />
  <product code="P12" description="T-Shirt" categoryId="APPAREL" price="12.00" />
  <product code="P13" description="Coat" categoryId="APPAREL" price="210.00" />
  <product code="P14" description="Screwdriver" categoryId="UTILS" price="7.00" />
  <product code="P15" description="Hairdryer" categoryId="UTILS" price="31.00" />
</products>
</store>
```

The provider Web Part that shows the categories will render a grid containing all the product categories along with a link button so that users can select a specific category. The products, or consumer, Web Part will render a grid of products, filtered by the selected category. Aside from the connection between the two Web Parts, their implementation is now trivial if you read Chapter 6; therefore, this discussion concentrates only on the code related to that connection. The provider and the consumer need to share a *communication contract*, which is an interface that will be implemented by the provider and consumed by the consumer. Thanks to the smart architecture of ASP.NET connectable Web Parts, you can define that interface freely, without any constraints on its properties, methods and signature. In addition, a typical interface for connecting Web Parts defines only properties that correspond to the data shared between provider and consumer. Listing 7-2 shows the interface defined for this example.

LISTING 7-2 The communication contract shared between the provider and the consumer Web Parts.

```
public interface ICategoriesProvider {
    String CategoryId { get; }
}
```

To make the connection available, you need to implement the interface in a custom type and include a public method in the provider Web Part that returns an instance of that type. Then, to make SharePoint and ASP.NET aware that the method can be assumed as a connection provider, you decorate it with the *ConnectionProviderAttribute* attribute. Listing 7-3 contains an excerpt of an example implementation of the provider Web Part.

LISTING 7-3 An excerpt of the provider Web Part.

```
public class CategoriesWebPart : WebPart, ICategoriesProvider {

    [WebBrowsable(true)]
    [Personalizable(true)]
    public String XmlDataSourceUri { get; set; }

    protected GridView gridCategories;

    protected override void CreateChildControls() {
        // ... code omitted ...
    }

    public String CategoryId {
        get {
                if (this.gridCategories.SelectedIndex >= 0) {
                    return (this.gridCategories.SelectedDataKey.Value as String);
                }
                else {
                    return (String.Empty);
                }
        }
    }

    [ConnectionProvider("Category")]
    public ICategoriesProvider GetCategoryProvider() {
        return (this);
    }

    // ... code omitted ...
}
```

As shown in Listing 7-3, the interface is generally implemented directly in the provider Web Part, returning an instance of the Web Part through the method decorated with the *ConnectionProvider* attribute. The *GetCategoryProvider* method simply returns *this* (the instance of the current Web Part), and is marked as *ConnectionProvider*, with a specific name for the data provided. That name will be shown to the end user while connecting Web Parts.

The other side of this connection—the consumer Web Part—looks like Listing 7-4.

LISTING 7-4 An excerpt of the consumer Web Part.

```
public class ProductsWebPart : WebPart {

    [WebBrowsable(true)]
    [Personalizable(true)]
    public String XmlDataSourceUri { get; set; }

    protected ICategoriesProvider _provider;
    protected GridView gridProducts;
    protected String categoryId;

    [ConnectionConsumer("Products of Category")]
    public void SetCategoryProvider(ICategoriesProvider categoriesProvider) {
        this._provider = categoriesProvider;
    }

    protected override void OnPreRender(EventArgs e) {
        if (this._provider != null) {
            this.categoryId = this._provider.CategoryId;

            if (!String.IsNullOrEmpty(this.categoryId)) {
                this.EnsureChildControls();
                // ... code omitted ...
            }
            else {
                this.Controls.Add(new LiteralControl(
                    "Please select a Product Category"));
            }
        }
        else {
            this.Controls.Add(new LiteralControl(
                "Please connect this Web Part to a Categories Data Provider"));
        }
            base.OnPreRender(e);
    }

    protected override void CreateChildControls() {
     // ... code omitted ...
    }
}
```

As its name implies, the consumer Web Part consumes the data presented by the provider Web Part through a specific public method, named *SetCategoryProvider*, which is decorated with the *ConnectionConsumerAttribute* attribute.

Under the covers, SharePoint matches the provider method, marked as *ConnectionProvider*, and the consumer method, marked as *ConnectionConsumer*, invoking the former to get a reference to the provider instance, and the latter to set the reference. This way, the consumer, which is in its *OnPreRender* event method, will be able to check if a reference to a specific data provider exists, and, if so, will query it to get back the currently selected product category.

Figure 7-1 shows the output of these Web Parts connected in a common Web Part Page.

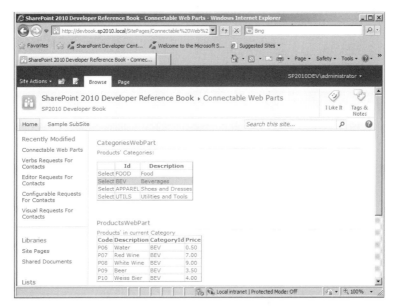

FIGURE 7-1 The output of the connected Web Parts within a SharePoint 2010 Web Part Page.

 Note It is strategic to query the data provider in the *OnPreRender* method of the consumer Web Part, instead of, for instance, invoking it in the *CreateChildControls* method. In fact, in the *CreateChildControls* method stage, the provider Web Part shouldn't be ready to provide the currently selected item, while in the *OnPreRender* stage the current selection, if any, will be available.

Figure 7-2 shows the configuration interface natively provided by SharePoint to connect a couple of connectable Web Parts.

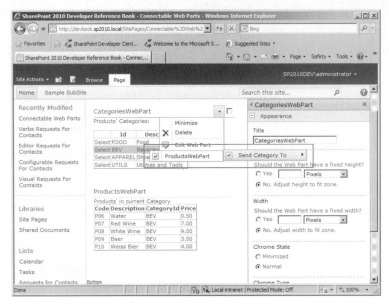

FIGURE 7-2 The native interface of SharePoint to connect a couple of connectable Web Parts.

Notice in Figure 7-2 how the Send Category To menu item goes into the ProductsWebPart item. The "Category" word is defined in the constructor of the *ConnectionProviderAttribute* in Listing 7-3.

In the interest of being thorough, Table 7-1 lists the configurable properties of *ConnectionProviderAttribute* and *ConnectionConsumerAttribute*. Some of these properties can be configured only through the constructors of these attributes.

TABLE 7-1 The Configurable Properties of *ConnectionProviderAttribute* and *ConnectionConsumerAttribute*

Property Name	Description
AllowsMultipleConnections	In both attributes, this indicates whether the connection point allows multiple connections.
ConnectionPointType	Represents a *Type* corresponding to the *ConnectionPoint* between the provider and the consumer. Generally, it is automatically assigned, however can be created and assigned using a custom type.
DisplayName	Represents the friendly name of the connection, used also in the browser UI when connecting Web Parts.
ID	Defines the unique ID of a connection provider and allows a provider to publish multiple unique connections, as well as a consumer to specify its target provider.

As is evident from the properties shown in Table 7-1, you can define a provider Web Part that provides data to multiple consumers, which can prove useful. As an example, if you build custom dashboards—typically for Business Intelligence solutions—you might have a provider Web Part that supplies the currently selected product, business unit, or whatever you need to monitor, and a set of consumer Web Parts that show detailed information about the currently selected item.

Microsoft SharePoint by itself provides some native interfaces that correspond to Web Parts' connections contracts, as listed in Table 7-2. However, these interfaces are considered obsolete, and you should rely on them only when you need to provide backward compatibility in your Web Parts.

TABLE 7-2 SharePoint's Native Connectable Interfaces

Interfaces	Description
ICellProvider, *ICellConsumer*	Contract to provide/consume a single value, like a field or a cell.
IRowProvider, *IRowConsumer*	Contract to provide/consume a single row, or a set of rows.
IListProvider, *IListConsumer*	Contract to provide/consume an entire list of items.
IFilterProvider, *IFilterConsumer*	Contract to provide/consume a filter in a master-detail scenario.
IParametersInProvider, *IParametersInConsumer*	Contract to provide/consume a set of parameters for a Web Part. In this situation the consumer gives the values of the parameters to the provider.
IParametersOutProvider, *IParametersOutConsumer*	Contract to provide/consume a set of parameters for a Web Part. In this situation the provider gives parameters' values to the consumer.

More Information Sometimes, you'll come across situations in which you would like to connect one provider Web Part, based on a specific provider contract interface, to another consumer Web Part that can't directly consume that contract—but can consume a different interface. The infrastructure of connectable Web Parts allows you to define interface transformers, which allow you to connect non-compatible interfaces. This book does not cover this topic; however, it is important to be aware of its existence.

Supporting AJAX

As you probably know, Asynchronous JavaScript and XML (AJAX) defines a technique to cause a webpage to react dynamically in response to programmatic events or user input, letting you load or replace portions of a webpage by communicating with the Web server in the background using XML and asynchronous HTTP requests—without the need to reload the entire page.

In previous versions of SharePoint, you had to manually update your Web application's web. config file and define some infrastructure controls in the page to enable AJAX support in SharePoint pages and Web Parts. Beginning with SharePoint 2010, however, SharePoint provides native support for ASP.NET AJAX. Now, to have an AJAX-enabled Web Part, you simply need to use the ASP.NET native controls, and everything will work seamlessly.

As a simple example, you can define a custom Web Part using an ASP.NET *UpdatePanel*, and load its contents with AJAX dynamically. Listing 7-4 shows the code for a "products" Web Part that loads the XML file containing the products and categories you saw in the previous section. This sample Web Part uses a tree view control that renders categories and products, grouped by category. When you expand a category, the ASP.NET AJAX library handles the tree outline in the background.

LISTING 7-4 An AJAX-enabled Web Part that renders a tree view of categories and products.

```
public class AjaxTreeProductsWebPart : WebPart {

    protected UpdatePanel ajaxPanel;
    protected TreeView treeProducts;
    private IEnumerable<CategoryItem> categoriesWithProducts;

    [WebBrowsable(true)]
    [Personalizable(true)]
    public String XmlDataSourceUri { get; set; }

    protected override void CreateChildControls() {
        if (!String.IsNullOrEmpty(this.XmlDataSourceUri)) {
            // ... code omitted ...
            this.treeProducts = new TreeView();

            foreach (var c in categoriesWithProducts) {
                treeProducts.Nodes.Add(new TreeNode(c.Description, c.Id)
                    { PopulateOnDemand = true });
            }

            this.treeProducts.ExpandDepth = 0;
            this.treeProducts.TreeNodePopulate += new
                TreeNodeEventHandler(treeProducts_TreeNodePopulate);

            this.ajaxPanel = new UpdatePanel();
            this.ajaxPanel.ContentTemplateContainer.Controls.Add(this.treeProducts);

            this.Controls.Add(this.ajaxPanel);
        }
        else {
            this.Controls.Add(new LiteralControl(
                "Please configure the Web Part data source URI"));
        }
    }
```

```
void treeProducts_TreeNodePopulate(object sender, TreeNodeEventArgs e) {
    EnsureChildControls();

    foreach (var p in categoriesWithProducts.First(c => c.Id ==
        e.Node.Value).Products) {
        e.Node.ChildNodes.Add(new TreeNode(p.Description, p.Code));
    }
}
// ... code omitted ...
}
```

Aside from the code that handles the *TreeView* control, which is not related to the current topic, the key point of Listing 7-4 is that it defines an *UpdatePanel* control as the only child control of the Web Part. All of the other controls, (the *TreeView* instance in this example) are defined inside the *UpdatePanel* instance

The *UpdatePanel* control is simple to use, but it's neither particularly efficient nor scalable. In fact, each time you invoke the server asynchronously via AJAX, on the server side, the web-page hosting the *UpdatePanel* must be rendered entirely from scratch; on the client side, the JavaScript related to the *UpdatePanel* grabs the area of the page that needs to be updated in the background and ignores all the other markup. In a real scenario, it would be better to use low-level AJAX events and code, to make the update process more efficient.

Connectable Web Parts with AJAX

In the previous section, you saw how to develop a couple of connected Web Parts. However, in that version, whenever you change the currently selected item in the provider Web Part, you experience a complete page reload to display the related products.

You could improve the fluency and user experience of these pages by using some AJAX code. To do that, you need to enable both the provider and consumer Web Parts for AJAX, which could be simple, because you can just wrap the controls of both the Web Parts with an *UpdatePanel* control instance. However, this is not enough to have a complete solution. In fact, adding an *UpdatePanel* control simply enables AJAX in the single Web Part, but you need to connect the reload of the consumer Web Part to the *SelectedIndexChanged* event of the *GridView* in the provider Web Part. To do that requires defining a custom trigger in the consumer Web Part related to the *SelectedIndexChanged* event of the *GridView* of the provider. Listing 7-5 defines a new public interface that is useful for creating a "hook" for an ASP.NET control and an event published by that control.

LISTING 7-5 An interface defining a hook for an ASP.NET control, together with a published event.

```
public interface IAjaxTriggerControlProvider {
    String TriggerControlID { get; }
    String TriggerEventName { get; }
}
```

This interface is implemented in the connection contract interface to make it aware of the AJAX connection between the provider and the consumer. Listing 7-6 shows the resulting *IAjaxCategoriesProvider* interface definition, which will be the communication contract between the two connectable Web Parts.

LISTING 7-6 The connection interface, together with the communication specific contract.

```
public interface IAjaxCategoriesProvider : IAjaxTriggerControlProvider {
    String CategoryId { get; }
}
```

Finally, the source code of the *AjaxCategoriesWebPart*, which is the AJAX-enabled Web Part providing categories, must be implemented to return the ID of the *GridView* instance as the value for *TriggerControlID*. It also returns the string "*SelectedIndexChanged*" as the value for the *TriggerEventName*, as shown in the code excerpt in Listing 7-7.

LISTING 7-7 An excerpt of the new *AjaxCategoriesWebPart* with cross-connection AJAX support.

```
public class AjaxCategoriesWebPart : WebPart, IAjaxCategoriesProvider {
    [WebBrowsable(true)]
    [Personalizable(true)]
    public String XmlDataSourceUri { get; set; }

    protected UpdatePanel ajaxPanel;
    protected GridView gridCategories;

    protected override void CreateChildControls() {
        // ... code omitted ...
    }

    public String CategoryId {
        get {
            // ... code omitted ...
        }
    }

    public string TriggerControlID {
        get { return(this.gridCategories.ID); }
    }
```

```
    public string TriggerEventName {
        get { return("SelectedIndexChanged"); }
    }

    [ConnectionProvider("Category")]
    public IAjaxCategoriesProvider GetCategoryProvider() {
        return (this);
    }
    // ... code omitted ...
}
```

The *AjaxProductsWebPart*, which is the AJAX-enabled consumer Web Part, has been implemented to support the new *IAjaxTriggerControlProvider* interface. Listing 7-8 shows the
resulting code.

LISTING 7-8 An excerpt of the *AjaxProductsWebPart* with cross-connection AJAX support.

```
public class AjaxProductsWebPart : WebPart {
    [WebBrowsable(true)]
    [Personalizable(true)]
    public String XmlDataSourceUri { get; set; }

    protected IAjaxCategoriesProvider _provider;
    protected UpdatePanel ajaxPanel;
    protected GridView gridProducts;
    protected String categoryId;

    [ConnectionConsumer("Products of Category")]
    public void SetCategoryProvider(IAjaxCategoriesProvider categoriesProvider) {
        this._provider = categoriesProvider;
    }

    protected override void OnPreRender(EventArgs e) {
        if (this._provider != null) {
            this.EnsureChildControls();

            this.categoryId = this._provider.CategoryId;

            this.ajaxPanel.Triggers.Add(new AsyncPostBackTrigger {
                ControlID = this._provider.TriggerControlID,
                EventName = this._provider.TriggerEventName
            });

            // ... code omitted ...
        }
        else {
            // ... code omitted ...
        }
        base.OnPreRender(e);
    }
```

```
    protected override void CreateChildControls() {
        if (!String.IsNullOrEmpty(this.XmlDataSourceUri)) {
            this.ajaxPanel = new UpdatePanel();
            this.gridProducts = new GridView();
            this.gridProducts.ShowHeader = true;
            this.gridProducts.AutoGenerateColumns = true;
            this.ajaxPanel.ContentTemplateContainer.Controls.Add(this.gridProducts);
            this.Controls.Add(this.ajaxPanel);
        }
        else {
            this.Controls.Add(new LiteralControl(
                "Please configure the Web Part data source URI"));
        }
    }
    // ... code omitted ...
}
```

The bold text in Listing 7-8 highlights the creation of the *UpdatePanel*, within the *CreateChildControls* method. The most interesting part of Listing 7-8, though, is the *OnPreRender* method implementation, which defines a custom AJAX trigger of type *AsyncPostBackTrigger* to connect the *UpdatePanel* of the consumer Web Part to the trigger event of the provider.

This is a tricky but smart solution that allows you to trigger cross-connection AJAX events between Web Parts.

Silverlight and External Applications

The big news in SharePoint 2010 is its native support for Microsoft Silverlight. To embed a Silverlight application into a SharePoint webpage, you simply need to insert a Silverlight Web Part instance into a Web Part Page or Wiki Page, defining the path of the .xap file to render. This is a considerable improvement with which you can create user-friendly interfaces with little effort and minimal knowledge of XAML.

As you have already seen in Chapter 5, "Client-Side Technologies," there is also a Silverlight-specific client object model that can interact with the back-end SharePoint server farm from a Silverlight client. Figure 7-3 shows a Silverlight application (Bing Maps) hosted in a SharePoint's Wiki Page.

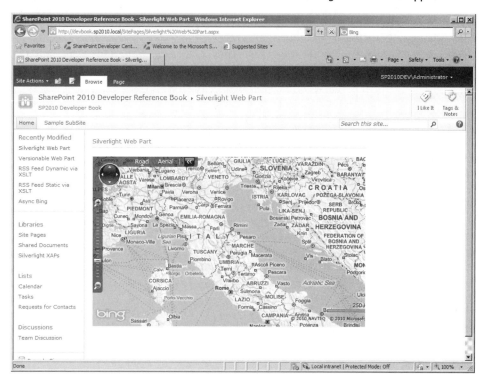

FIGURE 7-3 A Silverlight application hosted in the native Silverlight Web Part of SharePoint 2010.

Unfortunately, the Silverlight Web Part is a sealed class, so you cannot inherit from it to customize its behavior. However, if you need to host a Silverlight application with some custom behaviors or you need to host a Silverlight 4.0 control—which the native Silverlight Web Part does not support by default—you could simply define a custom Web Part, writing the code needed to host Silverlight in the browser (see Listing 7-9).

LISTING 7-9 The HTML code needed to embed a Silverlight application into a web browser.

```
<object data="data:application/x-silverlight-2" type="application/x-silverlight-2"
Height="650px" Width="800px" id="player">
    <param name="source" value="CustomApplication.xap">
    <param name="onError" value="onSilverlightError">
    <param name="background" value="transparent">
    <param name="windowless" value="true">
    <param name="minRuntimeVersion" value="4.0.50303">
    <param name="autoUpgrade" value="true">
    <a href="http://go.microsoft.com/fwlink/?LinkID=149156&v=4.0.50303.0"
      style="text-decoration: none">
        <img src="http://go.microsoft.com/fwlink/?LinkId=108181" alt="Get Microsoft
          Silverlight" style="border-style: none">
    </a>
</object>
```

The overall architecture of the Silverlight Web Part is based on a new environment provided by SharePoint Foundation to host non-SharePoint applications. Keep in mind though that hosting non-SharePoint applications has some constraints and side effects. First, you need to consider the security of the SharePoint environment, because the non-SharePoint application could access the data published by SharePoint; this is a concern about which you must think carefully. You can define some typical scenarios, such as:

- A SharePoint site hosting a non-SharePoint application published on the same domain.

- A SharePoint site hosting a non-SharePoint application published on a different domain, which does not access the SharePoint site's data.

- A SharePoint site hosting a non-SharePoint application published on a different domain, which accesses the SharePoint site's data.

In the first scenario, if the non-SharePoint application is based on .NET or Silverlight, you can take advantage of the Managed Client Object Model (for further details, see Chapter 5, "Client-Side Technologies") to read and write the SharePoint data. In this case, the data will be automatically accessed within the security context of the current user.

In the second scenario, you do not need to worry about security, because the non-SharePoint application does not access SharePoint's data.

The last scenario is the most complex from a security point of view; however, it is common because it allows you to share the same applications across many SharePoint sites, published through a unique shared domain.

For Silverlight applications, SharePoint 2010 provides a Silverlight Cross-Domain Data Access engine that allows you to define an application-specific principal to secure SharePoint's data on a per-application/per-domain basis. An "application principal" is a particular kind of *SPUser* that is used to assign specific permissions to an external Silverlight application. When a user adds a Web Part hosting, such as a Silverlight application, the permissions given to the external application will be the intersection of the permission granted to the application's principal and the permissions of the real user who opens the page hosting that Web Part.

In general, a non-SharePoint application hosted in a custom Web Part—not just Silverlight but any kind of external application—can use a new External Application Provider (EAP) environment. An EAP is an XML configuration that can be defined at the *SPWebService* level and is unique for each *SPWebService*. For security reasons an EAP can be deployed by a farm administrator only, and it must be provisioned programmatically.

The EAP declares the identity of the external application, together with the application principal mapped to it; information about the Web Part hosting the external application; and any other custom property useful for registering the external application. If you needed to, you could define your own EAP, a custom Web Part that hosts the external application, and of course, the external application itself.

More Information This book does not delve deeply into creating an EAP and a custom Web Part hosting an external application because the topic is beyond the scope of this book. However, the official SharePoint SDK contains a specific section that illustrates how to define a custom EAP and how to implement a custom Web Part that inherits from the base class *ClientApplicationWebPartBase*, to host a non-SharePoint external application.

Asynchronous Programming

Another useful topic for advanced custom Web Part development is making use of the ASP. NET asynchronous page rendering infrastructure. Beginning with version 1.*x*, the ASP.NET engine supports defining asynchronous handlers to improve scalability and efficiency of web applications.

Scalability, Performance, and Threading

To better understand this topic, it is useful to review some basic concepts. First, "scalable" does not mean "fast." A scalable software solution is a solution that performs the same—which could be slowly—regardless of the number of concurrently connected users. When the solution needs to support a larger number of users, you can simply add hardware, without changing any lines of code.

ASP.NET, along with many other server technologies, handles requests on a first-come, first-served basis, using a limited pool of threads. Each arriving request is placed in a queue, and any free threads in the pool take those requests from the queue and process them. When all the threads in the pool are busy serving requests, the queue will grow as new requests arrive. As soon as a working thread completes its work on its current request, it checks whether a new request exists in the queue, and if so, removes it from the queue and begins serving that request. The number of queued requests pending execution is a key indicator of the stress level of a server. Administrators can configure the size of the thread pool; however, it is not a good idea to increase thread pool size too much, because too many threads working concurrently perform worse than a smaller pool of threads with a well-defined pending queue.

Instead, it's better to improve thread efficiency by using and releasing worker threads as soon as possible, to free them so they're ready to serve other requests as quickly as possible. In cases where worker threads have to wait synchronously for an external resource, such as a DBMS query execution, or a SOAP Service request, or whatever else depends on an external CPU, the worker thread is idle—but not free. When too many worker threads are idle but not free, the pending queue will grow, reducing performance, and worse, reducing scalability.

> In many circumstances, it would be better to free the idled threads to serve other queued requests, moving external resources wait times to IO threads, and getting the worker thread back in the pool immediately after making the call to the external system/resource. ASP.NET has a standard way of handling such situations by utilizing asynchronous handlers and pages. You should investigate and use these capabilities to improve the overall scalability and response time of your applications.

As you have seen many times in this book so far, SharePoint is mainly a framework built on top of ASP.NET, so you can take advantage of native asynchronous programming techniques in SharePoint solutions as well—even when developing Web Parts. Imagine that you have a Web Part that queries an external resource, such as the Bing Search Engine. You might know that Bing is accessible via a specific SOAP service, which allows searching and querying websites, news, photos, and so on from any registered software application. In this section, you'll see how to build a custom Web Part that queries Bing for the latest news about a specific argument provided by the end user by using the Web Part user interface.

Figure 7-4 shows the final output of this sample Web Part; Listing 7-9 contains the corresponding source code.

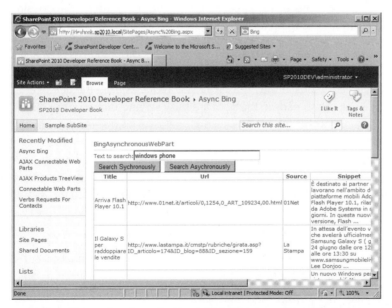

FIGURE 7-4 The user interface of a sample Web Part that queries Bing for news about a specific matter.

LISTING 7-9 An excerpt of the source code of the sample *BingAsynchronousWebPart*.

```
public class BingAsynchronousWebPart : WebPart {

    // ... code omitted ...

    private void ensureBingSearchClient() {
        if (this.bing == null || this.bing.State != CommunicationState.Opened) {
            this.bing = new LiveSearchPortTypeClient(new BasicHttpBinding(),
                new EndpointAddress(this.BingSearchServiceUri));
            this.bing.Open();
        }
    }

    IAsyncResult BeginSearch(Object sender, EventArgs e,
        AsyncCallback cb, Object state) {
        ensureBingSearchClient();

        SearchRequest request = new SearchRequest {
            AppId = this.AppID,
            Query = this.searchText.Text,
            UILanguage = "en-US",
            Options = new SearchOption[] { SearchOption.DisableLocationDetection },
            Sources = new SourceType[] { SourceType.News }
        };

        return (bing.BeginSearch(request, cb, state));
    }

    void EndSearch(IAsyncResult asyncResult) {
        SearchResponse response = bing.EndSearch(asyncResult);

        if (response.News != null && response.News.Results != null) {
            this.searchResults.DataSource = response.News.Results;
            this.searchResults.DataBind();
        }
    }

    void TimeoutSearch(IAsyncResult asyncResult) {
        this.Controls.Add(new LiteralControl("<br/>Timeout expired!"));
    }

    void searchCommandAsynchronously_Click(object sender, EventArgs e) {
        this.Page.RegisterAsyncTask(new PageAsyncTask(BeginSearch,
            EndSearch, TimeoutSearch, null));
        this.Controls.Add(new LiteralControl(
            String.Format("<br/>{0} - In the mean time I can do something else ...",
            DateTime.Now)));
    }
}
```

The Web Part can work both synchronously or asynchronously.

> **Note** The asynchronous version is the one discussed here; this is the only one we will comment on. The synchronous version is provided solely for your reference.

The *searchCommandAsynchronously_Click* event handler, which handles the *Click* event of the "Search Asynchronously" button, simply registers a *PageAsyncTask* at the current page level. This is a functionality provided by ASP.NET that allows registration of asynchronous tasks into a list of page-level asynchronous tasks. The underlying ASP.NET infrastructure guarantees that all these tasks will be executed before it completes the rendering of the page request. If a task takes a long time to complete, the worker thread assigned to the current page request will be returned to the pool of worker threads so that it can serve other requests in the meantime. When the *PageAsyncTask* has completed successfully—or when the timeout period expires, the ASP.NET infrastructure will queue the request completion, which will be handled as soon as a worker thread is available from the pool of worker threads.

It is important to notice that the *PageAsyncTask* class requires a *Begin** method to start the asynchronous task, and an *End** method to complete it, as well as a *Timeout** method to handle timeouts. The signatures of these methods are compliant with the more general .NET asynchronous design pattern so that every .NET library, even custom ones, can be used asynchronously if it defines a set of asynchronous methods in addition to the synchronous versions. The interesting part of this example is that, while the Web Part queries the Bing search service in the background, the worker thread returns to the pool to serve other requests; thus, reducing the overall execution time of the solution. *PageAsyncTask* is one of the three ways to manage asynchronous calls in ASP.NET; a full explanation of all these techniques is beyond the scope of this book .

> **Note** In the previous versions of SharePoint, there was a technique to develop asynchronous SharePoint Web Parts (those inheriting from *Microsoft.SharePoint.WebPartPages.WebPart*), based on the custom method *RegisterWorkItemCallback*. However, it is an obsolete and deprecated technique; it is better to use the ASP.NET asynchronous infrastructure.

XSLT Rendering

One of the main areas of investment when developing Web Parts is the user interface and the output of (X)HTML code. A Web Part needs to merge transparently into an existing page (Web Part Page or Wiki Page), adhering to the rich and user-friendly layout of the hosting site, which can be a public CMS solution. Nevertheless, until now the output of the Web Parts you have seen were defined in its *CreateChildControls* method or, for Visual Web Parts, in the ASCX code of the corresponding visual control. However, you cannot always predict where the Web Part will be hosted; thus, you cannot provide a layout that will be appropriate for *every* kind of output.

Of course, you can try to satisfy different layout requirements by just working with Cascading Style Sheets (CSS), but in general, there's no one-size-fits-all solution. This is an issue that Microsoft had to face when developing SharePoint itself. Consider how Web Parts such as the *SearchCoreResults* or the *XsltListViewWebPart* render their output, to name but a couple of examples. These native Web Parts accept an XSLT transformation as one of their main parameters and apply that transformation to an XML document that represents the real content of their output.

Often, in real SharePoint solutions that target not only intranet/extranet sites but also public Internet scenarios, you will need to develop custom Web Parts that follow these same basic principles. In this section, you'll see how to create a Web Part that generates its output using a configurable XSLT transformation, which is loaded from a document library in the current site. The example is an RSS Feed Viewer Web Part, (even though SharePoint already provides such a Web Part).

In Listing 7-10, you can see an excerpt of the source code for this *RSSFeedViewerWebPart*. The code highlighted in bold is the key part of the example. It loads the external XML source, which in an actual solution could be the output of a query against SharePoint's data, and then transforms it using an instance of the *XslCompiledTransform* class, which is available in the *System.Xml.Xsl* namespace. The output of the XSLT transformation is added to the collection of controls of the current Web Part, using a *LiteralControl*.

LISTING 7-10 The source code of the sample *RSSFeedViewerWebPart*.

```
public class RSSFeedViewerWebPart : WebPart {
    [WebBrowsable(true)]
    [Personalizable(true)]
    public String RSSFeedUri { get; set; }

    [WebBrowsable(true)]
    [Personalizable(true)]
    public String XsltUri { get; set; }

    protected override void CreateChildControls() {
        if (this.WebPartManager.DisplayMode == WebPartManager.BrowseDisplayMode) {
            if (!String.IsNullOrEmpty(this.RSSFeedUri) &&
            !String.IsNullOrEmpty(this.XsltUri)) {
                XslCompiledTransform xslt = new XslCompiledTransform();
                SPFile xsltFile = SPContext.Current.Web.GetFile(this.XsltUri);
                if (xsltFile != null) {
                  xslt.Load(new XmlTextReader(xsltFile.OpenBinaryStream()));
                  xslt.Load(this.XsltUri);
                  XmlReader xml = XmlReader.Create(
                      this.RSSFeedUri, new XmlReaderSettings {
                      CloseInput = true,
                      ValidationType = System.Xml.ValidationType.None,
                      XmlResolver = new XmlUrlResolver()});
```

```
                using (xml) {
                    StringWriter writer = new StringWriter();
                    xslt.Transform(xml, null, writer);

                    this.Controls.Add(new LiteralControl(writer.ToString()));
                  }
                }
                else {
                  this.Controls.Add(new LiteralControl(
                    "Please provide a valid XSLT file URI in the current site."));
                }
            }
          }
          else {
              this.Controls.Add(new LiteralControl(
                  "Please configure the Web Part."));
          }
        }
        else {
          this.Controls.Add(new LiteralControl(
              "This Web Part renders its output only in browsing mode."));
        }
      }
    }
}
```

Figure 7 5 shows the output in a browser. There is nothing especially exciting in this last example; in fact, the output is completely static. Dynamic behavior can be added only on the client side, at the browser level, by injecting some JavaScript/JQuery code into the output (X) HTML code. Listing 7-11 shows the XSLT used in this last example.

Note It is beyond the scope of this book to teach you what XSLT is and how to write an XSLT transformation. If you need further details about XSLT, try searching the Web and perhaps even attend a free online course at W3C School.

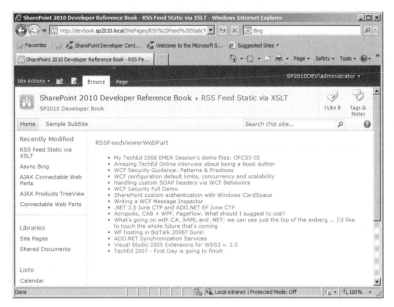

FIGURE 7-5 The output in the browser for the sample *RSSFeedViewerWebPart*.

LISTING 7-11 The XSLT used to transform the RSS with the *RSSFeedViewerWebPart*.

```xml
<?xml version="1.0" encoding="utf-8"?>
<xsl:stylesheet version="1.0" xmlns:xsl="http://www.w3.org/1999/XSL/Transform"
    xmlns:msxsl="urn:schemas-microsoft-com:xslt" exclude-result-prefixes="msxsl">
    <xsl:output method="xml" indent="yes"/>
    <xsl:template match="/">
      <ul>
        <xsl:for-each select="rss/channel/item">
          <li>
            <a href="{link}" target="_blank">
              <xsl:value-of select="title"/>
            </a>
          </li>
        </xsl:for-each>
      </ul>
    </xsl:template>
</xsl:stylesheet>
```

The real power of rendering the output of a Web Part using XSLT becomes evident if you think about a functionality provided by ASP.NET pages infrastructure: the capability to dynamically load ASPX/ASCX code at runtime, using the *ParseControl* method of the *Page* class.

If you change the code of Listing 7-9 slightly, adding some ASP.NET tags (those with "asp:" as the namespace prefix) instead of the HTML tags only, as shown in Listing 7-12, the output of the XSLT transformation could be a portion of ASPX code.

LISTING 7-12 The new XSLT used to transform the RSS within the RSS Feed Viewer Web Part.

```xml
<?xml version="1.0" encoding="utf-8"?>
<xsl:stylesheet version="1.0" xmlns:xsl="http://www.w3.org/1999/XSL/Transform"
    xmlns:asp="http://schemas.microsoft.com/AspNet/WebControls"
    xmlns:msxsl="urn:schemas-microsoft-com:xslt"
    exclude-result-prefixes="asp msxsl">
    <xsl:output method="xml" indent="yes"/>

    <xsl:template match="/">
      <asp:RadioButtonList ID="postsList" runat="server">
        <xsl:for-each select="rss/channel/item">
          <asp:ListItem Text="{title}" Value="{link}" />
        </xsl:for-each>
      </asp:RadioButtonList>
      <asp:Button ID="selectItemCommand" runat="server" Text="Select!" />
    </xsl:template>

</xsl:stylesheet>
```

Figure 7-6 shows the output of this new XSLT transformation. The XSLT transformation is not the only difference between the last two examples, though; the C# source code of the Web Part was also changed a little, as shown in Listing 7-13, which describes the new *RSSFeedDynamicViewerWebPart* control.

FIGURE 7-6 The output in the browser for the sample *RSSFeedViewerWebPart* with dynamic ASPX code in XSLT.

LISTING 7-13 An excerpt of the source code of the *RSSFeedDynamicViewerWebPart* control.

```csharp
public class RSSFeedDynamicViewerWebPart : WebPart {
    [WebBrowsable(true)]
    [Personalizable(true)]
    public String RSSFeedUri { get; set; }

    [WebBrowsable(true)]
    [Personalizable(true)]
    public String XsltUri { get; set; }

    protected IButtonControl selectItemCommand;
    protected ListControl postsList;

    protected override void CreateChildControls() {
        if (this.WebPartManager.DisplayMode == WebPartManager.BrowseDisplayMode) {
            if (!String.IsNullOrEmpty(this.RSSFeedUri) &&
            !String.IsNullOrEmpty(this.XsltUri)) {
                XslCompiledTransform xslt = new XslCompiledTransform();
                SPFile xsltFile = SPContext.Current.Web.GetFile(this.XsltUri);
                if (xsltFile != null) {
                  xslt.Load(new XmlTextReader(xsltFile.OpenBinaryStream()));

                  XmlReader xml = XmlReader.Create(this.RSSFeedUri,
                      new XmlReaderSettings {
                      CloseInput = true,
                      ValidationType = System.Xml.ValidationType.None,
                      XmlResolver = new XmlUrlResolver()
                  });

                  using (xml) {
                      StringWriter writer = new StringWriter();
                      xslt.Transform(xml, null, writer);

                      Control parsedControl =
                          this.Page.ParseControl(writer.ToString());
                      this.Controls.Add(parsedControl);

                      this.selectItemCommand =
                          this.FindControl("selectItemCommand") as IButtonControl;
                      this.postsList = this.FindControl("postsList") as ListControl;

                      if (this.selectItemCommand != null) {
                          this.selectItemCommand.Click +=
                              new EventHandler(selectItemCommand_Click);
                      }
                  }
                }
            }
            else {
              this.Controls.Add(new LiteralControl(
                "Please provide a valid XSLT file URI in the current site."));
            }
        }
    }
```

```
                else {
                    this.Controls.Add(new LiteralControl(
                                "Please configure the Web Part."));
                }
            }
            else {
                this.Controls.Add(new LiteralControl(
                            "This Web Part renders its output only in
                            browsing mode."));
            }
        }

        void selectItemCommand_Click(object sender, EventArgs e) {
            if (this.postsList != null) {
                if (this.postsList.SelectedValue != null) {
                    this.Page.Response.Redirect(this.postsList.SelectedValue);
                }
            }
        }
    }
}
```

The code highlighted in bold was changed to parse the output of the XSLT transformation, handling it as a graph of ASP.NET controls rather than a static block of (X)HTML. As you have already seen, the "magic" occurs through the *ParseControl* method of the Page class of ASP.NET, which isn't solely a SharePoint capability; it's an ASP.NET capability.

The *ParseControl* method accepts an input argument of type *String*, which will be parsed by the ASP.NET rendering engine and will return a graph of controls that is ready to be added to the controls collection of the current Web Part. If you define a naming and type convention for controls that you create through XSLT, the code will also be able to find controls created in XSLT, so you can attach event handlers to them. In fact, this example creates two ASP.NET controls with the IDs *postsList* and *selectItemCommand*, respectively. The former control is expected to be something that acts as a *ListControl*, such as a *RadioButtonList*, a *CheckBoxList*, a *DropDownList*, a *ListBox*, or a *BulletedList*. The latter control is expected to behave as an *IButtonControl*, so it will be a control that provides a *Click* event handler (*Button*, *ImageButton*, or *LinkButton*). The code in Listing 7-11 looks for these kind of controls and attaches an event handler to the *Click* event of the *IButtonControl*, to redirect the user's browser to the currently *SelectedValue* of the *ListControl* instance.

This technique is truly powerful because it lets you define a completely custom layout for Web Parts while still sharing common business logic and behavior, but it doesn't impose any specific constraints about the (X)HTML code to output, so it's often your best choice in real-world SharePoint Internet solutions.

Deployment, Security, and Versioning

The last topic covered in this chapter is a quick overview of Web Parts' deployment, taking a little bit of security and versioning into account as well. Chapter 8, "SharePoint Features and Solutions," thoroughly covers deployment of SharePoint solutions in general. Security is a fundamental part of deployment, as well. In Chapter 23, "Code Access Security and Sandboxed Solutions," you'll cover security in solution deployments, with the focus being on security features specific to Web Parts.

Deployment and Versioning

In SharePoint 2010, you can deploy a Web Part in three different locations:

- **Solution Gallery**   This is a new feature of SharePoint 2010, and it allows deploying Web Parts in a sandboxed environment (more on this in Chapter 23).

- **Bin directory of the hosting web application**   Using this deployment, you can release a Web Part locally to a specific web application, with local maintenance and configuration, and with a specific and limited set of permissions.

- **Global Assembly Cache (GAC)**   Code libraries and Web Parts are deployed here so that they can be shared by all the web applications in the current server farm. Code installed in the GAC has full trust rights on the hosting server.

Regardless of which deployment location you choose, as you saw in Chapter 6, a Web Part is deployed through a .webpart file that's either included in a SharePoint solution or manually deployed by an authorized user. However, deployment includes not only installing from scratch, but also upgrading from one version to another.

To upgrade a Web Part, one useful suggestion is to release upgrades only through strongly-named assemblies. A strongly-named assembly can be checked against its signature when .NET loads it, to prevent tampering. In addition, the strong name also declares the assembly version clearly, better supporting upgrade paths.

 Note The CLR checks the digital signature of a strongly-named assembly whenever it loads such an assembly deployed in the bin directory of the hosting application. However, the signature of an assembly deployed in the GAC is checked only when it's inserted into the GAC. This behavior may sound strange, but only Administrators (local or domain) can add assemblies to the GAC. If an Administrator inserts an assembly into the GAC, and that assembly has a valid signature, then only another user with administrative rights could change (tamper with) that binary file—so unless your Administrators become hackers, that situation should never happen!

If your upgrade process involves only internal code modification, but you did not change any public property of the Web Part, and you did not change the assembly version, you can simply substitute the assembly in the deployment location, and you are done. If you changed some of the public properties of the Web Part, you need to adapt older versions of your Web Part to the last version. If a Web Part Page or a Wiki Page contains an old instance of your Web Part, as soon as someone opens the page, the old Web Part will be loaded, and SharePoint infrastructure will look for its assembly and type. But if you have replaced the old one with a new version, SharePoint will not find the old assembly, and the type load would fail. Similarly, if you changed some properties—for example, if you renamed or removed a property—the serialization of the old Web Part will not match the new type.

To solve the assembly versioning issue, you can use the .NET native assembly binding redirect infrastructure. By manually adding a few lines of XML to the web.config of the web application, you can instruct the .NET CLR to load the new assembly in place of the old one. Listing 7-14 shows an example of assembly binding redirect.

LISTING 7-14 A excerpt of a web.config file with an assembly binding redirect directive.

```
<runtime>
  <assemblyBinding xmlns="urn:schemas-microsoft-com:asm.v1">
    <dependentAssembly>
      <assemblyIdentity name="DevLeap.SP2010.VersionableWebPart"
        publicKeyToken="6acae404adfa82c3" culture="neutral" />
      <bindingRedirect oldVersion="1.0.0.0" newVersion="2.0.0.0" />
    </dependentAssembly>
  </assemblyBinding>
</runtime>
```

This small piece of XML declares that when the CLR needs to load the assembly with name *DevLeap.SP2010.VersionableWebPart*, a *PublicKeyToken* value of *6acae404adfa82c3*, with neutral culture and version 1.0.0.0 (*oldVersion*), it should instead try to load version 2.0.0.0 (*newVersion*) of the same assembly. Of course the new assembly must be available in the web application bin folder or in the GAC.

On the other hand, migrating properties from one Web Part version into another is not a trivial feat. If you are upgrading an old SharePoint native Web Part to an ASP.NET Web Part, you can override the *AfterDeserialize()* method to migrate properties from the old version to the new one. This method will be invoked the first time SharePoint loads a page with an older version of your Web Part in it. For subsequent loads, the Web Part has already been upgraded and the *AfterDeserialize()* method will not be invoked again.

Keep in mind that when you are upgrading ASP.NET Web Parts, you cannot use this method. There is a specific interface for accomplishing versioning tasks for ASP.NET Web Parts, defined in the namespace *System.Web.UI.WebControls.WebParts*, called *IVersioningPersonalizable* that you can use for versioning personalization data. Listing 7-15 shows the signature of this interface.

LISTING 7-15 The *IVersioningPersonalizable* interface for Web Parts versioning.

```
namespace System.Web.UI.WebControls.WebParts {
    public interface IVersioningPersonalizable {
        void Load(IDictionary unknownProperties);
    }
}
```

The only method defined in this interface is *Load*, which receives a list of all the unknown properties that should be deserialized, but for which the Web Part environment does not know where to store their values. You can implement this interface to migrate personalization while the framework loads the Web Parts.

For clarity, consider the simple Web Part in Listing 7-16, which has one customizable property.

LISTING 7-16 A very simple Web Part to show how Web Parts versioning works.

```
namespace DevLeap.SP2010.VersionableWebPart.CustomWebPart {
    [ToolboxItemAttribute(false)]
    public class CustomWebPart : WebPart {

        [WebBrowsable(true)]
        [Personalizable(true)]
        public String TextToRender { get; set; }

        protected override void CreateChildControls() {
            this.Controls.Add(new LiteralControl(this.TextToRender));
        }
    }
}
```

This Web Part is deployed within an assembly with the following strong name:

```
DevLeap.SP2010.VersionableWebPart, Version=1.0.0.0, Culture=neutral,
PublicKeyToken=6acae404adfa82c3
```

Now suppose that you define a new version of this Web Part, changing the assembly version, renaming the public property *TextToRender* into *TextToRenderTimes*, and adding a new property, *NumberOfTimes*. First, you need to define a corresponding binding redirect in the web.config. Then you must install the new assembly into the GAC, and finally, you need to implement the versioning interface (*IVersioningPersonalizable*).

Listing 7-17 shows an example of a new Web Part that transparently migrates "unknown" properties.

LISTING 7-17 A simple Web Part, which is version two of Listing 7-16.

```
namespace DevLeap.SP2010.VersionableWebPart.CustomWebPart {

    [ToolboxItemAttribute(false)]
    public class CustomWebPart : WebPart, IVersioningPersonalizable {

        [WebBrowsable(true)]
        [Personalizable(true)]
        public String TextToRenderTimes { get; set; }

        [WebBrowsable(true)]
        [Personalizable(true)]
        public Int32 RepeatTimes { get; set; }

        protected override void CreateChildControls() {
            for (Int32 c = 0; c < this.RepeatTimes; c++) {
                this.Controls.Add(new LiteralControl(this.TextToRenderTimes));
            }
        }

        void IVersioningPersonalizable.Load(IDictionary unknownProperties) {
            foreach (DictionaryEntry entry in unknownProperties) {
                if (entry.Key.ToString() == "TextToRender") {
                    this.RepeatTimes = 1;
                    this.TextToRenderTimes = entry.Value.ToString();
                }
            }
        }
    }
}
```

The *Load* method of *IVersioningPersonalizable* receives a dictionary of all the unmatched properties, which lets you match or migrate them to the corresponding new property, if it exists.

SafeControls and Cross-Site-Scripting SafeGuard

From a security point of view, every Web Part acts in the context of the current user; thus, its security against SharePoint's data is based on the current user's permissions. However, SharePoint's data security may not be the ultimate measure of a secure solution. For example, a malicious user authorized to add custom Web Parts to a page could insert a Web Part that represents a risk for the client browser or for the server environment hosting the SharePoint solution. Imagine what would happen if a user uploads a custom Web Part that consumes a lot of CPU resources (perhaps 100%) due to a bug or even malicious intent. Any SharePoint front-end server that loads and executes this Web Part would block any further functionality—or at least have its performance seriously degraded. To avoid such issues, SharePoint provides a couple of answers: *sandboxed solutions* and *safe controls*. Sandboxed solutions are one of the most interesting new features of SharePoint 2010 for developers, and they deserve a dedicated chapter (Chapter 23), in which they are covered in detail.

SharePoint will load and execute only authorized Web Parts, based on a list of *SafeControls* declared in the web.config of the current web application. When you deploy a Web Part solution at the farm level, the Web Part class is marked as a *SafeControl* in the web.config of the site where the control is deployed. If you try to load a page that hosts a Web Part or a control not marked as a *SafeControl*, the load will fail, but the SharePoint environment will remain stable and secure. Listing 7-18 contains an example of a *SafeControl* declaration for one of the Web Parts defined previously in this chapter.

LISTING 7-18 A *SafeControl* declaration for the *RSSFeedDynamicViewerWebPart* control.

```
<SafeControl Assembly="DevLeap.SP2010.AdvancedWebParts, Version=1.0.0.0,
   Culture=neutral, PublicKeyToken=420cb6d9461e6c7c"
   Namespace="DevLeap.SP2010.AdvancedWebParts.RSSFeedDynamicViewerWebPart"
   TypeName="*" Safe="True" SafeAgainstScript="False" />
```

Notice that the *SafeControl* tag references the safe Web Part in terms of assembly, including its strong name, namespace and type name. The *SafeControl* tag also defines a *SafeAgainstScript* attribute with a *Boolean* value that allows configuring a new SharePoint 2010 feature called "Cross-site-scripting SafeGuard."

Beginning with SharePoint 2010, Web Parts can be customized by configuration properties only by users in the role of designers or higher. This means that now, by default, a site contributor cannot configure or customize Web Part properties, while in the past that was possible. You might be wondering why Microsoft changed this behavior. The answer is: for security reasons.

In SharePoint 2010, the client object model is available even in the web browser, via JavaScript. Imagine what would happen if a malicious user configures a Web Part property with some JavaScript code, invoking the Client Object Model to delete or change some data on the server, and that custom property is used to render the output of the Web Part (for instance a *Title* property). Of course, the Client Object Model acts in the context of the current user, so the injected JavaScript could do exactly what the current user can do. But what would happen if that same page were opened by a Site Collection Administrator, for example? What we just described is a new kind of cross-site-scripting (XSS) that is natively blocked by the "Cross-site-scripting SafeGuard" feature. This new feature impacts not only new Web Parts, but also any that were previously developed.

If—at your own risk—you want to continue to let a Web Part remain configurable, even by site contributors, you can change the SafeAgainstScript attribute of the SafeControl declaration for that Web Part. Figure 7-7 illustrates the user interface provided by Microsoft Visual Studio 2010 for changing this property.

A value of *true* instructs SharePoint to allow editing and configuration even by site contributors. There is also a new attribute, *RequiresDesignerPermissionAttribute,* which you can use to tag a property to make it configurable only by users with designer rights or higher. This last attribute overrides any configuration in the web.config, so if you declare a control as *SafeAgainstScript* but also define a property marked with *RequiresDesignerPermissionAttribute,* that property will still not be configurable by a contributor, and will require at least a designer role, regardless of the web.config configuration.

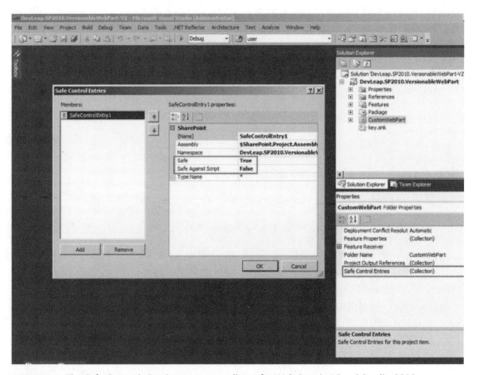

FIGURE 7-7 The Safe Controls Entries property editor of a Web Part in Visual Studio 2010.

Summary

This chapter showed you how to develop connectable Web Parts that take advantage of AJAX. In addition, it covered the native Silverlight support provided by SharePoint, as well as the External Application Provider framework on which the Silverlight support is built. You explored Web Part scalability using asynchronous programming in ASP.NET. The chapter also discussed developing Web Parts with an XSLT-based layout, which outputs (X)HTML code or (better) dynamic ASPX markup, ready to be parsed by the ASP.NET environment. Finally, you saw how to deploy Web Parts that support versioning and security.

PART IV

Extending Microsoft SharePoint 2010

Chapter 8
SharePoint Features and Solutions

Since version 2007, one of the most interesting capabilities of Microsoft SharePoint is the engine for managing custom features, together with the ability to deploy them through installation of solution packages. This chapter is the first within Part IV ("Extending Microsoft SharePoint 2010") of this book. It will walk you through the various kinds of features that you can define and about how to package SharePoint's solutions. Many of the features presented in this chapter will be covered in more detail in other chapters within this section. Thus, here the goal is to briefly describe all the available features, providing an overview but leaving detailed insights for discussion in upcoming chapters.

Features and Solutions

A *feature* is a customization or extension of the native environment that can be installed and activated selectively at various scope levels to deploy solutions modularly and granularly. For example, a feature could be used to deploy custom data structures, such as site columns, content types, list definitions, and so on. Additionally, a feature can be used to replace a standard UI control such as the search box (which appears in the upper-right corner of every standard SharePoint layout) with a custom search control. Another example of a feature might automate deployment of pages and Web Parts. The list of examples could be longer. Later in this section, you will see a more complete list of standard features offered by SharePoint.

In general, features let you develop customizations and extensions that take advantage of a native environment for deploying, upgrading, and managing them. The SharePoint Features engine supports automated deployment, automatic management of multiple load-balanced front-end web servers for reducing inconsistency issues, and automated upgrading to help avoid versioning issues. Each time you develop a feature, SharePoint at minimum creates an XML file, named Feature.xml and called the 7*feature manifest*, and stores it on every front-end web server of the farm in a subfolder of the SharePoint14_Root\TEMPLATE\FEATURES directory.

 Note SharePoint14_Root refers to the SharePoint root folder, which is typically located at C:\Program Files\Common Files\Microsoft Shared\Web Server Extensions\14.

Each feature has its own folder, whose name is that of the contained feature; thus, two features cannot share the same folder or the same name in a farm. Each feature's folder contains all the files required to implement that feature, together with the feature manifest file.

To deploy a feature, you need to install it (which means copying the feature's folder to each front-end web server), recycle the application pool, and then activate it. After you have deployed a feature, you can upgrade it for maintenance and versioning purposes. You can even deactivate and uninstall a feature.

Every feature has an activation scope that can assume one of the following values:

- *Farm*   The feature will target the entire SharePoint farm.

- *WebApplication*   The feature targets a single web application and all the contained Site Collections.

- *Site*   The feature will target a single Site Collection and all of its websites.

- *Web*   The feature targets a single website.

You can deploy a fixed set of standard features that are briefly described on page 246. Regardless the type of feature that you want to implement, every feature type shares the same feature manifest file structure, as illustrated in Listing 8-1.

LISTING 8-1 The SharePoint feature manifest file structure.

```
<Feature xmlns="http://schemas.microsoft.com/sharepoint/"
    ActivateOnDefault = "TRUE" | "FALSE"
    AlwaysForceInstall = "TRUE" | "FALSE"
    AutoActivateInCentralAdmin = "TRUE" | "FALSE"
    Creator = "Text"
    DefaultResourceFile =  "Text"
    Description = "Text"
    Hidden = "TRUE" | "FALSE"
    Id = "Text"
    ImageUrl = "Text"
    ImageUrlAltText = "Text"
    ReceiverAssembly = "Text"
    ReceiverClass = "Text"
    RequireResources = "TRUE" | "FALSE"
    Scope = "Text"
    SolutionId = "Text"
    Title = "Text"
    UIVersion = "Text"
    Version = "Text" >
    <ActivationDependencies>
        <ActivationDependency FeatureId = "Text" />
    </ActivationDependencies>
    <ElementManifests>
        <ElementManifest Location = "Text" />
        <ElementFile Location = "Text" />
    </ElementManifests>
    <Properties>
        <Property Key = "Text" Value = "Text" />
    </Properties>
```

```
<UpgradeActions ReceiverAssembly = "Text" ReceiverClass = "Text">
    <AddContentTypeField />
    <ApplyElementManifests />
    <CustomUpgradeAction />
    <MapFile />
    <VersionRange />
</UpgradeActions>
</Feature>
```

The *Feature* element shown in Listing 8-1 belongs to the *http://schemas.microsoft.com/share-point/* namespace. It is composed of a set of attributes, and accepts some optional child elements. Table 8-1 lists each available attribute along with a brief explanation.

TABLE 8-1 **Attributes Supported by the *Feature* Element**

Attribute Name	Description
ActivateOnDefault	An optional *Boolean* attribute with a default value of *True*. It applies only to *Farm*-scoped or *WebApplication*-scoped features and determines whether the feature will be activated by default during installation. For *WebApplication*-scoped features, if this attribute is set to *True*, the feature will also be activated when a new web application is created.
AlwaysForceInstall	This is an optional *Boolean* attribute with a default value of *False*. When set to *True*, it forces the feature to be installed—even if it is already installed.
AutoActivateInCentralAdmin	This is an optional *Boolean* attribute with a default value of *False*. It defines whether the feature will be activated by default in the Administrative website hosting the SharePoint Central Administration. It does not apply to *Farm*-scoped features.
Creator	This is an optional description of the feature's creator.
DefaultResourceFile	This is optional text that defines the name of a common resource file, usually shared with other features released by the same creator. By default, SharePoint will look for resources in a file in the path SharePoint14_Root\TEMPLATE\FEATURES*FeatureName*\Resources, with a file name such as Resources.*Culture*.resx (the *Culture* value can be any of the standard culture names defined by the Internet Engineering Task Force (IETF), such as *en-US*, *it-IT*, *fr-FR*, and so on). However, when you specify a name, for example *MySharedResources*, SharePoint will use that name, searching for a file named *MySharedResources.Culture*.resx in the shared path SharePoint14_Root\Resources.
Description	This is optional text that describes the feature in the features' management UI. You can define it using a resource string in the form *$Resources:ResourceName*. For example, if the feature description is a resource item with a key value of "FeatureDescription," the corresponding value should be *$Resources: FeatureDescription*.

Attribute Name	Description
Hidden	This is an optional *Boolean* attribute with a default value of *False*. When set to *True*, the feature will be hidden from the UI and can be activated or deactivated only through the command line tools or by using the Object Model.
Id	This is a required attribute of type text, which must contain an ID (GUID) that uniquely identifies the feature.
ImageUrl	This is optional text that defines the site-relative URL of an image used to render the feature in the UI.
ImageUrlAltText	This is optional text that defines alternate text for the image representing the feature in the UI (see *ImageUrl*). You can define this using a resource string, just like the *Description* property.
ReceiverAssembly	This is optional text that defines the strong name of an assembly that SharePoint will search for in the Global Assembly Cache (GAC) and that provides a receiver class to handle the feature's events.
ReceiverClass	This is optional text that defines the full class name of a receiver class to handle the feature's events. SharePoint will search for the receiver class name in the *ReceiverAssembly*.
RequireResources	This is an optional *Boolean* attribute with a default value of *False*. It determines whether SharePoint requires that resources exist for the language of the current website or Site Collection to make the feature visible in the UI. This attribute does not affect the capability to activate and manage the feature from the command line or from the object model.
Scope	This is a required text attribute. It defines the scope within which the feature can be activated. The possible values are: *Farm*, *WebApplication*, *Site*, and *Web*.
SolutionId	This is optional text that defines the ID of the solution to which the features belongs.
Title	This is optional text that defines the title of the feature and that is visible in the features' management UI. It is limited to a maximum length of 255 characters. You can define it using a resource string, as described in the *Description* property.
UIVersion	This is optional text that declares the UI version supported by the feature. The accepted values are *3* (for Windows SharePoint Services 3.0) and *4* (for Microsoft SharePoint Foundation 2010).
Version	This is optional text that defines the version of the feature. It can be made of up to four numbers, delimited by periods. For example, it might be *1.0.0.0*, *1.0.0.1*, and so on.

In addition, a *Feature* tag of a feature manifest can contain some child elements, such as:

- *ActivationDependencies*   Specifies a list of features on which activation of the current feature depends.

- *ElementManifests*   References a set of element manifests or element files, both declaring the definition of the feature.

- *Properties*   Provides a set of default values for the feature's properties, represented as a tuple of keys and values. For example, these properties are useful for deploying event receivers, which will be discussed in Chapter 12, "Event Receivers."

- *UpgradeActions*   Specifies any custom action to execute when the feature is upgraded.

The most important children are those declaring one or more elements that make up the feature. These elements correspond to zero or more *ElementManifest* tags, which are still defined through XML files, and zero or more *ElementFile* tags, which declare files supporting the feature. Both of these tags provide a *Location* attribute that references the target file as a path relative to the feature's folder. Listing 8-2 shows a feature manifest deploying a Web Part.

LISTING 8-2 A feature manifest file deploying a Web Part.

```
<Feature xmlns="http://schemas.microsoft.com/sharepoint/"
  Title="DevLeap Sample Web Part"
  Description="This feature deploys a sample Web Part."
  Id="c46c270e-e722-4aa0-82ba-b66c8dd61f4e" Scope="Site"
  Version="1.0.0.0">
  <ElementManifests>
    <ElementManifest Location="SampleWebPart\Elements.xml" />
    <ElementFile Location="SampleWebPart\SampleWebPart.webpart" />
  </ElementManifests>
</Feature>
```

The example feature manifest defines only the *Scope* and the *Id* for the feature, together with its *Title* and *Description*; meanwhile, the Web Part is referenced by the element manifest file located in the relative folder, SampleWebPart\Elements.xml. The Web Part deployment also requires a .webpart file, referenced by the *ElementFile* tag of the feature manifest.

Table 8-1 illustrated how you can support a multi-language user interface. To do that, you define a set of resource files for the feature, replacing text values with their corresponding resource key. Listing 8-3 shows the same feature manifest as Listing 8-2, but with resource strings instead of explicit values.

LISTING 8-3 A feature manifest supporting multi-language.

```
<Feature xmlns="http://schemas.microsoft.com/sharepoint/" Version="1.0.0.0"
Title="$Resources:FeatureTitle" Description="$Resources:FeatureDescription"
Id="c46c270e-e722-4aa0-82ba-b66c8dd61f4e" Scope="Site">
  <ElementManifests>
    <ElementManifest Location="SampleWebPart\Elements.xml" />
    <ElementFile Location="SampleWebPart\SampleWebPart.webpart" />
    <ElementFile Location="Resources\Resources.resx" />
    <ElementFile Location="Resources\Resources.it-IT.resx" />
  </ElementManifests>
</Feature>
```

The feature manifest declares the *Title* and *Description* properties as resources. It also includes a couple of resource files for the default invariant culture (Resources.resx) and for the Italian culture (Resources.it-IT.resx) in the feature deployment. These files are standard .resx files that you can define manually or by leveraging the tools in Visual Studio 2010.

Feature Element Types

Listing 8-2 and Listing 8-3 illustrated that the key information in every feature manifest file is the list of one or more element manifest files. Those files are based on the same XML schema as the feature manifest (*http://schemas.microsoft.com/sharepoint/*) and make use of a pre-defined set of tags, each of which corresponds to a specific feature type. The full schema for these XML files is defined in the wss.xsd document, available in the SharePoint14_Root\ TEMPLATE\XML folder. Table 8-2 shows a brief description of the main elements available in SharePoint 2010.

TABLE 8-2   THE MAIN STANDARD TYPES OF FEATURES THAT YOU CAN DEPLOY

Feature Element Name	Feature Description
ContentTypeBinding	Used to provision a content type on a list defined in a site template (see onet.xml in Chapter 14, "Site Templates"). Can be scoped to *Site*.
ContentType	Defines a content type, ready to be used in lists or libraries. Content types will be discussed in Chapter 10, "Data Provisioning." Can be scoped to *Site*.
Control	Used to customiz the configuration of an existing delegate control, or to declare a new delegate control to override SharePoint's standard controls. Delegate controls will be discussed in Chapter 9, "Extending the User Interface." Can be scoped to *Farm*, *WebApplication*, *Site*, and *Web*.
CustomAction	Defines an extension to the standard user interface. For example, you can use *CustomAction* to define a new button on a ribbon bar, a new menu item on a standard menu, or a new link on a site settings page. Custom actions will be discussed in Chapter 9. Can be scoped to *Farm*, *WebApplication*, *Site*, and *Web*.

Feature Element Name	Feature Description
CustomActionGroup	Groups custom actions. Custom actions groups will be discussed in Chapter 9. Can be scoped to *Farm*, *WebApplication*, *Site*, and *Web*.
DocumentConverter	Declares a document converter that can convert a document from a type X to a type Y. Requires some custom development, to implement the converter. Can be scoped to *WebApplication*.
FeatureSiteTemplateAssociation	Allows associating a feature to a specific site template definition for the purpose of provisioning the feature together with the site definition, when you create a new site with that definition. Can be scoped to *Farm*, *WebApplication*, and *Site*.
Field	Declares a Site Column definition. Site columns are discussed in Chapter 10. Can be scoped to *Site*.
HideCustomAction	Hides an existing custom action defined by another custom action or implemented by default in SharePoint. Hide custom actions will be discussed in Chapter 9. Can be scoped to *Farm*, *WebApplication*, *Site*, and *Web*.
ListInstance	Provisions an instance of a list definition, together with a specific configuration. Can be scoped to *Site* and *Web*.
ListTemplate	Defines a list template for the purpose of provisioning a custom lists' definitions. List templates are described in Chapter 10. Can be scoped to *Web*.
Module	Allows provisioning custom pages or files to a site. *Module* can also be used to deploy configured Web Parts, ListView Web Parts over existing or provisioned lists, NavBar links, custom Master Pages, and to configure properties of the target feature. Modules are discussed in Chapter 9 and Chapter 14. Can be scoped to *Site* and *Web*.
PropertyBag	Assigns properties and metadata to items (File, Folder, ListItem, Web) through features. Can be scoped to *Web*.
Receivers	Defines a custom event receiver. Event receivers are discussed in Chapter 12. Can be scoped to *Web*.
WebTemplate	Allows deploying a website template, even through a sandboxed solution so that it can create site instances based on that template. Site templates will be discussed in Chapter 14. Can be scoped to *Site*.
Workflow	Deploys a workflow definition on a target site. Workflows will be covered in the "Developing Workflows" section of this book. Can be scoped to *Site*.
WorkflowActions	Defines custom workflow actions for SharePoint Designer 2010. Custom actions for SPD2010 are described in Chapter 17, "Workflows with SharePoint Designer 2010." Can be scoped to *Farm*.
WorkflowAssociation	Associates a workflow with its target. Can be scoped to *Site*, *Web*.

Listing 8-4 presents an example of an element manifest file, declaring the Web Part referenced by the feature of Listing 8-3.

LISTING 8-4 An element manifest file that defines the Web Part deployed by Listing 8-3.

```xml
<?xml version="1.0" encoding="utf-8"?>
<Elements xmlns="http://schemas.microsoft.com/sharepoint/" >
  <Module Name="SampleWebPart" List="113" Url="_catalogs/wp">
    <File Path="SampleWebPart\SampleWebPart.webpart" Url="SampleWebPart.webpart"
      Type="GhostableInLibrary">
      <Property Name="Group" Value="DevLeap Web Parts" />
    </File>
  </Module>
</Elements>
```

Features and Solutions Deployment

As discussed in the previous section, to deploy a feature, you need to copy the feature's fold-er to the SharePoint14_Root\TEMPLATE\FEATURES path of every target server for the feature. When this is complete, you can use the STSADM.EXE command line tool to install and later activate the feature. The syntax to install and activate a feature via STSADM.EXE is illustrated in the following excerpt:

```
STSADM.EXE -o installfeature
           {-filename <relative path to Feature.xml from system feature directory> |
            -name <feature folder>}
           [-force]
STSADM.EXE -o activatefeature
           {-filename <relative path to Feature.xml> |
            -name <feature folder> |
            -id <feature Id>}
           [-url <url>]
           [-force]
```

 Note The STSADM.EXE command line tool can be found in the SharePoint14_Root\BIN folder.

If you want to forcibly install and activate the feature named *SampleWebPart*, you can use the following syntax:

```
STSADM.EXE -o installfeature -name SampleWebPart -force
STSADM.EXE -o activatefeature -name SampleWebPart -force -url http://server/site/subsite
```

Meanwhile, to deactivate a previously activated feature, you can use the following syntax:

```
STSADM.EXE -o deactivatefeature
           {-filename <relative path to Feature.xml> |
            -name <feature folder> |
            -id <feature Id>}
           [-url <url>]
           [-force]
```

Thus, here is the syntax to deactivate the *SampleWebPart* feature:

```
STSADM.EXE -o deactivatefeature -name SampleWebPart –force -url http://server/site/subsite
```

You can also uninstall an inactive feature by using the following STSADM.EXE command:

```
STSADM.EXE -o uninstallfeature
           {-filename <relative path to Feature.xml> |
            -name <feature folder> |
            -id <feature Id>}
           [-force]
```

The syntax for the *SampleWebPart* feature would be:

```
STSADM.EXE -o uninstallfeature -name SampleWebPart –force
```

If you prefer to use a Windows PowerShell script, which is the preferred tool starting from SharePoint 2010, to gain the same results, here is the brief syntax for installing and activating a feature:

```
Install-SPFeature FeatureFolderName
Enable-SPFeature FeatureFolderName -Url http://server/site/subsite
```

> **More Information** For a complete reference about all the available Windows PowerShell scripts for managing features and solutions, refer to this page on Microsoft TechNet at *http://technet.microsoft.com/en-us/library/ee906565.aspx.*

If you would like to deactivate and uninstall a feature you can use the following minimal scripts:

```
Disable-SPFeature FeatureFolderName -Url http://server/site/subsite
Uninstall-SPFeature FeatureFolderName
```

All of these scripts offer and support a wide set of parameters; for the sake of simplicity the examples are abridged.

Lastly, to simply activate and deactivate a feature, you can use the web browser UI, if you like to manage features remotely and/or to delegate features management tasks to other users who do not have access to the physical server farm. To manage features through the web browser interface, you need to go to the Site Settings page of the target site, select the Site Actions group, and then Manage Site Features. Here, you can manage website-level features. If you need to manage site collection features, under the Site Collection Administration group, select Site Collection Features. Both of these menu items will lead you to a features management page, from which you can activate or deactivate features.

Figure 8-1 shows the features management page, targeting the site collection features. If your features provide multi-language support, this page will give you the appropriate titles and descriptions, according to the languages configured for the current site and to the current user's language.

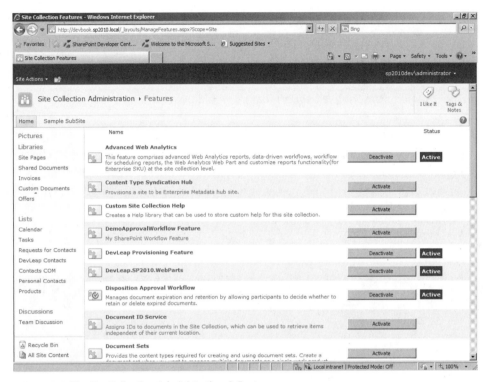

FIGURE 8-1 The Site Collection Administration & Features page.

Figure 8-1 illustrates a list of features that the page offers. You can click the Activate or Deactivate buttons to manage each of them.

You need to have the proper rights to execute these actions, regardless of whether you use the STSADM.EXE tool, or a Windows PowerShell script, or the web UI. Users can activate/ deactivate a feature at the website-level only if they are site owners or higher. To manage a feature targeting a Site Collection, you need to have a Site Collection administrator account. To manage a *WebApplication*-scoped or *Farm*-scoped feature, you need to be a farm administrator.

In the examples thus far, you have copied the features folders by hand to each server. However, it is not a good idea to manually copy these folders in this manner, because this is an error-prone practice. Instead, you can take advantage of a Solution Package, which is a new capability provided by SharePoint, since version 2007.

A Solution Package is a cabinet file (.cab compressed file) with an extension of .wsp—which stands for Windows SharePoint Services Solution Package—provided to automate the process of installing features and customizations. Through a .wsp package, you can deploy a set of one or more features, automatically copying the files and folders to every front-end server from a centralized management console. A .wsp contains a solution-specific manifest file, called solution manifest, which is yet another XML file that defines a set of information through some attributes and some child elements.

Listing 8-5 shows a sample XML file that demonstrates the structure of the solution manifest.

LISTING 8-5 The solution manifest file structure.

```
<Solution
    Description = "Text"
    DeploymentServerType = "ApplicationServer" | "WebFrontEnd"
    ResetWebServer = "TRUE" | "FALSE"
    ResetWebServerModeOnUpgrade = "Recycle" | "StartStop"
    SharePointProductVersion = "Text"
    SolutionId = "Text"
    Title = "Text" >
    <ActivationDependencies />
    <ApplicationResourceFiles />
    <Assemblies />
    <CodeAccessSecurity />
    <DwpFiles />
    <FeatureManifests />
    <Resources />
    <SiteDefinitionManifests />
    <RootFiles />
    <TemplateFiles />
</Solution>
```

The *Solution* element belongs to the same namespace as the *Feature* element, http://schemas.microsoft.com/sharepoint/. Table 8-3 gives a brief description of each attribute of the *Solution* element.

TABLE 8-3 The Attributes Supported by the *Feature* Element

Attribute Name	Description
Description	Optional text that briefly describes the solution.
DeploymentServerType	Describes whether the solution targets a front-end server or an application server. It can take the values *ApplicationServer* or *WebFrontEnd*.
ResetWebServer	An optional *Boolean* attribute with a default value of *False*. If the value is *True* and the package targets a front-end server, then the web server will be reset during deployment of the solution.
ResetWebServerModeOnUpgrade	Specifies the type of reset for the web server. Values are *Recycle*, for a complete recycle of the application pool, and *StartStop*, for a stop and start process. *ResetWebServerModeOnUpgrade* applies only if *ResetWebServer* has a value of *True*.
SharePointProductVersion	Defines the version of SharePoint Foundation in target for the current solution.
SolutionId	Defines the ID of the solution.
Title	Defines the title of the solution.

In addition, a *Solution* tag of a solution manifest can contain some child elements, such as:

- *ActivationDependencies* Specifies a list of solutions on which the activation of the current solutions depend.

- *ApplicationResourceFiles* Specifies the application resource files to include in the solution, referencing local or global resource files.

- *Assemblies* References a set of .NET assemblies, declared with their strong name, to include in the solution deployment. The referenced assemblies will be copied to all front-end servers when deploying the solution.

- *CodeAccessSecurity* Specifies custom code access security policies. To better understand this topic, refer to the "Security Infrastructure" section of this book. In particular, refer to Chapter 23, "Code Access Security and Sandboxed Solutions."

- *DwpFiles* Provides a list of Web Part deployment files (.dwp).

- *FeatureManifests* Provides a list of feature manifests to include in the solution deployment.

- *Resources* Specifies the resources to include in the solution.

- *SiteDefinitionManifests* Includes site definitions in the solution. To learn more about this topic, read Chapter 14.

- *RootFiles*   Declares a list of files to include in the solution that will also be deployed on every server of the farm, in a path relative to the SharePoint14_Root folder.

- *TemplateFiles*   Declares a list of files to include in the solution that will also be deployed on every server of the farm in a path relative to the SharePoint14_Root\TEMPLATE folder.

A .wsp package can be deployed using the STSADM.EXE command line tool by using the following syntax:

```
STSADM.EXE –o addsolution –filename filepath.wsp
```

Otherwise, you can use a Windows PowerShell script with syntax such as the following:

```
Add-SPSolution file.wsp
```

After installing a solution, you need to deploy it to be able to activate/deactivate and upgrade its features. Using the STSADM.EXE command line tool, you can invoke the following command:

```
STSADM.EXE -o deploysolution
        -name <Solution name>
        [-url <virtual server url>]
        [-allcontenturls]
        [-time <time to deploy at>]
        [-immediate]
        [-local]
        [-allowgacdeployment]
        [-allowcaspolicies]
        [-lcid <language>]
        [-force]
```

While using Windows PowerShell, the minimal script that you need to execute to deploy a solution on all web applications of the farm is as follows:

```
Install-SPSolution –Identity file.wsp –GACDeployment -AllWebApplications
```

However, once you have added a solution to the farm, you can also deploy it by using the web browser with the SharePoint Central Administration. Go to the System Settings page, and then click Manage Farm Solutions in the Farm Management group.

Note that regardless of the interface that you will use to deploy a solution, if your farm is not operating on a 24/7 basis, you can schedule the deployment at night to avoid any issues or failures during peak daytime usage. However, if your farm does operate on a 24/7 basis, you should have a set of front-end servers configured for network load balancing so that you can deploy and upgrade solutions on one server at a time, without any service interruption.

Just as you can install and deploy a solution, you can also retract and remove one. To retract a solution, you can still use the SharePoint Central Administration interface, or you can use a Windows PowerShell script, or the STSADM.EXE command line tool.

However, the most interesting thing to know is how to take advantage of solution versioning. Once you have deployed a solution, you can upgrade it through a standard and supported upgrade path. In the next section, you will find some useful information about upgrading solutions.

Finally, with SharePoint 2010, you can create more stable and solid sites by deploying solutions in a sandboxed environment. A sandboxed solution is a .wsp package deployed at the Site Collection level, by a Site Collection Administrator, without requiring an account with farm administrative rights. If a sandboxed solution has a bug or an issue that makes it unstable unsecure, or too demanding for the hardware of your farm, the environment will be able to disable it, keeping the overall Site Collection responsive and functional. Chapter 23 explores in greater depth how sandboxed solutions work in a restricted environment, with the capability to monitor resources consumption and to block unsafe solutions that, for example, consume too many resources, or throw too many unhandled exceptions.

Packaging with Visual Studio 2010

Microsoft Visual Studio 2010 natively provides some new tools that support developers in releasing SharePoint 2010 solutions. Whenever you create a SharePoint 2010 project within Visual Studio 2010, you can choose to manage the project deployment through the Package Explorer and the Package Designer. These tools give you the ability to graphically define the content of the package that will be compiled while building your solution. Figure 8-2 depicts the interface of the Package Explorer for a sample Web Part project.

The interface includes a tree view on the left, in which you can explore the package structure, as well as an editing interface in the body of Visual Studio. From the editing interface you can configure the name of the package, the features that will be put inside it (chosen from the whole set of features available in the current Visual Studio solution), and the order of installation of those features. At the bottom of the editor, there are three tabs (Design, Advanced, and Manifest) that you can use to change the display of the editing section of the Package Explorer. Figure 8-2 shows the editing section in Design view. In the Advanced view, you will be able to provide some custom .NET assemblies (DLLs) that will be deployed by the current package. In Manifest view, you will be able to see the auto-generated XML of the manifest, and you can customize the XML template that is used to generate it to provide any custom tag or attribute that's not defined by default. You can also take full control of the XML manifest content, replacing the auto-generated code with a completely manual version.

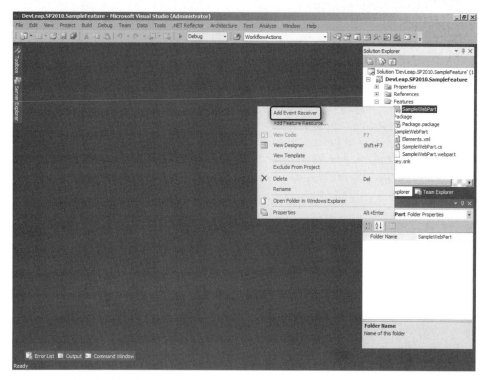

FIGURE 8-2 The Visual Studio 2010 Package Explorer interface.

As well as the Package Explorer, you also have the ability to manage the configuration of each feature included in the package. To configure a feature, double-click it in the Solution Explorer of Visual Studio, or you can click the Edit command available for each feature in the Package Explorer. The feature editor is where you can define the descriptive information of the feature, such as its title and description, as well as configuration and behavioral parameters including the target scope of the feature, the set of items that make up the feature, and any feature activation dependencies. A feature activation dependency gives you the ability to define a sequence of deployment for features. For example, you can create a sequence that prevents you from deploying one specific feature before another specific feature has been deployed. As with the Package Explorer, you can switch to Manifest view so that you can see the XML that describes the current feature. You can also customize the XML using a model or from scratch.

If you right-click a feature item in the Solution Explorer, you can also create custom resource files and you can add feature event receivers, which will be discussed on page 259.

Once you have defined a Package, right-click the Visual Studio project that contains it, and then deploy the .wsp by clicking Deploy. By default, Visual Studio will deploy the package on the server that you chose when you created the project. You can also simply create the package by clicking the Package menu item. The packaging command is useful whenever you need to deploy the .wsp into an external environment and you need to copy the .wsp file from your development environment to the target environment. Lastly, you can also retract a solution from the SharePoint server where you previously deployed it by clicking the Retract menu item. If you deploy a solution on a server where you have already deployed it—for example, because you fixed some bugs and you want to repeat solution testing—the deploy process offered by Visual Studio 2010 will automatically retract the old version and release the new one, deactivating the feature before retraction and activating it again during deployment. From the perspective of SharePoint, it would be better to upgrade the solutions, as you will see in the next section of this chapter. However for the sake of simplicity, Visual Studio retracts it and deploys it again.

Upgrading Solutions and Features

Often, while working in real projects, you need to upgrade your code and customize it during the course of a solution's lifetime. SharePoint 2010 provides a rich set of capabilities to support you while upgrading solutions and features. In fact, since the previous version of SharePoint, you can upgrade a solution to update a .wsp deployment from an older to a current version. To upgrade a solution, you can use the following STSADM.EXE command, as shown in the following:

```
STSADM.EXE -o upgradesolution
          -name <Solution name>
          [-filename <upgrade filename>]
          [-time <time to upgrade at>]
          [-immediate]
          [-local]
          [-allowgacdeployment]
          [-allowcaspolicies]
          [-lcid <language>]
```

Thus, for the *SampleWebPart* deployment package presented earlier in this chapter, the syntax would be the following:

```
STSADM.EXE -o upgradesolution -name SampleWebPart.wsp –allowGacDeployment
```

Otherwise, as usual, you can use a Windows PowerShell script, like the following:

```
Update-SPSolution -Identity file.wsp -LiteralPath c:\file_v2.wsp -GACDeployment
```

SharePoint will update the .wsp package stored in the configuration database and will synchronize every server in the farm with the content of the new package. For example, if your update includes some new files (DLLs, ASPX pages, XSLT files, and so on), the upgrade process will copy them to all of the servers within the farm. At the same time, if your upgrade removes some items that you will no longer use, the upgrade process will remove them from all of the servers.

Furthermore, SharePoint Foundation 2010 provides new elements for the feature's manifest that can be used to upgrade custom features through versioning and declarative upgrade actions. For this purpose, there are new types and members, in the server Object Model, that you will find useful when querying for features at different scopes (*SPWebService*, *SPWebApplcation*, *SPContentDatabase*, *SPSite*) and retrieving their current version. Listing 8-6 illustrates how to query a Site Collection for all the features that need to be upgraded.

LISTING 8-6 Using the new elements in SharePoint Foundation 2010 to query for features that need to be upgraded.

```
using(SPSite site = new SPSite("http://devbook.sp2010.local/")) {

    Boolean needsUpgrade = true;
    SPFeatureQueryResultCollection featuresToUpgrade =
        site.QueryFeatures(SPFeatureScope.Site, needsUpgrade);

    Boolean force = true;
    foreach (SPFeature feature in featuresToUpgrade) {
        feature.Upgrade(force);
    }
}
```

The *QueryFeatures* method of the *SPSite* class can search for features to upgrade, while the *Upgrade* method on each *SPFeature* instance upgrades it effectively. Now, the interesting part of the discussion is what happens during the upgrade process of a feature and how it works.

Every feature has a version number attribute specified in its manifest, so you can upgrade a feature by simply incrementing the version number; for example, you can use the property grid of the designer to release a new .wsp package to deploy the new version via an *upgradesolution* command. Beginning with SharePoint 2010, the feature's manifest has a section in which you can declare upgrade actions to execute during the *Upgrade* process. These upgrade actions are defined inside an *UpgradeActions* configuration element (see Listing 8-1), where you can define some custom actions to execute while upgrading a feature. You can use the *AddContentTypeField* element to define a field (for instance, a site column) that will be automatically added to a content-type, eventually pushing the modification to inheriting content types and lists. You can also specify some element manifests to apply during upgrade by using the *ApplyElementManifests* tag together with its children elements, *ElementFile* and *ElementManifest*. Using this last element, you could create some new contents like list definitions, site columns, content types, list instances, custom pages, an so forth. You can also specify a mapping between old and new files, using the *MapFile* element. Lastly, if you need to execute some custom code during the upgrade process, you can configure the *CustomUpgradeAction* tag, which will reference a custom upgrade action defined in a feature receiver. You will learn more about feature receivers in the next section.

Occasionally, you might need to release a version upgrade in various environments that requires different versions of the same feature. For example, imagine having a new feature with a current version of 2.0.0.0 that you want to update on a couple of customers' farms, called Farm1 and Farm2. Farm1 is currently version 1.0.0.0 of your feature, while Farm2 is running version 1.5.0.0. In such a scenario, you should define a new package with a path to upgrade your feature from version 1.0.0.0 to version 2.0.0.0, and from version 1.5.0.0 to version 2.0.0.0.

Luckily, the new features' manifest schema supports declaration of version ranges via the *VersionRange* element—a child of the *UpgradeActions* element. Thus, you can define two different upgrade paths, based on the initial version of the feature that you want to upgrade. Listing 8-7 shows an example of feature manifest that satisfies this scenario.

LISTING 8-7 A feature manifest that supports versioning with different upgrade paths for different versions.

```
<Feature xmlns="http://schemas.microsoft.com/sharepoint/" Version="1.0.0.0"
Title="$Resources:FeatureTitle" Description="$Resources:FeatureDescription"
Id="c46c270e-e722-4aa0-82ba-b66c8dd61f4e" Scope="Site">
  <UpgradeActions>
    <VersionRange BeginVersion="0.0.0.0" EndVersion="1.5.0.0">
      <MapFile FromPath="Old.aspx" ToPath="New.aspx" />
    </VersionRange>
    <VersionRange BeginVersion="1.5.0.0" EndVersion="2.0.0.0">
      <MapFile FromPath="New.aspx" ToPath="Latest.aspx" />
    </VersionRange>
  </UpgradeActions>
  <ElementManifests>
    <ElementManifest Location="SampleWebPart\Elements.xml" />
    <ElementFile Location="SampleWebPart\SampleWebPart.webpart" />
    <ElementFile Location="Resources\Resources.resx" />
    <ElementFile Location="Resources\Resources.it-IT.resx" />
  </ElementManifests>
</Feature>
```

The *VersionRange* element accepts two attributes for the *BeginVersion* and *EndVersion*. The former is a lower inclusive limit, while the latter is an upper exclusive limit. Thus, the first *VersionRange* defined in Listing 8-6 refers to features with a version greater than or equal to 0.0.0.0 and lower than 1.5.0.0, whereas the second *VersionRange* matches features with a version greater than or equal to 1.5.0.0 and lower than 2.0.0.0. In this example, the feature simply maps an old .aspx file to a newer one. Of course, during a feature's upgrade process, you can do whatever you want, because you can invoke custom SharePoint code using a custom feature receiver.

More Information For further details about upgrading features, read the section on MSDN Online at *http://msdn.microsoft.com/en-us/library/aa544511.aspx*.

Feature Receivers

A feature receiver is a class that executes some custom code upon the occurrence of specific lifecycle-related events, usually by making use of the SharePoint Server Object Model. Every feature receiver adheres to the architecture of the event receivers of SharePoint, which are described in Chapter 12 of this book. A feature receiver can trap the following events:

- **Feature Activation**   Occurs when a feature has been activated
- **Feature Deactivating**   Occurs while a feature is deactivating
- **Feature Installation**   Occurs when a feature has been installed
- **Feature Uninstalling**   Occurs while a feature is uninstalling
- **Feature Upgrading**   Occurs while a feature is upgrading

To implement your own feature receivers, you need to define a new class that inherits from the base abstract class, *SPFeatureReceiver*, which is defined in the *Microsoft.SharePoint* namespace. Listing 8-8 presents the definition of the *SPFeatureReceiver* abstract class.

LISTING 8-8 The definition of the base abstract class SPFeatureReceiver.

```csharp
public abstract class SPFeatureReceiver {
    public SPFeatureReceiver();

    public virtual void FeatureActivated(SPFeatureReceiverProperties properties);
    public virtual void FeatureDeactivating(SPFeatureReceiverProperties properties);
    public virtual void FeatureInstalled(SPFeatureReceiverProperties properties);
    public virtual void FeatureUninstalling(SPFeatureReceiverProperties properties);
    public virtual void FeatureUpgrading(SPFeatureReceiverProperties properties,
  string upgradeActionName, IDictionary<string, string> parameters);
}
```

Each of the virtual methods accepts an argument of type *SPFeatureReceiverProperties*, which allows accessing information about the target feature, its definition, and the current site. Listing 8-9 declares of the *SPFeatureReceiverProperties* class.

LISTING 8-9 The definition of the *SPFeatureReceiverProperties* class.

```csharp
public sealed class SPFeatureReceiverProperties : IDisposable {

    public SPFeatureDefinition Definition { get; internal set; }
    public SPFeature Feature { get; }
    public SPSite UserCodeSite { get; }
}
```

Through the properties of this class, you can do practically anything that you want, writing custom code to implement everything that is not already available through standard feature elements.

> **Note** Although the *SPFeatureReceiverProperties* class implements the *IDisposable* interface, you should not dispose of it directly; the infrastructure code of SharePoint Foundation already handles the disposal of instances of this type.

To create a feature receiver, you need to implement the receiver class, build its assembly, put it into the GAC, and declare the *ReceiverAssembly* and *ReceiverClass* attributes in a feature manifest XML file. Listing 8-10 illustrates an example of a feature manifest with a receiver declaration.

LISTING 8-10 The manifest of a feature with a custom feature receiver.

```xml
<Feature xmlns="http://schemas.microsoft.com/sharepoint/" Version="1.0.0.0"
Title="DevLeap Sample Web Part"
Description="This feature deploys a sample Web Part."
Id="c46c270e-e722-4aa0-82ba-b66c8dd61f4e"
ReceiverAssembly="DevLeap.SP2010.SampleFeature, Version=1.0.0.0,
  Culture=neutral, PublicKeyToken=b001133e0647953d"
ReceiverClass="DevLeap.SP2010.SampleFeature.SampleWebPartEventReceiver"
Scope="Site">
  <ElementManifests>
    <ElementManifest Location="SampleWebPart\Elements.xml" />
    <ElementFile Location="SampleWebPart\SampleWebPart.webpart" />
  </ElementManifests>
</Feature>
```

> **Note** Both the values of the *ReceiverAssembly* and the *ReceiverClass* attributes in Listing 8-10 need to be defined on a single of code.

Listing 8-11 shows you a sample feature receiver, creating a list instance when the feature is activated, and deleting the list instance while the feature is deactivating.

LISTING 8-11 A sample feature receiver that handles *FeatureActivated* and *FeatureDeactivating* events.

```csharp
public class SampleWebPartEventReceiver : SPFeatureReceiver {

    public override void FeatureActivated(SPFeatureReceiverProperties properties) {
        // Get the parent of the feature
        // Current feature has a Site scope, thus the Parent
        // should be a Site Collection
        SPSite site = properties.Feature.Parent as SPSite;
```

```
                if (site != null) {
                    SPWeb web = site.RootWeb;

                    // Check to see if the list already exists
                    try {
                        SPList targetList = web.Lists["Sample List"];
                    }
                    catch (ArgumentException) {
                        // The list does not exist, thus you can create it
                        Guid listId = web.Lists.Add("Sample List",
                            "Sample List for SampleWebPart", SPListTemplateType.Events);
                        SPList list = web.Lists[listId];
                        list.OnQuickLaunch = true;
                        list.Update();
                    }
                }
            }

            public override void FeatureDeactivating(SPFeatureReceiverProperties properties) {
                // Get the parent of the feature
                // Current feature has a Site scope, thus the Parent
                // should be a Site Collection
                SPSite site = properties.Feature.Parent as SPSite;

                if (site != null) {
                    SPWeb web = site.RootWeb;

                    // Check to see if the list already exists
                    try {
                        SPList list = web.Lists["Sample List"];
                        list.Delete();
                    }
                    catch (ArgumentException) {
                        // The list does not exist, thus you don't need to delete it
                    }
                }
            }
        }
```

Listing 8-11 illustrates that you should access the context of your feature through the *Feature. Parent* property of the current *SPFeatureReceiverProperties* argument. Depending on the scope of your feature, the *Parent* property could be the whole farm (*SPFarm*), a single web application (*SPWebApplication*), a Site Collection (*SPSite*), or a single website (*SPWeb*). It is up to you to know the target scope of your feature, and consequently determine the appropriate type to be hosted by the *Parent* property. In Listing 8-11, the scope of the feature is a Site Collection; thus, the *SPSite* property is used. If you are implementing a feature receiver that creates some contents during activation, it's a good habit to delete those contents while deactivating. However, there are times when it's a good idea to leave data upon deactivation of a feature so that you don't lose critical data for the end user. Additionally, if your feature is activated and deactivated many times during the lifecycle of your solutions, it's possible that you could activate it on a site where the contents created by the *FeatureActivated* event already exist. To prevent this, the code of Listing 8-11 checks for any previously existing list instance, prior to creating it.

Microsoft Visual Studio 2010 provides a shortcut for creating feature event receivers. To access it, go to the Solution Explorer and right-click a feature item within the Features folder of your SharePoint project to open the contextual menu. There, you can select the Add Event Receiver menu item, which will create all the plumbing code for you. You will only need to write the code of the receiver's methods. Figure 8-3 shows the contextual menu of a feature in the Solution Explorer.

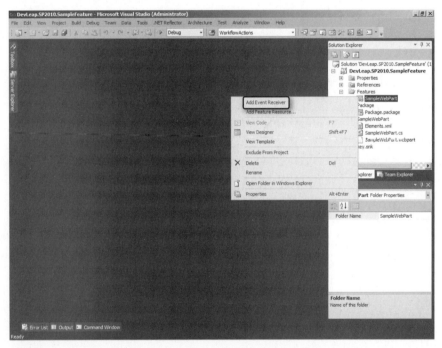

FIGURE 8-3 The Add Event Receiver menu item in the contextual menu of a feature in Microsoft Visual Studio 2010.

 Important Be very careful when you define error handling code, while implementing custom feature receivers. Any unhandled exception could lead to instability of your solution as well as blocking your feature deployment or removal.

Handling *FeatureUpgrading* Events

One feature receiver event that deserves a dedicated section is *FeatureUpgrading*. This is a new event, introduced in SharePoint 2010 for the purpose of handling features' upgrades. This method targets all situations in which you need to upgrade a feature executing some custom code. If you override the *FeatureUpgrading* method, you will receive an instance of the *SPFeatureReceiverProperties* type, as well as with all the other methods of the feature receivers. However, you will also get an argument of type *String* with name *upgrade-ActionName*, and an argument of type *IDictionary<String, String>* with name *parameters*. The values for these arguments can be defined in the feature manifest file, within the *UpgradeActions* section of the file schema (see Listing 8-7). The following is an example of this method in practice.

Suppose that you have deployed the *SampleWebPart* feature version 1.0.0.0 in your environment. Later, you want to upgrade it to version 2.0.0.0. This new version of your Web Part needs to change (by code) the configuration of the list instance that you created in the *FeatureActivated* event in Listing 8-11. Assume that your upgrade method changes the *OnQuickLaunch* status of the "Sample List," and configures the *ContentTypesEnabled* property. Listing 8-12 shows the feature manifest with the configuration of the custom upgrade action.

LISTING 8-12 The feature manifest file with the configuration of the custom upgrade action.

```
<Feature xmlns="http://schemas.microsoft.com/sharepoint/" Version="2.0.0.0"
Title="DevLeap Sample Web Part"
Description="This feature deploys a sample Web Part."
Id="c46c270e-e722-4aa0-82ba-b66c8dd61f4e" ReceiverAssembly="DevLeap.SP2010.
SampleFeature, Version=1.0.0.0, Culture=neutral, PublicKeyToken=b001133e0647953d"
ReceiverClass="DevLeap.SP2010.SampleFeature.Features.SampleWebPart.
SampleWebPartEventReceiver" Scope="Site">
  <UpgradeActions>
    <CustomUpgradeAction Name="UpgradeSampleList">
      <Parameters>
        <Parameter Name="ShowOnQuickLaunch">False</Parameter>
        <Parameter Name="EnableContentTypes">True</Parameter>
      </Parameters>
    </CustomUpgradeAction>
  </UpgradeActions>
  <ElementManifests>
    <ElementManifest Location="SampleWebPart\Elements.xml" />
    <ElementFile Location="SampleWebPart\SampleWebPart.webpart" />
  </ElementManifests>
</Feature>
```

Note Both the values of the *ReceiverAssembly* and the *ReceiverClass* attributes in Listing 8-12 need to be defined on a single of code.

The custom upgrade action is defined using a *Name* attribute and a set of *Parameter* elements. Meanwhile, Listing 8-13 demonstrates the implementation of the *FeatureUpgrading* method, which uses the custom upgrade action configuration.

LISTING 8-13 Using the *FeatureUpgrading* method implementation to handle the custom upgrade action.

```
public override void FeatureUpgrading(SPFeatureReceiverProperties properties,
    string upgradeActionName,
    System.Collections.Generic.IDictionary<string, string> parameters) {

    // Get the parent of the feature
    // Current feature has a Site scope, thus the Parent
    // should be a Site Collection
    SPSite site = properties.Feature.Parent as SPSite;

    if (site != null) {
        // Check the type of upgrade action
        if (upgradeActionName == "UpgradeSampleList") {
            // Extract and convert the properties
            Boolean showOnQuickLaunch =
                Boolean.Parse(parameters["ShowOnQuickLaunch"]);
            Boolean enableContentTypes =
                Boolean.Parse(parameters["EnableContentTypes"]);

            SPWeb web = site.RootWeb;

            // Check to see if the list already exists
            try {
                SPList list = web.Lists["Sample List"];
                list.OnQuickLaunch = showOnQuickLaunch;
                list.ContentTypesEnabled = enableContentTypes;
                list.Update();
            }
            catch (ArgumentException) {
                // The list does not exist, thus you cannot upgrade it
            }
        }
    }
}
```

The method invocation receives the *Name* attribute of the *CustomUpgradeAction* inside the *upgradeActionName* argument, and the set of *Parameter* elements through the parameters dictionary. Now the upgrade code can do whatever it needs to do to upgrade the feature, based on these arguments.

Summary

In this chapter, you have seen what features and solutions are and how to take advantage of them to deploy customization and custom code. Specifically, you have seen how to package features in .wsp packages and how to deploy them, as well as how to upgrade features using the new capabilities provided with SharePoint 2010. In future chapters, you will dig deeper into implementing some of the main features that are useful when developing and customizing SharePoint solutions.

Chapter 9
Extending the User Interface

This chapter describes how to extend the user interface of Microsoft SharePoint 2010. In particular, you will see how to customize menus, ribbons, controls, and pages. You will see also how to work with the new dialog framework. This chapter is important if you want to be able to provide your users or customers with a custom user interface that is compliant with the standard SharePoint behavior, while simultaneously satisfying the requirements of intranet and extranet solutions, as well as Internet publishing sites.

Custom Actions

The first area of customization that you will address is creating custom actions in the standard SharePoint user interface. Custom actions are features that can extend or change the standard behavior of any of the following items: menu items, link menus of administrative pages, and Ribbons. The Ribbon is important enough to warrant a dedicated section in this chapter (beginning on page 279); all other custom actions will be covered beginning here. Recall from Chapter 8, "SharePoint Features and Solutions," the types of custom action features that you can create are:

- *CustomAction* Creates a new custom action to define a new control on a Ribbon bar, a new menu item on a standard menu, or a new link on a settings page.

- *CustomActionGroup* Creates a new group of custom actions for better usability from the perspective of the end user.

- *HideCustomAction* Hides an existing custom action defined by another custom action or implemented by default in SharePoint.

In the following pages we will delve into these items.

The *CustomAction* Element

The definition of a *CustomAction* requires the declaration of a feature element manifest, based on the XML structure, as illustrated in Listing 9-1.

LISTING 9-1 The *CustomAction* element structure.

```
<CustomAction
  RequiredAdmin = "Delegated | Farm | Machine"
  ControlAssembly = "Text"
  ControlClass = "Text"
  ControlSrc = "Text"
  Description = "Text"
  FeatureId = "Text"
  GroupId = "Text"
  Id = "Text"
  ImageUrl = "Text"
  Location = "Text"
  RegistrationId = "Text"
  RegistrationType = "Text"
  RequireSiteAdministrator = "TRUE" | "FALSE"
  Rights = "Text"
  RootWebOnly = "TRUE" | "FALSE"
  ScriptSrc = "Text"
  ScriptBlock = "Text"
  Sequence = "Integer"
  ShowInLists = "TRUE" | "FALSE"
  ShowInReadOnlyContentTypes = "TRUE" | "FALSE"
  ShowInSealedContentTypes = "TRUE" | "FALSE"
  Title = "Text"
  UIVersion = "Integer">
    <UrlAction />
    <CommandUIExtension />
</CustomAction>
```

The *CustomAction* element is made of a set of attributes and accepts a couple of optional children elements. Table 9-1 describes each available attribute.

TABLE 9-1 The Attributes Supported by the *CustomAction* Element

Attribute Name	Description
RequiredAdmin	Optional *Text* attribute that specifies the rights required for the custom action to apply. Supported values are *Delegated*, *Farm*, and *Machine*.
ControlAssembly	Optional *Text* attribute used to declare a custom assembly full name, hosting a control for rendering the custom action with code running on the server side.
ControlClass	Used to declare a custom class, implementing a control for rendering the custom action with code running on the server side.
ControlSrc	Optional *Text* attribute that specifies the relative URL of an .ascx file that corresponds to the source of the custom action.
Description	Optional *Text* attribute with which you can provide a long description for the action.

Attribute Name	Description
FeatureId	Optional *Text* attribute that specifies the ID of the feature associated with the custom action.
GroupId	Optional *Text* attribute that declares the group that will contain the custom action. For a complete reference of all the available groups and locations, refer to MSDN online at *http://msdn.microsoft.com/en-us/library/bb802730.aspx*.
Id	Optional *Text* attribute that specifies the ID of the custom action. This can be a GUID or a string that uniquely identifies the custom action.
ImageUrl	Declares the relative URL of an image that represents an icon for the custom action.
Location	Specifies the location of the custom action. This is a value taken from a predefined list of locations or from a custom set of locations.
RegistrationId	Optional *Text* attribute that declares the ID of the target list, content type, or file type associated with the custom action.
RegistrationType	Optional *Text* attribute that declares the type of registration the action is targeting. *RegistrationType* works together with the *RegistrationId* attribute, and can assume one of the following values: *None*, *List*, *ContentType*, *ProgId*, or *FileType*.
RequireSiteAdministrator	Optional *Boolean* attribute that specifies whether the action will be displayed to all users, or only to site Administrators.
Rights	Optional *Text* attribute that defines the minimum set of rights required to view the current custom action. If it is not specified, the action will be visible to anyone. It can specify one or more rights, comma separated, selected from the list of available rights defined in standard base permission of SharePoint. Possible values are *ViewListItems*, *ManageAlerts*, *ManageLists*, and so on. For a complete reference of all the base permissions available in SharePoint, refer to the document, "SPBasePermissions Enumeration," on MSDN Online at *http://msdn.microsoft.com/en-us/library/microsoft.sharepoint.spbasepermissions.aspx*.
RootWebOnly	Optional *Boolean* attribute, valid only for sandboxed solutions, that specifies if the action must be only on root websites.
ScriptSrc	Optional *Text* attribute that defines the relative URL of a script to download and execute. *ScriptSrc* works only in conjunction with a *Location* attribute with a value of *ScriptLink*. It is very useful whenever you need to reference external JavaScript source files for implementing custom behaviors.
ScriptBlock	Optional *Text* attribute that defines the ECMAScript source code of a script to execute. *ScriptBlock* works only in conjunction with a *Location* attribute with a value of *ScriptLink*.
Sequence	Optional *Integer* attribute that defines the ordinal position of the custom action, within its group.

Attribute Name	Description
ShowInLists	Deprecated optional *Boolean* attribute that specifies whether the action will be shown in the page for managing content types.
ShowInReadOnlyContentTypes	Optional *Boolean* attribute that specifies whether the action will be displayed only for the page for managing read-only content types.
ShowInSealedContentTypes	Optional *Boolean* attribute that specifies whether the action will be displayed only for the page for managing sealed content types.
Title	Required *Text* attribute to specify the title of the action. *Title* will be used in the user interface to present the action to the end user.
UIVersion	Optional *Integer* value to define the version of the UI in which the action will be rendered.

In addition, a *CustomAction* tag can contain some children elements:

- *UrlAction* Defines a destination URL for when the end user clicks the custom action.

- *CommandUIExtension* Defines a complex UI extension, typically a Ribbon. This will be discussed in the next section, "Ribbons," beginning on page 279.

The most-used and basic attributes are those for defining the *Id*, the *Title*, the *Location* where you want the action to appear, and the *RegistrationType*, together with the *RegistrationId*. For example, if you want your action to be displayed when the end user clicks the contextual menu of a document (also called the Edit Control Block [ECB] menu), you can define a custom action for the document libraries of a site like the one illustrated in Listing 9-2.

LISTING 9-2 A *CustomAction* targeting the Edit Control Block of items in a Documents library.

```
<CustomAction
  Location="EditControlBlock"
  RegistrationType="List"
  RegistrationId="101"
  Id="DevLeap.CustomActions.DemoECB.SampleAction"
  Title="Sample Action"
  ImageUrl="/_layouts/images/DevLeap.SP2010.UIExtensions/SampleIcon.gif"
  Description="Sample custom action.">
  <UrlAction Url="javascript:window.alert('You clicked the Sample Action!');"/>
</CustomAction>
```

The *Location* attribute specifies that the action will be shown in the ECB menu. The *RegistrationType* attribute targets a specific *List*, while the *RegistrationId* explicitly defines the list type (101 = "Document Library"). Notice the child element, *UrlAction*, which defines a destination URL for when the end user clicks the menu item. In this first example, the custom action simply shows an alert. Figure 9-1 depicts how the action looks in the web browser.

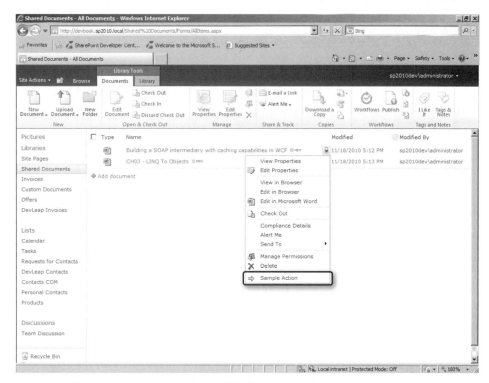

FIGURE 9-1 The custom action shown in the ECB of a document item.

Often, you need to define a custom action targeting not just a list, but a specific content type, regardless of the list in which it is contained. For example, suppose that you have a custom content type defining a document of type *invoice* (call it *DevLeapInvoice*). This content type needs to have an identifying unique ID, which in this example will have a value of 0x0101008D841CAC0C7F474288965287B30061DC.

> **Note** In Chapter 10, "Data Provisioning," you will learn how to programmatically define site columns, content types, and list definitions. You will also see what a content type ID is and how to define it. For the purpose of this chapter, simply assume that a content type ID is a unique ID for identifying a specific content type.

The *DevLeapInvoice* content type has some custom metadata fields to define the invoice number, a description, and a status that can assume some predefined values (*Draft*, *Approved*, *Sent*, and *Archived*). Figure 9-2 illustrates the edit form of this kind of document.

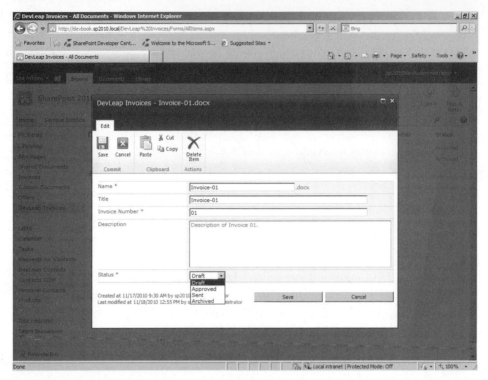

FIGURE 9-2 The edit form of a *DevLeapInvoice* item instance.

Listing 9-3 demonstrates a custom action, still targeting the ECB, that will be shown only in the ECB of items with a content type of *DevLeapInvoice*. The action allows archiving a single invoice, changing its *Status* field to a value of *Archived*.

LISTING 9-3 A *CustomAction* targeting the ECB of items with content type of *DevLeapInvoice*.

```
<CustomAction
  Location="EditControlBlock"
  RegistrationType="ContentType"
  RegistrationId="0x0101008d841cac0c7f474288965287b30061dc"
  Id="DevLeap.CustomActions.Invoices.Archive"
  Title="Archive Invoice"
  Rights="ViewListItems,EditListItems"
  ImageUrl="/_layouts/images/DevLeap.SP2010.UIExtensions/IconArchive.gif"
  Description="Approve this Invoice.">
  <UrlAction Url="~site/_layouts/DevLeap.SP2010.UIExtensions/
DevLeapInvoiceChangeStatus.aspx?ItemId={ItemId}&amp;ListId={ListId}&amp;
                                  Status=Archived" />
</CustomAction>
```

The only substantial difference between Listing 9-3 and Listing 9-2 is the *RegistrationType* attribute, which now targets a *ContentType*, as well as the *RegistrationId* that now defines the ID of the target content type instead of the ID of a list template. The code sample of Listing 9-3 also introduces the *Rights* attribute, with which you can archive invoices only to users who have the *ViewListItems* and *EditListItems* permissions assigned.

Additionally, the *UrlAction* child element defined in Listing 9-3 declares a URL of a custom application page, instead of a piece of JavaScript, such as in Listing 9-2. In the section, "Application Pages" on page 297, you will learn how to deploy custom application pages. Disregard the page itself and focus your attention on the *Url* attribute of the *UrlAction* element. This attribute can link to any kind of URL and can contain tokens that will be replaced by the environment during page rendering. These tokens are:

- *~site*   Website (*SPWeb*) relative link.

- *~sitecollection*   Site collection (*SPSite*) relative link.

- *{ItemId}*   Integer ID that represents the item within a list.

- *{ItemUrl}*   URL of the current item. This only works for documents in libraries.

- *{ListId}*   ID (GUID) of the list on which the action is currently working.

- *{SiteUrl}*   URL of the website (*SPWeb*).

- *{RecurrenceId}*   Recurrence index in when related to recurring event items.

Finally, you can use any valid JavaScript code block.

In Listing 9-3, the *Url* attribute uses the *{ItemId}* and *{ListId}* tokens, because it targets the ECB menu of a single item, so it passes the item ID and list ID to the target page as *QueryString* parameters.

The ECB menu isn't the only location suitable for defining custom actions. There are many other locations available. Table 9-2 lists the most useful ones.

> **More Information** For a complete list of all the available locations, refer to the document, "Default Custom Action Locations and IDs," on MSDN Online at *http://msdn.microsoft.com/en-us/library/bb802730.aspx*.

TABLE 9-2 The Most Useful Locations for Defining Custom Actions

Location	Group ID	Description
DisplayFormToolbar	Not applicable	Corresponds to the display form toolbar of lists.
EditControlBlock	Not applicable	Corresponds to the per-item ECB menu.
EditFormToolbar	Not applicable	Corresponds to the edit form toolbar of lists.
Microsoft.SharePoint.SiteSettings	Customization	Look And Feel section of the Site Settings page.
	Galleries	Galleries section of the Site Settings page.
	SiteAdministration	Site Administration section of the Site Settings page.
	SiteCollectionAdmin	Site Collection Administration section of the Site Settings page.
	UsersAndPermissions	Users And Permissions section of the Site Settings page.
Microsoft.SharePoint.StandardMenu	ActionsMenu	Actions menu in list and document library views.
	ActionsMenuForSurvey	Site Actions menu for surveys.
	NewMenu	New menu in list and document library views.
	SettingsMenu	Settings menu in list and document library views.
	SettingsMenuForSurvey	Site Settings links for surveys.
	SiteActions	Site Actions menu.
	UploadMenu	Upload menu in document library views.
	ViewSelectorMenu	View selection menu for changing views provided on the list editing tab of the Ribbon.
NewFormToolbar	Not applicable	Corresponds to the new form toolbar of lists.
ViewToolbar	Not applicable	Corresponds to the toolbar in list views.

Microsoft also documents the *Id* values for many of the previously-defined custom actions, with which you can override standard menu items with custom items of your own.

The *CustomActionGroup* Element

Another useful element for defining custom actions is the *CustomActionGroup*. Using this elements, you can define groups of actions; it is typically used when defining custom sections in the configuration pages, such as the Site Settings page or the pages of the Central Administration. In fact, you can also extend and override administrative pages, not only end user UI elements. Listing 9-4 shows the structure of the *CustomActionGroup* element.

LISTING 9-4 The *CustomActionGroup* element structure.

```
<CustomActionGroup
  Description = "Text"
  Id = "Text"
  Location = "Text"
  Sequence = "Integer"
  Title = "Text">
</CustomActionGroup>
```

The *CustomActionGroup* element is mainly descriptive (for the group it defines). It does not have any child element because the only purpose of this element is to declare a new group, which will be referenced by other custom actions. Table 9-3 presents a brief description of the available attributes.

TABLE 9-3 The Attributes Supported by the *CustomActionGroup* Element

Attribute Name	Description
RequiredAdmin	Optional *Text* attribute that specifies the rights required for the custom action group to apply. Values supported are *Delegated*, *Farm*, and *Machine*.
Description	Optional *Text* attribute with which you can provide a long description for the action group.
Id	Required *Text* attribute that specifies the ID of the custom action group. It can be a GUID or a string that uniquely identifies the custom action group.
ImageUrl	Optional *Text* attribute that declares the relative URL of an image representing an icon for the custom action.
Location	Required *Text* attribute that specifies the location of the custom action group. *Location* is a value taken from a predefined list of locations or from a custom set of locations.
Sequence	Optional *Integer* value that defines the ordinal position of the custom action group, within the set of groups.
Title	Required *Text* attribute that specifies the title of the action. *Title* will be used in user interface to present the action group to the end user.

Listing 9-5 illustrates how to use the *CustomActionGroup* element to define a new section in the "Site Settings" administrative page. Notice the *CustomAction* element that uses a value of *Microsoft.SharePoint.SiteSettings* for the *Location* attribute, and the value of the custom action group's *Id* for the *GroupId* attribute.

LISTING 9-5 A *CustomActionGroup* element extending the Site Settings administrative page.

```
<CustomActionGroup
  Location="Microsoft.SharePoint.SiteSettings"
  Id="DevLeap.CustomActions.Invoices.Settings"
  Description="View Invoices Settings"
  Title="Invoices Management"
  ImageUrl="/_layouts/images/DevLeap.SP2010.UIExtensions/DevLeap-Icon-48x48.png" />

<CustomAction
  Location="Microsoft.SharePoint.SiteSettings"
  GroupId="DevLeap.CustomActions.Invoices.Settings"
  Id="DevLeap.CustomActions.Invoices.SampleSettings"
  Title="Invoices Sample Settings Page"
  Description="Go to a custom page for managing Invoices' settings.">
  <UrlAction Url="~site/_layouts/DevLeap.SP2010.UIExtensions/InvoicesSettings.aspx" />
</CustomAction>
```

Figure 9-3 shows the customized Site Settings administrative page in action.

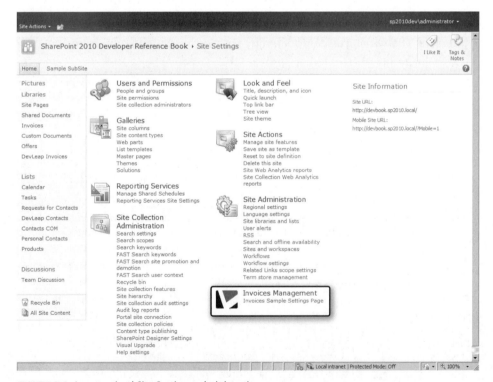

FIGURE 9-3 A customized Site Settings administrative page.

The *HideCustomAction* Element

The last element available for customizing UI actions is the *HideCustomAction.* Using this element, you can hide existing actions, regardless of whether they are standard and native actions or custom actions defined by you or someone else. Be aware though that not all native actions can be hidden. Listing 9-6 shows you the structure of the *HideCustomAction* element.

LISTING 9-6 The *HideCustomAction* element structure.

```
<HideCustomAction
  GroupId = "Text"
  HideActionId = "Text"
  Id = "Text"
  Location = "Text">
</HideCustomAction>
```

This element simply defines the information about the action to hide. Table 9-4 gives you a brief explanation of the available attributes.

TABLE 9-4 The Attributes Supported by the *HideCustomAction* Element

Attribute Name	Description
GroupId	Optional *Text* attribute that specifies the group to which the action to hide belongs.
HideActionId	Optional *Text* attribute that specifies the ID of the action to hide.
Id	Optional *Text* attribute that specifies the ID of the current hide custom action.
Location	Optional *Text* attribute that specifies the location of the custom action to hide.

Listing 9-7 presents an example of the *HideCustomAction* element being used to hide the Site Theme menu item in the Look And Feel group of the Site Settings page.

LISTING 9-7 The *HideCustomAction* element structure.

```
<HideCustomAction
  Id="DevLeap.CustomActions.HideThemeFromSettings"
  Location="Microsoft.SharePoint.SiteSettings"
  GroupId="Customization"
  HideActionId="Theme" />
```

In Listing 9-7, the *Location, GroupId,* and *HideActionId* attributes correspond to those identifying the Site Theme action. Figure 9-4 shows the result of this action, comparing the page before applying the customization, and then after.

FIGURE 9-4 The Look and Feel group before (left) and after (right) hiding the Site Theme action.

Server-Side Custom Actions

You can create custom actions that define their content dynamically by using server-side code, instead of using an XML declaration. To define these kind of actions, you need to declare a *CustomAction* element within a feature element manifest, providing a value for *ControlAssembly* and *ControlClass* attributes. These attributes will need to reference the assembly and the full type name of a class inheriting from the base class *System.Web.UI.WebControls.WebControl* and building a specific set of controls inside the *CreateChildControls* method override. Listing 9-8 illustrates an example of a custom action referencing a custom *ControlClass*.

LISTING 9-8 The *CustomAction* referencing a custom *ControlClass*.

```
<CustomAction
  Location="Microsoft.SharePoint.StandardMenu"
  GroupId="SiteActions"
  ControlAssembly="DevLeap.SP2010.UIExtensions, Version=1.0.0.0,
    Culture=neutral, PublicKeyToken=3b7c6076bf78362f"
  ControlClass="DevLeap.SP2010.UIExtensions.SwitchToMobileMode"
  Id="DevLeap.CustomActions.SwitchToMobileMode">
</CustomAction>
</CustomAction>
```

Note Both the values of the *ControlAssembly* and the *ControlClass* attributes in Listing 9-8 need to be defined on a single of code.

The action targets the Site Actions menu and allows switching the site to the mobile rendering mode. Of course, you could write this action without a custom class, but this is just to give you an example of the capability.

Listing 9-9 displays the sample implementation of the *ControlClass*, which internally generates the menu item.

LISTING 9-9 The class referenced by the *CustomClass* attribute of the custom action of Listing 9-8.

```
public class SwitchToMobileMode : System.Web.UI.WebControls.WebControl {
    protected override void CreateChildControls() {
        SPWeb web = SPControl.GetContextWeb(HttpContext.Current);

        MenuItemTemplate switchToMobile = new MenuItemTemplate();
        switchToMobile.Text = "Switch to mobile mode";
        switchToMobile.Description =
          "Switches the current site rendering mode to mobile";
        switchToMobile.ImageUrl =
          "/_layouts/images/DevLeap.SP2010.UIExtensions/Mobile32x32.png";
        switchToMobile.ClientOnClickNavigateUrl =
          String.Format("{0}?Mobile=1", web.Url);

        this.Controls.Add(switchToMobile);
    }
}
```

Listing 9-9 illustrates that you can instantiate a *MenuItemTemplate* class, which represents a single menu item. You can then configure its descriptive properties, such as *Text*, *Description*, *ImageUrl*, and so on. However, the fundamental properties are those related to the behavior of the menu item within the user interface. You can configure the *ClientOnClickNavigateUrl* if all you need is to define an URL to navigate to when the menu is clicked by the end user. Additionally, you can configure the *ClientOnClickScript* property to configure an ECMAScript code block to execute when the menu entry is clicked. Lastly, to set the control ID and parameter for a post-back event, you can assign the *ClientOnClickUsingPostBackEvent* property. In this last scenario, you should handle the post-back event yourself; for example, implementing the *System.Web.UI.IPostBackEventHandler* interface in the control class. Eventually, you can also configure the *ClientOnClickPostBackConfirmation* property to provide a confirmation message that will be displayed to the end user, just before handling the post-back event. Figure 9-5 shows the result of the sample in Listing 9-9.

FIGURE 9-5 The custom action defined using a *MenuItemTemplate* on the server side.

Another type of menu that you can instantiate within custom code is the *SubMenuTemplate*, which represents the parent of a hierarchical menu.

Regardless of the type of menu items you define within your *CustomClass* implementation, it is mandatory to define the class as a *SafeControl* for SharePoint. Details about *SafeControl* items were presented at the end of Chapter 7, "Advanced Web Parts."

> **Note**   While working with Microsoft Visual Studio 2010, Web Parts are automatically configured in the solution's manifest file as *SafeControl* items. However, the custom class shown in Listing 9-9, as well as any other control class that is not a Web Part, will not be automatically registered as a *SafeControl*. To force registration of the class as a *SafeControl*—using Visual Studio 2010— you can open the feature designer of any feature element of your package; for example, the one defining the custom actions. There, in the property grid panel, you will find a Safe Control Entries property of type *collection* that will support you in configuring one or more custom *SafeControl* entries.

Ribbons

The Ribbon is one of the most visible and evident new features of SharePoint 2010. Having a web-based solution with a command bar that makes use of Ribbons, such as Office clients do, is a great way to support and involve users who are already accustomed to using such tools.

SharePoint 2010 provides a native set of Ribbons, but any developer can define specific *CustomAction* elements to define his own Ribbon commands, groups, and tabs. In this section, you will learn how.

Ribbon Command

The first kinds of Ribbon elements that you can define are Ribbon commands. They represent single items to place in a previously existing Ribbon tab and group. For example, think about the code sample you saw in Listing 9-3. The goal of that custom action was to allow archiving a single invoice, changing its *Status* field to a value of *Archived*. However, expanding on the the idea of Ribbons and multiple selections of items in a list, it would be better to give users the opportunity to archive multiple invoices at the same time. The ECB extended with Listing 9-3 applies only to a single item per time. But a ribbon command could be applied to multiple items simultaneously, improving usability and overall user experience.

Let's start with a simple example. Listing 9-10 presents a Ribbon that displays an alert upon clicking it.

LISTING 9-10 A sample Ribbon that shows an alert upon clicking it.

```
<CustomAction
  RegistrationType="ContentType"
  RegistrationId="0x0101008D841CAC0C7F474288965287B30061DC"
  Id="DevLeap.CustomActions.Invoices.SampleRibbonCommand"
  Location="CommandUI.Ribbon.ListView">
  <CommandUIExtension>
    <CommandUIDefinitions>
      <CommandUIDefinition Location="Ribbon.Documents.Manage.Controls._children">
        <Button Id="SampleRibbonCommand"
                Alt="Shows an alert."
                Description="Shows an alert, just to make an example."
                Sequence="25"
                Command="ShowSampleAlert"
Image16by16="/_layouts/images/DevLeap.SP2010.UIExtensions/Baloon_16x16.png"
Image32by32="/_layouts/images/DevLeap.SP2010.UIExtensions/Baloon_32x32.png"
                LabelText="Show Alert"
                TemplateAlias="o1" />
      </CommandUIDefinition>
    </CommandUIDefinitions>
```

```
    <CommandUIHandlers>
      <CommandUIHandler Command="ShowSampleAlert"
                        CommandAction="javascript:
                        window.alert('This an alert from the ribbon');" />
    </CommandUIHandlers>
  </CommandUIExtension>
</CustomAction>
```

The *CustomAction* is almost the same as in the previous section, but the *Location* attribute targets a location with a value of *CommandUI.Ribbon.ListView*, which corresponds to the Ribbon menu of a *ListView*. Then, the action targets the *DevLeapInvoice* content type, through its content type ID, as with the ECB custom action defined earlier. Thus, the ribbon command will show up only while working on *DevLeapInvoice* items. However, instead of having a *UrlAction* child element, now there is a *CommandUIExtension* element, which defines a ribbon item. In particular, it defines a set of *CommandUIDefinition* elements, wrapped in a *CommandUIDefinitions* parent element, together with one or more *CommandUIHandler* elements, wrapped by a *CommadUIHandlers* parent tag. A *CommandUIDefinition* element defines the UI behavior of the command with its *Location* attribute, which in the code sample has a value of *Ribbon.Documents.Manage.Controls._ children* and declares that its child elements will be children of the *Manage* group of the *Documents* tab of the ribbon bar. In Listing 9-10, the command is represented as a *Button* element with a title, a description, a couple of images, sized 16 × 16 pixels and 32 × 32 pixels, and so on. Also in Listing 9-10, the *Button* element has a *Sequence* attribute with a value of 25, which means it will render between the second and third button of the target Ribbon group (Manage). For standard and native buttons, the *Sequence* attribute has a value that is a multiple of 10. Thus, the first button has a *Sequence* of 10, the second has a *Sequence* of 20, and so on.

Another interesting *Button* attribute is *TemplateAlias*, which defines the rendering behavior of the control. Native available templates are *o1*, which renders the 32 × 32 image form of the button, and *o2*, which renders the 16 × 16 image form. However, you can also define your own templates. Additionally, the *CommandUIHandler* element declares the code to execute upon clicking the commands. For example, in Listing 9-10, the *CommandAction* attribute of the *CommadUIHandler* element invokes a client-side *window.alert*, based on ECMAScript. In order to map the *Button* with its handler, there is a *Command* attribute whose value corresponds to the *Command* attribute of the *CommandUIHandler*. Figure 9-6 shows the results of listing 9-10 in action.

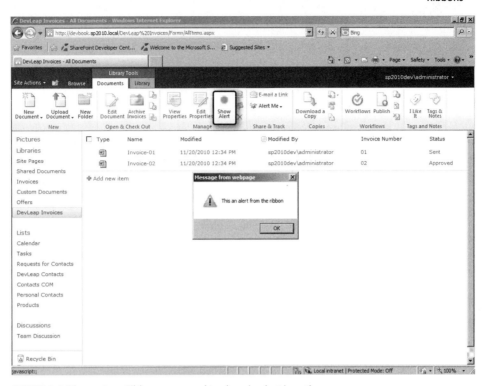

FIGURE 9-6 The custom Ribbon command to show in alert in action.

The *CommandUIDefinition* element can host a rich set of children elements. Table 9-5 presents a quick list of all the supported children elements, taken from the official product documentation on MSDN Online (*http://msdn.microsoft.com/en-us/library/ff458373.aspx*).

TABLE 9-5 The Children Elements of the *CommandUIDefinition* Element

Attribute Name	Description
Button	Defines a push button control. The main attributes are *Alt* for alternate text; the *Command* to execute on click; *Description* and *LabelText* for the UI; the various attributes to define images 16 × 16 and 32 × 32, eventually cropped from an image map; the *TemplateAlias* and the *Sequence* position of the button in the owner group; and the various attributes to define tooltip text and images.
CheckBox	Defines a check box control. *CheckBox* also has a *Command* to execute when clicked, as well as layout attributes regarding *Description*, images, and so on.
ComboBox	Defines a combo box control. *ComboBox* supports attributes for defining *AutoComplete*, *Command* to execute on click, command to execute on open, close, and preview.
ColorPicker	Defines a color picker control.
ContextualGroup	Defines a group of tabs that are presented when they are relevant. *ContextualGroup* allows defining a specific *Color* to use while showing the group.

Attribute Name	Description
ContextualTabs	Contains groups of tabs that are conditionally present. *ContextualTabs* is the container of one or more *ContextualGroup* elements.
Controls	Contains elements that define controls. *Controls* can contain elements of type: *Button, CheckBox, ComboBox, DropDown, FlyoutAnchor, GalleryButton, Label, MRUSplitButton, Spinner, SplitButton, TextBox,* and *ToggleButton*.
DropDown	Defines a control with which a user can select from a drop-down list. Supports almost the same attributes as the *ComboBox* element.
FlyoutAnchor	Defines the anchor point for a fly-out menu. Supports attributes for defining the *Command* to execute when the control is clicked, the various attributes for declaring images and tooltips, and some command to invoke in order to populate the menu dynamically.
Gallery	Defines a gallery. Supports attributes to define the dimension of child items. *Gallery* is made up of a set of *GalleryButton* children elements.
GalleryButton	Defines a gallery button. These are almost like standard buttons, except that they allow defining the dimension, according to the parent *Gallery*, and they support an *InnerHTML* attribute to define the HTML markup that illustrates the choice that the button represents.
GroupTemplate	Defines the scaling behavior for controls in a Group element. *GroupTemplate* can host *Layout* children elements and offers a *ClassName* attribute for defining a CSS to apply to the group.
Group	Defines a group of controls. Supports attributes for defining the *Description*, the various images, and the *Command* to execute when clicked.
Groups	Defines the groups of controls on a tab. Simply contains a set of children *Group* elements.
InsertTable	Defines a menu control for inserting a table that contains a variable number of cells. Provides a *Command* attribute for defining the code to execute when the table has to be inserted, as well as a *CommandPreview* and *CommandRevert* attributes to preview and revert the effect of the command.
Label	Defines a label control. *Label* supports a *ForId* attribute to declare the ID of the target control of the label, and some other attributes to define the images as well as the *LabelText*.
MRUSplitButton	Defines a control that combines a button and a drop-down menu to display a list of the most-recently used items. Provides some attributes to declare the code to execute for the purpose of populating the most recently used list, as well as to use when the user previews or reverts the selection, or effectively selects an item.
MaxSize	Specifies the maximum size for a group of controls. *MaxSize* offers a *Size* attribute to define the maximum allowed size for the group of controls.
Menu	Defines a menu control. *Menu* supports only a *MaxWidth* attribute.
MenuSection	Defines a section of a menu. *MenuSection* can host children elements of type *Controls* and *Gallery*. It also offers a *DisplayMode* attribute to define the sizing of the items, and a *Scrollable* attribute to declare if the menu section can be scrolled.

Attribute Name	Description
QAT	Defines a quick-access toolbar. *QAT* supports some attributes to declare images and CSS classes, and hosts a *Controls* child element.
Ribbon	Contains elements that define the Server ribbon user interface. *Ribbon* is the container of *Tabs* and *ContextualTabs* children elements. It supports many appearance attributes.
Scale	Defines how a group of controls on a tab is sized. *Scale* is the child of a *Scaling* element and supports *Size* and *PopupSize* attributes.
Scaling	Defines tab scaling. *Scaling* contains children elements of type *MaxSize* and *Scale*.
Spinner	Defines a spinner control. *Spinner* can contain a *Unit* child element and supports some appearance attributes as well as a *Command* to execute when the control is clicked.
SplitButton	Defines a control that combines a button and a drop-down menu. *SplitButton* can host a *Menu* child element. Supports many attributes to define various images, tooltips, and commands related to the drop-down menu.
Tab	Represents a tab control. *Tab* defines a *CssClass* to use while rendering the tab and the *Title* to show in the tab. It is the container of *Scaling* and *Groups* children elements.
Tabs	Contains elements that define tab controls. *Tabs* can host a set of *Tab* children elements.
TextBox	Defines a text box control. *TextBox* supports attributes for defining the appearance of the control as well as a *Command* to execute when it is clicked and *MaxLength* to define the maximum length in characters.
ToggleButton	Defines a button that is used to switch states. *ToggleButton* supports attributes for defining the appearance of the control as well as a *Command* to execute when it is clicked.

Recall that the goal of this particular section is to have a Ribbon with which a user can archive multiple items with content type *DevLeapInvoice* at the same time. Listing 9-11 shows the source code for such a Ribbon.

LISTING 9-11 Source code for a Ribbon that archives one or more items with a content type of *DevLeapInvoice*.

```
<CustomAction
  RegistrationType="ContentType"
  RegistrationId="0x0101008D841CAC0C7F474288965287B30061DC"
  Id="DevLeap.CustomActions.Invoices.ArchiveRibbon"
  Location="CommandUI.Ribbon.ListView">
  <CommandUIExtension>
    <CommandUIDefinitions>
      <CommandUIDefinition
        Location="Ribbon.Documents.EditCheckout.Controls._children">
```

```
        <Button Id="InvoiceArchiveRibbonButton"
                Alt="Changes the status of the Invoice to Archived."
                Description="Change the status of the Invoice to Archived."
                Sequence="25"
                Command="ChangeInvoiceStatusToArchived"
                Image16by16=
"/_layouts/images/DevLeap.SP2010.UIExtensions/IconArchive_16x16.gif"
                Image32by32=
"/_layouts/images/DevLeap.SP2010.UIExtensions/IconArchive_32x32.gif"
                LabelText="Archive Invoices"
                TemplateAlias="o1" />
      </CommandUIDefinition>
    </CommandUIDefinitions>
    <CommandUIHandlers>
      <CommandUIHandler Command="ChangeInvoiceStatusToArchived"
                        EnabledScript="javascript:
                        function checkInvoicesSelected() {
                          // Check the number of selected items
                          var items =
                            SP.ListOperation.Selection.getSelectedItems();
                          return (items.length >= 1);
                        }
                        checkInvoicesSelected();"
                        CommandAction="javascript:
                        // Shared variables
                        var ctx;
                        var itemsToArchive;
                        var notifyId = '';

                        // Function that archives the selected items
                        function archiveInvoices() {

                          // Notify the end user about the work in progress
                          this.notifyId =
                            SP.UI.Notify.addNotification(
                              'Archiving items...', true);

                          // Get the current ClientContext
                          this.ctx = new SP.ClientContext.get_current();

                          // Get the current Web
                          var web = this.ctx.get_web();

                          // Get the currently selected list
                          var listId =
                            SP.ListOperation.Selection.getSelectedList();
                          var sourceList = web.get_lists().getById(listId);

                          // Get the selected items and archive each of them
                          var items =
                            SP.ListOperation.Selection.getSelectedItems(
                              this.ctx);
```

```
                          var item;
                          this.itemsToArchive = new Array(items.length);
                          for(var i in items) {
                            item = items[i];

                            // Get each selected item
                            var listItem = sourceList.getItemById(item.id);
                            this.itemsToArchive.push(listItem);
                            this.ctx.load(listItem);
                          }

                          // Effectively load items from SharePoint
                          this.ctx.executeQueryAsync(
                            Function.createDelegate(this, onQuerySucceeded),
                            Function.createDelegate(this, onQueryFailed));
                        }

                        // Delegate called when server
                        // operation is completed upon success
                        function onQuerySucceeded(sender, args) {
                          // Mark each item as Archived
                          var item = null;
                          do {
                            item = this.itemsToArchive.pop();
                            if (item != null) {
                              item.set_item('DevLeapInvoiceStatus', 'Archived');
                              item.update();
                            }
                          } while (item != null);

                          // Effectively update items in SharePoint
                          this.ctx.executeQueryAsync(
                          Function.createDelegate(this, onUpdateSucceeded),
                          Function.createDelegate(this, onQueryFailed));
                        }

                        // Delegate called when server
                        // operation is completed upon success
                        function onUpdateSucceeded(sender, args) {
                          SP.UI.Notify.removeNotification(this.notifyId);
                          SP.UI.ModalDialog.RefreshPage(SP.UI.DialogResult.OK);
                        }

                        // Delegate called when server
                        // operation is completed with errors
                        function onQueryFailed(sender, args) {
                          alert('The requested operation failed: ' +
                            args.toString());
                        }
                        archiveInvoices();" />
            </CommandUIHandlers>
          </CommandUIExtension>
      </CustomAction>
```

Although Listing 9-11 is not short, it is actually quite simple. In fact, it takes advantage of the ECMAScript Client Object Model that was presented in Chapter 5, "Client-Side Technologies," within the code of the *CommandAction* attribute of the *CommandUIHandler* element. It creates a *ClientContext*, retrieves the selected items by using the *SP.ListOperation.Selection* class, and then updates them with a *Status* field value of *Archived,* invoking the asynchronous operation via the *executeQueryAsync* method of the *ClientContext.*

It is interesting to notice that the Ribbon is entirely defined in XML and ECMAScript, without the need for any kind of server-side code. Thus, it will work asynchronously in the web browser without requiring a post-back to the server. The only post-back is required at the end of the update process, to refresh the list of items and reflect the applied changes. You can see the invocation of the *SP.UI.ModalDialog.RefreshPage* method in the *onUpdateSucceeded* method. You can also include the ECMAScript code in an external .js file and reference it using a custom action with the *Location* attribute with a value of *ScriptLink*.

Another interesting aspect is the attribute *EnabledScript* of the element *CommandUIHandler.* This attribute is invoked on the client side, and it contains another ECMAScript script block to determine if the Ribbon command must be enabled or disabled. Internally, the script checks the number of selected items and returns *TRUE* only if there is at least one invoice selected in the result of the *SP.ListOperation.Selection.getSelectedItems()* method. As the sample code illustrates, the *SP.ListOperation.Selection.getSelectedItems()* method returns only the IDs of the selected items, not the whole item.

To complete the example, the *Location* attribute of the *CommandUIDefinition* element declares where to locate the new Ribbon. In this example, the ribbon is located in the Open & Check Out group of the Documents tab, which has a location of *Ribbon.Documents. EditCheckout.Controls.* Thus, the new command has a location value of *Ribbon.Documents. EditCheckout.Controls._children* to instruct the environment to show the item as a child of the Open & Check Out group.

 Note The complete list of locations can be found in the document, "Default Server Ribbon Customization Locations," which is available on MSDN Online at *http://msdn.microsoft.com/en-us/library/ee537543.aspx.*

The sample code of Listing 9-11 also uses the new Notification Area of SharePoint 2010, which will be discussed beginning on page 305. Figure 9-7 shows the Ribbon command in action.

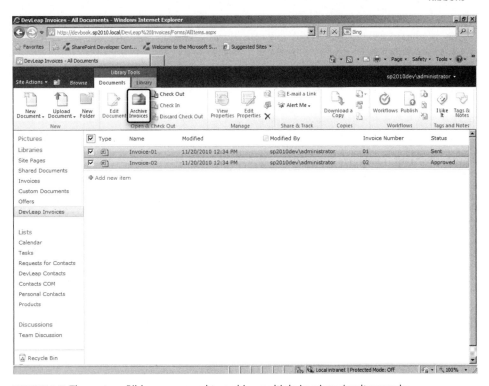

FIGURE 9-7 The custom Ribbon command to archive multiple invoices simultaneously.

Finally, consider that inside the code of the *CommandAction* attribute, you can use substitution tokens that are replaced by the environment before executing the script. The following are the available tokens:

- *{ItemId}*   ID (GUID) taken from the list view

- *{ItemUrl}*   Web-relative URL of the list item (Url)

- *{RecurrenceId}*   ID of a recurrent item (RecurrenceID)

- *{SiteUrl}*   The fully qualified URL to the site (Url)

- *{ListId}*   ID (GUID) of the list (ID)

- *{ListUrlDir}*   Server-relative URL of the site plus the list's folder

- *{Source}*   Fully qualified request URL

- *{SelectedListId}*   ID (GUID) of the list that is currently selected from a list view

- *{SelectedItemId}*   ID of the item that is currently selected from the list view

One last scenario to consider is the creation of a custom Ribbon tab. In fact, if you have multiple commands to support your custom content, it is good habit to define a Ribbon tab of your own, instead of extending an existing one. To define a new tab of Ribbons, you need to utilize the *Tab*, *Scaling*, *Groups*, and *Group* elements. Listing 9-12 demonstrates the declaration of a custom tab, which will show up only when selecting items with a content type of *DevLeapInvoice*. The tab will host three buttons that, for the sake of simplicity, just show an alert with a welcome message.

LISTING 9-12 A custom *Tab* of Ribbons for a content type of *DevLeapInvoice*.

```
<CustomAction
  RegistrationType="ContentType"
  RegistrationId="0x0101008D841CAC0C7F474288965287B30061DC"
  Id="DevLeap.CustomActions.Invoices.Tab"
  Location="CommandUI.Ribbon.ListView">
  <CommandUIExtension>
    <CommandUIDefinitions>
      <CommandUIDefinition
        Location="Ribbon.Tabs._children">
        <Tab
          Id="DevLeap.CustomActions.Invoices.Tab.One"
          Title="Invoices"
          Description="This tab holds custom commands for Invoices."
          Sequence="1000">
          <Scaling
            Id="DevLeap.CustomActions.Invoices.Tab.One.Scaling">
            <MaxSize
              Id="DevLeap.CustomActions.Invoices.Tab.One.Scaling.MaxSize"
              GroupId="DevLeap.CustomActions.Invoices.Tab.One.GroupOne"
              Size="OneLargeTwoSmall"/>
            <Scale
              Id="DevLeap.CustomActions.Invoices.Tab.One.Scaling.Scale"
              GroupId="DevLeap.CustomActions.Invoices.Tab.One.GroupOne"
              Size="OneLargeTwoSmall" />
          </Scaling>
          <Groups Id="DevLeap.CustomActions.Invoices.Tab.Groups">
            <Group
              Id="DevLeap.CustomActions.Invoices.Tab.One.GroupOne"
              Description="This is the first group."
              Title="First Group"
              Sequence="52"
              Template="DevLeap.CustomActions.Invoices.RibbonTemplate">
              <Controls Id="Ribbon.CustomTabExample.CustomGroupExample.Controls">
                <Button
                  Id="DevLeap.CustomActions.Invoices.Tab.One.ButtonOne"
                  Command="ButtonOneCommand"
                  Sequence="10"
                  Description="First sample command."
                  Image32by32=
                    "/_layouts/$Resources:core,Language;/images/formatmap32x32.png"
                  Image32by32Left="-160"
                  Image32by32Top="-256"
                  LabelText="First sample command!"
                  TemplateAlias="customOne"/>
```

```
            <Button
              Id="DevLeap.CustomActions.Invoices.Tab.One.ButtonTwo"
              Command="ButtonTwoCommand"
              Sequence="20"
              Description="Second sample command."
              Image16by16=
                "/_layouts/$Resources:core,Language;/images/formatmap16x16.png"
              Image16by16Left="-144"
              Image16by16Top="-32"
              LabelText="Second sample command!"
              TemplateAlias="customTwo"/>
            <Button
              Id="DevLeap.CustomActions.Invoices.Tab.One.ButtonThree"
              Command="ButtonThreeCommand"
              Sequence="30"
              Description="Third sample command."
              Image16by16=
                "/_layouts/$Resources:core,Language;/images/formatmap16x16.png"
              Image16by16Left="-96"
              Image16by16Top="-128"
              LabelText="Third sample command!"
              TemplateAlias="customThree"/>
          </Controls>
        </Group>
      </Groups>
    </Tab>
  </CommandUIDefinition>
  <CommandUIDefinition Location="Ribbon.Templates._children">
    <GroupTemplate Id="DevLeap.CustomActions.Invoices.RibbonTemplate">
      <Layout
        Title="OneLargeTwoSmall"
        LayoutTitle="OneLargeTwoSmall">
        <Section Alignment="Top" Type="OneRow">
          <Row>
            <ControlRef DisplayMode="Large" TemplateAlias="customOne" />
          </Row>
        </Section>
        <Section Alignment="Top" Type="TwoRow">
          <Row>
            <ControlRef DisplayMode="Small" TemplateAlias="customTwo" />
          </Row>
          <Row>
            <ControlRef DisplayMode="Small" TemplateAlias="customThree" />
          </Row>
        </Section>
      </Layout>
    </GroupTemplate>
  </CommandUIDefinition>
</CommandUIDefinitions>
<CommandUIHandlers>
  <CommandUIHandler
    Command="ButtonOneCommand"
    CommandAction="javascript:window.alert('You pressed CommandOne!');" />
```

```
        <CommandUIHandler
          Command="ButtonTwoCommand"
          CommandAction="javascript:window.alert('You pressed CommandTwo!');" />
        <CommandUIHandler
          Command="ButtonThreeCommand"
          CommandAction="javascript:window.alert('You pressed CommandThree!');" />
      </CommandUIHandlers>
    </CommandUIExtension>
  </CustomAction>
```

First, Listing 9-12 creates a new Ribbon tab that declares a *Location* value of *Ribbon.Tabs._children*, with a *Title* value of *Invoices*. It declares some *Scaling* information about how the ribbon will behave when the window is resized. Specifically, you must define a *MaxSize* element for each ribbon group, describing the rendering behavior at the maximum size. You also need to define at least one *Scale* element for each Ribbon group, providing information about how to scale the contents of the group. Both the *MaxSize* and *Scale* elements use a *Size* attribute with a value that references the *Title* attribute of the *Layout* elements defined in the *CommandUIDefinition* element, with a *Location* value of *Ribbon.Templates._children*. In the current example the *OneLargeTwoSmall* sizing layout describes a first *Section* with one row, and a second *Section* with two rows. The *Row* elements defined in the *Section* elements also declare a *TemplateAlias*, which the *Button* elements will reference. It is also important to underline the value of the *Location* attribute of the two *CommandUIDefinition* elements.

Another thing to notice is the way that the images of the buttons are defined. For performance reasons, SharePoint 2010 has images that are maps of multiple icons, rendered using CSS cropping. For example there are two image files with name formatmap16x16.png and formatmap32x32.png, which contain a rich set of icons used for rendering buttons of ribbons and menus with a size of 16 × 16 pixels or 32 × 32 pixels, respectively.

If you want to render a specific image, you need to reference the proper picture in the *Image16by16* or *Image32by32* attribute, depending on the size of the image you are looking for. Then, you need to provide the location of the top and left corners of the image to crop, using the attributes *Image16by16Top* and *Image16by16Left*, or *Image32by32Top* and *Image32by32Left*. These attributes require the offset as a negative value. Notice also that in Listing 9-12, the images URLs include the reference to the proper culture code, determined by querying the core resource strings. Figure 9-8 displays the output of Listing 9-12 as it appears in the web browser.

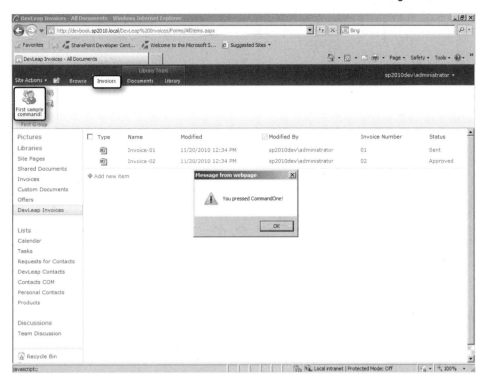

FIGURE 9-8 The custom tab of ribbons targeting the content type *DevLeapInvoice*.

Delegate Controls

Since version 2007, SharePoint allows you to extend native pages and mainly master pages, without having to modify them directly. If you take a look at one of the standard master pages, such as the v4.master or the default.master, you will see that there are many instances of a server control with the name *<SharePoint:DelegateControl />*. This is a control that defines a placeholder, with a *ControlId* attribute, unique within the page or the master page that will be replaced during page rendering with a proper ASP.NET server control, which can be configured using a *Control* feature.

For example, consider the small search box that is placed in the upper-right corner of every home page of a standard SharePoint layout (with master pages v4.master or default.master). This small search box is rendered by means of a delegate control, and it is defined in the v4.master master page, with the following syntax:

```
<SharePoint:DelegateControl runat="server" ControlId="SmallSearchInputBox" Version="4"/>
```

By default, this delegate control will be replaced by the native control defined by the class *Microsoft.SharePoint.Portal.WebControls.SearchBoxEx*, which is available in assembly *Microsoft.Office.Server.Search.dll*. If you prefer to override this default search box control, all you need to do is define a custom feature that includes a custom element manifest like the one shown in Listing 9-13.

LISTING 9-13 A feature element that overrides the default delegate control for the *SmallSearchInputBox*.

```xml
<?xml version="1.0" encoding="utf-8"?>
<Elements xmlns="http://schemas.microsoft.com/sharepoint/">
  <Control Id="SmallSearchInputBox"
    Sequence="10"
    ControlAssembly="DevLeap.SP2010.UIExtensions, Version=1.0.0.0, Culture=neutral,
      PublicKeyToken=3b7c6076bf78362f"
    ControlClass="DevLeap.SP2010.UIExtensions.CustomSmallSearchInputBox" />
</Elements>
```

> **Note** Both the values of the *ControlAssembly* and the *ControlClass* attributes in Listing 9-13 need to be defined on a single of code.

In Listing 9-13, the *Control* feature element declares to use the class with the name declared in the attribute *ControlClass*, available in the assembly with name *ControlAssembly*, whenever the *DelegateControl* references a control with a *ControlId* value of *SmallSearchInputBox*. There is also a *Sequence* attribute useful to define precedence while applying a delegate control replacement. In fact, the control with the smallest *Sequence* value will be used as the source for the *DelegateControl*. The *CustomSmallSearchInputBox* class in Listing 9-13 is a custom web control, which inherits from the standard *SearchBoxEx*. Through the declaration of a *Control* element, you can also reference an .ascx control instead of a compiled class, simply by defining a value for the *ControlSrc* attribute, such as in Listing 9-14.

> **Note** To use a custom control class as a source for a *DelegateControl* instance, you need to configure the control class as a *SafeControl* in the target SharePoint site.

LISTING 9-14 A feature element overriding the default delegate control for the *SmallSearchInputBox* with a custom .ascx template control.

```xml
<?xml version="1.0" encoding="utf-8"?>
<Elements xmlns="http://schemas.microsoft.com/sharepoint/">
  <Control Id="SmallSearchInputBox"
    Sequence="10"
    ControlSrc="/_controltemplates/CustomSmallSearchInputBox.ascx" />
</Elements>
```

Lastly, you can also use a *Control* element to simply customizing the configuration of an existing and eventually native control. The *Control* element accepts zero or more children elements with name *Property*, which allow configuring properties of the target delegate control. For example, Listing 9-15 shows you how to configure the native *SearchBoxEx* control to show a drop-down menu for selecting the target scope of the search, and to write a default text of "Write here your search ..." in the search textbox, which will have a width of 200 pixels.

LISTING 9-15 A feature element overriding the default delegate control for the *SmallSearchInputBox*.

```xml
<?xml version="1.0" encoding="utf-8"?>
<Elements xmlns="http://schemas.microsoft.com/sharepoint/">
  <Control Id="SmallSearchInputBox"
    Sequence="5"
    ControlClass="Microsoft.SharePoint.Portal.WebControls.SearchBoxEx"
    ControlAssembly="Microsoft.Office.Server.Search, Version=14.0.0.0, Culture=neutral,
PublicKeyToken=71e9bce111e9429c">
    <Property Name="FrameType">None</Property>
    <Property Name="DropDownMode">ShowDD</Property>
    <Property Name="TextBoxWidth">200</Property>
    <Property Name="ShowAdvancedSearch">false</Property>
    <Property Name="QueryPromptString">Write here your search ...</Property>
    <Property Name="SearchBoxTableClass">search-box</Property>
  </Control>
</Elements>
```

Note Both the values of the *ControlAssembly* and the *ControlClass* attributes in Listing 9-15 need to be defined on a single of code.

Figure 9-9 depicts the home page of a team site with the native control for the *SmallSearchInputBox*, customized as in Listing 9-15.

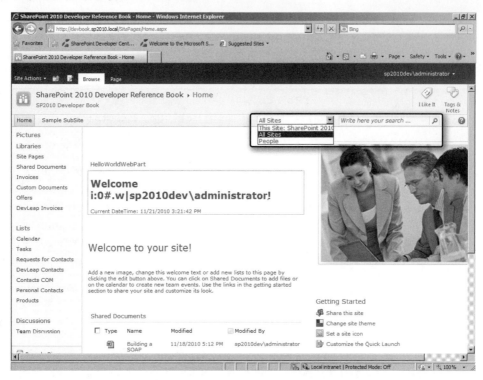

FIGURE 9-9 The standard *SmallSearchInputBox*, customized like in Listing 9-15.

> **Important** The *Control* element feature can target *Farm*, *WebApplication*, *Site*, or *Web*. Thus, you can use it to customize your users' experience at any level you like. For example, if you want to override the standard *SmallSearchInputBox* for every site, in every web application of the entire Farm, you can accomplish this simply by targeting the feature to the *Farm* scope.

Table 9-6 lists the most useful *ControlId* values available in default master pages of SharePoint 2010.

TABLE 9-6 The Main *Controlld* Values Available in SharePoint 2010

Controlld	Description
AdditionalPageHead	Defines additional headers for the page. *AdditionalPageHead* supports declaration of multiple delegate controls, which will be loaded inside the HTML header of the page. You can use it to provide custom metatags, headers, and scripts in the master page of your site.
GlobalNavigation	Defines a control that will be rendered at the top of the page, if you are using the v4.master master page. It can be used to provide the site with a custom global navigation bar.
SmallSearchInputBox	Defines a custom small search box.
TopNavigationDataSource	Defines a custom data source for the Top Navigation Bar.
PublishingConsole	Definesg a custom publishing console, which is the control that renders the page editing toolbar.
QuickLaunchDataSource	Defines a custom data source for the Quick Launch.
TreeViewAndDataSource	Defines a custom data source for the TreeView of the site.

Custom Contents

In the previous sections, some of the code listings referenced custom images and pages that were deployed on the farm together with the features that use them. In this section, you will learn how to deploy this kind of custom content by using features.

Images and Generic Content

The first kind of content that you will probably need to deploy is custom images. By default, SharePoint stores images in the SharePoint14_Root\TEMPLATE\IMAGES folder and makes them available through a virtual directory named *_layouts/images/*.

> **Note** SharePoint14_Root refers to the SharePoint root folder, which is typically located at C:\ Program Files\Common Files\Microsoft Shared\Web Server Extensions\14.

Working with Visual Studio 2010, you can deploy custom images in the proper folder by right-clicking the project, and then, from the contextual menu that appears (see Figure 9-10), selecting Add | SharePoint "Images" Mapped Folder. After you've done this, you will find a folder named Images in your project. By adding an image file to that folder, the file will be automatically deployed in SharePoint's images folder. To better organize files in SharePoint's folders, Visual Studio 2010 automatically creates a subfolder that uses the name of the current project and places the images there. For example, if your project name is *MyCustomProject*, and you add an image file with the name *MyImage.jpg*, then the image will be deployed under the path SharePoint14_Root\TEMPLATE\IMAGES\ MyCustomProject\MyImage.jpg, and will be available through the relative URI *./_layouts/ images/MyCustomProject/MyImage.jpg*.

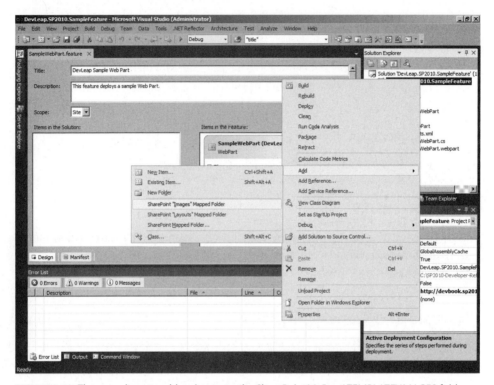

FIGURE 9-10 The menu item to add an image to the SharePoint14_Root\TEMPLATE\IMAGES folder.

If you need to deploy other kinds of generic content, such as .ascx controls, .css files, .js files, and so on, select the Add | SharePoint Mapped Folder from the project's contextual menu. You will be prompted with a pop-up window like the one shown in Figure 9-11. From there, you will be able to select any of the folders available under the SharePoint14_Root path.

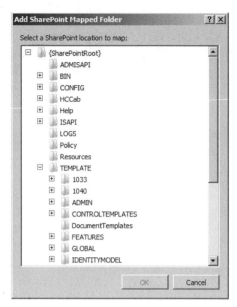

FIGURE 9-11 The pop-up window to select a SharePoint Mapped Folder.

Application Pages

Application pages are .aspx files that can be deployed to provide pages that are available for all sites of a farm, and deployed under the SharePoint14_Root\TEMPLATE\LAYOUTS folder. SharePoint makes them available through a virtual directory named _layouts. In general, these pages are defined to provide the user interface for administrative tasks or to implement custom application pages that will be used to support custom solutions. For example, in Part V of this book, "Developing Workflows," you use these kinds of pages to provide custom user interfaces to interact with your workflows. In Listing 9-3, there is an *UrlAction* element referencing a page called *DevLeapInvoiceChangeStatus.aspx*, which is a custom application page.

To create such pages using Visual Studio 2010 you can simply select to add a new item to the project, and then select an item of type Application Page, which is an .aspx file. A folder named Layouts will be added to the project, if it does not already exist. Within that folder a a subfolder will be created, using the name your project. The new .aspx file will be placed in that subfolder. The .aspx file will define a standard ASP.NET page, which you will be able to define using standard ASP.NET controls as well as custom SharePoint's controls, or custom controls of your own. By default, the page will have the *~masterurl/default.master* assigned, but you can freely change this behavior. In addition, the *CodeBehind* attribute of the page will reference a code file declaring a custom ASP.NET page that will inherit from the *LayoutsPageBase* class, which is defined in the *Microsoft.SharePoint.WebControls* namespace, and define the base and common behavior for every application page. The *LayoutsPageBase* base class provides some useful properties to directly access the *SPWeb* and *SPSite* instances of the current context.

Coming back to the example of Listing 9-3, the custom application page used in the *UrlAction* element was capable of changing the *Status* field of a single item with a content type of *DevLeapInvoice*, reading the target *ListId*, *ItemId*, and *Status* from the *QueryString*. Listing 9-16 reveals the source of the *CodeBehind* of that page.

LISTING 9-16 The *CodeBehind* of the *DevLeapInvoiceChangeStatus.aspx* page used in Listing 9-3.

```csharp
using System;
using Microsoft.SharePoint;
using Microsoft.SharePoint.WebControls;
using System.Web;
using Microsoft.SharePoint.Utilities;

namespace DevLeap.SP2010.UIExtensions.Layouts.DevLeap.SP2010.UIExtensions {
    public partial class DevLeapInvoiceChangeStatus : LayoutsPageBase {
        protected void Page_Load(object sender, EventArgs e) {

            String itemId = this.Request.QueryString["ItemId"];
            String listId = this.Request.QueryString["ListId"];
            String status = this.Request.QueryString["Status"];

            if (!String.IsNullOrEmpty(itemId) &&
                !String.IsNullOrEmpty(listId) &&
                !String.IsNullOrEmpty(status)) {
                SPWeb web = this.Web;

                try {
                    try {
                        SPList list =
                          web.Lists[new Guid(this.Request.QueryString["ListId"])];
                        SPListItem item =
                          list.GetItemById(
                            Int32.Parse(this.Request.QueryString["ItemId"]));

                        web.AllowUnsafeUpdates = true;
                        item[FieldsIds.DevLeapInvoiceStatus_ID] = status;
                        item.Update();
                        SPUtility.Redirect(
                          list.DefaultViewUrl,
                          SPRedirectFlags.Default,
                          HttpContext.Current);
                    }
```

```
                      finally {
                          web.AllowUnsafeUpdates = false;
                      }
                  }
                  catch (ArgumentException) {
                      throw new ApplicationException("Invalid List or Item ID!");
                  }
              }
          }
      }
  }
```

The .aspx code of the *DevLeapInvoiceChangeStatus.aspx* page is not terribly interesting because it has no content. However, a classic custom application page should define only the content regions to fill out the content place holders defined in the master page used by the target site.

> **Important** Application pages cannot be personalized or customized by the end user because they are defined on the file system. If you need to define custom pages that are also customizable, you need to refer to the next section.

Content Pages, Web Part Pages, and Galleries

Sometimes you need to deploy pages that do not need to be shared and available on any site of your farm. Instead, you simply need to deploy a custom page or a Web Part Page to a single target site, eventually supporting customization by the end user or by using Microsoft SharePoint Designer 2010.

To accomplish this task you can use the *Module* feature element, which allows deploying an item into the content database of a target site. Listing 9-17 shows the structure of the *Module* element, together with its children elements.

LISTING 9-17 The structure of the *Module* feature element, together with its children elements.

```
<Module
  HyperlinkBaseUrl = string
  IncludeFolders = "Text"
  List = "Integer"
  Name = "Text"
  Path = "Text"
  RootWebOnly = "TRUE" | "FALSE"
  SetupPath = "Text"
  Url = "Text">
```

```
<File
  DocumentTemplateForList = string
  DoGUIDFixUp = "TRUE" | "FALSE"
  IgnoreIfAlreadyExists = "TRUE" | "FALSE"
  Level = Draft
  Name = string
  NavBarHome = "TRUE" | "FALSE"
  Path = string
  Type = "Ghostable" | "GhostableInLibrary"
  Url = string>
    <AllUsersWebPart />
    <BinarySerializedWebPart />
    <NavBarPage />
    <Property />
    <View />
    <WebPartConnection />
  </File>
</Module>
```

The code in Listing 9-17 is made up of a small set of attributes, while the core part is made of the child *File* element. Table 9-7 provides explanations of the main attributes of the *Module* element.

TABLE 9-7 **The Main Attributes of the *Module* Element**

Attribute	Description
HyperlinkBaseUrl	Optional *Text* attribute that specifies an absolute URL to use as the base URL for hyperlinks.
List	Optional *Integer* attribute that specifies the type of the target list. The possible values are defined in the onet.xml file of the site template (more about this in Chapter 14, "Site Templates").
Name	Required *Text* attribute that specifies the name of the module.
Path	Optional *Text* attribute that specifies the path of the physical files, relative to the feature's folder SharePoint14_Root\TEMPLATE\FEATURES*FeatureName*.
RootWebOnly	Required *Boolean* attribute that specifies whether the files will be installed only on the top-level website of the current Site Collection.
SetupPath	Optional *Text* attribute that specifies the physical path to a folder, under the SharePoint14_Root\TEMPLATE\FEATURES*FeatureName* folder, that contains a file to include in the module.
Url	Optional *Text* attribute that specifies the virtual path of the folder in which to include the files to deploy. If *Path* is not specified, the value of *Url* will be used. If you provide a value that corresponds to a folder that does not exist, the folder will be created upon activation of the feature.

Table 9-8 provides explanations of each attribute available for the *File* element.

TABLE 9-8 The Attributes Supported by the *Module* Element

Attribute	Description
IgnoreIfAlreadyExists	Optional *Boolean* attribute that specifies whether to overwrite an already existing item (*true*) or not (*false*).
Name	Optional *Text* attribute that specifies the virtual path name for the file in the target site.
NavBarHome	Optional *Boolean* attribute that specifies whether to use the current content, in case it is a page, as the home link in the top navigation bar. In general it is used while defining custom site templates. For further details, see Chapter 14, "Site Templates."
Path	Optional *Text* attribute that specifies the path of the physical file, relative to the feature's folder SharePoint14_Root\TEMPLATE\FEATURES*FeatureName*.
Type	Optional *Text* attribute that specifies whether the file will be stored in a document library (*GhostableInLibrary*) or stored outside a document library (*Ghostable*).
Url	Required *Text* attribute that specifies the virtual path of the file in the target site. If the value of the *Name* attribute is specified, then it will be used as the virtual path. If the value of the *Path* attribute is not specified, the value of *Url* will be used, instead.

Listing 9-18 shows how to deploy a custom image into the Site Assets library of a SharePoint site by using the *Module* feature.

LISTING 9-18 A *Module* feature to deploy an image into the Site Assets library of a SharePoint site.

```xml
<?xml version="1.0" encoding="utf-8"?>
<Elements xmlns="http://schemas.microsoft.com/sharepoint/">
  <Module Name="SiteAssetsImage" Url="SiteAssets">
    <File IgnoreIfAlreadyExists="True"
          Path="SiteAssetsImage\SP2010-Developer-Reference.png"
          Url="SP2010-Developer-Reference.png"
          Type="GhostableInLibrary" />
  </Module>
</Elements>
```

You can also use the *Module* feature for deploying a content page, eventually made up of Web Parts. If you only need to deploy an .aspx content page, you can use an element manifest file, such as the one shown in Listing 9-19.

LISTING 9-19 A *Module* feature used to deploy a content page on a SharePoint site.

```xml
<?xml version="1.0" encoding="utf-8"?>
<Elements xmlns="http://schemas.microsoft.com/sharepoint/">
  <Module Name="SampleContentPage">
    <File IgnoreIfAlreadyExists="True"
          Path="SampleContentPage\SampleContentPage.aspx"
          Url="SampleContentPage.aspx" />
  </Module>
</Elements>
```

The code in Listing 9-19 provisions a page with a URL value of *SampleContentPage.aspx* under the root of the target site, reading the page content from a file stored in the feature's folder, under the relative path *SampleContentPage\SampleContentPage.aspx*. Listing 9-20 presents the source code of that page.

LISTING 9-20 The source code of the page *SampleContentPage.aspx* provisioned in Listing 9-19.

```aspx
<%@ Page language="C#" MasterPageFile="~masterurl/default.master" %>

<asp:Content ID="Content1" ContentPlaceHolderId="PlaceHolderPageTitle" runat="server">
    This is the SampleContentPage Title
</asp:Content>

<asp:Content ID="Content2" ContentPlaceHolderId="PlaceHolderPageTitleInTitleArea"
runat="server">
    This is the SampleContentPage Title in Title Area
</asp:Content>

<asp:Content ID="Content7" ContentPlaceHolderId="PlaceHolderPageDescription"
runat="server">
    This is the description of the SampleContentPage
</asp:Content>

<asp:Content ID="Content12" ContentPlaceHolderId="PlaceHolderMain" runat="server">
    This is the main body of the SampleContentPage
</asp:Content>
```

If the page you are going to provision is a Web Part Page, that means it is made up of Web Parts; the *File* element supports some children elements specifically available for including Web Parts in a Web Part Page. Now consider the .aspx page illustrated in Listing 9-21. It defines a page that includes a *WebPartZone* control with an ID of *MainWebPartZone* placed in the *PlaceHolderMain* content region.

LISTING 9-21 A Web Part Page provisioned through a *Module* feature.

```
<%@ Page language="C#" MasterPageFile="~masterurl/default.master"
Inherits="Microsoft.SharePoint.WebPartPages.WebPartPage,
Microsoft.SharePoint,Version=14.0.0.0,Culture=neutral,PublicKeyToken=71e9bce111e9429c" %>
<%@ Register Tagprefix="SharePoint" Namespace="Microsoft.SharePoint.WebControls"
Assembly="Microsoft.SharePoint, Version=14.0.0.0, Culture=neutral,
PublicKeyToken=71e9bce111e9429c" %>

<%@ Register Tagprefix="Utilities" Namespace="Microsoft.SharePoint.Utilities"
Assembly="Microsoft.SharePoint, Version=14.0.0.0, Culture=neutral,
PublicKeyToken=71e9bce111e9429c" %>
<%@ Register Tagprefix="WebPartPages" Namespace="Microsoft.SharePoint.WebPartPages"
Assembly="Microsoft.SharePoint, Version=14.0.0.0, Culture=neutral,
PublicKeyToken=71e9bce111e9429c" %>
<%@ Import Namespace="Microsoft.SharePoint" %>
<%@ Assembly Name="Microsoft.Web.CommandUI, Version=14.0.0.0, Culture=neutral,
PublicKeyToken=71e9bce111e9429c" %>

<asp:Content ID="Content1" ContentPlaceHolderId="PlaceHolderPageTitle" runat="server">
  <SharePoint:ListItemProperty ID="ListItemProperty1" Property="BaseName"
    maxlength="40" runat="server"/>
</asp:Content>

<asp:Content ID="Content12" ContentPlaceHolderId="PlaceHolderMain" runat="server">
  <table cellpadding="4" cellspacing="0" border="0" width="100%">
    <tr>
      <td id="_invisibleIfEmpty" name="_invisibleIfEmpty" valign="top" width="100%">
        <WebPartPages:WebPartZone runat="server" Title="loc:FullPage"
          ID="MainWebPartZone" FrameType="TitleBarOnly" />
      </td>
    </tr>
  </table>
</asp:Content>
```

Note The *@Register* directives at the top of Listing 9-21 must have the *Assembly* attribute defined on a unique line.

The *Module* element defined in Listing 9-22 automatically provisions the page from Listing 9-21 into the library Site Pages, adding two Web Parts into the *WebPartZone* with ID *MainWebPartZone*. The key point is the inclusion of the *AllUsersWebPart* children elements in the *File* element. The first one defines an instance of the standard *ImageWebPart* of SharePoint. The second child element references the *HelloWorldWebPart* that was defined at the beginning of Chapter 6, "Web Part Basics."

LISTING 9-22 The feature element manifest used to provision a Web Part Page, together with some Web Parts.

```xml
<?xml version="1.0" encoding="utf-8"?>
<Elements xmlns="http://schemas.microsoft.com/sharepoint/">
  <Module Name="SampleWebPartPage" Url="SitePages">
    <File IgnoreIfAlreadyExists="True"
          Path="SampleWebPartPage\SampleWebPartPage.aspx"
          Url="SampleWebPartPage.aspx"
          Type="GhostableInLibrary">
      <AllUsersWebPart WebPartZoneID="MainWebPartZone" WebPartOrder="1">
        <![CDATA[
          <WebPart xmlns="http://schemas.microsoft.com/WebPart/v2"
            xmlns:iwp="http://schemas.microsoft.com/WebPart/v2/Image">
              <Assembly>Microsoft.SharePoint, Version=12.0.0.0, Culture=neutral,
                PublicKeyToken=71e9bce111e9429c</Assembly>
              <TypeName>Microsoft.SharePoint.WebPartPages.ImageWebPart</TypeName>
              <FrameType>None</FrameType>
              <Title>$Resources:wp_SiteImage;</Title>
<iwp:ImageLink>/_layouts/images/homepageSamplePhoto.jpg</iwp:ImageLink>
              <iwp:AlternativeText>Home Page Sample Photo</iwp:AlternativeText>
          </WebPart>
        ]]>
      </AllUsersWebPart>
      <AllUsersWebPart WebPartZoneID="MainWebPartZone" WebPartOrder="2">
        <![CDATA[
          <webParts>
            <webPart xmlns="http://schemas.microsoft.com/WebPart/v3">
              <metaData>
                <type name="DevLeap.SP2010.WebParts.HelloWorldWebPart.
HelloWorldWebPart, DevLeap.SP2010.WebParts, Version=1.0.0.0, Culture=neutral, PublicKey
Token=cba640f292988abf" />
                <importErrorMessage>Cannot import this Web Part.</importErrorMessage>
              </metaData>
              <data>
                <properties>
                  <property name="Title" type="string">Hello World Web Part</property>
                </properties>
              </data>
            </webPart>
          </webParts>
        ]]>
      </AllUsersWebPart>
    </File>
  </Module>
</Elements>
```

Notice also that the two Web Parts are declared using two different syntaxes. In fact, the former is a legacy Web Part that supports the old-style .dwp Web Part deployment technique available in Microsoft SharePoint 2003, while the latter uses the syntax of the new .webpart deployment files.

The *File* element supports some other children elements. For example, there is the *View* child element, which can be used to instantiate a *ListView* into the target Web Part Page. Additionally, there is the *WebPartConnection* element to connect Web Parts directly during the provisioning process.

Status Bar and Notification Area

The Status Bar and the Notification Area are two new features introduced in SharePoint 2010. Both are based on ECMAScript code and some extra markup in the default master pages. You can implement these tools within your pages and code simply by using some specific classes provided by the ECMAScript Client Object Model.

There is the *SP.UI.Notify* class for managing the Notification Area, and the *SP.UI.Status* class for managing the Status Bar. Table 9-9 describes the methods of the *SP.UI.Notify* class.

TABLE 9-9 **The Methods Offered by the *SP.UI.Notify* Class**

Method	Description
addNotification	Used to add a notification to the Notification Area. Requires the text of the notification and a *Boolean* argument to specify if the notification will stay on the page until explicitly removed. *addNotification* returns an ID identifying the notification.
removeNotification	Removes a notification from the Notification Area. Requires the ID of the notification to remove.

To add a notification to the Notification Area, you can the following code:

```
var notifyId = SP.UI.Notify.addNotification("This is a Notification!", true);
```

To remove the notification, you use this code:

```
SP.UI.Notify.removeNotification(notifyId);
```

Table 9-10 describes the methods provided by the *SP.UI.Status* class.

TABLE 9-10 **The Methods Offered by the *SP.UI.Status* Class**

Method	Description
addStatus	Used to add a status to the Status Bar. Returns an ID identifying the status.
appendStatus	Appends text to an existing status message in the Status Bar.
removeAllStatus	Removes all the status messages from the Status Bar and hides the Status Bar.
removeStatus	Removes a status message from the Status Bar. Requires the ID of the status message that is being removed.
setStatusPriColor	Configures the color of the Status Bar.
updateStatus	Updates a status message. Requires the ID of the status message that is being updated.

To add a status message to the Status Bar using the red color, you use the following code:

```
var statusId = SP.UI.Status.addStatus("Critical Status!");
SP.UI.Status.setStatusPriColor(statusId, 'red');
```

To remove the status message, you use this code:

```
SP.UI.Status.removeStatus(statusId);
```

You can use these classes and methods whenever you need to interact with the end user, using the standard notification tools provided by SharePoint 2010. For example, the code in Listing 9-11 used the Notification Area to inform the end user about the process of archiving invoices. In Listing 9-23, there is a custom Ribbon tab that provides four commands to show and hide a notification message as well as to show and hide a status message.

LISTING 9-23 The code of a custom Ribbon tab that uses the *SP.UI.Notify* and *SP.UI.Status* classes.

```xml
<?xml version="1.0" encoding="utf-8"?>
<Elements xmlns="http://schemas.microsoft.com/sharepoint/">
  <CustomAction
    RegistrationType="ContentType"
    RegistrationId="0x0101008D841CAC0C7F474288965287B30061DC"
    Id="DevLeap.CustomActions.Invoices.Notifications"
    Location="CommandUI.Ribbon.ListView">
    <CommandUIExtension>
      <CommandUIDefinitions>
        <CommandUIDefinition
          Location="Ribbon.Tabs._children">
          <Tab
            Id="DevLeap.CustomActions.Invoices.NotificationsTab"
            Title="Notification &amp; Status"
            Description="This tab holds commands for Status and Notifications."
            Sequence="1000">
            <Scaling
              Id="DevLeap.CustomActions.Invoices.NotificationsTab.Scaling">
              <MaxSize
Id="DevLeap.CustomActions.Invoices.NotificationsTab.One.Scaling.MaxSize"
                GroupId="DevLeap.CustomActions.Invoices.NotificationsTab.GroupOne"
                Size="TwoLarge"/>
              <MaxSize
Id="DevLeap.CustomActions.Invoices.NotificationsTab.Two.Scaling.MaxSize"
                GroupId="DevLeap.CustomActions.Invoices.NotificationsTab.GroupTwo"
                Size="TwoLarge"/>
              <Scale
Id="DevLeap.CustomActions.Invoices.NotificationsTab.One.Scaling.Scale"
                GroupId="DevLeap.CustomActions.Invoices.NotificationsTab.GroupOne"
                Size="TwoLarge" />
              <Scale
Id="DevLeap.CustomActions.Invoices.NotificationsTab.Two.Scaling.Scale"
                GroupId="DevLeap.CustomActions.Invoices.NotificationsTab.GroupTwo"
                Size="TwoLarge" />
            </Scaling>
```

```
                    <Groups Id="DevLeap.CustomActions.Invoices.NotificationsTab.Groups">
                      <Group
                        Id="DevLeap.CustomActions.Invoices.NotificationsTab.GroupOne"
                        Description="This is the Notification Area group."
                        Title="Notification"
                        Sequence="10"
Template="DevLeap.CustomActions.Invoices.RibbonTemplate.Notification">
                        <Controls
Id="DevLeap.CustomActions.Invoices.NotificationsTab.GroupOne.Controls">
                          <Button
Id="DevLeap.CustomActions.Invoices.NotificationsTab.GroupOne.ShowNotification"
                            Command="ShowNotificationCommand"
                            Sequence="10"
                            Description="Show Notification command."
Image16by16="/_layouts/images/DevLeap.SP2010.UIExtensions/Baloon_16x16.png"
Image32by32="/_layouts/images/DevLeap.SP2010.UIExtensions/Baloon_32x32.png"
                            LabelText="Show Notification"
                            TemplateAlias="customOne"/>
                          <Button
Id="DevLeap.CustomActions.Invoices.NotificationsTab.GroupOne.HideNotification"
                            Command="HideNotificationCommand"
                            Sequence="20"
                            Description="Hide Notification command."
Image16by16="/_layouts/images/DevLeap.SP2010.UIExtensions/Baloon_16x16.png"
Image32by32="/_layouts/images/DevLeap.SP2010.UIExtensions/Baloon_32x32.png"
                            LabelText="Hide Notification"
                            TemplateAlias="customTwo"/>
                        </Controls>
                      </Group>
                      <Group
                        Id="DevLeap.CustomActions.Invoices.NotificationsTab.GroupTwo"
                        Description="This is the Status Area group."
                        Title="Status"
                        Sequence="20"
                        Template="DevLeap.CustomActions.Invoices.RibbonTemplate.Status">
                        <Controls Id="DevLeap.CustomActions.Invoices.NotificationsTab.
GroupTwo.Controls">
                          <Button
Id="DevLeap.CustomActions.Invoices.NotificationsTab.GroupTwo.ShowStatus"
                            Command="ShowStatusCommand"
                            Sequence="30"
                            Description="Show Status command."
Image16by16="/_layouts/images/DevLeap.SP2010.UIExtensions/Baloon_16x16.png"
Image32by32="/_layouts/images/DevLeap.SP2010.UIExtensions/Baloon_32x32.png"
                            LabelText="Show Status"
                            TemplateAlias="customThree"/>
                          <Button
Id="DevLeap.CustomActions.Invoices.NotificationsTab.GroupTwo.HideStatus"
                            Command="HideStatusCommand"
                            Sequence="40"
                            Description="Hide status command."
```

```
Image16by16="/_layouts/images/DevLeap.SP2010.UIExtensions/Baloon_16x16.png"
Image32by32="/_layouts/images/DevLeap.SP2010.UIExtensions/Baloon_32x32.png"
                    LabelText="Hide Status"
                    TemplateAlias="customFour"/>
            </Controls>
          </Group>
        </Groups>
      </Tab>
    </CommandUIDefinition>
    <CommandUIDefinition Location="Ribbon.Templates._children">
      <GroupTemplate Id="DevLeap.CustomActions.Invoices.RibbonTemplate.
Notification">
        <Layout
          Title="TwoLarge"
          LayoutTitle="TwoLarge">
          <Section Alignment="Top" Type="OneRow">
            <Row>
              <ControlRef DisplayMode="Large" TemplateAlias="customOne" />
              <ControlRef DisplayMode="Large" TemplateAlias="customTwo" />
            </Row>
          </Section>
        </Layout>
      </GroupTemplate>
    </CommandUIDefinition>
    <CommandUIDefinition Location="Ribbon.Templates._children">
      <GroupTemplate Id="DevLeap.CustomActions.Invoices.RibbonTemplate.Status">
        <Layout
          Title="TwoLarge"
          LayoutTitle="TwoLarge">
          <Section Alignment="Top" Type="OneRow">
            <Row>
              <ControlRef DisplayMode="Large" TemplateAlias="customThree" />
              <ControlRef DisplayMode="Large" TemplateAlias="customFour" />
            </Row>
          </Section>
        </Layout>
      </GroupTemplate>
    </CommandUIDefinition>
  </CommandUIDefinitions>
  <CommandUIHandlers>
    <CommandUIHandler
      Command="ShowNotificationCommand"
      CommandAction="javascript:
        this.notifyId = SP.UI.Notify.addNotification(
          'Notification message ...', true);" />
    <CommandUIHandler
      Command="HideNotificationCommand"
      CommandAction="javascript:
        SP.UI.Notify.removeNotification(this.notifyId);" />
```

```
        <CommandUIHandler
          Command="ShowStatusCommand"
          CommandAction="javascript:
            this.statusId = SP.UI.Status.addStatus('Status message ...');
            SP.UI.Status.setStatusPriColor(this.statusId, 'red');" />
        <CommandUIHandler
          Command="HideStatusCommand"
          CommandAction="javascript:
            SP.UI.Status.removeStatus(this.statusId);" />
      </CommandUIHandlers>
    </CommandUIExtension>
  </CustomAction>
  <CustomAction
    Location="ScriptLink"
    Id="DevLeap.CustomActions.Invoices.NotificationsTab"
    ScriptBlock="
      var notifyId = '';
      var statusId = '';
    "
    />
</Elements>
```

Take a look again at the last *CustomAction* element with a value of *ScriptLink* for the *Location* attribute. Notice that it instructs the SharePoint environment to include into the page the scripting code declared in the *ScriptBlock* attribute. As mentioned in Table 9-1, you can also reference an external script file, declaring the *ScriptSrc* attribute instead of the *ScriptBlock* attribute.

Dialog Framework

The last item you will learn about to extend the user interface is how to make use of the new Dialog Framework of SharePoint 2010, provided by the new class *SP.UI.ModalDialog* of the ECMAScript Client Object Model. Through this class, you can show pages inside modal dialog windows, and you can also pass information between the dialog window and the main window. Table 9-11 presents the main methods of the *SP.UI.ModalDialog* class.

TABLE 9-11 The Main Methods of the *SP.UI.ModalDialog* Class

Method	Description
close	Closes the current dialog window and returns a result value of type *SP.UI.DialogResult*. The *SP.UI.DialogResult* type can assume one of the following values: *invalid*, *cancel*, or *OK*.
commonModalDialogClose	Closes a modal dialog and returns a result value of type *SP.UI.DialogResult* and a custom return value of type *Object*. The *SP.UI.DialogResult* type can assume one of the following values: *invalid*, *cancel*, and *OK*.
commonModalDialogOpen	Opens a modal dialog and provides some input arguments, such as the URL of the content to show in the dialog, some options of type *SP.UI.DialogOptions*, a callback to a return function of type *SP.UI.DialogCallback*, and some extra arguments of type *Object*.
OpenPopUpPage	Opens a pop-up dialog page that provides some input arguments, such as the URL of the content to show in the pop-up page, a callback to a return function of type *SP.UI.DialogCallback*, and the *width* and *height* of the pop-up window.
RefreshPage	Reloads the current page for refreshing purposes.
showModalDialog	Shows a modal dialog that provides an input argument of type *SP.UI.DialogOptions*.
ShowPopupDialog	Shows a pop-up dialog that provides the URL of the content to show in the pop-up.
showWaitScreenSize	Shows a wait screen that provides some input arguments, such as the *title* of the window, the *message* to show while waiting, a *callbackFunc* delegate to a return function, and the *width* and *height* of the window.
showWaitScreenWithNoClose	The same as *showWaitScreenSize* but without a close button in the upper-right corner of the window. This kind of window must be closed by custom code.

Take a look at how some of these methods work. Suppose that you want to extend the list of invoices, providing a custom Ribbon command to open a pop-up window for changing the status of an item. Aside from the Ribbon command definition, which by now should be familiar to you, consider the scripting code defined in Listing 9-24 that shows a custom application page to manage the invoice status.

LISTING 9-24 The scripting code used to show a modal dialog for changing the status of an invoice.

```
// Function to open the dialog
function openChangeStatusDialog() {

    var ctx = SP.ClientContext.get_current();
    var selectedItem = SP.ListOperation.Selection.getSelectedItems(ctx)[0];
```

```
   var options = SP.UI.$create_DialogOptions();
   options.url = '/_layouts/DevLeap.SP2010.UIExtensions/' +
   'DevLeapInvoiceChangeStatusDialog.aspx' + '?ListId=' +
   SP.ListOperation.Selection.getSelectedList() +
   '&amp;ItemId=' + selectedItem.id;
   options.autoSize = true;
   options.dialogReturnValueCallback = Function.createDelegate(null,
dialogCloseCallback);
   this.dialog = SP.UI.ModalDialog.showModalDialog(options);
}

// Function to handle close callback
function dialogCloseCallback(result, returnValue) {
   if (result == SP.UI.DialogResult.OK) {
     window.alert('You clicked OK! And selected a status of: ' + returnValue);
   }
   if (result == SP.UI.DialogResult.cancel) {
     window.alert('You clicked Cancel!');
   }
   SP.UI.ModalDialog.RefreshPage(result);
}
```

Listing 9-24 demonstrates that the custom function *openChangeStatusDialog* creates a variable of type *SP.UI.DialogOptions* and provides it to the *SP.UI.ModalDialog.showModalDialog* method. The *SP.UI.DialogOptions* class is made of some members that are useful when creating a dialog window. These members are:

- *url*   The URL of the resource to load in the dialog window.

- *html*   Use this to include HTML content that you want to display in the dialog window, (in case you don't want to provide a URL). The content must be provided as a DOM graph of nodes and not as a simple text value.

- *title*   The title of the dialog window.

- *args*   Represents optional arguments that can be passed to the dialog window.

- *width*   The width of the dialog window.

- *height*   The height of the dialog window.

- *x*   Specifies the X-coordinate location of the upper-left corner of the dialog window.

- *y*   Specifies the Y-coordinate location of the upper-left corner of the dialog window.

- *autoSize*   A *Boolean* value that specifies whether the dialog framework will handle auto-sizing of the dialog window, based on its content.

- *allowMaximize*   A *Boolean* value that specifies whether the dialog window can be maximized.

- *showMaximized*   A *Boolean* value that specifies whether the dialog window will be opened maximized or not.

- *showClose*   A *Boolean* value that specifies whether the Close button will be shown or not.

- *dialogReturnValueCallback*   A delegate to a callback function to invoke when the dialog will be closed.

The callback function receives a *result* argument that allows determining whether the end user clicked the *cancel* button or the *OK* button to close the dialog. In addition, it also takes a *returnValue* argument, in case the dialog window returns something back to the main window. Notice that the code in Listing 9-25 defines the target *url* of the dialog window, including in the URL the *ListId* and *ItemId* of the current list and selected item, read using the Client Object Model. Figure 9-12 shows the dialog window in action.

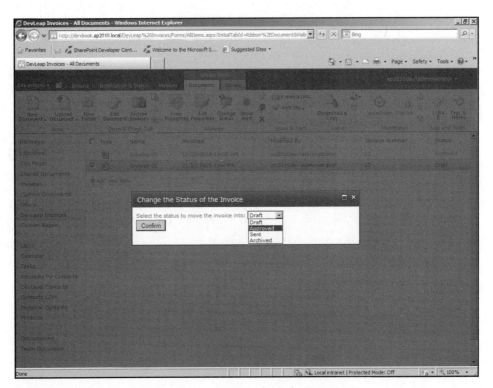

FIGURE 9-12 The dialog window to change the *Status* field of an invoice.

The target page is available in the source code samples, but it will not be explained here in detail because it is a standard application page, just as the one you have already seen in Listing 9-16 in the section, "Application Pages" on page 297. However, one particularly interesting piece of code of the *DevLeapInvoiceChangeStatusDialog.aspx* page opened in the dialog is the script used to close the dialog itself, which gives a feedback to the parent page. Listing 9-25 illustrates that code excerpt.

LISTING 9-25 The scripting code used to show a modal dialog for changing the status of an invoice.

```
// In case we are in a PopUp dialog, we need to close it
if ((SPContext.Current != null) && SPContext.Current.IsPopUI) {
    this.Context.Response.Write("<script type='text/javascript'>window.frameElement.
commonModalDialogClose(1, '" + statusDropDown.SelectedValue + "');</script>");
    this.Context.Response.Flush();
    this.Context.Response.End();
}
```

Notice that the current *SPContext* provides a property named *IsPopUI* to check if the current page is loaded in a pop-up dialog environment. If it is, the page writes to the ASP.NET *Response* a small piece of JavaScript code to close the dialog, returning a status of *SP.UI. DialogResult.OK* (= 1) and the value selected by the end user for the *Status* field.

Summary

In this chapter, you absorbed a lot of information about how to customize and extend the native SharePoint user interface. In particular, you have seen how to create features of type *CustomAction*, *CustomActionGroup*, and *HideCustomAction*. You learned how to create custom Ribbon commands and tabs, using the new Ribbon Model provided by SharePoint 2010. You also saw how to utilize the ECMAScript Client Object Model to implement the logic of your custom commands. You discovered how to use the *DelegateControl* class to customize the environment. You learned how to deploy contents by using *Module* features so you can provision images, custom content pages and custom application pages, as well as Web Part Pages and items in galleries. Finally, you saw how to improve the user experience by working with the Notification Area, the Status Bar, and the Dialog Framework.

Chapter 10
Data Provisioning

The previous chapters showed you how many SharePoint solutions use lists of items that contain data such as contacts, files, and so on. One main task when developing a SharePoint solution is to provision data structures for these lists of items. Whenever you need to develop a reusable and maintainable solution that will reside on many different site collections and with many different customers, you should formally define the data structures that you will use, rather than simply designing them through SharePoint's visual design interface from a web browser as an end user could do.

> **Note** Within the context of this book, the term "data structure" means the formal definition of custom List Definitions, Content Types, and Site Columns. Such formal definitions help to ensure data consistency across lists and sites.

This chapter explores the rules for custom lists and the tools that Microsoft SharePoint 2010 provides to accomplish these kinds of tasks. As a case study, you will see how to define a custom list of Contacts, based on two Content Types (Customer and Supplier), that use custom forms and are browsable through specific list views.

Site Columns

The first and main step in provisioning a custom data structure is to define Site Columns. A Site Column describes a reusable data type model that you can use in many different Content Types and lists definitions, across multiple SharePoint sites.

Unless you have never used SharePoint at all, you have already defined many Site Columns using a web browser, within the appropriate section of the Site Settings page; however, it is possible to define a Site Column using a feature element.

> **More Information** If you need a refresher, see Chapter 8, "SharePoint Features and Solutions," for further details about features and feature elements.

Listing 10-1 shows a very simple Site Column definition for a *Text* column that describes the "Company Name" of the sample Contact.

LISTING 10-1 A simple Site Column defined in a feature element

```xml
<?xml version="1.0" encoding="utf-8"?>
<Elements xmlns="http://schemas.microsoft.com/sharepoint/">
  <Field
    ID="{A8F24550-55CD-4d34-A015-811954C6CE24}"
    Name="DevLeapCompanyName"
    StaticName="DevLeapCompanyName"
    DisplayName="Company Name"
    Type="Text"
    Group="DevLeap Columns" />
</Elements>
```

Aside from the *Elements* tag itself (described in Chapter 8), the interesting part of the preceding column definition is the *Field* element. The most important feature of this element is the *ID* attribute, which is a GUID that uniquely identifies the Site Column. You can use this to reference this specific Site Column in each and every solution where you use it.

Listing 10-1 declares that the Company Name column will have an internal *Name* of "DevLeapCompanyName". *Name* is a required attribute, and like the *ID* attribute, it should also be unique, because it provides an alternative way to exclusively reference the column from code. In general, this example uses the company name value as a prefix to better ensure the uniqueness of this *Name*. The *Name* attribute value cannot contain spaces or directly contain any characters other than numbers (0–9) and letters (a–z; A–Z). Any other characters will be converted into the corresponding hexadecimal representation. For example, if you want to give a field the *Name* "Company Name," you must define it as *Company_x0020_ Name*. If you want to name a field "Revenue %," you must define it as *Revenue_x0020__ x0025_*. The last thing to keep in mind is that the *Name* attribute cannot be longer than 32 characters.

The preceding Site Column definition also defines the optional *StaticName* attribute, which is another way of defining the internal name. Finally, the Site Column definition defines the field's *DisplayName* attribute, whose value is the title that users will see in their browsers. This last attribute can take advantage of the multilanguage support provided by .NET in general, so declaring its value as a resource string reference ("*$Resources:<Assembly_ Name>,<Resource_Name>;*") instead of an explicit value will result in a multilanguage value.

Why Do You Need Three Attributes to Define Field Name Types?

You might be wondering why there are three attributes to define three kinds of names for a single field. The XML schema that we are using can be used by a developer, as we are doing here, but it is also used internally by SharePoint itself to represent a Site Column. When you define a column using the web browser interface, SharePoint automatically determines the internal name (for instance, *Name* and *StaticName*) based on the name (which becomes the *DisplayName*) that you give it, automatically converting any non-alpha and non-numeric characters to their corresponding hexadecimal representations, and then trimming the resulting string to 32 characters for the *Name* attribute, leaving the *StaticName* attribute value as long as needed. If a Site Column with the same *Name* already exists, SharePoint appends a number to the name, using a zero-based index.

If you later change the *DisplayName* of the field, SharePoint will keep both the *StaticName* and the *Name* unchanged. That scheme gives your Site Column three different values for the three attributes: the *DisplayName*, the *StaticName*, which is simply the original *DisplayName* with hexadecimal conversion of non-alphanumeric characters, and the *Name,* with hexadecimal conversion of non-alphanumeric characters trimmed to 32 characters.

Lastly, using the SharePoint Server Object Model (for further details, see Chapter 3, "Server Object Model") you can change the *StaticName*, but you cannot change the internal *Name* value. Therefore, when you have to define Site Columns using a feature element, I suggest that you assign the *Name* and the *StaticName* the same value, avoid using non-alphanumeric characters, and provide a descriptive value for the *DisplayName* attribute.

The *Type* attribute is mandatory for Site Column definitions. It defines the data type assigned to the field. This *Type* attribute value can be one of a predefined set of SharePoint field types (see Table 10-1), or it can be a custom field type that you have defined and deployed (refer to Chapter 11, "Developing Custom Fields"). Table 10-1 presents some of the main field types provided by SharePoint.

More Information For a complete list of field types, refer to the online product reference at *http://msdn.microsoft.com/en-us/library/ms437580(office.14).aspx.*

TABLE 10-1 Common Predefined Field Types

Field Type Name	Description
Boolean	Represents a Boolean value (*TRUE* or *FALSE*), stored as a *bit* in SQL Server and accessible as an *SPFieldBoolean* object through the Object Model.
Choice	Allows the user to select a single value from a predefined set of values. The XML schema of the *Field* must declare the values (for further details see Listing 10-2 on page 319). It is stored as an *nvarchar* in SQL Server, and is accessible as an *SPFieldChoice* object through the Object Model.
MultiChoice	Allows the user to select multiple values from a predefined set of values. The XML schema of the Field has to declare the values. It is stored as an *ntext* in SQL Server, and is accessible as an *SPFieldMultiChoice* object through the Object Model.
Currency	Defines a currency value. *Currency* is bound to a specific locale, using an *LCID* attribute. It can have constraints using *Min*, *Max* and *Decimals* attributes. It is stored as a *float* in SQL Server, and is accessible as an *SPFieldCurrency* object through the Object Model.
DateTime	Saves a date and time value. *DateTime* is stored as a *datetime* in SQL Server, and is accessible as an *SPFieldDateTime* object through the Object Model.
Lookup and *LookupMulti*	These field types behave almost the same as *Choice* and *MultiChoice*; however, the set of values to choose from is taken from another list of items within the same site. These field types are stored as *ints* in SQL Server, and are accessible as *SPFieldLookup* objects through the Object Model.
Note	Stores multiple lines of text. *Note* is stored as an *ntext* in SQL Server, and is accessible as an *SPFieldMultiLineText* object through the Object Model.
Number	Defines a floating point number. *Number* can have constraints using *Decimals*, *Div*, *Max*, *Min*, *Mult*, and *Percentage*. It is stored as a *float* in SQL Server, and is accessible as an *SPFieldNumber* object through the Object Model.
Text	Describes a single line of text of a configurable *MaxLength*. *Text* is stored as an *nvarchar* in SQL Server, and is accessible as an *SPFieldText* object through the Object Model.
URL	Defines a URL with a specific *LinkType* (*Hyperlink* or *Image*). *URL* is stored as an *nvarchar* in SQL Server, and is accessible as an *SPFieldUrl* object through the Object Model.
User and *UserMulti*	These field types describe a lookup for a single User, or for a set of Users. These are stored as an *ints* in SQL Server, and are accessible as *SPFieldUser* objects through the Object Model.

The last attribute defined in the Site Column example is the *Group* attribute, which simply defines a group membership to make it easier to find custom fields through the web browser administrative interface. *Group* is an optional attribute, but I suggest that you define it whenever you create a custom Site Column, to group your columns in personalized custom groups.

Table 10-2 shows some other interesting attributes that you can use when defining custom Site Columns.

TABLE 10-2 Interesting Optional *Boolean* Attributes Available for the Field Element

Field Attribute	Description
Hidden	The *Hidden* attribute can assume a value of *TRUE* or *FALSE*. When *TRUE*, the field will be completely hidden from the user interface and will be accessible only through code, using the Object Model.
ReadOnly	The *ReadOnly* attribute can assume a value of *TRUE* or *FALSE*. When *TRUE*, the field will not be displayed in *New* and *Edit* forms, but can be included in *Views*. It will remain accessible using the Object Model.
Required	The *Required* attribute can assume a value of *TRUE* or *FALSE*. Its name implies its role.
RichText	The *RichText* attribute can assume a value of *TRUE* or *FALSE*. It determines whether a text field will accept rich text formatting.
ShowInDisplayForm	The *ShowInDisplayForm* attribute can assume a value of *TRUE* or *FALSE*. When *FALSE*, the field will not be displayed in the display form of the item containing the field.
ShowInEditForm	The *ShowInEditForm* attribute can assume a value of *TRUE* or *FALSE*. When *FALSE*, the field will not be displayed in the editing form of the item containing the field.
ShowInNewForm	The *ShowInNewForm* attribute can assume a value of *TRUE* or *FALSE*. If it is *FALSE*, the field will not be displayed in the form to add a new item containing the field.

Note While you can declare many other attributes when defining a custom Site Column schema, the goal here is not to write an exhaustive keyword reference; instead, it's to provide you with sufficient information so that you can understand how SharePoint works and how to realize its potentials.

Listing 10-2 shows a more complex Site Column definition that declares a *MultiChoice* field used to select the Contact's country affiliation.

LISTING 10-2 A *MultiChoice* site column defined in a feature element.

```
<?xml version="1.0" encoding="utf-8"?>
<Elements xmlns="http://schemas.microsoft.com/sharepoint/">
  <Field
    ID="{149BF9A1-5BBB-468d-AA35-91ACEB054E3B}"
    Name="DevLeapCountry"
    StaticName="DevLeapCountry"
    DisplayName="Country"
    Type="Choice"
    Group="DevLeap Columns"
```

```
      Sortable="TRUE">
        <Default>Italy</Default>
        <CHOICES>
          <CHOICE>Italy</CHOICE>
          <CHOICE>USA</CHOICE>
          <CHOICE>Germany</CHOICE>
          <CHOICE>France</CHOICE>
        </CHOICES>
    </Field>
  </Elements>
```

This example shows how you can define a set of available values for a *Choice* field. Note that the list defines a *Default* element.

Another interesting task that you can accomplish when defining a Site Column is to declare a custom validation rule for its content. To do that, you simply define a *Validation* element as a child of the *Field* definition. The *Validation* element can have a *Message* attribute, which defines an error message to show to the end user when validation fails, and a *Script* attribute, which defines a JavaScript rule that performs the validation. Alternatively, you can define a rule using the *Formulas* syntax of SharePoint, putting the rule inside the *Validation* element.

> **More Information** For further details on Calculated Fields and Formulas in SharePoint, refer to the corresponding MSDN page at *http://msdn.microsoft.com/en-us/library/bb862071(office.14).aspx*.

Content Types

A Content Type schema defines a model for a specific SharePoint complex data type, and is based on a set of Site Column references, together with some other optional information related to forms, rendering templates, a specific document template (only in case of document items), and custom XML configuration.

Chapter 2, "Data Foundation," showed how SharePoint uses a hierarchical structure for defining Content Types, which consists of a base Content Type named *System* with a single child named *Item*. SharePoint then applies an inheritance paradigm (similar to OOP class inheritance) to define each and every Content Type descendant of *Item*. Figure 10-1 shows an excerpt of the hierarchical inheritance tree for native Content Types.

As a consequence of this behavior, provisioning Content Types also requires you to define inheritance information for any new Content Type that you declare. For more details, read the section, "Content Type IDs," on page 323.

Listing 10-3 provides an example of the Contact Content Type, defined by referencing a set of Site Columns.

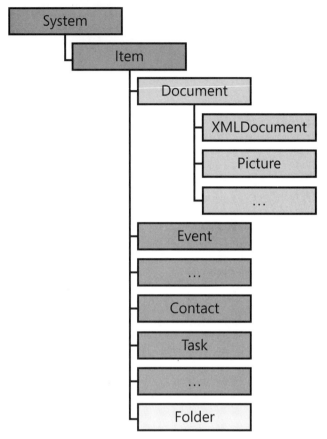

FIGURE 10-1 The Content Types inheritance hierarchy in SharePoint.

LISTING 10-3 A simple Content Type defined in a feature element, together with its Site Columns.

```xml
<?xml version="1.0" encoding="utf-8"?>
<Elements xmlns="http://schemas.microsoft.com/sharepoint/">
  <!-- Site Columns used by the Content Type -->
  <Field
    ID="{C7792AD6-F2F3-4f2d-A7E5-75D5A8206FD9}"
    Name="DevLeapContactID"
    StaticName="DevLeapContactID"
    DisplayName="Contact ID"
    Type="Text"
    Group="DevLeap Columns"
    Sortable="TRUE" />
  <Field
    ID="{A8F24550-55CD-4d34-A015-811954C6CE24}"
    Name="DevLeapCompanyName"
    StaticName="DevLeapCompanyName"
    DisplayName="Company Name"
    Type="Text"
    Group="DevLeap Columns"
```

```
          Sortable="TRUE" />
      <Field
        ID="{149BF9A1-5BBB-468d-AA35-91ACEB054E3B}"
        Name="DevLeapCountry"
        StaticName="DevLeapCountry"
        DisplayName="Country"
        Type="Choice"
        Group="DevLeap Columns"
        Sortable="TRUE">
          <Default>Italy</Default>
          <CHOICES>
            <CHOICE>Italy</CHOICE>
            <CHOICE>USA</CHOICE>
            <CHOICE>Germany</CHOICE>
            <CHOICE>France</CHOICE>
          </CHOICES>
      </Field>
      <!-- Parent ContentType: Item (0x01) -->
      <ContentType ID="0x0100a60f69c4b1304fbda6c4b4a25939979f"
                   Name="DevLeapContact"
                   Group="DevLeap Content Types"
                   Description="Base Contact of DevLeap"
                   Inherits="TRUE"
                   Version="0">
        <FieldRefs>
          <FieldRef
            ID="{fa564e0f-0c70-4ab9-b863-0177e6ddd247}"
            Name="Title"
            DisplayName="Full name" />
          <FieldRef
            ID="{C7792AD6-F2F3-4f2d-A7E5-75D5A8206FD9}"
            Name="DevLeapContactID"
            DisplayName="Contact ID"
            Required="TRUE" />
          <FieldRef
            ID="{A8F24550-55CD-4d34-A015-811954C6CE24}"
            Name="DevLeapCompanyName"
            DisplayName="Company Name" />
          <FieldRef
            ID="{149BF9A1-5BBB-468d-AA35-91ACEB054E3B}"
            Name="DevLeapCountry"
            DisplayName="Country" />
        </FieldRefs>
      </ContentType>
    </Elements>
```

The sample Content type listing contains a *ContentType* element, which defines some descriptive information, such as the *Name*, *Group*, and *Description*. The *ContentType* element also defines a *Version* attribute, which indeed is used for managing versioning as its name implies, but still reserved by Microsoft for future use. Last, but most important is the *ID* attribute, which defines the unique identifier for this Content Type in the Site Collection where it is defined. Inside the *ContentType* element you can see a *FieldRefs* element, which is the parent of a list of *FieldRef* or *RemoveFieldRef* elements. Each element in this list references a specific Site Column to be added or removed from this Content Type. You might notice that this example references all the Site Columns defined earlier in the feature element file. In fact, it's common to define the referenced Site Columns within the same feature element file—just before the Content Type that will use them.

Listing 10-3 also references a Site Column with the name "Title" and with the *ID {fa564e0f-0c70-4ab9-b863-0177e6ddd247}*. This is the SharePoint native Site Column that defines the *Title* field for each and every SharePoint item. In the Content Type example, we changed the *DisplayName* value from "Title," which still remains its internal name, to "Full name," which will be the displayed name for this Content Type. By default, the *Title* field is also used by SharePoint to render the Edit Control Block menu, which allows you to display, edit, and manage a list item from the list UI.

Content Type IDs

The *ID* attribute of a Content Type is not a simple GUID, as it was with the Site Columns definition; instead, it's a more complex value that describes the hierarchical inheritance of the type. In fact, every Content Type ID is composed of the *ID* of its hierarchical parent Content Type, followed by a hexadecimal value that's specific and unique to the current Content Type. You could say that a Content Type ID defines its genealogy. This logic is recursive, starting with the *System* Content Type, and extending all the way down to the current Content Type. Table 10-3 shows an excerpt of the base hierarchy of SharePoint Content Type IDs.

TABLE 10-3 An Excerpt of the Base Hierarchy of SharePoint Content Type IDs

Content Type	ID
System	0x
Item	0x01
Document	0x0101
XmlDocument	0x010101
Picture	0x010102
Event	0x0102
...	
Contact	0x0106
Task	0x0108
...	
Folder	0x0120

Table 10-3 demonstrates that the root Content Type is *System*, which is a special hidden Content Type with an *ID* value of *0x*. The *Item* Content Type is the only child of *System* and has an *ID* value of *0x01* (the *System ID + 01*). The *Document* Content Type, which is a child of *Item*, has an *ID* value of *0x0101*(the *Item ID + 01*), while its sibling Event has an *ID* of *0x0102* the *Item ID + 02*).

In general, the rule used to define Content Type IDs states that you can build an ID using two different techniques:

- Parent Content Type ID + two hexadecimal values (cannot be "00")
- Parent Content Type ID + "00" + hexadecimal GUID

Microsoft generally uses the first technique to define base Content Type IDs, while non-Microsoft developers typically use the latter technique to define custom Content Type IDs. If you want to define a hierarchy of custom Content Types of your own, you should:

1. Identify the base Content Type from which you want to inherit.
2. Add 00 at the end of the base Content Type ID.
3. Add a hexadecimal GUID just after the *00*.
4. Append two hexadecimal values to declare every specific child of your Content Type.

As a concrete example, suppose that you want to define a custom Content Type inherited from the *Document* base Content Type. You would start with *0x0101*, which is the *Document ID*, append *00* to it, and then append a hexadecimal GUID, making your *ID* something like ***0x010100****BDD3EC87EA65463AB9FAA5337907A3ED*

If you wanted to use your custom Content Type as a base for some other inherited Content Types, you would append *01*, *02*, and so on for each child Content Type, as in the following example:

- Base ID   0x010100BDD3EC87EA65463AB9FAA5337907A3ED
- Child 1   0x010100BDD3EC87EA65463AB9FAA5337907A3ED01
- Child 2   0x010100BDD3EC87EA65463AB9FAA5337907A3ED02

> **More Information**   Content type IDs have a maximum length of 512 bytes. Because every two hexadecimal characters correspond to a single byte, a Content Type ID has a maximum length of 1024 characters.

With that in mind, we can go back to the example custom Contact Content Type. First, you need to choose the base Content Type from which you want to inherit. For example purposes, assume that you decided to use the generic base *Item* as the parent Content Type. That means the custom Content Type ID will start with *0x01*, followed by *00* and then a hexadecimal GUID. The end result is the same as the ID highlighted in bold in Listing 10-3:

ID="**0x0100**a60f69c4b1304fbda6c4b4a25939979f"

The goal of the case study is to define a custom list that is based on a couple of Content Types (*Customer* and *Supplier*) inherited from this base Contact Content Type. Listing 10-4 shows the definitions of the *Customer* and *Supplier* Content Types.

LISTING 10-4 *Customer* and *Supplier* content type definitions.

```xml
<?xml version="1.0" encoding="utf-8"?>
<Elements xmlns="http://schemas.microsoft.com/sharepoint/">
  <Field
      ID="{AC689935-8E8B-485e-A45E-FF5A338DD92F}"
      Name="DevLeapCustomerLevel"
      StaticName="DevLeapCustomerLevel"
      DisplayName="Customer Level"
      Type="Choice"
      Group="DevLeap Columns">
    <Default>Level C</Default>
    <CHOICES>
      <CHOICE>Level A</CHOICE>
      <CHOICE>Level B</CHOICE>
      <CHOICE>Level C</CHOICE>
    </CHOICES>
  </Field>
  <Field
      ID="{A73DE518-B9B9-4e8d-9D94-6099B4603997}"
      Name="DevLeapSupplierAccount"
      StaticName="DevLeapSupplierAccount"
      DisplayName="Supplier Account"
      Type="User"
      Group="DevLeap Columns"
      Sortable="TRUE" />
  <ContentType ID="0x0100a60f69c4b1304fbda6c4b4a25939979f01"
              Name="DevLeapCustomer"
              Group="DevLeap Content Types"
              Description="Customer of DevLeap"
              Version="0">
    <FieldRefs>
      <FieldRef
          ID="{AC689935-8E8B-485e-A45E-FF5A338DD92F}"
          Name="DevLeapCustomerLevel"
          Required="TRUE" />
    </FieldRefs>
  </ContentType>
  <ContentType ID="0x0100a60f69c4b1304fbda6c4b4a25939979f02"
              Name="DevLeapSupplier"
              Group="DevLeap Content Types"
              Description="Supplier of DevLeap"
              Version="0">
```

```
    <FieldRefs>
      <FieldRef
          ID="{A73DE518-B9B9-4e8d-9D94-6099B4603997}"
          Name="DevLeapSupplierAccount"
          Required="TRUE" />
    </FieldRefs>
  </ContentType>
</Elements>
```

Both of these Content Types extend the base *Contact* Content Type; each adds a specific Site Column. The *Customer* Content Type adds a required field to define the "Customer Level" (A, B, or C) for each *Customer* instance, while the *Supplier* Content Type adds a field to reference a local *Account*, browsable as a SharePoint User.

Figure 10-2 shows a portion of the Site Content Types page of a Site Collection, where Listing 10-4 provisioned these three Content Types. The figure shows the inheritance hierarchy for the custom Content Types.

Site Content Type	Parent
DevLeap Content Types	
DevLeapContact	Item
DevLeapCustomer	DevLeapContact
DevLeapSupplier	DevLeapContact

FIGURE 10-2 The Site Content Types page of a site collection where the custom Content Types are provisioned.

Finally, consider that Microsoft Visual Studio 2010 automatically calculates the Content Type IDs when you add a new Content Type to a SharePoint project.

More about Content Types

There are some other interesting attributes available to you when defining custom Content Types. One is the *ReadOnly* attribute, which makes the Content Type read-only when its value is set to *TRUE*. Another is the *Sealed* attribute, which seals a Content Type so that only a Site Collection Administrator using the Object Model can unseal them for editing purposes. And last, there is a *Hidden* attribute, which is useful for making a Content Type invisible so that end users will not have the capability to create new items of this type in list views, but you will still have access to it through your custom code. If you want to declare a Content Type completely invisible, not only for end users but also for site collection administrators, you can make it belong to a special group named _Hidden.

In addition, you can configure a Content Type not only through *ContentType* element attributes, but also by declaring some child elements. One of these is the *FieldRefs* child element that you have already seen earlier in this chapter. Another useful element is *XmlDocuments*, with which you can define any kind of custom XML configuration to apply to the Content Type. SharePoint itself uses this element to declare custom controls and pages for the Content Type. Listing 10-5 shows how to use this element.

LISTING 10-5 This excerpt shows how to use the *XmlDocuments* element inside a Content Type definition.

```xml
<?xml version="1.0" encoding="utf-8"?>
<Elements xmlns="http://schemas.microsoft.com/sharepoint/">
  <ContentType ID="0x0100a60f69c4b1304fbda6c4b4a25939979f01"
               Name="DevLeapCustomer"
               Group="DevLeap Content Types"
               Description="Customer of DevLeap"
               Inherits="TRUE"
               Version="0">
    <FieldRefs>
      <FieldRef
        ID="{AC689935-8E8B-485e-A45E-FF5A338DD92F}"
        Name="DevLeapCustomerLevel"
        Required="TRUE" />
    </FieldRefs>
    <XmlDocuments>
      <XmlDocument NamespaceURI=
        "http://schemas.microsoft.com/sharepoint/v3/contenttype/forms">
        <FormTemplates xmlns=
          "http://schemas.microsoft.com/sharepoint/v3/contenttype/forms">
          <Display>DevLeapCustomerDisplay</Display>
          <Edit>DevLeapCustomerEdit</Edit>
          <New>DevLeapCustomerNew</New>
        </FormTemplates>
      </XmlDocument>
    </XmlDocuments>
  </ContentType>
</Elements>
```

Listing 10-5 shows that the *XmlDocuments* element is just a container for one or more *XmlDocument* elements. Every *XmlDocument* element can have a *NamespaceURI* attribute that declares the scope of the custom configuration defined. Listing 10-5 declares a configuration that defines custom ASCX controls that are used for rendering display, edit, and add forms for instances of the current Content Type. The ASCX controls referenced should be deployed inside the CONTROLTEMPLATES special folder of SharePoint. The content of each *XmlDocument* element derives from the referenced *NamespaceURI*. The only requirement is that the XML content must be valid against its declared XML schema.

When you consider that you can access any custom *XmlDocument* that you define while provisioning Content Types later through the Object Model, you can see that the model provides you with an extremely customizable environment.

Document Content Types

Content types inherited from the *Document* base Content Type (ID: *0x0101*) are a special case that you must analyze a bit more carefully. In fact, every document has numerous specific configurations that it must handle. For instance, in the section "Content Types," on page 47, you learned that a document can have a Document Template and/or a Document Information Panel.

Listing 10-6 shows the definition for a custom document Content Type that declares an Invoice document model.

LISTING 10-6 An example of the *Invoice* Content Type, inherited from the *Document* Content Type.

```xml
<?xml version="1.0" encoding="utf-8"?>
<Elements xmlns="http://schemas.microsoft.com/sharepoint/">
  <!-- Parent ContentType: Document (0x0101) -->
  <ContentType ID="0x010100a5fd8267a91945df9f3884d9eaa4f12f"
               Name="DevLeapInvoice"
               Group="DevLeap Content Types"
               Description="Invoice of DevLeap"
               Inherits="TRUE"
               Version="0">
    <FieldRefs>
      <!-- Field References here -->
    </FieldRefs>
    <DocumentTemplate TargetName="/_layouts/DevLeapInvoiceTemplate.dotx" />
  </ContentType>
</Elements>
```

The Document portion of the *ID* is highlighted in bold, to remind you of the underlying behavior of SharePoint. The *DocumentTemplate* element (also highlighted) has a *TargetName* attribute that defines the URL (absolute for the site collection) of the template item to use for every new *Invoice* instance. Listing 10-7 shows you how to define a custom Document Information Panel for a *Document* Content Type, assuming that you have already designed and deployed the panel.

LISTING 10-7 An example of an *Invoice* Content Type, inherited from the *Document* Content Type, with a custom Document Information Panel.

```xml
<?xml version="1.0" encoding="utf-8"?>
<Elements xmlns="http://schemas.microsoft.com/sharepoint/">
  <!-- Parent ContentType: Document (0x0101) -->
  <ContentType ID="0x010100a5fd8267a91945df9f3884d9eaa4f12f"
               Name="DevLeapInvoice"
               Group="DevLeap Content Types"
               Description="Invoice of DevLeap"
               Inherits="TRUE"
               Version="0">
```

```
    <FieldRefs>
      <!-- Field References here -->
    </FieldRefs>
    <XmlDocuments>
      <XmlDocument NamespaceURI=
        "http://schemas.microsoft.com/office/2006/metadata/customXsn">
        <xsnLocation>http://URL/customXsn.xsn</xsnLocation>
        <cached>False</cached>
        <openByDefault>True</openByDefault>
        <xsnScope>http://URL/documentLibrary</xsnScope>
      </XmlDocument>
    </XmlDocuments>
  </ContentType>
</Elements>
```

The example declares the absolute URL of the Document Information Panel by using the *xsnLocation* element. It also disables caching in the Microsoft Office client by setting the *cached* element to *FALSE*. Lastly, it defines how the document should behave relative to this new panel, through the *openByDefault* element, which is set to *TRUE*, meaning that the panel should open by default. The *xsnScope* element is required, but for now it is reserved by Microsoft for internal use only.

List Definitions

Now that we have defined our Content Types, we are ready to use them in a real list of Contacts, comprising Customers and Suppliers. In fact, generally, whenever you define a set of custom Content Types, you also define one or more list definitions that use these Content Types. A list definition is simply a formal representation, using an XML schema, of a list data model from which you are able to create one or more instances of items corresponding to that model.

In SharePoint 2010, a list definition is a combination of two files: a Schema.xml file, which defines the data structure and configuration of the list definition model, and a feature element file that describes the *ListTemplate*, which defines the information required for provisioning and deploying the list definition model.

List Schema File

The list schema file is an XML document that describes all the metadata for the list data structure. The main areas of the Schema.xml file for a list definition are:

- **Content Types**   This section defines the Content Types that will be available within the list definition.

- **Fields** This section declares the list-level Site Columns, which correspond to the entire set of Site Columns referenced by all the Content Types associated with the list definition.

- **Views** This section defines the views that will be available to the end user for navigating among the items of list template instances.

- **Forms** This section declares the ASPX pages that will be provided to the end user to add, display, and update items of a list instance based on the current list definition.

- **Validation** This section defines the validation rules for list items.

- **Toolbar** This section declares the type of toolbar that must be provided in the browser interface.

In addition to the preceding list, the complete XML schema contains some additional elements. Listing 10-8 shows an excerpt from a Schema.xml file that describes a list definition, together with these main sections.

LISTING 10-8 Excerpt of a List Definition Schema File

```xml
<?xml version="1.0" encoding="utf-8"?>
<List xmlns:ows="Microsoft SharePoint"
    Title="DevLeapContacts"
    FolderCreation="FALSE"
    Direction="$Resources:Direction;"
    Url="Lists/DevLeapContacts"
    BaseType="0"
    EnableContentTypes="TRUE"
    xmlns="http://schemas.microsoft.com/sharepoint/">
    <MetaData>
        <ContentTypes>
        <!-- Here are referenced the content types -->
        </ContentTypes>
        <Fields>
        <!-- Here are declared the list-level site columns -->
        </Fields>
        <Views>
        <!-- Here are defined the views -->
        </Views>
        <Forms>
        <!-- Here are declared the forms used to add, display, update items -->
        </Forms>
        <Validation>
        <!-- Here are declared the validation rules for list items -->
        </ Validation >
        <Toolbar />
        <!-- To define what kind of toolbar to use in the Web browser UI  -->
    </MetaData>
</List>
```

The *List* Element

The *List* element is the root of the schema file and declares some basic attributes for the list definition. The *Title* attribute defines the name of the list definition. The *BaseType* attribute defines the base list type to use for the current list definition. There is a *BaseTypes* element in the global Onet.xml file of SharePoint (for further details please read Chapter 14, "Site Templates") where all the possible integer values for the *BaseType* attribute are defined.

> **Note** The global ONET.XML file is located in the SharePoint14_Root\TEMPLATE\GLOBAL\XML folder.

The *BaseTypes* values available are:

- 0   Generic/Custom List
- 1   Document Library
- 2   Not used, may be reserved for future use
- 3   Discussion Forum (deprecated, use 0 instead)
- 4   Vote or Survey
- 5   Issues List

For example, Listing 10-8 used a *BaseType* with a value of *0* because we are defining a generic/custom list definition. The *Url* attribute is optional and defines the path to the root directory containing any ASPX file specific for the list definition. The *FolderCreation* attribute is also optional, and informs SharePoint whether to show (*TRUE*) or not to show (*FALSE*) the New Folder command in the list toolbar. Finally, the *Direction* attribute is optional and declares the reading direction: *RTL* (right-to-left), or *LTR* (left-to-right). In Listing 10-3, the *Direction* value is read from a resource string so the list will be compliant with the current locale settings of the site collection. Lastly, to make the users aware of the existence of the different Content Types available (*Contact*, *Customer*, and *Supplier*) when they are creating new items, we need to explicitly enable Content Types on the list definition, setting the *EnableContentTypes* attribute to a value of *TRUE*. There are many other attributes available for the *List* definition element; Table 10-4 shows some of them.

> **More Information** For a complete reference of all the available attributes for the List element, refer to the official product documentation on MSDN at *http://msdn.microsoft.com/en-us/library/ms415091(office.14).aspx*.

TABLE 10-4 **Some of the Main Attributes for the** *List* **Element of a Schema.xml List Definition File.**

Attribute	Description
DisableAttachments	Optional Boolean value to disable attachments on the list.
EnableMinorVersions	Optional Boolean value that controls versioning with major and minor version of items.
ModeratedList	Optional Boolean value to enable content approval on inserted items.
PrivateList	Optional Boolean value to specify that the list is private.
VersioningEnabled	Optional Boolean value to enable versioning on the list. This value can be changed when creating a list instance.

The *MetaData* Element

The main child element of *List* is the *MetaData* element, which wraps all the other elements in the Schema.xml file.

One of the main child nodes of *MetaData* is the *ContentTypes* element. This element declares the entire list of Content Types referenced by the current list definition. Listing 10-9 declares the *ContentTypes* element for the custom Contacts list.

LISTING 10-9 The *ContentTypes* section of metadata for the sample list definition.

```xml
<ContentTypes>
  <ContentType
    ID="0x0100a60f69c4b1304fbda6c4b4a25939979f"
    Name="DevLeapContact"
    Group="DevLeap Content Types"
    Description="Base Contact of DevLeap"
    Inherits="TRUE" Version="0" Hidden="TRUE">
    <FieldRefs>
      <FieldRef ID="{fa564e0f-0c70-4ab9-b863-0177e6ddd247}"
                Name="Title" DisplayName="Full name" Required="TRUE" />
      <FieldRef ID="{C7792AD6-F2F3-4f2d-A7E5-75D5A8206FD9}"
                Name="DevLeapContactID" DisplayName="Contact ID"
                Required="TRUE" />
      <FieldRef ID="{A8F24550-55CD-4d34-A015-811954C6CE24}"
                Name="DevLeapCompanyName" DisplayName="Company Name" />
      <FieldRef ID="{149BF9A1-5BBB-468d-AA35-91ACEB054E3B}"
                Name="DevLeapCountry" DisplayName="Country" />
    </FieldRefs>
  </ContentType>
  <ContentType
    ID="0x0100a60f69c4b1304fbda6c4b4a25939979f01"
    Name="DevLeapCustomer"
    Group="DevLeap Content Types"
    Description="Customer of DevLeap"
    Inherits="TRUE" Version="0">
```

```
     <FieldRefs>
       <FieldRef ID="{AC689935-8E8B-485e-A45E-FF5A338DD92F}"
                 Name="DevLeapCustomerLevel" Required="TRUE" />
     </FieldRefs>
     <XmlDocuments>
       <XmlDocument NamespaceURI=
         "http://schemas.microsoft.com/sharepoint/v3/contenttype/forms">
         <FormTemplates xmlns=
           "http://schemas.microsoft.com/sharepoint/v3/contenttype/forms">
           <Display>DevLeapCustomerDisplay</Display>
           <Edit>DevLeapCustomerEdit</Edit>
           <New>DevLeapCustomerNew</New>
         </FormTemplates>
       </XmlDocument>
     </XmlDocuments>
   </ContentType>
   <ContentType
     ID="0x0100a60f69c4b1304fbda6c4b4a25939979f02"
     Name="DevLeapSupplier"
     Group="DevLeap Content Types"
     Description="Supplier of DevLeap"
     Inherits="TRUE" Version="0">
     <FieldRefs>
       <FieldRef ID="{A73DE518-B9B9-4e8d-9D94-6099B4603997}"
                 Name="DevLeapSupplierAccount" Required="TRUE" />
     </FieldRefs>
   </ContentType>
 </ContentTypes>
```

Listing 10-9 defined all the Content Types already defined in the previous section, repeating their IDs to link these copies to the original definitions. You might be wondering why we would repeat these declarations instead of simply referencing them in some way, for example, by just linking their IDs. The reason for repeating the full declarations here is because, during a Content Type's lifetime, its structure might change. To prevent and avoid any data loss, SharePoint copies Content Type definitions inside the list definitions that use them. Doing so preserves data models and data instances even if someone later changes them. Imagine what would happen if you had a simple Content Type reference rather than a copy; if you were to provision a *Customer* Content Type and use it in a custom list, then a few months later, when you have thousands of customer instances in your list, you delete a column from the customer Content Type, or worse, delete the entire Content Type! Having a complete copy of the Content Type definition allows SharePoint to maintain your data, even when the original Content Type changes or is removed.

On the other hand, whenever you want to make a change to one of your provisioned Content Types and you want that change applied to each and every instance in a site collection, you need to explicitly force the update through the web browser Content Type administrative page, or through code using the Object Model, or by manually updating any references in all the provisioned XML files, including the schema.xml files for list definitions.

Listing 10-9 defines all three Content Types (*Contact, Customer,* and *Supplier*), and declares the base Contact as hidden, which forces users to explicitly create *Customer* or *Supplier* instances.

Another child of *MetaData* is the *Fields* element. It defines the list-level columns used to store metadata of items instances. These list-level columns are almost the same as the Site Columns defined in the first section of this chapter. Once again their definitions are duplicated rather than referenced, and for the same reasons: to support changes of the models without data loss during the Site Columns' lifetimes. The *Fields* section of the list definition contains all the columns used by any of the Content Types declared in the same Schema.xml file. Listing 10-10 shows the *Fields* element declared for the custom Contacts list.

LISTING 10-10 The *Fields* section of the *MetaData* element for the sample list definition.

```
<Fields>
  <Field ID="{c7792ad6-f2f3-4f2d-a7e5-75d5a8206fd9}"
         Name="DevLeapContactID"
         StaticName="DevLeapContactID"
         DisplayName="Contact ID"
         Type="Text"
         Group="DevLeap Columns"
         Sortable="TRUE" />
  <Field ID="{a8f24550-55cd-4d34-a015-811954c6ce24}"
         Name="DevLeapCompanyName"
         StaticName="DevLeapCompanyName"
         DisplayName="Company Name"
         Type="Text"
         Group="DevLeap Columns"
         Sortable="TRUE" />
  <Field ID="{149bf9a1-5bbb-468d-aa35-91aceb054e3b}"
         Name="DevLeapCountry"
         StaticName="DevLeapCountry"
         DisplayName="Country"
         Type="Choice"
         Group="DevLeap Columns"
         Sortable="TRUE">
  <Default>Italy</Default>
  <CHOICES>
    <CHOICE>Italy</CHOICE>
    <CHOICE>USA</CHOICE>
    <CHOICE>Germany</CHOICE>
    <CHOICE>France</CHOICE>
  </CHOICES>
  </Field>
  <Field ID="{ac689935-8e8b-485e-a45e-ff5a338dd92f}"
         Name="DevLeapCustomerLevel"
         StaticName="DevLeapCustomerLevel"
         DisplayName="Customer Level"
         Type="Choice"
         Group="DevLeap Columns">
```

```
        <Default>Level C</Default>
        <CHOICES>
          <CHOICE>Level A</CHOICE>
          <CHOICE>Level B</CHOICE>
          <CHOICE>Level C</CHOICE>
        </CHOICES>
      </Field>
      <Field ID="{a73de518-b9b9-4e8d-9d94-6099b4603997}"
            Name="DevLeapSupplierAccount"
            StaticName="DevLeapSupplierAccount"
            DisplayName="Supplier Account"
            Type="User"
            Group="DevLeap Columns"
            Sortable="TRUE" />
    </Fields>
```

Just as with the *ContentTypes* section, the *Fields* section is simply a wrapper for the copies of all the previously defined Site Columns. Notice that the *ID* values for the Site Columns are the same as those of the global Site Columns, serving to keep the global Site Columns linked to the local list-level columns.

Figure 10-3 shows how the List Settings page of a list based on the custom Contact List definition looks in a web browser. Note that all three Content Types and all the list-level columns are present.

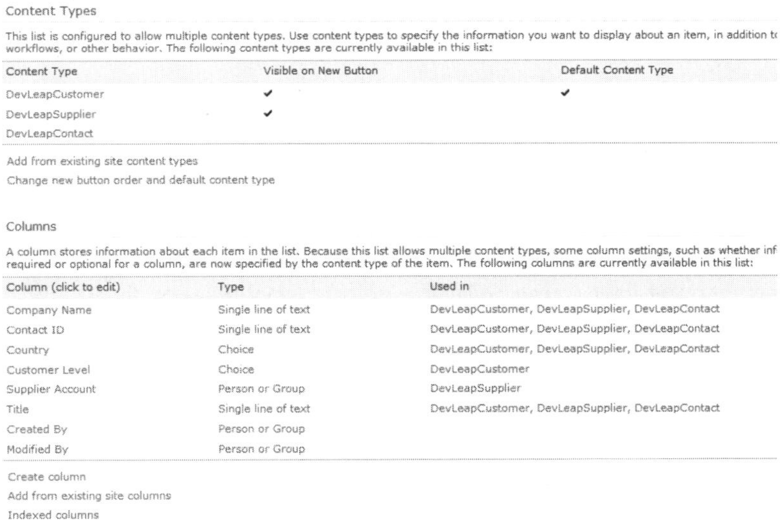

FIGURE 10-3 The List Settings page of a list instance based on the custom Contacts list definition.

Just after the *Fields* section, you'll see the *Views* element, which is a child of *MetaData*. This section is really interesting because here, we define the views on data that will be available to the end users in the web browser.

Each *View* element, child of *Views*, defines a data view declaring some configuration attributes that are illustrated in Table 10-5.

> **More Information**   For a complete list of all the available View attributes, refer to the official documentation on MSDN at *http://msdn.microsoft.com/en-us/library/ms438338(office.14).aspx*.

TABLE 10-5 Some of the Main Attributes for the *View* Element of a Schema.xml List Definition File

Attribute	Description
Type	The type of view. *Type* can be *HTML*, *Chart*, or *Pivot*.
BaseViewID	An *Integer* value that declares the ID of the view. *BaseViewID* must be unique within a Schema.xml file.
Url	The public URL to access the view from the browser.
DisplayName	The name of the view in the web browser.
DefaultView	A *Boolean* value that declares if the view is the default view for the current list.
MobileView	A *Boolean* value that specifies if the current view has to be made available to mobile devices, too.
MobileDefaultView	A *Boolean* value that declares if the view, enabled for mobile access, is the default view for mobile devices.
SetupPath	Defines the site-relative path to the ASPX file corresponding to the current view model. It allows provisioning a custom page for the current view.
WebPartZoneID	A string that declares the ID of the WebPartZone where the current view will be loaded, within the ASPX Web Part page.

The *View* element also allows you to declare some other configuration details using child elements. Listing 10-11 shows the default view definition for the list of contacts.

LISTING 10-11 The default *View* definition for the sample list.

```
<View BaseViewID="1" Type="HTML"
      WebPartZoneID="Main"
      DisplayName="$Resources:core,objectiv_schema_mwsidcamlidC24;"
      DefaultView="TRUE" MobileView="TRUE"
      MobileDefaultView="TRUE"
      SetupPath="pages\viewpage.aspx"
      ImageUrl="/_layouts/images/generic.png"
      Url="AllItems.aspx">
```

```
<Toolbar Type="Standard" />
<RowLimit Paged="TRUE">30</RowLimit>
<ViewFields>
  <FieldRef Name="Attachments">
  </FieldRef>
  <FieldRef Name="LinkTitle">
  </FieldRef>
</ViewFields>
<Query>
  <OrderBy>
    <FieldRef Name="ID">
    </FieldRef>
  </OrderBy>
</Query>
<XslLink>main.xsl</XslLink>
</View>
```

Listing 10-11 declared a *BaseViewID* with a value of *1*, and specified that this view will be the default (*DefaultView*) not only for classic web browsers, but also for mobile devices (*MobileDefaultView*). The *Url* to access the view will be *AllItems.aspx* and this page will be based on the *SetupPath* file *pages\viewpage.aspx* filling out the Web Part Zone whose *ID* is *Main*.

The child elements of the *View* tag in Listing 10-11 inform SharePoint to use the *Standard* value for the *Toolbar*. We set the maximum number of rows to return (*RowLimit*) to a value of *30*, enabling paging.

Note If not specified, the default *RowLimit* is *50*.

After these configuration elements, Listing 10-11 defines some other elements that determine the data to show, declaring a *Query* to filter and sort data, and a set of *ViewFields* to show, as well as some optional grouping rules.

The *Query* element is simply a CAML query that defines what values to extract from the source list, the ordering rule, and which of those to show in the current view. For example, Listing 10-11 queries all the items in the list, sorting them by the value of their *ID* fields.

Note CAML stands for "Collaborative Application Markup Language." This is an XML-based querying language that is useful to define filtering, sorting, and grouping on SharePoint data. The CAML language reference is available on MSDN at *http://msdn.microsoft.com/en-us/library/ms467521(office.14).aspx*.

Another important child section of the *View* element is the *ViewFields* element, which declares the fields to show in the resulting view. These fields are referenced by their internal names, using a specific *FieldRef* element.

The last child element we have in our *View* is the *XslLink* element. Beginning in SharePoint 2010, SharePoint renders views using XSLT transformations. The *XslLink* element specifies the path to the XSLT file used to render the view. This XSLT file path is relative to the folder *SharePoint14_Root\TEMPLATE\LAYOUTS\XSL*.

> **Note** SharePoint14_Root refers to the SharePoint root folder, which is typically located at C:\ Program Files\Common Files\Microsoft Shared\Web Server Extensions\14.

As an alternative to providing an explicit XSLT file path, you can use an *Xsl* element to simply declare the XSLT transformation inside the schema.xml file. However because you may want to reuse the XSLT transformation, it is better to reference an external file.

The *Forms* element is another important configuration section for the list definition, as shown in Listing 10-12.

LISTING 10-12 The Forms configuration section of the custom Contacts list definition.

```
<Forms>
  <Form Type="DisplayForm"
  Url="DispForm.aspx" SetupPath="pages\form.aspx" WebPartZoneID="Main" />
  <Form Type="EditForm"
  Url="EditForm.aspx" SetupPath="pages\form.aspx" WebPartZoneID="Main" />
  <Form Type="NewForm"
  Url="NewForm.aspx" SetupPath="pages\form.aspx" WebPartZoneID="Main" />
</Forms>
```

The *Forms* element contains a set of *Form* elements that declare the forms available to the end user. Each *Form* element requires a *Type* attribute that takes one of the following values:

- *DisplayForm*   The form to display a list item
- *EditForm*   The form to edit an existing list item
- *NewForm*   The form to add a new list item

Every form also requires a *Url* where it can be accessed, and might include an optional *SetupPath* from which to load the ASPX page model, and a *WebPartZoneID* attribute that specifies the *ID* of the Web Part zone used to load the rendering control of the form. As an alternative to the *SetupPath* attribute, you could have a *Path* attribute, which defines a physical file system path, relative to the *_layouts* folder for a template file, and a *Template* attribute that specifies the name of the template to use. You can also use CAML syntax to define the template for the body, buttons, opening section, and closing section of each of these forms, using these specific child nodes of the *Form* element: *ListFormBody*, *ListFormButtons*, *ListFormClosing*, and *ListFormOpening*.

The last configuration section shown is the *Validation* element. This is a new element introduced with SharePoint 2010 that supports defining validation rules that can apply to each item of the list. Listing 10-13 shows how to declare a custom validation rule together with a validation error message that end users will see if validation fails.

LISTING 10-13 A sample validation rule for the custom Contacts list definition items.

```
<Validation Message="Please check your data, there is something wrong!">
    =Title<>"Blank"
</Validation>
```

The validation rule forces the items to have a *Title* field with a value not equal to *Blank*. Figure 10-4 shows the validation error in a web browser.

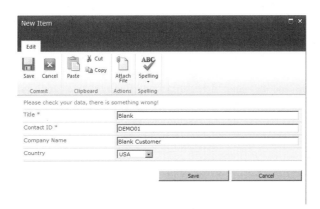

FIGURE 10-4 The New Item dialog form showing a custom validation error.

Notice that list-level validation rules work properly only with fields shared by all the Content Types of the list. If you enforce a rule against a field that is not defined in all the Content Types of the list, then your rule will always throw an error when applied to the wrong Content Types. For example, if you define a rule at the list level for the *DevLeapCustomerLevel* field of the Customer Content Type, you will not be able to add or update any Supplier instances, because the *DevLeapCustomer* field is not present in the Supplier Content Type. In such cases, you should instead define the validation rule at the Site Column level.

Defining a Custom View

When defining custom list definitions, it's also common to declare some custom views that correspond to the business rules of your data model. For example, the sample model could have one view that shows only Customers, and another that shows only Suppliers. In this section we will define only the former because the latter would be almost identical.

First, define a new *View* element under the *Views* element of the Schema.xml file. The new view will have a unique *BaseViewID*—in this example it will be *2*. The *DisplayName* will be "All Customers," the *Type* will be "HTML," and the *Url* will be "AllCustomers.aspx." All the other attributes values of the *View* element are trivial. You can see the complete definition of this view in Listing 10-14.

LISTING 10-14 A custom view definition for custom Contacts list definition.

```xml
<View BaseViewID="2" Type="HTML"
      WebPartZoneID="Main"
      DisplayName="All Customers"
      DefaultView="FALSE" MobileView="TRUE"
      MobileDefaultView="FALSE"
      SetupPath="pages\viewpage.aspx"
      ImageUrl="/_layouts/images/generic.png"
      Url="AllCustomers.aspx">
  <Toolbar Type="FreeForm" />
  <XslLink>Contacts_Main.xsl</XslLink>
  <RowLimit Paged="TRUE">20</RowLimit>
  <ViewFields>
    <FieldRef Name="Attachments">
    </FieldRef>
    <FieldRef Name="LinkTitle">
    </FieldRef>
    <FieldRef Name="DevLeapContactID">
    </FieldRef>
    <FieldRef Name="DevLeapCompanyName">
    </FieldRef>
    <FieldRef Name="DevLeapCountry">
    </FieldRef>
    <FieldRef Name="DevLeapCustomerLevel">
    </FieldRef>
  </ViewFields>
  <Query>
    <Where>
      <Eq>
        <FieldRef Name="ContentType" />
        <Value Type="Text">DevLeapCustomer</Value>
      </Eq>
    </Where>
    <OrderBy>
      <FieldRef Name="ID">
      </FieldRef>
    </OrderBy>
  </Query>
</View>
```

There are some areas of interest in this view definition. First, the code defined a *Query* to filter only items with a *ContentType* value of "DevLeapCustomer," and ordered the result by the item *ID*. Then it referenced all the fields of the Customer Content Type, defining a set of *FieldRef* elements within the *ViewFields* element. Lastly, a custom XSLT was defined for rendering the custom view. SharePoint will search for this XSLT file, Contacts_Main.xsl, in the *SharePoint14_Root\TEMPLATE\LAYOUTS\XSL* folder. The file is placed in that folder using the solution provisioning tools provided by Microsoft Visual Studio 2010. (For further details see Chapter 8, and Chapter 9, "Extending the User Interface.")

The XSLT file you reference in the *View* definition is a common XSLT transformation that will receive a wide range of parameters at runtime from SharePoint. In the XSLT code, for example, you can access the *XmlDefinition* variable, which provides the XML definition of the current *View*. To define an XSLT for a custom view, you must provide an XSLT template that matches the *BaseViewID* of the targeted view. For the Contacts example, the following template was defined:

```
<xsl:template match="View[@BaseViewID='2']" mode="full">
  <!-- Here is our custom XSLT transformation -->
</xsl:template>
```

The XSLT also receives a parameter named *Rows* that contains all the items to be rendered. In Listing 10-15, you can see an excerpt of the XML content of the *Rows* parameter. You can read it simply by using an XSLT template that copies the source content with an *<xsl:copy-of />* element.

LISTING 10-15 The content of the *Rows* parameter provided to a custom XSLT for rendering a list view.

```
<Rows>
  <Row ID="1" PermMask="0x7ffffffffffffff" Attachments="0"
  Title="Customer 01" FileLeafRef="1_.000" FileLeafRef.Name="1_"
  FileLeafRef.Suffix="000" FSObjType="0"
  Created_x0020_Date="1;#2010-02-13 16:24:12" Created_x0020_Date.ifnew="1"
  FileRef="/sites/SP2010DevRef/Lists/Test/1_.000"
  FileRef.urlencode="%2Fsites%2FSP2010DevRef%2FLists%2FTest%2F1%5F%2E000"
  FileRef.urlencodeasurl="/sites/SP2010DevRef/Lists/Test/1_.000"
  File_x0020_Type=""
  HTML_x0020_File_x0020_Type.File_x0020_Type.mapall="icgen.gif||"
  HTML_x0020_File_x0020_Type.File_x0020_Type.mapcon=""
  HTML_x0020_File_x0020_Type.File_x0020_Type.mapico="icgen.gif" ContentTypeId
="0x0100A60F69C4B1304FBDA6C4B4A25939979F010044C1B948A829E64CBD49ED3F42A868C7"
DevLeapContactID="C01" DevLeapCompanyName="Company 01"
  DevLeapCountry="Italy" DevLeapCustomerLevel="Level C"
  ContentType="DevLeapCustomer"></Row>
  <!-And many other rows here, one for each list item to show -->
</Rows>
```

Listing 10-15 illustrates that the *Rows* parameter provides each row along with its data columns, specified as attributes of a *Row* element. To output the content of the rows, you simply need to retreive the values of these attributes, wrapped into the graphical layout that you need to render. Teaching you XSLT is beyond the scope of this book; however, it is quite interesting to note that SharePoint 2010 opens up some great business opportunities, because it gives you the capability to display fully customized rendering of list views, meaning that your solutions can support fully-customized template layouts, even in extreme Web Content Management solutions.

The *ListTemplate* Definition File

The *ListTemplate* is the feature element file that declares all the deployment properties need- ed to provision the list definition. It must be provisioned into a custom feature together with the Schema.xml file discussed earlier in this chapter. Listing 10-16 shows the *ListTemplate* for the sample Contacts list definition.

LISTING 10-16 The *ListTemplate* feature element for the sample Contacts list definition.

```xml
<?xml version="1.0" encoding="utf-8"?>
<Elements xmlns="http://schemas.microsoft.com/sharepoint/">
    <ListTemplate
        Name="DevLeapContacts"
        Type="10001"
        BaseType="0"
        OnQuickLaunch="TRUE"
        SecurityBits="11"
        Sequence="410"
        DisplayName="DevLeap Contacts"
        Description="A list of Contact for DevLeap"
        Image="/_layouts/images/dlcon.png"/>
</Elements>
```

The *Type* attribute is the most important attribute in the *ListTemplate* element. *Type* takes an integer value that should be unique at the site collection level. The code sample uses a value of 10001, to avoid overlapping with values of out-of-the-box list templates. In general, you should give it a big integer value, to avoid overlapping with SharePoint. The uniqueness of this attribute allows you to define custom user interface extensions that will target the entire set of lists with that *Type* value. The other attributes are straightforward. The *BaseType* attribute states the base type for the current list definition. The *Name* attribute represents the internal name of the list, while the *DisplayName* is the text shown to end users, together with the *Description* and the *Image*. You can load the values of these descriptive attributes from external resource strings, to provision list definitions in a multilanguage environment. The *OnQuickLaunch Boolean* attribute value controls whether SharePoint shows any instance of the list in the Quick Launch menu. If you also provision a list instance through a cus- tom feature, this value can be overridden by the *ListInstance* element that you will use. The *Sequence* attribute defines the ordinal position of the list template in the page to create new list instances.

Finally, the *SecurityBits* attribute defines the security behavior of the list. This is a two-digit string, where the first digit controls whether users can read all items (*1*) or only their own items (*2*). The second digit defines edit access permissions. The possible values are: users can edit any item (*1*), users can edit only their own items (*2*), or users cannot edit items (*4*). For example, a value of *22* for the *SecurityBits* attribute means that users can see and edit only their own items, while the default value of *11* means that users can see and edit all the items in the list.

There are some other minor attributes available for the *ListTemplate* element, however we've covered the important and useful attributes.

 More Information For a complete list of attributes for the *ListTemplate* element, refer to the official product documentation on MSDN at *http://msdn.microsoft.com/en-us/library/ms462947(office.14).aspx*.

Summary

In this chapter, you have seen how to define XML files to provision SharePoint data models and structures. In particular, you have seen how to use feature element files to deploy Site Columns, Content Types and List Definitions. These files, together with custom fields, custom pages, and UI extensions, means that you can define complete custom site definitions (see Chapter 14, "Site Templates") autonomously for all your customers. These features promise a great return on investment, and a common maintenance plan. All the XML files you learned about in this chapter can also be defined using Visual Studio 2010, which provides you some useful tools and wizards to automatically generate XML code, and deploy it on a target site collection.

Chapter 11

Developing Custom Fields

One of the most useful extensibility areas of Microsoft SharePoint 2010 is its capability to create custom fields to enrich the native set of data types that are available to define the columns of list items.

In Chapter 10, "Data Provisioning," you learned how to provision a SharePoint solution, taking advantage of Content Types and List Definitions. You also saw how to define Site Columns based on specific SharePoint native columns types, such as *Text*, *Number*, *Choice*, *Lookup*, and so on. Under the covers each of these SharePoint field types is a .NET class, inherited from the base *SPField* class defined in the SharePoint Server Object Model. For example, a Site Column of type *Text* references a class of type *SPFieldText*, while a Site Column of type *Lookup* references a class of type *SPFieldLookup*. You're not limited to the existing field types. Just as Microsoft did with the SharePoint native class framework, you can define your own custom field types that use the same Object Model.

In this chapter, you'll see how to develop such custom field types and how to reference them in Site Columns, Content Types, and List Definitions.

Fields Type Basics

A custom field type consists of a set of .NET classes and some optional supporting files. The main class that each and every field type needs is the field type itself, which inherits from either *SPField* or from one of the classes that inherits from *SPField*. In fact, you can either define a completely new field type that inherits from the very basic *SPField*, or you can simply customize an already existing field type, inheriting from its definition class and changing various aspects of its behavior. Table 11-1 shows some of the main field types provided by the SharePoint 2010 native class framework.

TABLE 11-1 Some of the Main Field Types Provided by SharePoint 2010

Field Type	Description
SPField	Defines the base abstract class for any kind of field type.
SPFieldAttachments	Describes a file attachment.
SPFieldBoolean	Represents a *Boolean* value (*TRUE* or *FALSE*).
SPFieldCalculated	A calculated field based on a formula.
SPFieldChoice	Allows the user to select a single value from a predefined set of values.
SPFieldComputed	A computed field based on the value of another field.
SPFieldCrossProjectLink	Represents a link between an event and a related Meeting Workspace site.

Field Type	Description
SPFieldCurrency	Defines a currency value.
SPFieldDateTime	Saves a date and time value.
SPFieldFile	Represents a field that contains a File.
SPFieldGuid	Describes a field containing a GUID.
SPFieldLookup	Behaves almost the same as *Choice* and *MultiChoice*; however, the set of values from which users choose comes from another list of items within the same site.
SPFieldMultiChoice	Allows users to select multiple values from a predefined set of values.
SPFieldMultiColumn	Defines the base abstract class for multivalue/multicolumn field types.
SPFieldMultiLineText	Stores multiple lines of text.
SPFieldNumber	Defines a floating point number.
SPFieldPageSeparator	Defines a page separation in a survey.
SPFieldRecurrence	Defines a recurrence pattern in a Calendar.
SPFieldText	Describes a single line of text.
SPFieldUrl	Defines a URL with a specific *LinkType* (*Hyperlink* or *Image*).
SPFieldUser	Describes a lookup for a single user or set of users.

The SharePoint 2010 native class framework also contains other more specific field types that inherit from the field types shown in Table 11-1. For instance the *SPFieldUser* type, which is useful for looking up a user instance, inherits from the *SPFieldLookup* type.

Every custom field is made up of a set of classes, some of which are optional. These classes are:

- **Field Type**   The main class that defines the field type. This class is mandatory.

- **Field Rendering Control**   This control renders the field in a browser. It acts almost like any common ASP.NET server control. This class is optional, but often needed.

- **Field Mobile Rendering Control**   This control renders the field in mobile devices. It is optional.

- **Field Value Type**   This defines the class that holds the value of each instance of the custom field type, such as the field rendering control. While not mandatory, this class is very useful and commonly included.

- **Field Editor Type/Control**   Defines the control that allows advanced users to configure instances of the custom field type. This class is optional.

To deploy a custom field, you build a new class library made up of some of these classes, and deploy it into the Global Assembly Cache (GAC) of every SharePoint server in the farm. You can do this using a SharePoint solution.

> **More Information** For details about deploying SharePoint solutions, refer to Chapter 8,
> "SharePoint Features and Solutions."

You must reference every field type in an XML definition file that must reside in the
SharePoint14_Root\TEMPLATE\XML folder. In addition, the file must be named using the
structure FLDTYPES_*.XML, where the asterisk (*) is replaced with a unique and descriptive
name related to the specific custom field type or to a group of custom field types that share
the same XML definition file. Finally, there could be some ASP.NET ASCX controls and/or XSLT
files that can help define how the field renders in a browser. You'll see in-depth information
about custom field rendering on page 358.

The SPField Class

Listing 11-1 shows some of the main public and protected members of the *SPField* class.

LISTING 11-1 Some of the main public and protected members of the *SPField* class.

```
public class SPField {
    // Properties to define the custom field set of names
    public string InternalName { get; }
    public string StaticName { get; set; }
    public string Title { get; set; }

    // Methods to handle field value
    public virtual object GetFieldValue(string value);
    public virtual string GetFieldValueAsHtml(object value);
    public virtual string GetFieldValueAsText(object value);
    public virtual string GetFieldValueForEdit(object value);
    public virtual string GetValidatedString(object value);
    public virtual void ParseAndSetValue(SPListItem item, string value);

    // Properties to define custom field related rendering controls
    public virtual BaseFieldControl FieldRenderingControl { get; }
    public virtual SPMobileBaseFieldControl FieldRenderingMobileControl { get; }
    public virtual Type FieldValueType { get; }

    // Methods to handle custom field configuration properties
    public object GetCustomProperty(string propertyName);
    public void SetCustomProperty(string propertyName, object propertyValue);

    // Events handlers to track and manage
    // field adding/deleting/updating tasks
    public virtual void OnAddingToContentType(SPContentType contentType);
    public virtual void OnAdded(SPAddFieldOptions op);
    public virtual void OnDeleting();
    public virtual void OnDeletingFromContentType(SPContentType contentType);
    public virtual void OnUpdated();
```

```
// Methods to track and manage field adding/deleting/updating tasks
public virtual void Update();
public void Update(bool pushChangesToLists);

// Properties to define the custom field behavior in rendering UI
public bool? ShowInDisplayForm { get; set; }
public bool? ShowInEditForm { get; set; }
public bool? ShowInListSettings { get; set; }
public bool? ShowInNewForm { get; set; }
public bool? ShowInViewForms { get; set; }
public bool ShowInVersionHistory { get; set; }

// Properties to define the custom field behavior in rendering UI
public bool Required { get; set; }
public bool EnforceUniqueValues { get; set; }
public bool ReadOnlyField { get; set; }
public virtual bool NoCrawl { get; set; }
}
```

The *SPField* class exposes many properties and methods that define the field features and behavior. For instance, the *InternalName*, *StaticName,* and *Title* properties are used to configure field instances in lists and Content Types. Another group of methods—*GetFieldValue*, *GetFieldValueAsHtml*, *GetFieldValueAsText*, *GetFieldValueForEdit*, *GetValidatedString*—are, as their names imply, useful for retrieving the value of a specific field instance. As a counterpart, the *ParseAndSetValue* method supports setting the value of a specific field instance.

Three read-only properties define the custom .NET types related to the field. The *FieldValueType* property returns the type of the value stored in each specific field instance. The *FieldRenderingControl* and *FieldRenderingMobileControl* properties return the types of the ASP.NET controls that will render the field in a web browser and in a mobile device, respectively.

Often, a field has a set of configuration properties that can be configured by the end user through the UI. These can be managed through the *GetCustomProperty* and *SetCustomProperty* methods. You will learn more about this on page 351.

You can override the virtual method *OnAddingToContentType* and *OnAdded* to intercept when the field is going to be added to a specific Content Type or has been added to a list definition, respectively. Similarly, override *OnDeletingFromContentType* or *OnDeleting* to intercept when the field is going to be deleted from a specific Content Type or from a list definition. Lastly, override the virtual method *OnUpdated* to intercept a field update, which happens when the *Update* method fires. You'll find these virtual methods particularly useful when managing the field custom configuration editors that are in the examples in the last part of this chapter.

Every field also has a set of public properties that are useful to define where to show the field in the various SharePoint item forms. For instance, the *ShowInDisplayForm* property defines whether the field will be shown in the *DisplayForm* of an item, in the *EditForm* (*ShowInEditForm*), in the *AddNewForm* (*ShowInNewForm*), in the *ViewForm* (*ShowInViewForms*), in the list settings page (*ShowInListSettings*), and in the history of the item (*ShowInVersionHistory*), when the list currently hosting the field has history enabled.

Lastly, there are some properties that determine whether the field defines unique constraints (*EnforceUniqueValues*), to declare that the field is mandatory (*Required*), read-only (*ReadOnlyField*), or that it should not be crawled (*NoCrawl*) by the Search Engine crawler.

Whenever you define a custom field, you should override some of these methods and properties to specify the custom behavior for the field you plan to deploy.

Developing Custom Field Types

In this section, you will see how to develop two field types that are useful in some common scenarios and that fulfill customers' requirements.

A Basic E-Mail Field Type

First you'll develop a simple field type that provides regular expression validation for its content. SharePoint 2010 now includes field-level validation rules (see Chapter 10 for more details about this); however, they don't include regular expressions.

To begin, create a new Microsoft Visual Studio 2010 SharePoint Empty project. Next, choose to deploy it as a farm solution, because the output of this kind of project needs to be shared in the GAC. Add a new class to the project for implementing the field type.

To develop such a class, you could start from scratch, inheriting the *SPField* type; however, in this case, the goal is to accept text values and validate them against a configured regular expression, so it's more convenient to inherit the new custom field from the already existing *SPFieldText* field type, and simply change its validation behavior.

Listing 11-2 shows the main class (*RegExTextField*) for the custom field.

LISTING 11-2 The main class of the custom *RegExTextField*.

```
using System;
using System.Collections.Generic;
using System.Text;
using Microsoft.SharePoint;
using System.Text.RegularExpressions;
```

```
namespace DevLeap.SP2010.CustomFields {
    public class RegExTextField : Microsoft.SharePoint.SPFieldText {
        public RegExTextField(SPFieldCollection fields, String fieldName)
            : base(fields, fieldName) {
            this.Init();
        }
        public RegExTextField(SPFieldCollection fields, String typeName,
        String displayName) : base(fields, typeName, displayName) {
            this.Init();
        }
        private void Init(){
            Object regularExpressionValue =
            GetCustomProperty("RegularExpression");
            if (regularExpressionValue != null)
                this.RegularExpression = regularExpressionValue.ToString();
            else
                this.RegularExpression = String.Empty;

            Object errorMessageValue = GetCustomProperty("ErrorMessage");
            if (errorMessageValue != null)
                this.ErrorMessage = errorMessageValue.ToString();
            else
                this.ErrorMessage = String.Empty;
        }

        private String _regularExpression;
        public String RegularExpression {
        get { return (this._regularExpression); }
        set { this._regularExpression = value; }
        }

        private String _errorMessage;
        public String ErrorMessage {
            get { return (this._errorMessage); }
            set { this._errorMessage = value; }
        }

        public override string GetValidatedString(Object value)
        {
            if (value == null)
                return String.Empty;

            String textValue = value.ToString();
            Regex regex = new Regex(this.RegularExpression,
            RegexOptions.IgnoreCase);

            if (!regex.IsMatch(textValue)) {
                throw new SPFieldValidationException(this.ErrorMessage);
            }
            else {
                return textValue;
            }
        }
    }
}
```

In Listing 11-2, the custom field constructors simply invoke the base constructors to ensure the proper initialization of the field environment, and then call the private *Init* method. The constructor parameters are somewhat self-explanatory: the first parameter references the collection of fields that are siblings of the current field, in case you need to make some calculation based on them, while the others supply its *fieldName*, *typeName*, and *displayName* respectively.

For now, the important part of the field code is the overridden *GetValidatedString* method. This method takes the field value as an input parameter of type *Object* and returns a variable of type *String*. The remainder of the method defines a *Regex* instance, populates it with a custom regular expression rule, and then checks the input value against the rule. If the value matches the regular expression, then the method returns the *ToString* value of the input variable; otherwise, it throws a new *SPFieldValidationException* with a specific validation error message. The *SPFieldValidationException* class is specific for field validation errors and provides a default rendering UI for these kind of errors.

> **Note** The .NET Framework also contains an abstract base class named *ValidationRule* that you can use to define custom validation rules to check the validity of user input. If you want, you can define a custom *RegExValidationRule* class that inherits from *ValidationRule* and invoke it from the *GetValidatedString* method. However, for the sake of simplicity, the example invokes the *RegEx* instance directly, within the validation method of the field type.

To make sense of the custom field, you need a way to configure the regular expression it uses to check the field value. You also need a custom error message to show the end user when the content of the field does not match the rule. You can make these available to site designers and administrators as configuration parameters, set through the field configuration panel in the browser UI (see Figure 11-1).

The *Init* method provides access to the configured values inside the custom field code; it's invoked by the constructors, as you have already seen. The *Init* method uses the *GetCustomProperty* method of the *SPField* base class to access the custom configuration properties, in this case, using their names: "RegularExpression" and "ErrorMessage." In the interest of thoroughness and code clarity, the code also defines two class properties that map the custom configuration properties.

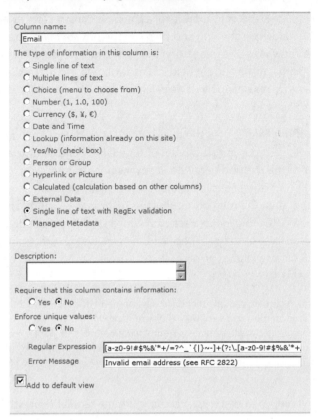

FIGURE 11-1 The custom field configuration panel in the browser UI.

You might be wondering how SharePoint knows how to make these properties available for configuration in the browser UI. It discovers them through an XML definition file that you ship along with the class library that holds the custom field definition.

To deploy it, add a SharePoint mapped folder to your current project, targeting the SharePoint14_Root\TEMPLATE\XML folder. The file you deploy must be named using the structure FLDTYPES_*.XML, where the asterisk (*) is replaced with a unique name for your field or for a group of custom fields.

Note Every custom field definition, from all over the world, will have a corresponding FLDTYPES_*.XML file in the SharePoint14_Root\TEMPLATE\XML folder. Therefore, your file names should include the name of your company or organization, to distinguish them from those of other custom solutions providers.

Listing 11-3 shows the XML definition file for the custom field example.

LISTING 11-3 The XML definition file for the custom field example (fldtypes_DevLeapRegExField.xml).

```xml
<?xml version="1.0" encoding="utf-8" ?>
<FieldTypes>
    <FieldType>
        <Field Name="TypeName">DevLeapRegExField</Field>
        <Field Name="TypeDisplayName">Single line of text with
                RegEx validation</Field>
        <Field Name="ParentType">Text</Field>
        <Field Name="UserCreatable">TRUE</Field>
        <Field Name="FieldTypeClass">DevLeap.SP2010.CustomFields.RegExTextField,
            DevLeap.SP2010.CustomFields, Version=1.0.0.0, Culture=neutral,
            PublicKeyToken=bc0e225f606933d3</Field>
        <Field Name="Sortable">TRUE</Field>
        <Field Name="Filterable">TRUE</Field>
        <Field Name="AllowBaseTypeRendering">TRUE</Field>
        <PropertySchema>
            <Fields>
                <Field Name="RegularExpression"
                        DisplayName="Regular Expression"
                        MaxLength="255"
                        DisplaySize="50"
                        Type="Text">
                    <Default></Default>
                </Field>
                <Field Name="ErrorMessage"
                        DisplayName="Error Message"
                        MaxLength="255"
                        DisplaySize="50"
                        Type="Text">
                    <Default></Default>
                </Field>
            </Fields>
        </PropertySchema>
    </FieldType>
</FieldTypes>
```

Listing 11-3 defines a set of custom *FieldType* elements, each made up of a set of *Field* elements with a *Name* attribute. One of the main *Field* tags is the *TypeName*, which represents the internal name that SharePoint will use to reference this custom field type in content types, list columns, CAML queries, and so forth. This name should be unique, so you should use your company or organization name (or a part of it) to make it unique. Also, the *ParentType* element is important, because it defines the inheritance pattern of the field. This example states that *DevLeapRegExField* inherits from the *Text* field (*SPFieldText*). For further details, refer to Table 10-1 and Table 11-1. The *FieldTypeClass* element declares the fully qualified name of the .NET type that corresponds to this custom field type. The *Filterable*, *Sortable*, and *UserCreatable* elements are self-explanatory.

The *AllowBaseTypeRendering* element instructs SharePoint to render this field using the rendering pattern of its parent field type (*SPFieldText*).

You can define some other configuration fields in the XML definition file, but they are not relevant to this example. You'll see more about some of them later.

> **More Information** For a complete list of available *Field* configuration elements, refer to the official product documentation on MSDN at *http://msdn.microsoft.com/en-us/library/ aa544201(office.14).aspx*.

One last interesting section of the XML definition file is the *PropertySchema* element and its child nodes. The *PropertySchema* element defines the configuration parameters that SharePoint makes available in the browser UI (see Figure 11-1). You can read the values using the base *GetCustomProperty* method. Each configuration property is defined as a *Field* element in a collection of *Fields*, and each *Field* has a set of attributes defining its *Name*, *DisplayName*, and behavioral configuration. For example, in the Init method, you could write:

```
GetCustomProperty("RegularExpression")
```

The preceding code references the value of the *RegularExpression* field defined in the *PropertySchema* of the FLDTYPES_*.XML file. You'll see more about this topic toward the end of this chapter. Figure 11-2 shows the field in action, applying the validation rule against an invalid field value.

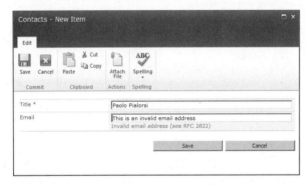

FIGURE 11-2 The custom field in action, displaying a validation error in a field value.

A Multicolumn Field Type

Another common type of custom field holds a set of values, instead of a single value. For example, Europeans use a unique code that identifies a bank account, called IBAN (International Bank Account Number). The code consists of a set of meaningful parts. Here's an explanation of the structure of an IBAN:

		IBAN			
			BBAN		
Country code (ISO 3166)	Check digit	CIN	ABI	CAB	Account Number
IT	12	A	12345	12345	123456789012

Now suppose that you want to store an IBAN for a set of contacts in SharePoint 2010, both customers and suppliers. You could store each IBAN as a single string; however, storing the IBAN parts separately provides easier usage and richness of information. Thus, you need to acquire and store each IBAN part separately: Country Code; Check Digit; CIN; ABI; CAB; and Account Number.

To define a custom field to hold an IBAN code, you first need to declare the value type that hosts the composite value. Listing 11-3 shows the structure of such a type.

LISTING 11-3 The value type for a custom *IBANFieldValue*

```
namespace DevLeap.SP2010.CustomFields {
    public class IBANFieldValue : SPFieldMultiColumnValue {
        private const Int32 columnsCount = 6;
        public IBANFieldValue()
            : base(columnsCount) { }

        public IBANFieldValue(string value)
            : base(value) { }

        public String CountryCode {
            get { return (this[0]); }
            set { this[0] = value; }
        }
        public String CheckDigit {
            get { return (this[1]); }
            set { this[1] = value; }
        }
        public String CIN {
            get { return (this[2]); }
            set { this[2] = value; }
        }
        public String ABI {
            get { return (this[3]); }
            set { this[3] = value; }
        }
        public String CAB {
            get { return (this[4]); }
            set { this[4] = value; }
        }
        public String AccountNumber {
            get { return (this[5]); }
            set { this[5] = value; }
        }
    }
}
```

The *IBANFieldValue* class inherits its behavior and configuration from the SharePoint base class named *SPFieldMultiColumnValue*. Essentially, the class divides the parts of an IBAN code into a set of smaller pieces and then leverages the capabilities of the base class—*SPFieldMultiColumnValue*—to hold them. This base class needs to know the total number of pieces in its constructor; the custom constructor for *IBANFieldValue* simply calls the base *constructorm*, passing a static *columnsCount* variable of type *Int32*. Internally, the *SPFieldMultiColumnValue* keeps the values of each part in a private member of type *List<String>*, and stores the values in the content database as an *ntext* column.

Aside from the field value, you also need to define the field type itself (see Listing 11-4).

LISTING 11-4 The custom *IBANField* field type definition.

```
namespace DevLeap.SP2010.CustomFields {
    public class IBANField : SPFieldMultiColumn {
        public IBANField(SPFieldCollection fields, String fieldName)
            : base(fields, fieldName) { }

        public IBANField(SPFieldCollection fields, String typeName,
        String displayName) : base(fields, typeName, displayName) { }

        public override Type FieldValueType {
            get { return (typeof(IBANFieldValue)); }
        }

        public override object PreviewValueTyped {
            get {
                IBANFieldValue previewValue = new IBANFieldValue(
                            ";#IT;#12;#A;#12345;#12345;#123456789012;#");
                return(previewValue);
            }
        }

        public override BaseFieldControl FieldRenderingControl {
            get {
                BaseFieldControl renderingControl =
                  new IBANFieldControl ();
                renderingControl.FieldName = this.InternalName;
                return renderingControl;
            }
        }

        public override object GetFieldValue(string value) {
            if (!String.IsNullOrEmpty(value))
                return (new IBANFieldValue(value));
            else
                return (null);
        }
```

```
        public override string GetFieldValueAsText(object value) {
            IBANFieldValue typedValue;
            if (value == null) {
                return string.Empty;
            }
            if (value is IBANFieldValue) {
                typedValue = (IBANFieldValue)value;
            }
            else {
                if (!(value is string)) {
                    throw new ArgumentException();
                }
                typedValue = new IBANFieldValue(
    ((string)value).Replace(" ", ";#"));
            }
            return (String.Format("{0} {1} {2} {3} {4} {5}",
                typedValue.CountryCode, typedValue.CheckDigit,
                typedValue.CIN, typedValue.ABI, typedValue.CAB,
                typedValue.AccountNumber ));
        }
    }
}
```

Notice that the class uses a base class of type *SPFieldMulticolumn*, which informs SharePoint that this field will hold a set of values in a multicolumn layout.

Another key point is that the class overrides the *FieldValueType* read-only property. The property returns the *IBANFieldValue* type defined previously, which informs SharePoint about the type of the value stored in each field instance.

The overridden *FieldRenderingControl* read-only property returns an instance of a custom field rendering control that you still need to define. You'll see how to do that in the next section of this chapter.

Moreover, there is a *PreviewValueTyped* read-only property, which provides a sample preview typed value for the field.

Lastly, there are two methods related to the value of an instance of this field. The *GetFieldValue* method returns the value of the current field instance as a typed object, compliant with the value of the *FieldValueType* property. The *GetFieldValueAsText* method returns the value of an instance of this field, formatted as a simple string. SharePoint invokes this last method by SharePoint when it renders a list of items; thus, it is useful when customizing the layout of a data list.

Field Rendering Control

The field rendering control is an ASP.NET server control that renders the UI of a custom SharePoint field in several different situations, including displaying a field (Display), editing a field (Edit), or adding a field (New). Microsoft has proposed a suggested naming convention by which you should name a field rendering control using the syntax *[FieldName]FieldControl*. Thus, the field rendering control for the custom *IBANField* is defined as the *IBANFieldControl* class.

Figure 11-3 shows how the *IBANFieldControl* class behaves while displaying an item.

FIGURE 11-3 The custom field rendering in Display mode.

Figure 11-4 shows how SharePoint renders the *IBANField* in Edit/New mode.

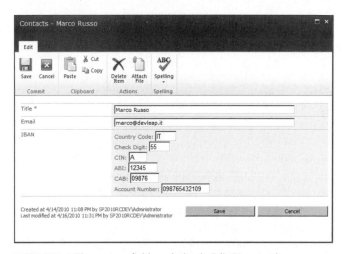

FIGURE 11-4 The custom field rendering in Edit/New mode.

You control the rendering behavior illustrated in Figures 11-3 and 11-4 in the *IBANFieldControl* class code, as shown in Listing 11-5.

LISTING 11-5 The custom *IBANFieldControl* definition.

```
namespace DevLeap.SP2010.CustomFields {
    public class IBANFieldControl: BaseFieldControl {
        private InputFormTextBox countryCode;
        private InputFormTextBox checkDigit;
        private InputFormTextBox CIN;
        private InputFormTextBox ABI;
        private InputFormTextBox CAB;
        private InputFormTextBox accountNumber;

        protected override void CreateChildControls() {
            base.CreateChildControls();

            if ((this.ControlMode == SPControlMode.Edit) ||
            (this.ControlMode == SPControlMode.New)) {
                this.countryCode = new InputFormTextBox();
                this.countryCode.Columns = 2;
                this.countryCode.MaxLength = 2;
                this.Controls.Add(new LiteralControl("Country Code: "));
                this.Controls.Add(this.countryCode);

                this.checkDigit = new InputFormTextBox();
                this.checkDigit.Columns = 2;
                this.checkDigit.MaxLength = 2;
                this.Controls.Add(new LiteralControl("<br />Check Digit: "));
                this.Controls.Add(this.checkDigit);

                this.CIN = new InputFormTextBox();
                this.CIN.Columns = 1;
                this.CIN.MaxLength = 1;
                this.Controls.Add(new LiteralControl("<br />CIN: "));
                this.Controls.Add(this.CIN);

                this.ABI = new InputFormTextBox();
                this.ABI.Columns = 5;
                this.ABI.MaxLength = 5;
                this.Controls.Add(new LiteralControl("<br />ABI: "));
                this.Controls.Add(this.ABI);

                this.CAB = new InputFormTextBox();
                this.CAB.Columns = 5;
                this.CAB.MaxLength = 5;
                this.Controls.Add(new LiteralControl("<br />CAB: "));
                this.Controls.Add(this.CAB);

                this.accountNumber = new InputFormTextBox();
                this.accountNumber.Columns = 12;
                this.accountNumber.MaxLength = 12;
                this.Controls.Add(new LiteralControl("<br />Account Number: "));
                this.Controls.Add(this.accountNumber);
            }
        }
```

```
public override object Value {
    get {
        return new IBANFieldValue {
            CountryCode = this.countryCode.Text,
            CheckDigit = this.checkDigit.Text,
            CIN = this.CIN.Text,
            ABI = this.ABI.Text,
            CAB = this.CAB.Text,
            AccountNumber = this.accountNumber.Text,
        };
    }
    set {
        IBANFieldValue typedValue =value as IBANFieldValue;

        if (typedValue != null) {
            if (this.countryCode != null)
                this.countryCode.Text = typedValue.CountryCode;
            if (this.checkDigit != null)
                this.checkDigit.Text = typedValue.CheckDigit;
            if (this.CIN != null)
                this.CIN.Text = typedValue.CIN;
            if (this.ABI != null)
                this.ABI.Text = typedValue.ABI;
            if (this.CAB != null)
                this.CAB.Text = typedValue.CAB;
            if (this.accountNumber != null)
                this.accountNumber.Text = typedValue.AccountNumber;
        }
    }
}
```

Both the field class and the field rendering control class are based on a class hierarchy. In fact, you can inherit the *BaseFieldControl* base class to define a custom field rendering control. However, you can reuse some existing rendering behaviors by inheriting from the *TextField* class (to render a field of type *SPTextField*) or the *DateTimeField* class (to render a field of type *SPDateTimeField*). Depending on your needs, you can inherit many of the base field types.

The *BaseFieldControl* base class provides a *Field* property that holds a reference to the corresponding field instance that it renders. Internally, it manages all the code useful for rendering a field in Display and Edit/Add forms.

In Listing 11-5, the custom class inherits directly from the *BaseFieldControl* base class, and just as with any other ASP.NET server control, it defines its child controls tree within the *CreateChildControls* method. The only difference here is that the field changes its behavior depending on the rendering mode (Display, Edit, New). When rendering the field in Edit/Add mode, the *CreateChildControls* method creates a controls tree composed of labels and textboxes to manage input/output of values. In Display mode, the control does not need to explicitly define a control tree (unless you want to define a specific behavior), because the default implementation of the *BaseFieldControl* base class will output the text value of the current field instance.

Another very interesting part of code in the class shown in Listing 11-5 is the *Value* property, which defines *get* and *set* operations to either return a typed *IBANFieldValue* object (*get*), or to read the *IBANFieldValue* instance (*set*), to populate the ASP.NET controls in the UI.

It's useful to know that the *BaseFieldControl* class implements the *System.Web.UI.IValidator* interface, which provides a hook for the ASP.NET forms validation infrastructure. In fact, you can override the *Validate* method to provide a custom validation rule. Whenever a user shows the custom field in Edit/Add mode, the ASP.NET validation infrastructure will invoke the field rendering control validation logic, making it possible to apply custom validation to the field content.

Finally, you can do whatever you need in custom rendering controls to implement a user-friendly UI. For example, you can provide code to use AJAX style controls, for the purpose of making the user experience more fluent. The richness of the rendering control is completely up to your imagination.

Field Rendering Templates

The previous section showed how to implement the UI for the rendering control by creating an ASP.NET controls tree inside the *CreateChildControls* method. Although it is absolutely possible to define a rendering control in such a manner, it is useful to know that the *BaseFieldControl* base class internally inherits from the SharePoint *TemplateBasedControl* class, which holds a reference to a set of *ITemplate* instances. Each of these templates is just a hook to a section of an ASCX control deployed in the SharePoint14_Root\TEMPLATE\ CONTROLTEMPLATES folder. There you can find and deploy as many ASCX files as you like. Each is made up of a set of *RenderingTemplate* controls instances, which themselves have a specific and unique *ID*. Listing 11-6 shows an excerpt of a custom rendering template for the *IBANField* type.

LISTING 11-6 A custom ASCX file with some specific rendering templates for the *IBANField* type.

```
<SharePoint:RenderingTemplate id="DevLeapIBANFieldDisplay" runat="server">
    <Template>
        <nobr><asp:label id="IBANValue" runat="server" /></nobr>
    </Template>
</SharePoint:RenderingTemplate>
```

```
<SharePoint:RenderingTemplate id="DevLeapIBANFieldEditAdd" runat="server">
    <Template>
        <table>
            <tr>
                <td>Country Code:</td>
                <td><SharePoint:InputFormTextBox id="countryCode" Columns="2"
                    runat="server" /></td>
            </tr>
            <tr>
                <td>Check Digit:</td>
                <td><SharePoint:InputFormTextBox id="checkDigit" Columns="2"
                    runat="server" /></td>
            </tr>
            <tr>
                <td>CIN:</td>
                <td><SharePoint:InputFormTextBox id="CIN" Columns="1"
                    runat="server" /></td>
            </tr>
            <tr>
                <td>ABI:</td>
                <td><SharePoint:InputFormTextBox id="ABI" Columns="5"
                    runat="server" /></td>
            </tr>
            <tr>
                <td>CAB:</td>
                <td><SharePoint:InputFormTextBox id="CAB" Columns="5"
                    runat="server" /></td>
            </tr>
            <tr>
                <td>Account Number:</td>
                <td><SharePoint:InputFormTextBox id="AccountNumber"
                    Columns="12" runat="server" /></td>
            </tr>
        </table>
    </Template>
</SharePoint:RenderingTemplate>
```

The code in Listing 11-6 defines two different templates. The first template, which has an *ID* value of *DevLeapIBANFieldDisplay*, is the template for rendering the field in Display mode, using an ASP.NET *Label*. The second, with the ID value *DevLeapIBANFieldEditAdd*, is the template for rendering the field in Edit/Add mode. It uses a set of SharePoint *InputFormTextBox* controls.

To use these templates, you need to reference their IDs in the field rendering control code. For example, to reference the Display template, you override the *DisplayTemplateName* property value; for the Edit/Add template, you override the *DefaultTemplateName*. Listing 11-7 shows a revised edition of the *IBANFieldControl* code that supports template-based rendering.

LISTING 11-7 The *IBANFieldControl* class, revised to support template-based rendering.

```
namespace DevLeap.SP2010.CustomFields {
    public class IBANFieldControl: BaseFieldControl {

        private InputFormTextBox countryCode;
        private InputFormTextBox checkDigit;
        private InputFormTextBox CIN;
        private InputFormTextBox ABI;
        private InputFormTextBox CAB;
        private InputFormTextBox accountNumber;
        private Label IBANValue;

        public IBANFieldRenderingControl() : base() {
            this.DisplayTemplateName = "DevLeapIBANFieldDisplay";
        }

        protected override void CreateChildControls() {
            base.CreateChildControls();
            if ((this.ControlMode == SPControlMode.Edit) ||
            (this.ControlMode == SPControlMode.New)) {
                this.countryCode =
                    (InputFormTextBox)TemplateContainer.FindControl("countryCode");
                this.checkDigit =
                    (InputFormTextBox)TemplateContainer.FindControl("checkDigit");
                this.CIN = (InputFormTextBox)TemplateContainer.FindControl("CIN");
                this.ABI = (InputFormTextBox)TemplateContainer.FindControl("ABI");
                this.CAB = (InputFormTextBox)TemplateContainer.FindControl("CAB");
                this.accountNumber = (InputFormTextBox)
                    TemplateContainer.FindControl("accountNumber");
            }
            else {
                this.IBANValue = (Label)TemplateContainer.FindControl("IBANValue");
            }
        }

        protected override void RenderFieldForDisplay(HtmlTextWriter output) {
            this.EnsureChildControls();
            if (this.IBANValue != null)
                this.IBANValue.Text = this.Field.GetFieldValueAsText(
                    this.ListItemFieldValue).Replace(" ", "-");
            base.RenderFieldForDisplay(output);
        }

        protected override string DefaultTemplateName {
            get {
                return "DevLeapIBANFieldEditAdd";
            }
        }
    }
```

```
public override object Value {
    get {
        return new IBANFieldValue {
            CountryCode = this.countryCode.Text,
            CheckDigit = this.checkDigit.Text,
            CIN = this.CIN.Text,
            ABI = this.ABI.Text,
            CAB = this.CAB.Text,
            AccountNumber = this.accountNumber.Text,
        };
    }
    set {
        IBANFieldValue typedValue = value as IBANFieldValue;

        if (typedValue != null) {
            if (this.countryCode != null)
                this.countryCode.Text = typedValue.CountryCode;
            if (this.checkDigit != null)
                this.checkDigit.Text = typedValue.CheckDigit;
            if (this.CIN != null)
                this.CIN.Text = typedValue.CIN;
            if (this.ABI != null)
                this.ABI.Text = typedValue.ABI;
            if (this.CAB != null)
                this.CAB.Text = typedValue.CAB;
            if (this.accountNumber != null)
                this.accountNumber.Text = typedValue.AccountNumber;
        }
    }
}
```

There are some key differences between the original code shown in Listing 11-5, which is based on code-only rendering, and the new code in Listing 11-7, which is based on templates. First, the new code version defines a constructor that configures the *DisplayTemplateName* property so that it matches the corresponding *RenderingTemplate* control in the custom ASCX file. Note that *CreateChildControls* method no longer creates the controls instances; instead, it populates them by invoking the *FindControl* method of the *TemplateContainer*, which represents a reference to the current rendering template. Of course, to make this code work correctly and without errors, the rendering template should be compliant with the code in the rendering control; otherwise, the *FindControl* method will return a *null* reference. Lastly, the new version customizes the *RenderFieldForDisplay* method to initialize the template controls with values coming from the field instance.

Figure 11-5 shows the output of the new rendering template, replacing the code-based rendering control.

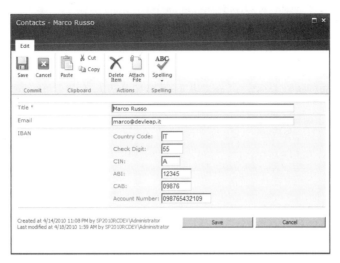

FIGURE 11-5 The new layout of the field rendering template for the custom IBANField.

And finally, keep in mind that field rendering templates apply to display, add, and edit forms only; they do not apply to list view rendering.

Field Rendering Using CAML

Sometimes you need to provide custom field behavior just to render content—without any real interaction with the end user, and without any business logic, validation rules, and so on. Often, this is exactly what you need to render read-only content in Display mode and in List views. To accomplish this behavior without having to write too much custom code, SharePoint provides a set of *RenderingPatterns* that you can define in the field type definition XML file (the FLDTYPES_*.xml file), using a specific XML syntax called Collaborative Application Markup Language (CAML). This technique is available for backward compatibility with previous versions of SharePoint. However, you should opt to render fields using XSLT (as you will see in the next section).

> **Note** CAML is an XML-based query language that is useful for defining filtering, sorting, and grouping operations on SharePoint data. The CAML language reference is available on MSDN at *http://msdn.microsoft.com/en-us/library/ms467521(office.14).aspx*.

Table 11-2 lists all the types of rendering patterns provided by SharePoint 2010.

TABLE 11-2 The Available Field Rendering Patterns Provided by SharePoint 2010

Field Type	Description
HeaderPattern	Defines column header rendering on list view pages.
DisplayPattern	Defines field rendering for the View (list item) form and for list view pages.
EditPattern	Defines field rendering for the Edit (list item) form.
NewPattern	Defines field rendering for the New (list item) form.
PreviewDisplayPattern	Defines a preview of how the field will look in Display mode, available for tools such as Microsoft Office SharePoint Designer 2010.
PreviewEditPattern	Defines a preview of how the field will look in Edit mode, available for tools such as Microsoft Office SharePoint Designer 2010.
PreviewNewPattern	Defines a preview of how the field will look in New mode, available for tools such as Microsoft Office SharePoint Designer 2010.

Listing 11-8 contains a new version of the fldtypes_DevLeapIBANField.xml definition file that declares a custom rendering pattern for displaying *IBANField* instances. Also in Listing 11-8, note the *CAMLRendering* element (highlighted in bold). This element is new in SharePoint 2010. When declared with a *TRUE* value, it instructs SharePoint to render the field using the CAML rendering patterns defined in the file. This example defines a "DisplayPattern" that simply switches the current field value: when the value is null or empty, it does nothing; when the field has a value, it displays the main parts of an IBAN code separating them with an HTML "hard space."

> **Note** The "DisplayPattern" rendering is used for displaying both item pages and list view pages. By using a field rendering control you can provide a custom rendering pattern for the display item page, overriding the *RenderFieldForDisplay* method of the base *BaseFieldControl* class; however, the list view page will still refer to the "DisplayPattern" when rendering the field because field controls and templates target forms rendering only.

LISTING 11-8 A new version of the fldtypes_DevLeapIBANField.xml definition file.

```xml
<?xml version="1.0" encoding="utf-8" ?>
<FieldTypes>
  <FieldType>
    <Field Name="TypeName">DevLeapIBANField</Field>
    <Field Name="TypeDisplayName">International Bank Account Number</Field>
    <Field Name="ParentType">MultiColumn</Field>
    <Field Name="UserCreatable">TRUE</Field>
    <Field Name="FieldTypeClass">DevLeap.SP2010.CustomFields.IBANField,
DevLeap.SP2010.CustomFields, Version=1.0.0.0, Culture=neutral,
PublicKeyToken=86505f09458f0c4c</Field>
    <Field Name="Sortable">TRUE</Field>
    <Field Name="Filterable">TRUE</Field>
    <Field Name="AllowBaseTypeRendering">FALSE</Field>
    <Field Name="CAMLRendering">TRUE</Field>
```

```
<RenderPattern Name="DisplayPattern">
  <Switch>
    <Expr>
      <Column/>
    </Expr>
    <Case Value="">
    </Case>
    <Default>
      <Column SubColumnNumber="0" HTMLEncode="TRUE"/>
      <HTML><![CDATA[ ]]></HTML>
      <Column SubColumnNumber="1" HTMLEncode="TRUE"/>
      <HTML><![CDATA[ ]]></HTML>
      <Column SubColumnNumber="2" HTMLEncode="TRUE"/>
      <HTML><![CDATA[ ]]></HTML>
      <Column SubColumnNumber="3" HTMLEncode="TRUE"/>
      <HTML><![CDATA[ ]]></HTML>
      <Column SubColumnNumber="4" HTMLEncode="TRUE"/>
      <HTML><![CDATA[ ]]></HTML>
      <Column SubColumnNumber="5" HTMLEncode="TRUE"/>
    </Default>
  </Switch>
</RenderPattern>
    </FieldType>
</FieldTypes>
```

The CAML elements you can use in a *RenderPattern* are taken from the list of CAML markup available in the "View Schema."

More Information For a complete reference of CAML elements defined in the "View Schema," refer to the official page at *http://msdn.microsoft.com/en-us/library/ms439798(office.14).aspx*.

Teaching you the CAML syntax is beyond the scope of both this chapter and this book, not only because a thorough exploration of CAML would require a dedicated book, but also because SharePoint 2010 offers some interesting alternatives to CAML rendering patterns.

Note Whenever a field does not have a specific *RenderPattern* in its field type definition file (the FLDTYPES_*.xml file), it inherits the *RenderPattern* from its base field configuration.

Field Rendering Using XSLT

One of the most interesting features introduced in SharePoint Foundation 2010 is its support for XSLT in list views and fields rendering patterns. In fact, starting with SharePoint 2010, every field has a rendering based on XSLT by default, and only when it uses an explicit declaration (*CAMLRendering = TRUE*) will SharePoint render that field using a CAML *RenderPattern*.

At the SharePoint14_Root\TEMPLATE\LAYOUT\XSL path, you'll find some XSLT files named with the pattern "fldtypes_*.XSL" that define fields rendering patterns through XSLT code.

The rendering engine of SharePoint picks up all the files with that name mask (fldtypes_*.XSL), merges all the XSLT templates they define, and then uses those templates to render fields in the browser UI.

> **Note** To deploy a "fldtypes_*.XSL" file, you simply need to define a SharePoint mapped folder in your Microsoft Visual Studio 2010 project, adding your own custom XSL file to that folder. The deployment features of Microsoft Visual Studio 2010 for SharePoint 2010 will do the rest for you.

The key point of this new feature is that it lets you define an XSLT that targets a specific field. The solution is quite simple, every XSLT template element should match its target field using its name, ID, or anything else that uniquely identifies that field. You specify the field properties to render as XML attributes of an XML element named *FieldRef*. For example, Listing 11-9 defines a custom XSLT template for the *IBANField*.

LISTING 11-9 A custom XSLT file for rendering a field.

```
<?xml version="1.0" encoding="utf-8" ?>
<xsl:stylesheet version="1.0" xmlns:xsl="http://www.w3.org/1999/XSL/Transform">

  <xsl:template match="FieldRef[@Name='DevLeapIBANField']" mode="Note_body">

    Value: <xsl:value-of select="translate(., ';#', ' ')"
        disable-output-escaping="yes" />

  </xsl:template>

</xsl:stylesheet>
```

The XSLT template defined in Listing 11-9 matches any field reference (*FieldRef* element) corresponding to a field with a name (*@Name* attribute) of *DevLeapIBANField*—the custom field name. Then it renders the value of the field using the <xsl:value-of /> construct of XSLT, reading the value of the current context node, which is represented by the dot ("."). Note the *mode* attribute, applied to the template XSLT element. SharePoint uses this attribute to better target templates, by using their relationship with their base SharePoint field type. In fact, the *IBANField* example type inherits from *SPFieldMultiColumn*, which inherits from the base field "Note." Thus, the XSLT defines a mode with a value of *Note_body* to instruct SharePoint Foundation that it targets the rendering of the body of a field named *DevLeapIBANField*, of type *Note* (or inherited from *Note*). There are many other modes available for XSLT rendering templates. Table 11-3 shows a list of the main mode values that the SharePoint XSLT templates engine supports natively.

TABLE 11-3 The Main XSLT Mode Values Supported by SharePoint XSLT Templates

Field Type	Description
DateTime_body	Matches a DateTime field value.
Computed_body	Matches a Computed field column.
Attachments_body	Matches an attachments field.
User_body	Matches a User of an SPFieldUser.
Note_body	Matches the content of a Note field.
Text_body	Matches the content of a Text field.
Number_body	Matches the content of a Number or Currency field.
Lookup_body	Matches the content of a Lookup field.
URL_body	Matches a URL field.
CrossProjectLink_body	Matches a field describing a link between an event and a related Meeting Workspace site.
Recurrence_body	Matches a Recurrence field in a meeting.
AllDayEvent_body	Matches the "all day event" field in a meeting.
CAMLRendering_body	Matches all fields that have an "old-style" CAML-based rendering.

You can use even more mode values and XSLT template matching rules in your XSLT layouts, but discussing them all is beyond the scope of this chapter.

Supporting Mobile Devices

SharePoint 2010 supports custom rendering of fields on mobile devices. To add mobile custom rendering, override the *FieldRenderingMobileControl* property of the *SPField* base class, within the custom field definition class—just as you did in the previous section with the *FieldRenderingControl* property. Listing 11-10 shows how you might change the *IBANField* class to support mobile rendering.

LISTING 11-10 An excerpt of the *IBANField* class, with the *FieldRenderingMobileControl* definition.

```
namespace DevLeap.SP2010.CustomFields {
    public class IBANField : SPFieldMultiColumn {

        // Code hidden for the sake of simplicity

        public override SPMobileBaseFieldControl FieldRenderingMobileControl {
            get {
                return(new IBANMobileFieldControl());
            }
        }

        // Code hidden for the sake of simplicity

    }
}
```

The preceding excerpt simply returns an instance of a custom type (you'll see how to develop it in this section), which is the counterpart of the standard field rendering control, but that targets mobile devices rather than standard browsers on classic computers. Listing 11-11 defines the *IBANMobileFieldControl*.

LISTING 11-11 The source code of the *IBANMobileFieldControl* class.

```
using System;
using System.Collections.Generic;
using System.Linq;
using System.Text;
using Microsoft.SharePoint.MobileControls;
using Microsoft.SharePoint.Utilities;
using Mobile = System.Web.UI.MobileControls;

namespace DevLeap.SP2010.CustomFields {
    public class IBANMobileFieldControl: SPMobileBaseFieldControl {

        private Mobile.TextBox countryCode;
        private Mobile.TextBox checkDigit;
        private Mobile.TextBox CIN;
        private Mobile.TextBox ABI;
        private Mobile.TextBox CAB;
        private Mobile.TextBox accountNumber;

        protected override Mobile.MobileControl CreateControlForDisplay() {
            return (this.CreateControlAsLabel());
        }

        protected override Mobile.MobileControl CreateControlForEdit() {
            Mobile.MobileControl control = null;
            if (this.Item != null) {
                control = this.CreateControlForNew();
            }
            return control;
        }

        protected override Mobile.MobileControl CreateControlForNew() {
            if (this.ReadOnly) {
                return (this.CreateControlForDisplay());
            }
            else {
                return (this.CreateUIControls());
            }
        }

        protected override Mobile.MobileControl CreateControlAsLabel() {
            Mobile.MobileControl result = this.CreateControlForView();
            result.BreakAfter = this.BreakAfter;
            return(result);
        }
```

```
        protected override Mobile.MobileControl CreateControlForView() {
            this.LabelControl.Text =
                this.Field.GetFieldValueAsText(
                this.ItemFieldValue).Replace(" ", "-");
            return this.LabelControl;
        }

        public override object Value {
            get {
                return new IBANFieldValue {
                    CountryCode = this.countryCode.Text,
                    CheckDigit = this.checkDigit.Text,
                    CIN = this.CIN.Text,
                    ABI = this.ABI.Text,
                    CAB = this.CAB.Text,
                    AccountNumber = this.accountNumber.Text,
                };
            }
        }
    }
}
```

There are several differences. First, the class inherits from the *SPMobileBaseFieldControl* base class, which provides a set of virtual methods that you can override to define the behavior of the mobile rendering controls. These methods are:

- *CreateControlForDisplay*   Defines a custom rendering behavior for the field in display (read-only) mode. Typically, this method simply calls the *CreateControlAsLabel*.

- *CreateControlForView*   Defines the output for the field when it is rendered in a list view. Typically, this method simply calls the *CreateControlAsLabel*.

- *CreateControlAsLabel*   Renders the field in read-only mode, using a predefined *Label* control that has the value of the field as its text.

- *CreateControlForNew*   Defines the rendering behavior for the field in a new item form.

- *CreateControlForEdit*   Defines the rendering behavior for the field in an edit item form. Quite often this method shares its implementation with the *CreateControlForNew* method.

While the three methods for displaying the field share almost the same implementation, based on the *CreateControlAsLabel* implementation, the two remaining methods invoke a private implementation (*CreateUIControls*), as shown in Listing 11-12.

LISTING 11-12 The *CreateUIControls* method of the *IBANMobileFieldControl* class.

```
private Mobile.MobileControl CreateUIControls() {

    Mobile.Panel panel = new Mobile.Panel();

    Mobile.LiteralText literalText = new Mobile.LiteralText();
    literalText.BreakAfter = true;
    panel.Controls.Add(literalText);

    Mobile.Label countryCodeLabel = new Mobile.Label();
    countryCodeLabel.Text = "Country Code:";
    panel.Controls.Add(countryCodeLabel);
    this.countryCode = new Mobile.TextBox();
    this.countryCode.MaxLength = 2;
    this.countryCode.BreakAfter = true;
    panel.Controls.Add(this.countryCode);

    Mobile.Label checkDigitLabel = new Mobile.Label();
    checkDigitLabel.Text = "Check Digit:";
    panel.Controls.Add(checkDigitLabel);
    this.checkDigit = new Mobile.TextBox();
    this.checkDigit.MaxLength = 2;
    this.checkDigit.BreakAfter = true;
    panel.Controls.Add(this.checkDigit);

    Mobile.Label CINLabel = new Mobile.Label();
    CINLabel.Text = "CIN:";
    panel.Controls.Add(CINLabel);
    this.CIN = new Mobile.TextBox();
    this.CIN.MaxLength = 1;
    this.CIN.BreakAfter = true;
    panel.Controls.Add(this.CIN);

    Mobile.Label ABILabel = new Mobile.Label();
    ABILabel.Text = "ABI:";
    panel.Controls.Add(ABILabel);
    this.ABI = new Mobile.TextBox();
    this.ABI.MaxLength = 5;
    this.ABI.BreakAfter = true;
    panel.Controls.Add(this.ABI);

    Mobile.Label CABLabel = new Mobile.Label();
    CABLabel.Text = "CAB:";
    panel.Controls.Add(CABLabel);
    this.CAB = new Mobile.TextBox();
    this.CAB.MaxLength = 5;
    this.CAB.BreakAfter = true;
    panel.Controls.Add(this.CAB);
```

```
Mobile.Label AccountNumberLabel = new Mobile.Label();
AccountNumberLabel.Text = "Account Number:";
panel.Controls.Add(AccountNumberLabel);
this.accountNumber = new Mobile.TextBox();
this.accountNumber.MaxLength = 12;
this.accountNumber.BreakAfter = true;
panel.Controls.Add(this.accountNumber);

this.Controls.Add(panel);

IBANFieldValue typedValue = this.ItemFieldValue as IBANFieldValue;
if (typedValue != null) {
    if (this.countryCode != null)
        this.countryCode.Text = typedValue.CountryCode;
    if (this.checkDigit != null)
        this.checkDigit.Text = typedValue.CheckDigit;
    if (this.CIN != null)
        this.CIN.Text = typedValue.CIN;
    if (this.ABI != null)
        this.ABI.Text = typedValue.ABI;
    if (this.CAB != null)
        this.CAB.Text = typedValue.CAB;
    if (this.accountNumber != null)
        this.accountNumber.Text = typedValue.AccountNumber;
}
return (panel);
}
```

The main point of this method is that it creates a set of mobile controls, taken from the *System.Web.UI.MobileControls* namespace, so you need to reference the System.Web.Mobile. dll assembly in your solution. For instance, in a classic rendering control, where you would create instances of *System.Web.UI.WebControls.TextBox* or *Microsoft.SharePoint.WebControls. InputFormTextBox* controls, in a mobile control you instead create instances of *System.Web. UI.MobileControls.TextBox* controls. Additionally, for field editing, the end of this method retrieves the current value to show from the *ItemFieldValue* property, inherited from the base class. Figure 11-6 presents the output of this newly defined mobile rendering control, in both list view and in edit mode.

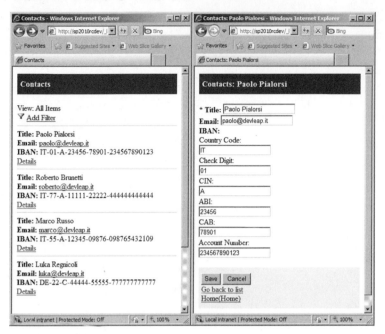

FIGURE 11-6 The output of the mobile rendering control of IBANField, in both list view and in edit mode.

Field Rendering Mobile Templates

Just as with field rendering controls for standard computers, mobile rendering controls can also take advantage of ASCX templates. For a mobile control, you need to define an ASCX control that will be deployed into the SharePoint14_Root\TEMPLATE\CONTROLTEMPLATES folder, with a definition of a *RenderingTemplate* control instance that targets the field type using a specific control ID. You must define the ID by merging a set of values so that SharePoint can uniquely identify the target field to render. Here's the structure of the ID:

MobileCustomListField_ListTypeID_FieldType_Field

This kind of ID can be segmented into four tokens (IDs). The first ID has a fixed value of *MobileCustomListField* and simply instructs SharePoint Foundation 2010 that the target of this template is a mobile custom list field. The second ID (*ListTypeID*) specifies the list type that will use the custom field type; its value can be either the name of one of the native List Template definitions available in SharePoint Foundation (see the following Note), or the numeric ID of the List Template you are targeting.

> **More Information** You can find the complete list of available values for this set of List Template definitions in the official product documentation at *http://msdn.microsoft.com/en-us/ library/microsoft.sharepoint.splisttemplatetype(office.14).aspx*.

Using the numeric ID is particularly useful when working with custom fields deployed in custom lists, because such lists do not have an official List Template name in the standard enumeration provided by SharePoint; using the ID is the only way to reference them. The third ID (*FieldType*), references the target field type, and can be either one of the native field types (such as *Text*, *DateTime*, *Number*, and so forth), or it can be the name specified for the custom field type in its XML definition file (the FLDTYPES_*.xml file). The fourth and last ID is the internal name of the field in the current list instance. After reading this paragraph, you could probably argue that's it not so easy to define a custom mobile rendering template targeting a field instance designed using the browser UI, even if it is possible. On the other hand, this way of working was mainly meant to support developers, who define custom fields, content types, and list definitions using the tools and techniques discussed in Chapter 10 and in this chapter.

Here's a concrete example. Consider the mobile rendering template illustrated in Listing 11-13.

LISTING 11-13 The mobile rendering template for the *IBANField* field type.

```
<%@ Register TagPrefix="GroupBoardMobile"
Namespace="Microsoft.SharePoint.Applications.GroupBoard.MobileControls"
Assembly="Microsoft.SharePoint,Version=14.0.0.0, Culture=neutral,
PublicKeyToken=71e9bce111e9429c" %>
<%@ Assembly Name="Microsoft.SharePoint, Version=14.0.0.0, Culture=neutral,
PublicKeyToken=71e9bce111e9429c" %>
<%@ Register TagPrefix="mobile" Namespace="System.Web.UI.MobileControls"
Assembly="System.Web.Mobile, Version=1.0.3300.0, Culture=neutral,
PublicKeyToken=b03f5f7f11d50a3a" %>
<%@ Register TagPrefix="SharePoint" Namespace="Microsoft.SharePoint.WebControls"
Assembly="Microsoft.SharePoint, Version=14.0.0.0, Culture=neutral,
PublicKeyToken=71e9bce111e9429c" %>
<%@ Register TagPrefix="DevLeap" Namespace="DevLeap.SP2010.CustomFields"
Assembly="DevLeap.SP2010.CustomFields, Version=1.0.0.0, Culture=neutral,
PublicKeyToken=86505f09458f0c4c" %>

<SharePoint:RenderingTemplate
    id="MobileCustomListField_GenericList_DevLeapIBANField_IBAN" runat="server">
 <Template>
  <table>
   <tr>
    <td colspan="2">
     <mobile:Panel RunAt="Server" Alignment="Center" EnableViewState="False">
      <mobile:DeviceSpecific RunAt="Server">
       <Choice Filter="IsMicrosoftMobileExplorer">
        <ContentTemplate>
        We are in Microsoft Mobile Internet Explorer
        </ContentTemplate>
       </Choice>
       <Choice Filter="IsHtml32">
        <ContentTemplate>
        We have support for HTML 3.2
        </ContentTemplate>
       </Choice>
```

```
      <Choice Filter="IsXhtmlMp">
       <ContentTemplate>
       We have support for XHTML Mobile Profile
       </ContentTemplate>
      </Choice>
      <Choice>
       <ContentTemplate>
       Everything else
       </ContentTemplate>
      </Choice>
     </mobile:DeviceSpecific>
    </mobile:Panel>
   </td>
  </tr>
  <tr>
   <td>
    <DevLeap:IBANMobileFieldControl id="IBANFieldControl" runat="server" />
   </td>
  </tr>
 </table>
 </Template>
</SharePoint:RenderingTemplate>
```

In Listing 11-13, the ID of the *RenderingTemplate* has a value of *MobileCustomListField_ GenericList_DevLeapIBANField_IBAN*, and declares that the template should be applied to any *IBANField* instance whose internal name is *IBAN*, and defined in any SharePoint custom list of items (*GenericList = 100*).

Internally, the *RenderingTemplate* definition uses some mobile-specific controls to determine the client platform available (*<mobile:DeviceSpecific />*), and it uses the original mobile rendering control to render the field. In general, you can define whatever you want in this template so that the output will be compliant with the mobile device consumer.

Note To investigate this topic in greater detail, take a look at the native mobile rendering templates provided by SharePoint by inspecting the MobileDefaultTemplates.ascx file within the SharePoint14_Root\TEMPLATE\CONTROLTEMPLATES folder.

Custom Field Editor

So far, you have seen how to develop a custom field type, focusing on rendering patterns for the end user's UI. However there is another interesting area where you can define a custom rendering pattern: the field editor section. In fact, whenever you create a new column instance in a list definition or define a new site column using a custom field type, you can also configure some custom information about the field instance. You declare this information in the XML field definition file using the *PropertySchema* section of the FLDTYPES_*.XML file, just as you did earlier in this chapter. Alternatively, you can define it using a specific editor control.

The *PropertySchema* section uses CAML syntax to define configuration properties, so it works only with limited or low profile solutions—for simple properties such as text, numbers, check boxes, and so on that do not require any kind of business logic or validation rule. When you need to provide a completely customizable field editor to a user configuring a new instance of your field, you should declare a dedicated ASCX control.

There are many reasons you might want to do that; for example, when you need to provide a custom validation rule to the configuration values provided by the user, or when you need to data bind some controls in the editor UI. In such cases, you need to write some custom .NET code to look up external data sources.

To develop a custom field editor control, you need to define a field editor class and a field editor ASCX. The class acts as the code-behind for the ASCX control. It must implement the *IFieldEditor* interface, available in SharePoint Foundation, and must also inherit from the *UserControl* class of ASP.NET, or a class derived from it. Microsoft's proposed naming convention for this control type suggests that you name the field editor class using the pattern *[FieldName]FieldEditor*, and the ASCX control file using the pattern [FieldName]FieldEditor. ASCX. Following this convention, the field editor control for the custom *IBANField* example should be named *IBANFieldEditor* and the ASCX file should be IBANFieldEditor.ASCX. Lastly, you must deploy the ASCX file in the well-known SharePoint14_Root\TEMPLATE\ CONTROLTEMPLATES folder, for example, using SharePoint mapped folders of Visual Studio 2010.

For educational purposes, imagine that the *IBANField* requires a custom editor that configures a SharePoint list to perform lookup operations for trusted banks, using their ABI and CAB codes. The original *IBANField* class has been extended with a new property called *BankListID*, which represents the ID of the target list of trusted banks. The sample code defines this lookup list as a list definition, based on a custom content type; however, this chapter does not cover that part of the solution, it focuses only on the custom field editor.

Figure 11-7 demonstrates the look and feel of the custom editor that you'll develop in the following pages. Notice the custom property with which users can configure the lookup list for banks.

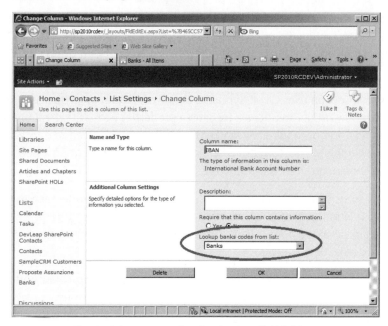

FIGURE 11-7 The UI of the custom editor for the *IBANField* field type.

The first part of code that we will examine is the ASCX editor control, which you can see in Listing 11-14.

LISTING 11-14 The source code of the IBANFieldEditor.ASCX control.

```
<%@ Control Language="C#" AutoEventWireup="true"
Inherits="DevLeap.SP2010.CustomFields.IBANFieldEditor, DevLeap.SP2010.CustomFields,
  Version=1.0.0.0, Culture=neutral, PublicKeyToken=86505f09458f0c4c" %>
<%@ Assembly Name="$SharePoint.Project.AssemblyFullName$" %>
<%@ Assembly Name="Microsoft.Web.CommandUI, Version=14.0.0.0, Culture=neutral,
  PublicKeyToken=71e9bce111e9429c" %>
<%@ Import Namespace="Microsoft.SharePoint" %>
<%@ Register Tagprefix="SharePoint" Namespace="Microsoft.SharePoint.WebControls"
  Assembly="Microsoft.SharePoint, Version=14.0.0.0, Culture=neutral,
  PublicKeyToken=71e9bce111e9429c" %>
<%@ Register Tagprefix="Utilities" Namespace="Microsoft.SharePoint.Utilities"
  Assembly="Microsoft.SharePoint, Version=14.0.0.0, Culture=neutral,
  PublicKeyToken=71e9bce111e9429c" %>
<%@ Register Tagprefix="asp" Namespace="System.Web.UI"
  Assembly="System.Web.Extensions, Version=3.5.0.0, Culture=neutral,
  PublicKeyToken=31bf3856ad364e35" %>
<%@ Register Tagprefix="WebPartPages" Namespace="Microsoft.SharePoint.WebPartPages"
  Assembly="Microsoft.SharePoint, Version=14.0.0.0, Culture=neutral,
  PublicKeyToken=71e9bce111e9429c" %>
<%@ Register TagPrefix="wssuc" TagName="InputFormControl"
  src="~/_controltemplates/InputFormControl.ascx" %>
```

```
<wssuc:InputFormControl LabelText="Lookup banks codes from list:" runat="server">
    <Template_Control>
        <asp:DropDownList id="banksLookupList" runat="server" />
    </Template_Control>
</wssuc:InputFormControl>
```

This is a very simple ASCX control that merely registers a set of controls and classes from the SharePoint Foundation infrastructure. From the ASCX markup point of view, the control is made up of a SharePoint *InputFormControl* that hosts a template based on a *DropDownList*, which effectively looks up lists in the current website. The control defines an *InputFormControl* as the root of the markup, because you want to insert the custom field editor in the main configuration section of the field. If you wanted to place the editor in a dedicated section, you would instead use an *InputFormSection* control as the root for its markup.

All the business logic and behaviors for this control are in the *IBANFieldEditor* class from which the control inherits. This class implements the *IFieldEditor* interface. That's a good place to start examining the code, shown in Listing 11-15.

LISTING 11-15 The *IFieldEditor* interface, provided by SharePoint Foundation framework.

```
public interface IFieldEditor {
    void InitializeWithField(SPField field);
    void OnSaveChange(SPField field, bool isNewField);
    bool DisplayAsNewSection { get; }
}
```

SharePoint Foundation invokes the first method (*InitializeWithField*) to configure the controls of the editor control, reading the configuration from the associated field instance. The second method (*OnSaveChanges*) is invoked whenever the user saves the configuration for the custom field. There is also a *DisplayAsNewSection* property, which simply instructs the SharePoint rendering engine whether to render the editor as a new configuration section in the standard field configuration page, or to render within the native configuration section. Listing 11-16 shows the full source code for the *IBANFieldEditor* class.

LISTING 11-16 The complete source code for the *IBANFieldEditor* class.

```
public class IBANFieldEditor: UserControl, IFieldEditor {
    private IBANField _IBANField;
    protected DropDownList banksLookupList;

    public bool DisplayAsNewSection {
        get { return(false); }
    }
```

```
public void InitializeWithField(Microsoft.SharePoint.SPField field) {
    this._IBANField = field as IBANField;

    if (!Page.IsPostBack) {
        BindLookupList();

        if ((this._IBANField != null) &&
        (this._IBANField.BanksListID != Guid.Empty)) {
            var item = this.banksLookupList.Items.FindByValue(
                this._IBANField.BanksListID.ToString());
            if (item != null) {
                this.banksLookupList.ClearSelection();
                item.Selected = true;
            }
        }
    }
}

public void OnSaveChange(Microsoft.SharePoint.SPField field, bool isNewField) {
    IBANField targetField = field as IBANField;
    if (targetField != null) {
        targetField.BanksListID = new Guid(this.banksLookupList.SelectedValue);
    }
}

private void BindLookupList() {
    SPWeb web = SPContext.Current.Web;



    foreach (SPList list in web.Lists) {
        this.banksLookupList.Items.Add(new ListItem(
            list.Title, list.ID.ToString()));
    }
}
}
```

In the preceding code, the *InitializeWithField* method simply takes the current field instance, if it exists, and configures it according to the selected item in the lookup list.

> **Note** The preceding sentence uses "if it exists" because whenever you create a new field instance, the field editor will receive a *null* variable. That occurs because the field still does not exist at that time.

The initialization method also invokes a private *BindLookupList* method that loads all the available lists from the current website into the *DropDownList* instance.

The *OnSaveChange* method is the counterpart of the previous method; it simply saves the selected configuration into the field instance.

Custom Properties Persistence

The editor control itself is just a UI element built on top of the field type; in fact, it is the field type that takes care of effectively saving the configuration.

Moreover, whenever you add a new field, the field editor control gets a field object that is not already plugged into the list definition that will host it. The field is added to the *Fields* collection of the list immediately after the editor control invocation.

As with field configuration updating, the save operation is defined in the field type code.

You need to save the field configuration by using the set of virtual methods provided by *SPField*, which you have seen at the beginning of this chapter. In fact, you might remember that the *SPField* class provides a set of virtual methods to handle adding a field (*OnAdded*), field configuration updating (*OnUpdated*), and field deleting (*OnDeleting*). These are where you implement the custom properties persistence code.

First, it's important to understand that every field in SharePoint stores its configuration in an XML format, and every field instance can read its own configuration by simply retrieving the *SchemaXml* property value, which is of type *String*. To save the custom properties, you simply need to write a portion of this *SchemaXml* node set, and to read the configuration, you just need to read the XML nodes from the *SchemaXml* property. Behind the scenes, SharePoint Foundation will read and write that XML from and to the content database of the current site. Listing 11-17 shows a sample XML node set that describes the configuration for an instance of the *IBANField*.

LISTING 11-17 A sample XML node set that describes the configuration of an instance of *IBANField*.

```xml
<Field Type="DevLeapIBANField" DisplayName="IBAN" Required="FALSE"
    ID="{e004c98c-6cb3-4344-ac69-a75b25530bbe}"
    SourceID="{465cc570-4357-4273-913e-16dbb45058fe}" StaticName="IBAN"
    Name="IBAN" ColName="ntext2" RowOrdinal="0" Group="" Version="1748"
    BanksListID="e0b85f6f-8dd8-4e52-8814-f2a6808707e3" AddFieldOption="Default">
  <Customization>
    <ArrayOfProperty>
      <Property>
        <Name>BanksListID</Name>
      </Property>
    </ArrayOfProperty>
  </Customization>
</Field>
```

The preceding XML contains an attribute named *BanksListID*, and a node set of elements declaring that this attribute is a custom property of the field. For complex configuration properties, you can store their values into the *Customization* section of the XML, with a *Value* element for each custom *Property*, using some custom code to read and write the *SchemaXml* node set. Listing 11-18 shows an excerpt from the *IBANField* class code that supports the persistence of custom properties.

LISTING 11-18 An excerpt from the *IBANField* class source code that manages the persistence of custom properties.

```
private Guid _banksListID;

public Guid BanksListID {
    get {
        if (this._banksListID == Guid.Empty) {
            String currentBanksListIDPropertyValue = this.GetProperty("BanksListID");
            if (!String.IsNullOrEmpty(currentBanksListIDPropertyValue))
                this._banksListID = new Guid(currentBanksListIDPropertyValue);
        }
        return (this._banksListID);
    }
    set {
        this._banksListID = value;
        SetPropertyOnThread("BanksListID", this._banksListID);
    }
}

private void SetPropertyOnThread(string propertyName, Object value) {
    Thread.SetData(Thread.GetNamedDataSlot(propertyName), value);
}

private TProperty GetPropertyFromThread<TProperty>(string propertyName) {
    return (TProperty)Thread.GetData(Thread.GetNamedDataSlot(propertyName));
}

private void CleanThreadLocalStorage() {
    Thread.FreeNamedDataSlot("BanksListID");
}

private bool savingSchemaXml;

public override void OnAdded(SPAddFieldOptions op) {
    if (!this.savingSchemaXml) {
        this.savingSchemaXml = true;
        base.SchemaXml = this.CreateOrUpdateFieldSchemaXml(op);
        this.CleanThreadLocalStorage();
    }
}

public override void OnUpdated() {
    SPAddFieldOptions op = SPAddFieldOptions.Default;
```

```
        String addFieldOptionPropertyValue = this.GetProperty("AddFieldOption");
        if (!String.IsNullOrEmpty(addFieldOptionPropertyValue)) {
            op = (SPAddFieldOptions)Enum.Parse(typeof(SPAddFieldOptions),
                this.GetProperty("AddFieldOption"), true);
        }
        if (!this.savingSchemaXml) {
            this.savingSchemaXml = true;
            base.SchemaXml = this.CreateOrUpdateFieldSchemaXml(op);
            this.CleanThreadLocalStorage();
        }
    }

    public override void OnDeleting() {
        base.OnDeleting();
    }

    private string CreateOrUpdateFieldSchemaXml(SPAddFieldOptions op) {
        XElement schemaXmlElement = XElement.Parse(this.SchemaXml);
        schemaXmlElement.SetAttributeValue("BanksListID",
            this.GetPropertyFromThread<Guid>("BanksListID"));
        schemaXmlElement.SetAttributeValue("AddFieldOption", op.ToString());

        return (schemaXmlElement.ToString());
    }
```

The code defines a custom property named *BanksListID* that holds the ID, of type *Guid*, of the currently selected lookup list, if one is selected. The *get/set* property accessors read or write a private field. The setter accessor also stores the actual property value into the slot of the currently running thread. That's because SharePoint creates two different instances of the field internally: one while it's being configured, and another when it adds the configured instance to the *Fields* collection of the target list.

There are many techniques for sharing such configuration information across different object instances. For example, in ASP.NET, you could use the Session object or something similar. However, using the current thread store guarantees that these parameters are kept alive for the lifetime of the current thread, regardless of the specific platform executing the code (ASP. NET, Windows Forms, WPF, and so on). In addition, if you take a look at the internal implementation of native editor controls in SharePoint Foundation, you will see that Microsoft also uses the thread local store for this purpose.

Whenever a user configures the field, the SharePoint infrastructure invokes the *OnAdded* or *OnUpdate* methods, depending on the action the user performed. In those methods, you write or update the *SchemaXml* property content, using a private method called *CreateOrUpdateFieldSchemaXml*. That method uses LINQ to XML to store the configuration properties within the *SchemaXml* content. In Listing 11-18, the method starts by reading the already existing *SchemaXml* value. It then changes the values of the target custom attributes, and returns the resulting XML to the invoker.

For the sake of completeness, Listing 11-19 shows the implementation of the *Validate* method of the *IBANFieldControl*, where the lookup list is used to search for the configured bank via ABI/CAB.

LISTING 11-19 The implementation of the Validate method of the *IBANFieldControl*.

```
public override void Validate() {
    IBANField currentField = this.Field as IBANField;
    if (currentField != null) {
        SPWeb web = SPContext.Current.Web;

        try {
            SPList lookupList = web.Lists[currentField.BanksListID];

            SPQuery query = new SPQuery();
            query.Query = String.Format(
                "<Where><And><Eq><FieldRef Name=\"DevLeapBankABI\" />" +
                "<Value Type=\"Number\">{0}</Value></Eq><Eq>" +
                "<FieldRef Name=\"DevLeapBankCAB\" />" +
                "<Value Type=\"Number\">{1}</Value></Eq></And></Where></Query>",
                this.ABI.Text, this.CAB.Text);
            SPListItemCollection items = lookupList.GetItems(query);

            if (items.Count == 0) {
                this.IsValid = false;
                this.ErrorMessage = "Invalid ABI/CAB values";
            }
        }
        catch (IndexOutOfRangeException) {
            this.IsValid = false;
            this.ErrorMessage = "Invalid Banks lookup list ID";
        }
    }
}
```

The implementation of this validation method is trivial. It uses the SharePoint Server Object Model (for further details, read Chapter 3, "Server Object Model") using an *SPQuery* to search for an item (*SPListItem*) in the target lookup list (*SPList*) that has the ABI/CAB values provided by the user. When the bank does not exist, the field control raises a validation error.

Summary

In this chapter, you have seen how to create custom field types that extend the SharePoint native data model. You have seen how to create both simple text-based fields and more complex fields that hold multiple values. You have also seen the tools and techniques available in SharePoint to customize the field rendering in both standard and mobile-device browsers. Finally, you have seen how to develop custom field editors for advanced solutions.

Chapter 12
Event Receivers

Often, real SharePoint solutions need to catch events and user actions to subsequently execute some custom code. Whenever you need to start business processes related to such events and user actions, you would probably need to develop custom workflows (see Part V, "Developing Workflows"). However there are many situations in which a workflow is overkill. In such cases, it suffices to execute a small piece of code that executes quickly and might not always be critical to the business. Suppose, for example, that you want to trigger an event just after a document check-out user action. In this situation, you can define a custom event receiver that executes your custom code whenever the check-out operation happens.

To satisfy these situations, Microsoft SharePoint 2010 provides a standard way to develop *event receivers* (known in early SharePoint versions as event sinks), by inheriting from common base classes and registering the corresponding libraries into the target environment.

Types of Receivers

Event receivers are just custom classes, inherited from a base class specific to a particular set of events. There are event receivers related to single SharePoint items (*SPListItem*), which inherit from the *SPItemEventReceiver* base class. There are event receivers for trapping events related to list instances that inherit from *SPListEventReceiver*. There are receivers that catch events raised by webs, which are inherited from *SPWebEventReceiver*. There are events related to workflows instances, which inherit from *SPWorkflowEventReceiver*. There are receivers (*SPEmailEventReceiver*) that trigger whenever an e-mail–enabled document library receives an e-mail message. Lastly there are receivers for features deployment, which inherit from the *SPFeatureReceiver* base class, as you have seen in the "Feature Receivers" section of Chapter 8, "SharePoint Features and Solutions."

All of these receiver base classes (except for *SPEmailEventReceiver* and *SPFeatureReceiver*) inherit from a common base class named *SPEventReceiverBase*, which provides the very basic infrastructure for events management. In addition, all of these classes provide a set of virtual methods that developers should override when implementing events.

One key feature of SharePoint event receivers is the availability of "Before" and "After" events. The Before events are those that happen just after the event occurred, but before SharePoint writes any data to the SharePoint content database. Such events are useful for custom validation, rules checking, and cancelation of users' actions. The After events are those that happen after SharePoint commits the data to the SharePoint content database. These After event handlers cannot cancel the current action/operation, but they are guaranteed to execute only after specific actions. These two categories of events are also referred to as *synchronous* (Before) and *asynchronous* (After) events.

One last important thing to know is that Before events run in the same process and thread as the current action, while After events by default run in a background thread; however, you can force them to run synchronously, that means within the same process and thread of the current action. You'll see more about this topic starting on page 398 in the section "Event Synchronization."

Item-Level Event Receivers

The events related to *SPListItem* instances are defined in classes that inherit from *SPItemEventReceiver*. Table 12-1 shows an alphabetical list of events (virtual methods) provided by this base class.

TABLE 12-1 The Events Provided by the *SPItemEventReceiver* Base Class

Event Name	Description
ItemAdded	Occurs after an item has been added to a list.
ItemAdding	Occurs before an item is going to be added to a list.
ItemAttachmentAdded	Occurs after an attachment has been added to a list item.
ItemAttachmentAdding	Occurs before an attachment is going to be added to a list item.
ItemAttachmentDeleted	Occurs after an attachment has been deleted from a list item.
ItemAttachmentDeleting	Occurs before an attachment is going to be deleted from a list item.
ItemCheckedIn	Occurs after an item has been checked into a list.
ItemCheckedOut	Occurs after an item has been checked out from a list.
ItemCheckingIn	Occurs before an item is going to be checked into a list.
ItemCheckingOut	Occurs before an item is going to be checked out from a list.
ItemDeleted	Occurs after an item has been deleted from a list.
ItemDeleting	Occurs before an item is going to be deleted from a list.
ItemFileConverted	Occurs after a file has been converted using document conversion services.
ItemFileMoved	Occurs after an item has been moved.
ItemFileMoving	Occurs before an item is going to be moved.
ItemUncheckedOut	Occurs after an item has been unchecked out from a list.
ItemUncheckingOut	Occurs before an item is going to be unchecked out from a list.
ItemUpdated	Occurs after an item has been updated from a list.
ItemUpdating	Occurs before an item is going to be updated from a list.
ContextEvent	The item received a context event.

Listing 12-1 shows an example of an event receiver that triggers whenever an item is going to be changed (Before) by the end user, and whenever an item has been added (After). This event receiver targets a standard list of Contacts of a SharePoint Team Site. The core implementation of the events checks the Email field of the current *SPListItem* against a regular expression provided through the configuration of the event receiver when an item is changed. It then sends an alert e-mail to the registered contact, whenever the contact has been added.

Beginning on page 397, you'll see how to provide a custom configuration for an event receiver instance; here, we simply use a custom static utility class that is out of scope in the context of this first example.

LISTING 12-1 An event receiver that traps *ItemUpdating* Before and *ItemAdded* After events.

```
namespace DevLeap.SP2010.EventReceivers {

    public class ContactItemEventReceiver : SPItemEventReceiver {

        public override void ItemUpdating(SPItemEventProperties properties) {
            // Get configuration for the current EventReceiver instance
            ContactItemEventReceiverConfiguration configuration =
            XmlSerializationUtility.
                    Deserialize<ContactItemEventReceiverConfiguration>(
                        properties.ReceiverData);

            // If we have the specific configuration
            if ((configuration != null) &&
                (configuration.validation != null)) {

                // Prepare a Regex to validate the email of the contact
                Regex regex = new Regex(configuration.validation.emailRegEx,
                        RegexOptions.IgnoreCase);

                String newEmail = (String)properties.AfterProperties["Email"];

                // Validate the email
                if (!regex.IsMatch(newEmail)) {
                    // If it is not valid, cancel the current operation
                    properties.Cancel = true;
                    properties.ErrorMessage = "Invalid email value!";
                }
            }
        }

        public override void ItemAdded(SPItemEventProperties properties) {
            // Get configuration for the current EventReceiver instance
            ContactItemEventReceiverConfiguration configuration =
            XmlSerializationUtility.
                    Deserialize<ContactItemEventReceiverConfiguration>(
                        properties.ReceiverData);
```

```
            // If we have the specific configuration
            if ((configuration != null) &&
                (configuration.smtp != null)) {

                // Send an email to alert the target contact
                SmtpClient smtp = new SmtpClient();
                smtp.Send(configuration.smtp.from,
                    (String)properties.AfterProperties["Email"],
                    configuration.smtp.subject,
                    configuration.smtp.body);
            }
        }
    }
}
```

To create this event receiver, you can start from scratch, writing a custom class that inherits from *SPItemEventReceiver*, or you can create a new Visual Studio 2010 project, selecting the "SharePoint 2010 – Event Receiver" project template. This particular project template prompts you with a wizard to choose the target project type (farm or sandboxed solution), the target SharePoint site, the target list, and the type of event receivers you want to develop. Figure 12-1 shows an example of this wizard screen. This example shows a list of Contacts as the target list and "An item is being updated" and "An item was added" as the events to handle.

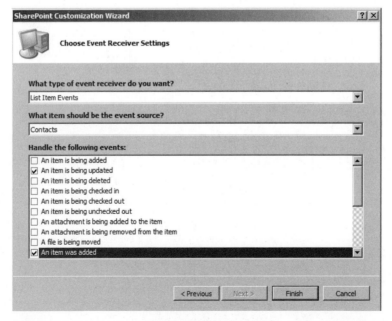

FIGURE 12-1 The wizard provided by Visual Studio 2010 for creating custom event receivers.

The key point of this example, as well as of any item-level event receiver, is the argument of type *SPItemEventProperties* that is passed to the event handling methods. This class inherits from *SPEventPropertiesBase*. It provides the event receiver instance with all the useful information about the event, the source item, the before and after properties of the list item, the *SPWeb* and *SPSite* where the event occurred, and the custom configuration for the receiver instance. Table 12-2 presents the main members of its base class.

TABLE 12-2 **The Main Members of the *SPEventPropertiesBase* Class**

Member Name	Description
EventType	Describes the kind of event that occurred, using a *SPEventReceiverType* event type enumeration.
EventUserToken	Corresponds to the current user token (*SPUserToken*) at the time the event is fired.
OriginatingUserToken	Corresponds to the user token (*SPUserToken*) of the user that makes the request.
Cancel	*Boolean* property with which you cancel the current event in Before events.
ErrorMessage	The error message that will be displayed to the end user if the event is cancelled.
Status	Defines the status (*SPEventReceiverStatus*) of the current event. It can assume values of: *Continue*, to continue with the event; *CancelNoError*, to cancel the event without throwing any kind of error; *CancelWithError*, to cancel the event and throw an error; *CancelWithRedirectUrl*, to cancel the event and redirect the user to a specific *RedirectUrl*.
RedirectUrl	Defines the URL to redirect the user to, when the *Status* value is *CancelWithRedirectUrl*.
SiteId	Returns the *ID* of the *SPSite* that contains the event source list item.
ReceiverData	Returns a *String* that represents the configuration of the current event receiver instance.

Table 12-3 lists the members of the *SPItemEventProperties* implementation.

TABLE 12-3 **The Main Members of the *SPItemEventProperties* Class**

Member Name	Description
InvalidateListItem	Invalidates (sets the corresponding variable to *NULL*) the list item that represents the source of the event.
InvalidateWeb	Invalidates (sets the corresponding variables to *NULL*) the list item, the list, and the website that represent the source of the event. Internally, this method also disposes of the *SPWeb* instance related to the event, if any such instance exists.
OpenSite	Returns an instance of the *SPSite* that corresponds to the current event source, impersonating the current user at the time the event is fired, if any user is available; otherwise, it uses the current user.

Member Name	Description
OpenWeb	Returns an instance of the *SPWeb* corresponding to the current event source, impersonating the current user at the time the event is fired, if any user is available; otherwise, it uses the current user.
Dispose	Disposes the current *SPSite* and *SPWeb* instances. Internally, it also invokes the *InvalidateWeb* method.
CurrentUserId	Returns the *ID* of the user who caused the event to fire.
UserDisplayName	Returns the *DisplayName* of the user who caused the event to fire.
UserLoginName	Returns the *LoginName* of the user who caused the event to fire.
AfterProperties	References a hash table of tuples (*String/Object*) describing the properties (columns) of the source list item after the event occurred.
AfterUrl	Represents the URL of the source list item after the event occurred. For item file rename or move operations, this is the new file name.
BeforeProperties	References a hash table of tuples (*String/Object*) describing the properties (columns) of the source list item before the event occurred.
BeforeUrl	Represents the URL of the source list item before the event occurred. For item file rename or move operations, this is the old file name.
List	Returns a reference to the *SPList* that contains the event source list item.
ListId	Returns the *ID* of the list that contains the event source list item.
ListItem	Returns a reference to the *SPListItem* that represents the event source item.
ListItemId	Returns the *ID* of the event source item.
ListTitle	Returns the *Title* of the list that contains the event source list item.
Web	Returns a reference to the *SPWeb* that contains the event source item.
WebUrl	Returns the absolute URL of the *SPWeb* that contains the event source item.
RelativeWebUrl	Returns the server-relative URL of the *SPWeb* that contains the event source item.
Zone	Returns the Zone of the website that contains the event source list item.
Versionless	Provides the option to instruct SharePoint to handle the event without changing the version number of the current source list item.

The *SPItemEventProperties* class is fundamental to implementing the logic of a custom event receiver because it is the link to the context of the event itself. When using this logic, it is important to remember that the class implements *IDisposable*; thus, if you reference any *SPWeb* or *SPSite* instance in the event properties members, you will need to dispose of them to release unmanaged objects.

List-Level Event Receivers

Another set of useful events are those related to lists. SharePoint offers a base class named *SPListEventReceiver* with which you can trap changes to the fields of an existing list as well as actions related to adding or deleting lists instances. Table 12-4 shows the events provided by *SPListEventReceiver*.

TABLE 12-4 The Events Provided by the *SPListEventReceiver* Base Class

Event Name	Description
FieldAdded	Occurs after a field has been added to a list definition.
FieldAdding	Occurs before a field is going to be added to a list definition.
FieldDeleted	Occurs after a field has been removed from a list definition.
FieldDeleting	Occurs before a field is going to be removed from a list definition.
FieldUpdated	Occurs after a field has been updated to a list definition.
FieldUpdating	Occurs before a field is going to be updated to a list definition.
ListAdded	Occurs after a new list has been added to a *SPWeb* instance.
ListAdding	Occurs before a new list is added to a *SPWeb* instance.
ListDeleted	Occurs after a list has been deleted from a *SPWeb* instance.
ListDeleting	Occurs before a list is deleted from a *SPWeb* instance.

As with item-level events, all list-level events methods also receive a single argument that inherits from *SPEventPropertiesBase* and represents the context of the event that will occur (Before) or has occurred (After). For list-level events, the argument is a *SPListEventProperties* type, and provides the small set of members listed in Table 12-5.

TABLE 12-5 The Main Members of the *SPListEventProperties* Class

Member Name	Description
InvalidateList	Invalidates (sets the corresponding variable to *NULL*) the list and/or the field that represents the source of the event.
InvalidateWeb	Invalidates (sets the corresponding variables to *NULL*) the list, the field, and the website that represent the source of the event. Internally, this method also disposes of the *SPWeb* instance related to the event, if any such instance exists.
Dispose	Disposes the current *SPSite* and *SPWeb* instances. Internally, it also invokes the *InvalidateWeb* method.
FeatureId	Returns the GUID of the SharePoint feature that created the list instance for *ListAdding* and *ListAdded* event types.
Field	References the field that is the source of the current event.
FieldName	References the name of the field that is the source of the current event.

Member Name	Description
FieldXml	Returns the XML definition of the field that is the source of the current event.
List	Returns a reference to the *SPList* instance that is the source of the event.
ListId	Returns the *ID* of the *SPList* instance that is the source of the event.
ListTitle	Returns the *Title* of the *SPList* instance that is the source of the event.
TemplateId	Returns the ID of the list template that is related to the list instance that is the source of the event.
UserDisplayName	Returns the *DisplayName* of the user who caused the event to fire.
UserLoginName	Returns the *LoginName* of the user who caused the event to fire.
Web	Returns a reference to the *SPWeb* that contains the event source list.
WebId	Returns a reference to the ID of the *SPWeb* that contains the event source list.
WebUrl	Returns the absolute URL of the *SPWeb* that contains the event source list.

Listing 12-2 shows a list-level event receiver example that traps and cancels changes to the fields of a list definition, if that list is a specific custom type provisioned through a WSP solution.

LISTING 12-2 A list-level event receiver that traps field events.

```
namespace DevLeap.SP2010.EventReceivers {

    public class ContactsListEventReceiver : SPListEventReceiver {
        public override void FieldAdding(SPListEventProperties properties) {
            // Check if the list template is our custom list template
            if (properties.TemplateId == 10001) {
                properties.Cancel = true;
                properties.ErrorMessage =
                "You cannot change this list definition through the web browser";
            }
            base.FieldAdding(properties);
        }

        public override void FieldDeleting(SPListEventProperties properties) {
            // Almost the same code as FieldAdding event
        }

        public override void FieldUpdating(SPListEventProperties properties) {
            // Almost the same code as FieldAdding event
        }
    }
}
```

You should be aware that field events do not occur whenever the events are related to a content type's actions. For example, if you add a new field to a list definition directly, the

FieldAdding and *FieldAdded* events will occur; however, if you add a Content Type to a list definition, the field events will not occur—even if the Content Type requires registration of new fields.

> **Note** In general, list event receivers are useful for intercepting user actions against list definitions, to enforce validation rules and policies and help avoid chaos to a website's structure. For example, you can enforce common naming conventions or common sets of validation rules to each and every list created from a web browser; thus, leaving the end users free to provision contents and lists, but still monitored and constrained by rules defined in the lists' event receivers.

Web-Level Event Receivers

At the web level, you can catch some events related to Site Collection deletion, both before and after the action, and for website creation, deletion, moving, and provisioning. To trap such events, you need to implement a custom class that inherits from *SPWebEventReceiver*. Table 12-6 lists the available web-level events.

TABLE 12-6 The Events Provided by the *SPWebEventReceiver* Base Class

Event Name	Description
SiteDeleted	Occurs after a Site Collection has been deleted.
SiteDeleting	Occurs before a Site Collection is being deleted.
WebAdding	Occurs before an *SPWeb* is being added to a list collection.
WebDeleted	Occurs after an *SPWeb* has been removed from a Site Collection.
WebDeleting	Occurs before an *SPWeb* is going to be removed from a Site Collection.
WebMoved	Occurs after an *SPWeb* has been renamed or moved to another location.
WebMoving	Occurs before an *SPWeb* is being renamed or moved to another location.
WebProvisioned	Occurs after an *SPWeb* has been provisioned into a Site Collection.

Web-level event receivers are usually most useful for enforcing custom policies, custom layout templates, or checking naming conventions, similar to list-events receivers. Another common use for web-level event receivers is to deny site or web deletion of specific websites—even if the current user has the rights to provision and unprovision contents and sites. The unique argument for the web-level event receiver methods is of type *SPWebEventProperties*, which provides an entry point to the context Web, the context site, and their URLs. Table 12-7 shows the *SPWebEventProperties* public members.

TABLE 12-7 The Main Members of the *SPWebEventProperties* Class

Member Name	Description
InvalidateWeb	Invalidates (sets the corresponding variables to *NULL*) the website that represents the source of the event. Internally, this method also disposes of the *SPWeb* instance related to the event, if any instance exists.
Dispose	Disposes of the current *SPSite* and *SPWeb* instances. Internally, it invokes the *InvalidateWeb* method.
FullUrl	Returns the absolute URL of the source *Web* on which the event occurred.
NewServerRelativeUrl	Represents the URL of the site after it has been moved.
ParentWebId	Returns the GUID of the current *SPWeb* instance.
ServerRelativeUrl	Represents the URL of the site before it has been moved.
UserDisplayName	Returns the *DisplayName* of the user who caused the event to fire.
UserLoginName	Returns the *LoginName* of the user who caused the event to fire.
Web	Returns a reference to the *SPWeb* that contains the event source list.
WebId	Returns a reference to the ID of the *SPWeb* that contains the event source list.

Not all the members listed in Table 12-7 are always available; for example, the *Web* property will not be accessible for *WebDeleted* or *SiteDeleted* events. If you try to access them, you will get a *FileNotFoundException*. Similarly, when handling a *WebAdding* event, you will not have access to the current *Web* instance; for that, you need to wait until the *WebProvisioned* event fires.

Workflow Event Receivers

SharePoint provides workflow event receivers so that you can intercept events related to running workflows. For instance, you can trap the *WorkflowCompleted* event to execute a custom action whenever a workflow instance completes. Table 12-8 lists all the available events, which are provided by the base class, *SPWorkflowEventReceiver*.

TABLE 12-8 The Events Provided by the *SPWorkflowEventReceiver* Base Class

Event Name	Description
WorkflowCompleted	Occurs after a workflow instance is completed.
WorkflowPostponed	Occurs after a workflow instance has been postponed.
WorkflowStarted	Occurs after a workflow instance has been started.
WorkflowStarting	Occurs after a workflow instance is starting.

All the virtual methods in Table 12-8 receive a parameter of type *SPWorkflowEventProperties* that provides an entry point to the event context. Table 12-9 shows the most important members of this *SPWorkflowEventProperties* class.

TABLE 12-9 The Main Members of the *SPWorkflowEventProperties* Class

Member Name	Description
ActivationProperties	Represents the properties to start a new workflow instance. For example, it contains the *InitiationData* for the workflow. For further details about workflow instances, go to Part V, "Developing Workflows."
AssociationData	Contains the workflow association data.
CompletionType	Contains information about the real outcome of the workflow. In fact, whenever the workflow completes, you can read the *CompletionType* property from within the *WorkflowCompleted* event. The property might have any of the following values: ■ Completed ■ *Errored* ■ *ExternallyTerminated* ■ *FailedOnStart* ■ *InternallyTerminated* ■ *NotApplicable*
ErrorException	Returns the current exception instance, if defined.
InitiationData	Contains the workflow initiation data.
InstanceId	Represents the ID of the instance.
PostponedEvent	Signals whether the workflow has been postponed for *Load* or for *Start*.
RelativeWebUrl	Returns the relative URL of the *SPWeb* that contains the source.
TerminatedByUserId	The *UserID* of the user who terminated the workflow, for a terminated workflow instance.
WebUrl	Returns the URL of the *SPWeb* that contains the source.

E-Mail Event Receivers

The e-mail event receivers support e-mail–enabled list instances, and allow you to intercept events when the list receives e-mail messages. These event receivers are based on a class that inherits from *SPEmailEventReceiver*, and they override the *EmailReceived* virtual method. Listing 12-3 shows an example.

LISTING 12-3 An sample e-mail event receiver.

```
namespace DevLeap.SP2010.EventReceivers {
    public class EmailEventReceiver : SPEmailEventReceiver {
        private List<String> validSenders;

        static EmailEventReceiver() {
            // Code omitted ...
        }

        public override void EmailReceived(SPList list,
            SPEmailMessage emailMessage, String receiverData) {

            if (!validSenders.Contains(emailMessage.Sender))
                throw new Exception("Invalid sender email");

            base.EmailReceived(list, emailMessage, receiverData);
        }
    }
}
```

In Listing 12-3, the method signature differs from previous event receivers, because it simply receives a reference to the current target list (*SPList*), the e-mail message in a variable of type *SPEmailMessage*, and a *ReceiverData* string that could hold some configuration parameters. This code simply checks whether the sender of the e-mail exists in a trusted list of senders. Another useful scenario could be the extraction of attachments from a received e-mail. In fact, the *SPEmailMessage* class also provides an *Attachments* collection property that you can configure to extract all the *SPEmailAttachment* instances together with their content. This is available through the *ContentStream* property.

Avoiding Event Loops

Whenever you implement a custom event receiver—for example, with code that changes the list item on which the event fired—you should first disable event firing to avoid becoming trapped in a loop. That's because if you simply change an item inside an event receiver, such as *ItemUpdated* event, the event will fire again, and you could unexpectedly create a loop. To disable event firing, all the event receivers inherit a *Boolean* property named *EventFiringEnabled* from the *SPEventPropertiesBase* base class, which you saw earlier in this chapter. Setting this property to *false* disables event firing for the current event; this permits your code to change the current item without firing a new event receiver. It's good practice to always set this flag to *false* at the beginning of your event receiver code, and then set it back to *true* at the end of code execution.

Event Deployment and Binding

You can deploy event receivers by using a couple of different techniques. The first technique uses a SharePoint feature that provisions the receiver via WSP deployment. Listing 12-4 displays a feature element that installs an event receiver for a list.

LISTING 12-4 A feature element file for provisioning a custom item-level event receiver.

```xml
<?xml version="1.0" encoding="utf-8"?>
<Elements xmlns="http://schemas.microsoft.com/sharepoint/">
  <Receivers ListTemplateId="105">
    <Receiver>
      <Name>EventReceiver1ItemUpdating</Name>
      <Type>ItemUpdating</Type>
      <Assembly>$SharePoint.Project.AssemblyFullName$</Assembly>
      <Class>DevLeap.SP2010.EventReceivers.EventReceiver1.EventReceiver1</Class>
      <Data>Custom configuration</Data>
      <SequenceNumber>10000</SequenceNumber>
    </Receiver>
    <Receiver>
      <Name>EventReceiver1ItemAdded</Name>
      <Type>ItemAdded</Type>
      <Assembly>$SharePoint.Project.AssemblyFullName$</Assembly>
      <Class>DevLeap.SP2010.EventReceivers.EventReceiver1.EventReceiver1</Class>
      <SequenceNumber>10000</SequenceNumber>
    </Receiver>
  </Receivers>
</Elements>
```

Notice that in the *Data* tag of the *Receiver* element you can define a custom configuration text that will be provided to the event receiver via the *ReceiverData* property of the *SPEventPropertiesBase* base class, whenever the receiver is invoked. In general, you supply this configuration element/property with a custom XML node set, so you can deserialize the content inside the event receiver code. Keep in mind, however, that the length of the content of the *Data* element is limited to 255 characters.

The second deployment technique is based on custom code. It can be useful when you want to deploy your receiver using some custom parameters, thus you prefer to publish a deployment page or a custom deployment tool that—using custom .NET code—will effectively configure the receiver against its intended target, whether that's a list, a site, or anything else. Listing 12-5 shows an example of this deployment technique.

LISTING 12-5 A custom item-level event receiver deployed using code.

```csharp
using (SPSite site = new SPSite("http://sp2010dev/")) {
    using (SPWeb web = site.OpenWeb())  {

        ContactItemEventReceiverConfiguration config = new
            ContactItemEventReceiverConfiguration();
```

```
        // Omissis ...
        SPList list = web.Lists["Contacts"];
        var newReceiver = list.EventReceivers.Add();

        Assembly asm =
            Assembly.LoadFrom(@"..\..\DevLeap.SP2010.EventReceivers.dll");
        newReceiver.Assembly = asm.FullName;
        newReceiver.Class = asm.GetType(
          "DevLeap.SP2010.EventReceivers.ContactItemEventReceiver").FullName;
        newReceiver.Name = "Contact Receiver";
        newReceiver.Type = SPEventReceiverType.ItemUpdating;
        newReceiver.SequenceNumber = 100;
        newReceiver.Data = XmlSerializationUtility.Serialize
          <ContactItemEventReceiverConfiguration>(config);
        newReceiver.Update();
    }
}
```

One of the main innovations of SharePoint 2010 is the ability to deploy an event receiver not only at the web level, but also at the Site Collection level. In fact, *all* of the event receivers except the *SPEmailEventReceiver* can be deployed at the Site Collection level, so you can share their behavior across all the websites within that Site Collection. For instance, you can share at the Site Collection level, a list-level event receiver that checks list provisioning and/ or custom fields using a unique deployment step.

Another interesting deployment feature introduced with SharePoint 2010 is the ability to bind an event receiver to a list template, using its *ListTemplateId* property, and then apply that event receiver to every list instance based on that *ListTemplateId*.

Event Synchronization

In SharePoint, all the Before events are executed synchronously within the same process and thread of the current user request, while all After events are executed asynchronously, on a background thread and potentially in a process different from the current user request.

However, there might be circumstances for which you want to execute an After event, such as *ItemUpdated*, and make it wait to execute as if it were a synchronous event. To support this, SharePoint provides a *deployment configuration property* that allows you to specify the *Synchronization* of the event receiver. The property can assume one of the following values:

- *Default*   Before events are synchronous; After events are asynchronous.
- *Synchronous*   The current event is executed synchronously.
- *Asynchronous*   The current event is executed asynchronously.

To configure this property, you can define it in the feature element XML file, as shown in Listing 12-6.

LISTING 12-6 A feature element file provisioning a custom item-level "After" event receiver synchronously.

```xml
<?xml version="1.0" encoding="utf-8"?>
<Elements xmlns="http://schemas.microsoft.com/sharepoint/">
  <Receivers ListTemplateId="105">
      <Receiver>
        <Name>EventReceiver1ItemAdded</Name>
        <Type>ItemAdded</Type>
        <Assembly>$SharePoint.Project.AssemblyFullName$</Assembly>
<Class>DevLeap.SP2010.EventReceivers.EventReceiver1.EventReceiver1</Class>
        <SequenceNumber>10000</SequenceNumber>
        <Synchronization>Synchronous</Synchronization>
      </Receiver>
  </Receivers>
</Elements>
```

Another option is to configure the *Synchronization* property in code, as shown in Listing 12-7.

LISTING 12-7 A code excerpt that provisions a custom item-level "After" event receiver as *Synchronous*.

```csharp
using (SPSite site = new SPSite("http://sp2010dev/")) {
    using (SPWeb web = site.OpenWeb()) {

        ContactItemEventReceiverConfiguration config = new
            ContactItemEventReceiverConfiguration();

        // Omissis ...
        SPList list = web.Lists["Contacts"];
        var newReceiver = list.EventReceivers.Add();

        Assembly asm = Assembly.LoadFrom(
            @"..\..\DevLeap.SP2010.EventReceivers.dll");
        newReceiver.Assembly = asm.FullName;
        newReceiver.Class = asm.GetType(
            "DevLeap.SP2010.EventReceivers.ContactItemEventReceiver")
            .FullName;
        newReceiver.Name = "Contact Receiver";
        newReceiver.Type = SPEventReceiverType.ItemUpdated;
        newReceiver.SequenceNumber = 110;
        newReceiver.Data = XmlSerializationUtility.Serialize
            <ContactItemEventReceiverConfiguration>(config);
        newReceiver.Synchronization =
            SPEventReceiverSynchronization.Synchronous;
        newReceiver.Update();
    }
}
```

It's up to you whether to define the event and its synchronization model using a feature or custom code.

Event Security

By default, all events in SharePoint run under the context of the user who raised the event. For example, if Bob is changing a list item, the *ItemUpdating* event will be executed under the same context as Bob. However, there are some situations, such as in custom SharePoint workflows, in which code needs to execute under the System Account. In such cases, SharePoint has the *SPSecurity* class, which provides some security methods, including the famous *RunWithElevatedPrivileges*, which let you run a SharePoint process impersonating the system account. But be aware that if your receiver executes *another* event receiver, it would run with system account privileges, as well—and as you can imagine, that's not a good idea for security reasons. To avoid such issues, you can leverage the new *OriginatingUserToken* property, which is available in any event receiver through the *SPEventPropertiesBase* base class. Using this token, you can create a new and independent instance of *SPSite* and/or *SPWeb*, impersonating the originating user. Listing 12-8 shows an example of code that executes some activities by impersonating the originating user in this manner.

LISTING 12-8 Using the *OriginatingUserToken* to impersonate the originating user.

```
public override void ItemUpdated(SPItemEventProperties properties) {
    using (SPSite site = new SPSite(properties.SiteId,
                properties.OriginatingUserToken)) {
        using (SPWeb web = site.OpenWeb(properties.RelativeWebUrl)) {
            // Do something here impersonating the originating user token
        }
    }
    base.ItemUpdated(properties);
}
```

Summary

In this chapter, you've seen how to develop custom event receivers that trap events related to list items, lists, Webs and workflows. Keep in mind that you should use these event receivers only for quick and small activities, not for business-critical tasks. In fact, the execution of an event receiver could be stopped unexpectedly, such as for *SPSite* application pool recycling, which would cause you to lose all the inserted data and the event state. If you must implement business processes in response to events, consider using SharePoint Workflows instead, and read the related Part V, "Developing Workflows."

Chapter 13
Document Management

This chapter covers some topics related to document management. In particular, the first part will be focused on some new features introduced in Microsoft SharePoint 2010, such as Document Sets and the Document Id. Later in the chapter, the focus will move to the new Word Automation Services available with Microsoft SharePoint Server 2010.

 Note This is the first chapter covering topics that are available only in the Standard and Enterprise editions of SharePoint Server 2010. If you own a Microsoft SharePoint Foundation 2010 license, or you plan to deploy your solution on SharePoint Foundation, you will not be able to make use of features presented here.

Document Sets

Document sets are one of the great improvements offered by SharePoint 2010 for managing sets of documents. Many times customers ask to use SharePoint document libraries to store not only single documents, but also multiple documents belonging to the same project, customer, work order, and so on. A document set is a special Content Type that holds multiple documents in a unique container. However, it is not simply a folder. Similar to a folder, a document set can have metadata of its own, but it also has a custom user interface based on a dedicated welcome page, dedicated versioning of the entire set, specific workflows, synchronization of metadata between the document set and the items that it contains, and custom behaviors in general.

As an example, consider the processing of a typical work order for a product. You have some documentation about the work order, such as the quote you sent to the customer with all the specifications of the products, the order received by the customer, the specifications of all the work items, a timeline scheduling, the quality check outputs, the testing results, and the delivery documents. You likely will have many other documents, but for the sake of simplicity, these will suffice. The work order itself will probably have a protocol number, an estimated delivery date, a reference to the target customer, and so on. In all probability, you will have a workflow process that will monitor and manage the whole procedure. A document set could hold all of the information in a unique SharePoint item, functionally equivalent to the legacy idea of folder in a library, but with custom behaviors and appearance that can be defined by code.

Figure 13-1 presents the default welcome page of a standard document set, in this case, made up of a couple of documents. Notice the dedicated Document Set tab in the Ribbon.

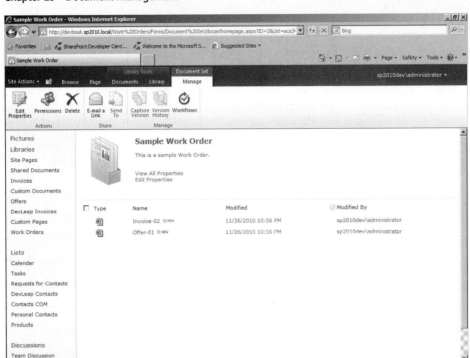

FIGURE 13-1 The default welcome page of a sample document set.

Under the hood, a document set is a special Content Type, inherited from the folder content type (ID 0x0120). You can extend it in nearly the same manner as you can extend a standard Content Type. The basic ID of the Document Set content type is 0x0120D520, because it is inherited from the Document Collection Folder content type (ID 0x0120D5).

> **Note** For further details about Content Type IDs, refer to the "Content Type IDs " section on page 323 of Chapter 10, "Data Provisioning."

To implement document sets in your sites, you first need to activate the corresponding feature in the Site Collection Features management page. Then you will be able to add the *Document Set* Content Type to an existing library, or you can create a new Content Type of your own, inheriting from the *Document Set* Content Type.

From the perspective of a SharePoint designer, a document set can be designed using the web browser or SharePoint Designer 2010. To design a new document set, you simply need to create a new Content Type via the Site Content Types page, inheriting from the basic Document Set Content Type, which is available in the Document Set Content Types group.

From a developer's perspective, a document set can be defined in Microsoft Visual Studio 2010, inheriting a new Content Type from the base *Document Set* Content Type.

No matter which method you use to create a document set, you will be able to customize the following areas:

- **Metadata schema**   Defines the metadata fields describing the root document set.

- **Workflow associations**   Associates workflows definitions to the document set.

- **List of allowed child content types**   Defines the content types of items that can be added into the document set.

- **Metadata to synchronize with items in the document set**   Defines which metadata fields of the root document set will be replicated on documents contained in the set.

- **Default contents of the document set**   Defines a pre-defined set of documents to load in every new instance of the document set.

- **New page**   The page presented to the end user while creating a new instance of the document set. It can be customized.

- **Welcome page**   The page presented to the end user while showing/editing a document set. It is a Web Part Page and can be customized, too.

Provisioning Document Sets

If you are configuring the document set using the web browser, there is a dedicated page for managing these configurations, which is available in the configuration page of any content type inherited from the document set. If you like to work within Visual Studio 2010, you can define a custom XML element for provisioning the document set (see Chapter 10, "Data Provisioning).

Listing 13-1 shows an XML code excerpt that defines a "Work Order Document Set" created in Visual Studio 2010 as a custom Content Type that uses automated provisioning capabilities.

LISTING 13-1 A document set Content Type defined in an XML provisioning file.

```xml
<?xml version="1.0" encoding="utf-8"?>
<Elements xmlns="http://schemas.microsoft.com/sharepoint/">
  <!-- Site Columns used by the Content Type -->
  <Field
    ID="{EA8DC9E7-0EA8-4F5C-961D-4CCFBC6C8407}"
    Name="DevLeapWorkOrderID"
    StaticName="DevLeapWorkOrderID"
    DisplayName="Work Order ID"
    Type="Text"
    Group="DevLeap Columns"
```

```xml
              Sortable="TRUE" />
<Field
  ID="{D54685EC-C28E-46F7-9200-63F182162A66}"
  Name="DevLeapCustomerName"
  StaticName="DevLeapCustomerName"
  DisplayName="Customer Name"
  Type="Text"
  Group="DevLeap Columns"
  Sortable="TRUE" />
<Field
  ID="{3AD0914C-410B-42C6-8C38-8CCDA18CC9D3}"
  Name="DevLeapWorkOrderStatus"
  StaticName="DevLeapWorkOrderStatus"
  DisplayName="Status"
  Type="Choice"
  Group="DevLeap Columns"
  Sortable="TRUE">
  <Default>Created</Default>
  <CHOICES>
    <CHOICE>Created</CHOICE>
    <CHOICE>In Progress</CHOICE>
    <CHOICE>Completed</CHOICE>
  </CHOICES>
</Field>

<!-- Parent ContentType: Document Set (0x0120D520) -->
<ContentType ID="0x0120D52000d18b61fc3fae4ef7a089a8586bbbaa13"
             Name="DevLeapWorkOrderDocumentSet"
             Group="DevLeap Content Types"
             Description="Content Type for describing a Work Order"
             Inherits="False"
             Version="2"
             ProgId="SharePoint.DocumentSet">
  <Folder TargetName="_cts/DevLeapWorkOrderDocumentSet" />
  <FieldRefs>
    <FieldRef
      ID="{EA8DC9E7-0EA8-4F5C-961D-4CCFBC6C8407}"
      Name="DevLeapWorkOrderID" />
    <FieldRef
      ID="{D54685EC-C28E-46F7-9200-63F182162A66}"
      Name="DevLeapCustomerName" />
    <FieldRef
      ID="{3AD0914C-410B-42C6-8C38-8CCDA18CC9D3}"
      Name="DevLeapWorkOrderStatus" />
  </FieldRefs>
  <XmlDocuments>
    <XmlDocument NamespaceURI="http://schemas.microsoft.com/sharepoint/events">
      <spe:Receivers xmlns:spe="http://schemas.microsoft.com/sharepoint/events">
        <Receiver>
          <Name>DocumentSet ItemUpdated</Name>
          <Synchronization>Synchronous</Synchronization>
          <Type>10002</Type>
          <SequenceNumber>100</SequenceNumber>
          <Assembly>Microsoft.Office.DocumentManagement, Version=14.0.0.0,
```

```
                          Culture=neutral, PublicKeyToken=71e9bce111e9429c</Assembly>
                    <Class>
                     Microsoft.Office.DocumentManagement.DocumentSets.DocumentSetEventReceiver
                    </Class>
                    <Data></Data>
                    <Filter></Filter>
                  </Receiver>
                  <Receiver>
                    <Name>DocumentSet ItemAdded</Name>
                    <Synchronization>Synchronous</Synchronization>
                    <Type>10001</Type>
                    <SequenceNumber>100</SequenceNumber>
                    <Assembly>Microsoft.Office.DocumentManagement, Version=14.0.0.0,
                       Culture=neutral, PublicKeyToken=71e9bce111e9429c</Assembly>
                    <Class>
                       Microsoft.Office.DocumentManagement.DocumentSets.
DocumentSetItemsEventReceiver
                    </Class>
                    <Data></Data>
                    <Filter></Filter>
                  </Receiver>
               </spe:Receivers>
            </XmlDocument>
            <XmlDocument NamespaceURI=
               "http://schemas.microsoft.com/office/documentsets/allowedcontenttypes">
               <act:AllowedContentTypes xmlns:act=
                 "http://schemas.microsoft.com/office/documentsets/allowedcontenttypes"
                 LastModified="11/26/2010 22:49:18">
                 <!-- Document -->
                 <AllowedContentType id="0x0101" />
                 <!-- Picture -->
                 <AllowedContentType id="0x010102" />
                 <!-- DevLeapInvoice -->
                 <AllowedContentType id="0x0101008D841CAC0C7F474288965287B30061DC" />
               </act:AllowedContentTypes>
            </XmlDocument>
            <XmlDocument NamespaceURI=
               "http://schemas.microsoft.com/office/documentsets/sharedfields">
               <sf:SharedFields xmlns:sf=
                 "http://schemas.microsoft.com/office/documentsets/sharedfields"
                 LastModified="11/26/2010 22:49:18">
                 <!-- Work Order ID-->
                 <SharedField id="EA8DC9E7-0EA8-4F5C-961D-4CCFBC6C8407" />
                 <!-- Status -->
                 <SharedField id="3AD0914C-410B-42C6-8C38-8CCDA18CC9D3" />
               </sf:SharedFields>
            </XmlDocument>
            <XmlDocument NamespaceURI=
               "http://schemas.microsoft.com/office/documentsets/defaultdocuments">
               <dd:DefaultDocuments xmlns:dd=
                 "http://schemas.microsoft.com/office/documentsets/defaultdocuments"
                 LastModified="11/26/2010 22:49:18" AddSetName="True">
                 <DefaultDocument name="Invoice-01.docx" idContentType="0x0101" />
                 <DefaultDocument name="Offer-01.docx" idContentType="0x0101" />
               </dd:DefaultDocuments>
```

```
        </XmlDocument>
        <XmlDocument NamespaceURI=
          "http://schemas.microsoft.com/office/documentsets/welcomepagefields">
          <wpf:WelcomePageFields xmlns:wpf=
            "http://schemas.microsoft.com/office/documentsets/welcomepagefields"
            LastModified="11/26/2010 22:49:18">
            <WelcomePageField id="EA8DC9E7-0EA8-4F5C-961D-4CCFBC6C8407" />
            <WelcomePageField id="3AD0914C-410B-42C6-8C38-8CCDA18CC9D3" />
          </wpf:WelcomePageFields>
        </XmlDocument>
        <XmlDocument NamespaceURI=
          "http://schemas.microsoft.com/sharepoint/v3/contenttype/forms">
          <FormTemplates xmlns=
            "http://schemas.microsoft.com/sharepoint/v3/contenttype/forms">
            <Display>DocSetDisplayForm</Display>
            <Edit>ListForm</Edit>
            <New>DocSetDisplayForm</New>
          </FormTemplates>
        </XmlDocument>
        <XmlDocument NamespaceURI=
          "http://schemas.microsoft.com/sharepoint/v3/contenttype/forms/url">
          <FormUrls xmlns=
            "http://schemas.microsoft.com/sharepoint/v3/contenttype/forms/url">
            <New>_layouts/NewDocSet.aspx</New>
          </FormUrls>
        </XmlDocument>
      </XmlDocuments>
    </ContentType>
  </Elements>
```

The content type definition in Listing 13-1 is nearly the same as those defined in Chapter 10. However, it is interesting to underline that the *ContentType* element must have an *Inherits* attribute set to *False* to break inheritance from the base *Document Set* Content Type, giving a custom behavior, appearance, and configuration to this new custom document set. Another key configuration defined in the sample Content Type is the *ProgId* attribute, which has a value of *SharePoint.DocumentSet* to give an appearance and behavior of document set to items based on this new Content Type. Then there is a *Folder* child element that defines the root folder for the content related to the current Content Type. This folder maps to a URL under the *_cts* folder, which is a hidden resource folder for SharePoint, specifically defined to host Content Type models, templates, and items in general. This folder organizes content in separate subfolders for each Content Type. In the current example, the folder has a value of *_cts/DevLeapWorkOrderDocumentSet*.

The big difference from a classic Content Type is the long list of *XmlDocument* elements in the *XmlDocuments* extension section of the Content Type definition. Table 13-1 lists the supported extension elements and their meaning. Listing 13-1 then shows an example of content for these elements.

TABLE 13-1 The Extension Elements Supported by a File Provisioning a Document Set

Element and Namespace	Description
WelcomePageView *http://schemas.microsoft.com/office/documentsets/welcomepageview*	Defines the data view that will be shown in the welcome page.
Receivers *http://schemas.microsoft.com/sharepoint/events*	Defines one or more event receivers. By default, a document set, which replicates some of its metadata fields on its child items, will have a couple of receivers (*ItemUpdated* and *ItemAdded*).
AllowedContentTypes *http://schemas.microsoft.com/office/documentsets/allowedcontenttypes*	Defines the list of allowed Content Types. *AllowedContentTypes* references each allowed Content Type through its Content Type ID.
SharedFields *http://schemas.microsoft.com/office/documentsets/sharedfields*	Defines the list of metadata fields that will be replicated to the child items. The fields are references through their site column ID.
DefaultDocuments *http://schemas.microsoft.com/office/documentsets/defaultdocuments*	Defines the default documents to include in every instance of the document set. The documents must be deployed under the _cts/ {ContentTypeName} folder of the current site.
WelcomePageFields *http://schemas.microsoft.com/office/documentsets/welcomepagefields*	Defines the metadata fields of the document set that will be shown in the welcome page.
FormTemplates *http://schemas.microsoft.com/sharepoint/v3/contenttype/forms*	Declares the forms templates to use while displaying, listing, and editing items, based on the current content type.
FormUrls *http://schemas.microsoft.com/sharepoint/v3/contenttype/forms/url*	Declares the forms URLs to browse to while displaying, adding, updating items, based on the current content type.

The sample document set (*DevLeapWorkOrderDocumentSet*), created by the code sample attached to this chapter, defines three custom metadata fields (*DevLeapWorkOrderID*, *DevLeapCustomerName*, *DevLeapWorkOrderStatus*) and provisions a couple of default documents, together with a custom welcome page. To deploy the default documents and the custom welcome page, it uses a *Module* feature, which you saw in Chapter 9, "Extending the User Interface." Listing 13-2 shows the source code of the *Module* feature.

LISTING 13-2 The *Module* element feature used to deploy the default documents and the custom welcome page for the custom document set defined in Listing 13-1.

```xml
<?xml version="1.0" encoding="utf-8"?>
<Elements xmlns="http://schemas.microsoft.com/sharepoint/">
  <Module Name="DefaultDocuments" Url="_cts/DevLeapWorkOrderDocumentSet">
    <File Path="DefaultDocuments\Invoice-01.docx" Url="Invoice-01.docx" />
    <File Path="DefaultDocuments\Offer-01.docx" Url="Offer-01.docx" />
    <File Path="DefaultDocuments\docsethomepage.aspx" Url="docsethomepage.aspx">
      <AllUsersWebPart WebPartZoneID="WebPartZone_TopLeft" WebPartOrder="1">
        <![CDATA[
          <WebPart xmlns="http://schemas.microsoft.com/WebPart/v2"
            xmlns:iwp="http://schemas.microsoft.com/WebPart/v2/Image">
            <Assembly>Microsoft.SharePoint, Version=14.0.0.0, Culture=neutral,
              PublicKeyToken=71e9bce111e9429c</Assembly>
            <TypeName>Microsoft.SharePoint.WebPartPages.ImageWebPart</TypeName>
            <FrameType>None</FrameType>
            <Title>$Resources:wp_SiteImage;</Title>
<iwp:ImageLink>/_layouts/images/docset_welcomepage_big.png</iwp:ImageLink>
            <iwp:AlternativeText>Work Order Document Set</iwp:AlternativeText>
          </WebPart>
        ]]>
      </AllUsersWebPart>
      <AllUsersWebPart WebPartZoneID="WebPartZone_Top" WebPartOrder="2">
        <![CDATA[
          <WebPart xmlns:xsi="http://www.w3.org/2001/XMLSchema-instance"
            xmlns:xsd="http://www.w3.org/2001/XMLSchema"
            xmlns="http://schemas.microsoft.com/WebPart/v2">
            <Assembly>Microsoft.Office.DocumentManagement, Version=14.0.0.0,
Culture=neutral, PublicKeyToken=71e9bce111e9429c</Assembly>
<TypeName>Microsoft.Office.Server.WebControls.DocumentSetPropertiesWebPart</TypeName>
            <Title>Document Set Properties</Title>
            <FrameType>Default</FrameType>
            <Description>Displays the properties of the Document Set.</Description>
            <IsIncluded>true</IsIncluded>
          </WebPart>
        ]]>
      </AllUsersWebPart>
      <AllUsersWebPart WebPartZoneID="WebPartZone_CenterMain" WebPartOrder="2">
        <![CDATA[
          <WebPart xmlns:xsi="http://www.w3.org/2001/XMLSchema-instance"
            xmlns:xsd="http://www.w3.org/2001/XMLSchema"
            xmlns="http://schemas.microsoft.com/WebPart/v2">
            <Assembly>Microsoft.Office.DocumentManagement, Version=14.0.0.0,
              Culture=neutral, PublicKeyToken=71e9bce111e9429c</Assembly>
```

```
<TypeName>Microsoft.Office.Server.WebControls.DocumentSetContentsWebPart</TypeName>
            <Title>Document Set Contents</Title>
            <FrameType>Default</FrameType>
            <Description>Displays the contents of the Document Set.</Description>
            <IsIncluded>true</IsIncluded>
        </WebPart>
      ]]>
      </AllUsersWebPart>
    </File>
  </Module>
</Elements>
```

The welcome page is a Web Part Page, and the *Module* element configures the Web Parts of this page via the *AllUsersWebPart* child element. For the sake of simplicity, the welcome page in this example was defined almost the same as the standard welcome page. However, you could define fully customized welcome pages using exactly the same tools and techniques. Figure 13-2 displays the custom welcome page created by Listing 13-1.

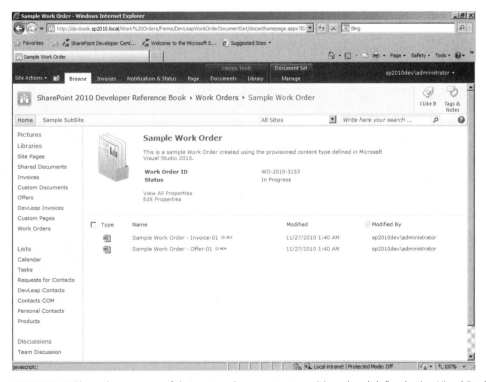

FIGURE 13-2 The welcome page of the custom document set provisioned and defined using Visual Studio.

Handling Document Sets by Code

Document sets can also be defined and managed by code. For example, if you would like to manage a library made up of document sets, you can take a reference to each folder (document set) of the library and use it through the *DocumentSet* class, which is defined in the *Microsoft.Office.DocumentManagement.DocumentSets* namespace and represents a document set in the Server Object Model. Table 13-2 describes the main members of the *DocumentSet* class.

TABLE 13-2 The Main Members of the *DocumentSet* Class

Member Name	Description
Create	Creates a *DocumentSet* instance object within an existing *SPFolder* instance.
Export	Exports the current *DocumentSet* into a packaged (ZIP compressed) file.
GetDocumentSet	Static method that gets the *DocumentSet* object from a specified *SPFolder* object.
Import	Static method that imports a *DocumentSet* from a package previously exported via the *Export* method.
Provision	Provisions a *DocumentSet* instance, placing the default documents into the document set.
SendToOfficialFile	Sends a *DocumentSet* instance to a records repository. This is useful in enterprise level scenarios.

You can use this class in your own custom code. For example, Listing 13-3 demonstrates code with which you can export the entire content of a document as a compressed .ZIP file.

LISTING 13-3 Exporting a document set into a .ZIP file.

```
using (SPSite site = new SPSite("http://devbook.sp2010.local/")) {
    using (SPWeb web = site.OpenWeb()) {
        SPList library = web.Lists["Work Orders"];

        // Search for items of type Document Set
        foreach (SPListItem item in library.Items) {
            // In case the ContentTypeId of the item inherits from a DocumentSet
            if (DocumentSetTemplate.Id.IsParentOf(item.ContentTypeId)) {
                // Get a reference to the DocumentSet instance
                DocumentSet ds = DocumentSet.GetDocumentSet(item.Folder);
                // Export the item as a .ZIP content
                Byte[] package = ds.Export();
```

```
            using (FileStream fs = new FileStream(ds.Item.Title + ".zip",
               FileMode.CreateNew, FileAccess.Write, FileShare.None)) {
                 using(BinaryWriter bw = new BinaryWriter(fs)) {
                     bw.Write(package);
                     bw.Flush();
                 }
             }
          }
       }
    }
}
```

The *Microsoft.Office.DocumentManagement.DocumentSets* namespace hosts some other classes for managing document set templates, allowed Content Types, default document collections, shared fields, welcome page fields, and document set versioning. As usual, you can accomplish provisioning with code nearly the same as using the web browser or XML.

Document ID

Another new and interesting feature introduced with SharePoint Server 2010 is the Document ID feature. This is a provider-based identifier generator that creates unique identifiers for documents in libraries so that they can be used to retrieve documents independently from their location. In previous editions of SharePoint, referencing contents with a unique URL was a well-known issue, because the URL of an item was only related to its container library and moving a document from one folder to another would change its URL and break any already existing reference to it. Now, with the Document ID feature you can move documents wherever you want, unless you do not change the Site Collection, and they will maintain a unique URL—called a static URL—which will redirect the web browser to the current URL of the document. This is based on a Site Collection-level feature, called "Document ID Service," which must be activated to be used. This will add some infrastructural columns to the documents Content Types as well as a static URL field for every document. Also, be aware that the Document ID feature works only with documents; it does not generate IDs for other types of list items.

The Document ID feature provides also an administrative page (Figure 13-3), which you can access on the Site Settings page, under the Site Collection Administration group.

FIGURE 13-3 The administrative page of the Document ID feature.

You can use the administrative page for defining a common prefix to use for every generated Document ID and to reset any previously assigned IDs, to use a defined prefix.

Note the disclaimer located at the top of the page in Figure 13-3. It states that the "Configuration of the Document ID feature is scheduled to be completed by an automated process." This is because the Document ID engine works with some automated timer job work-items. By default these jobs are scheduled for execution on a daily basis. There is a job with the title "Document ID enable/disable job" that executes daily at 9:30 PM which propagates Content Type changes across all sites in case of any configuration changes. There is also another job with the title "Document ID assignment job," which assigns Document IDs to all items in the site collection. If you want to speed up the activation process of the Document ID feature, you can start these jobs manually, using the SharePoint Central Administration.

When you activate the feature, the Document Content Type and the Document Set Content Type, if you enabled the Document Set feature, will be extended with some new site columns, declaring the following fields: *DocID*, *Static URL*, and *PersistID*. The *DocID* site column stores the unique ID for the current document. The *Static URL* column stores the unique URL to access the item, wherever it is stored. The *PersistID* column is hidden and simply determines whether the current *DocID* value must be regenerated after copying the current document into a new location or not.

Note Even if you deactivate the Document ID feature on a Site Collection, the documents will keep the additional columns that were used by the Document ID feature's infrastructure. In addition, the static URL will stop working and anyone trying to access a document through its static URL will get back a generic error message.

Whenever you upload or create a new document in a site collection with the Document ID feature activated, the Document ID engine, using a synchronous event receiver (the *ItemAdded* event), will give the document a unique ID. If you move the document from one library to another within the same site collection, the ID will not change. If you copy a document, the copied document will have a new ID of its own. Figure 13-4 illustrates a detail view of a document with the Document ID field configured and assigned.

More Information For details about event receivers, refer to Chapter 12, "Event Receivers."

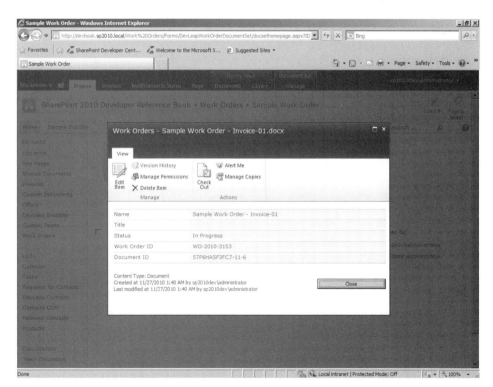

FIGURE 13-4 The detail view of a document with the Document ID field configured and assigned.

In Figure 13-4, the Document ID field is represented as a hyperlink. When you click it, your browser will be redirected to the following URL:

```
http://{your site URL}/_layouts/DocIdRedir.aspx?ID={Document ID Value}
```

The *DocIdRedir.aspx* page internally resolves the current location of the file with the provided ID and redirects the browser to the corresponding URL, if the ID corresponds to an existing file.

To retrieve a document using its Document ID, the SharePoint engine by default will first use the search engine to look up the document with that specific Document ID value. If it does not find the document, it will try to invoke an internal lookup implementation provided by the current Document ID provider. You can also use the ID to retrieve documents by invoking the methods *FindUrlById* and *FindUrlsById* of the *DocumentId* class, which is available in the *Microsoft.Office.DocumentManagement* namespace of the Server Object Model.

Custom Document ID Provider

The Document ID engine is based on a provider model. You can implement your own providers by implementing a class that inherits from the base abstract class *DocumentIdProvider* declared in the *Microsoft.Office.DocumentManagement* namespace. Listing 13-4 shows the *DocumentIdProvider* base abstract class definition.

LISTING 13-4 The *DocumentIdProvider* base abstract class definition.

```
namespace Microsoft.Office.DocumentManagement {

    public abstract class DocumentIdProvider {

        protected DocumentIdProvider();

        public abstract bool DoCustomSearchBeforeDefaultSearch { get; }

        public abstract string GenerateDocumentId(SPListItem listItem);

        public abstract string[] GetDocumentUrlsById(SPSite site,
            string documentId);

        public abstract string GetSampleDocumentIdText(SPSite site);
    }
}
```

The abstract methods and properties are:

- *DoCustomSearchBeforeDefaultSearch* Determines whether the Document ID engine has to search the document by looking in the provider first and then in the search engine. By default the search engine lookup occurs before the provider.

- *GenerateDocumentId* Generates a unique Document ID for a provided *SPListItem*.

- *GetDocumentUrlsById* Implements a custom lookup search method and returns an array of URLs pointing to documents with a specified Document ID value.

- *GetSampleDocumentIdText*   Generates a sample Document ID for documentation purposes. For example, the returned value will be initially displayed in the Document ID search Web Part.

Listing 13-5 demonstrates implementation of a custom Document ID Provider.

LISTING 13-5 A sample implementation of a custom *DocumentIDProvider.*

```csharp
using System;
using System.Collections.Generic;
using System.Linq;
using System.Text;
using Microsoft.Office.DocumentManagement;
using Microsoft.SharePoint;

namespace DevLeap.SP2010.SampleDocumentIDProvider {
    public class GuidDocumentIdProvider : DocumentIdProvider {
        public override bool DoCustomSearchBeforeDefaultSearch {
            get { return(false); }
        }

        public override string GenerateDocumentId(
          Microsoft.SharePoint.SPListItem listItem) {
            return(String.Format("ID{0}", Guid.NewGuid().ToString("N")));
        }

        public override string[] GetDocumentUrlsById(
          Microsoft.SharePoint.SPSite site, string documentId) {
            List<String> urls = new List<string>();

            foreach (SPWeb web in site.AllWebs) {
                using (web) {
                    foreach (SPList list in web.Lists) {
                        SPDocumentLibrary library = list as SPDocumentLibrary;
                        if (library != null) {
                          foreach (SPListItem item in list.Items) {
                              try {
                                  if ((String)item["Document ID"] == documentId) {
                                      urls.Add(String.Format("{0}/{1}",
                                          web.Url, item.Url));
                                  }
                              }
                              catch (ArgumentException) {
                                  // Invalid field
                              }
                          }
                        }
                    }
                }
            }
            return (urls.ToArray());
        }
```

```
        public override string GetSampleDocumentIdText(
          Microsoft.SharePoint.SPSite site) {
            return (String.Format("ID{0}", Guid.NewGuid().ToString("N")));
        }
      }
    }
```

Be aware that the *GetDocumentUrlsById* method implementation in this example is horribly inefficient, because it browses each document in all of the libraries within the entire Site Collection—but it is useful for a short simple example. To implement a class such as the one shown in Listing 13-5, you need to create a class library project, targeting .NET Framework 3.5 with x64 or Any CPU, and strongly-named, because you will need to deploy it in the Global Assembly Cache (GAC). Then you will need to reference the *Microsoft.Office. DocumentManagement* assembly.

> **Important** A custom Document ID Provider should generate Document ID values that are unique and human readable/writable, because an end user should be able to write them in the location toolbar of the web browser.

After implementing a custom Document ID Provider, you need to register it to make it the default provider. In the following example, you can see the syntax for registering a custom Document ID Provider using Windows PowerShell:

```
$site = Get-SPSite http://{your site URL}/
[System.Reflection.Assembly]::LoadWithPartialName("Microsoft.Office.DocumentManagement")
$assembly = [System.Reflection.Assembly]::Load("DevLeap.SP2010.SampleDocumentIDProvider,
Version=1.0.0.0, Culture=neutral, PublicKeyToken=ceede85c5f9eff7e");
$type = $assembly.GetType("DevLeap.SP2010.SampleDocumentIDProvider.GuidDocumentIdProvider");
$provider = [System.Activator]::CreateInstance($type);
[Microsoft.Office.DocumentManagement.DocumentId]::SetProvider($site, $provider);
```

You need to load the assembly and the type representing your custom Document ID Provider. Then you need to create an instance of the provider and give it to the *DocumentId. SetProvider* method, where the *DocumentId* class is defined in the *Microsoft.Office. DocumentManagement* namespace. Alternatively, you can use a WSP package to deploy the assembly into the GAC and configure the provider with a feature receiver.

> **Important** The default Document ID Provider offered by SharePoint is implemented in the class *Microsoft.Office.DocumentManagement.Internal.OobProvider*. If you want to revert your site collection back to the default provider, you can invoke the *DocumentId.SetDefaultProvider* method. To accomplish this, you can either use a Windows PowerShell script or a piece of custom code.

File Conversion Services

Since Microsoft Office SharePoint Server 2007, in SharePoint there are document conversion services that support developers and site builders in developing automated document conversion solutions. For example, you can deploy a Word .DOC or .DOCX file into a document library and use a document converter to generate an HTML page for web publishing. Or perhaps you have external software generating an XML file that contains the list of your company's products. You can use a document converter to transform that XML into a published HTML page, using a custom XSLT. The list of samples could be very long, because the document conversion engine of SharePoint is extensible. You can implement you own document converters, deploy them into the farm, and then start converting documents.

> **Note** Implementing a custom document converter is an uncommon task and beyond the scope of this book. However, if you are interested in developing a custom document converter of your own, you can read the document, "Document Converter Framework Sample," available on MSDN Online at *http://msdn.microsoft.com/en-us/library/bb897921.aspx*. If you are simply looking for an overview of the document conversion engine, you can read the document, "Document Converter Services Overview," available on MSDN Online at *http://msdn.microsoft.com/en-us/library/aa979484.aspx*.

In the fields of document conversion, beginning with SharePoint 2010, there is a fresh new engine, called Word Automation Services, which helps to manage and convert Microsoft Word documents. In the next section, you will learn how to make use of this new service.

Word Automation Services

Word Automation Services can be used to automate and manage unattended server-side conversion processes. It can work with all the main input file formats supported by Microsoft Word, and can also output any supported output file format. For example, you can use it to convert a .doc or .docx document into an .xps or .pdf file. The following list shows the supported input formats:

- Open XML File Format documents (.docx, .docm, .dotx, .dotm)
- Word 97-2003 documents (.doc, .dot)
- Rich Text Format files (.rtf)
- Webpages (.htm, .html, .mht, .mhtml)
- Word 2003 XML Documents (.xml)

And the supported output formats are:

- Open XML File Format documents (.docx, .docm, .dotx, .dotm)

- Word 97-2003 documents (.doc, .dot)

- Rich Text Format files (.rtf)

- Webpages (.htm, .html, .mht, .mhtml)

- Word 2003 XML Documents (.xml)

- Portable Document Format (.pdf)

- Open XML Paper Specification (.xps)

The service can be installed on one or more SharePoint servers in a farm, and can be configured using the SharePoint Central Administration. Figure 13-5 depicts the configuration page of the service.

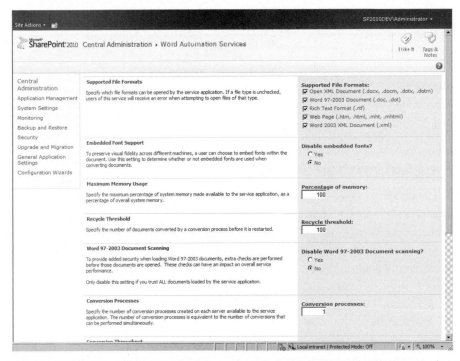

FIGURE 13-5 The Word Automation Services configuration page in the SharePoint Central Administration.

Using the service configuration page, you can define the following parameters:

- **Supported File Formats**   Specifies the supported input file formats.

- **Embedded Font Support**   Preserve visual fidelity across different machines by embedding fonts into documents during conversion process.

- **Maximum Memory Usage**   Specifies the percentage of overall system memory that will be used for executing the conversion processes.

- **Recycle Threshold**   Specifies the number of conversions to execute with a conversion process before recycling it.

- **Word 97-2003 Document Scanning**   Disables the scanning of Word 97-2003 documents while loading them.

- **Conversion Processes**   Determines the number of processes to use for concurrent conversion on a single server in the farm. Configure this parameter with a value no greater than the number of processors, minus one available on the smallest server in the farm and running the conversion engine. For example if your smallest server, hosting the Word Automation Services, has 4 processors, then configure this parameter with a value of 3.

- **Conversion Throughput**   Defines the number of conversion processes to start concurrently and the frequency to use for starting groups of conversion processes.

- **Job Monitoring**   Specifies the length of time before conversions are monitored and, if necessary, restarted.

- **Maximum Conversion Attempts**   Determines the maximum number of retries for a conversion process that failed.

The interesting thing to notice about the Word Automation Services is that the service must be used through user code. In fact, it is exposed through a Server Object Model that you can use in your own code, but an end user cannot use it directly, unless you provide some code within custom Ribbons, pages, Web Parts, and so forth.

Listing 13-6 converts a document from .DOC to .XPS by using the Server Object Model of the Word Automation Services, impersonating the current user while executing the conversion job.

LISTING 13-6 Converting a document from .DOC to .XPS using the Word Automation Services.

```
String siteUrl = "http://devbook.sp2010.local/";
String wordAutomationServiceName = "Word Automation Services";

using (SPSite site = new SPSite(siteUrl)) {
    using (SPWeb web = site.OpenWeb()) {
        SPFile sourceFile = web.GetFile("Shared%20Documents/Source.doc");

        ConversionJob job = new ConversionJob(wordAutomationServiceName);
        job.UserToken = site.UserToken;
        job.Settings.UpdateFields = true;
        job.Settings.OutputFormat = SaveFormat.XPS;
```

```
        String sourceUrl = web.Url + "/" + sourceFile.Url;
        String destinationUrl = web.Url + "/" +
          sourceFile.Url.Replace(".doc", ".xps");

        job.AddFile(sourceUrl, destinationUrl);
        job.Start();
    }
}
```

Listing 13-6 retrieves a reference to the source document, using the *GetFile* method of the *SPWeb* class. Then, it creates a new instance of the *ConversionJob* class, provided by the Word Automation Services' engine and available in assembly *Microsoft.Office.Word. Server*. This assembly can be referenced in a Visual Studio 2010 project by selecting the item named Microsoft Office 2010 Component from the Add Reference window, as illustrated in Figure 13-6.

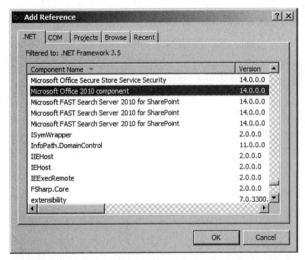

FIGURE 13-6 The Word Automation Services assembly selected in the Add Reference window of Visual Studio.

Note As with any other .NET application working with the SharePoint 2010 Server Object Model, when you work with the Word Automation Services, you need to create a Visual Studio 2010 project targeting .NET 3.5 and x64 or Any CPU.

The *ConversionJob* class defines a conversion job item that can be configured and then executed using a timer job. Table 13-3 describes the members available in the *ConversionJob* class.

TABLE 13-3 **The Main Members of the *ConversionJob* Class**

Member Name	Description
AddFile	Adds a file to the conversion job, declaring also the name of the output file.
AddFolder	Adds all the files, eventually recursively, of an input folder (*SPFolder*) to the conversion job, declaring also the name of the output folder (*SPFolder*).
AddLibrary	Adds all the files of a document library (*SPList*) to the conversion job, declaring also the name of the output document library (*SPList*).
Cancel	Cancels a conversion job in progress
CancelJob	Static method to cancel a conversion job by using its *JobId*.
Start	Starts a conversion job.
Canceled	Read-only property that indicates whether the current conversion job has been canceled.
JobId	Read-only property that returns the ID of the current conversion job.
Name	Property to set and get a friendly name for the conversion job.
Settings	Property to define the settings of the conversion job, using a complex type named *ConversionJobSettings*. Through this property, you can configure many settings. The most interesting are: ■ Whether to add a thumbnail to the converted document ■ The compatibility mode (Word 2003, Word 2007, Word 2010) for an Open XML output document ■ The language to use by the Word Automation Service to resolve language-dependent ambiguities ■ Whether to embed system fonts in the output file ■ Whether to embed fonts in the output file ■ The output format to use for the converted file ■ The output save behavior (append, overwrite, and so on) for the converted file ■ How to manage revisions (final, final showing markup, original, original showing markup) in the output document ■ Whether to update fields in the document or not
Started	A read-only property that indicates whether the current conversion job has been started.
UserToken	Property to set and get the user token (*SPUserToken*) of the user on behalf of whom to execute the conversion.

Another useful type provided by the Word Automation Services library is the *ConversionJobStatus* class with which you can monitor the execution of a conversion job. It provides some static methods to retrieve a reference to the status of all the running jobs. Alternatively, you can use its constructor to monitor a specific conversion job providing its *JobId*. Listing 13-7 illustrates how to monitor the status of a specific conversion job.

LISTING 13-7 How to monitor the status of a conversion job.

```
static void MonitorJob(Guid jobId) {
    ConversionJobStatus job = new ConversionJobStatus(
        "Word Automation Services", // Name of the service instance
        jobId, // The JobId to monitor
        null); // Guid of the subscription in case of multiple servers

    Console.WriteLine("Job name: {0}", job.Name);
    Console.WriteLine("Total job activities:\t\t{0}", job.Count);
    Console.WriteLine("Job activities succeeded:\t\t{0}", job.Succeeded);
    Console.WriteLine("Job activities failed:\t\t{0}", job.Failed);
    Console.WriteLine("Job activities in progress:\t\t{0}", job.InProgress);
    Console.WriteLine("Job activities canceled:\t\t{0}", job.Canceled);
    Console.WriteLine("Job activities not started:\t\t{0}", job.NotStarted);
}
```

Using the *ConversionJobStatus* class, you could write a custom page to show the status of all the running conversion jobs.

Summary

In this chapter, you learned how to manage set of documents by using the Document Set feature. You also learned how to create custom document sets, defining custom Content Types of type document set and provisioning their configuration and pages through custom features and package solutions. You were also introduced to the Document Id feature, and shown how to use it in your solutions and how to define a custom Document Id provider of your own. Lastly, you learned how to use the Word Automation Services to convert documents on the server side, eventually monitoring the conversion jobs using the Server Object Model provided by the Word Automation Services.

Chapter 14
Site Templates

In the previous chapters of this section, you have seen how to extend SharePoint in various ways by using features. In many cases, to satisfy the requirements of a project, it will suffice to provide your customers with packages of features and activate them selectively. However, there are situations in which it would be better to create a ready-to-go site from the ground up, starting from a template. SharePoint natively provides a set of site models that satisfy the most common scenarios. Some of these site templates are: Blank Site, Team Site, Document Workspace, Meeting Workspace, and so on. But in many cases, these are too broad and designed for more general purposes. For those circumstances, you will need to create site definitions or site templates of your own.

For example, imagine a situation in which you want to create an extranet site collection to host a set of sites, where each site represents the private extranet of a customer. It is likely that every customer's site will have a common set of contents and features, such as the library of orders, the library of invoices, a discussion area, and many others. Furthermore, it would be completely crazy to create each site starting from one of the natively provided site models, and then manually provision the content using features. Clearly, it would be better to have a new custom site model defining the structure of a customer's extranet site, and creating every site instance starting from that model.

SharePoint 2010 provides many ways for defining site models. You could have a site definition, which is a site model defined on the file system and stored under the folder SharePoint14_Root\TEMPLATE\SiteTemplates of every front-end server. Otherwise, you could create a web template either using Microsoft Visual Studio 2010 or saving an already existing site instance through a specific page available in the Site Settings page (under the menu item Save Site As Template in the Site Actions menu group). A web template can also be exported from SharePoint Designer 2010 as a .WSP package.

 Note In Microsoft Office SharePoint Server 2007, a site template was an .STP file. This format is no longer supported.

In this chapter, you will learn how to create, deploy, and manage these kinds of site models using Visual Studio 2010.

Native Site Definitions

First, it's useful to see the list of site definitions that are natively available in SharePoint 2010. In fact, while creating custom site models, you could use one of the existing models and simply extend them. To choose the right model to get started though, you need to know what they are. As already stated, the native site definitions are stored in the file system of the servers, in the SharePoint14_Root\TEMPLATES\SiteTemplates folder. There, you will find a subfolder for every base site definition or group of site definitions. Whenever you create a new Site Collection or a new subsite under an existing Site Collection, SharePoint provides a list of available site templates from which you can choose the model to use for your new site. Figure 14-1 shows the standard dialog for choosing the template for a new subsite.

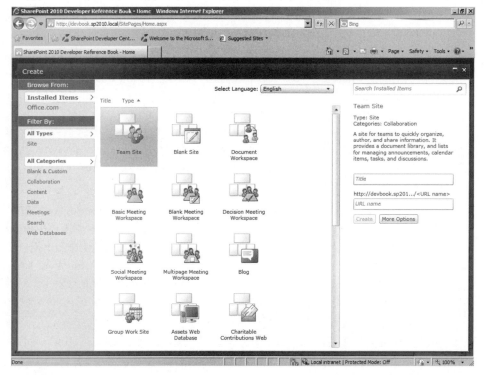

FIGURE 14-1 The standard dialog for choosing the template for a new subsite, with the Silverlight plug-in installed.

Under the cover, SharePoint loads the list of available models, reading all the available files with a name like WEBTEMP*.XML in the SharePoint14_Root\TEMPLATE\{*IdCulture*}\XML folder, where *IdCulture* corresponds to the currently selected language in the create site dialog window. For example, 1033 stands for English, 1040 for Italian, and so forth. The WEBTEMP*. XML files enumerate one or more site models, together with their name, configuration, and folder. In Listing 14-1, the content of the main and standard WEBTEMP.XML file is set for the English language.

LISTING 14-1 The content of the standard webtemp.xml file, set for English.

```xml
<?xml version="1.0" encoding="utf-8"?>
<!-- _lcid="1033" _version="14.0.4762" _dal="1" -->
<!-- _LocalBinding -->
<Templates xmlns:ows="Microsoft SharePoint">
  <Template Name="GLOBAL" SetupPath="global" ID="0">
    <Configuration ID="0" Title="Global template" Hidden="TRUE" ImageUrl=""
Description="This template is used for initializing a new site." ></Configuration>
  </Template>
  <Template Name="STS" ID="1">
    <Configuration ID="0" Title="Team Site" Hidden="FALSE" ImageUrl="/_layouts/
images/stts.png" Description="A site for teams to quickly organize, author, and share
information. It provides a document library, and lists for managing announcements,
calendar items, tasks, and discussions." DisplayCategory="Collaboration">
</Configuration>
    <Configuration ID="1" Title="Blank Site" Hidden="FALSE" ImageUrl="/_layouts/
images/stbs.png" Description="A blank site for you to customize based on your
requirements." DisplayCategory="Collaboration"
AllowGlobalFeatureAssociations="False"></Configuration>

    <!-- Code omitted for the sake of brevity -->

  </Template>

<!-- Code omitted for the sake of brevity -->

</Templates>
```

The file provides a list of *Template* items, each with a *Name* attribute and an optional *SetupPath* attribute. Each *Template* element is the parent of one or more *Configuration* elements, which provide a custom configuration for that specific template. For example, the STS template is available in three different configurations: STS#0, STS#1, and STS#2. The syntax of {TemplateName}#{Configuration ID}, which has just been introduced, is common in SharePoint. Table 14-1 lists the main available site definitions with the corresponding configurations, described as they are in SharePoint.

TABLE 14-1 The Main Native Site Definitions Available in SharePoint 2010

Title	Base Definition	Config.	Description
Team Site	STS	0	A site for teams to quickly organize, author, and share information.
Blank Site	STS	1	A blank site for you to customize, based on your requirements.
Document Workspace	STS	2	A site for colleagues to work together on a document.
Basic Meeting Workspace	MPS	0	A site for planning, organizing, and capturing the results of a meeting.

Title	Base Definition	Config.	Description
Blank Meeting Workspace	MPS	1	A blank meeting site for you to customize, based on your requirements.
Decision Meeting Workspace	MPS	2	A site for meetings that track status or make decisions.
Social Meeting Workspace	MPS	3	A site to plan social occasions.
Multipage Meeting Workspace	MPS	4	A site for planning, organizing, and capturing the results of a meeting.
Central Admin Site	CENTRALADMIN	0	Used to create the SharePoint Central Administration site. This template is hidden.
Blog	BLOG	0	Defines a new blog site.
Group Work Site	SGS	0	Provides a groupware solution with which teams can create, organize, and share information quickly and easily.
Assets Web Database	ACCSRV	1	Creates an assets database to keep track of assets, including asset details and owners.
Charitable Contributions Web Database	ACCSRV	3	Creates a database to track information about fundraising campaigns, including donations made by contributors, campaign related events, and pending tasks.
Contacts Web Database	ACCSRV	4	Creates a contacts database to manage information about people that your team works with, such as customers and partners.
Issues Web Database	ACCSRV	6	Creates an issues database to manage a set of issues or problems.
Projects Web Database	ACCSRV	5	Creates a project tracking database to track multiple projects, and assign tasks to different people.
Document Center	BDR	0	A site to centrally manage documents in your enterprise.
Records Center	OFFILE	1	Creates a site designed for records management.
PowerPoint Broadcast Site	PowerPointBroadcast	0	Used for hosting PowerPoint broadcasts.
Business Intelligence Center	BICenterSite	0	A site for presenting Business Intelligence Center.

Title	Base Definition	Config.	Description
Personalization Site	SPSMSITE	0	A site for delivering personalized views, data, and navigation from this site collection into My Site.
Publishing Site	CMSPUBLISHING	0	A blank site for expanding your website and quickly publishing webpages.
Publishing Site with Workflow	BLANKINTERNET	2	A site for publishing webpages on a schedule by using approval workflows.
Publishing Portal	BLANKINTERNETCONTAINER	0	A starter site hierarchy for an Internet-facing site or a large intranet portal.
Enterprise Wiki	ENTERWIKI	0	A site for publishing knowledge that you capture and want to share across the enterprise.
Enterprise Search Center	SRCHCEN	0	A site for delivering the search experience.
Basic Search Center	SRCHCENTERLITE	0	A site for delivering the search experience.
FAST Search Center	SRCHCENTERFAST	0	A site for delivering the FAST search experience.
Visio Process Repository	visprus	0	A site for teams to quickly view, share, and store Visio process diagrams.

The availability of some of these site definitions depends on your SharePoint 2010 license. For example, the *PowerPointBroadcast* site requires you to have Office Web Applications licensed and installed. There are some other site definitions provided by default. However, they are hidden and available only for backward compatibility. When you create a site instance by code, you can reference the site definition using the syntax {TemplateName}#{Configuration ID}. For example STS#0 means Team Site, while BLOG#0 means a Blog Site, and so forth.

The WEBTEMP*.XML files are just directories of site templates' configurations. The actual configuration is included in an XML file, named ONET.XML, which is located in the XML subfolder of every site definition. For example, consider the group of templates defined in the STS site definition. The corresponding ONET.XML file declares some common configuration items, such as the document templates, the list templates, the navigation bar groups, and the custom pages and Web Part Pages to deploy. Then it defines some *Configuration* elements, each one corresponding to a specific configuration for the STS template. Listing 14-2 shows the ONET.XML of the STS template, defining the configuration for STS#0.

LISTING 14-2 The ONET.XML file for the standard STS site template defining STS#0.

```
<Configuration ID="0" Name="Default" MasterUrl="_catalogs/masterpage/v4.master">
  <Lists>
    <List FeatureId="00BFEA71-E717-4E80-AA17-D0C71B360101" Type="101"
      Title="$Resources:core,shareddocuments_Title;"
      Url="$Resources:core,shareddocuments_Folder;"
      QuickLaunchUrl="$Resources:core,shareddocuments_Folder;/Forms/AllItems.aspx" />
    <List FeatureId="00BFEA71-6A49-43FA-B535-D15C05500108" Type="108"
      Title="$Resources:core,discussions_Title;"
      Url="$Resources:core,lists_Folder;/$Resources:core,discussions_Folder;"
      QuickLaunchUrl="$Resources:core,lists_Folder;/$Resources:core,discussions_
        Folder;/AllItems.aspx" EmailAlias="$Resources:core,discussions_EmailAlias;" />
    <!-- Code omitted for the sake of brevity -->
  </Lists>
  <Modules>
    <Module Name="Default" />
  </Modules>
  <SiteFeatures>
    <!-- BasicWebParts Feature -->
    <Feature ID="00BFEA71-1C5E-4A24-B310-BA51C3EB7A57" />
    <!-- Three-state Workflow Feature -->
    <Feature ID="FDE5D850-671E-4143-950A-87B473922DC7" />
  </SiteFeatures>
  <WebFeatures>
    <!-- TeamCollab Feature -->
    <Feature ID="00BFEA71-4EA5-48D4-A4AD-7EA5C011ABE5" />
    <!-- MobilityRedirect -->
    <Feature ID="F41CC668-37E5-4743-B4A8-74D1DB3FD8A4" />
    <!-- WikiPageHomePage Feature -->
    <Feature ID="00BFEA71-D8FE-4FEC-8DAD-01C19A6E4053" />
  </WebFeatures>
</Configuration>
```

The configuration declares the list instances that will be created into the target site, the modules that will be provisioned (the pages that will be created), the site-level and Web-level features that will be activated. Additionally, consider that all of the site definitions inherit from a common and global definition named GLOBAL, which is defined in the SharePoint14_Root\ TEMPLATE\GLOBAL folder. There, in the ONET.XML file in the XML folder, are defined all the base lists templates and list types used by the other site definitions.

Site Definitions

If you want to define your own site definitions, you can start by using what you have just read in the previous section. To manually create a custom site definition, you could simply copy an existing folder and change the ONET.XML file to select the lists definition to use for creating list instances, the modules to provision, and the features to activate. Then you should define

a custom WEBTEMP*.XML file and copy it into the proper folder, within SharePoint14_Root\
TEMPLATES\{IdCulture}\XML. Just after recycling the application pool of your target web
application or after executing IISRESET, to reset the entire IIS environment, you will be able to
use the new site definition.

For example, copy the SharePoint14_Root\TEMPLATES\SiteTemplates\Blog folder and name
it **MyBlog**. Then open the ONET.XML file in the XML subfolder of MyBlog and change the
Configuration section according to your goal. Suppose that you want to add a "Shared
Documents" list, which is not present in a standard Blog site. To accomplish this, you need to
add a *List* element to the *Lists* element of the *Configuration* tag in the ONET.XML file. Here is
the *List* element to add:

```
<List FeatureId="00BFEA71-E717-4E80-AA17-D0C71B360101" Type="101" Title="$Resources:core,shareddo
cuments_Title;" Url="$Resources:core,shareddocuments_Folder;" QuickLaunchUrl="$Resources:core,s
hareddocuments_Folder;/Forms/AllItems.aspx" />
```

The values for the *FeatureId* and *Type* attributes are those corresponding to the base list
definition of the Document Library, as it is declared in the *DocumentLibrary* feature in the
SharePoint14_Root\TEMPLATES\FEATURES\DocumentLibrary folder.

To make the site template available for creating new site instances, you need to define a
custom WEBTEMP*.XML file; for example, call it WEBTEMPMYBLOG.XML and copy it into the
SharePoint14_Root\TEMPLATES\{IdCulture}\XML folder. Listing 14-3 shows the source code of
such a file.

LISTING 14-3 The source code of the custom WEBTEMPMYBLOG.XML file for the custom MyBlog site
definition.

```
<?xml version="1.0" encoding="utf-8"?>
<!-- _lcid="1033" _version="14.0.4762" _dal="1" -->
<!-- _LocalBinding -->
<Templates xmlns:ows="Microsoft SharePoint">
 <Template Name="MYBLOG" ID="10001">
    <Configuration ID="0" Title="My Blog" Hidden="FALSE" ImageUrl="/_layouts/images/
stbg.png" Description="A site for a person or team to post ideas, observations,
and expertise that site visitors can comment on. It provides also a list of shared
documents." DisplayCategory="DevLeap" SupportsMultilingualUI="FALSE" >    </
Configuration>
 </Template>
</Templates>
```

Notice the *ID* value of 10001 used in the *Template* definition. In custom site templates you
should use values equal to or greater than 10000 for the *ID* attribute, to avoid overriding the
IDs of native templates.

That's all! You have just created a site template with the name MYBLOG#0. To use it, you need to recycle the application pool of the target web application where you want to create a new site, based on this template. You can also reset IIS, invoking the IISRESET command, to make the template available on all the web applications. Recycling the application pool or resetting the IIS process are required because SharePoint loads the site templates once at startup and then caches them for performance reasons. Figure 14-2 displays the new site template available in the list of templates.

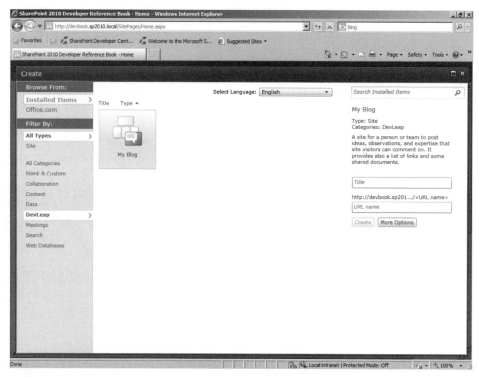

FIGURE 14-2 The standard dialog for choosing the template for a new subsite, with the new custom site template, when the Silverlight plug-in is installed.

Just after recycling IIS, you will be able to create a new site starting from the My Blog site template. Figure 14-3 illustrates the home page of a site created using the new template, with the Shared Documents library at the top of the page.

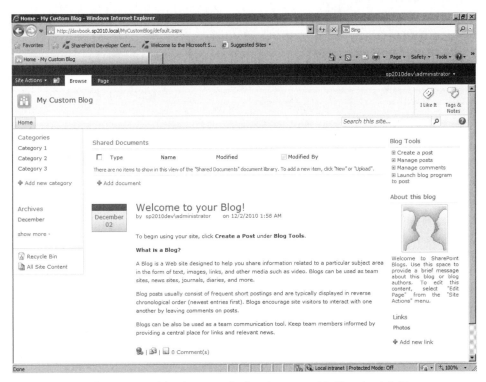

FIGURE 14-3 The home page of the site created using the custom My Blog site definition.

To have the list view showing the document library in the home page, you need to add a *View* element inside the *Module* element that is provisioning the default.aspx page, in the ONET.XML file of your site definition. You'll see more about this last topic in the next section.

Site Definitions with Visual Studio

What you have just done is completely functional and supported. However, it requires a great effort if you have many servers in a farm, because you must copy the files and folders on to each server to use your custom site definition. Also, in the previous sample of My Blog, you used features already available in the farm. However, quite often you need to define a custom site template to take advantage of custom features and custom contents, which you need to deploy together with your site definition. Figure 14-4 shows the New Project window of Visual Studio 2010, with the proper project template selected.

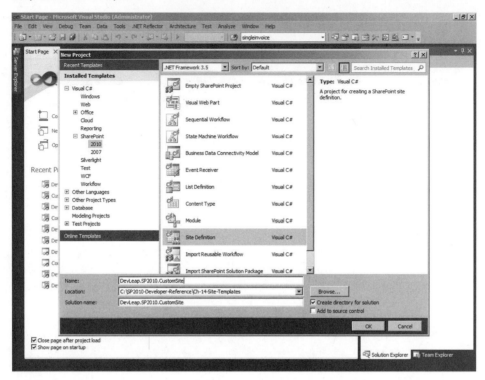

FIGURE 14-4 The New Project window of Visual Studio 2010 with the Site Definition project template highlighted.

Luckily, Visual Studio 2010 provides a project template specifically defined for creating .WSP packages in order to automate deployment of custom site definitions, including provisioning of custom contents and features. To design a site definition, you should start Visual Studio 2010 and create a new project of type Site Definition.

More Information For further information about creating a custom site definition within Visual Studio 2010, you can read the document, "How to: Create a Custom Site Definition and Configuration," available on MSDN Online at *http://msdn.microsoft.com/en-us/library/ms454677. aspx*.

Important Each time you define a project in Visual Studio, it builds and deploys an assembly. However, in general a site definition is a code-less solution, unless you do not write custom code to support your custom features or you implement a custom feature receiver. Thus, in case you do not have custom code, you can simply exclude the assembly from being deployed and avoid having an empty assembly deployed on the farm. To exclude an assembly from deployment, you need to set the value of the Include Assembly In Package property for the current project to *False*, using the Visual Studio property grid.

Once you choose the project template, Visual Studio 2010 prompts you with the common window, asking for the target site URL and the type of deployment (farm solution or sandboxed solution). For the site definition, your only choice is a farm solution deployment. This is because the site definition must be stored on the file system of the farm's servers; thus, the sandboxed deployment is not available. The template project outline is made up of the minimal contents for defining a site definition: an ONET.XML file, a WEBTEMP*.XML file, and a default.aspx home page. To define your site definition, you simply need to add features (as you did in previous chapters), package the solution, and then deploy it.

For example, suppose that you want to deploy a new site definition for managing work projects, with a custom list definition, based on a new content type describing a Project item, and a corresponding list instance of Projects. Additionally, you want to have a Web Part to show the content of that list of Projects in the home page (default.aspx) of the site.

First, you need to edit the WEBTEMP*.XML file, providing a *Name* and an *ID* for the *Template* element, as well as a value for the attributes *Title*, *Description*, and *DisplayCategory* of the *Configuration* element. Listing 14-4 presents the WEBTEMP*.XML file corresponding to the sample Projects site definition.

LISTING 14-4 The content of the WEBTEMP*.XML file related to the sample Projects site definition.

```xml
<?xml version="1.0" encoding="utf-8"?>
<Templates xmlns:ows="Microsoft SharePoint">
  <Template Name="DLPROJECTS" ID="10002">
    <Configuration ID="0" Title="DevLeap Projects" Hidden="FALSE"
ImageUrl="/_layouts/images/CPVW.gif"
Description="A custom site for managing projects." DisplayCategory="DevLeap">
    </Configuration>
  </Template>
</Templates>
```

In Listing 14-4, the *Name* of the *Template* is *DLPROJECTS*, the *ID* has a value of *10002*, and the *Configuration ID* is *0*, which means it is the first configuration. So, if you want to reference that site definition configuration by code, you should use the name *DLPROJECTS#0*.

Also, because the name assigned to the template is *DLPROJECTS*, you should change the deployment location for the ONET.XML, default.aspx, and any other file of the site definition, to target the folder SiteTemplates*DLPROJECTS*. For example, because the ONET.XML file needs to be deployed in the XML folder of the site definition, its deployment location should be SiteTemplates*DLPROJECTS*\\Xml\\. To carry this out, you need to edit the "Deployment Location" property value in the property grid of each target item, after selecting it in the Solution Explorer.

Just after defining the WEBTEMP*.XML file, you should work on the ONET.XML, which is the main schema file for the custom site definition. You could define the Projects list within the ONET.XML by using the *ListTemplate* element and a *List* instance element. Be aware that if you provision data through the ONET.XML file, you will not be able to extend or maintain it over the course of the site's lifetime. In fact, data provisioned with a site definition cannot be upgraded, and you would need to write custom code of your own to upgrade them. Instead, you could add the Content Type, the list definition, and the list instance defining the Projects data structure by using feature elements, which can be upgraded and maintained during the lifecycle of your site. (You should already know how to manage this; if not, refer to Chapter 10, "Dava Provisioning".) In addition, if you use features, you can add features activation directives to the ONET.XML file. For example, suppose that you have a feature provisioning a new list instance of Projects, based on a custom list definition and a custom content type. Listing 14-5 shows a sample ONET.XML deploying that list of Projects, using a custom feature and the custom default.aspx page.

LISTING 14-5 The content of the ONET.XML file related to the sample Projects site definition.

```xml
<?xml version="1.0" encoding="utf-8"?>
<Project Title="DevLeap.SP2010.CustomSite" Revision="2" ListDir=""
        xmlns:ows="Microsoft SharePoint"
        xmlns="http://schemas.microsoft.com/sharepoint/">
  <NavBars>
  </NavBars>
  <Configurations>
    <Configuration ID="0" Name="DEFPROJECTS">
      <Lists>
      </Lists>
      <SiteFeatures>
      </SiteFeatures>
      <WebFeatures>
        <Feature ID="13957dde-9510-4216-8e15-9b769ff73bcd" />
      </WebFeatures>
      <Modules>
        <Module Name="DefaultWithProjects" />
      </Modules>
    </Configuration>
  </Configurations>
  <Modules>
    <Module Name="DefaultWithProjects" Url="" Path="">
      <File Url="default.aspx" IgnoreIfAlreadyExists="TRUE">
        <View List="Lists/Projects" BaseViewID="1"
          WebPartZoneID="CentralZone" WebPartOrder="1">
          <![CDATA[
            <webParts>
              <webPart xmlns="http://schemas.microsoft.com/WebPart/v3">
                <metaData>
                  <type name="Microsoft.SharePoint.WebPartPages.XsltListViewWebPart,
Microsoft.SharePoint,Version=14.0.0.0,Culture=neutral,
PublicKeyToken=71e9bce111e9429c" />
                  <importErrorMessage>Cannot import this Web Part.
                  </importErrorMessage>
                </metaData>
```

```
            <data>
              <properties>
                <property name="AllowConnect" type="bool">True</property>
                <property name="ChromeType" type="chrometype">None</property>
                <property name="AllowClose" type="bool">False</property>
              </properties>
            </data>
          </webPart>
        </webParts>
      ]]>
    </View>
  </File>
  </Module>
 </Modules>
 <ServerEmailFooter>Email from DevLeap Projects Site</ServerEmailFooter>
</Project>
```

The first thing to notice in the ONET.XML file is the *Configuration* element, which corresponds to the one defined in the WEBTEMP*.XML file. Then, to use the content defined by your custom provisioning feature, you need to put a *Feature* element within the *WebFeatures* element. The feature provisioning the list instance of Project, together with site columns, content types, and list definition is a Web-scoped feature. Additionally, there is a *Module* element for the *Configuration*, referencing one of the available *Module* elements defined in the *Modules* section of the ONET.XML file.

The syntax of the *Module* element used here is almost the same as the one discussed in Chapter 9, in the section "Content Pages, Web Part Pages, and Galleries" on page 299. In fact, the *Module* provisioning the default.aspx page also declares a *View* element, which includes a Web Part of type *XsltListViewWebPart* that renders the items of the list of Projects, with path "Lists/Projects", into the *WebPartZone* with *ID CentralZone*, defined in the source code of default.aspx. Listing 14-6 illustrates the source code of the default.aspx page provisioned with the custom site definition.

LISTING 14-6 The source of the default.aspx page provisioned with the sample Projects site definition.

```
<%@ Page language="C#" MasterPageFile="~masterurl/default.master" Inherits="Microsoft.
SharePoint.WebPartPages.WebPartPage,Microsoft.SharePoint,Version=14.0.0.0,Culture=neut
ral,PublicKeyToken=71e9bce111e9429c"  %>
<%@ Register Tagprefix="SharePoint" Namespace="Microsoft.SharePoint.WebControls"
  Assembly="Microsoft.SharePoint, Version=14.0.0.0, Culture=neutral,
  PublicKeyToken=71e9bce111e9429c" %>
<%@ Register Tagprefix="Utilities" Namespace="Microsoft.SharePoint.Utilities"
  Assembly="Microsoft.SharePoint, Version=14.0.0.0, Culture=neutral,
  PublicKeyToken=71e9bce111e9429c" %>
<%@ Register Tagprefix="asp" Namespace="System.Web.UI" Assembly="System.Web.
Extensions, Version=3.5.0.0, Culture=neutral, PublicKeyToken=31bf3856ad364e35" %>
```

```
<%@ Register Tagprefix="WebPartPages" Namespace="Microsoft.SharePoint.WebPartPages"
  Assembly="Microsoft.SharePoint, Version=14.0.0.0, Culture=neutral,
  PublicKeyToken=71e9bce111e9429c" %>
<%@ Import Namespace="Microsoft.SharePoint" %>
<%@ Import Namespace="Microsoft.SharePoint.ApplicationPages" %>
<%@ Assembly Name="Microsoft.Web.CommandUI, Version=14.0.0.0, Culture=neutral,
  PublicKeyToken=71e9bce111e9429c" %>

<asp:Content ContentPlaceHolderId="PlaceHolderPageTitle" runat="server">
  <SharePoint:ProjectProperty Property="Title" runat="server"/>
</asp:Content>

<asp:Content ID="ContentMain" ContentPlaceHolderId="PlaceHolderMain" runat="server">
  <table id="MSO_ContentTable" MsoPnlId="layout" cellpadding="4" cellspacing="0"
border="0" width="100%">
    <tr>
      <td>
        <table cellpadding="0" cellspacing="0" style="width:100%;padding:
          5px 10px 10px 10px;">
          <tr>
            <td valign="top">
              <WebPartPages:WebPartZone runat="server" FrameType="TitleBarOnly"
                ID="CentralZone" Title="loc:CentralZone"
                AllowPersonalization="false" />
            </td>
          </tr>
        </table>
      </td>
    </tr>
  </table>
</asp:Content>
```

To deploy the site definition, you can simply select the Deploy command in Visual Studio. However, before deploying the site definition, I suggest that you change the deployment configuration from Default to No Activation in the project's properties, under the SharePoint properties page (see Figure 14-5). This will avoid activating the features into the deployment target site, as well.

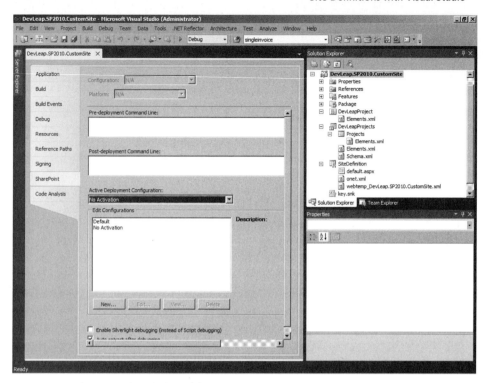

FIGURE 14-5 The Properties window of the project provisioning the sample site definition.

Just after deploying the site definition, you will find its corresponding folder in the SharePoint14_Root\TEMPLATES\SiteTemplates folder, and you will be able to create new site instances by using the new custom site template. Figure 14-6 displays the new site definition available in the list of creatable site definitions, while Figure 14-7 presents the home page of a site of Projects created using the new site definition.

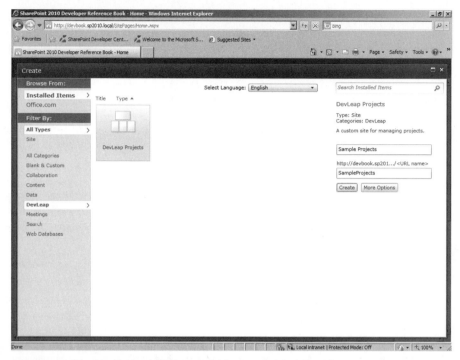

FIGURE 14-6 The sample site definition available as a model while creating a new site instance.

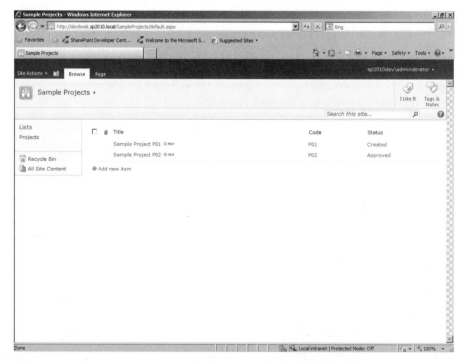

FIGURE 14-7 The home page of a site of Projects created using the new sample site definition.

Custom Web Templates

When you create a new site instance from the UI of SharePoint, you are prompted to select a model, as shown in Figure 14-6. The list of available site models is made up of site definitions and web templates. The former have been discussed in the previous section, while the latter will be discussed here.

A custom web template is created by exporting the definition of an existing site instance, with or without its content, and storing the result into the content database as a sandboxed solution. To export an existing site definition you can use SharePoint Designer 2010, or you can use the web browser, navigating to the Save Site As Template page, located under the Site Actions group on the Site Settings page of the current website.

Regardless of how you save the web template, the result will be a .WSP package with a feature element specifically introduced in SharePoint 2010 for managing deployment of custom web templates. The corresponding element is the *WebTemplate* element. To have a look at its structure you can simply export an existing site instance, save the .WSP generated file, and then rename it as .CAB. You can then extract the element manifest declaring the *WebTemplate* feature. Listing 14-7 reveals the structure of the *WebTemplate* element.

LISTING 14-7 The *WebTemplate* element structure.

```
<WebTemplate
  AdjustHijriDays = "Integer"
  AlternateCssUrl = "Text"
  AlternateHeader = "Text"
  BaseTemplateID = "Integer"
  BaseTemplateName = "Text"
  BaseConfigurationID = "Integer"
  CalendarType = "Integer"
  Collation = "Integer"
  ContainsDefaultLists = "TRUE" | "FALSE"
  CustomizedCssFiles = "Text"
  CustomJSUrl = "Text"
  Description = "Text"
  ExcludeFromOfflineClient = "TRUE" | "FALSE"
  Locale = "Integer"
  Name = "Text"
  ParserEnabled = "TRUE" | "FALSE"
  PortalName = "Text"
  PortalUrl = "Text"
  PresenceEnabled = "TRUE" | "FALSE"
  ProductVersion = "Integer"
  QuickLaunchEnabled = "TRUE" | "FALSE"
  Subweb = "TRUE" | "FALSE"
  SyndicationEnabled = "TRUE" | "FALSE"
  Time24 = "TRUE" | "FALSE"
```

```
    TimeZone = "Integer"
    Title = "Text"
    TreeViewEnabled = "Text"
    UIVersionConfigurationEnabled = "TRUE" | "FALSE">
</WebTemplate>
```

The *WebTemplate* element comprises a set of attributes, which are described in Table 14-2.

TABLE 14-2 The Attributes Supported by the *WebTemplate* Element

Attribute Name	Description
AdjustHijriDays	Optional *Integer* attribute that specifies the number of days to extend or reduce the current month in Hijri (Islamic) calendars used on the target website.
AlternateCssUrl	Optional *Text* attribute that specifies the URL for an alternative cascading style sheet (CSS).
AlternateHeader	Optional *Text* attribute that provides the name of a custom .ASPX page. *AlternateHeader* defines a custom alternative header for provisioned pages. It should be available in the SharePoint14_Root\ TEMPLATE\LAYOUTS folder.
BaseTemplateID	Required *Integer* attribute that specifies the *ID* of the parent site definition. *BaseTemplateID* contains the value of the *ID* attribute of the *Template* element in the WEBTEMP*.XML file that defines the parent site definition.
BaseTemplateName	Required *Text* attribute that specifies the *Name* of the parent site definition. *BaseTemplateName* contains the value of the *Name* attribute of the *Template* element in the WEBTEMP*.XML file that defines the parent site definition.
BaseConfigurationID	Required *Integer* attribute that specifies the *ID* of the configuration of the parent site definition. *BaseConfigurationID* contains the value of the *ID* attribute of the *Configuration* element in the WEBTEMP*.XML file that defines the parent site definition.
CalendarType	Optional *Integer* attribute that specifies the type of the default calendar type for calendars created on the target website.
Collation	Optional *Integer* attribute that specifies the collation to use for the target website.
ContainsDefaultLists	Optional *Boolean* attribute that specifies whether the parent site definition contains lists that are defined in the ONET.XML file of the GLOBAL site definition.
CustomizedCssFiles	Optional *Text* attribute that specifies custom CSS files.
CustomJSUrl	Optional *Text* attribute that provides a custom JavaScript file located in the SharePoint14_Root\TEMPLATE\LAYOUTS folder, which will be executed within the target website.

Attribute Name	Description
Description	Optional *Text* attribute that specifies a description for the site template.
ExcludeFromOfflineClient	Optional *Boolean* attribute that specifies whether the site must be downloaded during client offline synchronization.
Locale	Optional *Integer* attribute that specifies the locale ID of the language/culture for the target website.
Name	Required *Text* attribute that specifies the internal name of the web template.
ParserEnabled	Optional *Boolean* attribute that specifies whether the values of columns in document libraries will be automatically added to documents added to libraries of the target website.
PortalName	Optional *Text* attribute that provides the name of the portal associated with the website.
PortalUrl	Optional *Text* attribute that specifies the URL of the portal associated with the target website.
PresenceEnabled	Optional *Boolean* attribute that specifies whether online presence will be enabled for users of the target website.
ProductVersion	Optional *Integer* attribute that specifies the version of SharePoint Foundation used to create the web template.
QuickLaunchEnabled	Optional *Boolean* attribute that determines if the QuickLaunch area will be enabled on the target website.
Subweb	Optional *Boolean* attribute that specifies whether the web template has been created from a child *Web* or from the root *Web* of a site collection.
SyndicationEnabled	Optional *Boolean* attribute that determines if RSS syndication will be enabled on the target website.
Time24	Optional *Boolean* attribute that specifies whether to use the 24-hour format to represents hours.
TimeZone	Optional *Integer* attribute that specifies the default time zone for the target website.
Title	Optional *Text* attribute that provides the title for the web template.
TreeViewEnabled	Optional *Text* attribute that specifies whether the TreeView in the left navigation area of pages will be enabled. *TreeViewEnabled* can only take *TRUE* or *FALSE* text values.
UIVersionConfigurationEnabled	Optional *Boolean* attribute that specifies whether users can change the UI version of the target website.

Listing 14-8 shows an example of a *WebTemplate* instance, generated by exporting an instance of the sample site for managing Projects, which you saw in the previous section.

LISTING 14-8 The *WebTemplate* element feature generated from the sample Projects site definition instance.

```
<Elements xmlns="http://schemas.microsoft.com/sharepoint/">
  <WebTemplate AdjustHijriDays="0"
               AlternateCssUrl=""
               AlternateHeader=""
               BaseTemplateID="10002"
               BaseTemplateName="DLPROJECTS"
               BaseConfigurationID="0"
               CalendarType="1"
               Collation="25"
               ContainsDefaultLists="TRUE"
               CustomizedCssFiles=""
               CustomJSUrl=""
               ExcludeFromOfflineClient="FALSE"
               Locale="1033"
               Name="SampleProjects"
               ParserEnabled="TRUE"
               PortalName=""
               PortalUrl=""
               PresenceEnabled="TRUE"
               ProductVersion="4"
               QuickLaunchEnabled="TRUE"
               Subweb="TRUE"
               SyndicationEnabled="TRUE"
               Time24="FALSE"
               TimeZone="4"
               Title="SampleProjects"
               TreeViewEnabled="FALSE"
               UIVersionConfigurationEnabled="FALSE" />
</Elements>
```

Note in Listing 14-8 how the *WebTemplate* references its parent site definition (*10002, DLPROJECTS#0*). In fact, all the three attributes—*BaseTemplateID*, *BaseTemplateName*, and *BaseConfigurationID*—reference the site definition created in the previous section. For this reason, Microsoft does not support changing or removing a site definition after having used it for creating sites. If a referenced site definition is changed or removed, elements such as the *WebTemplate* feature in Listing 14-8 will no longer work.

The easiest way to create a *WebTemplate* feature using Visual Studio is to design the site in the browser. Then you can save it as a template and export the resulting .WSP package file, downloading it from the Solution Gallery page of the Site Collection. From there, you simply need to import the .WSP into Visual Studio, creating a new project of type "Import SharePoint Solution Package." Now you can select to define a sandboxed solution, because the *WebTemplate* feature has been implemented by Microsoft specifically to satisfy the requirement of deploying web templates through sandboxed solutions. Visual Studio will start a wizard that will prompt you to choose the .WSP file, and then it will analyze the .WSP and generate a list of items that will be imported. In general, you should accept the proposed list, unless you prefer to exclude some content from the web template. When you click the wizard's Finish button, you will have a new Visual Studio project, complete with a SharePoint package full of features and elements that correspond to the structure of the original site that was used to generate the web template.

To customize the web template project, you can manually open the imported ONET.XML file and change its contents. Figure 14-8 illustrates the interface of Visual Studio, while editing an imported web template.

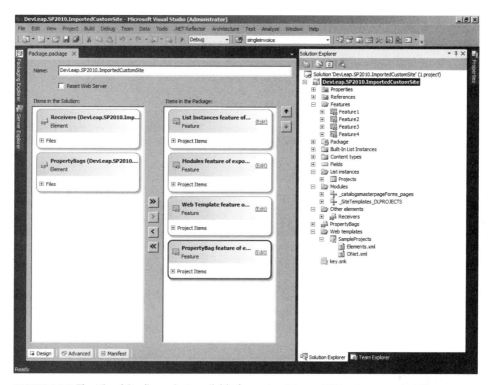

FIGURE 14-8 The Visual Studio project available for customizing a .WSP auto-generated file.

There are a lot of features and elements that are not really needed by the application. The only important elements are the list of Projects and the custom home page.

Of course, you could also create a project for a web template from scratch, manually adding items to the corresponding folders and creating a project structure like the one shown in Figure 14-8. However, usually it's easier to start from an existing .WSP, customizing it as needed in Visual Studio.

Site Definitions versus Web Templates

It is important to understand that creating a site definition or a web template is an uncommon and complex task. In general, you should create features and solutions to deploy custom data structures and content. Features and solutions are more flexible, modular, and more easily maintained than site definitions or web templates, and they are typically the easiest to define.

If you decide that you need to create a new site model, you will need to make a choice between creating a site definition or a web template. In such situations, you should factor in the following:

- Deploying a web template requires only the proper rights to upload the .WSP file into the solution gallery of the target site collection. A site definition requires physical access to the file system of the servers in the farm. In fact, a web template is a sandboxed solution.

- A site definition cannot be deployed in a cloud environment (SharePoint Online or Office 365), while a web template can be deployed and used in the cloud.

- A web template can be versioned without affecting existing site instances, created from a previous version.

- When you change the pages defined in a web template, those changes will be available only in new sites, while changing the layout of pages provisioned through a site definition will also affect previously deployed sites.

- A web template can do almost everything you can do with a site definition.

- The only elements that you can define exclusively using a site definition are: document templates, not related to a specific Content Type; custom e-mail footers, which are not available in web templates; and custom components to process files or security.

Thus, I highly suggest that you favor web templates and avoid using site definitions, unless you really do need them.

Summary

In this chapter, you learned what a site definition is and how to create one of your own, both manually and with Visual Studio. You also learned what a web template is and how to define it within Visual Studio. Finally, you were presented with some important characteristics to consider when deciding whether to create a site definition or web template.

Chapter 15
Developing Service Applications

Service applications are undoubtedly one of the most powerful and interesting new features of Microsoft SharePoint 2010. In this chapter, you will learn how service applications work and how to develop a custom service application of your own. The contents of this chapter are not trivial, and you should continue on only if you really need to understand the service applications' architecture and you need to develop a custom service application. Otherwise, use a bookmark and refer back to this later, if circumstances dictate that you need to.

Service Application Architecture

Service applications are the evolution of the Shared Services Provider (SSP) infrastructure, as it was known in SharePoint 2007. A service application is a middle-tier service that can be shared between multiple web application instances of the same farm or even across multiple farms. A service application provides a functionality or capability to SharePoint's infrastructure, taking advantage of its native scalable, maintainable, and extensible framework. For example, a service application could be a service to share business data, to provide complex calculations or algorithms, to manage long running processes, and so on.

All the native services of SharePoint 2010 are implemented as service applications. For instance, the Search Service is a service application that can be shared across multiple web applications and multiple farms. The Business Connectivity Services, with which you can consume and manage third-party data within the SharePoint UI, is another service application. With the User Profile Service, you can manage users profiles, personalization, my sites, and so on. The list could be very long: the entire architecture of SharePoint 2010 is based on service applications.

Figure 15-1 presents the architectural schema of SharePoint 2010, based on various native service applications.

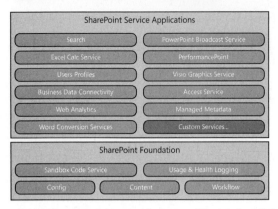

FIGURE 15-1 The architectural schema of SharePoint 2010, based on various native service applications.

Figure 15-1 shows that the architecture is natively capable of hosting third-party service applications. In this chapter, you will develop a service application that will be completely integrated with the environment. Figure 15-2 depicts a representation of the architecture of a single service application.

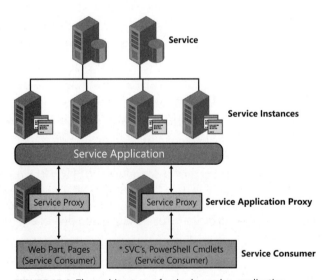

FIGURE 15-2 The architecture of a single service application.

Every service application is made up of a set of elements that are a requirement to satisfy the scalability, extensibility, and maintainability capabilities of the service applications' architecture. The elements that make up a service application are:

- **Service**   This is the actual service, with its own engine, data storage, and infrastructure. It can be hosted on a specific server of the farm, or it can be a third-pary service. For example, this could be an external ERP, or it can be a software component that will be installed in the farm.

- **Service Instance**   Represents a single instance of the service, running on a server of the farm. There can be multiple instances of a service running on multiple application servers. The service application architecture gives you the ability to provide services in a scalable, multi-server configuration, with a load balancer to dispatch requests to the servers.

- **Service Application**   This is a logical layer that makes the back-end infrastructure available to the farm. Whenever you use a service application, you do not care about where and how it is exposed. You do not care about the number and location of the physical service instances. You simply access the service application as a logical service.

- **Service Application Proxy**   This is the proxy that virtualizes the access to the service application. In general, it is used on front-end servers of the farm and allows accessing the service application transparently and independently from its actual location.

- **Service Consumer**   This is a page, a Web Part, or whatever else that runs on a server of the farm, consuming a service application through its service application proxy.

This architecture makes it possible to have a fully scalable and extensible environment, where consumers of service applications do not know where the real services are or how they function. Instead, they interact through a proxy that transparently communicates with one of the configured service instances. In addition, this architecture allows consuming services that are published by remote farms, not just those that are available in the current farm. In fact, by using the transparent proxy model, the service application can be on a third-party farm, sharing a critical service between multiple farms. You could even publish a service application on your farm and share it with third-party farms, too. The communication infrastructure at the very base of the service application architecture is secure and reliable by default, taking advantage of the communication framework provided by Windows Communication Foundation (WCF) of Microsoft .NET Framework 3.5.

Figure 15-3 demonstrates a sample schema of a service shared across multiple farms.

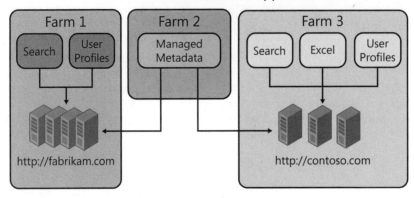

FIGURE 15-3 A service application shared across multiple farms.

By default, SharePoint 2010 installs and preconfigures a couple of service applications that are fundamental to the whole environment of all the other service applications. These services are:

- **Application Discovery and Load Balancer Service Application**   Use this service application to manage service applications, discover service instances, and implement load balancing requests across multiple service instances. This is a fundamental service and the service application architecture could not work without it.

- **Security Token Service Application**   This is the service application that supervises all the authentication processes. It makes use of WCF to secure communication, authentication, and identity delegation between front-end servers and the application servers that host service instances. You will learn more about security issues such as these in Chapter 22, "Claims-Based Authentication and Federated Identities."

To manage the service applications environment, you can use the SharePoint Central Administration. To access this, select the Manage Service Applications menu under the Application Management group. A window appears that contains a listing of all the services installed in the farm. In addition to managing an existing service, you can install new services or connect to a service published by a third-party farm.

Note that neither the Application Discovery And Load Balancer Service Application nor the Security Token Service Application can be managed from the SharePoint Central Administration.

Service Application Framework

Service applications are extensible, and you can build and deploy services of your own, integrated with the native environment. There is a framework of classes from which you can inherit to build your custom service applications. This framework is called Service Application Framework.

Through the Service Application Framework, you have a shared set of tools with which you can concentrate on the real business logic of your service, employing a common set of types and tools for implementing the common tasks of every service application. For example, every service application in general needs to publish a service through a dedicated Internet Information Services (IIS) web application; quite often this requires that you have a dedicated database for storing state and data; a backup and restore engine (a commonly-needed capability); integration with the SharePoint Central Administration (a mandatory capability); as well as support for management through Windows PowerShell. This group of tasks can be accomplished using the basic tools provided by the Service Application Framework.

Creating a Service Application

A custom service application includes many components, which you will need to implement to provide a solid and professional service application experience to your customers. The main and fundamental components of a service application are:

- The service engine, which in general can be implemented as a WCF service. However, from a Service Application Framework viewpoint, it is not mandatory to use WCF. If you do not use WCF as the communication framework under the cover of your service application, you will probably lose the capability to integrate with the secure communication environment offered by WCF and supported by SharePoint 2010.

- The service database, which is not mandatory (if one is needed, it is used to store data related to the service). In general, the database is stored in the SQL Server database instance that is used by the whole SharePoint farm.

- A set of custom rights for configuring security and authorization for the service application.

- Some administrative pages that are useful to deploy, maintain, and publish the service application.

- Some management scripts for the Windows PowerShell management console.

- A proxy library for consuming the service application.

- Some administrative pages that are useful to register and consume a service application published by a third-party farm.

- A consumer page, Web Part, or component to use in sites where you want to use the service application.

In the following sections, you will learn how to implement each of these components by using Microsoft Visual Studio 2010 and the Service Application Framework. To understand the concepts illustrated from here to the end of the chapter, I strongly recommend that you know what WCF is and how it works. If you are not familiar with WCF, it might be better to skip the following sections.

Custom Protocol Service Application

The service application that you will learn to build is a "Protocol Service Application," which implements the business logic to integrate SharePoint 2010 with an external protocol engine. For example, you would like to consume this sample service application from a custom Document ID provider. For more details about Document ID providers, you can read Chapter 13, "Document Management."

Before moving to the code of the custom service application, it's probably a good idea to explain the goal you're trying to attain so that you have a clear idea of what you are going to build. Figure 15-4 shows the SharePoint Central Administration page for managing and configuring service applications.

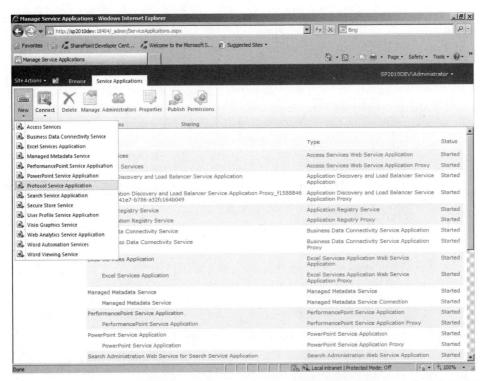

FIGURE 15-4 The service applications' management page available in SharePoint Central Administration.

On the Ribbon, click New, and then select Protocol Service Application from the list that appears (which includes the other native service applications). Figure 15-5 shows the administrative page to configure a new service instance.

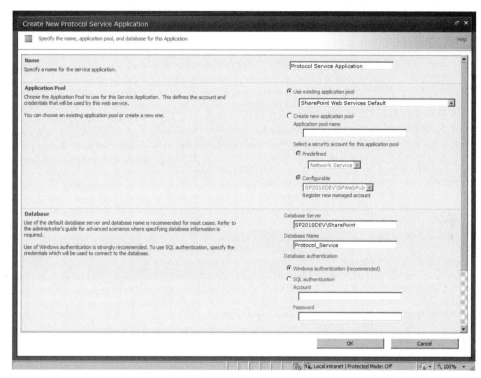

FIGURE 15-5 The custom service applications' management page, available in SharePoint Central Administration.

In the following sections, you will learn how to define such a page. The page requires some configuration parameters to deploy and publish the service application instance, as do many other service applications configuration pages. The configuration parameters are:

- **Name**   The name that the service application will have in the farm. This is free, but should be unique.

- **Application Pool**   Specifies where the service application will be instantiated. As you have already seen, the service application, in general, is a WCF service. Thus, it will run in a virtual directory of IIS under a specific application pool. Here, you need to determine the application pool to use, or you can create a new application pool from scratch.

- **Database** Specifies the database server name and the database file name to use for storing the service application data, if needed. Here, you can also determine the authentication model and credentials to use for accessing the SQL Server database engine. You can also provide an optional failover SQL Server database, for high-availability service applications.

- **Add To Default Proxy List** Determines whether to add the service application to the list of default services available in every web application.

Upon clicking the OK button, you will see the Protocol Service Application in the list of configured services. However, to use the service you will need to start it on a server of the farm. To do this, you can go to the Manage Services On Servers page (Figure 15-6), which is available under the Application Management menu of the SharePoint Central Administration. There you will find the list of all the service instances available on every server of the farm, and you will have the opportunity to start the service on one or more servers.

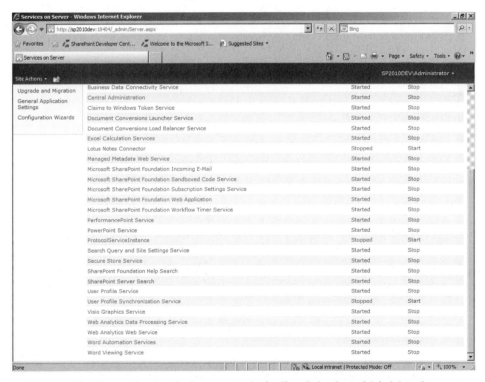

FIGURE 15-6 The Manage Services On Servers page in the SharePoint Central Administration.

After you activate a service instance on a specific server, the Application Discovery And Load Balancer Service Application will begin announcing the availability of that service instance through that specific server, and you will be ready to consume it. For the purposes of demonstration in this chapter, assume that the consumer will be a Web Part running on a front-end server.

Solution Outline

To develop the service application, you need to define a new solution in Visual Studio 2010. You should create at least four projects, as described in the following list:

- **The service application**   This project defines the service, the service application, and all the management pages and scriptlets. It is based on an "Empty SharePoint Project."

- **The service contracts**   If you decide to implement the service application as a WCF service, you will need to isolate the communication contracts to share them between the service application and the service application proxy. This project is based on a "Class Library" project targeting .NET Framework 3.5 for x64 or anyCPU platforms.

- **The service application proxy**   This project implements the code to invoke the service via the base service application proxy. It is based on an "Empty SharePoint Project."

- **The service consumer**   This project will host the consumer's controls, such as Web Parts, Web Part Pages, and so on. It is based on an "Empty SharePoint Project."

All of these projects, with the exception of the service contracts, will be created starting from empty SharePoint 2010 projects. Figure 15-7 shows the solution outline in Visual Studio 2010.

FIGURE 15-7 The solution outline in Visual Studio 2010 for the Protocol Service Application.

Service Application

The first piece of code to evaluate is the WCF protocol service by itself. Here, you will have the real application logic. All the other pieces of code will be plumbing for supporting the environment of SharePoint service applications. Listing 15-1 presents the definition of the WCF service contract for the *protocol* service.

LISTING 15-1 The WCF service contract of the *protocol* service.

```
namespace DevLeap.SP2010.ProtocolServiceAppContracts {
  [ServiceContract(
    Namespace = "http://schemas.devleap.com/services/ProtocolService")]
  public interface IProtocolService {

    [OperationContract]
    String GenerateProtocolNumber(String contentUri);
  }
}
```

This is a standard WCF service contract, without any kind of special case or particularity. The service accepts a document URI as an input argument of type *String* and returns a protocol number, still as a *String*. Later, you will see the concrete service implementation, based on this service contract.

The first class to implement in the service application project is the service from the perspective of SharePoint. In the sample solution, it corresponds to the *ProtocolService* class. This class should inherit from the *SPIisWebService* abstract class, which is illustrated in Listing 15-2, and which inherits from the more general *SPService* class.

LISTING 15-2 The *SPIisWebService* base abstract class.

```
[Guid("F36F7F8B-5E93-4F79-8E08-29FDEC543E3A")]
public abstract class SPIisWebService : SPService {
  protected SPIisWebService();
  protected SPIisWebService(SPFarm farm);
  public override void Update();
}
```

To support the administrative engine of SharePoint, each service application should implement the interface *IServiceAdministration*. Listing 15-3 illustrates and defines the methods for creating and managing a service application instance.

LISTING 15-3 The *IServiceAdministration* interface for implementing management of a service application.

```
public interface IServiceAdministration {
  SPServiceApplication CreateApplication(string name, Type serviceApplicationType,
SPServiceProvisioningContext provisioningContext);
  SPServiceApplicationProxy CreateProxy(string name, SPServiceApplication
serviceApplication, SPServiceProvisioningContext provisioningContext);
  SPPersistedTypeDescription GetApplicationTypeDescription(Type
serviceApplicationType);
  Type[] GetApplicationTypes();
  SPAdministrationLink GetCreateApplicationLink(Type serviceApplicationType);
  SPCreateApplicationOptions GetCreateApplicationOptions(Type serviceApplicationType);
}
```

For example, the *IServiceAdministration* interface defines a couple of methods for creating the application and the application proxy. Listing 15-4 shows the *ProtocolService* class, which implements the *CreateApplication* method of the *IServiceAdministration* interface in the concrete protocol service application.

LISTING 15-5 An excerpt of the *IServiceAdministration* interface implementation in the *ProtocolService* class.

```
public SPServiceApplication CreateApplication(string name, Type serviceApplicationType,
SPServiceProvisioningContext provisioningContext) {
  if (provisioningContext == null)
    throw new ArgumentNullException("provisioningContext");
  if (serviceApplicationType != typeof(ProtocolServiceApplication))
    throw new NotSupportedException(
        "Invalid Service Application type, expected ProtocolService");

  ProtocolServiceApplication application =
    this.Farm.GetObject(
      name,
      this.Id,
      serviceApplicationType) as ProtocolServiceApplication;

  if (application == null) {
    SPDatabaseParameters databaseParameters =
      SPDatabaseParameters.CreateParameters(
        name,
        SPDatabaseParameterOptions.GenerateUniqueName);

    application = ProtocolServiceApplication.Create(
      name,
      this,
      provisioningContext.IisWebServiceApplicationPool,
      databaseParameters);
  }
  return (application);
}
```

The method checks the farm for the existence of a service with the name of the service that it is going to create. If one does not already exist, then the new service will be created. Creating a service means also creating a service dedicated database, if needed, and then creating the service by itself. At the same time, a class implementing the *IServiceAdministration* interface will need to provide some descriptive properties and methods so it can return descriptive information for the administrative UI of SharePoint. Notice the *GetCreateApplicationLink* method, used to return the URL of a custom administrative page that will be prompted to the administrative users while creating the service application. This is the page illustrated in Figure 15-5, which must be defined and deployed (more about this later). Take a look also at the *GetApplicationTypeDescription* method, which is useful for returning descriptions for the service. Both the *GetCreateApplicationLink* and *GetApplicationTypeDescription* methods are illustrated in Listing 15-6.

LISTING 15-6 Implementing the *GetCreateApplicationLink* and *GetApplicationTypeDescription* methods in the *ProtocolService* class.

```
public SPPersistedTypeDescription GetApplicationTypeDescription(Type
serviceApplicationType) {
    if (serviceApplicationType != typeof(ProtocolServiceApplication))
        throw new NotSupportedException(
            "Invalid Service Application type, expected ProtocolService");

    return new SPPersistedTypeDescription("Protocol Service Application",
        "A custom protocol service");
}

public override SPAdministrationLink GetCreateApplicationLink(
    Type serviceApplicationType) {
    return new SPAdministrationLink(
        "/_admin/ProtocolService/ProtocolServiceCreate.aspx");
}
```

Service Application Database

To create the database, you can configure a class of type *SPDatabaseParameters*. In Listing 15-5, notice in particular the method *SPDatabaseParameters.CreateParameters*, which is used to prepare a configuration for creating the database and providing it a unique name. To effectively create the service database, you need to implement a specific class, inheriting from the base class *SPDatabase*, which provides all the plumbing code for managing a service database. For example, the *SPDatabase* class provides code for managing backup and restore of the database, targeting a Microsoft SQL Server database. The sample code of this section defines a *ProtocolServiceDatabase* class which overrides the *Provision* and *Unprovision* methods of the base class, as illustrated in Listing 15-7.

LISTING 15-7 The *ProtocolServiceDatabase* class that represents the specific service database for the protocol service.

```csharp
using System;
using System.Collections.Generic;
using System.Linq;
using System.Text;
using Microsoft.SharePoint.Administration;
using Microsoft.SharePoint.Utilities;
using System.Security.Principal;

namespace DevLeap.SP2010.ProtocolServiceApp {
  [System.Runtime.InteropServices.Guid("139CA8FC-0AAA-4599-AC86-21E9D62A3BD7")]
  internal sealed class ProtocolServiceDatabase: SPDatabase {
    #region Constructors
    public ProtocolServiceDatabase()
      : base() { }

    internal ProtocolServiceDatabase(SPDatabaseParameters parameters)
      : base (parameters) {
      this.Status = SPObjectStatus.Disabled;
    }
    #endregion

    #region SPDatabase
    public override void Provision() {
      if (this.Status == SPObjectStatus.Online)
        return;

      this.Status = SPObjectStatus.Provisioning;
      this.Update();

      Dictionary<String, Boolean> options = new Dictionary<string, bool>(1);
      options.Add(SqlDatabaseOption[(int)DatabaseOptions.AutoClose], false);

      SPDatabase.Provision(
        this.DatabaseConnectionString,
      SPUtility.GetGenericSetupPath(@"Template\SQL\ProtocolServiceApplication.sql"),
      options);

      this.Status = SPObjectStatus.Online;
      this.Update();
    }

    public override void Unprovision() {
      base.Unprovision();
    }
    #endregion
```

```
    #region Internal methods
    internal void GrantApplicationPoolAccess(SecurityIdentifier
processSecurityIdentifier) {
        this.GrantAccess(processSecurityIdentifier, "db_owner");
    }
    #endregion
  }
}
```

The interesting portions of code in Listing 15-7 are the invocation of the *Provision* method of the base class. This is invoked providing a SQL script for creating the database, together with the *GrantApplicationPoolAccess* method, which gives the right permissions to the application pool user to access the SQL Server database instance. The SQL code to generate the database is trivial; however, it's interesting to notice that it is defined in the same project as the service application, and it is deployed in the SharePoint14_Root\TEMPLATE\SQL folder, where all of the custom and infrastructural SQL scripts are stored. In Listing 15-7, the code retrieves the physical installation path of SharePoint (the SharePoint14_Root folder) by using the *GetGenericSetupPath* method of the *SPUtility* helper class.

Service

To create the service application based on the newly-created database, the code sample offers a public and static method named *Create*, from a *ProtocolServiceApplication* class, which is the real service that implements the WCF service contract. This class also inherits from the *SPIisWebServiceApplication* base abstract class. This infrastructural class inherits from the more general *SPServiceApplication* class, which is provided for those service applications that are not based on a web service.

The *Create* method of the *ProtocolServiceApplication* class is interesting because it also registers the protocol bindings for the WCF listeners of the service. Listing 15-8 illustrates the implementation of the *ProtocolServiceApplication.Create* method.

LISTING 15-8 The *ProtocolServiceApplication.Create* method.

```
public static ProtocolServiceApplication Create(string name, ProtocolService
service, SPIisWebServiceApplicationPool applicationPool, SPDatabaseParameters
databaseParameters) {

  // Parameters validation
  if (name == null)
    throw new ArgumentNullException("name");
  if (service == null)
    throw new ArgumentNullException("service");
  if (applicationPool == null)
    throw new ArgumentNullException("applicationPool");
```

```
    if (databaseParameters == null)
      throw new ArgumentNullException("databaseParameters");

    // Register the database
    ProtocolServiceDatabase database =
      new ProtocolServiceDatabase(databaseParameters);
    database.Update();

    // Create and persist the service application
    ProtocolServiceApplication serviceApplication = new ProtocolServiceApplication(
      name,
      service,
      applicationPool,
      database);
    serviceApplication.Update();

    // Register endpoints
    serviceApplication.AddServiceEndpoint("http", SPIisWebServiceBindingType.Http);
    serviceApplication.AddServiceEndpoint("https", SPIisWebServiceBindingType.Https,
    "secure");

    return (serviceApplication);
  }
```

Notice the final instructions of the method, which register one http endpoint and one https endpoint. You could also register net.tcp, net.pipe, and whatever other endpoint listeners you need.

In addition, the *ProtocolServiceApplication* class implements the WCF service contract. Even if the internal implementation of the protocol service by itself is trivial and not fundamental to the discussion about implementing a custom service application, in the interest of being thorough, Listing 15-9 gives you the sample implementation of the service contract, anyway.

LISTING 15-9 The service concrete implementation.

```
[OperationBehavior(Impersonation = ImpersonationOption.Allowed)]
public string GenerateProtocolNumber(string contentUri) {

    DemandAccess(ProtocolServiceAccessRights.Request);

    return (String.Format("{0}-{1}",
        Guid.NewGuid(),
        contentUri));
}
```

Of interest here is the *DemandAccess* method invoked at the very beginning of the *GenerateProtocolNumber* method implementation. It is a method provided by the *SPIisWebServiceApplication* base class, expecting an argument of type *SPIisWebServiceApplicationRights* representing a specific service right.

In fact, every service application can define its own rights and permissions, configurable for the end users of the service, overriding the *AccessRights* read-only property. There is also an *AdministrationAccessRights* read-only property for defining rights targeting the administrative users. The sample service application defined in this chapter declares a set of custom end users access rights named *ProtocolServiceAccessRights*, which are illustrated in Listing 15-10. The sample defines the right to *Request* a new protocol number to the protocol service, and, due to the *DemandAccess* method invocation in Listing 15-9, only users having this specific right will be able to request protocol numbers.

LISTING 15-10 The *ProtocolServiceAccessRights* class.

```
internal static class ProtocolServiceAccessRights {
  public const SPIisWebServiceApplicationRights Request =
    (SPIisWebServiceApplicationRights)0x1;
}
```

You can define as many rights as you like, and then check for them by invoking the *DemandAccess* method within the service application. The SharePoint management environment, for example, within the SharePoint Central Administration UI, will support you while configuring and assigning rights to the users. Figure 15-8 shows the administrative page provided by the SharePoint Central Administration for configuring end users' access rights. Notice the *Request* custom access right.

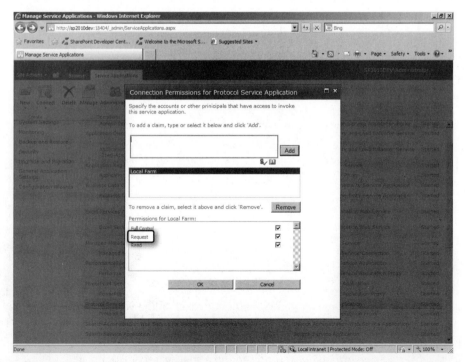

FIGURE 15-8 The administrative page for configuring user access rights to the service application.

There are some other methods and properties in the *SPIisWebServiceApplication* base class, which allow defining the links to .ASPX pages for managing and administering the service, the link of the service endpoint, the methods to execute while provisioning or unprovisioning the service, and so on. For the sake of brevity, not all of these methods will be discussed here. However, you can find their complete implementation in the complementary code samples to this chapter. Listing 15-11 presents the implementation of some of these methods and properties.

LISTING 15-11 The *ProtocolServiceAccessRights* class.

```
protected override string DefaultEndpointName {
  get { return ("http"); }
}

public override string TypeName {
  get { return ("Protocol Service Application"); }
}

protected override string InstallPath {
  get { return Path.GetFullPath(
    SPUtility.GetGenericSetupPath(@"WebServices\ProtocolService")); }
}

protected override string VirtualPath {
  get {
    return "ProtocolService.svc";
  }
}

public override Guid ApplicationClassId {
  get { return (new Guid("C7E904DA-9DF0-4038-9806-025EEA58C437")); }
}

public override Version ApplicationVersion {
  get { return (new Version("1.0.0.0")); }
}

public override void Provision() {
  base.Status = SPObjectStatus.Provisioning;
  this.Update();

  this._database.Provision();
  base.Provision();
}

public override void Unprovision(bool deleteData) {
  base.Status = SPObjectStatus.Unprovisioning;
  this.Update();
```

```
      base.Unprovision(deleteData);
      if (deleteData && (this._database != null)) {
        this._database.Unprovision();
      }

      base.Status = SPObjectStatus.Disabled;
      this.Update();
    }

    public override SPAdministrationLink ManageLink {
      get {
        return new SPAdministrationLink(
          String.Format("/_admin/ProtocolService/ProtocolServiceManage.aspx?appid=",
            this.Id));
      }
    }

    public override SPAdministrationLink PropertiesLink {
      get {
        return new SPAdministrationLink(
          String.Format("/_admin/ProtocolService/ProtocolServiceProperties.aspx?appid=",
            this.Id));
      }
    }

    protected override SPNamedCentralAdministrationRights[] AdministrationAccessRights {
      get {
        return base.AdministrationAccessRights;
      }
    }

    protected override SPNamedIisWebServiceApplicationRights[] AccessRights {
      get {
        return new SPNamedIisWebServiceApplicationRights[] {
          SPNamedIisWebServiceApplicationRights.FullControl,
            new SPNamedIisWebServiceApplicationRights("Request",
              ProtocolServiceAccessRights.Request),
                SPNamedIisWebServiceApplicationRights.Read,
        };
      }
    }
}
```

In Listing 15-11, the *ApplicationClassId* and *ApplicationVersion* properties are very important because they will be referenced by the service application proxy to uniquely identify the target service application.

Also, the *InstallPath* and *VirtualPath* properties deserve a special note. These properties define where the WCF service will be deployed on the target farm. In fact, the WCF service needs an .SVC file for listening at the published endpoints. These properties define where the .SVC file will be located in the file system of the servers, relative to the SharePoint14_Root folder, as well as the name of the .SVC file. By default, every native or custom service in SharePoint 2010 must be deployed in the SharePoint14_Root\WebServices folder, defining a subfolder for each service or group of services. For example, the protocol service application solution deploys a ProtocolService.SVC file and a specific web.config file in the SharePoint14_Root\WebServices\ProtocolService folder. Additionally, to deploy the .SVC file in the appropriate folder, you can use the Add Mapped Folder functionality of Visual Studio 2010. For further details, you can take a look at Figure 15-7, which illustrates the SharePoint mapped folders defined in the solution. Listing 15-12 reveals the content of the web.config file related to the ProtocolService.SVC service file.

LISTING 15-12 The web.config related to the ProtocolService.SVC service file.

```xml
<?xml version="1.0" encoding="utf-8" ?>
<configuration>
  <system.serviceModel>
    <services>
      <service name="DevLeap.SP2010.ProtocolServiceApp.ProtocolServiceApplication"
               behaviorConfiguration="ProtocolServiceBehavior" >
        <endpoint
            address=""
            binding="customBinding"
            bindingConfiguration="ProtocolServiceHttpBinding"
            behaviorConfiguration="EndpointBehavior"
            contract="DevLeap.SP2010.ProtocolServiceAppContracts.IProtocolService"/>
        <endpoint
            address="secure"
            binding="customBinding"
            bindingConfiguration="ProtocolServiceHttpsBinding"
            behaviorConfiguration="EndpointBehavior"
            contract="DevLeap.SP2010.ProtocolServiceAppContracts.IProtocolService"/>
      </service>
    </services>
    <bindings>
      <customBinding>
        <binding name="ProtocolServiceHttpsBinding" maxBufferPoolSize="1073741824"
          maxReceivedMessageSize="1073741824" sendTimeout="1:00:00">
          <security authenticationMode="IssuedTokenOverTransport" />
          <textMessageEncoding>
            <readerQuotas
              maxStringContentLength="1073741824"
              maxArrayLength="1073741824"
              maxBytesPerRead="1073741824" />
          </textMessageEncoding>
          <httpsTransport
            maxBufferPoolSize="1073741824"
            maxReceivedMessageSize="1073741824"
            useDefaultWebProxy="false"
            transferMode="Streamed"
            authenticationScheme="Anonymous"/>
        </binding>
```

```
          <binding name="ProtocolServiceHttpBinding" maxBufferPoolSize="1073741824"
            maxReceivedMessageSize="1073741824" sendTimeout="1:00:00">
            <security authenticationMode="IssuedTokenOverTransport"
             allowInsecureTransport="true"/>
            <textMessageEncoding>
              <readerQuotas
                maxStringContentLength="1073741824"
                maxArrayLength="1073741824"
                maxBytesPerRead="1073741824" />
            </textMessageEncoding>
            <httpTransport
              maxBufferPoolSize="1073741824"
              maxReceivedMessageSize="1073741824"
              useDefaultWebProxy="false"
              transferMode="Streamed"
              authenticationScheme="Anonymous"/>
          </binding>
        </customBinding>
      </bindings>
      <behaviors>
        <serviceBehaviors>
          <behavior name="ProtocolServiceBehavior" >
            <serviceMetadata httpGetEnabled="true" />
          </behavior>
        </serviceBehaviors>
        <endpointBehaviors>
          <behavior name="EndpointBehavior">
            <dispatcherSynchronization maxPendingReceives="10" />
          </behavior>
        </endpointBehaviors>
      </behaviors>
    </system.serviceModel>
    <system.web>
      <httpRuntime maxRequestLength="204800"/>
    </system.web>
    <system.webServer>
      <security>
        <authentication>
          <anonymousAuthentication enabled="true" />
          <windowsAuthentication enabled="false" />
        </authentication>
      </security>
    </system.webServer>
  </configuration>
```

Notice in Listing 15-12 that both the *http* and *https* bindings registered for the corresponding endpoints use a custom binding definition. In fact, they need to use some customized bindings. For example, the http-based service endpoint uses a new security model, introduced in WCF 3.5 Service Pack 1 and mandatory for SharePoint 2010, which allows using an unsecure transport. (Note the *allowInsecureTransport* attribute in the custom binding named

ProtocolServiceHttpBinding.) In addition, both the custom bindings use a security authentication mode of type *IssuedTokenOverTransport*, which is useful to support the claims-based
authentication and authorization model, natively supported by SharePoint 2010. Lastly,
both the service endpoints share a common endpoint behavior, which applies the *dispatcher-
Synchronization* behavior to the communication environment. This behavior enables a service
to send replies asynchronously, using multiple threads for better performances.

The service implementation illustrated in the sample protocol service application also uses
custom implementations of both a *ServiceHost* and a *ServiceHostFactory* classes. These custom types are defined to support the claims-based authentication model.

Service Instance

The architectural overview of the service applications showed that the service application
needs one or more service instances to make a service accessible. Thus, you also need to
implement a service instance class. It is a very simple class that simply describes the service
application for the purpose of being configurable from the SharePoint Central Administration
UI, or from any other management tool such as the Windows PowerShell. Listing 15-13 shows
the *ProtocolServiceInstance* class, defined in the sample solution. Notice that the class inherits
from the *SPIisWebServiceInstance* base abstract class.

LISTING 15-13 The *ProtocolServiceInstance* class definition.

```
namespace DevLeap.SP2010.ProtocolServiceApp {
  [System.Runtime.InteropServices.Guid("4FD10153-8B94-48d3-ACB1-46EA2F1F9DED")]
  public class ProtocolServiceInstance : SPIisWebServiceInstance {

    #region Constructors
    public ProtocolServiceInstance()
      : base() { }

    internal ProtocolServiceInstance(SPServer server, ProtocolService service)
      : base(server, service) { }

    internal ProtocolServiceInstance(string name, SPServer server,
      ProtocolService service)
      : base(server, service) {
        this.Name = name;
    }
    #endregion

    #region SPIisWebServiceInstance
    public override string DisplayName {
      get { return (this.GetType().Name); }
    }
```

```
    public override string TypeName {
      get { return(this.GetType().Name); }
    }
    #endregion
  }
}
```

Administrative Pages

The last step for creating the service side of the sample application is to implement the administrative pages for creating and managing the service application. These pages are common administrative pages, which can be defined and deployed as demonstrated in Chapter 9, "Extending the User Interface." The only interesting thing to see is the source code of the service application creation page. An excerpt of the .ASPX code of that page is illustrated in Listing 15-14.

LISTING 15-14 The ASPX source code of the ProtocolServiceCreate.aspx service creation page.

```
<wssuc:InputFormSection
  Title="Name"
  Description="Specify a name for the service application."
  runat="server">
    <Template_InputFormControls>
      <wssuc:InputFormControl LabelText="" LabelAssociatedControlID="m_asAppName"
runat="server">
        <Template_control>
          <wssawc:InputFormTextBox title="Name" class="ms-input"
            ID="m_asAppName" Columns="35" Runat="server" MaxLength=256 />
          <wssawc:InputFormRequiredFieldValidator ID="m_asAppNameValidator"
            ControlToValidate="m_asAppName"
            ErrorMessage="Specify a name for the service application."
            width='300px' Runat="server"/>
          <wssawc:InputFormCustomValidator ID="m_uniqueNameValidator"
            ControlToValidate="m_asAppName"
            OnServerValidate="ValidateUniqueName"
            runat="server" />
        </Template_control>
      </wssuc:InputFormControl>
    </Template_InputFormControls>
</wssuc:InputFormSection>

<wssuc:IisWebServiceApplicationPoolSection
    id="m_applicationPoolSection" runat="server" />

<wssuc:ContentDatabaseSection
    id="ProtocolServiceAppDBSection" title="Database"
    IncludeSearchServer="false" IncludeFailoverDatabaseServer="true"
    runat="server"/>
```

```
<wssuc:InputFormSection
  Title="Add to default proxy list"
  Description="The setting makes this service application available by default for web
applications in this farm to use. Do not check this setting if you wish to specify
manually which web applications should use this service application."
  runat="server">
    <Template_InputFormControls>
      <wssuc:InputFormControl LabelText=""
        LabelAssociatedControlID="m_default" runat="server">
        <Template_control>
          <asp:CheckBox ID="m_default" Runat="server"
            Checked="True"
  Title="Add this service application's proxy to the farm's default proxy list."
  Text="Add this service application's proxy to the farm's default proxy list." />
        </Template_control>
      </wssuc:InputFormControl>
    </Template_InputFormControls>
</wssuc:InputFormSection>

<SharePoint:FormDigest id="formDigest" runat=server/>
```

This example uses some custom controls, defined in the standard control templates
folder of SharePoint (SharePoint14_Root\TEMPLATE\ControlTemplates). For example, the
IisWebServiceApplicationPoolSection and the *ContentDatabaseSection* controls provide a
simplified way for prompting the administrative users with questions about the application pool to use for the service application and the content database name and location.
The *FormDigest* control is used for security reasons, and you can read more about it in
"AllowUnsafeUpdates and *FormDigest"* sections of Chapter 3, "Server Object Model." Lastly,
the *InputFormSection* control provides a standard layout for an input section in a web form.
The code beside the .ASPX page simply handles the click event on the OK button and creates
a new protocol service application (using the SharePoint Server Object Model) by using the
classes and methods for provisioning the service application that you have just read about in
the previous sections. You can view this in the accompanying sample code to this chapter.

Service Application Deployment

There is no feature to automatically deploy a service application. Instead, you carry out
deployment through a custom feature receiver. Listing 15-15 illustrates the source code
of the custom feature receiver you need to implement for deploying the protocol service
application.

More Information To learn how to create a custom feature receiver, read Chapter 8,
"SharePoint Features and Solutions."

LISTING 15-15 The feature receiver code for deploying the protocol service application.

```
namespace DevLeap.SP2010.ProtocolServiceApp.Features.ProtocolServiceApp {
  [Guid("9cba5093-a97b-40e3-8a4e-b2272ad0a86a")]
  public class ProtocolServiceAppEventReceiver : SPFeatureReceiver {
    public override void FeatureActivated(SPFeatureReceiverProperties properties) {
      SPFarm farm = SPFarm.Local;
      SPServer server = SPServer.Local;

      ProtocolService service = ProtocolService.CurrentInstance;

      if (service == null) {
        service = new ProtocolService(farm);
        service.Update();
      }

      ProtocolServiceInstance serviceInstance =
        server.ServiceInstances.GetValue<ProtocolServiceInstance>();

      if (serviceInstance == null) {
        serviceInstance = new ProtocolServiceInstance(server, service);
        serviceInstance.Update(true);
      }
    }

    public override void FeatureDeactivating(
      SPFeatureReceiverProperties properties) {
      SPFarm farm = SPFarm.Local;
      SPServer server = SPServer.Local;

      ProtocolService service = ProtocolService.CurrentInstance;
      if (service != null) {
        ProtocolServiceInstance serviceInstance =
          server.ServiceInstances.GetValue<ProtocolServiceInstance>();
        if (serviceInstance != null) {
          server.ServiceInstances.Remove(serviceInstance.Id);
        }
        farm.Services.Remove(service.Id);
      }
    }
  }
}
```

The methods implemented by the feature receiver are those for activating and deactivating
the feature. During feature activation, the sample code creates a new *ProtocolService* instance
related to the current *SPFarm* and links it to a *ProtocolServiceInstance*. To deactivate the feature, the event receiver removes the service instance and the service from the *SPFarm*.

After you have deployed, configured, and activated a service instance on a server, you will be
able to find the custom service application's database created in the farm's database server,

and you will find a new virtual directory in the IIS Manager. This new directory uses a GUID as its name and is published on the site named "SharePoint Web Services," which is in the application servers where the service instance is running. Figure 15-9 illustrates the virtual directory configured by SharePoint for the protocol service instance.

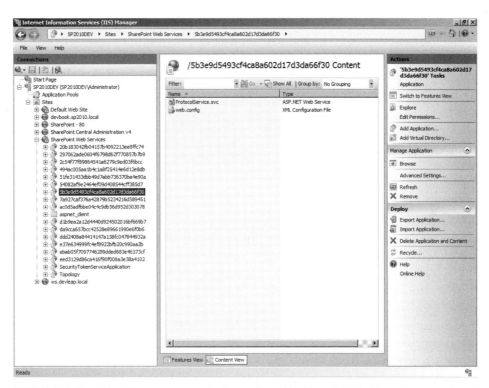

FIGURE 15-9 The virtual directory automatically configured by SharePoint for the protocol service instance.

Service Application Proxy

The service application proxy is simpler than the service and takes advantage of a few custom classes. The first class to look at is the *ProtocolServiceClient*, which is a utility class that makes it easier to use the *ProtocolService* from a client viewpoint. It simply uses the current *SPServiceContext* to retrieve a reference to the service application environment, and from there to get a proxy corresponding to the protocol service application. This class offers a *GenerateProtocolNumber* method, which wraps invocation of the service method, providing a simple and user-friendly interface. Listing 15-16 presents the definition of the *ProtocolServiceClient* class.

LISTING 15-16 The definition of the *ProtocolServiceClient* class.

```
public sealed class ProtocolServiceClient {

  private SPServiceContext _serviceContext;

  public ProtocolServiceClient(SPServiceContext serviceContext) {
    if (serviceContext == null)
      throw new ArgumentNullException("serviceContext");
    this._serviceContext = serviceContext;
  }

  public String GenerateProtocolNumber(String contentUri, ExecuteOptions options) {
    String result = String.Empty;

    ProtocolServiceApplicationProxy.Invoke(_serviceContext,
      proxy => result = proxy.GenerateProtocolNumber(contentUri, options));
    return (result);
  }
}
```

The *GenerateProtocolNumber* method internally uses an instance of the *ProtocolService ApplicationProxy* class, which is the second custom class defined on the consumer side of the service application. This class inherits from the base abstract class *SPIisWebServiceApplicationProxy*, which provides the proxy-side plumbing for invoking the remote WCF service by using the service application infrastructure and architecture. In fact, in the implementation of this class, there is the code to create the *ChannelFactory* to invoke the service as well as the code that uses the "Application Discovery and Load Balancer Service Application" to discover the service location and the instance to invoke, based on the configured load balancing protocol, which by default is implemented by a class inheriting from the *SPServiceLoadBalancer* class. As usual, you can inherit from this class and override the internal logic of the load balancer, or you can use the default load balancer provided by SharePoint and implemented in the *SPRoundRobinServiceLoadBalancer* class. As its name implies, the *SPRoundRobinServiceLoadBalancer* class uses a Round Robin logic for load balancing service requests. The inner implementation of the *ProtocolServiceApplicationProxy* class is not trivial and requires a solid knowledge of WCF to be mastered, thus it is not presented here and it is only available in the accompanying code sample to this chapter.

The third and last class to implement on the proxy side is the *ProtocolServiceProxy*, which inherits from *SPIisWebServiceProxy* and implements the *IServiceProxyAdministration* interface. The former class implements the basic logic for implementing the proxy, while the latter provides the methods and properties for administering the proxy. In fact, similar to any service, the proxy can be defined using the management tools of SharePoint. In this chapter's complementary example, the proxy is automatically generated while creating a service. However, there could be situations in which you want to only create and manage the proxy layer, for example, because the service layer is published by a third-party farm and you simply need to handle the consumer side of the service's topology.

The most interesting part of the code defining the *ProtocolServiceProxy* class is the type declaration, which is illustrated in Listing 15-17.

LISTING 15-17 The declaration of the *ProtocolServiceProxy* class.

```
namespace DevLeap.SP2010.ProtocolServiceAppProxy {
  [System.Runtime.InteropServices.Guid("0DDA776A-932B-45d0-8330-70C022CFEEAF")]
  [SupportedServiceApplication("C7E904DA-9DF0-4038-9806-025EEA58C437",
    "1.0.0.0", typeof(ProtocolServiceApplicationProxy))]
  public sealed class ProtocolServiceProxy :
    SPIisWebServiceProxy, IServiceProxyAdministration {

    // Implementation omitted for the sake of simplicity

  }
}
```

The *ProtocolServiceProxy* class is decorated with a *SupportedServiceApplication* attribute, which is specific to the service application proxy environment. This attribute declares that this proxy is valid for a service application with an *ApplicationClassId* and an *ApplicationVersion* that correspond to those defined in Listing 15-11.

The last thing to do on the proxy side is to declare a service client configuration. On the service side you saw in Listing 15-12 that the service required a custom web.config for declaring bindings and behaviors specific for the service communication infrastructure. On the consumer side, you need to have a corresponding configuration.

SharePoint 2010 provides a folder for hosting configuration file for invoking remote services. This folder is the SharePoint14_Root\WebClients, and the service application proxy project deploys a client.config file into that folder. Listing 15-18 displays the content of that file.

LISTING 15-18 The client.config related to the *ProtocolServiceProxy*.

```
<?xml version="1.0" encoding="utf-8" ?>
<configuration>
  <system.serviceModel>
    <client>
      <endpoint
        name="http"
        contract="DevLeap.SP2010.ProtocolServiceAppContracts.IProtocolService"
        binding="customBinding" bindingConfiguration="ProtocolServiceHttpBinding" />
      <endpoint
        name="https"
        contract="DevLeap.SP2010.ProtocolServiceAppContracts.IProtocolService"
        binding="customBinding" bindingConfiguration="ProtocolServiceHttpsBinding"/>
    </client>
```

```
    <bindings>
      <customBinding>
        <binding name="ProtocolServiceHttpsBinding" maxBufferPoolSize="1073741824"
          maxReceivedMessageSize="1073741824" sendTimeout="1:00:00">
          <security authenticationMode="IssuedTokenOverTransport" />
          <textMessageEncoding>
            <readerQuotas
              maxStringContentLength="1073741824"
              maxArrayLength="1073741824"
              maxBytesPerRead="1073741824" />
          </textMessageEncoding>
          <httpsTransport
            maxBufferPoolSize="1073741824"
            maxReceivedMessageSize="1073741824"
            useDefaultWebProxy="false"
            transferMode="Streamed"
            authenticationScheme="Anonymous"/>
        </binding>
        <binding name="ProtocolServiceHttpBinding" maxBufferPoolSize="1073741824"
          maxReceivedMessageSize="1073741824" sendTimeout="1:00:00">
          <security authenticationMode="IssuedTokenOverTransport"
            allowInsecureTransport="true"/>
          <textMessageEncoding>
            <readerQuotas
              maxStringContentLength="1073741824"
              maxArrayLength="1073741824"
              maxBytesPerRead="1073741824" />
          </textMessageEncoding>
          <httpTransport
            maxBufferPoolSize="1073741824"
            maxReceivedMessageSize="1073741824"
            useDefaultWebProxy="false"
            transferMode="Streamed"
            authenticationScheme="Anonymous"/>
        </binding>
      </customBinding>
    </bindings>
  </system.serviceModel>
</configuration>
```

Notice the *security* elements highlighted in bold. They both declare that the WCF bindings related to the current service will use an authentication method based on an issued token. The former custom binding supports an HTTPS secure transport, while the latter provides a clear-text HTTP transport, which is suitable for intra-farm communication, to speed up the communication process by removing transport-level encryption.

The service client endpoints use a configuration that is exactly the same as the one defined on the service-side. It is interesting to notice that the client endpoints do not have an end-point address attribute. However, this is correct, because it will be up to the load balancer to determine the correct address to which to send messages.

Service Application Consumer

The service consumer in this chapter's complementary sample code is a very simple Web Part that invokes the *GenerateProtocolNumber* method exposed by the *ProtocolServiceClient* class. Nevertheless, you can consume the service application with any kind of consumer, such as a page, a workflow, an event receiver, and so forth. Listing 15-19 illustrates an excerpt of the sample Web Part implementation.

LISTING 15-19 Implementing the Web Part that consumes the protocol service application.

```
void getProtocolNumber_Click(object sender, EventArgs e) {
  ProtocolServiceClient psc = new ProtocolServiceClient(SPServiceContext.Current);
  this.result.Text = psc.GenerateProtocolNumber(
    this.contentUri.Text, ExecuteOptions.None);
}
```

When viewed against the considerable effort that a developer expends to implement the whole service application infrastructure, the consumer code is really simple and anyone implementing the consumer can ignore the complexity under the cover.

Service Application Proxy Deployment

The service application proxy is also deployed using a custom feature receiver. Listing 15-20 shows the activating and deactivating events of that feature receiver.

LISTING 15-20 The feature receiver for deploying the custom service application proxy.

```
public override void FeatureActivated(SPFeatureReceiverProperties properties) {
  SPFarm farm = SPFarm.Local;
  SPServer server = SPServer.Local;

  ProtocolServiceProxy serviceProxy =
    farm.ServiceProxies.GetValue<ProtocolServiceProxy>();

  if (serviceProxy == null) {
    serviceProxy = new ProtocolServiceProxy(farm);
    serviceProxy.Update(true);
  }
}

public override void FeatureDeactivating(SPFeatureReceiverProperties properties) {
  SPFarm farm = SPFarm.Local;
  SPServer server = SPServer.Local;

  ProtocolServiceProxy serviceProxy =
    farm.ServiceProxies.GetValue<ProtocolServiceProxy>();
```

```
    if (serviceProxy != null) {
        farm.ServiceProxies.Remove(serviceProxy.Id);
    }
}
```

The code for activating the feature registers the service application proxy into the farm, while the code for deactivating the feature simply removes the proxy registration.

> **Important** To implement a complete and professional solution, you should provide your customers with a set of CmdLet scripts for installing, uninstalling, activating and deactivating the service application, as well as the service application proxy, by using Windows PowerShell. Internally, these CmdLet scripts should utilize the types defined in this chapter. In the code sample attached to this chapter, you will find a sample implementation of a CmdLets script.

Final Thoughts

As you have just seen, implementing a service application is not a trivial task. You should implement a service application only when you really need one. Otherwise, the effort required would be too big, particularly when compared with other simpler solutions. In general, a service application in general should be implemented in the following situations:

- When you need to share business logic and/or some data across multiple web applications or multiple SharePoint farms.

- When you need to implement long-running activities and tasks that can be executed on the back-end, monitored and managed from multiple sites, eventually involving remote processes.

- When you need a natively scalable and manageable infrastructure that takes advantage of an existing architecture.

- When you need to use the claims-based authentication for user's credentials delegation and authorization.

Conversely, you should not implement a service application in the following situations:

- When you need to share some data across sites or site collections within the same web application.

- When you do not need to interact with data sources or components external to a single web application.

- When you need to implement a simple logic that will need to interact with the end-user UI.

- When you can achieve your goal simply by implementing a workflow, or a Web Part, or a custom event receiver.

Lastly, it's important to underline that a service application can be implemented as a WCF service, and I strongly suggest that you use WCF as the communication infrastructure. However, it is not mandatory to use WCF, and you could implement a service application communicating with any kind of protocol and communication infrastructure that you like. Of course, if you choose to not use WCF, you will probably lose the capability to make use of the claims-based authentication and authorization capabilities offered by SharePoint.

Summary

In this chapter, you learned what a service application is. You also learned what the overall architecture of the service applications and of the service application framework is. Then you learned how to implement a service application of your own, through a step-by-step concrete example.

PART V
Developing Workflows

Chapter 16
SharePoint Workflows Architecture

This is the first chapter of the "Developing Workflows" section, which focuses on the Microsoft SharePoint 2010 integrated workflow engine: Windows Workflow Foundation. In this chapter, you will learn about the overall architecture of Windows Workflow Foundation 3.5, together with SharePoint 2010, while in the next chapters, you will learn how to create custom workflows using Microsoft SharePoint Designer 2010 or Microsoft Visual Studio 2010.

Workflow Foundation Overview

Microsoft Windows Workflow Foundation (also known as WF) is the first release of the workflow engine proposed by Microsoft since .NET Framework 3.0. The basic idea behind WF is to provide a workflow engine to .NET developers that gives them the ability to integrate workflow capabilities into their own software solutions. To be precise, WF is not a workflow engine ready to use out of the box, and it is not an application server for dedicated workflow solutions. More accurately, as its name implies, WF is the foundation for creating custom workflow-enabled solutions.

Note The most current version of Workflow Foundation (also known as WF4) is the one that is shipped together with Microsoft .NET Framework 4.0. It is a completely fresh new engine, which is absolutely not compatible with the previous versions of WF (WF 3.0/WF 3.5, or WF 3.*x*). However, SharePoint 2010 still uses the previous version of the workflow engine, so you will not learn about the newest version of WF in this chapter.

More Information For a complete coverage of Windows Workflow Foundation 3.*x*, read the book *Microsoft Windows Workflow Foundation Step by Step*, by Kenn Scribner (Microsoft Press, 2007; ISBN: 978-0-7356-2335-4).

You can use WF whenever you need to implement custom algorithms using a workflow paradigm, or when you need to offer to your end users the capability to design and customize some business logics of your software, using flow diagrams.

Workflow Foundation Architecture

From an architectural viewpoint, a WF workflow is a set of elements called activities. An activity is the smallest, most fundamental piece of a workflow that you can execute. A workflow is an activity, too. Regardless of the number of activities that make up your workflow definition, sooner or later the workflow will become a .NET class. In fact, WF handles workflows as types, and workflow instances are instances of those types. Executing an activity, which also means executing a workflow, requires you to employ a workflow engine, which is based on a set of runtime services. The workflow engine must be hosted in a workflow hosting application, which is your responsibility to implement. However, the workflow runtime engine and some default and common runtime services are already provided by the native infrastructure of WF. Figure 16-1 presents a simplified overall architecture of WF 3.x.

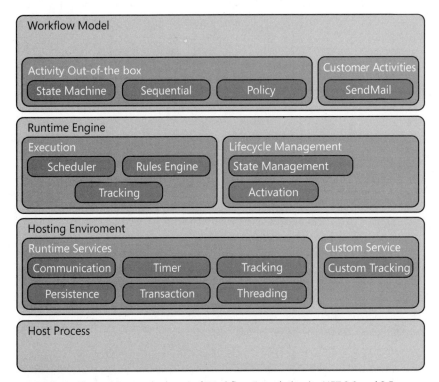

FIGURE 16-1 The architectural schema of Workflow Foundation in .NET 3.0 and 3.5.

A runtime service is a service that supports the runtime engine while managing and executing workflows instances. For example, whenever you create a custom workflow and execute it in one of your applications, you must load the workflow definition into memory; this is handled by a loader runtime service. If your workflow defines a long-running process, it's likely that the workflow instances will be idle at certain points. You could persist these instances on persistence storage instead of keeping them in memory, which you can manage by using a persistence runtime service. The main and native runtime services offered by WF 3.x are:

- **Loader** This service loads a workflow definition to create a new workflow type. In WF 3.x the native loader service can load a workflow from a class library or from an XAML markup file.

- **Scheduler**   This service allocates and manages threads for executing workflow instances. By default, the scheduler executes each workflow instance with no more than a single thread. Also by default, the overall number of threads available to the runtime engine for executing workflow instances is very low; for a single core machine, you will have 5 threads, for a multicore machine, you will have 4 (= 5 * 0.8) threads for each core.

- **Persistence**   This service manages persistence and reloading of workflow instances. In general, it persists a workflow instance when it is idle, and then reloads it when there is something to do.

- **Tracking**   This service tracks events and messages while the workflow process of a workflow instance evolves. It can be used to monitor execution of workflows as well as for analyzing previously-executed processes.

- **Commit Work Batch**   This service manages transactional persistence storage of information together with the current state of a workflow instance.

- **Communication**   These services support communication between a workflow instance and the hosting environment. For example, if you have a workflow instance that needs to interact with an end user, you will probably need to make the workflow instance invoke the UI, and then you will need the workflow to wait for events fired by the UI.

If you do not like the behavior or the implementation of these services, you can implement custom services of your own, replacing the default services.

> **Important**   Although WF architecture is very open and extensible, while using WF with SharePoint 2010, you will not have the opportunity to customize each and every runtime service. In fact, some runtime services, when using WF with SharePoint 2010, have already been customized by Microsoft, so you can't change them.

The activities natively offered by WF are just for the most common and useful tasks. Table 16-1 lists the native activities offered by WF in .NET 3.5, together with a brief explanation.

TABLE 16-1 The Native Activities Offered by WF in .NET 3

Activity Name	Description
CallExternalMethod	An activity with which you can invoke a method on a registered external instance class. *CallExternalMethod* is used to communicate from the workflow instance to the host.
Code	Defines and executes some custom code. The code is written using a .NET language and is compiled as an event handler within the class defining the workflow.
Compensate	An activity that supports long-running transaction scenarios. *Compensate* allows compensating an activity, which is already executed and completed, after a while if something else in the long-running transaction fails.

Activity Name	Description
CompensatableSequence	A container of other activities, which will be executed in sequence, and that can be compensated by a *Compensate* activity instance.
ConditionedActivityGroup	A complex activity to define an iterative and constraint-based block of conditioned activities (such as a *While*). When each step of the iteration occurs, the *ConditionedActivityGroup* (CAG) checks the condition of every contained activity, and executes only those where the condition is *True*. The iteration will be repeated until an *UntilCondition* property of CAG becomes *True* or all the child activities' conditions evaluate to *False*.
Delay	Introduces a time-based delay in the flow execution. While the workflow waits for the delay to elapse, the workflow is idle and can be persisted on the persistence storage.
EventDriven	Wraps an activity with an event-driven execution.
EventHandlingScope	Defines the scope of child activities related to a specific event.
FaultHandler	Handles a fault (an exception).
HandleExternalEvent	An activity that allows handling an event raised by a registered external instance class. *HandleExternalEvent* is used to communicate from the host to the workflow instance.
IfElse	Defines a standard *If ... Else* block with which you can execute conditional steps in the workflow.
InvokeWebService	Invokes an external SOAP service. Internally, it utilizes the ASP.NET Web Services engine. (I recommend instead using *SendActivity* and *ReceiveActivity*, introduced with .NET 3.5 and based on WCF.)
InvokeWorkflow	Executes another workflow instance. *InvokeWorkflow* executes the instance asynchronously and you do not have control on the other instance.
Listen	Defines a set of event listeners and makes the workflow wait for any of the events to occur before the workflow proceeds.
Parallel	It declares branches of activities that will be logically executed in parallel.
Policy	A complex activity, used to define chains of rules that will be evaluated and eventually re-evaluated until a stable state or an exit condition occurs.
Replicator	Executes a prototype of activities for a given group of input elements. For example, *Replicator* can submit the same approval task to a group of approvers.
Sequence	Executes a set of activities in an ordered sequence.
Suspend	Suspends the current workflow instance.
SynchronizationScope	Represents a section of a workflow that requires controlled access to shared variables.
Terminate	Terminates the current workflow instance.
Throw	Throws an exception.

Activity Name	Description
TransactionScope	Represents a section of a workflow that will execute activities under a unique transactional context.
CompensatableTransactionScope	Represents a section of a workflow that will execute activities under a unique transactional context and that can be compensated by a *Compensate* activity in case of failure of a long running transaction.
WebServiceInput	Allows receiving request data from the outside using an ASP.NET .ASMX Web Service interface.
WebServiceOutput	Sends response data to the outside using an ASP.NET .ASMX Web Service interface.
WebServiceFault	Sends a SOAP fault response to the outside using an ASP.NET .ASMX Web Service interface.
While	Runs a child activity iteratively, as long as a defined condition is *True*.
ReceiveActivity	Receives data by using a WCF channel and a specific service contract. *ReceiveActivity* was introduced with .NET 3.5.
SendActivity	Sends data by using a WCF channel and a specific service contract. *SendActivity* was introduced with .NET 3.5.

You might have noticed that there are no domain specific activities. This is because it is your responsibility to perform a complete analysis of your software requirements and define domain specific activities to support your scenario. For example, there are no data or SQL management activities. There are no activities to send e-mails or to save files. In fact, all of these are domain-specific tasks. Thus, a real workflow solution is made up of one or more workflow definitions and a set of custom activities that are generally implemented in shared libraries of activities.

Workflow Types

A single workflow definition can be declared either by using some markup code, which is called eXtensible Application Markup Language (XAML), or with a classic .NET class. Microsoft Visual Studio 2010 supports both options. No matter which language (XAML, C#, VB.NET, and so on) you will use to define a workflow, by default, each workflow instance can be defined as a sequential workflow or as a state machine workflow.

A sequential workflow, as its name implies, is a workflow that defines a chronologically-ordered flow, with an explicit start and an explicit end. A sequential workflow cannot move backward in its definition; it can only move forward, from the starting activity to the ending activity. A sequential workflow is a good choice for those scenarios in which you do not need user interaction, or where you need to drive the users, in a closed schema of interaction. Internally, a sequential workflow is a class inheriting from the base type *SequentialWorkflowActivity*.

By contrast, a state machine workflow represents a state machine, which can assume a specific state as a consequence of a flow evolution. The set of possible states can be defined by you while designing the flow. Then, there are rules for moving between one state and another. Every time a state machine workflow moves into a specified state, it can execute a custom sequence of steps before moving to the next state. Every state machine workflow will necessarily have a begin state, but the ending state is optional. A state machine workflow without an ending state will run indefinitely. Internally, a state machine workflow is a class inheriting from the base type *StateMachineWorkflowActivity*.

Theoretically, using a sequential workflow you can define any state machine workflow; however, it is not a trivial undertaking to make a sequential workflow behave like a more complex state machine flow. From a practical viewpoint, a sequential workflow is the ideal candidate for developing workflows for data-intensive activities, machine interaction, conversion processes, and so on. Meanwhile, a state machine is the ideal candidate for developing workflows for document approval, multi-step process approval, order processing, and so on.

From the architectural point of view of WF 3.x, you can define extra workflow models, simply by using the foundation types and creating custom base classes and designers of your own.

> **More Information** To view some examples of custom designers and workflow models for defining the flow of pages in a classic wizard-like application, go to *http://www.codeplex.com*.

Workflows Definition

To define a workflow, you need to create a workflow project, a workflow library project, for example, and then design the workflow definition using the workflow designer provided by Visual Studio.

> **Important** To write workflows with WF 3.5 using Visual Studio 2010, you need to explicitly select .NET Framework 3.5 as the target framework while creating your projects. Otherwise, by default Visual Studio 2010 will lead you to create WF4 workflows, which are not supported by SharePoint 2010.

A point that you might find interesting is that the workflow designer of Visual Studio can be re-hosted in your own applications. Thus, you can provide your end users the capability to customize and design workflow definitions within the UI of your application, without having a Visual Studio license. Figure 16-2 shows what the workflow designer looks like while designing a sequential workflow definition.

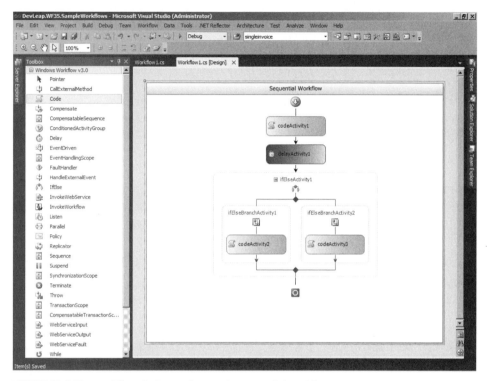

FIGURE 16-2 The workflow designer of a sample sequential workflow.

The sample workflow in Figure 16-2 consists of a *Code* activity, followed by a *Delay*, and an *IfElse* activity. Inside both of the branches of the *IfElse* activity there is a *Code* activity. In Figure 16-3, the designer is editing a state machine workflow for a very basic approval flow.

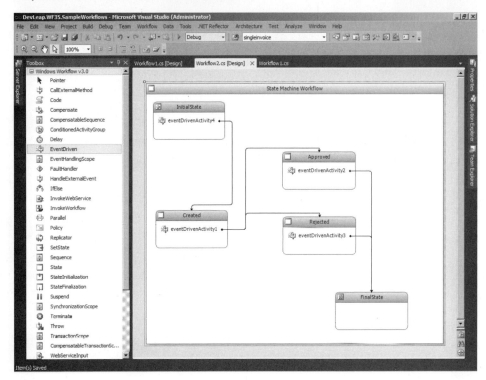

FIGURE 16-3 The workflow designer of a sample state machine workflow.

Here, you can see five states. The first is called *InitialState*; the last is called the *FinalState*. To move from the beginning to the end, the flow moves into the *Created* state as soon as it begins, then it can move to the *Approved* state or to the *Rejected* state. Both of these states can only move into the *FinalState*.

Custom Activities

The sample workflows illustrated in Figures 16-2 and 16-3 are based on standard and native activities. However, as you have already seen in previously, a real workflow solution requires that you define a library of custom and domain specific activities.

Custom activities are just classes, ultimately inheriting from a base class called *Activity* and defined in namespace *System.Workflow.ComponentModel* of the homonym assembly. Thus, a custom activity can be defined by code in much the same manner as any other .NET type. Listing 16-1 shows an excerpt of the definition of the base *Activity* class.

LISTING 16-1 The definition of the *Activity* base class.

```
public class Activity : DependencyObject {
  protected internal virtual ActivityExecutionStatus Cancel(
    ActivityExecutionContext executionContext);
```

```
    protected internal virtual ActivityExecutionStatus Execute(
      ActivityExecutionContext executionContext);

    protected internal virtual ActivityExecutionStatus HandleFault(
      ActivityExecutionContext executionContext, Exception exception);

    protected internal virtual void Initialize(IServiceProvider provider);

    protected internal virtual void Uninitialize(IServiceProvider provider);

    // Code omitted for the sake of simplicity ...
}
```

The core virtual method of the *Activity* class is the *Execute* method, which is invoked whenever an activity instance is invoked and executed. It is there that you should define the internal logic of your custom activity. There are some other useful virtual methods, as well. For example, there is the *HandleFault* method that is used to handle any kind of unexpected fault. There are the *Initialize* and *Uninitialize* methods for managing initialization and uninitialization tasks while loading and persisting the activities during workflow execution. Lastly, there is a *Cancel* virtual method that handles cancellation of the current activity.

Each activity internally works as a state machine by itself; the available states are described in Figure 16-4.

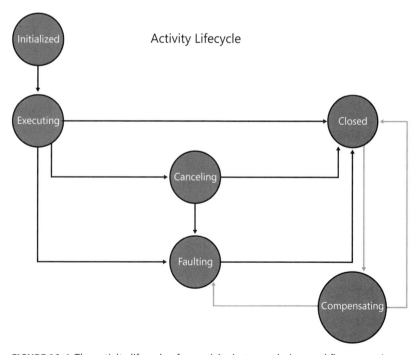

FIGURE 16-4 The activity lifecycle of an activity instance during workflow execution.

When an activity is created it is placed in a state of *Initialized*. The only state available after initialization is the *Executing* state. Here, the activity is executing the *Execute* method or is working asynchronously, using a background worker service.

During execution an activity could fail, moving into the *Faulting* state. Alternatively, an activity could also be cancelled by a third-party activity, and so could move into the *Canceling* state. Finally, if the execution completes correctly without cancellation or faults, the activity will move into the *Closed* state, which is generally the final state for a standard non-compensatable activity. Even in the event of a cancellation or faulting, the activity will move into the *Closed* state.

However, there are situations in which an activity that supports compensation can move from the *Closed* state into a *Compensating* state, as the consequence of a compensation request from an external *Compensate* activity. In that case, the activity in the *Compensating* state can correctly compensate and come back to the *Closed* state, or it can fail during compensation. In this last situation, the state will move to *Faulting*, for handling the occurred fault, and then will come back to *Closed*. The compensation flow can occur only once, so a compensatable activity that has already performed compensation and is in the *Closed* state has definitely completed its lifecycle. Listing 16-2 presents an example of a custom activity writing a message to the console, for the sake of simplicity.

LISTING 16-1 An excerpt of the definition of the *Activity* base class.

```
public class ConsoleWriterActivity: Activity {

  public String Message { get; set; }

  protected override ActivityExecutionStatus Execute(
    ActivityExecutionContext executionContext) {

      Console.WriteLine(this.Message);
      return (ActivityExecutionStatus.Closed);
  }
}
```

The *Execute* method receives an argument of type *ActivityExecutionContext*, which represents the execution context of the current activity and is the entry point for communicating with the workflow runtime engine and the workflow host, as well as to interact with child activities in case your custom activity is a container of other activities.

In Chapter 20, "Advanced Workflows," you will learn more about creating real-world custom activities.

Note You can also define custom activities using a graphical designer and aggregating existing activities. However, this is just a kind of graphical composition and it is not the best solution for developing professional libraries of activities.

Workflow Execution Model

The previous section showed that a single activity is like a state machine, moving across states and terminating its lifecycle in the *Closed* state. Also, each workflow is an activity. In fact, both the sequential workflow (*SequentialWorkflowActivity*) and the state machine workflow (*StateMachineWorkflowActivity*) are based on classes that ultimately inherit from the *Activity* base class. Thus, every workflow internally works as a state machine.

When the workflow runtime engine of WF 3.*x* loads and runs a workflow, internally it loads the workflow definition, by default validates its definition schema, and then schedules its execution through the configured scheduler service. As soon as the scheduler has resources (meaning at least one thread) for executing the workflow instance, it will be invoked by the *Execute* method of that workflow activity instance. Typically, each container activity in its *Execute* method schedules execution of its child activities. The default workflow scheduler will execute every workflow with a single thread, avoiding concurrency issues, and will execute each individual activity sequentially. If activity B is just after activity A, then the scheduler will not execute B until A is in the *Closed* state. When all the activities of the workflow are in the *Closed* state, including the workflow activity itself, then the workflow instance will be considered completed. Of course, if the workflow instance execution fails or it executes a *Terminate* activity, then the scheduler still considers the instance completed with fault or terminated.

Workflows in SharePoint

From the perspective of SharePoint 2010, a workflow is exactly the same as what you have just seen in the previous section. SharePoint 2010 is just another hosting process, which hosts workflow instances targeting SharePoint contents and making use of a set of custom activities explicitly defined to integrate with SharePoint contents and capabilities. However, the team of SharePoint 2010 also customized some runtime services of WF to better integrate it with SharePoint. Figure 16-5 illustrates how the architecture of WF within SharePoint 2010 is based on some customized runtime services that change the standard behavior of WF.

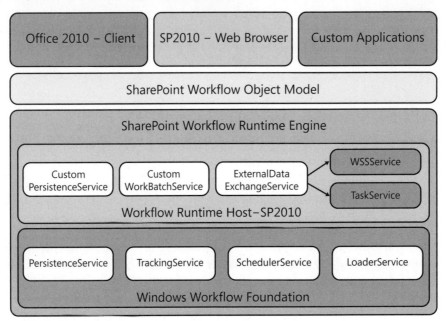

FIGURE 16-5 The architectural schema of Workflow Foundation 3.*x* hosted in SharePoint 2010.

There is a custom persistence service, which persists the status of any workflow instance into the content database of the SharePoint Site Collection in which the workflow is running. There is a custom Work Batch Service, which assists in managing transactional scenarios and state persistence. There is a dedicated communication service to manage communication and events related to SharePoint by itself and tasks of SharePoint. In fact, in SharePoint, a workflow communicates with the hosting environment and with the end user through tasks.

On top of this customized runtime engine, there is a set of SharePoint specific activities, which are defined to support the most common tasks while working with SharePoint content. For example, there are activities for checking-in and checking-out a document, for creating a task, for sending an e-mail message, and so on. In the section "SharePoint 2010 Custom Activities," on page 492, you can see the complete list of SharePoint 2010 custom activities.

SharePoint also provides a specific object model for managing, executing, and monitoring workflow instances. This object model is integrated with the standard Server Object Model of SharePoint. For example, every object of type *SPListItem* has a *Workflows* property, which allows browsing for workflow instances currently running on that specific list item. Chapter 20 presents some examples that use these workflow-related classes in the section "Workflow Management by Code" on page 576.

At the very top of the SharePoint workflow architecture there are the consumers, which can be the standard web browsers, but can also be the Microsoft Office 2010 client platform or a custom software developed by you, utilizing the Server Object Model or a specific ASMX web service called workflow.asmx, which is provided to start and control workflow execution from a remote software or location.

Workflow Targets and Association

In SharePoint 2010, a workflow definition can be associated with three different targets:

- **List** or **Library**   A list or library can have one or more associated workflow definitions. The workflow definition will be available and eventually executed for each item of the list or library, upon item creation, updating, or even manually depending on the activation configuration you will provide.

- **Content Type**   A Content Type can have one or more associated workflow definitions. The workflows will be executed against any item having that content type, regardless of the list or folder that contains that item.

- **Site**   A site workflow is simply a workflow that is not associated with a specific item, but works at the level of the entire site collection. For example, it can be used for scheduled maintenance tasks. This is a new feature of SharePoint 2010.

When you design a workflow and want to associate it to any of the three possible targets, you will need to declare a name for that workflow association, the target list of tasks to use for communication, and the target history list that will eventually be used for logging and tracing purposes. Figure 16-6 displays a schema that describes the types of associations supported by SharePoint 2010.

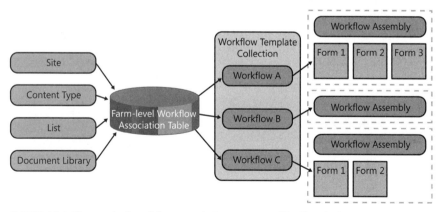

FIGURE 16-6 The types of workflow associations supported by SharePoint 2010.

A workflow associated with a list, library, or content type can be executed manually by the end user, or it can be started automatically upon item creation or modification. An item can have multiple workflow instances of different workflow definitions running concurrently. However, there can be only one workflow instance for each specific workflow definition.

Each workflow definition comprises an XML definition file, the workflow itself, the assemblies required for the correct workflow execution, and any UI form to interact with the workflow from the end user point of view, as well as from the administrative point of view. In addition, depending on the version of the product you can define custom forms simply using ASP. NET custom .ASPX pages, if you are using SharePoint Foundation 2010, or you can also use InfoPath Forms, if you are using SharePoint Server 2010.

SharePoint supports both sequential workflows and state machine workflows. But no matter which type of workflow you define, internally SharePoint 2010 uses a custom scheduler that executes the workflows within the front-end process and using front-end threads while it requires interacting with the end user. Similarly, if a running workflow becomes idle and is persisted by the runtime engine, if it resumes execution without the need to interact with any end user, SharePoint 2010 will resume execution in an external process owned by the OWSTIMER.EXE service, which is the process of the "SharePoint 2010 Timer" Windows' service.

SharePoint 2010 Custom Activities

As stated previously, SharePoint 2010 is a domain specific context for workflows of WF 3.5. Thus, there are custom activities and services that support you while developing workflows targeting SharePoint 2010. Table 16-2 describes the custom activities available in SharePoint 2010 workflows. These activities are defined in the assembly with name *Microsoft.SharePoint. WorkflowActions*, available in the SharePoint14_Root\ISAPI folder. Many of the activities illustrated make use of custom runtime services registered by the custom runtime engine of SharePoint 2010.

TABLE 16-2 The Custom Activities for WF 3.5 Offered by SharePoint 2010

Activity Name	Description
ApplyActivation	Declares an activity that is used to update the initial properties of the workflow.
CompleteTask	Marks a task as completed and sets an optional outcome for the task.
CreateTask	Creates and assigns a new task.
CreateTaskWithContentType	Creates and assigns a new task using a custom content type for the task definition.
DeleteTask	Deletes a task.
EnableWorkflowModification	Enables workflow modifications. As a consequence of executing this activity, the UI of SharePoint will allow authorized users to change the configuration of the running workflow. Any modification that will occur will be notified to the workflow instance through the *OnWorkflowModified* event activity.
InitializeWorkflow	Allows invoking an initialization method in the local service of the workflow engine.

Activity Name	Description
LogToHistoryListActivity	Logs an event to the history list configured for the current workflow.
OnTaskChanged	Raises an event, coming from the SharePoint hosting process, whenever a specific task is changed.
OnTaskCreated	Raises an event, coming from the SharePoint hosting process, whenever a task is created.
OnTaskDeleted	Raises an event, coming from the SharePoint hosting process, whenever a specific task is deleted.
OnWorkflowActivated	Raises an event, coming from the SharePoint hosting process, whenever the workflow instance is activated. This is always the first activity of any workflow targeting SharePoint. Through this activity you can get a reference to the execution context of the current workflow instance. *OnWorkflowActivated* will be covered in Chapter 18, "Workflows with Visual Studio 2010."
OnWorkflowItemChanged	Raises an event, coming from the SharePoint hosting process, when the item, on which the workflow is running on, is changed.
OnWorkflowIdemDeleted	Raises an event, coming from the SharePoint hosting process, when the item, on which the workflow is running on, is deleted.
OnWorkflowModified	Raises an event, coming from the SharePoint hosting process, when the configuration of the current workflow instance is changed. *OnWorkflowModified* works together with the *EnableWorkflowModification* activity.
RollbackTask	Rolls a workflow task back to its last accepted state.
SendEmail	Sends an email using the mail engine of SharePoint.
SetState	Sets the state of the current workflow instance. *SetState* uses a *State* property defined in SharePoint and useful to monitor the workflow lifecycle.
UpdateAllTasks	Updates all the incomplete tasks that are associated with the current workflow instance.
UpdateTask	Updates some properties of a specific task that is associated with the current workflow instance.
CheckInItemActivity	Checks a document into its document library.
CheckOutItemActivity	Checks a document out of its document library.
CopyItemActivity	Copies an item from one list to another.
CreateItemActivity	Creates a new item in a specified target list.
DeleteItemActivity	Deletes an item from a specified target list.
UpdateItemActivity	Updates the properties of an item in a specified list.

Even if the list of custom activities is not short and there are activities supporting you in many of the most common tasks, the list could still be longer. For example, quite often you need to assign or change permissions to a specific item and there isn't a custom activity for this purpose. In many real workflows, you need to convert a document using, for instance, the Word Conversion Services that is described in Chapter 13, "Document Management," and there isn't an out-of-the-box activity for that. Thus, you will probably still need to develop some custom activities that will be reusable in many projects and solutions.

Summary

In this chapter, you saw a quick overview of what Windows Workflow Foundation is and how its architecture is organized. Next, you saw how SharePoint 2010 integrates with WF 3.x as well as what are the targets of association for a workflow in SharePoint. In the next chapters, you will see how to implement real workflows by using SharePoint 2010 and WF 3.x.

Chapter 17
Workflows with SharePoint Designer 2010

In this chapter, you will learn how Microsoft SharePoint Designer 2010 supports you while developing workflows, and what features are offered to help you design them. Specifically, you will see how to define a simple order approval workflow.

Caution The code samples that accompany this chapter contain files and workflow definitions that are provided solely so you can inspect them with a text editor; if you want to test the workflows described in this chapter, you should create them from scratch, following the chapter guidelines instead of importing the code samples into an existing SharePoint environment.

SharePoint Designer 2010 Workflows

Beginning with SharePoint 2010, the SharePoint Designer 2010 is a free tool that can be used by developers, not just by site builders or designers. In fact, there are many capabilities and features offered by SharePoint Designer 2010 that are very useful for developers, too. Undoubtedly, workflow development, together with the definition of Business Connectivity Services models (covered in Chapter 25, "Business Connectivity Services") are the main areas of interest from a developer's perspective.

Using SharePoint Designer 2010 you can create three types of workflows:

- **List Workflow**   These are workflows that target a specific list instance. They cannot be reused and they are applied to all the items of that list.

- **Reusable Workflow**   These are workflows that can be associated to many lists or Content Types. When associated with a list, they will run on every item in the list. When associated with a Content Type, they will run on every instance of that Content Type, regardless of its container list.

- **Site Workflow**   These are workflows that are associated to a site and that can be started from the Site Workflows menu item, which is located in the View All Site Contents page. They run without a specific target list item.

No matter what type of workflows you want to define, you will probably use SharePoint Designer 2010 to design them, and in this section you will learn how to do that.

Workflow Designer

When you begin the process of creating a workflow definition using SharePoint Designer 2010, you will be presented with a fresh new designer that can be used to define workflows in a sequence of ordered steps. In fact, under the cover, SharePoint Designer creates a sequential workflow. Each step can consist of conditions to verify and actions to execute. You can define steps, conditions, and actions using a "point-and-click" approach, or you can type their names manually, of course, taking advantage of auto-complete and IntelliSense-based behavior offered by the designer. Figure 17-1 displays the new user interface of the workflow designer of SharePoint Designer 2010.

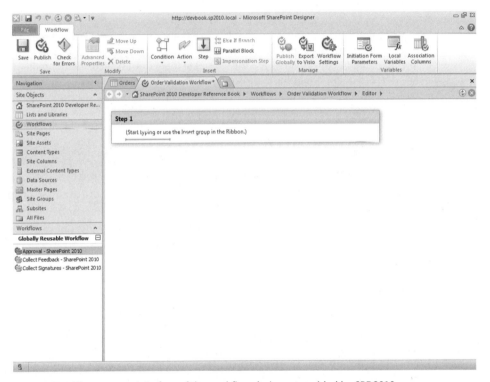

FIGURE 17-1 The new user interface of the workflow designer provided by SPD2010.

Take a look at the Ribbon at the top of the window illustrated in Figure 17-1. You can see that there are some interesting commands, which I'll describe here:

- **Save**   Saves the current workflow definition. However, unless you publish it, the workflow will not be available to the end users.

- **Publish**   Saves and publishes the current workflow definition.

- **Check for Errors**   Checks the structure of the workflow for errors.

- **Advanced Properties**   Defines viewing and editing properties of actions with an advanced approach.

- **Move Up**   Moves the currently selected item up into the workflow definition schema.

- **Move Down**   Moves the currently selected item down into the workflow definition schema.

- **Delete**   Deletes the currently selected item.

- **Condition**   Inserts a condition, which is a fundamental part of a workflow. There are conditions for checking the value of a field in a specified item, the value of a variable, and so on.

- **Action**   Inserts an action, which is another fundamental part of a workflow.

- **Step**   Inserts a new step into the flow.

- **Else-If Branch**   Adds an *Else-If* branch into an already existing *If* branch.

- **Parallel Block**   Inserts a parallel block of actions to execute actions in parallel.

- **Impersonation Ste**p   Creates a step whose actions will be executed impersonating the last user who edited the workflow.

- **Publish Globally**   Publishes a reusable workflow in the root site of a site collection, making it available for the whole site collection.

- **Export to Visio**   Exports the current workflow to Microsoft Visio 2010.

- **Workflow Settings**   Changes some configuration parameters for the current workflow definition.

- **Initiation Form Parameters**   Defines the parameters that will be presented to the end users when they manually start the workflow.

- **Local Variables**   Declares variables that will be scoped locally to the current workflow definition.

- **Association Columns**   Defines one or more columns that will be attached to items in target for the current workflow. These columns could be the container of metadata that is required somewhere else in the overall project you are working on.

In addition, a new feature introduced with SharePoint 2010 and SharePoint Designer 2010 is the capability to import and export workflows from Visio 2010. Thus, you can design your workflows using Visio and then import them into SharePoint via a specific command of SharePoint Designer 2010. Otherwise, you can design the workflow in SharePoint Designer 2010 and then export its schema to Visio, for documentation purposes. This topic will be covered in more detail in the section "Visio 2010 Integration" on page 510.

Conditions and Actions

The core engine of SharePoint Designer 2010 workflows are the conditions and actions available in the workflow designer. In SharePoint Designer 2010 there is an abundant set of native actions and conditions, but if you need more, you can extend the engine with custom elements developed using Microsoft Visual Studio 2010. You will learn how to do this in Chapter 20, "Advanced Workflows." Additionally, conditions and actions support some SharePoint 2010 specific properties and methods and by default are inserted into a sequential workflow definition. Figure 17-2 shows the native conditions in the selection menu of SharePoint Designer 2010.

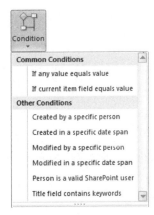

FIGURE 17-2 The SharePoint Designer 2010 menu for inserting native conditions.

Conditions are used to define a fork or a decision that needs to be made in the path of the workflow. For example, there are conditions for checking values of fields or information about the user who created or modified the current item. Table 17-1 lists the native conditions along with a brief explanation of each.

TABLE 17-1 The Native Conditions Offered by SharePoint Designer 2010

Condition Title	Explanation
If any value equals value	Compares a value of any item available in the current context with another value of another item. Items in the context could be the current item on which is running the workflow, any parameter or variable of the current workflow, or any list available in the current site.
If current item field equals value	Compares a value of a field of the current item with that of another item in the current context.
Created by a specific person	Checks if the current item has been created by a specific person.
Created in a specific date span	Checks if the current item has been created between two specific dates.
Modified by a specific person	Checks if the current item has been modified by a specific person.

Condition Title	Explanation
Modified in a specific date span	Checks if the current item has been modified between two specific dates.
Person is a valid SharePoint user	Checks if a person is a valid SharePoint user.
Title field contains keywords	Checks if the *Title* field of the current item contains specific keywords.

The other components of steps are actions. These are used to execute commands or to wait for events in the workflow. For example, there are actions to send an e-mail, or to submit a task, or to wait for a field changed event, and so on. Table 17-2 presents the list of native actions. Following that, Figure 17-3 displays the native actions in the selection menu of SharePoint Designer 2010.

TABLE 17-2 **The Native Actions Offered by SharePoint Designer 2010**

Action Title	Explanation
Add a Comment	Adds a comment to the current workflow definition. *Add a Comment* is useful for people designing the workflow, not for the end users.
Add Time to Date	Adds a specified number of minutes, hours, days, months, or years to a date.
Do Calculation	Performs a calculation.
Log to History List	Logs a message to the History List associated with the current workflow.
Pause for Duration	Pauses the current workflow for a specified delay.
Pause until Date	Pauses the current workflow until a specified date.
Send an Email	Sends an e-mail message. You can also define To, CC, Subject, and the Body of the e-mail. Subject and Body can be defined dynamically, mixing fixed text with context variables.
Set Time Portion of Date/ Time Field	Changes the time portion of a Date/Time field.
Set Workflow Status	Sets the status of the workflow. The default values of the workflow status field are: *Canceled*, *Approved*, and *Rejected*. However, you can create custom status values for a specific workflow, if needed.
Set Workflow Variable	Sets the value of a variable defined in the context of the workflow.
Stop Workflow	Stops the current workflow and logs a message.
Capture a version of the Document Set	Saves a version of a Document Set, if the workflow is running against a Document Set. This action is available only with Microsoft SharePoint Server 2010.
Send Document Set to Repository	Sends the current Document Set, if the workflow is running against a Document Set, to a destination address with an explanatory text. This action is available only with SharePoint Server 2010.
Set Content Approval Status for Document Set	Sets the content approval status for a Document Set, if the workflow is running against a Document Set. This action is available only with SharePoint Server 2010.

Action Title	Explanation
Start Document Set Approval Process	Starts the approval process for a Document Set, if the workflow is running against a Document Set. This action is available only with SharePoint Server 2010.
Check In Item	Checks an item into its document library.
Check Out Item	Checks an item out of its document library.
Copy List Item	Copies a list item from a source list to a target list.
Create List Item	Creates a new list item into a target list, setting its fields' values.
Declare Record	Declares an item as Record, if you are working in a records management solution. This action is available only with SharePoint Server 2010.
Delete Item	Deletes an item from a list, providing item selection criteria.
Discard Check Out Item	Discards check-out on an item from its document library.
Set Content Approval Status	Sets content approval status for an item under content approval.
Set Field in Current Item	Sets the value of a field for the current item.
Undeclare Record	Undeclares an item as Record, if you are working in a records management solution. This action is available only with SharePoint Server 2010.
Update List Item	Updates an item in a list, providing fields' values to update and item selection criteria.
Wait for Field Change in Current Item	Suspends the workflow, waiting for a field in the current item to change.
Lookup Manager of a User	Lookup for a manager of a user, reading in the organization diagram if it is defined. This action is available only with SharePoint Server 2010.
Assign a Form to a Group	Assigns a form to a group of users.
Assign a To-do Item	Assigns a to-do item to one or more users or groups of users.
Collect Data from a User	Collects some data from a target user, using a custom .ASPX page that will be presented to the end user.
Start Approval Process	Starts the approval process for an item under content approval. This action is available only with SharePoint Server 2010.
Start Custom Task Process	Creates a task process and assigns it to a set of users. This action is available only with SharePoint Server 2010.
Start Feedback Process	Starts a feedback process and assigns it to a set of users. This action is available only with SharePoint Server 2010.
Extract Substring from End of String	Extracts a substring from the end of a provided input string.
Extract Substring from Index of String	Extracts a substring from a provided input string, starting at a specified start index character.
Extract Substring from Start of String	Extracts a substring from the beginning of a provided input string.
Extract Substring of String from Index with Length	Extracts a substring from a provided input string, starting at a specified start index character and for a provided length.
Find Interval Between Dates	Finds the interval duration between two provided dates, in minutes, hours, or days.

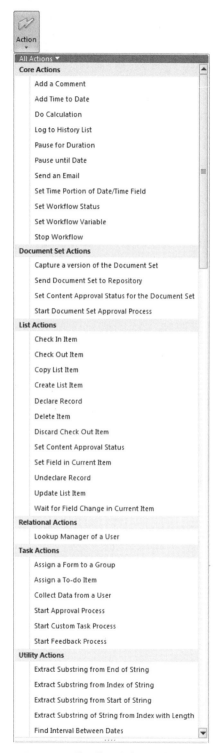

FIGURE 17-3 The SharePoint Designer 2010 menu for inserting native actions.

It's pretty clear that the set of native actions provided by SharePoint Designer 2010 is considerably more extensive than the list of activities for WF 3.*x* described in the previous chapter. And in Chapter 20, you will learn how to extend the native environment with yet more actions and conditions.

Structure of a Published Workflow

Once you have defined a workflow in SharePoint Designer 2010, you need to save and publish it to make it available to end users. SharePoint 2010, under the cover, saves a set of files in the virtual path with the name *Workflows*, under the root of the current site, isolating each workflow definition in a specific auto-generated folder. These files are organized as follows:

- [Workflow Name].xoml   This is an .XOML file, which is the real workflow definition. The activities of the workflow are declared inside this file (which is an XML file).

- [Workflow Name].xoml.rules   This is another XOML file, which defines the rules, if any, that are used in conditions. For example, a rule could be the formal representation of A > B, where A should be a field of the current item, and B could be a workflow's local variable.

- [Workflow Name].xoml.wfconfig.xml   This is an XML configuration file, which contains declaration of initiation variables, interaction forms, and every custom content type used by the workflow.

- Some .ASPX or .XSN files, respectively defining pages for the various forms of the current workflow.

- [Workflow Name]_vN.vdw   Optionally there could be a workflow definition file useful for rendering the workflow in Visio 2010 and in the browser, using the Visio services. The name of the file contains the version (_vN) of the flow to better support versioning.

These kinds of workflows are easy to define, deploy, and maintain, because there are no compiled assemblies or referenced assemblies, and the files described previously are stored in the content database of the current site collection. Thus, a backup/restore process will also preserve these workflow definitions.

Designing a Workflow

In this section, you will learn how to define a simple workflow using SharePoint Designer 2010. Suppose that you have a custom list of orders, and each order has the following custom fields:

- *Title*   The standard and common descriptive field of every item in SharePoint.

- *OrderID*   A site column for storing the order ID, which is an alphanumeric field.

- *OrderEuroAmount*   The amount of the order expressed in currency of your choice. For the purposes of the example in this section, this will be the Euro.

- *OrderDeliveryDate*   The estimated date and time of delivery for the current order.

Suppose you have a workflow for orders validation called "Order Validation Workflow." The workflow should validate orders based on the value of the *OrderEuroAmount* field. Figure 17-4 shows the Visio diagram of the target workflow; the procedure for generating the Visio diagram will be discussed later in the section "Visio 2010 Integration," on page 510.

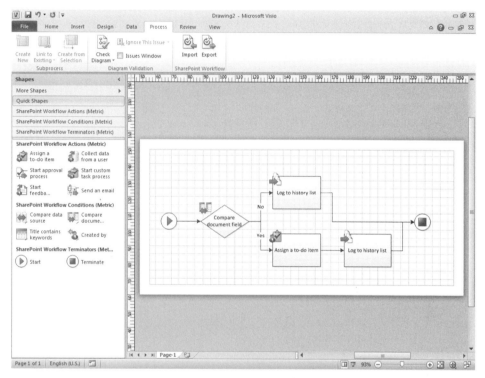

FIGURE 17-4 The Visio diagram of the target Order Validation Workflow.

The workflow will start comparing the *OrderEuroAmount* field with a reference upper-bound value. If the *OrderEuroAmount* field value is greater than the upper-bound, the order will require an explicit approval. Thus, the workflow will assign a to-do item to an approver and log the pending approval request to the history list of the workflow. Otherwise, it will log that the order has been automatically approved.

Workflow Outline Definition

First, to implement such a workflow, you need to determine if it will be a reusable workflow or a list-bound workflow so that you can select the proper type of workflow from which to begin. Then, you will need to define a couple of parameters: one to hold the upper-bound, and another for the e-mail of the approver, in case approval is needed.

These properties should be acquired during workflow startup, because they are fundamental for the correct process execution. Thus, you can define a couple of Initiation Form Parameters by clicking the corresponding menu action on the Ribbon menu. (If you need to, refer back to the "Workflow Designer" section, on page 496 to review the commands available on the Ribbon.) Figure 17-5 presents the dialog window to define such parameters.

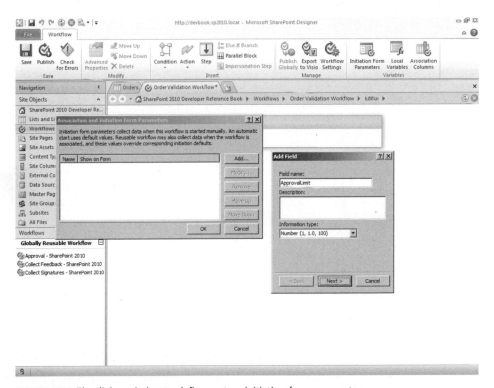

FIGURE 17-5 The dialog window to define custom initiation form parameters.

In the complementary sample workflow to this chapter, the following parameters have been defined:

- *ApprovalLimit*   A variable of type *Number*, with a default value of 0 (zero) and a minimum value allowed of 0 (zero).

- *ApproverEmail*   A variable of type *Text*, single line.

After you have defined the initiation parameters, you can design the workflow. Figure 17-6 illustrates the final workflow definition.

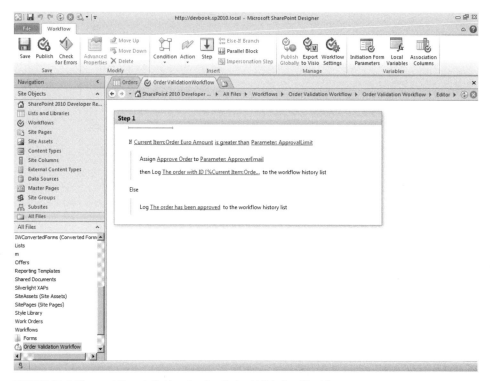

FIGURE 17-6 The workflow definition for the Order Validation Workflow.

The designer uses text to define exactly what the workflow does; it is exactly the same work-flow illustrated in the Visio diagram of Figure 17-4. You might have noticed the layout of the designer and the expressiveness of the text-based user experience offered by SharePoint Designer 2010. In fact, the workflow can be read as a natural language description. The first line, "If Current Item:Order Euro Amount is greater than Parameter: ApprovalLimit," repre-sents a comparison condition and utilizes a condition of type "If any value equals value". Figure 17-7 shows how this has been defined the right part of the comparison, looking up for the currency value to which to compare the *OrderEuroAmount* field.

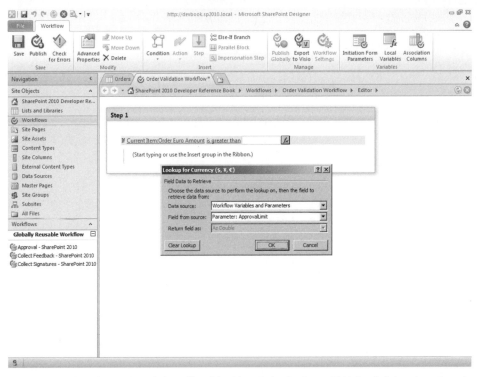

FIGURE 17-7 The value lookup dialog offered by S harePoint Designer 2010 for defining the value of a comparison condition.

You can use the lookup dialog to lookup values in the current item on which the workflow is running, in the workflow parameters and variables, or in any list existing in the current site.

The two lines executed in case the condition of the first line is true are actions. The first action is of type "Assign a to-do item," and uses the *ApproverEmail* parameter as the target user for the to-do item. The second action is of type "Log to History List," and defines the body of the log message dynamically, mixing fixed text with context values. The message content is defined as follows:

```
The order with ID [%Current Item:Order ID%] has been submitted for approval to
[%Parameter:ApproverEmail%] because the Order Euro Amuount exceeds the limit of
[%Parameter:ApprovalLimit%]
```

The values wrapped by the *[%* and *%]* characters are context values. If the order does not require explicit approval, it invokes another "Log to History List" action with a default message value of "The order has been approved."

Workflow Settings

When you click the Workflow Settings tab on the Ribbon menu, you can see the settings page for the current sample workflow. Figure 17-8 illustrates the page corresponding to the sample "Order Validation Workflow."

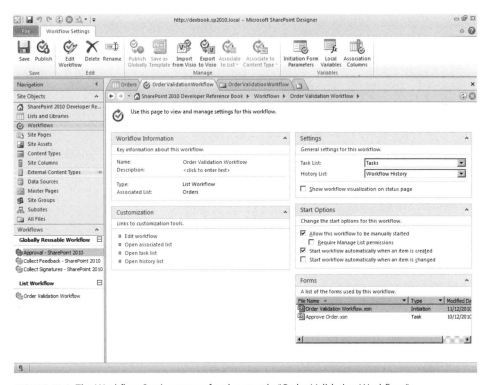

FIGURE 17-8 The Workflow Settings page for the sample "Order Validation Workflow."

On this page, you can manage the following configuration sections:

- **Workflow Information**   Here, you can define the *Name* and *Description* of the current workflow definition.

- **Customization**   You can use quick access commands to edit the workflow definition, to open the target list, or the target task list, or the target history list.

- **Settings**   From this section, you can define the target task and history lists of the workflow definition. You can also determine if the workflow status page of the instances running for the current workflow will show a Visio diagram of the workflow status. This will be covered in further detail in the section "Visio 2010 Integration," beginning on page 510.

- **Start Options** Here, the startup options for the current workflow are defined. For example, you can determine if the workflow will support manual start, eventually only by users with the permission to manage the target list. You can also decide if the workflow will start automatically for newly-created items, or for changed items.

- **Forms** Use this to view and edit the InfoPath forms or the ASPX pages associated with the workflow and its tasks.

From the Ribbon command bar, you can invoke commands to edit, publish, import from and export to Visio, as well as define parameters, variables, and managed columns. In addition, you can also associate a reusable workflow to a list or to a Content Type.

Workflow User Experience

After having designed, saved, and published a workflow definition, your end users will be able to use it. If the workflow is configured for manual startup, it can be executed from the edit control box contextual menu of every item in target, simply by selecting the Workflows menu item (Figure 17-9). You can also start the workflow from the Ribbon bar.

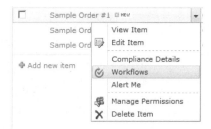

FIGURE 17-9 The ECB menu with the Workflows menu item highlighted.

The menu will lead the user to the page for managing workflows for the current item. That page is shown in Figure 17-10.

From the management page, you can start a new workflow instance, but you can also monitor the status of running workflows as well as the history of completed workflows, which have been executed in the past against the current list item.

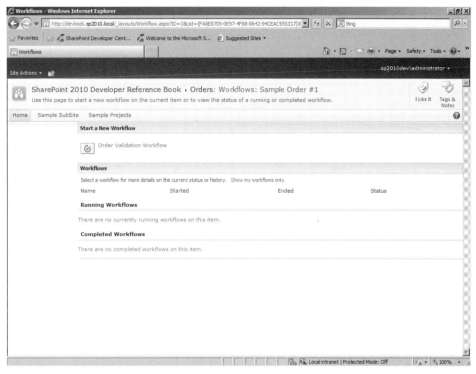

FIGURE 17-10 The workflow status page for the sample Order Validation Workflow..

When you click the workflow to start, the SharePoint workflow engine will check if the selected workflow requires any initiation parameters. If parameters are required, SharePoint will prompt the user with an initiation form page, which in the current example corresponds to the Order Validation Workflow.xsn InfoPath form, available in the list of "Forms" in the lower-right corner of the Workflow Settings page (refer to Figure 17-8). The form will ask the end user to provide a value for every initiation parameter defined while designing the workflow. Figure 17-11 depicts the form in action for the sample "Order Validation Workflow."

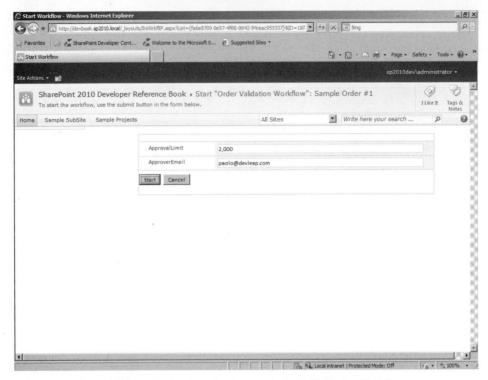

FIGURE 17-11 The workflow initiation form for the sample Order Validation Workflow.

After clicking Start, the workflow will commence and your end user will have the opportunity to check its status with the infrastructural Workflow Status page (shown in Figure 17-12, in the next section).

Visio 2010 Integration

The contents of this section are suitable only if you have an Enterprise Edition of SharePoint Server 2010. Thus, if you have Microsoft SharePoint Foundation 2010 or SharePoint Server 2010 Standard Edition, you will not be able to execute what is illustrated.

Beginning with SharePoint 2010, there is a native integration capability between Visio 2010 and SharePoint. You can use Visio diagrams to render portions of pages dynamically, eventually reading data from an external and trusted data source, and you can use Visio as a workflow designer. In addition, SharePoint natively supports rendering workflow status using a dynamic Visio diagram. Figure 17-12 shows how a workflow status looks when rendered in a Visio diagram.

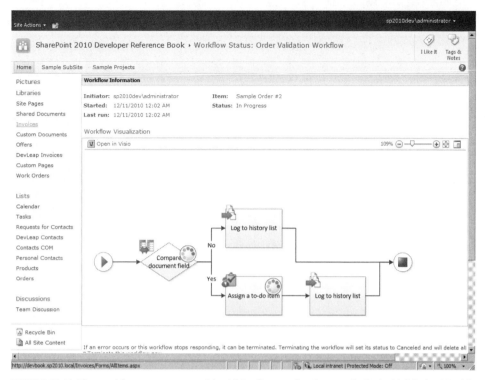

FIGURE 17-12 The workflow status page with a Visio diagram for the sample Order Validation Workflow.

The Visio diagram is interactive and takes advantage of a Silverlight control to support pan, zoom, and move. If the client browser does not support Silverlight, the status diagram will be rendered as a PNG static image.

If you have Microsoft Visio 2010 Premium Edition on the client side, you can also use it to design workflows or to import definitions of existing workflows that were created with SharePoint Designer 2010. If you use Visio to design a workflow from scratch, you should select to create a file of type "Microsoft SharePoint Workflow," available under the Flowchart group of item templates. Figure 17-13 displays the menu to create a new item template of that type.

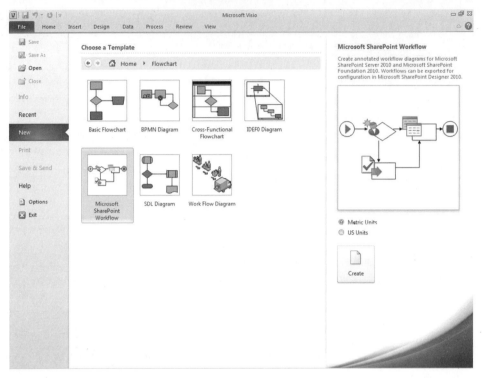

FIGURE 17-13 The create New item menu of Visio 2010, while creating a new SharePoint Workflow.

Through the Visio designer, you can define the workflow, using shapes specific for the work-flow context. You have available to you three groups of dedicated shapes:

- **SharePoint Workflow Actions**   These shapes correspond to the native actions available in SharePoint Designer 2010.

- **SharePoint Workflow Conditions**   These shapes correspond to the native conditions provided by SharePoint Designer 2010.

- **SharePoint Workflow Terminators**   The only shapes available in this group are the Start and Terminate shapes, corresponding to the beginning and ending steps of the sequential workflow that you can define in SharePoint Designer 2010.

You can refer back to Figure 17-4 to see how the workflow designer provided by Visio appears.

Keep in mind that the Visio designer does not support setting properties and details of shapes. You can only connect them, give a label to the connections, and assign a description to each single shape. Thus, after you have designed the workflow in Visio, you need to export it, using the appropriate Export menu command under the Process Ribbon menu, and then import the resulting file into SharePoint Designer 2010 where you can configure its properties. The export command produces a file with a .vwi extension, which under the cover is a

ZIP file containing one or more of the files that are normally published in the SharePoint site under the Workflows folder. This file will be the natural input for the Import From Visio menu item available in SharePoint Designer 2010.

Summary

In this chapter, you saw the capabilities offered by SharePoint Designer 2010 in the area of workflow design. You also saw how to implement a simple workflow using the tools provided by SharePoint Designer 2010. Finally, you saw how to make use of Visio 2010 integration to design workflows and to monitor the status of running workflows from the web browser.

Chapter 18
Workflows with Visual Studio 2010

This chapter covers developing workflows using Microsoft Visual Studio 2010. In particular, you will focus on designing a document approval workflow using the standard tools provided by Visual Studio 2010. The contents of this chapter are based on the architecture illustrated in Chapter 16, "SharePoint Workflows Architecture," which you should consider a requirement for understanding the topic.

Workflow Modeling

Beginning with version 2008, Visual Studio has supported designing workflow solutions for Microsoft SharePoint. The development environment provides two project templates, under the "SharePoint" group of projects, supporting sequential and state machine workflows, respectively. Both project templates are configured for designing a workflow definition, providing also deployment capabilities.

Imagine that you want to design a document approval sequential workflow using Visual Studio. For example, the goal of the workflow will be to approve or reject offers before sending them to the target customers. In this chapter, the outcome of the workflow will be related to the content of the document, assuming that the approver will read the contents of each document pending approval. In Chapter 19, "Workflow Forms," you will learn how to create a parametric workflow, determining the workflow outcome based on the total amount of each offer, evaluated against a specified approval upper limit.

Creating the Workflow Project

First, you need to create a new SharePoint workflow project. When you create a new project of this kind, the environment will ask you to provide the URL of a debugging site, for testing purposes. However, it will not ask you to choose between farm and sandboxed deployment, because by default, a workflow project will be deployed as a farm solution. Workflow projects also require installing assemblies in the Global Assembly Cache (GAC).

Note If you like to develop a solution wider than a single workflow design, you can start from an "Empty SharePoint" project template and then add one or more workflow items, together with all the other SharePoint items you will to include in the whole solution. Keep in mind that the project will need to be configured as a farm solution and not a sandboxed one.

The next step is providing a name for the workflow and a target, and choosing between a list workflow and a site workflow. As you have already seen, a list workflow runs against a specific item of a list or with a specified Content Type, while a site workflow will run for the overall site, without a target list item.

Figure 18-1 shows the second step of the SharePoint Customization Wizard for creating a new workflow definition in Visual Studio 2010.

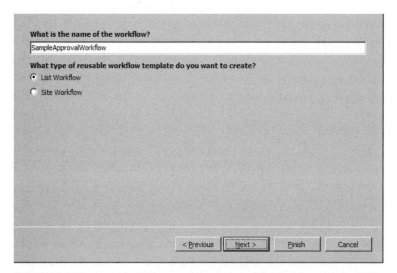

FIGURE 18-1 The second step for creating a new workflow in Visual Studio 2010.

If you try to create a new workflow project against a blank site or against a site that does not have the minimum requirement of a target list, a task list, and an history list, the wizard will raise an exception (Figure 18-2), and you will not be able to continue.

FIGURE 18-2 An invalid target site exception raised by Visual Studio 2010.

After you provide a name and target for your workflow, the Customization Wizard asks you to select the lists to use for debugging (Figure 18-3), which include the history list, the task list, and, if you selected a workflow targeting a list, you will need to choose that target list, too. Otherwise, the target list will be skipped. Again, all of these configuration parameters are just for testing purposes; you will be able to manually associate your workflow to many other lists.

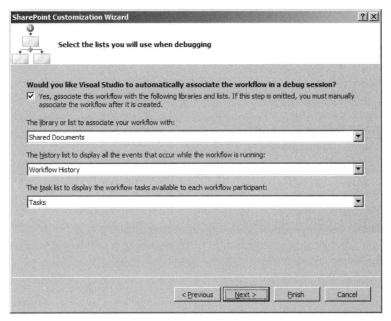

FIGURE 18-3 Step three for creating a new workflow in Visual Studio 2010.

Figure 18-3 shows that also you have the option to skip association of the workflow to a target list altogether. Select this option if you prefer to manually associate the workflow for testing and debugging purposes.

In the last step, you select when the workflow will be started (Figure 18-4). You can choose to start it automatically upon items creation or modification, or you can also choose to start the workflow manually. Again, this choice is just for testing purposes, so it is not fundamental and final.

> **Note** If you find that you need to change some of the choices that you made during setup, right-click the workflow item in the project, and then click Workflow Debug Settings from the contextual menu, which will re-run the main steps of the wizard.

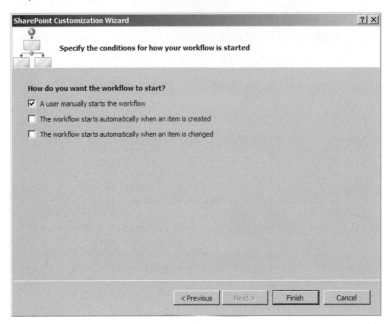

FIGURE 18-4 The fourth and final step for creating a new workflow in Visual Studio 2010.

Upon completion of the setup, you will have a Visual Studio 2010 project with a set of files ready to go. The project template creates a project with a workflow item named *Workflow1*, a feature for deployment purposes, and some useful references to other workflow infra-structural assemblies. In addition, the project will reference the family of *System.Workflow.** assemblies and the *Microsoft.SharePoint.WorkflowActions* assembly, which contains the cus-tom workflow activities for SharePoint.

At this point, the workflow item will contain only a startup activity of type *OnWorkflowActivated*. Figure 18-5 displays the startup environment, just after a new workflow project has been created.

Note By default, the name of the workflow item created by the project template will be *Workflow1*. If you prefer another name, you can rename the item by using Visual Studio and its refactoring capabilities. However, if you use refactoring, you should also enable replacement in strings. Also, you will need to manually fix the Elements.xml file associated with the item. So, if you want to rename a workflow, you should try to do so at the very beginning of the workflow design process; renaming it at the end of the design process will be error prone and difficult due to all the occurrences of the workflow name in code and strings. Instead, it would be better to start from a "SharePoint Empty Project" template and then add a workflow item with a name of your choice.

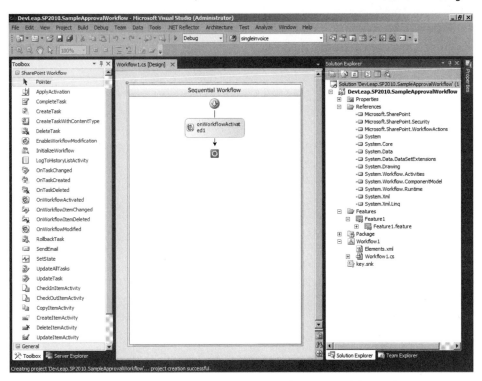

FIGURE 18-5 The startup environment of Visual Studio 2010 for a new workflow project.

Workflow Outline

Every workflow targeting SharePoint must have the *OnWorkflowActivated* activity as its first and startup activity (this is mandatory). This activity is responsible for providing some contextual and infrastructural information to the workflow. For example, through this activity you have access to a property called *WorkflowProperties*, of type *SPWorkflowActivationProperties*, which will provide you some useful information about the current workflow context. Table 18-1 presents the main members of the *SPWorkflowActivationProperties* type.

TABLE 18-1 The Main Members of the *SPWorkflowActivationProperties* Type

Member Name	Description
AssociationData	A *String* that provides some configuration data that can be defined while associating the workflow with its target. To provide association data to your workflow, you need custom forms. These will be covered in Chapter 19.
Context	An *Object* that represents the object on which the workflow instance is running. You can cast it to the type of the workflow's target.
HistoryList	An *SPList* corresponding to the History List associated with the workflow.
HistoryListId	A *Guid* corresponding to the ID of the History List associated with the workflow.

Member Name	Description
HistoryListUrl	A *String* corresponding to the URL of the History List associated with the workflow.
InitiationData	A *String* providing some configuration data that can be passed to the current workflow instance during startup. To provide initiation data to your workflow, you need custom forms. These will be covered in Chapter 19.
Item	An *SPListItem* corresponding to the list item on which the workflow is running.
ItemId	An *Int32* corresponding to the ID of the list item on which the workflow is running.
ItemUrl	A *String* corresponding to the URL of the list item on which the workflow is running.
List	It is an *SPList* corresponding to the List containing the item on which the workflow is running.
ListId	A *Guid* corresponding to the ID of the List containing the item on which the workflow is running.
ListUrl	It is a *String* corresponding to the URL of the List containing the item on which the workflow is running.
Originator	A *String* corresponding to the user name of the user who initiated the workflow instance.
OriginatorEmail	A *String* corresponding to the e-mail of the user who initiated the workflow instance.
OriginatorUser	An *SPUser* corresponding to the user who initiated the workflow instance.
Site	An *SPSite* corresponding to the site on which the workflow is located.
SiteId	A *Guid* corresponding to the ID of the site on which the workflow is located.
SiteUrl	A *String* corresponding to the URL of the site on which the workflow is located.
TaskList	An *SPList* corresponding to the Task List associated with the workflow.
TaskListId	A *Guid* corresponding to the ID of the Task List associated with the workflow.
TaskListUrl	It is a *String* corresponding to the URL of the Task List associated with the workflow.
TemplateName	A *String* representing the name of the workflow association from which the workflow instance was created.
Web	An *SPWeb* corresponding to the website on which the workflow is located.
WebId	A *Guid* corresponding to the ID of the website on which the workflow is located.
WebUrl	A *String* corresponding to the URL of the website on which the workflow is located.
Workflow	An *SPWorkflow* corresponding to the workflow instance.
WorkflowId	A *Guid* corresponding to the ID of the workflow instance.

To use this activity, you can double-click it while you are in the designer surface. The designer displays the code of the workflow, and in particular, you will have the opportunity to write the code of an event handler, corresponding to the *Invoked* event, which will be raised when the *OnWorkflowActivated* activity is invoked. There you can access the *WorkflowProperties* property and execute some custom code. For example, you can save the information available through the *WorkflowProperties* property in some local variables. You'll see more on this later in the chapter.

Before you continue, here is a brief description of the sample workflow that accompanies this chapter. Suppose that you want to assign an approval task to a user of the site, and that you want to take advantage of the content approval engine already available in SharePoint for approving or rejecting the item. To do this, you can add an instance of the *CreateTask* activity to your workflow definition, properly configured, and then wait for the current item to change, declaring an instance of the *onWorkflowItemChanged* activity. As soon as the current item is modified, you can determine if the modification is an approval, a rejection, or whatever else and you will write as the outcome to the History List, as a comment. Figure 18-6 illustrates the outline of this workflow definition.

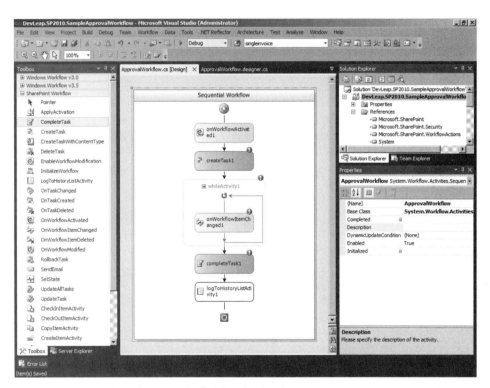

FIGURE 18-6 The outline of the sample workflow for this chapter.

The workflow has a *createTask1* activity, followed by a *While* activity that will execute until the *onWorkflowItemChanges1* event raises a changing event of interest. When that occurs, the workflow completes the pending task by using the *completeTask1* activity and moves to the *LogToHistoryListActivity1* to log the outcome.

To better understand the behavior of SharePoint workflows, take a few moments to analyze each activity in the flow. First, notice in Figure 18-6 that many of the activities added to the designer are under an error condition. The workflow designer validates activities upon insertion in the flow and most of the SharePoint workflow activities have some requirements to satisfy for a proper configuration. The error condition in the current designer exists because the activities have not yet been configured. For example, for the *createTask1* activity to work properly, you must first configure the following members:

- A property with the name CorrelationToken, which is discussed further beginning on page 533.

- A property with the name TaskId, which is a Guid that must be created as a unique value in the code of the workflow.

- A property with the name TaskProperties, which holds the properties of the task that is going to be created.

The *TaskId* and *TaskProperties* members can be assigned with an explicit value in the designer, or they can be bound to a workflow's variables. In general, the latter is the most useful. To bind a member of an activity to a workflow's variable, you can make use of the native property binding capabilities of the workflow designer.

For example, select the *createTask1* activity and take a look at the properties declaration in the Properties pane. You will see that there are some properties with a yellow cylinder adjacent to their declaration. These are called dependency properties and you will learn how to create them in Chapter 20, "Advanced Workflows." Figure 18-7 shows the Properties pane of the designer for the *createTask1* activity.

FIGURE 18-7 The Properties pane of the *createTask1* activity with boundable properties highlighted.

Double-click one of the yellow cylinders to display the Bind 'TaskID' To An Activity's Property dialog window, in which you can select the data source that provides the value for that property, as shown in Figure 18-8.

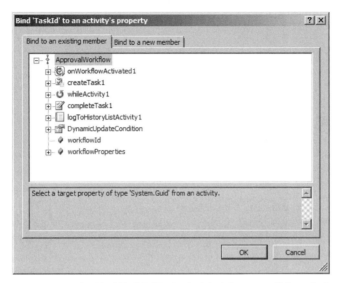

FIGURE 18-8 The Bind 'TaskID' To An Activity's Property dialog window that you use to bind the *TaskId* property of the *createTask1* activity.

You can select any existing property with a data type compliant with the expected value for the property you are configuring. In this example, you can choose any property or field with a data type of *Guid*. If you do not find a suitable member, you can create a new one by clicking the Bind To A New Member tab. You will need to provide the name type (field or property) of the new member that will be created. Under the cover, the designer will create some code for you, declaring a member to hold the variable. Suppose that choose a property with the name *ApprovalTaskId*. Do the same for the *TaskProperties* member, creating a new data bound property with the name *ApprovalTaskProperties*. Now the *createTask1* activity is configured correctly. If you double-click it while in the designer surface, you will be prompted with the code of an event called *createTask1_MethodInvoking*, which can be used to configure properties and fields just before task creation.

> **Note** The *CreateTask* is an activity that invokes the workflow host, such as SharePoint, to create a new task. As with every standard activity used to invoke the host from the workflow instance, the activity is displayed in the designer using a light-blue color. In general, you can double-click light-blue activities that communicate with the host and write some code that will be executed while invoking (method invoking) the host.

Moving forward in the workflow, you now need to configure the *While* activity, providing a looping condition. In Workflow Foundation a condition can be expressed in a couple of ways:

- **Code Condition**　This represents a condition expressed in code. You need to implement an event-driven method, which receives an event argument of type *ConditionalEventArgs* and that defines a Boolean property with the name Result that will be evaluated by the While activity to determine whether to repeat execution or not.

- **Declarative Rule Condition**　This is an expression, defined using a designer, which represents a condition without the need to write too much code. Every workflow definition could have a set of declarative rule conditions, all saved within the same .xoml.rules file.

Regardless of which type of condition you choose, you will need to wait for the current item to change before checking the approval status and deciding whether to repeat the loop or not. For this purpose there is the *onWorkflowItemChanged1* activity, which is an event-based activity that simply requires a mandatory *CorrelationToken* property, and then raises an event whenever the item on which the workflow is running changes. The event can be handled by code, writing a specific event handler procedure.

> **Note**　The *OnWorkflowItemChanged* is an activity that receives an asynchronous event from the workflow host, such as SharePoint. As with every standard activity used to handle events from the host to the workflow instance, the activity is displayed in the designer using a light-green color. In general, you can double-click light-green activities that communicate with the host and write some code that will be executed when the event will be invoked (method invoked) by the host.

Listing 18-1 displays the workflow's code, describing all the initialization code for the activities.

LISTING 18-1 The sample workflow's code.

```
public sealed partial class ApprovalWorkflow : SequentialWorkflowActivity {
  public ApprovalWorkflow() {
    InitializeComponent();
  }

  public Guid workflowId = default(System.Guid);
  public SPWorkflowActivationProperties workflowProperties =
    new SPWorkflowActivationProperties();

  private void onWorkflowActivated_Invoked(object sender, ExternalDataEventArgs e) {
    // Here you could write some initialization code
  }
```

```
// ApprovalTaskId and ApprovalTaskProperties members declaration
// omitted for the sake of brevity

private void createApprovalTask_MethodInvoking(object sender, EventArgs e) {
    // Assign a unique ID to the ApprovalTask
    this.ApprovalTaskId = Guid.NewGuid();

    // Configure the properties of the ApprovalTask
    this.ApprovalTaskProperties = new SPWorkflowTaskProperties();
    this.ApprovalTaskProperties.AssignedTo = "SP2010DEV\\DemoUser";
    this.ApprovalTaskProperties.Description = "Please approve this offer";
    this.ApprovalTaskProperties.DueDate = DateTime.Now.AddDays(10);
    this.ApprovalTaskProperties.SendEmailNotification = true;
    this.ApprovalTaskProperties.Title = "Please approve this offer";
}

private void waitForOutcome(object sender, ConditionalEventArgs e) {
    // This method is invoked for every loop of the While activity
    e.Result = repeatWhile;
}

public Boolean repeatWhile = true;
public String currentModerationStatusText;

private void onOfferItemChanged_Invoked(object sender, ExternalDataEventArgs e) {
    this.currentModerationStatusText =
        SPFieldModStat.TextFieldValueFromValue(
        this.workflowProperties.Item[FieldsIds.ModerationStatusFieldId]);

    if ((this.currentModerationStatusText == "Approved") ||
      (this.currentModerationStatusText == "Rejected")) {
        this.repeatWhile = false;
    }
    else {
        this.repeatWhile = false;
    }
  }
}
```

Listing 18-1 illustrates how the method *onWorkflowActivated_Invoked* could execute some
initialization code based on the *AssociationData* and *InitiationData* of the *WorkflowProperties*
property. However, in this first workflow, the initialization code is omitted for the sake
of simplicity. Then there is the *createApprovalTask_MethodInvoking*, which initializes the
ApprovalTaskId and *ApprovalTaskProperties* properties. Due to the lack of a configuration
form for this first sample, the code statically provides an assignee and a due date for the
approval task. If you would like to deploy this workflow in a testing environment, you need
to change these values or to make them configurable. In Chapter 19, "Workflow Forms," you
will see how to use configurable values. Lastly, the *onOfferItemChanged_Invoked* method is

invoked whenever the current item changes. The code of this method extracts the value of the Approval Status field, and if it is "Approved" or "Rejected," it stops the loop of the *While* activity by setting the *repeatWhile* member to *false*. The *waitForOutcome* method associated as the Code Condition of the *While* activity returns a *Result* corresponding to the value of the *repeatWhile* member.

To complete the workflow design, you simply need to configure the *completeTask1* activity so it completes the approval task, and then you need to configure the *logToHistoryListActivity1* to write an event log in the History List. The *completeTask1* activity provides the configuration of the following properties:

- *CorrelationToken* This will be discussed in detail on page 533. However, it must correspond to the same value assigned to the activity used for creating the task that this activity completes.

- *TaskId* A Guid that corresponds to the ID of the task to complete. In the current example, it is the ApprovalTaskId.

- *TaskOutcome* This is an optional property that can be used to write a specific outcome text in the Outcome field of the task.

The *logToHistoryListActivity1* allows configuring the following properties:

- *EventId* Assumes a value that defines the type of event you are going to log. For example, it can assume values of type WorkflowComment, WorkflowError, Workflow-Started, WorkflowCompleted, and so on.

- *HistoryDescription* The text to write to the history list item.

- *HistoryOutcome* The outcome related to the history list item.

- *OtherData* Used to store extra data and information related to the current event.

- *UserId* The numeric ID of the user who executed the event.

Figure 18-9 shows the designer for the sample workflow in its final state. The activities in this final layout have been renamed to better describe their purpose.

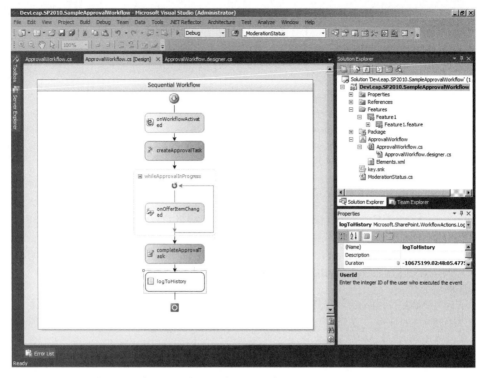

FIGURE 18-9 The designer of the sample workflow in its final state.

The workflow you have just seen is rudimentary, but it gives you a good understanding of the fundamental elements of a workflow for SharePoint, which are:

- The startup activity of type OnWorkflowActivated.

- The usage and flow of SharePoint related activities.

- The correlation tokens (which will be covered in the next section).

- The custom code behind each activity.

Of course, a workflow designed in Visual Studio 2010 often requires a set of custom activities to interact with external systems such as an Enterprise Resource Planning (ERP) system or third-party SOAP services. Using only the standard and default activities offered by SharePoint often is not enough, and you will need to develop custom activities of your own, specifically designed to run in a SharePoint workflow. This is covered in greater detail in Chapter 20.

A real workflow solution also interacts with the end users through custom forms, which will be explored in Chapter 19.

Workflow Deployment

Once you have developed your workflow, to deploy and test the solution on your development environment, you simply need to select the Deploy Solution item under the Build menu of Visual Studio 2010. The deployment process creates a .WSP solution package, activates the feature, and associates the workflow with the target list that you chose during the initial configuration of the project. However, when you're ready to release your workflow solution to a customer's site, you will need to install it manually, using the .WSP. For final deployment, you should switch the solution build configuration to Release. Then, you can select the Package menu item (also under the Build menu) to generate a finalized, ready-to-go .WSP in the bin\ release folder of the current workflow project. Using that .WSP file, you will be ready to install the solution, deploy it on one or more web applications, and activate the corresponding feature in the sites where you want to implement the workflow.

Internally, the feature for deploying a workflow uses a *Workflow* feature element, which has a structure similar to that illustrated in Listing 18-2.

LISTING 18-2 The *Workflow* feature element structure.

```
<Workflow
  Title="Text"
  Name="Text"
  CodeBesideAssembly="Text"
  CodeBesideClass="Text"
  Description="Text"
  Id="Text"
  EngineClass="Text"
  EngineAssembly="Text"
  AssociationUrl="Text"
  InstantiationUrl="Text"
  ModificationUrl="Text"
  StatusUrl="Text"
  TaskListContentTypeId="Text" >
  <AssociationData />
  <MetaData />
  <Categories />
</Workflow>
```

The *Workflow* element accepts several attributes and three child elements. Table 18-2 provides a description of each available attribute.

TABLE 18-2 The Main Attributes of the *Workflow* Feature Element

Attribute	Description
Title	Optional *Text* attribute that describes the title of the workflow.
Name	Required *Text* attribute that defines the name of the workflow, and that will be used to reference the workflow in the SharePoint UI.
CodeBesideAssembly	Required *Text* attribute that defines the strong name of the assembly containing the workflow definition. By default, Visual Studio 2010 uses the token $assemblyname$, which will be replaced during deployment with the proper assembly name.
CodeBesideClass	Required *Text* attribute defining the full name of the type containing the workflow definition.
Description	Optional *Text* attribute that describes the workflow.
Id	A required *Text* attribute that defines the unique ID (GUID) of the workflow definition.
EngineClass	Reserved by Microsoft for future use.
EngineAssembly	Reserved by Microsoft for future use.
AssociationUrl	Optional *Text* attribute that defines the URL of a custom association form. For details about custom forms, refer to Chapter 19.
InstantiationUrl	Optional *Text* attribute that defines the URL of a custom initiation form. For details about custom forms, refer to Chapter 19.
ModificationUrl	Optional *Text* attribute that defines the URL of a custom modification form. For details about custom forms, refer to Chapter 19.
StatusUrl	Obsolete *Text* attribute. Avoid using *StatusUrl*.
TaskListContentTypeId	Optional *Text* attribute That specifies the ID of the custom task content type that will be assigned to the workflow's tasks list.

The *AssociationData* child element allows defining custom association data to pass to the workflow during association with its target. The *MetaData* child element contains any valid XML metadata for defining custom forms, custom statuses, custom status page, and so on. For example, through the *AssociationCategories* child element of the *MetaData* element, you can define the target associations for your custom workflow. Lastly, the *Categories* element is reserved by Microsoft for future use. Listing 18-3 illustrates a *Workflow* feature element for deploying a workflow that targets only lists.

LISTING 18-3 The *Workflow* feature element for deploying a list-only workflow definition.

```
<?xml version="1.0" encoding="utf-8" ?>
<Elements xmlns="http://schemas.microsoft.com/sharepoint/">
  <Workflow
    Name="SampleApprovalWorkflow"
    Description="My SharePoint Workflow"
    Id="faad7421-538f-475b-85ec-7488c628c486"
    CodeBesideClass="DevLeap.SP2010.SampleApprovalWorkflow.ApprovalWorkflow"
    CodeBesideAssembly="DevLeap.SP2010.SampleApprovalWorkflow, Version=1.0.0.0,
```

```
Culture=neutral, PublicKeyToken=9719971a17e963bb">
    <Categories/>
    <MetaData>
      <AssociationCategories>List</AssociationCategories>
      <StatusPageUrl>_layouts/WrkStat.aspx</StatusPageUrl>
    </MetaData>
  </Workflow>
</Elements>
```

 Note The value of the *CodeBesideAssembly* should appear on a single line in your XML code; it's divided in two lines here due to typographic display constraints.

Workflow Association

To associate the workflow with a target list, you need to do some manual work through the management UI of SharePoint. First, browse to the Settings page of the target list and select the Workflow Settings menu item, under the Permissions And Management menu group. (You can also click the Workflow Settings button on the Settings Ribbon.) If your list does not have any associated workflows, the Add A Workflow page appears; otherwise, if the list already has one or more workflow associations, a page for managing those associations (or for creating a new one) appears. Figure 18-10 depicts the Add A Workflow page.

You need to provide the target of the workflow by selecting all the contents or a specific Content Type only. Next, you need to select the workflow to associate with the current list. There are also two sections for selecting the task list and the history list to use for the workflow association infrastructure. You can select existing lists, or you can ask SharePoint to create new list instances for you. Finally, you must choose the Start Options, as you do with workflows defined in SharePoint Designer 2010. You can allow users who have edit permissions to start the workflow manually; optionally, you can restrict manual workflow start only to users with the permissions to manage the current list. You can also decide to start the workflow automatically for newly-created items, or for changed items.

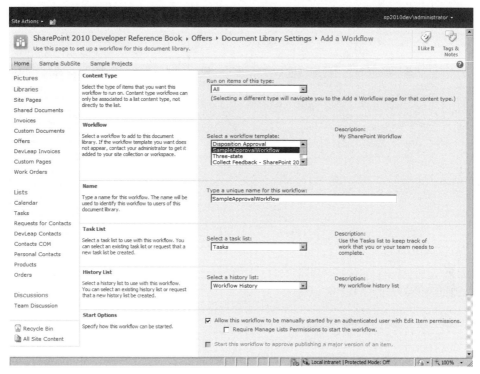

FIGURE 18-10 The Add A Workflow page for a list.

When you click the OK button in the current page, you will either see the custom association page, if your workflow has one, or if not, the workflow association process will be completed, and you will be able to use your workflow.

After you associate a workflow instance with a target list, you will be able to come back to the Workflow Settings page and manage the association by selecting it in the list of available workflows.

Workflow Versioning

The Workflow Settings page gives you the option to remove an existing workflow association. This is an interesting task, because when you remove one, you must choose what will happen to the running instances of that workflow. Figure 18-11 shows the Remove Workflows page that displays when you choose to remove an association.

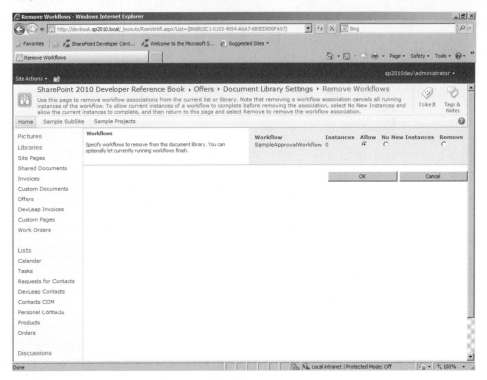

FIGURE 18-11 The Remove Workflows page for a list.

You have the option to force workflow association removal, interrupting any running instance, by selecting the Remove option. Otherwise, you can select the No New Instances option, which allows the running instances to complete, but disables the capability to create new instances of that workflow. Usually, these options are very useful when performing workflow maintenance or an upgrade. Recall that an idle workflow instance is persisted in the content database of the current Site Collection and will be reloaded in memory when execution starts again as the result of a user's task change, a delay expiration, and so on.

When this occurs, you have no guarantee that the same workflow version will be still available on the current environment. For example, there could be a newer version, potentially different from the original one used during instance creation.

If you decide to forcibly remove the workflow association without waiting for any running instances to conclude, the workflow engine of SharePoint will terminate running instances immediately, and thus avoid any kind of issues related to workflow versioning. Of course, you will lose any data or information status about the running workflow instances.

On the other hand, if you decide to prevent new instances of the workflow, but you leave all the running instances in their state, you will have the opportunity to wait for their completion. Just after the completion of all the running instances, you can forcibly remove the association from the target list. In the meantime, you can already associate a new version of the workflow and start using it on the other items of the target list. Of course, in this last situation, you need to deploy the new version with a new package instead of upgrading the existing one.

Correlation Tokens

In the sample illustrated in Figure 18-9, you can see that the workflow has a *CorrelationToken* property defined in the *OnWorkflowActivated* activity instance. Both the *createApprovalTask* activity and the *completeApprovalTask* activity have a *CorrelationToken* property, too. In addition, the sample workflow is configured to share the same value for the *CorrelationToken* property between both the task-related activities, but with a bounded variable different than that used for the correlation token of the *OnWorkflowActivated* activity instance. This may be leading you to wonder what exactly a correlation token is.

You might think about a correlation token as a unique identifier that correlates activities in the workflow together and with the hosting environment. In fact, when the hosting environment receives an event targeting a specific workflow instance, the target instance is identified by the workflow instance ID and—in case of a workflow for SharePoint—by a workflow specific correlation token, too. The hosting environment determines the right workflow instance to deliver the event to, based on that instance ID and the correlation token, searching an in memory or a persisted instance with that instance ID and serving that correlation token.

When you design a new SharePoint workflow, you have a correlation token defined in the *OnWorkflowActivated* activity instance, and you should use that correlation token variable for each activity that works at the workflow level. If you have activities with a scope tighter than the whole workflow and that need to work against the same context, like activities for managing a specific task (*CreateTask*, *UpdateTask*, *CompleteTask*, *OnTaskChanged*, and so on), you should define a correlation token specific for these activities.

As an example, consider a workflow definition for managing a document approval process submitted in parallel to multiple approvers. You might have at least two document approvers with a specific approval task assigned to each of them. When the workflow hosting environment (for instance, SharePoint) needs to notify to the target workflow instance that one of these two tasks has been completed, it uses the workflow instance ID to identify the target workflow instance. However, the instance ID will not suffice to make the workflow instance aware of the task that has been completed or about the *OnTaskChanged* activity that it needs to wake up. Using a correlation token that correlates all the activities related to a specific task will help the runtime and the workflow instance to uniquely identity the target task inside the workflow and the corresponding target activity for the event. That is why each specific task in the workflow needs to have its own correlation token, sharing it with each activity related to the same specific task.

Site Workflows

There might be times when you need to design a workflow for executing a site-level task, for example, for changing a field on every item of a list, or for updating a field in some items in any list of a site, and so on. Before SharePoint 2010, one possibility to satisfy this need was to create a custom dummy list with fake items, to associate a workflow to that list, and to execute instances of the workflow against a fake item, but ignoring it. Beginning with SharePoint 2010, concept of site-level workflows was introduced to address these kinds of needs.

A site-level workflow is almost the same as an item-level workflow, but it doesn't need an associated list item to work against. Because site-level workflows do not have an associated list item, you need to start them manually. To start such workflows, go to the View All Site Content page and select the Site Workflows command. A list of the available workflows appears that offers exactly the same user experience as that of item-level workflows. For example, you can start the workflow, provide initiation parameters (if there is an initiation form page), and monitor the workflow status page and history list.

One last thing to consider when working with site-level workflows; in the workflow design, you will not have a reference to the current target item, because there isn't a target list item. Thus, your code needs to find its context on its own by using the SharePoint Server Object Model and probably by working with some *CodeActivity* instances.

Summary

In this chapter, you saw how to develop a custom workflow definition by using Visual Studio 2010. In particular, you learned about the very basic outline of a workflow definition, the fundamental activities provided by SharePoint, and the deployment and versioning of a workflow definition. In addition, you saw what correlation tokens are and how to use them during workflow design. Lastly, you learned about site-level workflows.

Chapter 19

Workflow Forms

Chapter 18, "Workflows with Visual Studio 2010," covered the requirements for developing a basic workflow, one with only the bare minimum of realistic user interaction. In this chapter, you will learn how to create custom .ASPX forms so that your workflows can interact realistically with end users.

 Important You can create custom workflow forms using .ASPX pages or Microsoft InfoPath 2010, using Microsoft InfoPath Services on the server side. However, the InfoPath method requires you to have Microsoft SharePoint Server 2010. If you implement custom forms as .ASPX pages, you can use the same workflow solution with both Microsoft SharePoint Foundation 2010 and Microsoft SharePoint Server 2010. Therefore, this chapter will cover .ASPX forms only.

Management Forms

The first group of forms that you can define to extend a workflow user interface combines the association, initiation, and modification forms. They are nearly the same in their structure and definition. These forms also give you an opportunity to provide some configuration and initialization parameters to the workflow instances when they are started. However, the association form typically targets an administrative user and is used while associating a workflow definition to a target list, Content Type, or site. The initiation form targets end users and is presented to them when they manually start a workflow instance. If a workflow association is configured for automatic startup, the initiation form will not be invoked and the workflow instance will receive only association data. That is why an initiation form usually allows configuring a subset of the parameters available in the association form. Thus, the initiation form is used to customize the behavior of a specific workflow instance manually started, while the association form provides the default configuration parameters for automatic startup. Finally, the modification form is useful when you need to change the configuration of a workflow instance that is already running.

For example, suppose that you need to extend and improve the offers approval workflow introduced in Chapter 18. To begin, you could define a custom content type to model a custom concept of Offer. Listing 19-1 shows how it is defined using a sample Content Type named *DevLeapOffer*. For further details about creating and provisioning custom content types, read Chapter 10, "Data Provisioning." Keep in mind though that creating a custom Content Type is not mandatory for supporting workflow forms. So, the sample code for this chapter defines a custom *DevLeapOffer* Content Type just for the sake of thoroughness and to respect SharePoint 2010 best practices.

LISTING 19-1 The XML code for provisioning a custom *DevLeapOffer* Content Type.

```xml
<?xml version="1.0" encoding="utf-8"?>
<Elements xmlns="http://schemas.microsoft.com/sharepoint/">
  <!-- Site Columns used by the Content Type -->
  <Field ID="{43A5D26C-8924-44A5-80F5-E24131838E90}"
    Name="DevLeapOfferCode" StaticName="DevLeapOfferCode" DisplayName="Offer Code"
    Type="Text" Group="DevLeap Columns" Sortable="TRUE" />
  <Field ID="{54C4A2FF-D9F4-495F-B18B-AFB32A58F78A}"
    Name="DevLeapOfferEuroAmount" StaticName="DevLeapOfferEuroAmount"
    DisplayName="Euro Amount" Type="Currency" LCID="1040"
    Group="DevLeap Columns" Sortable="TRUE" />
  <Field ID="{12DAC41E-3E7C-4A1B-83FB-557E8120305D}"
    Name="DevLeapOfferStatus" StaticName="DevLeapOfferStatus"
    DisplayName="Status" Type="Choice" Group="DevLeap Columns"
    Sortable="TRUE">
    <Default>Inserted</Default>
    <CHOICES>
      <CHOICE>Inserted</CHOICE>
      <CHOICE>Approved</CHOICE>
      <CHOICE>Rejected</CHOICE>
    </CHOICES>
  </Field>
  <!-- Parent ContentType: Document (0x0101) -->
  <ContentType ID="0x0101001c5496fe0188439099e8a0b19007fb27"
               Name="DevLeapOffer"
               Group="DevLeap Content Types"
               Description="DevLeap Offer Content Type"
               Inherits="TRUE"
               Version="0">
    <FieldRefs>
      <FieldRef ID="{43A5D26C-8924-44A5-80F5-E24131838E90}"
        Name="DevLeapOfferCode" Required="TRUE" />
      <FieldRef ID="{54C4A2FF-D9F4-495F-B18B-AFB32A58F78A}"
        Name="DevLeapOfferEuroAmount" Required="TRUE" />
      <FieldRef ID="{12DAC41E-3E7C-4A1B-83FB-557E8120305D}"
        Name="DevLeapOfferStatus" ShowInEditForm="False" ShowInNewForm="False" />
    </FieldRefs>
  </ContentType>
</Elements>
```

In this code, each offer is characterized by a *DevLeapOfferEuroAmount* field with a value of type *Currency*. For educational reasons, you will review the offers approval workflow that you defined in Chapter 18, which was designed to automatically approve offers with an amount lower than a parametric lower-level bound. Every offer above that limit will require a manager's explicit approval and the assignment of an approval task to an "Offer Manager." Figure 19-1 displays the outline of the custom offers approval workflow presented in this chapter.

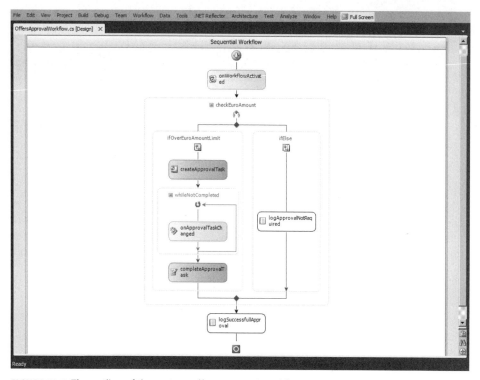

FIGURE 19-1 The outline of the custom offers approval workflow.

Association Form

Working within the context of the workflow presented in Figure 19-1, to acquire the lower level bound value along with the name of the user that will be the offer manager in case of approval requirement, the workflow will need an association form. Through this form you will accept the default values for both the lower-level bound and the manager's username.

Figure 19-2 shows a preview of the association form, which represents the goal of this section. Remember that it will be presented to the administrative users while associating the workflow with its target list or Content Type.

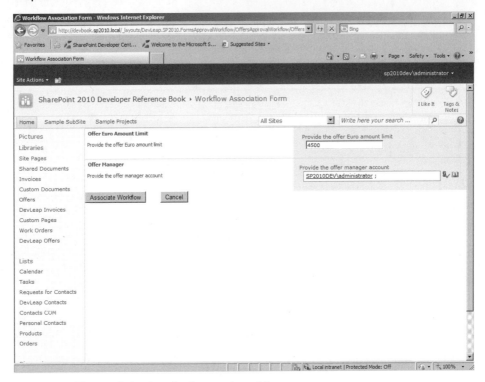

FIGURE 19-2 The association form for the sample workflow.

The form is a common ASP.NET page, but it is deployed as an application page of SharePoint. In Chapter 9, "Extending the User Interface," you saw how to develop and deploy an application page, so it will be not covered here again in detail. But it is interesting to understand the underlying infrastructure for that page.

You can create this page by using Microsoft Visual Studio 2010. To do so, right-click a workflow item in the Solution Explorer (within a SharePoint project of course) then select Workflow Association Form, which represents a skeleton for an association page. After you add an item based on that model, an .aspx page appears that contains some useful content, ready to use. This page will be provisioned in the Layouts folder of SharePoint and will behave as a normal application page. Listing 19-2 illustrates the code template for the .aspx page.

LISTING 19-2 The code template for the .ASPX page of an association form.

```
<%@ Assembly Name="$SharePoint.Project.AssemblyFullName$" %>
<%@ Assembly Name="Microsoft.Web.CommandUI, Version=14.0.0.0, Culture=neutral,
PublicKeyToken=71e9bce111e9429c" %>
<%@ Import Namespace="Microsoft.SharePoint" %>
<%@ Import Namespace="Microsoft.SharePoint.ApplicationPages" %>
<%@ Register Tagprefix="SharePoint" Namespace="Microsoft.SharePoint.WebControls"
```

```
Assembly="Microsoft.SharePoint, Version=14.0.0.0, Culture=neutral,
  PublicKeyToken=71e9bce111e9429c" %>
<%@ Register Tagprefix="Utilities" Namespace="Microsoft.SharePoint.Utilities"
Assembly="Microsoft.SharePoint, Version=14.0.0.0, Culture=neutral,
  PublicKeyToken=71e9bce111e9429c" %>
<%@ Register Tagprefix="asp" Namespace="System.Web.UI"
  Assembly="System.Web.Extensions, Version=3.5.0.0, Culture=neutral,
  PublicKeyToken=31bf3856ad364e35" %>

<%@ Page Language="C#"
    DynamicMasterPageFile="~masterurl/default.master"
    AutoEventWireup="true"
Inherits="DevLeap.SP2010.FormsApprovalWorkflow.OffersApprovalAssociationForm"
    CodeBehind="OffersApprovalAssociationForm.aspx.cs" %>

<asp:Content ID="Main" ContentPlaceHolderID="PlaceHolderMain" runat="server">
    <asp:Button ID="AssociateWorkflow" runat="server"
      OnClick="AssociateWorkflow_Click" Text="Associate Workflow" />
          
    <asp:Button ID="Cancel" runat="server" Text="Cancel" OnClick="Cancel_Click" />
</asp:Content>

<asp:Content ID="PageTitle" ContentPlaceHolderID="PlaceHolderPageTitle" runat="server">
    Workflow Association Form
</asp:Content>

<asp:Content ID="PageTitleInTitleArea" runat="server"
  ContentPlaceHolderID="PlaceHolderPageTitleInTitleArea">
    Workflow Association Form
</asp:Content>
```

This is a standard SharePoint .aspx page, with a content place holder for the main content region (*PlaceHolderMain*) of the master page and some other content placeholders. If you wish to extend the content of the page, you should be careful to adhere to the standard style and presentation of controls of SharePoint 2010. To better present content and fields, you should take advantage of the native controls available in the SharePoint14_Root\TEMPLATES\ CONTROLTEMPLATES shared folder. For example, imagine that you want to configure the lower-level bound for the *DevLeapOfferEuroAmount* field, and you also want to request who is the default "Offer Manager" to ask for approval. You need a custom association form to carry this out. Listing 19-3 presents the *PlaceHolderMain* content region that makes this form possible.

LISTING 19-3 The *PlaceHolderMain* content region for a custom association form.

```
<asp:Content ID="Main" ContentPlaceHolderID="PlaceHolderMain" runat="server">
  <table border="0" cellspacing="0" cellpadding="0" class="ms-propertysheet">

    <wssuc:InputFormSection runat="server" Title="Offer Euro Amount Limit"
    Description="Provide the offer Euro amount limit">
      <Template_InputFormControls>
        <tr valign="top">
          <td class="ms-authoringcontrols" width="10"> </td>
          <td class="ms-authoringcontrols" colspan="4">
            Provide the offer Euro amount limit<br/>
            <table border="0" cellspacing="1">
              <tr>
                <td> </td>
                <td class="ms-authoringcontrols">
                  <input size="25" class="ms-input" type="TexL"
                  name="OfferEuroAmountLimit" ID="OfferEuroAmountLimit"
                  runat="server" maxlength="15" />
                </td>
              </tr>
            </table>
          </td>
        </tr>
      </Template_InputFormControls>
    </wssuc:InputFormSection>

    <wssuc:InputFormSection runat="server" Title="Offer Manager"
      Description="Provide the offer manager account">
      <Template_InputFormControls>
        <tr valign="top">
          <td class="ms-authoringcontrols" width="10">& nbsp;</td>
          <td class="ms-authoringcontrols" colspan="4">
            Provide the offer manager account<br/>
            <table border="0" cellspacing="1">
              <tr>
                <td> </td>
                <td class="ms-authoringcontrols">
                  <SharePoint:PeopleEditor ID="OfferManager" runat="server"
                  width="350px" AllowEmpty="false" MultiSelect="false"
                  SelectionSet="User" />
                </td>
              </tr>
            </table>
          </td>
        </tr>
      </Template_InputFormControls>
    </wssuc:InputFormSection>
  </table>

  <asp:Button ID="AssociateWorkflow" runat="server"
    OnClick="AssociateWorkflow_Click" Text="Associate Workflow" />
          
  <asp:Button ID="Cancel" runat="server" Text="Cancel" OnClick="Cancel_Click" />
</asp:Content>
```

The page makes use of a classic HTML input control of type *Text* to acquire the lower-level bound for the *DevLeapOfferEuroAmount* field. Then, it uses a *PeopleEditor* control of SharePoint to browse for the default "Offer Manager" user. Both the *textbox* and the *PeopleEditor* controls are wrapped by an *InputFormSection* control. The *PeopleEditor* and the *InputFormSection* controls are not standard ASP.NET server controls, but they are part of the native SharePoint environment, as you have seen in Chapter 15, "Developing Service Applications."

The association page has a code-behind class inheriting from the base class *Microsoft. SharePoint.WebControls.LayoutsPageBase*, which is one of the standard base classes for SharePoint custom pages. Listing 19-4 shows the template-based code of the code-behind class.

LISTING 19-4 The C# code behind the out-of-the-box association form page.

```
public partial class OffersApprovalAssociationForm : LayoutsPageBase {
  // Private fields declaration omitted for the sake of simplicity

  protected void Page_Load(object sender, EventArgs e) {
    InitializeParams();
  }

  private void PopulateFormFields(SPWorkflowAssociation existingAssociation) {
      // Optionally, add code here to pre-populate your form fields.
  }

  // This method is called when the user clicks
  // the button to associate the workflow.
  private string GetAssociationData() {
    // TODO: Return a string that contains the association data that
    // will be passed to the workflow. Typically, this is in XML format.
    return string.Empty;
  }

  protected void AssociateWorkflow_Click(object sender, EventArgs e) {
    // Optionally, add code here to perform additional steps
    // before associating your workflow
    try {
      CreateTaskList();
      CreateHistoryList();
      HandleAssociateWorkflow();
      SPUtility.Redirect("WrkSetng.aspx", SPRedirectFlags.RelativeToLayoutsPage,
        HttpContext.Current, Page.ClientQueryString);
    }
    catch (Exception ex) {
      SPUtility.TransferToErrorPage(String.Format(
        CultureInfo.CurrentCulture, workflowAssociationFailed, ex.Message));
    }
  }
}
```

```
    protected void Cancel_Click(object sender, EventArgs e) {
      SPUtility.Redirect("WrkSetng.aspx", SPRedirectFlags.RelativeToLayoutsPage,
        HttpContext.Current, Page.ClientQueryString);
    }

    // Code omitted for the sake of brevity and simplicity
  }
```

Most of the code in the code-behind file is plumbing that you do not need to be concerned with. The only points of interest for you are the *PopulateFormFields* method, which can be used to populate form fields with defaults or suggested values, and the *GetAssociationData* method, which is the core method of this class.

When a user associates a workflow definition with a target, if you have an association form, the *GetAssociationData* method will be invoked to extract the values configured in the page. The result of this method will be assigned to the *AssociationData* property of the workflow association. Then, whenever a workflow instance is created for that association, SharePoint will pass the value of the *AssociationData* to the workflow instance via the *WorkflowProperties* property of the *OnWorkflowActivated* activity.

Because the association data is just a string, usually it is formatted and used as a string representation of an XML data structure. For example, you can design your workflow association configuration as an XML Schema, such as the one shown in Listing 19-5.

LISTING 19-5 The XML Schema of a hypothetical configuration for an association page.

```
<?xml version="1.0" encoding="utf-8"?>
<xsd:schema id="AssociationDataConfiguration"
    targetNamespace="http://schemas.devleap.com/AssociationDataConfiguration"
    elementFormDefault="qualified"
    xmlns="http://schemas.devleap.com/AssociationDataConfiguration"
    xmlns:xsd="http://www.w3.org/2001/XMLSchema">
  <xsd:element name="AssociationDataConfiguration">
    <xsd:complexType>
      <xsd:sequence>
        <xsd:element name="OfferEuroAmountLimit" type="xsd:decimal" />
        <xsd:element name="OfferManager" type="xsd:string" />
      </xsd:sequence>
    </xsd:complexType>
  </xsd:element>
</xsd:schema>
```

Note that two elements are defined for holding the *OfferEuroAmountLimit* and the *OfferManager* parameters.

Now, using tools such as XSD.EXE or SVCUTIL.EXE (both available in the SDK of Microsoft .NET Framework), you can create a .NET class-based representation of that XML data structure. Here is the sample syntax for invoking the XSD.EXE command line tool:

```
xsd -c AssociationDataConfiguration.xsd /n:DevLeap.SP2010.FormsApprovalWorkflow
```

If you serialize an instance of the *AssociationDataConfiguration* generated class, the serializer will produce the expected XML, while if you already have XML, you can create a class instance deserializing data with that structure. Thus, in your *GetAssociationData* method you simply need to create an instance of the serializable type that you created from the XSD of Listing 19-4, configure it, and serialize it using the proper serializer. The result of the serialization process will be returned to the SharePoint workflow environment as a *String* and will be deserialized during workflow execution, to come back to an instance of the *AssociationDataConfiguration* class. Listing 19-6 shows the definition of the *AssociationDataConfiguration* class.

LISTING 19-6 The *AssociationDataConfiguration* class definition.

```
[System.CodeDom.Compiler.GeneratedCodeAttribute("xsd", "4.0.30319.1")]
[System.SerializableAttribute()]
[System.Diagnostics.DebuggerStepThroughAttribute()]
[System.ComponentModel.DesignerCategoryAttribute("code")]
[System.Xml.Serialization.XmlTypeAttribute(AnonymousType=true,
  Namespace="http://schemas.devleap.com/AssociationDataConfiguration")]
[System.Xml.Serialization.XmlRootAttribute(
Namespace="http://schemas.devleap.com/AssociationDataConfiguration", IsNullable=false)]
public partial class AssociationDataConfiguration {

    private decimal offerEuroAmountLimitField;
    private string offerManagerField;

    public decimal OfferEuroAmountLimit {
        get { return this.offerEuroAmountLimitField; }
        set { this.offerEuroAmountLimitField = value; }
    }

    public string OfferManager {
        get { return this.offerManagerField; }
        set { this.offerManagerField = value; }
    }
}
```

Listing 19-7 illustrates an implementation of the *GetAssociationData* method, using an *XmlSerializer*.

LISTING 19-7 The code of a sample *GetAssociationData* method.

```
// This method is called when the user clicks the button to associate the workflow.
private string GetAssociationData() {
  // Define an instance of the serializable type holding the AssociationData
  AssociationDataConfiguration associationData = new AssociationDataConfiguration();

  // Set the value for the OfferEuroAmountLimit field
  associationData.OfferEuroAmountLimit =
    Decimal.Parse(this.OfferEuroAmountLimit.Value);

  // Validate the content of the PeopleEditor in order
  // to populate the list of Entities
  this.OfferManager.Validate();

  // If there are selected entities
  if (this.OfferManager.Entities.Count > 0) {
    // Set the currently selected value for the OfferManager field
    associationData.OfferManager =
      ((PickerEntity)this.OfferManager.Entities[0]).Description;
  }

  // Return the AssociationData serialized as an XML String
  return WorkflowUtility.SerializeData(associationData);
}
```

The method implementation retrieves selected values from the ASP.NET server controls configured on the page.

Initiation Form

After implementing an association form, you will probably also need an initiation form, if you would like to allow end users to provide some custom parameters while starting the workflow instance. An initiation form can also be used to override values of parameters configured during workflow association. An initiation form is nearly the same as an association form, except that it is rendered during the startup phase of a single workflow instance.

In Visual Studio, there is an item template, just as there is for the association form. To access it, right-click a workflow item in the Solution Explorer, and then select Workflow Initiation Form. After you have added that item, an .ASPX page appears, containing the base skeleton of the initiation form. This page is almost the same as the one presented in Listing 19-2. Inside the .ASPX code, you must define the ASP.NET server controls for rendering the user interface of the form. The code-behind this class is slightly different from that of the association form. This is because an initiation form has the option to load the values to show within its controls from the current workflow association definition, and then give them back to the SharePoint environment as soon as the end user starts the workflow instance. Listing 19-8 displays the out-of-the-box code-behind of an initiation form.

LISTING 19-8 The C# code behind the out-of-the-box initiation form page.

```
public partial class OffersApprovalInitiationForm : LayoutsPageBase {
  protected void Page_Load(object sender, EventArgs e) {
    InitializeParams();
    // Optionally, add code here to pre-populate your form fields.
  }

  // This method is called when the user clicks the button to start the workflow.
  private string GetInitiationData() {
    // TODO: Return a string that contains the association data that
    // will be passed to the workflow. Typically, this is in XML format.
    return string.Empty;
  }
  protected void StartWorkflow_Click(object sender, EventArgs e) {
    // Optionally, add code here to perform additional steps
    // before starting your workflow
    try {
      HandleStartWorkflow();
    }
    catch (Exception) {
      SPUtility.TransferToErrorPage(
        SPHttpUtility.UrlKeyValueEncode("Failed to Start Workflow"));
    }
  }

  protected void Cancel_Click(object sender, EventArgs e) {
    SPUtility.Redirect("Workflow.aspx", SPRedirectFlags.RelativeToLayoutsPage,
      HttpContext.Current, Page.ClientQueryString);
  }

  // Code omitted for the sake of brevity and simplicity
}
```

The base class is still the *Microsoft.SharePoint.WebControls.LayoutsPageBase* class. However, here the method to implement is *GetInitiationData*, which behaves exactly the same as the *GetAssociationData* method of the association form.

Listing 19-9 shows a sample implementation of this method for an initiation form page that targets the offers approval workflow.

LISTING 19-9 Implementing the *GetInitiationData* method.

```
// This method is called when the user clicks the button to start the workflow.
private string GetInitiationData() {
  // Define an instance of the serializable type holding the InitiationData
  InitiationDataConfiguration initiationData = new InitiationDataConfiguration();

  // Validate the content of the PeopleEditor in order to populate
  // the list of Entities
  this.OfferManager.Validate();
```

```
  // If there are selected entities
  if (this.OfferManager.Entities.Count > 0) {
    // Set the currently selected value for the OfferManager field
    initiationData.OfferManager =
      ((PickerEntity)this.OfferManager.Entities[0]).Description;
  }

  // Set the value for the ApprovalRequestNotes field
  initiationData.ApprovalRequestNotes = this.ApprovalRequestNotes.Text;

  // Return the InitiationData serialized as an XML String
  return WorkflowUtility.SerializeData(initiationData);
}
```

Optionally, you can also customize the *Page_Load* method to preconfigure values of server controls, eventually loading their content from the workflow *AssociationData*. This is particularly useful when your initiation form prompts the end users with parameters that have already been configured during the workflow's association, but you would like set them up so that their values can be overridden by the end users. Listing 19-10 presents a sample implementation of the *Page_Load* method that behaves in this manner.

LISTING 19-10 A customized *Page_Load* method.

```
protected void Page_Load(object sender, EventArgs e) {
  InitializeParams();

  // Optionally, add code here to pre-populate your form fields.
  if (!this.IsPostBack) {
    this.associationGuid = Request.Params["TemplateID"];

    // Retrieve the current AssociationData configuration
    if ((association != null) && !String.IsNullOrEmpty(association.AssociationData))
    {
      SPWorkflowAssociation association =
        this.workflowList.WorkflowAssociations[new Guid(this.associationGuid)];
      AssociationDataConfiguration associationData =
        WorkflowUtility.DeserializeData<AssociationDataConfiguration>(
        association.AssociationData);

      // Set the current value for the PeopleEditor control
      this.OfferManager.CommaSeparatedAccounts = associationData.OfferManager;
      // And validate that value
      this.OfferManager.Validate();
    }
  }
}
```

Modification Form

Whenever you have a workflow instance already running, and you'd like to change its configuration, you need to use a modification form. For example, when you start a new instance of the offers approval workflow, you also provide the username of an "Offer Manager." If the selected offer manager is out of office for vacation, you could use a modification form to change the currently selected Offer Manager account, without stopping the current workflow instance and starting another one for such a temporary circumstance. To support this scenario, you need to enable modification on your workflow by using the *EnableWorkflowModification* activity and providing a *ModificationID* that identifies the modification context as well as a *ContextData* property, which represents any custom context information that you want to give to the modification form. Then you need to wait for the modification to complete, utilizing the *OnWorkflowModified* activity and reading the *ContextData* property of type string for the new configuration of the workflow instance. Having modification enabled and supported in a workflow implies having a modification form, which is not provided as a native page template in Visual Studio 2010. However, a modification form is almost the same as an instantiation form.

Task Forms

Task forms are the most interesting and useful forms that you can build for a workflow. In fact, trough tasks, you can define custom forms for interacting with the various users of a workflow instance. As you have already seen in Chapter 16, "SharePoint Workflows Architecture," a workflow interacts with the end users through a list of tasks, and every time a workflow needs to query its users, it assigns them a task. Then, when the users edit or complete that task, the *TaskService* runtime service—internally corresponding to the *SPWinOETaskService* class—raises an event into the workflow instance.

Workflow Tasks

Beginning with SharePoint version 2007, there is a native Content Type named Workflow Task, which has an ID of 0x010801 and is hidden and reserved for custom developments. However, the Workflow Task provides a standard user interface as well as standard fields, such as *Predecessors*, *Priority*, *Status*, *% Complete*, and so on. In a real workflow solution, you probably need to prompt end users with a custom user interface and with custom fields. With SharePoint, you can provision custom Content Types with specific fields and management forms. Thus, you can consider defining custom workflow tasks, inheriting from the base workflow task Content Type. Listing 19-10 illustrates the XML code provisioning a custom workflow task that supports the offers approval workflow.

LISTING 19-10 XML code provisioning a custom *OfferApprovalTask* Content Type.

```xml
<?xml version="1.0" encoding="utf-8"?>
<Elements xmlns="http://schemas.microsoft.com/sharepoint/">

  <!-- Site Columns used by the Content Type -->
  <Field ID="{4675B905-38E1-4277-BD13-D13FEADCC87F}"
    Name="DevLeapApprovalTaskNotes" StaticName="DevLeapApprovalTaskNotes"
    DisplayName="Approval Task Notes" Type="Note"
    RichText="FALSE" Group="DevLeap Columns" Sortable="TRUE" />
  <Field ID="{841410DE-EFEB-49B3-8A8E-0D006FFCE879}"
    Name="DevLeapApprovalTaskOutcome" StaticName="DevLeapApprovalTaskOutcome"
    DisplayName="Approval Task Outcome" Type="Choice"
    Group="DevLeap Columns" Sortable="TRUE">
    <Default>Pending Approval</Default>
    <CHOICES>
      <CHOICE>Pending Approval</CHOICE>
      <CHOICE>Approved</CHOICE>
      <CHOICE>Rejected</CHOICE>
    </CHOICES>
  </Field>

  <!-- Parent ContentType: Workflow Task (0x010801) -->
  <ContentType ID="0x010801001ee27bf9c4974b87b1c0f25fa677d6f8"
               Name="OfferApprovalTask" Group="DevLeap Content Types"
               Description="Offer Approval Task Content Type"
               Inherits="FALSE" Version="0">
    <FieldRefs>
      <FieldRef ID="{4675B905-38E1-4277-BD13-D13FEADCC87F}"
        Name="DevLeapApprovalTaskNotes" />
      <FieldRef ID="{841410DE-EFEB-49B3-8A8E-0D006FFCE879}"
        Name="DevLeapApprovalTaskOutcome" />
    </FieldRefs>
    <XmlDocuments>
      <XmlDocument
        NamespaceURI="http://schemas.microsoft.com/sharepoint/v3/contenttype/forms/url">
        <FormUrls
          xmlns="http://schemas.microsoft.com/sharepoint/v3/contenttype/forms/url">
<Display>_layouts/FormsApprovalWorkflow/OfferApprovalTaskForm.aspx</Display>
<Edit>_layouts/FormsApprovalWorkflow/OfferApprovalTaskForm.aspx</Edit>
        </FormUrls>
      </XmlDocument>
    </XmlDocuments>
  </ContentType>

</Elements>
```

The first thing you might have noticed is that the content type inherits from the standard Workflow Task ID 0x010801. Next, there is the *Inherits* attribute with a value of *FALSE*, which is mandatory to have a custom user interface for the custom task. By default, when you add a new Content Type definition, Visual Studio 2010 declares the *Inherits* attribute with a value of *TRUE*. However, this configuration disables rendering of any custom form for the Content Type. In addition, the content type has a couple of fields, one to provide an outcome regarding the offer approval process, and another for leaving some notes about the approval. Finally, the Content Type declares a custom *XmlDocuments* section, which in general can be used to define any kind of custom XML configuration items. In the event of a content type with a custom set of forms, you can employ the *FormUrls* element to define the URLs of customized forms for rendering your Content Type. The *NamespaceURI* attribute applied to the *XmlDocument* element is required in order to instruct SharePoint about the target schema that will be defined inside the *XmlDocument*. Then, the *Display* element defines the URL of the display form; the *Edit* element defines the URL of the edit form; lastly, you can define a *New* element, so that you can provide a custom form URL for adding items.

More Information To learn more about custom forms for Content Types, read the "FormUrls Schema Overview" document available at *http://msdn.microsoft.com/en-us/library/ms473210. aspx*.

In Listing 19-10, the custom Content Type has the same URL for rendering both the edit and the display forms. The code sample does not define a *New* form because the workflow task will always be created by the workflow, and not by the end user through the web interface. That URL corresponds to a custom application page that you have to define by yourself. Unfortunately, there isn't a custom Task Form project item template natively provided by Visual Studio. However, you can find many templates on the network. Otherwise, you can create a standard application page, just implementing some plumbing code by yourself, eventually defining a custom base class inheriting from the standard *LayoutsPageBase* and adding the plumbing code to that class. Figure 19-3 illustrates the custom user interface defined for the *OfferApprovalTask* content type of Listing 19-10.

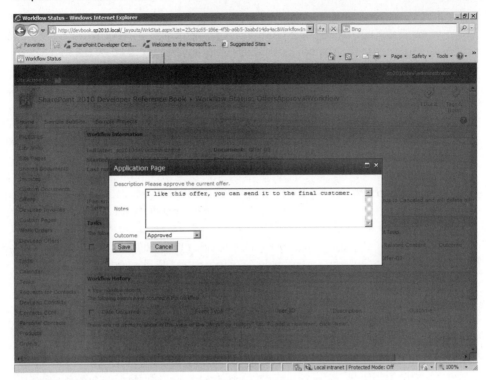

FIGURE 19-3 The custom edit form for the *OfferApprovalTask* custom Content Type.

Listing 19-11 displays the .ASPX code of the *PlaceHolderMain* content region of the sample edit form.

LISTING 19-11 The .ASPX code defining the *PlaceHolderMain* region of the custom *OfferApprovalTask* form.

```
<table>
  <tr>
    <td>Description</td>
    <td><asp:Label ID="DevLeapApprovalTaskDescription" runat="server" /></td>
  </tr>
  <tr>
    <td>Notes</td>
    <td><asp:TextBox ID="DevLeapApprovalTaskNotes" TextMode="MultiLine"
      Columns="60" Rows="5" runat="server" /></td>
  </tr>
  <tr>
    <td>Outcome</td>
```

```
   <td>
      <asp:DropDownList ID="DevLeapApprovalTaskOutcome" runat="server">
         <asp:ListItem Value="Pending Approval" Text="Pending Approval" />
         <asp:ListItem Value="Approved" Text="Approved" />
         <asp:ListItem Value="Rejected" Text="Rejected" />
      </asp:DropDownList>
   </td>
 </tr>
</table>

<asp:Button ID="SaveApprovalTask" runat="server"
  OnClick="SaveApprovalTask_Click" Text="Save" />
        
<asp:Button ID="Cancel" runat="server" Text="Cancel" OnClick="Cancel_Click" />
```

In Listing 19-11, the .ASPX code is simple and fairly common. It defines some ASP.NET server controls for managing the interaction with the end user and rendering the interface illustrated in Figure 19-3. However, the code-behind of the custom form page deserves more attention. Listing 19-12 presents the code-behind of the form.

LISTING 19-12 The code-behind the custom *OfferApprovalTask* form.

```
public partial class OfferApprovalTaskForm : LayoutsPageBase {

   protected SPList targetTasksList;
   SPListItem targetTask;
   protected SPWorkflow workflowInstance;
   protected SPWorkflowModification workflowModification;

   protected void Page_Load(object sender, EventArgs e) {
      // Retrieve the current task list and task item
      targetTasksList = Web.Lists[new Guid(Request.Params["List"])];
      targetTask = targetTasksList.GetItemById(int.Parse(Request.Params["ID"]));

      if (!this.Page.IsPostBack) {
         // Populate fields on the form
         this.DevLeapApprovalTaskDescription.Text =
            targetTask[FieldsIds.DevLeapApprovalTaskDescription_Id] != null ?
            targetTask[FieldsIds.DevLeapApprovalTaskDescription_Id].ToString() :
            String.Empty;
         this.DevLeapApprovalTaskNotes.Text =
            targetTask[FieldsIds.DevLeapApprovalTaskNotes_Id] != null ?
            targetTask[FieldsIds.DevLeapApprovalTaskNotes_Id].ToString() : String.Empty;

         ListItem outcomeToSelect = this.DevLeapApprovalTaskOutcome.Items.FindByValue(
            targetTask[FieldsIds.DevLeapApprovalTaskOutcome_Id].ToString());

         if (outcomeToSelect != null) {
            this.DevLeapApprovalTaskOutcome.ClearSelection();
            outcomeToSelect.Selected = true;
         }
      }
   }
```

```
    protected void UpdateTaskFromControls(SPListItem targetTask,
System.Collections.Hashtable taskProperties) {
  // Update task item fields
  taskProperties[FieldsIds.DevLeapApprovalTaskStatus_Id] = "Completed";
  taskProperties[FieldsIds.DevLeapApprovalTaskNotes_Id] =
    this.DevLeapApprovalTaskNotes.Text;
  taskProperties[FieldsIds.DevLeapApprovalTaskOutcome_Id] =
    this.DevLeapApprovalTaskOutcome.SelectedValue;
}

#region Infrastructural code

protected void SaveApprovalTask_Click(object sender, EventArgs e) {
  try {
    Hashtable taskProperties = new Hashtable();
    UpdateTaskFromControls(targetTask, taskProperties);
    SPWorkflowTask.AlterTask(targetTask, taskProperties, false);
  }
  catch (Exception exception) {
    SPUtility.Redirect("Error.aspx", SPRedirectFlags.RelativeToLayoutsPage,
      HttpContext.Current,
      "ErrorText=" + SPHttpUtility.UrlKeyValueEncode(exception.Message));
  }
  ClosePopup();
}

protected void Cancel_Click(object sender, EventArgs e) {
  ClosePopup();
}

private void ClosePopup() {
  this.Response.Clear();
  this.Response.Write("<html><body>Closing ...<script type='text/javascript'>" +
    "window.frameElement.commitPopup();</script></body></html>");
  this.Response.Flush();
  this.Response.End();
}

#endregion
}
```

The *Page_Load* method implementation is trivial. It simply initializes the form controls and retrieves from the current page URL using some *querystring* parameters, which are automatically provided by SharePoint and represent a reference to the current task list (*List*) and task item (*ID*). The *UpdateTaskFromControls* method configures the target task fields populating a *Hashtable* with the values currently provided in the form controls. The *SaveApprovalTask_Click* event handler method is more interesting, because it invokes the *SPWorkflowTask.AlterTask* method, which leverages some infrastructural code provided by the SharePoint

Server Object Model so that it can manage updates to workflows' tasks. This method accepts a target task item, a *Hashtable* of fields' values, and a *Boolean* argument to determine if the update will occur synchronously (*true*) or in background (*false*). Also of interest is the implementation of the *ClosePopup* method, which injects some JavaScript code into the browser that closes the current pop-up window.

Forms Deployment

In order to deploy custom management forms, you need to configure the proper attributes in the *Workflow* feature element that provisions your custom workflow. In Chapter 18, you were introduced to the *AssociationUrl* and *InstantiationUrl* attributes for the *Workflow* element. Listing 19-13 shows the feature element provisioning the workflow illustrated in this chapter, together with its custom management forms.

> **Note** In Listing 19-13, all of the XML attributes that reference types, namespaces, full assembly names, and so forth, should be written on a unique line. Here, the lines are divided due to typographic constraints.

LISTING 19-13 The *Workflow* feature element deploying the sample offers approval workflow.

```xml
<?xml version="1.0" encoding="utf-8" ?>
<Elements xmlns="http://schemas.microsoft.com/sharepoint/">
  <Workflow
      Name="OffersApprovalWorkflow"
      Description="Offers Approval Workflow"
      Id="21574cc5-97d2-4929-8679-f430c39544a2"
CodeBesideClass="DevLeap.SP2010.FormsApprovalWorkflow.OffersApprovalWorkflow.
OffersApprovalWorkflow"
      CodeBesideAssembly="DevLeap.SP2010.FormsApprovalWorkflow, Version=1.0.0.0,
Culture=neutral, PublicKeyToken=442facc71ca68eec"
AssociationUrl="_layouts/DevLeap.SP2010.FormsApprovalWorkflow/OffersApprovalWorkflow/
OffersApprovalAssociationForm.aspx"
InstantiationUrl="_layouts/DevLeap.SP2010.FormsApprovalWorkflow/OffersApprovalWorkflow/
OffersApprovalInitiationForm.aspx">
    <Categories/>
    <MetaData>
      <AssociationCategories>General</AssociationCategories>
      <StatusPageUrl>_layouts/WrkStat.aspx</StatusPageUrl>
    </MetaData>
  </Workflow>
</Elements>
```

As you can see the workflow definition targets both lists and Content Types, and the *AssociationCategories* element defines a value of *General*. Moreover, the *Workflow* feature element defines the URLs of the custom association and instantiation forms.

More Information To learn more about the possible values for the *AssociationCategories* element, read the document, "AssociationCategories Element (Workflow)," which is available online at *http://msdn.microsoft.com/en-us/library/aa543430.aspx*.

To deploy a custom workflow task, you simply need to use the standard provisioning tools available for deploying any kind of custom content. In addition, you need to add your custom workflow task Content Type to the target task list that you will use while associating the workflow to its target list, content type or site. To automate these tasks, you can define a custom provisioning feature to provide the Content Type and bind it to a target list of tasks using a *ContentTypeBinding* feature element. If the workflow task Content Type that you created is the only one used by the workflow definition, you can also use the *TaskListContentTypeId* attribute (see Table 18-2).

Summary

In this chapter, you learned how to create custom workflow forms for managing workflow instances, as well as for rendering custom workflow tasks. Furthermore, you saw how to define custom .ASPX forms so that you can deploy your solutions on both SharePoint Foundation 2010 and SharePoint Server 2010.

Chapter 20

Advanced Workflows

In this last chapter of the "Developing Workflows" section, you will learn about some advanced topics and some new features introduced with Microsoft SharePoint 2010. Reading this chapter is not necessary, especially if you are working with SharePoint workflows for the first time. It would probably be better to read this chapter after having had some experience with standard workflows features.

Custom Actions and Conditions

One of the main areas of extensibility for every workflow solution—not just SharePoint solutions—is developing custom activities. In Chapter 16, "SharePoint Workflows Architecture," you learned to create custom activities simply by defining a custom class that inherits from the *System.Workflow.ComponentModel.Activity* base class. However, depending on your implementation, your custom activities will behave differently. For example, to have a custom activity available in Microsoft SharePoint Designer 2010, you need to carry out some specific tasks. In this section, you will see how to develop custom activities targeting both SharePoint Designer 2010 and Microsoft Visual Studio 2010.

 Note Remember that every workflow is basically an activity. Thus, much of the information you will read about in this chapter applies to workflows, too.

Dependency Properties

The first topic to cover is that of dependency properties. Recall from previous chapters in this section that there are activities with properties that are boundable in the designer user interface. In Chapter 18, "Workflows with Visual Studio 2010," Figure 18-7 showed those properties marked with a yellow cylinder. These are also called dependency properties and they all share the same kind of declaration in code. A dependency property is a property that makes use of a shared repository for the workflow's state. They are based on type *DependencyObject*, which is defined in the *System.Workflow.ComponentModel* namespace, and which internally is a kind of hash table, storing all the values of any dependency property defined in a type. When you implement a custom activity, and you want to provide a designer-bindable property, you need to define that property as a dependency property. Dependency properties of an activity instance can be bound to instance data of the current workflow and are evaluated during runtime. Under the cover, the workflow persistence engine will persist the centralized *DependencyObject*, optimizing persistence workload. Dependency properties can be defined in three ways:

- **Standard Property**   Instance properties that share a common repository provided by the centralized *DependencyObject*.

- **Metadata Property**   Instance properties that are immutable at runtime and that can be assigned with a literal value during design time.

- **Attached Property**   Instance properties that are not defined in the target type, but are attached to the target type by a parent type.

In this chapter, you will focus on standard dependency properties. Listing 20-1 shows you how to define a dependency property with the name *Username* and a value of type *String*.

LISTING 20-1 Defining a sample dependency property.

```
public class AssignUserToGroup: Activity {

  public static DependencyProperty UserNameProperty =
    DependencyProperty.Register("UserName", typeof(String),
    typeof(AssignUserToGroup));

  [System.ComponentModel.Description("UserName")]
  [System.ComponentModel.Category("Custom Properties")]
  [System.ComponentModel.Browsable(true)]
  [System.ComponentModel.DesignerSerializationVisibility(
  System.ComponentModel.DesignerSerializationVisibility.Visible)]
  public String UserName {
    get {
        return ((String)(base.GetValue(AssignUserToGroup.UserNameProperty)));
    }
    set {
        base.SetValue(AssignUserToGroup.UserNameProperty, value);
    }
  }
}
```

This code declares a public static property with the name *UsernameProperty* of type *DependencyProperty*. The name is formed by appending "Property" to the name of the actual property (for instance, *Username*). Next, the static property must be initialized with the factory static method *Register* that is provided by the *DependencyProperty* type. This method is available with multiple overloads. The one used in Listing 20-1 declares the real name of the target property (*Username*), the type of the target property (*String*), and the type of the container activity, which in Listing 20-1 is *AssignUserToGroup*.

Of course, there is a real *Username* property of type *String*. This property, inside its implementation of the *get* and *set* methods, works with methods provided by the *base* class, which is the *Activity* class, to set the value or to get the value of the current property through the static dependency property *UsernameProperty*. The *SetValue* and *GetValue* methods of the base class are available through the *DependencyObject* type, which is the base class of the *Activity* class.

The syntax in Listing 20-1 is not very developer friendly. However, Visual Studio 2010 offers a code snippet called "wdp" (workflow dependency property) that can be used to automatically define a new dependency property.

When you bind a dependency property to another instance data, you can target any of the following data sources:

- A field
- A property
- Another dependency property
- A method

Internally, the workflow designer will save an *ActivityBind* instance within the dependency property, which is an object that stores the name of the data source and the path to the member of the data source.

Custom Actions for SharePoint Designer 2010

The set of actions available in SharePoint Designer 2010 is extensible and you can write custom workflow activities of your own, making them available as custom actions in SharePoint Designer 2010, too. However, one of the main requirements for a custom activity targeting SharePoint Designer 2010 is to have all the properties defined as dependency properties. This way, you can configure them in the user interface of the workflow designer.

Suppose that you need to create a custom activity to assign a user to a specific group. If that user does not exist in the current site, you also need to create him. First, you need to create a strongly-named assembly project, which can also be a "SharePoint Empty Project," and reference some infrastructural assemblies such as *Microsoft.SharePoint.dll* and *Microsoft.SharePoint.WorkflowActions.dll*, both of which are available in the SharePoint14_Root\ISAPI folder.

Next, recall from Chapter 16 that you can implement a custom activity, which is a class inheriting from the base class *Activity*, and the main code of every custom activity is the implementation of the *Execute* method. If the custom activity is intended to place a user within a specific group, the *Execute* method will use the SharePoint Server Object Model to register the user and assign him to the target group. The username and the target group will be dependency properties of the custom activity. Listing 20-2 presents the code of that activity.

LISTING 20-2 The code of a custom activity to assign a user to a group.

```
public class AssignUserToGroup : Activity {
  public static DependencyProperty UserNameProperty =
    DependencyProperty.Register("UserName", typeof(String),
    typeof(AssignUserToGroup));

  [System.ComponentModel.Description("UserName")]
  [System.ComponentModel.Category("Custom Properties")]
  [System.ComponentModel.Browsable(true)]
  [System.ComponentModel.DesignerSerializationVisibility(
    System.ComponentModel.DesignerSerializationVisibility.Visible)]
  public String UserName {
    get {
      return ((String)(base.GetValue(AssignUserToGroup.UserNameProperty)));
    }
    set {
      base.SetValue(AssignUserToGroup.UserNameProperty, value);
    }
  }

  public static DependencyProperty GroupProperty =
    DependencyProperty.Register("Group", typeof(String),
    typeof(AssignUserToGroup));

  [System.ComponentModel.Description("Group")]
  [System.ComponentModel.Category("Custom Properties")]
  [System.ComponentModel.Browsable(true)]
  [System.ComponentModel.DesignerSerializationVisibility(
    System.ComponentModel.DesignerSerializationVisibility.Visible)]
  public String Group {
    get {
      return ((String)(base.GetValue(AssignUserToGroup.GroupProperty)));
    }
    set {
      base.SetValue(AssignUserToGroup.GroupProperty, value);
    }
  }

  public static DependencyProperty __ContextProperty =
    DependencyProperty.Register("__Context", typeof(WorkflowContext),
    typeof(AssignUserToGroup));

  [System.ComponentModel.Description("__Context")]
  [System.ComponentModel.Category("__Context Category")]
  [System.ComponentModel.Browsable(true)]
  [System.ComponentModel.DesignerSerializationVisibility(
    System.ComponentModel.DesignerSerializationVisibility.Visible)]
  public WorkflowContext __Context {
    get {
    return ((WorkflowContext)(base.GetValue(AssignUserToGroup.__ContextProperty)));
    }
```

```
    set {
      base.SetValue(AssignUserToGroup.__ContextProperty, value);
    }
  }

  protected override ActivityExecutionStatus Execute(
    ActivityExecutionContext executionContext) {
    // Execute the code with elevated privileges
    SPSecurity.RunWithElevatedPrivileges(
      delegate() {
        // Get a reference to the current SPSite
        using (SPSite site = new SPSite(this.__Context.Site.ID)) {
          // Open the current SPWeb
          using (SPWeb web = site.OpenWeb(this.__Context.Web.ID)) {
            // Ensure the user
            SPUser user = web.EnsureUser(this.UserName);
            // Add him to the target group
            web.Groups[this.Group].AddUser(user);
          }
        }
      });
    return (ActivityExecutionStatus.Closed);
  }
}
```

Listing 20-2 illustrates that there are two dependency properties of type *String* to get the target *Username* and *Group*. There is also another dependency property, *__Context*, which has a conventional name. SharePoint Designer 2010 will automatically populate this property with an instance of type *Microsoft.SharePoint.WorkflowActions.WorkflowContext*. The *WorkflowContext* class represents the context of the current workflow and gives you information about the current site, web, item, list, and workflow instance. The *Execute* method uses this to reference the current site and web to check if the target user exists and to associate him with the target group. The *Execute* method executes its code impersonating a high-privileged account to ensure that it has the proper permissions to create a new user and assign that user to a group. Finally, the *Execute* method returns a value of *ActivityExecutionStatus.Closed* to signal that it has completed its job.

 Note The *__Context* dependency property of type *WorkflowContext* is not mandatory if you plan to develop a custom activity for use only in workflows designed in Visual Studio.

A custom action such as the one you have just defined can be deployed to SharePoint by copying the strongly-named assembly into the Global Assembly Cache (GAC) and by defining a specific XML manifest file. You can do this by defining a SharePoint 2010 project. The manifest is a language-dependent file that has an .ACTIONS extension. It must be deployed in the SharePoint14_Root\TEMPLATE\[*Locale-ID*]\Workflow folder, where *Locale-ID* is the locale ID of the language that you want to support.

> **More Information** For a complete list of all available locale IDs, read the document, "Locale IDs assigned by Microsoft," which is available at *http://msdn.microsoft.com/en-us/goglobal/ bb964664*.

For example, to target the en-US culture, use a Locale ID value of 1033; therefore, you deploy an .ACTIONS file in the SharePoint14_Root\TEMPLATE\1033\Workflow folder. If you also want to support the Italian language (Locale ID 1040), you must deploy another .ACTIONS file in the SharePoint14_Root\TEMPLATE\1040\Workflow folder. Each language-dependent file will have text messages translated in its specific language. Listing 20-3 displays a sample .ACTIONS file targeting the en-US culture for deploying the *AssignUserToGroup* sample action.

LISTING 20-3 The .ACTIONS file used to deploy the *AssignUserToGroup* action.

```xml
<?xml version="1.0" encoding="utf-8"?>
<WorkflowInfo Language="en-us">
  <Actions Sequential="then" Parallel="and">
    <Action Name="Assign User to Group"
      ClassName="DevLeap.SP2010.Activities.AssignUserToGroup"
      Assembly="DevLeap.SP2010.Activities, Version=1.0.0.0, Culture=neutral,
        PublicKeyToken=5fac8a683d6301bf"
      Category="DevLeap Actions"
      AppliesTo="all">
      <RuleDesigner Sentence="Assign %1 to %2">
        <FieldBind Field="UserName" Text="user" Id="1" DesignerType="TextBox" />
        <FieldBind Field="Group" Text="group" Id="2" DesignerType="Person" />
      </RuleDesigner>
      <Parameters>
        <Parameter Name="__Context"
          Type="Microsoft.SharePoint.WorkflowActions.WorkflowContext,
          Microsoft.SharePoint.WorkflowActions"
          Direction="In" DesignerType="Hide" />
        <Parameter Name="UserName" Type="System.String, mscorlib" Direction="In" />
        <Parameter Name="Group" Type="System.String, mscorlib" Direction="In" />
      </Parameters>
    </Action>
  </Actions>
</WorkflowInfo>
```

> **Note** In Listing 20-3, the *Assembly* attribute value and the *<Parameter>* tag's *Type* attribute value should appear on a single code line. They're wrapped here due to typographic constraints.

The file has a *WorkflowInfo* document element with a *Language* attribute to declare the target culture. Then it defines an *Actions* element, which consists of one or more *Action* elements. Each *Action* element defines the main information about the custom action that you're deploying. For example, there are attributes to declare the *Name*, *ClassName*, and

Assembly of the custom action. In addition, there is the *AppliesTo* attribute, which declares the target of the current custom action. Valid values for the *AppliesTo* attribute are *list*, *doclib*, and *all*, which target lists, document libraries, or everything, respectively. Each *Action* element wraps a *RuleDesigner* element, which defines how the action will behave in the SharePoint Designer 2010 workflow designer. Finally, there is a *Parameters* element, which binds the user interface parameters to the dependency properties of the custom action. As usual, in your real solutions, all the XML attributes referencing assemblies, namespaces, and so on will need to be on a unique line.

For example, in the *AssignUserToGroup* action, the *RuleDesigner* element defines a sentence with a value of *Assign %1 to %2*, which will be rendered in the workflow designer. The token *%1* corresponds to the *FieldBind* element with an *ID* value of *1*, which is the *Username* field. The token *%2* corresponds to the *FieldBind* element with an *ID* value of *2*, which is the *Group* field. The value of the *Text* attribute of each of the *FieldBind* elements will be rendered as a placeholder for the two fields in the workflow designer interface. The *DesignerType* attribute defines how the field will be rendered. For example, a *DesignerType* value of *TextBox* will render a textbox, while a value of *Person* will render a people/group picker. Table 20-1 lists the values for the *DesignerType* attribute, available by default in SharePoint 2010.

TABLE 20-1 Values for the *DesignerType* Attribute

Value	Description
Boolean	A *Boolean* field with the choices *True/False*, rendered with a drop-down list.
ChooseDoclibItem	An item selector for an item in a document library.
ChooseListItem	An item selector for an item in a list.
CreateListItem	An advanced control for describing a list item to create.
Date	A *DateTime* selector.
Dropdown	A drop-down list with a list of *Option* values.
Email	An advanced control for creating an e-mail message.
FieldNames	A drop-down list populated with the list of all the fields available in the current target list or document library.
Float	A floating-point field value.
Hyperlink	An hyperlink field with a URL builder user interface.
Integer	An *Integer* field value.
ListNames	A drop-down list populated with the names of all the lists and document libraries available in the current website.
Operator	A drop-down list populated with the operator available to evaluate two sides of an operation.
ParameterNames	A drop-down list populated with all the local variables defined in the current workflow definition.
Person	An advanced control for selecting a person or group.
SinglePerson	An advanced control for selecting a single person or group.
StringBuilder	A string builder control.

Value	Description
Survey	An advanced control for creating a to-do item.
TextBox	A textbox control.
TextArea	A multiline textbox control.
UpdateListItem	An advanced control for updating a list item.
WritableFieldNames	A drop-down list populated with the fields that can be edited in the current list or document library.

When SharePoint Designer 2010 starts designing a workflow definition, it retrieves the list of all the available .ACTIONS files from the target SharePoint server and loads their definitions so that their actions are available in the designer.

Figure 20-1 depicts the workflow designer of SharePoint Designer 2010 as it renders the custom *AssignUserToGroup* action, while searching for the target group.

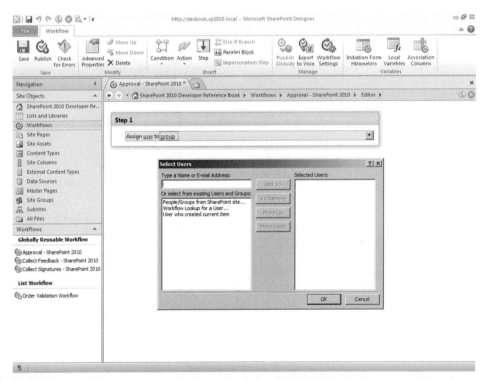

FIGURE 20-1 The workflow designer of SharePoint Designer 2010 rendering the custom *AssignUserToGroup* action.

Lastly, you need to authorize your custom action to be loaded and executed by the SharePoint workflow engine. For security reasons, SharePoint loads only authorized actions. To authorize your action, you need to edit the web.config file of the web application where you like to use the new custom activity, adding an *authorizedType* element, using the following path:

configuration/System.Workflow.ComponentModel.WorkflowCompiler/authorizedTypes

In the sample *AssignUserToGroup* action, the *authorizedType* element is as follows:

```
<authorizedType Assembly="DevLeap.SP2010.Activities, Version=1.0.0.0, Culture=neutral,
  PublicKeyToken=5fac8a683d6301bf" Namespace="DevLeap.SP2010.Activities"
  TypeName="*" Authorized="True" />
```

In the section "Workflow Service Deployment," beginning on page 573, you will learn how to automate the web.config modification process using a custom feature.

Custom Conditions for SharePoint Designer 2010

Another extensible area for the SharePoint Designer 2010 workflow designer is the development of custom conditions. A custom condition is just a logical condition that allows the workflow to perform a specific action only if the condition evaluates to *true*. To implement a custom condition you need to create a new project for building a strongly-named assembly. Next, you need to reference *Microsoft.SharePoint.dll* and *Microsoft.SharePoint. WorkflowActions.dll*, as you do with custom actions. Alternatively, you can start from an "Empty SharePoint Project" template and simply add a reference to *Microsoft.SharePoint. WorkflowActions.dll*. To implement custom conditions, you simply need to define one or more static methods in a public class. Each static method corresponds to a condition, and it needs to adhere to some requirements in order to be used correctly by SharePoint Designer 2010. Listing 20-4 illustrates a custom condition that checks the file name extension of the current document. This condition applies to document libraries only.

LISTING 20-4 A custom condition to check the file name extension of the current document.

```
public class DevLeapConditions {
  public static Boolean FileNameExtension(WorkflowContext context,
    String listId, Int32 itemId, String extension) {

    // Retrieve the current web
    using (SPWeb web = context.Web) {
      // Retrive the current list instance
      SPList list = web.Lists[Helper.GetListGuid(context, listId)];

      // Retrieve the single item
      SPListItem item = list.GetItemById(itemId);

      // Check the filename extension
      if (item.File != null && item.File.Name.ToUpper().EndsWith(extension))
        return (true);
      else
        return (false);
    }
  }
}
```

The static method returns a *Boolean* result. It receives three predefined arguments that correspond to the current workflow context, the list ID, and the item ID in target. After these three arguments, you can define more arguments of your own following these three. For example, in Listing 20-4, the *extension* argument is introduced to check for a file name extension. From there, the method implementation is trivial. To deploy a custom action you need to add some specific elements to the same .ACTIONS file that you saw in the previous section.

Listing 20-5 shows an .ACTIONS file deploying the sample custom condition.

LISTING 20-5 An .ACTIONS file that deploys the sample custom condition.

```xml
<?xml version="1.0" encoding="utf-8"?>
<WorkflowInfo Language="en-us">
  <Condition Name="File extension a of specific type"
    FunctionName="FileNameExtension"
    ClassName="DevLeap.SP2010.Activities.DevLeapConditions"
    Assembly="DevLeap.SP2010.Activities, Version=1.0.0.0, Culture=neutral,
PublicKeyToken=5fac8a683d6301bf"
    AppliesTo="doclib"
    UsesCurrentItem="true">
    <RuleDesigner Sentence="current document has an extension of %1">
      <FieldBind Id="1" Field="_1_" Text="file extension" DesignerType="Dropdown">
        <Option Name=".DOCX" Value=".DOCX" />
        <Option Name=".DOC" Value=".DOC" />
        <Option Name=".XPS" Value=".XPS" />
        <Option Name=".XLSX" Value=".XLSX" />
        <Option Name=".XLS" Value=".XLS" />
        <Option Name=".PDF" Value=".PDF" />
      </FieldBind>
    </RuleDesigner>
    <Parameters>
      <Parameter Name="_1_" Type="System.String, mscorlib" Direction="In" />
    </Parameters>
  </Condition>
</WorkflowInfo>
```

As with any custom action, custom conditions contain a *RuleDesigner* element, whose child elements define the behavior of the condition's parameters in the user interface. They also contain a *Parameters* section to map designer fields to arguments of the method implementing the condition. Notice that the value if the *Field* attribute of the *FieldBind* element in the *RuleDesigner* is the same as the value of the *Name* attribute of the *Parameter* element. In this example the *FieldBind* element has a *DesignerType* attribute with a value of *Dropdown*. Thus, there is a list of *Option* elements inside the *FieldBind* that declares all of the available file extensions for which to check.

Figure 20-2 displays the new condition working in a workflow designed in SharePoint Designer 2010.

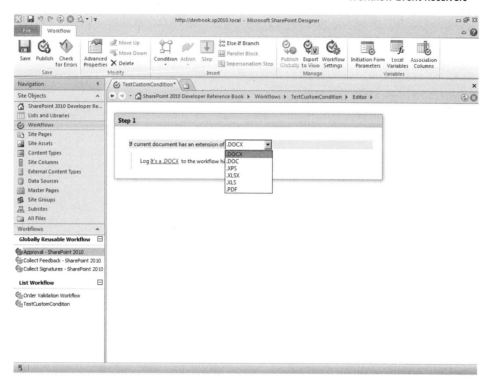

FIGURE 20-2 The user interface of SharePoint Designer 2010 rendering the sample custom condition.

Workflow Event Receivers

In Chapter 12, "Event Receivers," you learned that SharePoint 2010 now gives you the capability to develop custom event receivers for workflows, too. Here in this section, you explore the topic in greater depth by looking at a brief example of a workflow event receiver.

A workflow event receiver is a custom class that inherits from the *SPWorkflowEventReceiver* base class and overrides one or more of the virtual methods offered by that base class. Table 12-8 introduced these methods to you, which are:

- *WorkflowStarting*   Occurs after a workflow instance is starting.

- *WorkflowStarted*   Occurs after a workflow instance has been started.

- *WorkflowPostponed*   Occurs after a workflow instance has been postponed.

- *WorkflowCompleted*   Occurs after a workflow instance is completed.

All of these methods receive an argument of type *SPWorkflowEventProperties*, which provides some information about the current workflow, its context, and so on. Listing 20-6 lays out a sample event receiver that executes some custom code whenever a workflow is starting against an item of a document library.

LISTING 20-6 A workflow event receiver.

```
public class DevLeapOffersWFReceiver : SPWorkflowEventReceiver {
  public override void WorkflowStarting(SPWorkflowEventProperties properties) {
    if (properties.ActivationProperties != null) {
      SPUtility.SendEmail(properties.ActivationProperties.Web,
        false, false,
        properties.ActivationProperties.Site.Owner.Email,
        "Workflow Starting",
        String.Format("Is starting a workflow on item {0}.",
          properties.ActivationProperties.Item.Title), false);
    }
  }
}
```

The instance of the *SPWorkflowEventProperties* class provides an entry point to the current activation context through the *ActivationProperties* property. In particular, you have access to the current *SPListItem*, *SPList*, *SPWeb*, *SPSite*, history list, and task list.

> **Important** The *ActivationProperties* property is available only during the *WorkflowStarting* event. If you decide to intercept more than one workflow events within the same event receiver class, consider that each event will be handled by a specific event receiver instance. Thus, you cannot share data or activation properties within an instance variable, because every event will have its own instance.

In Listing 20-6, the code retrieves a reference to the current item so that it can send an e-mail to the Site owner, informing him that a new workflow instance is starting on a specific item.

In general, you can think about using a workflow event receiver as a tool for managing extra code that works behind the workflow. For example, a workflow event receiver could be used to notify external systems about the runtime status of the workflow, without explicitly correlating the workflow instance with the external system.

Workflow Services

There are situations in which you need to define a workflow that interacts with an external system, for example, external Line of Business solutions, an ERP, a CRM, and so on. In these cases, you cannot use a custom workflow event receiver, because it can be executed only when the workflow is starting, is started, is postponed, or is completed. As an example, consider a reviewed version of the offers approval workflow illustrated in Chapter 18 and Chapter 19, "Workflow Forms." Whenever an offer has been approved, you need to send it to an external CRM to get a reference code for the offer. However, the reference code requires some manual intervention to be generated, so there is an unpredictable time delay between sending the offer to the CRM and getting the code back. In such circumstances, you have the opportunity to create custom activities to interact with the CRM. However, the CRM is an external system and even though calling it directly through a custom activity is not terribly complex, it would be better to have an infrastructural service that decouples the communication between the workflow and the CRM. In addition, the time delay spent waiting for the offer code from the external CRM shouldn't burden the workflow engine. This is a typical situation in which the workflow instance should be idled while waiting for the external CRM, with the workflow instance persisted on the back-end persistence storage, and then retrieve the instance later when the CRM code is available.

To satisfy this requirement, you could communicate with the external CRM using a SOAP service, taking advantage of the *SendActivity* and *ReceiveActivity* activities available in Workflow Foundation since .NET 3.5. However, these activities assume that your external system is available through a SOAP service.

Beginning with SharePoint 2010, you can now develop custom workflow services that will allow your workflows to communicate with external systems by using the external data exchange infrastructure offered by Workflow Foundation 3.*x*. The external data exchange infrastructure makes use of the *CallExternalMethod* and *HandleExternalEvent* activities (introduced in Table 16-1). *CallExternalMethod* invokes a method in the workflow host and waits synchronously for its execution. *HandleExternalEvent* waits for an event that will be raised by the workflow host. While waiting for the event, the workflow instance will be automatically put in the *Idle* state and will be persisted on the persistence storage. Since version 2007, by default, a workflow hosted in SharePoint can handle events related to the current workflow item or the tasks list associated with the current workflow association. Beginning with SharePoint 2010, you now have the capability to develop custom infrastructural services that you can plug into the runtime engine of SharePoint 2010, making them available to your workflows. Figure 20-3 demonstrates the offers approval workflow, extended with the CRM integration.

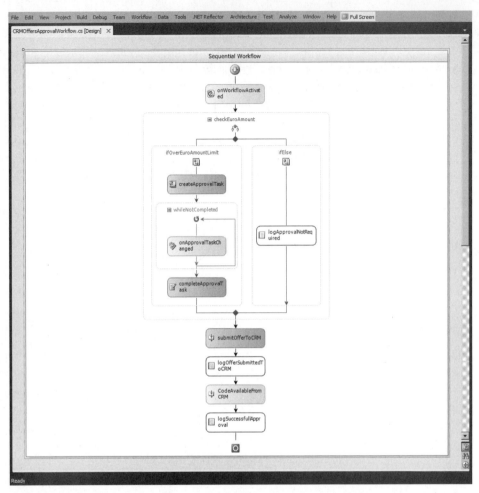

FIGURE 20-3 The offers approval workflow, extended with the CRM integration.

Notice in the last part of the workflow shown in Figure 20-3 that there is an activity that invokes the external CRM, submitting the approved offer. Then there is an event-based activity that waits for the availability of the offer code generated by the CRM. In the following pages you will see how to implement this scenario.

Implementing the Service

When developing a custom SharePoint workflow service, the first thing to do is to define a custom class that inherits from the base type *SPWorkflowExternalDataExchangeService*, which is available in the *Microsoft.SharePoint.Workflow* namespace of Microsoft.SharePoint.dll assembly. The custom service class must also implement a custom communication interface; this is the decoupling link between the workflow host engine and the external system. Listing 20-7 shows how the CRM communication interface is defined.

LISTING 20-7 The CRM communication interface for a custom SharePoint workflow service.

```
[ExternalDataExchange]
public interface ICRMService {
    void SubmitOffer(Offer item);
    event EventHandler<CRMCodeEventArgs> CRMCodeAvailable;
}

[Serializable]
public class Offer {
    public String SharePointCode { get; set; }
    public Decimal EuroAmount { get; set; }
}

[Serializable]
public class CRMCodeEventArgs : ExternalDataEventArgs {
    public CRMCodeEventArgs(Guid instanceId)
        : base(instanceId) { }

    public String CRMCode { get; set; }
}
```

The *ICRMService* interface defines a *SubmitOffer* method that the workflow instance invokes to submit the approved offer to the external CRM. The interface also defines a *CRMCodeAvailable* event that the external CRM raises when the offer code is available. The *SubmitOffer* method accepts an argument of type *Offer*, which is a custom entity hypothetically corresponding to a CRM offer entity. Additionally, the *ICRMService* interface is marked with the attribute *ExternalDataExchange*, which is defined in namespace *System.Workflow. Activities* and is part of the standard Workflow Foundation infrastructure. This attribute tells to the workflow engine that the interface can be used to exchange data with an external system. Without this attribute definition, the interface would serve no purpose to the workflow external data exchange. The *Offer* entity class must be marked as *Serializable*. This way, in the event of workflow persistence, the arguments passed to external data exchange service could be persisted too, and the persistence engine by default uses the runtime serialization to save the workflow state. Also, the *CRMCodeAvailable* event uses a specific *EventArgs* argument of type *CRMCodeEventArgs*, inherited from the *ExternalDataEventArgs* base class and marked as *Serializable*. The *Serializable* attribute is mandatory as a result of the need to serialize the state of the workflow. The inheritance from the base class *ExternalDataEventArgs*, defined in namespace *System.Workflow.Activities*, is an infrastructural requirement of the standard Workflow Foundation infrastructure. In fact, the *ExternalDataEventArgs* class provides some properties and a base constructor that serve the external communication engine. For example, the constructors of the *ExternalDataEventArgs* class accept an argument of type *Guid*, which represents the workflow instance ID of the target workflow for the raised event.

Once you have defined the communication interface with all the required methods and events to communicate with your external system, you can implement it in the concrete workflow service. Listing 20-8 presents the implementation of a custom *CRMService*.

LISTING 20-8 Implementing a custom *CRMService*.

```
class WorkflowContextState {
    public SPWeb Web { get; set; }
    public Guid InstanceId { get; set; }
}

public class CRMService : SPWorkflowExternalDataExchangeService, ICRMService {
    public void SubmitOffer(Offer item) {
        // Simulate an external CRM engine
        ThreadPool.QueueUserWorkItem(delegate(Object state) {
            WorkflowContextState workflowState = state as WorkflowContextState;

            if (workflowState != null) {
                // Simulate a random workload
                Random rnd = new Random();
                Thread.Sleep(TimeSpan.FromSeconds(rnd.Next(1, 60)));

                RaiseEvent(
                    workflowState.Web,
                    workflowState.InstanceId,
                    typeof(ICRMService),
                    "CRMCodeAvailable",
                    new Object[] { String.Format("CRM_CODE_{0:0000}",
                        rnd.Next(1, 1000)) });
            }
        }, new WorkflowContextState {
            Web = this.CurrentWorkflow.ParentWeb,
            InstanceId = WorkflowEnvironment.WorkflowInstanceId
        });
    }

    public event EventHandler<CRMCodeEventArgs> CRMCodeAvailable;

    public override void CallEventHandler(Type eventType, string eventName,
        object[] eventData, SPWorkflow workflow, string identity,
        System.Workflow.Runtime.IPendingWork workHandler, object workItem) {
        // Prepare the custom ExternalDataEventArgs instance
        CRMCodeEventArgs args = new CRMCodeEventArgs(workflow.InstanceId) {
            WorkHandler = workHandler,
            WorkItem = workItem,
            Identity = identity,
            // Get the result from the Object[] with name EventData
            CRMCode = eventData[0].ToString(),
        };
        this.OnOfferApprovalOutcomeAvailable(args);
    }
```

```
protected virtual void OnOfferApprovalOutcomeAvailable(CRMCodeEventArgs args) {
    if (this.CRMCodeAvailable != null) {
        // Pass null as the event source to avoid having
        // serialization issues during workflow persistence
        this.CRMCodeAvailable(null, args);
    }
}
}

public override void CreateSubscription(
  System.Workflow.Activities.MessageEventSubscription subscription) {
    throw new NotImplementedException();
}

public override void DeleteSubscription(Guid subscriptionId) {
    throw new NotImplementedException();
}
}
```

The implementation of the *SubmitOffer* method uses the standard *ThreadPool* class of .NET to simulate a delay for processing the request by sending the execution of a background thread into a queue. Within the background thread, the code will elapse after a random delay, simulating a CRM workload and operator intervention, and then raise the *CRMCodeAvailable* callback event. To raise the event, the code uses a *RaiseEvent* static method provided by the *SPWorkflowExternalDataExchangeService* class. This method provides a couple of overloads that accept the following arguments:

- An *SPWeb* instance corresponding to the current website.

- An *Int32* variable corresponding to the current user ID. There is an overload without this argument.

- A *Guid* that is the instance ID of the target workflow for the event to be raised.

- The *Type* of the event that will be raised, and corresponds to the type of the communication interface. In the current example it is *typeof(ICRMService)*.

- A *String* defining the name of the event that will be raised. It should be an event published by the *Type* defined in the previous argument.

- An array of *Object* that will hold any custom data that will be provided to the code raising the event. Here, you can include any result that you want to return to the workflow instance.

- An enumerated argument of type *SPWorkflowRunOptions* to determine how the event will be run. The available values are *Asynchronous*, *Synchronous*, and *SynchronousAllowPostpone*.

Important The *RaiseEvent* method is static and public, thus you can invoke it from outside the workflow service implementation. For example, you could develop a custom Web Part or a custom application page in which you invoke the *RaiseEvent* method in the code-behind. This would allow you to provide a communication interface, hosted in SharePoint, but accessible to end users without the need to have a workflow task. Moreover, you could also develop a custom Windows Communication Foundation (WCF) service accessible from outside SharePoint, and invoke the *RaiseEvent* method in the service implementation. This last scenario would allow an external system to communicate with SharePoint, interacting with running workflow instances.

Notice that the sample implementation of the *SubmitOffer* method passes a private variable of type *WorkflowContextState* to the background thread. This variable has been defined to hold some information about the current workflow context. In particular, it is used to pass the current *SPWeb* instance and the current workflow instance ID to the background thread.

When the *RaiseEvent* method raises the target event, the *CallEventHandler* method is invoked. This method overrides an abstract method of the *SPWorkflowExternalDataExchange-Service* base class and receives a rich set of arguments that will be used to properly configure the custom *ExternalDataEventArgs* class before invoking the real target event. First, the *CallEventHandler* method must determine the event to invoke. To do this, it can evaluate the *EventName* argument. In the current example the raised event will always be the *CRMCodeAvailable* event. Next, the *CallEventHandler* method constructs the proper *ExternalDataEventArgs* instance, which in the current example will be a variable of type *CRMCodeEventArgs*. Notice the assignment of the *CRMCode* variable, reading the content of the *eventData* array of *Object*.

The *SPWorkflowExternalDataExchangeService* base class also provides a couple of abstract methods called *CreateSubscription* and *DeleteSubscription*, which must be overridden. They are provided by the standard Workflow Foundation infrastructure, through the base abstract class *WorkflowSubscriptionService*. These methods supervise management of events subscriptions, so you can use them to create and delete events subscriptions, or to persist some contextual information into a persistence store that will be accessible by external systems.

In the current example you do not need them, thus the sample code throws a *NotImplementedException* if they are invoked. Meanwhile, the native workflow run-time service that supervises the communication with the workflow's tasks (corresponding to the class *SPWinOETaskService*), uses these methods to monitor events related to the tasks associated with a workflow instance. The *CreateSubscription* method implementation in *SPWinOETaskService* defines an event receiver (see Chapter 12) of type *SPWinOEItemEventReceiver*, which is an internal class of SharePoint and will wait for the proper events occurring on the tasks related to the current workflow. Conversely, the *DeleteSubscription* method implementation of the *SPWinOETaskService* class deletes the event receiver defined during execution of the *CreateSubscription* method.

Workflow Service Deployment

The deployment of a workflow service requires you to build a strongly-named assembly in order to install the assembly file into the GAC. Next, you need to configure the workflow service in the web.config of the web application, where you will use it. Listing 20-9 presents the XML configuration for activating a workflow service.

> **Note** The following code should appear on individual lines in your code. They're wrapped here due to typographic constraints.

LISTING 20-9 The XML configuration for activating a workflow service.

```
<WorkflowServices>
  <WorkflowService Assembly="Microsoft.SharePoint, Version=14.0.0.0, Culture=neutral,
PublicKeyToken=71e9bce111e9429c"
Class="Microsoft.SharePoint.Workflow.SPWinOEWSSService"></WorkflowService>
  <WorkflowService Assembly="Microsoft.SharePoint, Version=14.0.0.0, Culture=neutral,
PublicKeyToken=71e9bce111e9429c" Class="Microsoft.SharePoint.Workflow.
SPWinOETaskService"></WorkflowService>
  <WorkflowService Assembly="DevLeap.SP2010.ExternalCRMService, Version=1.0.0.0,
Culture=neutral, PublicKeyToken=665aaca1c91d20cb" Class="DevLeap.SP2010.
ExternalCRMService.CRMService"></WorkflowService>
</WorkflowServices>
```

The code highlighted in bold shows the *WorkflowService* element that is related to the current sample workflow service (*CRMService*) as well as the two default and standard workflow services defined in any SharePoint 2010 environment (*SPWinOEWSSService* and *SPWinOETaskService*). The configuration must be defined in the following XPath of the web. config file:

```
configuration/SharePoint/WorkflowServices
```

If you like to provide your customers with an automated deployment of the custom workflow service, you can create a project starting from the "Empty SharePoint" project template. Then you can deploy the assembly into the GAC, configuring the output .wsp using the solution package designer of Visual Studio 2010. Finally, you can define a feature receiver with a *WebApplication* scope to automatically configure the web.config file. The SharePoint Server Object Model provides a class named *SPWebConfigModification* specifically for the purpose configuring the contents of the web.config file automatically. Listing 20-10 shows this feature receiver.

LISTING 20-10 A feature receiver that configures and removes a custom workflow service from the web.config by using the *SPWebConfigModification* class.

```
public class CRMServiceFeatureEventReceiver : SPFeatureReceiver {
  public override void FeatureActivated(SPFeatureReceiverProperties properties) {
    // The parent of this feature receiver is an SPWebApplication
    SPWebApplication webApplication = properties.Feature.Parent as
      SPWebApplication;

    if (webApplication != null) {
      // Define the web.config modification
      SPWebConfigModification modification =
        new SPWebConfigModification() {
          Name = "CRMWorkflowService",
          Path = "configuration/SharePoint/WorkflowServices",
          Owner = "DevLeap",
          Sequence = 0,
          Type =
            SPWebConfigModification.SPWebConfigModificationType.EnsureChildNode,
          Value = "<WorkflowService
          Assembly=\"DevLeap.SP2010.ExternalCRMService,
          Version=1.0.0.0, Culture=neutral, PublicKeyToken=665aaca1c91d20cb\"
          Class=\"DevLeap.SP2010.ExternalCRMService.CRMService\">
          </WorkflowService>"
      };

      // Apply it to the web.config of the current SPWebApplication
      webApplication.WebConfigModifications.Add(modification);
      webApplication.Update();
      webApplication.WebService.ApplyWebConfigModifications();
    }
  }

  public override void FeatureDeactivating(
    SPFeatureReceiverProperties properties) {
    // The parent of this feature receiver is an SPWebApplication
    SPWebApplication webApplication = properties.Feature.Parent
      as SPWebApplication;

    if (webApplication != null) {
      // Search the modification to remove
      var modification =
        (from m in webApplication.WebConfigModifications
        where m.Name == "CRMWorkflowService"
        select m).FirstOrDefault();

      // If any
      if (modification != null) {
        // Remove it to the web.config of the current SPWebApplication
        webApplication.WebConfigModifications.Remove(modification);
        webApplication.Update();
        webApplication.WebService.ApplyWebConfigModifications();
      }
    }
  }
}
```

Listing 20-10 illustrates how you can create an instance of the *SPWebConfigModification* class, configure the *Path* (XPath) of the configuration to create or update, define a *Value* for the node to configure, and declare the *Type* of configuration by using an enumerated value of type *SPWebConfigModificationType*. In addition, you can configure a *Name* for the configuration, an ordinal *Sequence*, and an *Owner*. The *Name* is useful because it can be used later to retrieve the configuration and eventually remove it. In fact, the *SPWebConfigModification* instance can be added to or removed from the *WebConfigModifications* collection property of the current *SPWebApplication*. However, because you could have multiple front-end servers in your farm, you need to invoke the *ApplyWebConfigModifications* method to propagate the configuration changes on all the front-end servers of the farm.

Communication Activities

Now that you have a custom workflow service configured in your environment, you need to take advantage of it within your workflow definition. As you have already seen, an external data exchange service can be used to declare a *CallExternalMethod* activity, if you choose to invoke a method published by the service, or it can declare an *HandleExternalEvent* activity, if you prefer to wait for an event raised by the external service. However, both of these native Workflow Foundation activities require a manual and not insignificant configuration to define the communication interface, the method or event names, the arguments, and so on. Fortunately, the SDK of .NET 3.*x* provides a command line tool called WCA.EXE. This tool, which by default is available in the C:\Program Files (x86)\Microsoft SDKs\Windows\v7.0A\Bin folder, is capable of automatically generating the code for preconfigured custom activities to make use of an external data exchange service communication interface. In the following command line, you can see the syntax to invoke the tool, applied to the sample workflow service defined in this chapter:

```
WCA.EXE DevLeap.SP2010.ExternalCRMService.dll
```

The tool accepts the path of a .NET assembly, declaring one or more interfaces marked with the attribute *ExternalDataExchangeAttribute*. By default, the output of the tool is a set of .cs files (or .vb if you specify the */language:VB* command line argument) generated in the current working folder and declaring one activity for every method or event published by the target interfaces. If you use the *and*, the output will be an *ICRMService.Invokes.cs* file that declares the activities to invoke the service, and an *ICRMService.Sinks.cs* file that declares the activities for handling external events raised by the service. For the sake of brevity, this chapter does not illustrate the auto-generated code in detail. However, you can consider that the *SubmitOffer* method will have a corresponding *SubmitOffer* activity, inherited from the *CallExternalMethodActivity* standard activity. Likewise, the *CRMCodeAvailable* event will have a corresponding *CRMCodeAvailable* activity, inherited from the *HandleExternalEventActivity* standard activity.

Figure 20-3 showed these activities in the designer context. The interesting part of this topic is that the activities will provide to the workflow some dependency properties to bind their input and output arguments and parameters in the workflow designer context. For example, the *SubmitOffer* activity provides a dependency property of type *Offer*, which accepts a reference to the offer to submit to the CRM. Similarly the *CRMCodeAvailable* activity provides a *CRMCode* dependency property to get the CRM Code back into the workflow instance.

Workflow Management by Code

Another advanced topic with regard to developing workflow solutions is how to manage workflows and interact with them by code. You can do that either by using the Server Object Model on a SharePoint server, or remotely using a specific SOAP service published by every SharePoint front-end server. In Chapter 19, you used the workflow Server Object Model while developing custom association, initiation, and modification forms of workflows.

Workflow Server Object Model

The Server Object Model of SharePoint provides a number of classes for managing workflow instances, definitions, task, and so on. You can start a workflow by code, using syntax such as that shown in Listing 20-11.

LISTING 20-11 Using the *SPWorkflowManager* to start a workflow instance on every item in a library.

```
// Retrieve e reference to the target SPSite and SPWeb
using (SPSite site = new SPSite("http://devbook.sp2010.local/")) {
  using (SPWeb web = site.OpenWeb()) {
    // Retrieve e reference to the target library
    SPList listOffers = web.Lists["DevLeap CRM Offers"];

    // Retrieve a reference to the workflow association to start
    var wfAssociation =
        (from SPWorkflowAssociation wfa in listOffers.WorkflowAssociations
            where wfa.Name == "CRMOffersApprovalWorkflow"
            select wfa).FirstOrDefault();

    // If any
    if (wfAssociation != null) {
        // Prepare Initiation Data
        CRMInitiationDataConfiguration initData =
            new CRMInitiationDataConfiguration {
                OfferManager = "SP2010DEV\\Administrator",
                ApprovalRequestNotes = "Please approve this offer",
            };

        String initDataText =
        WorkflowUtility.SerializeData<CRMInitiationDataConfiguration>(initData);
```

```
            // For each item in the list, start the workflow
            // unless it is not already running
            foreach (SPListItem item in listOffers.Items) {
                var workflowAlreadyRunning =
                    (from SPWorkflow wf in item.Workflows
                        where wf.AssociationId == wfAssociation.Id
                        && wf.InternalState == SPWorkflowState.Running
                        select wf).Count();

                if (workflowAlreadyRunning == 0) {
                    // Start a new workflow instance
                    SPWorkflow wf = site.WorkflowManager.StartWorkflow(
                    item, wfAssociation, initDataText);
                    Guid wfInstanceId = wf.InstanceId;

                    Console.WriteLine("Started instance {0} on item {1}",
                        wfInstanceId, item.Title);
                }
            }
        }
    }
}
```

The code sample starts a workflow instance on every item of a target library on which one is not already running. Notice how it uses the *SPWorkflowManager* class, which can be used to control workflow instances, to start a new workflow instance invoking the method *StartWorkflow*. Similarly, the class *SPWorkflowManager* can also be used to retrieve all the workflow instances running on a specific item. Listing 20-12 shows the code to produce this result.

LISTING 20-12 Getting the list of workflow instances running on a specific item.

```
// Retrieve e reference to the target SPSite and SPWeb
using (SPSite site = new SPSite("http://devbook.sp2010.local/")) {
    using (SPWeb web = site.OpenWeb()) {
        // Retrieve e reference to the target library
        SPList listOffers = web.Lists["DevLeap CRM Offers"];
        SPListItem item = listOffers.Items[0];

        SPWorkflowCollection runningWorkflows =
            site.WorkflowManager.GetItemActiveWorkflows(
            item);

        Console.WriteLine("There are {0} workflow instances running on item {1}",
            runningWorkflows.Count, item.Title);
    }
}
```

Furthermore, you can also use the *SPWorkflowManager* class to retrieve pending tasks related to a running workflow instance, eventually filtered based on their status or *assignedTo* user. Listing 20-13 illustrates the code to retrieve the pending tasks for a specific workflow instance.

LISTING 20-13 Getting the list of pending tasks for a running workflow instance.

```
// Retrieve e reference to the target SPSite and SPWeb
using (SPSite site = new SPSite("http://devbook.sp2010.local/")) {
  using (SPWeb web = site.OpenWeb()) {

    // Retrieve e reference to the target library
    SPList listOffers = web.Lists["DevLeap CRM Offers"];
    SPListItem item = listOffers.Items[0];

    // Retrieve the running workflow instances
    SPWorkflowCollection runningWorkflows =
        site.WorkflowManager.GetItemActiveWorkflows(
        item);

    // Get the first running instance
    SPWorkflow runningInstance = runningWorkflows[0];

    // Define a filter to retrieve only pending tasks
    SPWorkflowFilter filter = new SPWorkflowFilter(
        SPWorkflowState.Running, SPWorkflowState.None,
        SPWorkflowAssignedToFilter.None);

    // Retrieve pending tasks
    SPWorkflowTaskCollection pendingTasks =
        site.WorkflowManager.GetWorkflowTasks(
        item, runningInstance.InstanceId, filter);

    Console.WriteLine("There are {0} pending tasks running on " +
        "item {1} for workflow
    instance {2}", pendingTasks.Count, item.Title, runningInstance.InstanceId);
  }
}
```

The ability to retrieve the pending tasks could be useful whenever you need to manage or complete those tasks by code. You can use the *SPWorkflowTask* class and its *AlterTask* method to update the task item. You have already seen an example of code leveraging the *AlterTask* method in Chapter 19, within the custom task form. Listing 20-14 shows how to complete by code a pending task related to an offer approval workflow instance.

LISTING 20-14 Completing a pending task for a running workflow instance.

```
// Retrieve e reference to the target SPSite and SPWeb
using (SPSite site = new SPSite("http://devbook.sp2010.local/")) {
  using (SPWeb web = site.OpenWeb()) {
```

```
// Retrieve e reference to the target library
SPList listOffers = web.Lists["DevLeap CRM Offers"];
SPListItem item = listOffers.Items[0];

// Retrieve the running workflow instances
SPWorkflowCollection runningWorkflows =
    site.WorkflowManager.GetItemActiveWorkflows(item);

// Get the first running instance
SPWorkflow runningInstance = runningWorkflows[0];

// Define a filter to retrieve only pending tasks
SPWorkflowFilter filter = new SPWorkflowFilter(
    SPWorkflowState.Running, SPWorkflowState.None,
    SPWorkflowAssignedToFilter.None);

// Retrieve pending tasks
SPWorkflowTaskCollection pendingTasks =
    site.WorkflowManager.GetWorkflowTasks(
    item, runningInstance.InstanceId, filter);

if (pendingTasks.Count == 1) {
    // Get the target task, if any
    SPWorkflowTask targetTask = pendingTasks[0];

    // Complete the task
    Hashtable taskProperties = new Hashtable();
    taskProperties[FieldsIds.DevLeapCRMApprovalTaskStatus_Id] = "Completed";
    taskProperties[FieldsIds.DevLeapCRMApprovalTaskNotes_Id] =
      "Automatically approved!";
    taskProperties[FieldsIds.DevLeapCRMApprovalTaskOutcome_Id] = "Approved";

    SPWorkflowTask.AlterTask(targetTask, taskProperties, true);

    Console.WriteLine("Pending task automatically completed!");
    }
  }
}
```

There are many other classes and methods that you can use to interact with your workflows by code; however, those just presented are most useful or frequently used.

Workflow Web Service

The Server Object Model is useful whenever your code runs on a SharePoint server. However, there are situations in which you would like to manage workflows remotely, from a smart client or a remote server/system. Fortunately, SharePoint offers a SOAP service that can be used to interact with workflows from a remote site. The service is available at the following URL:

```
http://<site_url>/_vti_bin/workflow.asmx
```

This service publishes a small set of operations, which are described in Table 20-2.

TABLE 20-2 The List of Operations Published by the Workflow.asmx Service

Value	Description
AlterToDo	Updates properties of a specific workflow task for a given SharePoint item.
ClaimReleaseTask	Claims or releases a specific workflow task for a given SharePoint item.
GetTemplatesForItem	Retrieves the list of workflow templates available for a given SharePoint item.
GetToDosForItem	Retrieves the list of running tasks for a given SharePoint item and assigned to the current user or group to which the workflow task belongs.
GetWorkflowDataForItem	Retrieves the workflow data for a given SharePoint item and for the current user or group to which the workflow belongs.
GetWorkflowTaskData	Retrieves the data of a task based on its ListID and ItemID.
StartWorkflow	Starts a new workflow instance for a given SharePoint item

Internally, these operations make use of the SharePoint Server Object Model and the classes and methods you have just seen in the previous section. Thus, you could use the workflow. asmx to start and manage a workflow instance from a remote site. Listing 20-15 presents the code to retrieve the list of available workflow templates for a current item in order to start a new instance of the offers approval workflow.

> **Important** The workflow.asmx SOAP service is available only in SharePoint Server edition. If you are using SharePoint Foundation 2010, you will not be able to take advantage of the features in this section.

LISTING 20-15 Starting a new instance of a workflow using the workflow SOAP service.

```
// Configure the service proxy
WorkflowService.Workflow wfSoapService =
    new WorkflowService.Workflow();
wfSoapService.Credentials = System.Net.CredentialCache.DefaultCredentials;

// Configure the URL of the target specific item
String itemUrl = "http://devbook.sp2010.local/DevLeap%20CRM%20Offers/Offer-01.docx";

// Retrieve the workflow templates associated with the target item
XmlNode templates = wfSoapService.GetTemplatesForItem(itemUrl);

// Retrieve the templateId of the workflow to start
XmlNamespaceManager ns = new XmlNamespaceManager(templates.OwnerDocument.NameTable);
ns.AddNamespace("wf", "http://schemas.microsoft.com/sharepoint/soap/workflow/");
```

```
XmlNode templateIdNode = templates.SelectSingleNode("//wf:WorkflowTemplate[@Name =
'CRMOffersApprovalWorkflow']/wf:WorkflowTemplateIdSet/@TemplateId", ns);
Guid templateId = new Guid(templateIdNode.Value);

XmlDocument initiationData = new XmlDocument();
initiationData.LoadXml("<?xml version=\"1.0\" encoding=\"utf-16\"?>
  <CRMInitiationDataConfiguration
    xmlns:xsi=\"http://www.w3.org/2001/XMLSchema-instance\"
    xmlns:xsd=\"http://www.w3.org/2001/XMLSchema\"
    xmlns=\"http://schemas.devleap.com/CRMInitiationDataConfiguration\">
    <OfferManager>SP2010DEV\\Administrator</OfferManager>
    <ApprovalRequestNotes>Please approve this offer
    </ApprovalRequestNotes></CRMInitiationDataConfiguration>");

XmlNode startResult = wfSoapService.StartWorkflow(
  itemUrl, templateId, initiationData);
```

> **Note** The long XML line in the preceding listing should appear in your code on a single line. It's wrapped here due to typographic constraints.

Notice that the *GetTemplatesForItem* and *StartWorkflow* operations require an argument of type *String* that corresponds to the URL of the target item. Also, the *StartWorkflow* operation requires also the ID (GUID) of the workflow template to start, and an *XmlNode* with the XML serialization of the initiation data. The template ID can be retrieved by using XPath from the *XmlNode* that results from the invocation of the *GetTemplatesForItem* operation.

Once you have started a workflow instance, you can utilize the *GetWorkflowDataForItem* operation to retrieve the status of the workflows for the current item. Here is the syntax:

```
XmlNode wfDataForItem = wfSoapService.GetWorkflowDataForItem(itemUrl);
```

The output of the operation will be an *XmlNode* with the structure illustrated in Listing 20-16.

LISTING 20-16 The structure of the XML returned by the *GetWorkflowDataForItem* operation.

```
<WorkflowData xmlns="http://schemas.microsoft.com/sharepoint/soap/workflow/">
  <ToDoData>
  </ToDoData>
  <TemplateData>
    <Web Title="SharePoint 2010 Developer Reference Book"
      Url="http://devbook.sp2010.local" />
    <List Title="DevLeap CRM Offers"
      Url="http://devbook.sp2010.local/DevLeap CRM Offers" />
    <WorkflowTemplates>
      <WorkflowTemplate Name="CRMOffersApprovalWorkflow"
        Description="My SharePoint Workflow">
```

```
InstantiationUrl="http://devbook.sp2010.local/_layouts/DevLeap.SP2010.
CRMOffersApproval/CRMOffersApprovalWorkflow/CRMOffersApprovalInitiationForm.
aspx?List=66e774b2-3c5b-4acb-b333-699860c5772b&amp;ID=1&amp;TemplateID={4ceea64b-cdcf-
4450-b066-ea610a41d832}&amp;Web={49245065-f375-4be0-be4f-d6a8c757d275}">
        <WorkflowTemplateIdSet TemplateId="4ceea64b-cdcf-4450-b066-ea610a41d832"
          BaseId="d3a2dc00-6c59-40c1-9c74-e7053009be96" />
        <AssociationData>
          <string>
            &lt;?xml version="1.0" encoding="utf-16"?&gt;
            &lt;CRMAssociationDataConfiguration
            xmlns:xsi="http://www.w3.org/2001/XMLSchema-instance"
            xmlns:xsd="http://www.w3.org/2001/XMLSchema"
            xmlns="http://schemas.devleap.com/CRMAssociationDataConfiguration"&gt;
            &lt;OfferEuroAmountLimit&gt;4500&lt;/OfferEuroAmountLimit&gt;
            &lt;OfferManager&gt;SP2010DEV\administrator&lt;/OfferManager&gt;
            &lt;/CRMAssociationDataConfiguration&gt;
          </string>
        </AssociationData>
        <Metadata />
      </WorkflowTemplate>
    </WorkflowTemplates>
  </TemplateData>
  <ActiveWorkflowsData>
    <Workflows>
      <Workflow StatusPageUrl="http://devbook.sp2010.local/_layouts/WrkStat.aspx?List
=%7B66E774B2%2D3C5B%2D4ACB%2DB333%2D699860C5772B%7D&amp;WorkflowInstanceID=%7B56e0ff
f6%2D6a8d%2D4c83%2Dadf5%2D012096c522b5%7D" Id="56e0fff6-6a8d-4c83-adf5-012096c522b5"
TemplateId="4ceea64b-cdcf-4450-b066-ea610a41d832"
ListId="66e774b2-3c5b-4acb-b333-699860c5772b"
SiteId="a6219f45-d457-48ee-afc6-4a1de6ca5ef0"
WebId="49245065-f375-4be0-be4f-d6a8c757d275" ItemId="1"
ItemGUID="26252f8b-ad4d-414c-b651-74153132f9dd"
TaskListId="50c9bdc6-bd15-4167-9514-5e6e873a3908" AdminTaskListId="" Author="1"
Modified="20101227 10:08:25" Created="20101227 10:08:25" StatusVersion="0" Status1="2"
Status2="" Status3="" Status4="" Status5="" Status6="" Status7="" Status8=""
Status9="" Status10="" TextStatus1="" TextStatus2="" TextStatus3="" TextStatus4=""
TextStatus5="" Modifications="" ActivityDetails="System.Byte[]" InstanceData=""
InstanceDataSize="0" InternalState="2" ProcessingId="" />
    </Workflows>
  </ActiveWorkflowsData>
  <DefaultWorkflows>
  </DefaultWorkflows>
</WorkflowData>
```

Note The *StatusPageUrl* attribute in the preceding listing should appear on a single line in your code. It's wrapped here due to typographic constraints.

Notice that the XML provides access to the web and list of the provided SharePoint item, as well as information about available workflow templates and information about active workflows. In particular, you have access to the URLs for accessing the workflow status page, and any running task. If you are interested only in retrieving currently running tasks, you can use the following syntax:

```
XmlNode toDosForItem = wfSoapService.GetToDosForItem(itemUrl);
```

The output of the operation will be another *XmlNode*, structured as shown in Listing 20-17.

LISTING 20-17 The structure of the XML returned by the *GetToDosForItem* operation.

```
<ToDoData xmlns="http://schemas.microsoft.com/sharepoint/soap/workflow/">
  <xml xmlns:s="uuid:BDC6E3F0-6DA3-11d1-A2A3-00AA00C14882"
    xmlns:dt="uuid:
    C2F41010-65B3-11d1-A29F-00AA00C14882"
    xmlns:rs="urn:schemas-microsoft-com:rowset"
    xmlns:z="#RowsetSchema">
    <rs:data ItemCount="1">
      <z:row xmlns:z="#RowsetSchema"
      ows_ContentTypeId=
    "0x010801005964A1099DCA407C960D1CADECF6CB4B00E6B8C0A0BD176146931B5B8D1BB377D4"
        ows_Title="Please approve offer Offer-01"
        ows_Predecessors="" ows_Priority="(2) Normal"
        ows_Status="Not Started" ows_AssignedTo="3;#SP2010DEV\Administrator"
        ows_Body="Please approve this offer" ows_StartDate="2010-12-27 11:08:25"
        ows_DueDate="2011-01-06T10:08:25+00:00"
        ows_WorkflowLink=
          "http://devbook.sp2010.local/DevLeap CRM Offers/Offer-01.docx, Offer-01"
        ows_WorkflowName="CRMOffersApprovalWorkflow" ows_TaskType="0"
        ows_HasCustomEmailBody="0" ows_SendEmailNotification="1" ows_Completed="0"
        ows_WorkflowListId="{66E774B2-3C5B-4ACB-B333-699860C5772B}"
        ows_WorkflowItemId="1" ows_GUID="{F6174F06-943E-4ACB-A20F-00245A5742DD}"
        ows_WorkflowInstanceID="{56E0FFF6-6A8D-4C83-ADF5-012096C522B5}"
        ows_DevLeapCRMApprovalTaskOutcome="Pending Approval" ows_ID="29"
        ows_ContentType="CRMOfferApprovalTask" ows_Modified="2010-12-27 11:08:25"
        ows_Created="2010-12-27 11:08:25" ows_Author="1;#sp2010dev\administrator"
        ows_Editor="1073741823;#System Account" ows_owshiddenversion="1"
        ows_WorkflowVersion="1" ows__UIVersion="512" ows__UIVersionString="1.0"
        ows_Attachments="0" ows__ModerationStatus="0"
        ows_LinkTitleNoMenu="Please approve offer Offer-01"
        ows_LinkTitle="Please approve offer Offer-01"
        ows_LinkTitle2="Please approve offer Offer-01"
        ows_SelectTitle="29" ows_Order="2900.00000000000"
        ows_FileRef="29;#Lists/Tasks/29_.000"
        ows_FileDirRef="29;#Lists/Tasks"
        ows_Last_x0020_Modified="29;#2010-12-27 11:08:25"
        ows_Created_x0020_Date="29;#2010-12-27 11:08:25"
        ows_FSObjType="29;#0" ows_SortBehavior="29;#0"
        ows_PermMask="0x7fffffffffffffff" ows_FileLeafRef="29;#29_.000"
        ows_UniqueId="29;#{BE263F50-B1E8-4E72-94DB-EE0AA4BD2B8C}"
        ows_ProgId="29;#" ows_ScopeId="29;#{4556BF50-FDF2-432B-803A-7AA6E4A0033C}"
        ows__EditMenuTableStart="29_.000" ows__EditMenuTableStart2="29"
        ows__EditMenuTableEnd="29" ows_LinkFilenameNoMenu="29_.000"
        ows_LinkFilename="29_.000" ows_LinkFilename2="29_.000"
```

```
        ows_ServerUrl="/Lists/Tasks/29_.000"
        ows_EncodedAbsUrl="http://devbook.sp2010.local/Lists/Tasks/29_.000"
        ows_BaseName="29_"
        ows_MetaInfo="29;#WorkflowCreationPath:SW|4ceea64b-cdcf-4450-b066-
ea610a41d832;&#xD;&#xA;"
        ows__Level="1" ows__IsCurrentVersion="1" ows_ItemChildCount="29;#0"
        ows_FolderChildCount="29;#0"
        ows_TaskListId="50c9bdc6-bd15-4167-9514-5e6e873a3908"
        ows_EditFormURL="http://devbook.sp2010.local/_layouts/DevLeap.SP2010.
          CRMOffersApproval/CRMOfferApprovalTaskForm.aspx?ID=29&amp;
          List=50c9bdc6-bd15-4167-9514-5e6e873a3908"
        ows_WorkflowFormURL="" ows_FormData="" />
    </rs:data>
  </xml>
</ToDoData>
```

The structure is a *Rowset* with a *z:row* element for each task. You can extract information about each of the tasks by using XPath rules. The code highlighted in bold shows some of the most important attributes, such as the *ows_Status*, *ows_AssignedTo*, *ows_DueDate*, *ows_WorkflowInstanceId*, *ows_EditFormURL*, *ows_ID*, *ows_TaskListID*, and custom fields.

If you want to complete the task from the remote site, you can invoke the *AlterToDo* operation by using syntax such as the following:

```
XmlNode alterToDoResult = wfSoapService.AlterToDo(itemUrl, taskItemID, taskListID, taskData);
```

The *itemUrl* is the full URL of the target item. The *taskItemID* and *taskListID* arguments can be retrieved from the XML illustrated in Listing 20-17, reading the values of attributes *ows_ID* and *ows_TaskListID*. Lastly, the fourth argument is an *XmlNode*, with the XML data representing the updated content of the task.

Listing 20-18 illustrates the code for completing and approving the approval task of an offers approval workflow instance.

LISTING 20-18 Completing and approving a task using the *AlterToDo* operation.

```
XmlDocument taskData = new XmlDocument();
taskData.LoadXml("<fields/>");
taskData.DocumentElement.AppendChild(
  taskData.CreateElement("DevLeapCRMApprovalTaskNotes"));
taskData.DocumentElement.LastChild.InnerText =
  "Task approved by remote smart client!";
taskData.DocumentElement.AppendChild(
  taskData.CreateElement("DevLeapCRMApprovalTaskOutcome"));
taskData.DocumentElement.LastChild.InnerText = "Approved";
taskData.DocumentElement.AppendChild(taskData.CreateElement("Status"));
taskData.DocumentElement.LastChild.InnerText = "Completed";
XmlNode alterToDoResult = wfSoapService.AlterToDo(itemUrl, taskItemID, taskListID,
taskData);
```

The *taskData* variable has a structure similar to the XML illustrated in Listing 20-19.

LISTING 20-19 Completing and approving a task using the *AlterToDo* operation.

```
<fields>
  <DevLeapCRMApprovalTaskNotes>Task approved by remote smart client!
  </DevLeapCRMApprovalTaskNotes>
  <DevLeapCRMApprovalTaskOutcome>Approved</DevLeapCRMApprovalTaskOutcome>
  <Status>Completed</Status>
</fields>
```

The XML document has a root element with a name that you can freely choose. Then you should define a child element for every field that you want to update, assigning to each element the name of the target field. Substantially, it is an XML serialization of an hashtable of fields.

SPTimer Service and Workflows

One last important topic to be aware of is that SharePoint can execute workflow instances in one of two processes. The first and most common process is the W3WP.EXE process of the current front-end web server. Whenever you start a workflow instance from the browser user interface, or you interact with a workflow task using the browser, or more in general your last action was related to a user input within the browser, then the workflow instance will be executed in the front-end process of the front-end server that served the last request. However, whenever a workflow resumes from a delay, or handles an event coming from an external system, the workflow instance executes in the context of the SPTimer Service of SharePoint. The SPTimer Service corresponds to the OWSTIMER.EXE process and is an operating system service installed and activated on every SharePoint server. It is important to be aware of this behavior because whenever your workflow definition relies on the hosting environment for its execution, it is important to know that the execution environment could be doubled. For example, if your service uses a custom configuration section in the web.config of the hosting web application, you will need to replicate the configuration also in the configuration file of the OWSTIMER.EXE process, which is located at SharePoint14_Root\BIN\OWSTIMER.EXE. config.

Note Starting from SharePoint 2010 you can also choose to define a preferred server for running the SPTimer service.

Summary

In this chapter, you learned how to define a custom workflow activity, eventually targeting SharePoint Designer 2010 so that you can provide custom actions or custom conditions. Then, you learned how to develop a custom workflow event receiver and a custom workflow service. Additionally, you saw how to manage workflows programmatically by using the Server Object Model on a SharePoint server, or by utilizing a SOAP service available only in SharePoint Server editions. Finally, you were introduced to the two processes by which workflows are executed when they are defined in SharePoint.

PART VI

Security Infrastructure

Chapter 21
Authentication and Authorization Infrastructure

This first chapter in the "Security Infrastructure" section covers the main topics about authentication and authorization in Microsoft SharePoint 2010 fields. In particular, you will learn how both classic and claims-based authentication work. You will also learn how SharePoint authorizes users after having authenticated them.

Authentication Infrastructure

SharePoint 2010 supports multiple authentication methods, which can be configured against a web application or a zone using the SharePoint Central Administration.

> **Note** A SharePoint zone provides the ability to publish the same web application with multiple endpoints (URLs). Available since version 2007, the goal of this feature is to give you a method to share a common application configuration and common content databases between multiple IIS sites that otherwise would have required customizing the web.config files of each zone with specific configurations of authentication, authorization, and security in general.

The supported authentication methods are:

- **Windows Authentication** Uses the Windows infrastructure, providing support for NTML, Kerberos, Anonymous, Basic, and Digest authentication. X.509 Certificate authentication is not supported, unless you manually configure a users' certificate mapping rules within Internet Information Services (IIS).

- **Forms-Based Authentication (FBA)** Utilizes a username and password HTML form that queries a membership provider in the back-end. By default, there are providers for LDAP and SQL Server; however, you can develop custom providers of your own. FBA is based on the standard forms authentication provided by Microsoft ASP.NET, which resides at the very core of SharePoint.

- **SAML token-based Authentication** Uses an external identity provider that supports SAML 1.1 and WS-Federation Passive profile. SAML token-based Authentication includes Active Directory Federation Services v. 2.0 (AD FS 2.0), LDAP, or custom third-party identity providers.

Whenever you create a new web application, you have the opportunity to choose between using the classic or claims-based authentication mode. Depending on your choice, you will be able to make use of one or more of these three authentication methods.

The classic mode supports only the Windows Authentication, while the claims-based mode supports all the three available authentication methods.

If you are migrating an existing SharePoint solution to the latest SharePoint 2010, you should carefully consider the authentication mode to choose. If you are creating a fresh new web application based on SharePoint 2010, you should always choose the claims-based mode, which is a super-set of the classic-mode. Figure 21-1 displays the Create New Web Application dialog box, in which you can choose the authentication mode.

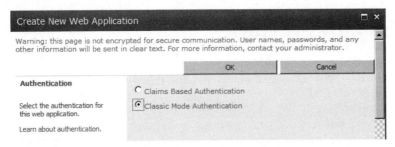

FIGURE 21-1 The Create New Web Application dialog box, in which you choose the authentication mode.

In the following sections, you will learn the main differences between these two modes.

Classic Mode Authentication

The classic mode authenticates users via Windows Authentication, either against the local users' repository of the server, for a single-server deployment, or against the Active Directory repository,for a more common farm deployment with a Windows Domain. The users' account will be treated as an Active Directory Domain Services account, and you will be able to query the current user's identity and principal as *WindowsIdentity* and *WindowsPrincipal* instances. This authentication mode supports all of the available Windows Authentication methods: NTLM, Kerberos, Anonymous, Basic, and Digest.

This mode natively supports integrated authentication, based on NTLM or Kerberos. Thus, a user accessing a SharePoint site published with this authentication mode will not be prompted for his credentials and can access the site with the user's credentials used for running the Internet Explorer process. If the user's identity is not registered in the target SharePoint site, then the browser will prompt the user for alternative credentials.

NTLM-integrated authentication is easier to configure—it's a matter of a couple of mouse clicks—but it is more limited in capabilities. For instance, NTLM-integrated authentication does not allow you to use multi-hop delegation scenarios, when a front-end server needs to access a resource from a back-end server, using the identity of the user calling the front-end. Unfortunately, NTLM is not capable of satisfying this scenario, because internally, NTLM is based on the user's password hash and the front-end server does not have the user's password.

Conversely, Kerberos-integrated authentication utilizes a ticketing infrastructure that is not based on the user's password. Of course, the end user must authenticate with a domain controller during logon, but he will not need his password any further while using network resources. He will only need to get tickets from a Key Distribution Center (KDC). Also, the front-end server will have the capability to request a ticket to a KDC on behalf of the end user. Thus, the front-end server will be able to delegate the user's identity to the back-end server. Of course, Kerberos requires a bit more configuration and some modeling with the assistance of a system administrator.

Claims-Based Authentication

The claims-based authentication mode was introduced with SharePoint 2010. It employs the concept of claims identity, representing each user's identity as tokens made of claims. A claim is a statement, asserted by an issuer, about a subject which is assumed to be true by the reader, due to a trust relationship between the reader and the issuer. The statement can be about any kind of information. For example, it could be the name, the identity, a role membership, a user preference, or anything else. Claims are issued by a Claim Provider and packaged into a Security Token, which is emitted by a Security Token Service, also known as an Identity Provider. The target of the Security Token is a Service Provider, which can be a website, a web service, or whatever else. The entity described by the Security Token is called Subject; in general, this is a user, a server, a service, or anything else that can have an identity of his own.

Each claim consists of a *ClaimType*, which in general is a URI that uniquely defines the type of the claim; a *ClaimValue*, which is the real content of the claim; and a *ClaimValueType*, which defines the data type of the *ClaimValue*. Each claim can also be described by some other information, such as the *Issuer* and the target *Subject*.

The capability to describe an identity as a set of claims (a set of true information) allows supporting any kind of authentication mechanism. In fact, with the claims-based mode, you can still use Windows Authentication, but you can also use FBA or any third-party trusted Identity Provider.

If you use Windows Authentication, under claims-based authentication mode, the Windows identities will be converted to a set of claims representing the current user. You can still take advantage of integrated authentication, because the Windows identity of the current user will be translated into claims at no cost to you. In addition, a Windows user authenticated by using classic mode is almost the same as a user authenticated with claims-based, because internally the user identity is the same. In the back-end SharePoint 2010 always uses claims identities—regardless of the mode you selected on the front-end—to communicate between the front-end servers and the servers (within the same farm) hosting service applications.

In your code, the current user's identity and principal will be instances of type *ClaimsIdentity* and *ClaimsPrincipal*, available in the assembly *Microsoft.IdentityModel* released with Windows Identity Foundation 1.0 (WIF).

> **More Information** For further details about Windows Identity Foundation 1.0, read the book, *Programming Windows Identity Foundation*, by Vittorio Bertocci (Microsoft Press, 2010; ISBN: 978-0-7356-2718-5).

Claims-Authentication Types

The classic mode is provided for compatibility reasons only, but in new installations of SharePoint 2010, you should always choose the claims-based mode. In this section, you will see how this mode supports the various authentication methods, focusing your attention on Windows Authentication and FBA. In Chapter 22, "Claims-Based Authentication and Federated Identities," you will learn more about Trusted Identity Providers.

In the meantime, one important thing to notice is that with the new claims-based mode you can enable multiple authentication methods within the same zone. In previous editions of SharePoint, you had to create one zone for each different authentication method. Now you can have a unique zone—and thus a unique URL—to access your site, but your users will be able to provide their credentials choosing between multiple authentication methods.

When you configure claims-based mode with a unique authentication method, SharePoint will authenticate the end users directly with that unique method. However, if you configure multiple authentication methods, your users will be prompted with a specific page for selecting the authentication method to use. Figure 20-2 depicts the authentication method selection page, configured to support both Windows Authentication and FBA.

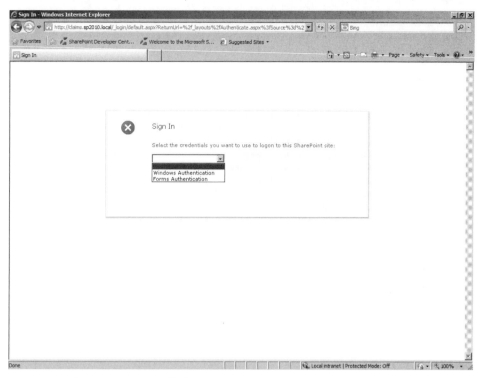

FIGURE 21-2 The Sign In page, in which end users select the authentication method when multiple authentication methods are configured on the same zone.

Under the cover, the authentication engine of SharePoint normalizes all the users' identities into *SPUser* instances, converting every identity into a set of claims. The users' identities normalization process involves invoking a native service application of SharePoint, called Security Token Service. Figure 21-3 shows a functional schema of the identity normalization process managed by SharePoint 2010.

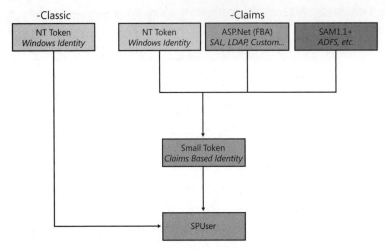

FIGURE 21-3 A functional schema of the identity normalization process managed by SharePoint 2010.

Windows Authentication

As discussed earlier, in terms of capabilities, this is almost the same as the classic mode. However, under the cover the user's identity is translated into a set of claims. If you develop a custom control or Web Part for writing a user's identity, you will see that the current user's identity is a *ClaimsIdentity*. The set of claims that comprise the user's identity by default is presented in the following list:

- *http://schemas.xmlsoap.org/ws/2005/05/identity/claims/nameidentifier*   A claim with a value of type *String* that defines the user name.

- *http://schemas.microsoft.com/ws/2008/06/identity/claims/primarysid*   A claim with a value of type *String* that defines the Security Identifier (SID) of the user.

- *http://schemas.microsoft.com/ws/2008/06/identity/claims/primarygroupsid*   A claim with a value of type *String* that defines the SID of the primary group of the users.

- *http://schemas.microsoft.com/sharepoint/2009/08/claims/userlogonname*   A claim with a value of type *String* that defines the logon name of the user.

- *http://schemas.microsoft.com/sharepoint/2009/08/claims/userid*   A claim with a value of type *String* that defines the user ID of the current user. For Windows Authentication, it assumes a value of "0#.w|*[Username]*", where the string "0#.w|" is a trailer and *[Username]* is the user name of the user. The "w" stands for Windows Authentication.

- *http://schemas.xmlsoap.org/ws/2005/05/identity/claims/name*   A claim with a value of type *String* that defines the name of the user, assuming a syntax like that of the previously described claim (*userid*).

- *http://schemas.microsoft.com/sharepoint/2009/08/claims/identityprovider*   A claim with a value of type *String* that defines the name of the identity provider. For Windows Authentication, it assumes a value of *windows*. This is a SharePoint-specific claim.

- *http://sharepoint.microsoft.com/claims/2009/08/isauthenticated*   A claim with a value of type *String* and an inner value of *True* or *False*, which is used to indicate whether the current user is authenticated. This is a SharePoint-specific claim.

- *http://schemas.microsoft.com/sharepoint/2009/08/claims/farmid*   A claim with a value of type *String* that defines the ID of the current SharePoint Farm. This is a SharePoint-specific claim.

- *http://sharepoint.microsoft.com/claims/2009/08/tokenreference*   A claim with a value of type *String* that defines a reference to the user token. This is a SharePoint-specific claim.

- *http://schemas.microsoft.com/ws/2008/06/identity/claims/groupsid*   A claim with a value of type *String* that defines the SID of a group to which the current user belongs. There could be many claims of this type in a single *ClaimsIdentity*, depending on the number of groups to which the current user belongs.

- *http://schemas.microsoft.com/ws/2008/06/identity/claims/authenticationmethod*   A claim with a value of type *String* that defines the configured authentication method. When using Windows Authentication, it assumes a value of *http://schemas.microsoft. com/ws/2008/06/identity/authenticationmethod/windows*.

- *http://schemas.microsoft.com/ws/2008/06/identity/claims/authenticationinstant*   A claim with a value of type *DateTime* that defines the date and time the token was issued.

To extract the value of the claims, you can use code such as that illustrated in Listing 21-1.

LISTING 21-1 Extracting claims from a current user's identity.

```
ClaimsIdentity ci = this.Page.User.Identity as ClaimsIdentity;
if (ci != null) {
    this.Controls.Add(new LiteralControl("<h2>Claims</h2>"));
    foreach (Claim c in ci.Claims) {
        this.Controls.Add(new LiteralControl(
            String.Format(
                "<div>ClaimType: {0} - ClaimValue: {1} - ClaimValueType: {2}</div>",
                c.ClaimType, c.Value, c.ValueType)));
    }
}
```

In this example, it suffices to cast the current user's identity (*this.Page.User.Identity*) to the *ClaimsIdentity* type of the *Microsoft.IdentityModel* namespace. Assuming the cast is successful, you will be able to enumerate the *Claims* property and extract each individual *Claim* instance.

Forms-Based Authentication

When you configure FBA, you will have the capability to authenticate your users against an external repository of users, which by default can be an LDAP or a Microsoft SQL Server database built by using the standard SQL Membership Provider of ASP.NET. Of course, you can also develop custom membership providers of your own, querying any kind of users' repository. Beginning on page 597, you will see how to configure SharePoint 2010 to support FBA with the standard SQL Membership Provider. The list that follows presents the default set of claims that make up the user's identity when using FBA:

- *http://schemas.xmlsoap.org/ws/2005/05/identity/claims/nameidentifier*   This is the same as in Windows Authentication.

- *http://schemas.microsoft.com/ws/2008/06/identity/claims/role*   A claim with a value of type *String* that defines the name of a role to which the current user belongs. There could be many claims of this type in a single *ClaimsIdentity*, depending on the number of roles to which the current user belongs.

- *http://schemas.microsoft.com/sharepoint/2009/08/claims/userlogonname*   This is the same as in Windows Authentication.

- *http://schemas.microsoft.com/sharepoint/2009/08/claims/userid*   A claim with a value of type *String* that defines the user ID of the current user. For FBA, it assumes a value of *"0#.f|[MembershipProvider]|[Username]"*, where the string *"0#.f|"* is a trailer, *[MembershipProvider]* is the name of the configured Membership Provider, and *[Username]* is the username of the user. The "f" stands for FBA.

- *http://schemas.xmlsoap.org/ws/2005/05/identity/claims/name*   A claim with a value of type *String* that defines the name of the user, assuming a syntax like that of the previously-described claim (*userid*).

- *http://schemas.microsoft.com/sharepoint/2009/08/claims/identityprovider*   A claim with a value of type *String* that defines the name of the identity provider. For FBA, it assumes a value of *forms:[MembershipProvider]*, where *[MembershipProvider]* is the name of the configured Membership Provider. This is a SharePoint-specific claim.

- *http://sharepoint.microsoft.com/claims/2009/08/isauthenticated*   A claim with a value of type *String* and an inner value of *True* or *False*, which is used to indicate whether the current user is authenticated. This is a SharePoint-specific claim.

- *http://schemas.microsoft.com/sharepoint/2009/08/claims/farmid*   A claim with a value of type *String* that defines the ID of the current SharePoint Farm. This is a SharePoint-specific claim.

- *http://sharepoint.microsoft.com/claims/2009/08/tokenreference*   A claim with a value of type *String* that defines a reference to the user token. This is a SharePoint-specific claim.

Configuring FBA with SQL Membership Provider

In this section, you will learn how to configure a SharePoint 2010 web application to support FBA against a SQL Server database.

Configuring the SQL Server Database

To configure SharePoint to support FBA with SQL Membership Provider, you first need to create a SQL Server database file that supports your environment. To do this, you can take advantage of a tool provided by ASP.NET called ASPNET_REGSQL.EXE, which is available in the Microsoft .NET Framework folder. You can invoke ASPNET_REGSQL.EXE within the Visual Studio Command Prompt and have it create a SQL Server database file. The tool is organized as a wizard (see Figure 21-4), with its main steps being as follows:

- **Welcome Screen**   There is nothing more to do here than simply press the Next button.

- **Select A Setup Option**   In this step, you select whether to configure a new database or to remove an existing one. Choose the Configure SQL Server For Application Services option.

- **Select The Server And Database**   Here, you can select the target SQL Server where the database file will be created, together with the authentication method that will be used to communicate with the server and the name of the database file that will be created.

- **Confirm Your Settings**   This is simply a summary of what you selected in the previous two steps.

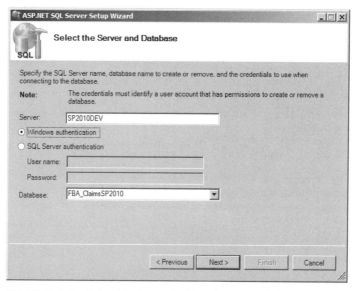

FIGURE 21-4 The Select The Server And Database step of the ASPNET_REGSQL.EXE Wizard.

Note Inspecting the content of this database is beyond the scope of this book; however, you can search the Internet for many articles and blogs about this topic.

After you create the database, you need to configure some users and groups to use in SharePoint. For this purpose—and for the sake of simplicity—you can create a new "ASP.NET Empty Web Site" project in Visual Studio.

 Important Remember that SharePoint 2010 is based on Microsoft .NET Framework 3.5. Therefore, your website should be created using the same target version of .NET Framework to avoid issues with varying assembly versions.

You can configure the website by going to Website | ASP.NET Configuration, which brings up the ASP.NET Web Site Administration Tool. This is a well-known tool with which every ASP.NET developer should be familiar. From there, you can use the Security Setup Wizard to configure your site for supporting FBA using the previously created SQL database. You can also manually configure the web.config, if you like. After completing this task the web.config of the sample site will look like the XML excerpt illustrated in Listing 21-2.

 More Information If you are not familiar with the Web Site Administration Tool site, you can read the document, "Web Site Administration Tool Overview," which is available on MSDN Online at *http://msdn.microsoft.com/en-us/library/yy40ytx0.aspx*.

LISTING 21-2 The web.config of the sample site for configuring FBA in Visual Studio.

```xml
<configuration>
  <connectionStrings>
    <add name="FBASP2010" connectionString="server=SP2010DEV\SQLEXPRESS;database=FBA_
ClaimsSP2010;integrated security=SSPI;"/>
  </connectionStrings>

  <system.web>
    <membership defaultProvider="FBASQLMembershipProvider">
      <providers>
        <add connectionStringName="FBASP2010" applicationName="/"
             passwordAttemptWindow="5" enablePasswordRetrieval="false"
             enablePasswordReset="false" requiresQuestionAndAnswer="true"
             requiresUniqueEmail="true" passwordFormat="Hashed"
             name="FBASQLMembershipProvider"
             type="System.Web.Security.SqlMembershipProvider, System.Web,
Version=2.0.3600.0, Culture=neutral, PublicKeyToken=b03f5f7f11d50a3a" />
      </providers>
    </membership>
```

```
    <roleManager enabled="true" defaultProvider="FBASQLRoleManager">
      <providers>
        <add connectionStringName="FBASP2010" applicationName="/"
            name="FBASQLRoleManager"
            type="System.Web.Security.SqlRoleProvider, System.Web, Version=2.0.3600.0,
Culture=neutral, PublicKeyToken=b03f5f7f11d50a3a" />
      </providers>
    </roleManager>

    <authentication mode="Forms" />
    <authorization>
      <deny users="?"/>
    </authorization>

    <!-- Configuration omitted for the sake of brevity -->

  </system.web>
</configuration>
```

 Note The *type* attribute values in the preceding listing should appear on a single line in your code. They're wrapped here due to typographic constraints.

Those configuration elements will be useful when configuring SharePoint 2010 for FBA. While you're in the Security Setup Wizard, you can also configure some users and groups, for testing purposes. In the sample code that accompanies this chapter, the following roles have been created:

- Admins
- Managers
- Users

In addition, the following users have been created:

- SampleAdmin01
- SampleManager01
- SampleUser01

As their names imply, each user belongs to the corresponding role. You should test your authentication infrastructure writing a couple of sample pages for logging in and logging out.

Configuring SharePoint web.config Files

Now that you have a working configuration for you site, you are ready to apply that configuration to SharePoint. First, you need to locate the web.config of the web application where you will configure FBA. By default, the root folder of a SharePoint web application is located in the C:\inetpub\wwwroot\wss\VirtualDirectories folder of every front-end server.

> **Note** For the sake of simplicity, you could create a new web application by using the SharePoint Central Administration and configure it to use the claims-based authentication mode and then proceed with the following steps.

Next, you need to copy the *connectionStrings/add* element that defines your SQL Server Membership database into the *connectionStrings* element of the target web.config. If the *connectionStrings* section is missing, you must create it from scratch, adding it after the *configSections* element of the web.config, as shown in the following:

```
<connectionStrings>
  <add name="FBASP2010" connectionString="server=SP2010DEV;database=FBA_
ClaimsSP2010;integrated security=SSPI;"/>
</connectionStrings>
```

Then you need to locate the *Membership* and *RoleProvider* sections, within the system.web section of the target web.config. There, you need to copy only the providers' configuration, without changing the default providers that were already configured by SharePoint. The result should look like the following:

```
<membership defaultProvider="i">
  <providers>
    <add name="i" type="Microsoft.SharePoint.Administration.Claims.
SPClaimsAuthMembershipProvider, Microsoft.SharePoint, Version=14.0.0.0, Culture=neutral,
    PublicKeyToken=71e9bce111e9429c" />
    <add connectionStringName="FBASP2010" applicationName="/"
         passwordAttemptWindow="5" enablePasswordRetrieval="false"
         enablePasswordReset="false" requiresQuestionAndAnswer="true"
         requiresUniqueEmail="true" passwordFormat="Hashed"
         name="FBASQLMembershipProvider"
         type="System.Web.Security.SqlMembershipProvider, System.Web, Version=2.0.3600.0,
Culture=neutral, PublicKeyToken=b03f5f7f11d50a3a" />
  </providers>
</membership>
```

```
<roleManager defaultProvider="c" enabled="true" cacheRolesInCookie="false">
  <providers>
    <add name="c" type="Microsoft.SharePoint.Administration.Claims.SPClaimsAuthRoleProvider,
Microsoft.SharePoint, Version=14.0.0.0, Culture=neutral, PublicKeyToken=71e9bce111e9429c" />
    <add connectionStringName="FBASP2010" applicationName="/"
         name="FBASQLRoleManager"
         type="System.Web.Security.SqlRoleProvider, System.Web, Version=2.0.3600.0,
Culture=neutral, PublicKeyToken=b03f5f7f11d50a3a" />
  </providers>
</roleManager>
```

Note The *type* attribute values in the preceding listing should appear on a single line in your code. They're wrapped here due to typographic constraints.

In the previous example, the code highlighted in bold shows that SharePoint 2010 already has a default Membership Provider named "i" and a default Role Provider named "c." These are the providers that manage the claims-based infrastructure.

After you have configured the web.config of the target web application, you should also configure the web.config of the SharePoint Central Administration web application in the same way, as well as the web.config of the internal Security Token Service (STS) of SharePoint. The SharePoint Central Administration web application must be configured so that you can manage users defined in the FBA database from within the administrative pages, as well. You can still find its web.config in a folder in the C:\inetpub\wwwroot\wss\VirtualDirectories path of every front-end server. The STS web application needs to have access to the FBA database in order to retrieve claims and information about the authenticated users during identity normalization. You can find the STS service of SharePoint and its web.config in the SharePoint14_Root\WebServices\SecurityToken folder.

Configuring SQL Server Permissions

To take full advantage of the authentication infrastructure that you just configured, the Application Pools of SharePoint need to have access to the SQL Server Database you configured for FBA. Thus, you need to properly configure the database's permissions. This is a simple but fundamental task. To carry it out, you need to enable the Windows identities configured for:

- SharePoint Central Administration Application Pool
- Security Token Service Application Pool
- Target Web Application Application Pool

All of them need to have the following database role memberships:

- aspnet_Membership_FullAccess
- aspnet_Roles_FullAccess

Configuring SharePoint

You are almost done. Now you simply need to configure the FBA providers through the SharePoint Central Administration interface. To access the list of all the available web applications, click Application Management, Manage Web Applications, choose the FBA target, and then, on the Ribbon, click the Authentication Providers command. In the window that appears, click the Default Configuration hyperlink. The Edit Authentication configuration page opens.

Select the Enable Forms Based Authentication (FBA) check box, and then provide the name for the Membership Provider and Role Provider to use. Figure 21-5 shows the configuration dialog, completed with information based on the current sample scenario.

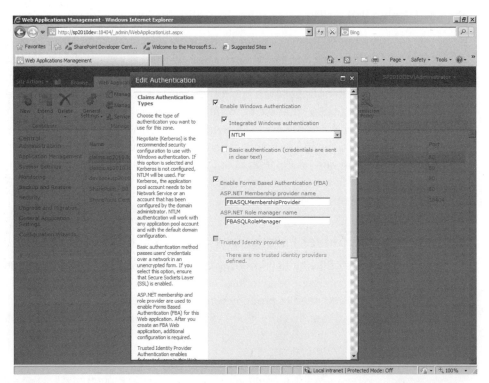

FIGURE 21-5 The Edit Authentication configuration page of the SharePoint Central Administration.

Enabling FBA Users or Roles

The last step in configuring FBA is to enable some users or roles to access the Site Collections defined in your target web application. You can accomplish this task either from the SharePoint Central Administration or from the People And Groups page of the target site.

Notice that if you now try to browse for users or roles, you will be able to browse both Windows and FBA users within the same browsing windows. As is shown in Figure 21-6, from the perspective of SharePoint 2010, all the users are claims identities, regardless of the authentication provider that was used. Notice how searching for "Users" returns one result in the Role: Forms Auth repository and three more results in the Security Group: All Users repository.

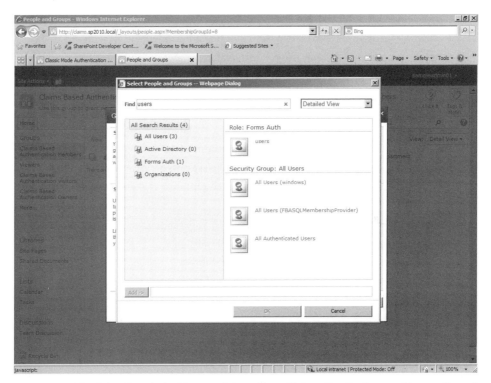

FIGURE 21-6 The Select People And Groups dialog with multiple authentication providers configured.

Authorization Infrastructure

No matter which authentication mode and methods you choose, authorization in SharePoint is always managed the same way. This is a great feature that really improves the quality of life of SharePoint administrators, because they do not need to care about the front-end authentication environment.

Authorization in SharePoint is based on Permissions Levels, which are a formal definition of a set of Permissions. Permission Levels can be assigned to users (*SPUser*) or groups (*SPGroup*). The permission is the low-level item from an authorization viewpoint. There are many permissions defined in SharePoint. Table 21-1 presents the full list, as they are defined in the SharePoint management interface. Consider that these permissions cannot be customized or extended. However, it's unlikely that you would need to customize them because they cover a very wide range of needs.

TABLE 21-1 The List of Permissions Defined in SharePoint 2010

Permission	Description
Manage Lists	Create and delete lists, add or remove columns in a list, and add or remove public views of a list.
Override Check Out	Discard or check in a document which is checked out to another user.
Add Items	Add items to lists and add documents to document libraries.
Edit Items	Edit items in lists, edit documents in document libraries, and customize Web Part Pages in document libraries.
Delete Items	Delete items from a list and documents from a document library.
View Items	View items in lists and documents in document libraries.
Approve Items	Approve a minor version of a list item or document.
Open Items	View the source of documents with server-side file handlers.
View Versions	View past versions of a list item or document.
Delete Versions	Delete past versions of a list item or document.
Create Alerts	Create alerts.
View Application Pages	View forms, views, and application pages. Enumerate lists.
Manage Permissions	Create and change permission levels on the website and assign permissions to users and groups.
View Web Analytics Data	View reports on website usage.
Create Subsites	Create subsites such as team sites, Meeting Workspace sites, and Document Workspace sites.
Manage Web Site	Grants the ability to perform all administration tasks for the website as well as manage content.
Add and Customize Pages	Add, change, or delete HTML pages or Web Part Pages, and edit the website using a Microsoft SharePoint Foundation-compatible editor.
Apply Themes and Borders	Apply a theme or borders to the entire website.
Apply Style Sheets	Apply a style sheet (.CSS file) to the website.
Create Groups	Create a group of users that can be used anywhere within the Site Collection.
Browse Directories	Enumerate files and folders in a website using SharePoint Designer and Web DAV interfaces.
Use Self-Service Site Creation	Create a website using Self-Service Site Creation.

Permission	Description
View Pages	View pages in a website.
Enumerate Permissions	Enumerate permissions on the website, list, folder, document, or list item.
Browse User Information	View information about users of the website.
Manage Alerts	Manage alerts for all users of the website.
Use Remote Interfaces	Use SOAP, Web DAV, the Client Object Model or SharePoint Designer interfaces to access the website.
Use Client Integration Features	Use features which launch client applications. Without this permission, users will have to work on documents locally and upload their changes.
Open	Allows users to open a website, list, or folder in order to access items inside that container.
Edit Personal User Information	Allows a user to change his or her own user information, such as adding a picture.
Manage Personal Views	Create, change, and delete personal views of lists.
Add/Remove Personal Web Parts	Add or remove personal Web Parts on a Web Part Page.
Update Personal Web Parts	Update Web Parts to display personalized information.

A Permission Level is made of a set of permissions, selected from the list in Table 21-1. By default, SharePoint 2010 defines a default set of Permission Levels, which are described in the following list:

- **View Only**   View pages, list items, and documents. Document types with server-side file handlers can be viewed in the browser but not downloaded.

- **Limited Access**   View specific lists, document libraries, list items, folders, or documents when given permissions.

- **Read**   View pages and list items, and download documents.

- **Contribute**   View, add, update, and delete list items and documents.

- **Design**   View, add, update, delete, approve, and customize.

- **Full Control**   Full control.

Chapter 2, "Data Foundation," showed how an out-of-the-box SharePoint site configures four groups of users: Viewers, Site Visitors, Site Members, and Site Owners.

To configure Permission Levels you need to browse to the Site Permissions page, which you can access on the Site Actions menu, on the Site Settings page. Click the Permission Levels ribbon command to display a page in which you can create new Permission Levels.

To create and configure groups, go to the People And Groups page, which you can reach through the Site Settings page.

When you enable Anonymous Access for a site, you will able to configure also permissions for anonymous users. Figure 21-7 demonstrates that an anonymous user can have access to Nothing (no access), to Lists And Libraries, where anonymous users have been explicitly enabled, or to the Entire Web Site. Consider that an anonymous user does not have any claim assigned, but he is still represented by a *ClaimsIdentity* and a *ClaimsPrincipal*, in case of claims-based authentication mode.

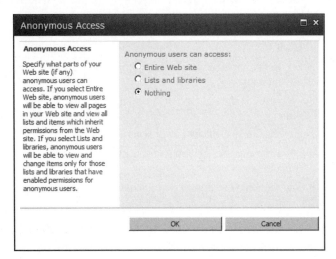

FIGURE 21-7 The Anonymous Access dialog page for configuring anonymous access permissions.

 Note Anonymous Access can be configured from the SharePoint Central Administration via the Authentication Providers page. You used this page earlier in this chapter to configure the authentication providers for a web application.

Once you have defined permission levels and have assigned them to users or groups, you can also override default permissions at the list or library level, or even at the single item level. Because webpages are items, as well as documents or general list items, you can configure permission at the single page level, too.

Summary

In this chapter, you learned how SharePoint 2010 authenticates and authorizes users. In particular, you have seen that there are two authentication modes: classic and claims-based. You can choose three authentication methods, which are: Windows Authentication, Forms-Based Authentication, and Trusted Identity Provider. You also saw how to configure both the claims-based mode and Forms-Based Authentication to authenticate users against a SQL Server database. Finally, you learned how SharePoint manages authorizations and permissions.

Chapter 22

Claims-Based Authentication and Federated Identities

In this chapter, you will take a detailed look at claims-based authentication. You will start with a general overview, focusing your attention on web and HTTP-based scenarios. Then, you will see how to use Windows Identity Foundation (the official Microsoft claims-based framework) to implement a simple Security Token Service of your own. Lastly, you will register that Security Token Service in Microsoft SharePoint 2010 so that you can share a common, single sign-on infrastructure between multiple SharePoint sites and even third-party sites.

Claims-Based Authentication and WS-Federation

Today's software solutions always require user authentication and authorization. However, quite often each application implements its own authentication method and users are obliged to remember and manage many different credentials. Think about a typical day in your life: you log on to your domain network when you turn on your computer; you log on to Facebook, as do so many people the first thing in the morning, using Facebook's specific credentials; next, you move to *www.live.com* where you log on using your Windows Live ID credentials; then, if you need to access your home banking system, you provide another set of credentials specific for that system, too; and so on. The list of examples could be very long, indeed.

The problem is evident; you and everyone else in today's digital world have too many sets of credentials to remember, manage, and keep safe! There's no doubt that it would be a great improvement to decouple applications and software solutions from their authentication environment, taking advantage of a shared set of credentials, and thus avoiding entering authentication information so often. In the ideal digital world, you should authenticate once, at the very beginning of the day, and use a worldwide single sign-on infrastructure.

Now consider the scenario of the emerging cloud computing offerings. Quite often you have some services on premises, such as domain controllers, file servers, ERP, and so forth, and some other online services, such as Microsoft Office 365 (Office, Exchange Online, SharePoint Online, Lync Online), Microsoft CRM Online, and some services built on top of the Windows Azure platform. Of course, users of your internal network's domain should authenticate on the internal network as well as online, and you should avoid multiplying users' credentials and authentications. In the ideal world, you should federate your internal network with the

607

online services, providing a single sign-on experience to your users, utilizing a federated trust between your network on premises and the online services in the cloud.

Furthermore, from a developer's perspective, it is hard to implement the authentication and authorization logic for each and every software solution she implements. It would be better to externalize the authentication infrastructure, concentrating the software implementation on the business logic and rules, eventually providing a custom authorization environment only.

Many software solutions authenticate their users just because they need to authorize access to resources or functionalities based on users' identities. However, they do not really need to collect and maintain users' credentials. From an authorization viewpoint, it suffices to have some information about the users to cluster them in groups or audiences and authorize access to resources based on their properties.

Pushed by these ideas, a few years ago the software market started working on the goal of defining an authentication infrastructure that could be externalized and that could identify every user as a digital identity. Chapter 21, "Authentication and Authorization Infrastructure," shows that a digital identity can be considered as a set of claims. Remember that a claim is a statement that is asserted by an issuer about a subject which is assumed to be true by the reader, due to a trust relationship between the reader and the issuer. The externalized authentication provider is generally defined as the Identity Provider (IP) and often publishes a Security Token Service (STS). The application or software solution externalizing the authentication process is called Service Provider (SP) or Relying Party (RP). The consumer, who uses the SP authenticating with the IP is generally called the Subject. Figure 22-1 portrays an extremely simplified schema of a typical authentication architecture employed by a software solution that uses externalized authentication.

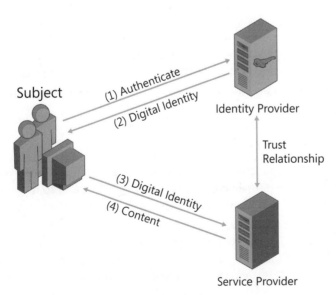

FIGURE 22-1 A simplified schema showing the architecture of a system with externalized authentication.

From a technology viewpoint these concepts use specifications like WS-Security, WS-Trust, and WS-*. The final goal of these specifications is to allow implementing a token-based authentication and authorization system, where tokens can be issued by third parties.

In December 2006, an international and multi-vendor working group defined a specification called Web Services Federation Language 1.1 (WS-Federation), which "defines mechanisms to allow different security realms to federate, such that authorized access to resources managed in one realm can be provided to security principals whose identities are managed in other realms" (quote from WS-Federation 1.1 specification).

 Note If you are interested, you can download the full WS-Federation specification document from *http://specs.xmlsoap.org/ws/2006/12/federation/ws-federation.pdf.*

From a practical viewpoint, WS-Federation defines extensions to the WS-Security and WS-Trust specifications that support exchange of authentication and authorization claims between federated partners, identities brokering, and protection of claims during their transmission across partners. One of the most interesting features of WS-Federation is the capability to provide federation techniques that you can utilize in SOAP-based communication, via WS-Security and WS-Trust, as well as in web browser-based environments. The SOAP scenario is often called "Active Requestor," while the web browser based scenario is referred to as "Passive Requestor."

From the perspective of SharePoint and web/HTTP, the Passive Requestor scenario is the one in which you should be interested.

 Note The Active Scenario (SOAP-oriented) is used by SharePoint 2010 in the service applications' communication infrastructure. However, providing complete coverage of all the WS-Federation scenarios is beyond the scope of this book.

Figure 22-2 illustrates a sequence diagram related to the functional schema of WS-Federation in the Passive Requestor scenario.

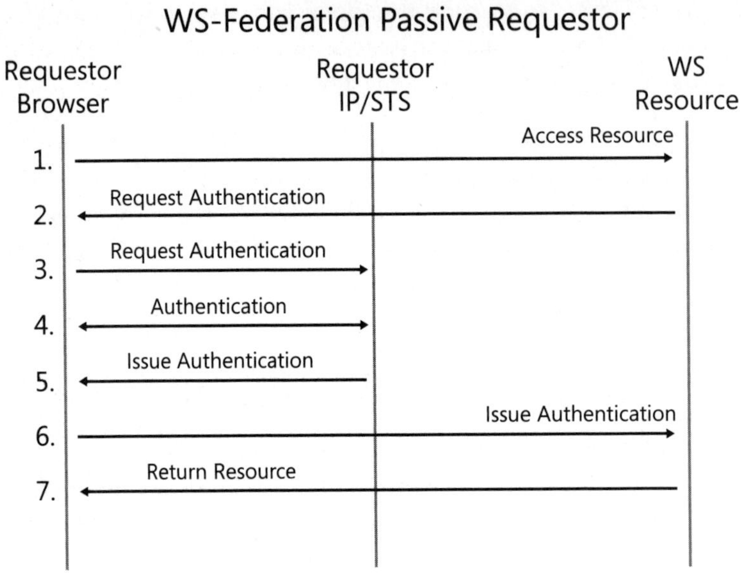

WS-Federation Passive Requestor

FIGURE 22-2 The sequence diagram of WS-Federation for the Passive Requestor scenario.

In the Figure 22-2, the passive requestor scenario walks through the following steps:

- The web browser (Subject) sends a request for a resource to the web server (SP).

- The SP returns a request for authentication and redirects the browser to the STS of the IP.

- The end user authenticates within the IP/STS.

- If the credentials are valid, it receives back an issued token.

- The browser sends (via automatic HTTP POST) the issued token to the SP.

- The SP receives the issued token, validates it against the list of trusted IPs; if the token has been issued by a trusted IP, it marks the end user as authenticated and eventually authorized.

- If the user recognized by the IP/STS is valid, the SP accepts the request and returns the originally requested resource.

The term "Passive" derives from the fact that the web browser is unconsciously and automatically redirected to the IP/STS and then automatically POSTs the token to the SP. Thus, the browser is passive during the authentication process.

If you share the same IP/STS for two or more sites, once an end user has authenticated with the IP/STS, she will be able to obtain issued tokens for all of the federated sites without authenticating again. This is a single-sign-on scenario.

Furthermore, when you log on to SharePoint 2010 using claims-based authentication mode, the front-end does not redirect you to an external IP/STS for authentication. Instead, it communicates in the back-end with the internal IP/STS of SharePoint, using SOAP as the communication protocol.

If you want to realize a complete WS-Federation scenario, you need to register an external IP, together with all the information about its STS. Then, you will be able to authenticate with third-party solutions, whereupon you will experience WS-Federation Passive Requestor concretely.

Implementing an STS with Windows Identity Foundation

Windows Identity Foundation (WIF) is a framework provided by Microsoft that supports .NET developers while developing claims-based solutions. Using WIF you can implement claims consumers (SP or RP) solutions as well as claims providers (IP/STS) solutions of your own. WIF is available both for .NET 3.5 and .NET 4.0, and you need to download and install it as an add-on to your standard development environment. If you simply need to develop a smart client that consumes a claims-based service, you do not necessarily need WIF; the standard implementation of the client stack of WCF will suffice.

> **Note** If you prefer to use WIF without developing custom solutions, you can simply download the WIF runtime engine, which is available as a free download from *http://www.microsoft.com/ downloads/en/details.aspx?FamilyID=eb9c345f-e830-40b8-a5fe-ae7a864c4d76*. However, if you need to develop custom solutions, you should download the WIF SDK, which is available at *http://www.microsoft.com/downloads/en/details.aspx?FamilyID=c148b2df-c7af-46bb-9162- 2c9422208504*. To work with the code samples that accompany this chapter, you must install the WIF SDK.

In the next section, you will learn how to leverage WIF to implement a claims provider solution, which can be used to implement a web-based Passive Requestor scenario, suitable for realizing a single-sign-on user experience shared across multiple sites, whether or not they are implemented with SharePoint.

Building a Security Token Service

Imagine that you have a company with a shared repository of credentials that is based on the standard ASP.NET Membership Providers infrastructure for authenticating users and which will be used both for a SharePoint site and for a classic ASP.NET site. First, you need to create a new project in Microsoft Visual Studio 2010. If you installed WIF SDK, you will have some project templates dedicated to WIF development. To implement new STS, you can start from a new website project of type ASP.NET Security Token Service Web Site. Figure 22-3 shows the new IP/STS site being set up in the New Web Site Wizard.

> **Important** If you installed WIF SDK for .NET 4.0 on top of Microsoft Visual Studio 2010, you will need to choose .NET 4.0 as the target framework for the custom STS website.

FIGURE 22-3 The New Web Site Wizard, shown configured for creating the new IP/STS site.

The project template will prepare a new website project with a couple of .ASPX pages, some code for the STS plumbing, and a *FederationMetadata* folder. Figure 22-4 displays the resulting project outline.

FIGURE 22-4 The project outline for the new STS site based on the ASP.NET Security Token Service Web Site template.

In the illustration, you can see that the Default.aspx and Login.aspx pages are standard ASP. NET pages with a front-end ASPX portion and a code-behind file. The Default.aspx file could be used as is; it simply implements the entry point for sign-in and sign-out logic of the STS. The Login.aspx page implements the logon code, and you should change it, together with the web.config file of the website so that you can implement the authentication method that you want to offer. As it relates of the sample code that accompanies this chapter, the web. config has been configured to use Forms-Based Authentication (FBA) with the same backend ASP.NET Membership database that you used in Chapter 21. The Login.aspx page simply provides the user interface for logging in the end users, utilizing an ASP.NET *Login* control.

The App_Code folder hosts some infrastructural code files that implement the real business logic of the STS, implementing and overriding some native types available in WIF. The main class is defined in the CustomSecurityTokenService.cs code file. In fact, that file implements the core STS engine, inheriting from the *SecurityTokenService* base abstract class, available in the *Microsoft.IdentityModel.SecurityTokenService* namespace, provided by the Microsoft. IdentityModel.dll assembly.

The main areas of intervention that you use to customize the STS implementation are in this class. First, you need to choose whether the STS will serve requests for everyone, or if it will provide claims only to trusted, relying parties. In the latter case, you need to open the CustomSecurityTokenService.cs code file and change the *enableAppliesToValidation* static *Boolean* variable to a value of *true*. In addition, you will also need to define the list of trusted relying parties. By default, the STS uses another static variable, also defined in the *CustomSecurityTokenService* class, named *PassiveRedirectBasedClaimsAwareWebApps* which represents an array of *String*, where each *String* instance is the URL of a trusted relying party. Listing 22-1 demonstrates the class file modified so that it trusts a couple of relying parties.

LISTING 22-1 The *CustomSecurityTokenService* class modified to trust relying parties.

```
public class CustomSecurityTokenService : SecurityTokenService {
    // TODO: Set enableAppliesToValidation to true to enable only the RP Url's
    // specified in the PassiveRedirectBasedClaimsAwareWebApps
    // array to get a token from this STS
    static bool enableAppliesToValidation = true;

    // TODO: Add relying party Url's that will be allowed to get token from this STS
    static readonly string[] PassiveRedirectBasedClaimsAwareWebApps = {
        "http://claims.sp2010.local/_trust/default.aspx",
        "http://ws.devleap.local/DevLeapSite/" };

    // Code omitted for the sake of brevity ...
}
```

Any custom implementation of the *SecurityTokenService* class can override a bunch of abstract methods. However, there are two methods that are fundamental for implementing a real STS. These methods are:

- *GetScope*   This method returns the configuration for the token issuance. For example, here you can determine if the resulting token will be encrypted and/or signed. If encryption or signing is designated, you can choose the digital certificates to use.

- *GetOutputClaims*   This method returns the claims that will be issued to the relying party within the security token. The result of the method is a variable that implements the interface *IClaimsIdentity*, which is available in the runtime of WIF.

In the sample STS that accompanies this chapter, the *GetOutputClaims* method has been overridden to return the following claims:

- *http://schemas.xmlsoap.org/ws/2005/05/identity/claims/name*   Defines the name of the Subject.

- *http://schemas.xmlsoap.org/ws/2005/05/identity/claims/emailaddress*   Defines the e-mail of the Subject.

- *http://schemas.devleap.com/Claims/Username*   Defines the username of the Subject.

- *http://schemas.microsoft.com/ws/2008/06/identity/claims/role*   Defines one role to which the Subject belongs. In the event that a Subject belongs to multiple roles, there will be multiple instances of this claim, one for each distinct role.

Listing 22-2 presents the *GetOutputClaims* method custom implementation.

LISTING 22-2 A custom implementation of *GetOutputClaims*.

```
protected override IClaimsIdentity GetOutputClaimsIdentity(IClaimsPrincipal principal,
RequestSecurityToken request, Scope scope) {
    if (null == principal) {
        throw new ArgumentNullException("principal");
    }

    ClaimsIdentity outputIdentity = new ClaimsIdentity();

    // Issue custom claims.

    // Retrieve the current MembershipUser and his/her Roles
    MembershipUser currentUser = Membership.GetUser();
    String[] roles = Roles.GetRolesForUser();

    // Emit the output claims
    outputIdentity.Claims.Add(new Claim(
        System.IdentityModel.Claims.ClaimTypes.Name, principal.Identity.Name));
```

```
        outputIdentity.Claims.Add(new Claim(
            System.IdentityModel.Claims.ClaimTypes.Email, currentUser.Email));
        outputIdentity.Claims.Add(new Claim(
            "http://schemas.devleap.com/Claims/Username", currentUser.UserName));

        foreach (var role in roles) {
            outputIdentity.Claims.Add(new Claim(ClaimTypes.Role, role));
        }
        return outputIdentity;
    }
```

In the code sample, the *GetOutputClaims* method emits claims based on the current *MembershipUser* instance and his roles. Each emitted claim has a type corresponding to an existing claim type, like *Name* and *EMail*, or custom, like the *Username.*

Lastly, the *FederationMetadata* folder publishes an XML file (*FederationMetadata.xml*), which is the manifest of the IP/STS. Internally, the file defines the endpoints published by the STS as well as the claims offered by the claims provider. By default the project template will provide the following claims:

- *http://schemas.xmlsoap.org/ws/2005/05/identity/claims/name* Defines the name of the authenticated Subject.

- *http://schemas.microsoft.com/ws/2008/06/identity/claims/role* Defines the role of the authenticated Subject.

In the current example, the claims have been customized and you need to change the content of the FederationMetadata.xml file according to the custom implementation of the *CustomSecurityTokenService* class. However, the FederationMetadata.xml file is digitally signed and you cannot change it manually. Instead, you should change or generate it using some infrastructural classes offered by WIF.

> **Note** You can also evaluate a third-party tool called "Federation Metadata Generator," which was developed by Thinktecture and is freely distributed at *http://static.thinktecture.com/chris-tianweyer/FederationMetadataGenerator_1.0.zip*. Otherwise, you can also try the "STS Starter Kit" project, which is also implemented and freely distributed by Thinktecture at *http://start-ersts.codeplex.com/*. In this section's example, you will work with standard .NET tools, except for the generation of the FederationMetadata.xml file, which will be made using the "Federation Metadata Generator" tool, for the sake of convenience.

Lastly, you should consider the web.config file of the auto-generated STS project. For an STS website, the web.config file defines some *appSettings* items related to the STS internal implementation. Listing 22-3 displays the web.config file of the current sample.

LISTING 22-3 The *web.config* file of the current sample STS.

```
<appSettings>
  <add key="IssuerName" value="PassiveSigninSTS"/>
  <add key="SigningCertificateName" value="CN=STSTestCert"/>
  <add key="EncryptingCertificateName" value=""/>
</appSettings>
```

In this listing, there is an *IssuerName* setting that simply defines the description of the current STS. Then, there is the *SigningCertificateName* setting, which defines the subject name of the certificate that will be used to digitally sign the security tokens issued by the STS. In addition, there is an *EncryptingCertificateName* setting, which defines the subject name of the certificate that will be used to encrypt the security tokens. In real solutions, these are valid certificates and they are different; the signing certificate identifies the token issuer, while the encrypting certificate should be specific for each different relying party.

By default, WIF uses an auto-generated signing certificate named "STSTestCert." This certificate is also automatically added to the machine certificate store. In addition, the encrypting setting is left blank, in order to disable encryption. However, in production environments you should avoid using the STSTestCert, and you should also encrypt issued tokens.

 Important You should ensure that the user identity for the application pool of IIS running your STS code has the proper rights to access the private key of the signing certificate.

Depending on the type of authentication method you would like to use, the web.config file might also have some configuration items related the authentication method. In the current example, the STS implements authentication using FBA and ASP.NET Membership. Thus, the web.config file has the sections illustrated in Listing 22-4.

LISTING 22-4 A code excerpt of the web.config file related to the authentication configuration.

```
<system.web>
  <membership defaultProvider="FBASQLMembershipProvider">
    <providers>
      <add connectionStringName="FBASP2010" applicationName="/"
           passwordAttemptWindow="5" enablePasswordRetrieval="false"
           enablePasswordReset="false" requiresQuestionAndAnswer="true"
           requiresUniqueEmail="true" passwordFormat="Hashed"
           name="FBASQLMembershipProvider"
           type="System.Web.Security.SqlMembershipProvider, System.Web,
Version=2.0.3600.0, Culture=neutral, PublicKeyToken=b03f5f7f11d50a3a" />
    </providers>
  </membership>
```

```
    <roleManager enabled="true" defaultProvider="FBASQLRoleManager">
      <providers>
        <add connectionStringName="FBASP2010" applicationName="/"
              name="FBASQLRoleManager"
              type="System.Web.Security.SqlRoleProvider, System.Web, Version=2.0.3600.0,
Culture=neutral, PublicKeyToken=b03f5f7f11d50a3a" />
      </providers>
    </roleManager>
    <!-- FBA -->
    <authentication mode="Forms">
      <forms loginUrl="Login.aspx" protection="All" timeout="30" name=".ASPXAUTH"
path="/" requireSSL="false" slidingExpiration="true" defaultUrl="default.aspx"
cookieless="UseDeviceProfile" enableCrossAppRedirects="false" />
    </authentication>

    <!-- Deny Anonymous users. -->
    <authorization>
      <deny users="?" />
    </authorization>

    <!-Configuration omitted for the sake of brevity -->

</system.web>
```

Note The *type* attribute values in the preceding listing should appear on one line in your code; they're wrapped here due to typographic constraints.

In the web.config file, there is a custom location section to enable free access from the outside to the FederationMetadata.xml file.

Building a Relying Party

To test the IP/STS that you have just implemented, you can add a new website project of type "Claims-aware ASP.NET Web Site" to the current solution. This kind of project is a common ASP.NET website, with the addition of some references to libraries and *HttpModule* instances provided by the infrastructure of WIF. To configure the site to consume claims provided by the custom IP/STS, you can use the Add STS Reference menu extension provided in Visual Studio 2010 by the WIF SDK (see Figure 22-5).

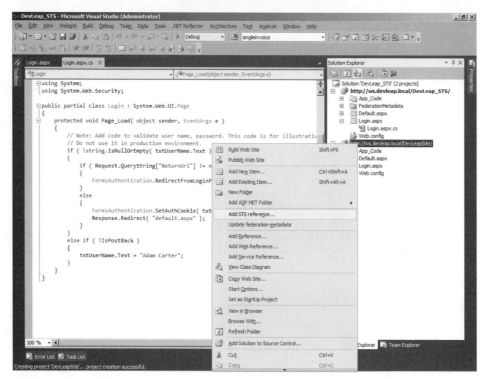

FIGURE 22-5 The menu extension to Add STS Reference to an ASP.NET website project.

This menu extension opens a wizard that collects information from you about the target IP to use. The wizard steps are the following:

- **Welcome To The Federation Utility Wizard**   Here, you can choose the web.config that will be used to support an external STS. This is usually the path to the web.config file of the current web project. In addition, you need to provide the URL of the current site, which is used as a parameter for the target STS during invocation.

- **Security Token Service**   Here, you can disable any previously-configured STS, you can register a new STS, including the corresponding project creation, or you can register an existing STS, providing the URL of its FederationMetada.xml file.

- **Security Token Encryption**   During this step, you can determine whether the STS will issue encrypted tokens or clear tokens. For encrypted tokens, you will need to provide the digital certificate to use for decryption.

- **Offered Claims**   This step summarizes a read-only view of the claims provided by the remote STS.

- **Summary**   This last step provides a summary of the setup. From this step you can also configure a timer job for periodically refreshing the reference to the STS.

Once you have completed the wizard steps, your ASP.NET website will be ready for authenticating users, taking advantage of the custom IP/STS. By pressing F5 or by navigating to the Default.aspx page of the site, you will be redirected to the STS logon page. There, you will be able to authenticate and, in case of valid credentials, you will get back a security token with all the custom claims defined in Listing 22-2. Figure 22-6 shows the logon page of the STS.

FIGURE 22-6 The logon page of the custom IP/STS site.

Take a closer look at the web.config file after it has been modified by the Add STS Reference Wizard. First, notice that a new configuration section named *microsoft.identityModel* has been defined that targets the WIF infrastructure. The standard ASP.NET authentication method has been set to *None*, because authentication events will be intercepted by an *HttpModule* of WIF called *WSFederationAuthenticationModule*, available in the *Microsoft. IdentityModel.Web* namespace. There are also two more modules registered that correspond to the classes *SessionAuthenticationModule* and *ClaimsPrincipalHttpModule*. The former avoids repeating authentication against the STS for each request, storing the session security token in a cookie stored securely and locally for the current web application. The latter is defined in case your website does not relate to an external STS for authentication, but you still want to use claims during authentication and authorization.

Listing 22-5 shows the configuration of the *microsoft.identityModel* section of the XML configuration file.

LISTING 22-5 An excerpt of the web.config file related to the *microsoft.identityModel* section.

```xml
<microsoft.identityModel>
  <service>
    <audienceUris>
      <add value="http://ws.devleap.local/DevLeapSite/" />
    </audienceUris>
    <federatedAuthentication>
      <wsFederation passiveRedirectEnabled="true"
        issuer="http://ws.devleap.local/DevLeap_STS/"
        realm="http://ws.devleap.local/DevLeapSite/" requireHttps="false" />
      <cookieHandler requireSsl="false" />
    </federatedAuthentication>
    <applicationService>
      <claimTypeRequired>
        <claimType
          type="http://schemas.xmlsoap.org/ws/2005/05/identity/claims/name"
          optional="true" />
        <claimType
          type="http://schemas.xmlsoap.org/ws/2005/05/identity/claims/emailaddress"
          optional="true" />
        <claimType
          type="http://schemas.devleap.com/Claims/Username" optional="true" />
        <claimType
          type="http://schemas.microsoft.com/ws/2008/06/identity/claims/role"
          optional="true" />
      </claimTypeRequired>
    </applicationService>
    <issuerNameRegistry type="Microsoft.IdentityModel.Tokens.
ConfigurationBasedIssuerNameRegistry, Microsoft.IdentityModel, Version=3.5.0.0,
Culture=neutral, PublicKeyToken=31bf3856ad364e35">
      <trustedIssuers>
        <add thumbprint="E9BDE461E8774F4D7EA4D393ED4DA2DC7536CEAE"
          name="http://ws.devleap.local/DevLeap_STS/" />
      </trustedIssuers>
    </issuerNameRegistry>
  </service>
</microsoft.identityModel>
```

The key points of this listing are highlighted in bold and summarized in the following list:

■ The list of the audience URIs, which are the URLs that represent the relying party (RP).

■ A federated Authentication element, which defines the configuration details of the WS-Federation protocol. For example, here you can enable the passive requestor profile, the URI of the token issuer, and the realm of the relying party. Remember that the realm will be evaluated by the STS to determine whether the current site (RP) has been authorized to request tokens issuing or not.

■ The list of claims that will be requested to the IP/STS for the purpose of acquiring information about an authenticated user.

- The list of trusted issuers, which are the token issuers that are trusted by the current website. Each trusted issuer is identified by the thumbprint of its certificate. It is important to update this value when moving from a development environment, based on a test certificate, to a production environment using a real certificate.

If you try to log on to the sample website, using the just-configured IP/STS, you will see that the Default.aspx page automatically included in the site based on the project of type Claims-aware ASP.NET Web Site will show you all the claims related to the current user. Figure 22-7 depicts a sample home page of the test site after it has authenticated an administrative test user.

FIGURE 22-7 The home page of the custom claims-consumer website, just after a user's authentication.

SharePoint Trusted Identity Providers

As you have already seen in Chapter 21, SharePoint 2010 uses WIF and the WS-Federation specification as a kind of authentication provider. Thus, the IP/STS you have implemented in the previous section can be registered in SharePoint 2010 as a trusted identity provider. To do this, you must complete some configuration steps.

Trusting the IP/STS

To begin, you need to trust the identity provider from the perspective of SharePoint. So, you need to retrieve the certificate of the IP/STS and register it in the list of trusted issuers of SharePoint. If you are consuming an STS published by a third-party IP, then you can extract the public key of the certificate from the FederationMetadata.xml file, selecting the following XPath node:

```
EntityDescriptor/RoleDescriptor/KeyDescriptor/KeyInfo/X509Data/X509Certificate
```

You can simply copy the content of that XML node into a text file and save it with a .cer file extension.

Otherwise, if you are working with an STS published by the same machine on which you are running SharePoint, you can export the .cer certificate file from the local machine certificate store. Also, if you implemented the STS with WIF, keep in mind that by default WIF uses an auto-generated *STSTestCert* certificate. Figure 22-8 shows a screenshot of the Certificate Manager tool, in which you can see the *STSTestCert* certificate. You can export that *STSTestCert* certificate by using the Certificate Manager tool options.

Once you have the .cer file you can import it into the private SharePoint 2010 certificate store either by using a Windows PowerShell script or the UI of the SharePoint Central Administration. The following is the syntax of the cmdlet for Windows Powershell:

```
$cert = New-Object System.Security.Cryptography.X509Certificates.
X509Certificate2("STSTestCert.cer")
New-SPTrustedRootAuthority -Name "DevLeap custom STS certificate" -Certificate $cert
```

As the previous code shows, it suffices to retrieve an instance of the *X509Certificate2* class, referencing the .cer file path, and then load it by invoking the *New-SPTrustedRootAuthority* cmdlet specific of SharePoint 2010.

If you prefer to use the UI of the SharePoint Central Administration, browse to the Security section, select Manage Trust, and then under the General Security group, add a new item by providing a name and the path to the .cer file into the Establish Trust Relationship page, as shown in Figure 22-9.

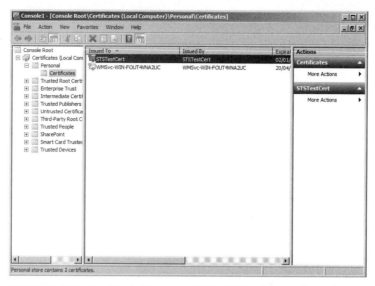

FIGURE 22-8 The Certificate Manager with the STSTestCert certificate (auto-generated by WIF) selected.

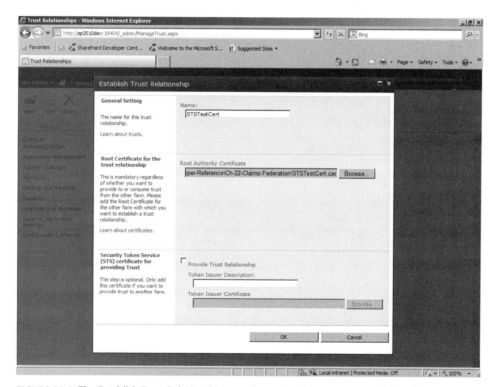

FIGURE 22-9 The Establish Trust Relationship page for registering a new trust relationship.

Registering the Identity Provider and Mapping Claims

Now you are ready to register the custom IP into SharePoint 2010. To begin, you need to define the claims that you would like to manage, and then map them to claims that will be available on the SharePoint side. In fact, each time you authenticate a subject by using an external IP, you have the capability to map the claims emitted by the STS in the security token to claims of the SharePoint side. For example, the custom IP/STS that you implemented returns a claim of type *http://schemas.devleap.com/Claims/Username*, which represents the *username* of the current user from a DevLeap_STS viewpoint. In SharePoint, you will have the opportunity to map this claim to another claim type, or you can leave it as is. The claims-based authentication infrastructure of SharePoint will translate claims for you during user authentication.

> **Important** The claims mapping capability is really useful and important, because you could have multiple IPs registered for a single web application, and the capability to translate claims from one type to another allows SharePoint to normalize claims during authentication. You also have the capability to implement custom claim providers, inheriting from the class *SPClaimProvider*, to augment claims of a current principal during the authentication phase. However, for the sake of brevity, this chapter will not cover this topic. Nevertheless, if you are interested you can read the document "Claims Walkthrough: Writing Claims Providers for SharePoint 2010" available on MSDN Online at *http://msdn.microsoft.com/en-us/library/ff699494. aspx*.

To register claims mapping you can use a few commands in Windows PowerShell. Here are the commands for mapping the claims issued by the custom DevLeap_STS:

```
$map1 = New-SPClaimTypeMapping -IncomingClaimType "http://schemas.devleap.com/Claims/
Username" -IncomingClaimTypeDisplayName "UserName"
-SameAsIncoming
$map2 = New-SPClaimTypeMapping -IncomingClaimType "http://schemas.xmlsoap.org/ws/2005/05/
identity/claims/emailaddress" -IncomingClaimTypeDisplayName "Email" -LocalClaimType "http://
schemas.xmlsoap.org/claims/EmailAddress"
$map3 = New-SPClaimTypeMapping -IncomingClaimType "http://schemas.microsoft.com/ws/2008/06/
identity/claims/role" -IncomingClaimTypeDisplayName "Role" -SameAsIncoming
```

For example, in the previous excerpt, any *username* claim is left way it is as it comes in (see the argument *-SameAsIncoming*) as well as any *role* claim. While, any claim describing the *emailaddress* of the authenticated subject will be translated from a claim type value of *http:// schemas.xmlsoap.org/ws/2005/05/identity/claims/emailaddress* into a claim type value of *http://schemas.xmlsoap.org/claims/EmailAddress*.

The last step for registering an external IP is to create a new entry for the identity provider in the list of available providers. Again, you can use a Windows PowerShell script to accomplish this. Here is a sample command excerpt:

```
$realm = "http://claims.sp2010.local/_trust/default.aspx"
$signinurl = "http://ws.devleap.local/DevLeap_STS/default.aspx"
New-SPTrustedIdentityTokenIssuer -Name "DevLeap STS" -Description "DevLeap custom STS"
-Realm $realm -ImportTrustCertificate $cert -ClaimsMappings $map1,$map2,$map3
-SignInUrl $signinurl -IdentifierClaim $map1.InputClaimType
```

The preceding script defines the *$realm* variable, corresponding to the *realm* of the claims-consumer site. The value of this URL (*/_trust/default.aspx* relative to the target SharePoint site) corresponds to a page that will be automatically added to the root folder of your SharePoint web application when you activate a trusted identity provider as an authentication technique. That page will be almost empty in terms of ASP.NET markup, and it will inherit its behavior from the page *TrustedProviderSignInPage*, defined in the *Microsoft.SharePoint.IdentityModel. Pages* namespace. This page will only redirect the user's browser to the IP/STS logon page.

Another variable defined in the script is the URL of the logon page of the IP/STS (*$signinurl*). Finally, the script registers a new *SPTrustedIdentityTokenIssuer* instance by invoking the cmd-let *New-SPTrustedIdentityTokenIssuer*. The arguments provided to this cmdlet in the previous example are: a *Name* and a *Description* for the new identity provider; the *realm* of the target SharePoint site; the X.509 certificate of the IP/STS and the sign-in URL; the claims mappings and the type of the claim that will be considered as the identifier claim for the authenticated subject.

Configuring the Target Web Application

To complete the configuration process you need to add the new identity provider to the list of authentication providers for the target web application. On to the SharePoint Central Administration page, under the Application Management section, click Manage Web Applications. A window appears that presents the list of all the available web applications. Choose the web application for which you want to enable the IP/STS as one of the authentication methods. Next, on the Ribbon, click the Authentication Providers command. In the window that appears, click the Default Configuration hyperlink. The Edit Authentication configuration page opens, as shown in Figure 22-10. Here, you can select the new identity provider.

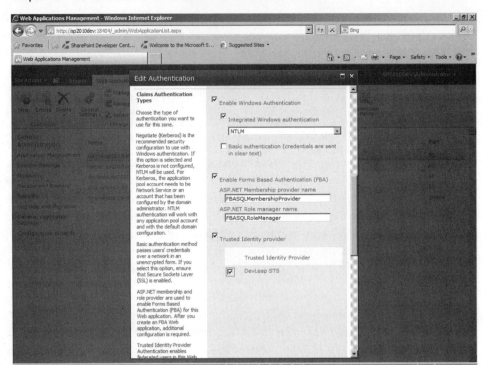

FIGURE 22-10   The Edit Authentication configuration page of the SharePoint Central Administration.

That's it! Now you're ready to authenticate your users by using the custom IP/STS. Figure 22-11 shows the authentication options that are presented to any end user willing to authenticate.

FIGURE 22-11   The authentication options displayed to any end user willing to authenticate.

Notice the third option, DevLeap STS, which will redirect the user to the logon page of the IP/STS. Of course, if you configure the identity provider as the unique authentication provider, your users will be redirected automatically to the IP/STS without stepping into the authentication method selection page.

Now you will also be able to configure users authenticated by the IP as specific SharePoint users or to give them specific permissions. Figure 22-12 shows the Select People And Groups dialog window, with a search result obtained by searching against the currently configured IP.

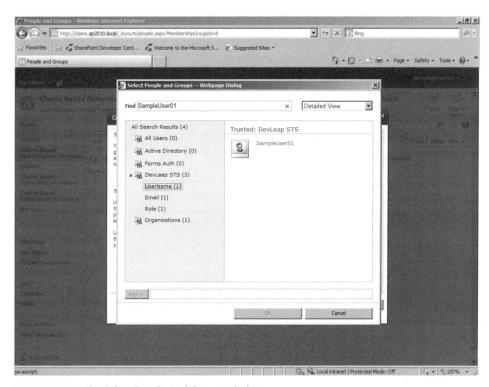

FIGURE 22-12   The Select People And Groups window.

If you try to access the sample site you defined earlier in this chapter in the section, "Building a Relying Party" on page 617, you will see that you will be automatically authenticated and you will have access to the site. Thus, you are experiencing a real single-sign-on user experience.

Summary

In this chapter, you learned about what a claims-based environment is, what WS-Federation is (from a general viewpoint), and how to use WIF to develop an STS for a custom Identity Provider. You also saw how to register an STS implemented with WIF into SharePoint for the purpose of authenticating SharePoint users through an external and trusted IP.

Chapter 23

Code Access Security and Sandboxed Solutions

Beginning with the first edition of Microsoft .NET, Code Access Security has been the foundation of security. Because Microsoft SharePoint 2010 is completely based on Microsoft .NET, it natively takes advantage of Code Access Security capabilities. In this chapter, you'll learn the general principles of how Code Access Security works in .NET, then in Microsoft ASP. NET applications, and finally, in SharePoint solutions. In addition, you will also see how Code Access Security has been employed in architecting a completely new and awesome feature of SharePoint 2010: sandboxed solutions. You will learn what sandboxed solutions are, what permissions are granted to sandboxed code, and how to define solution validators and sandbox full-trust proxies.

Code Access Security

Code Access Security (CAS) is at the very heart of .NET and supersedes the execution of any code within the .NET CLR. When you load a .NET assembly to execute its code, the CLR asks to the CAS engine to check whether that assembly has the permission to work or not. In fact, whenever you load a .NET assembly, under the cover, the .NET CLR environment retrieves all the available information about that assembly: the author, the publisher, the Internet zone from which the code comes from, and so on. This information is called evidence, and based on the evidence of an assembly, the .NET CLR determines its corresponding execution permissions. At the same time, the .NET CLR determines the *PermissionSet* that is assigned to the target assembly and consequently authorizes or denies code execution, access to resources, networking permissions, or even code loading.

 Important Complete coverage of CAS is beyond the scope of this book. If you are interested in more information, read the book, *.NET Security*, by Jason Bock, Peter Stromquist, Tom Fischer, and Nathan Smith (APress, 2002; ISBN: 978-1-5905-9053-9). You should also consider that beginning with .NET 4.0, Microsoft has changed some of the basic behaviors of CAS. Thus, you should also read the article, "Exploring the .NET Framework 4 Security Model," available at *http://msdn. microsoft.com/en-us/magazine/ee677170.aspx*. And finally, keep in mind that the examples and topics covered in this chapter target .NET Framework 3.5, because SharePoint is based on .NET Framework 3.5.

As its name implies, a *PermissionSet* is a set of permissions, wherein each permission is a .NET class defining a specific permission. Table 23-1 lists the very basic permissions available in .NET, together with a pair of permissions that are specific to SharePoint (highlighted in bold).

TABLE 23-1 Some of the Main Permissions Available in .NET and SharePoint

Permission Name	Description
AspNetHostingPermission	Controls access permissions in environments hosted by ASP.NET. It defines a *Level* attribute, which can assume the following values: *None, Minimal, Low, Medium, High,* and *Unrestricted.*
ConfigurationPermission	Defines a permission that allows methods or classes to access configuration files.
DnsPermission	Defines a permission that allows methods or classes to access DNS servers on the network.
EnvironmentPermission	Defines a permission, which controls access to system and user environment variables.
FileIOPermission	Defines a permission that controls access to file system folders and files.
IsolatedStorageFilePermission	Specifies the right to use and the quota of usage for a private virtual file system.
PrintingPermission	Defines a permission, which controls access to printers.
ReflectionPermission	Controls access to the reflection APIs.
RegistryPermission	Defines a permission that controls the ability to access the system registry.
SecurityPermission	Defines permissions that will be applied to code. *SecurityPermission* uses a set of *Flags* defined with a homonym attribute, and that can assume the following values: *NoFlags, Assertion, UnmanagedCode, SkipVerification, Execution, ControlThread, ControlEvidence, ControlPolicy, SerializationFormatter, ControlDomainPolicy, ControlPrincipal, ControlAppDomain, RemotingConfiguration, Infrastructure, BindingRedirects,* and *AllFlags.*
SharePointPermission	Defines a custom permission that controls the access to SharePoint by code.
SmtpPermission	Defines a permission that allows methods or classes to access SMTP servers on the network.
SocketPermission	Defines a permission that allows methods or classes to manage sockets on the network.
SqlClientPermission	Defines a permission that allows methods or classes to access SQL servers on the network.
UIPermission	Controls access to the user interface and to the Clipboard.
WebPartPermission	Defines a custom permission that controls the access to Web Parts resources.
WebPermission	Defines a permission that allows methods or classes to access HTTP resources and servers on the network.

.NET permissions are extensible. This can be a tremendous benefit, because you can develop .NET classes of your own, representing custom permissions, and use them while defining a *PermissionSet.* A *PermissionSet* can be assigned to code groups, which are groups of assemblies sharing some common evidences, or they can be assigned to code executed by a .NET process.

Partially Trusted ASP.NET Code

The capability to execute ASP.NET code in a sandboxed environment has been available since ASP.NET 1.1. This gives you the ability to select the policy level with which to execute the code. By default, every ASP.NET solution has a policy level of type Full Trust, which means that the web application can do whatever it wants, being only subject to Windows security policies. However it is possible—and suggested—to change the Full Trust policy level to a safer level, with a limited set of permissions that are really needed by the current application. ASP.NET provides some native policies, such as Minimal Trust, Low Trust, Medium Trust, and High Trust. Each policy defines a specific set of permissions, and you should choose the right one for your specific needs on a per-application basis. For example, if a web application does not need to access the file system of the hosting server, why should you give the application permission to do that? A web application with more permissions than what it really needs is just a convenient access point for a hacker.

You can change the trust level of a web application to the proper level for your needs by editing the web.config file. Listing 23-1 illustrates the web.config file for a web application based on .NET 3.5 and configured for a Minimal Trust level.

LISTING 23-1 A *web.config* file of a web application configured for Minimal Trust level.

```xml
<?xml version="1.0" encoding="utf-8" ?>
<configuration>
  <system.web>

    <!-- Configuration omitted for the sake of simplicity -->

    <trust level="Minimal" originUrl="" />

    <!-- Configuration omitted for the sake of simplicity -->

  </system.web>
</configuration>
```

If you are working with .NET 3.5 on a 64-bit machine (as does SharePoint 2010), the default trust levels are defined in dedicated XML files, which are available in the %WINDIR%\Microsoft.NET\Framework64\v3.5\Config folder. The reference files are:

- *web_hightrust.config* Defines the High Trust level. Use the value *High* for the level attribute.

- *web_mediumtrust.config* Defines the Medium Trust level. Use the value *Medium* for the level attribute.

- *web_lowtrust.config* Defines the Low Trust level. Use the value *Low* for the level attribute.

- *web_minimaltrust.config* Defines the Minimal Trust level. Use the value *Minimal* for the level attribute.

The Full Trust level does not have a dedicated policy file, because it is a native system policy level. Keep in mind that if you need to assign wider permissions to a specific class or library, you should not enlarge the permissions for the entire web application. Similarly, you can define a custom policy level, which is a custom XML policy file copied from an existing one, adding a *PermissionSet* that targets your custom code only. In the following section, you will learn how to accomplish this task, for those times when you are working in a SharePoint solution.

If you need to configure a custom policy level in a web application, you must register the custom policy file and reference it in the web.config. Listing 23-2 demonstrates a web.config registering a custom policy level for a web application.

LISTING 23-2 A *web.config* file registering a custom policy level.

```xml
<?xml version="1.0" encoding="utf-8" ?>
<configuration>
  <system.web>
    <securityPolicy>
      <trustLevel name="CustomLevel" policyFile="custom_policy.config" />
    </securityPolicy>
    <trust level="CustomLevel" originUrl="" />

    <!-- Configuration omitted for the sake of simplicity -->

  </system.web>
</configuration>
```

While in Listing 23-3 you can see the content of a sample policy file.

LISTING 23-3 The content of a sample policy file (web_minimaltrust.config of .NET 3.5).

```xml
<configuration>
  <mscorlib>
    <security>
      <policy>
        <PolicyLevel version="1">
          <SecurityClasses>
            <SecurityClass Name="AllMembershipCondition"
             Description="System.Security.Policy.AllMembershipCondition,
               mscorlib, Version=2.0.0.0, Culture=neutral,
               PublicKeyToken=b77a5c561934e089"/>
            <SecurityClass Name="AspNetHostingPermission"
              Description="System.Web.AspNetHostingPermission, System,
              Version=2.0.0.0, Culture=neutral,
              PublicKeyToken=b77a5c561934e089"/>

            <!-- XML code omitted for the sake of brevity -->
```

```xml
          <SecurityClass Name="SecurityPermission"
            Description="System.Security.Permissions.SecurityPermission,
            mscorlib, Version=2.0.0.0, Culture=neutral,
            PublicKeyToken=b77a5c561934e089"/>

          <!-- XML code omitted for the sake of brevity -->

        </SecurityClasses>
        <NamedPermissionSets>
          <PermissionSet class="NamedPermissionSet" version="1"
            Unrestricted="true" Name="FullTrust"
            Description="Allows full access to all resources" />
          <PermissionSet class="NamedPermissionSet" version="1"
            Name="Nothing"
            Description="Denies all resources, including the right to execute" />
          <PermissionSet class="NamedPermissionSet" version="1" Name="ASP.Net">
            <IPermission class="AspNetHostingPermission" version="1"
              Level="Minimal" />
            <IPermission class="SecurityPermission" version="1"
              Flags="Execution" />
          </PermissionSet>
        </NamedPermissionSets>
        <CodeGroup class="FirstMatchCodeGroup" version="1"
          PermissionSetName="Nothing">
          <IMembershipCondition class="AllMembershipCondition" version="1" />
          <CodeGroup class="UnionCodeGroup" version="1"
            PermissionSetName="ASP.Net">
            <IMembershipCondition class="UrlMembershipCondition" version="1"
              Url="$AppDirUrl$/*" />
          </CodeGroup>
          <CodeGroup class="UnionCodeGroup" version="1"
            PermissionSetName="ASP.Net">
            <IMembershipCondition class="UrlMembershipCondition" version="1"
              Url="$CodeGen$/*" />
          </CodeGroup>
          <CodeGroup class="UnionCodeGroup" version="1"
            PermissionSetName="Nothing">

            <!-- XML code omitted for the sake of brevity -->

          </CodeGroup>
        </CodeGroup>
        </PolicyLevel>
      </policy>
    </security>
  </mscorlib>
</configuration>
```

 Note The *Description* attribute values in the preceding code should appear on a single line in your code. They're wrapped here due to typographic constraints.

At the very top of the file there is the declaration of all the permissions classes that will be referenced in the policy file. Each permission item corresponds to a *SecurityClass* element. Next, there are some *PermissionSet* elements, declaring groups of permissions. Each permission is defined through an *IPermission* element. The *PermissionSet* instances will be assigned to their target *CodeGroup* elements, which are defined just after the *PermissionSet* elements. Each *CodeGroup* indetifies its members, declaring elements of type *IMembershipCondition*.

SharePoint and CAS

The structural architecture of SharePoint is deeply rooted in the principle of *secure by default*, so it enforces a very tight base-level security policy, which is a customization of the Minimal Trust level, called WSS_Minimal. There is also a WSS_Medium policy level, if you need to slightly escalate constraints. If you would like to inspect these policy levels, you can look at the files wss_mediumtrust.config and wss_minimaltrust.config, which are available in the SharePoint14_Root\CONFIG folder and are referenced in the web.config of every SharePoint web application.

Table 22-2 compares these two policy levels. Consider as well that any permission that is not illustrated in Table 22-2 is forbidden in any of the two policy levels.

TABLE 22-2 Comparison of WSS_Minimal and WSS_Medium Policy Levels (source: SharePoint 2010 SDK)

Permission	WSS_Medium	WSS_Minimal
AspNetHostingPermission	Medium	Minimal
DnsPermission	Unrestricted	None
EnvironmentPermission	Read: TEMP, TMP, OS, USERNAME, COMPUTERNAME	None
FileIOPermission	Read, Write, Append, PathDiscovery:Application Directory	None
IsolatedStoragePermission	AssemblyIsolationByUser, Unrestricted UserQuota	None
PrintingPermission	Default printing	None
SecurityPermission	Execution, Assertion, ControlPrincipal, ControlThread, RemotingConfiguration	Execution
SharePointPermission	ObjectModel = true	None
SqlClientPermission	AllowBlankPassword=false	None
WebPartPermission	Connections = true	Connections = true
WebPermission	Connect to origin host (if configured)	None

As an example, in Table 22-2 you can see that a SharePoint web application with the default WSS_Minimal policy level cannot host .NET code that accesses a SQL Server database

(*SqlClientPermission* = None). In addition, a .NET class deployed on a SharePoint site by default cannot access the SharePoint Server Object Model, based on the argument for *SharePointPermission* in the WSS_Minimal policy. On the contrary, when you deploy farm-level solutions, you will not see any issue related to these strict defaults. In fact, by default, a farm-level solution deploys assemblies in the Global Assembly Cache (GAC) and any .NET assembly deployed in the GAC is automatically assigned a Full Trust permission set.

> **Important** There are many SharePoint developers who deploy their solutions at the farm level, simply to avoid addressing of the consequent security topics. However, this is a bad practice, and they expose their sites and customers to the risk of security breaches. You should never give Full Trust permissions to custom code running in SharePoint—just for the sake of simplicity. Quite to the contrary, you should always assign each assembly exactly the permissions it needs: no more, no less. Beginning on page 645, you will see how to develop sandboxed solutions, which are a new capability of SharePoint 2010, designed exactly to help you to avoid leaving custom assemblies with Full Trust permissions just because they were deployed in the GAC. In addition, if you develop solutions targeting Microsoft Office 365, you cannot deploy farm-level solutions; you can only deploy sandboxed solutions.

However, often virtue is in the middle, and it is not correct to deploy everything into the GAC, just for the sake of simplicity. Nevertheless, if you try to deploy a Web Part such as the one show in Listing 23-4 at the web application level (for instance, in the */bin* folder of the target web application) by using a custom WSP package that targets a single web application, you will trigger an exception of type *System.Security.SecurityException* with the following error message:

```
Request for the permission of type 'Microsoft.SharePoint.Security.SharePointPermission,
    Microsoft.SharePoint.Security, Version=14.0.0.0, Culture=neutral,
    PublicKeyToken=71e9bce111e9429c' failed
```

This exception arises as the result of using of the Server Object Model (highlighted in bold).

LISTING 23-4 A Web Part that requires a custom permission level to run.

```
public class ShowWelcome : WebPart {
    protected override void CreateChildControls() {
        SPWeb web = SPControl.GetContextWeb(HttpContext.Current);

        LiteralControl literal = new LiteralControl(
            String.Format("Welcome {0}", web.CurrentUser.Name));
        this.Controls.Add(literal);
    }
}
```

To solve this issue, you can create a sandboxed solution, as you will learn beginning on page 645. Otherwise, you should raise the trust level of the full web application, which is a bad solution, or you could define a custom policy level for your assembly and deploy it through a

WSP SharePoint Solution. Chapter 8, "SharePoint Features and Solutions," described what a WSP is and how to deploy custom developments with features and solutions. Listing 8-5 illustrates that a *Solution* element manifest can have a child element of type *CodeAccessSecurity*, which specifies custom code access security policies. Here you will dive into details of declaring that element. The *CodeAccessSecurity* element can contain one or more *PolicyItem* elements, which internally declare a subset of a security policy. Listing 23-5 presents a custom *Solution* element with a *CodeAccessSecurity* child element declared.

LISTING 23-5 A WSP manifest with custom security policy deployment.

```
<Solution xmlns="http://schemas.microsoft.com/sharepoint/" SolutionId="399bfa99-73b8-
42cd-a096-f879ef125ffb" SharePointProductVersion="14.0">
  <CodeAccessSecurity>
    <PolicyItem>
      <PermissionSet
        class="NamedPermissionSet" version="1" Name="CustomPolicyWebPart">
        <IPermission class="AspNetHostingPermission" version="1" Level="Medium" />
        <IPermission class="SecurityPermission" version="1"
          Flags="Execution, ControlPrincipal" />
        <IPermission class="Microsoft.SharePoint.Security.SharePointPermission,
          Microsoft.SharePoint.Security, Version=14.0.0.0, Culture=neutral,
          PublicKeyToken=71e9bce111e9429c" version="1" ObjectModel="True" />
      </PermissionSet>
      <Assemblies>
        <Assembly Name="DevLeap.SP2010.CustomPolicyWebPart"
          PublicKeyBlob="002400000048000009400000060200000024000052534131300
            04000001000100e3fc0594d6d003a10368fbca704d93fe3d2ca67777e985369c
            8503924bc0b70f54e02be59b2cb133139880b2356fd67016d9a4a2c99c416e32c
            49bafe766deb05ae9d2fea2a81096ca496b1a594c8430ca37a93a0fa0e31cec21
            8f8beb1c6db1a109dec860fda78ad5f864674cf1fc4babf4f5fce7cfc5dcb6766
            70c714c68ea" Version="1.0.0.0" />
      </Assemblies>
    </PolicyItem>
  </CodeAccessSecurity>
  <Assemblies>
    <Assembly Location="DevLeap.SP2010.CustomPolicyWebPart.dll"
      DeploymentTarget="WebApplication">
      <SafeControls>
        <SafeControl Assembly="DevLeap.SP2010.CustomPolicyWebPart, Version=1.0.0.0,
          Culture=neutral, PublicKeyToken=e11ce962f93bfe29"
          Namespace="DevLeap.SP2010.CustomPolicyWebPart.ShowWelcome" TypeName="*" />
      </SafeControls>
    </Assembly>
  </Assemblies>
  <FeatureManifests>
    <FeatureManifest
      Location="DevLeap.SP2010.CustomPolicyWebPart_DeployShowWelcome\Feature.xml" />
  </FeatureManifests>
</Solution>
```

Note The long *class*, *PublicKeyBlob*, and *Assembly* attribute values in the preceding listing should appear on one line in your code. They're wrapped here due to typographic constraints.

The source code illustrates that the *PolicyItem* defines a *PermissionSet* element, which targets one or more assemblies, defined in the *Assemblies* element. The *PermissionSet* element is almost the same as it was in Listing 23-3. Each *Assembly* element references a .NET assembly using its name, version, and public key blob. The public key blob can be obtained by using the SN.EXE command line tool, invoked by the following syntax:

```
SN.EXE –Tp assemblyfile.dll
```

The output of this command is illustrated in the following excerpt:

```
Microsoft (R) .NET Framework Strong Name Utility  Version 4.0.30319.1
Copyright (c) Microsoft Corporation.  All rights reserved.

Public key is
0024000004800000940000000602000000240000525341310004000001000100e3fc0594d6d003
a10368fbca704d93fe3d2ca67777e985369c8503924bc0b70f54e02be59b2cb133139880b2356f
d67016d9a4a2c99c416e32c49bafe766deb05ae9d2fea2a81096ca496b1a594c8430ca37a93a0f
a0e31cec218f8beb1c6db1a109dec860fda78ad5f864674cf1fc4babf4f5fce7cfc5dcb676670c
714c68ea

Public key token is e11ce962f93bfe29
```

The public key blob portion is highlighted in bold. You should copy it, put it on a unique line and paste the result into the *PublicKeyBlob* attribute of the target *Assembly* element.

Note This technique of declaring a custom security policy through a *Solution* manifest is often employed while deploying custom Web Parts that cannot be installed via sandboxed solutions, but that you do not want to deploy into the GAC.

When you deploy a solution with a custom policy item, the SharePoint engine warns you that the solution contains a CAS policy, as illustrated in Figure 23-1. You must explicitly accept to apply a custom policy; otherwise, it could reduce the security of your environment. Even using the STSADM.EXE command line tool, while invoking the *deploysolution* operation you will need to provide the *–allowCasPolicies* attribute while deploying the solution. If you don't, the engine will block deployment for security reasons. Also, when using Windows PowerShell, you need to provide the *–CASPolicies* parameter to the *Install-SPSolution* cmdlet.

Note Unfortunately, with the RTM version of Visual Studio 2010 there is a known issue that causes the package deployment to fail when you use a custom policy. However, there is a knowledge base article that describes how to solve this problem, which is available at *http://support.microsoft.com/kb/2022463*. If you want to avoid the problem, you can deploy the package manually.

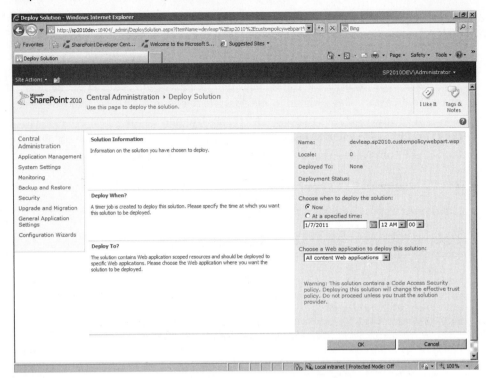

FIGURE 23-1 The SharePoint Central Administration alerts you about a WSP with a Code Access Security policy.

After deploying your WSP on a target site, you will see that the assembly has been copied into the */bin* folder of the web application root that hosts the target site. Furthermore, the web.config file of the web application has been backed up and changed. The new copy of the file defines a new *trustLevel* element that declares a custom security configuration file. Lastly, the *trust* element will have a *level* attribute with a value of *WSS_Custom*. If you deploy two or more solutions on the same web application, all with a custom CAS policy configuration, the deployment engine of SharePoint will merge the policies into a unique custom file.

Listing 23-6 shows the web.config modified so that applies the new policy.

LISTING 23-6 The web.config file, modified to apply the new policy.

```
<?xml version="1.0" encoding="UTF-8" standalone="yes"?>
<configuration>

  <!-- Configuration omitted for the sake of simplicity  -->

  <system.web>
    <securityPolicy>
      <trustLevel name="WSS_Medium" policyFile="C:\Program Files\Common Files\
Microsoft Shared\Web Server Extensions\14\config\wss_mediumtrust.config" />
```

```
      <trustLevel name="WSS_Minimal" policyFile="C:\Program Files\Common Files\
Microsoft Shared\Web Server Extensions\14\config\wss_minimaltrust.config" />
      <trustLevel name="WSS_Custom" policyFile="C:\Program Files\Common Files\
Microsoft Shared\Web Server Extensions\14\config\wss_custom_wss_minimaltrust.config"
/>
    </securityPolicy>

    <!-- Configuration omitted for the sake of simplicity  -->

    <trust level="WSS_Custom" originUrl="" />

    <!-- Configuration omitted for the sake of simplicity  -->

  </system.web>

  <!-- Configuration omitted for the sake of simplicity  -->

</configuration>
```

 Note The *policyFile* attribute values in the preceding listing should appear on one line in your code. They're wrapped here due to typographic constraints.

Sandboxed Solutions Overview

The first half of this chapter clearly shows that deploying a SharePoint solution with the proper security rights is not always a simple matter. Moreover, a GAC deployment often is not the best choice from a security viewpoint and is invasive for the target farm, and although a WSP with a custom policy is safer, it's still invasive because it requires you to copy files onto the target file system and to change the web.config of the target web applications. In the era of cloud computing and online hosted services, you should not rely on deployment techniques that are so invasive of the target farm.

Fortunately, Microsoft SharePoint Foundation 2010 introduced the concept of sandboxed solutions. Sandboxed solutions are WSP solutions that can be uploaded and deployed by authorized users at the Site Collection level, running within a safe and limited execution context. All the sandboxed solutions are stored in a dedicated solution gallery, which is persisted in the content database of the current Site Collection. Thus, backup and restore policies also gain the benefits of this new capability.

The code executing within a sandboxed solution can use only a limited subset of the available types and namespaces of the SharePoint Server Object Model. This is done to avoid having users deploying Trojan Horses.

Sandboxed solutions can be monitored and validated by farm administrators, giving them the ability to monitor memory consumption, CPU execution time, exceptions count, database queries, and so on. If a sandboxed solution deployed by a user consumes too many resources, an administrator can deactivate it, and avoid stressing the environment.

Figure 23-2 depicts the user interface of the Solution Gallery, which is the page available for managing all the sandboxed solutions of the current Site Collection. You can access this via the Site Settings page of the current Site Collection.

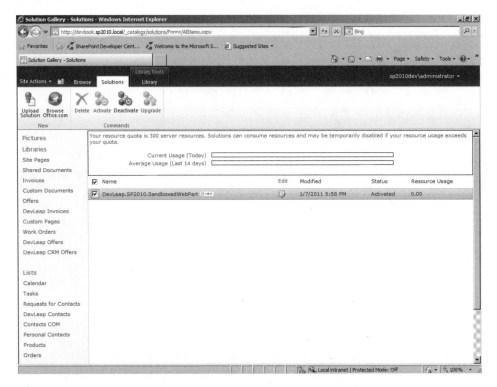

FIGURE 23-2 The Solution Gallery user interface.

Sandboxed Solutions Architecture

A sandboxed solution is a WSP package that is deployed in the solution gallery, at the Site Collection level. The deployment process comprises the following steps:

- **Upload** Uploads into the Solution Gallery.
- **Activation** Activates a previously-uploaded solution. During activation the solution is validated, and any Site Collection–level feature is activated, too.

Once you have activated a solution, you can process the following management steps:

- **Deactivation** Deactivates an active solution. This can be done manually by an authorized user or automatically if the solution consumes too many resources.

- **Deletion** Deletes the WSP package from the Solution Gallery.

- **Upgrade** Occurs whenever you upload a WSP into the Solution Gallery that has the same solution identifier of a previously-existing solution, but with a different file hash code (a different file content). During this phase, any feature upgrade actions are executed, as well. See Chapter 8 for further details about this topic.

A sandboxed solution is executed in a dedicated .NET application domain, which runs on a dedicated and isolated process with a restricted set of permissions. When a front-end server receives a request targeting a sandboxed solution, it utilizes an Execution Manager engine, which routes the request to the SharePoint User Code Service (SPUCHostService.exe). The User Code Service routes the request to the target application domain, which runs in a dedicated process called SPUCWorkerProcess.exe. Because every sandboxed solution acts in a restricted environment, every request targeting the SharePoint API will be routed to a third process called SPUCWorkerProcessProxy.exe, which is responsible for effectively invoking SharePoint. You can inspect the configuration and behavior of these processes by browsing the SharePoint14_Root\UserCode folder.

Figure 23-3 displays a functional schema of the sandboxed solutions in SharePoint 2010.

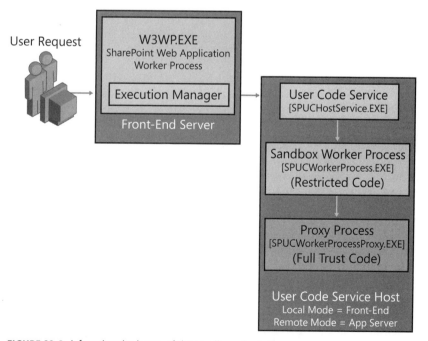

FIGURE 23-3 A functional schema of the sandboxed solutions.

Lastly, you can configure the farm to run sandboxed solutions in either local or remote mode. In local mode, each sandboxed solution runs on the front-end that receives the request; in remote mode, each sandboxed solution runs on back-end application servers that are dedicated to running sandboxed solutions. When using remote mode, there is also a native load balancing engine that will route requests to the least loaded server, if there are multiple application servers.

 Important It is fundamental to know the names of the worker processes that run sandboxed solutions, because you will need to attach to them when you debug.

By default every sandboxed solution runs under a trust level called WSS_Sandbox and defined by a CAS policy. This CAS policy file is not directly referenced by the web.config of a SharePoint web application. Instead, it is referenced by the process of the Sandboxed Solutions engine.

Listing 23-7 illustrates the *PermissionSet* defined in the corresponding policy file.

LISTING 23-7 An excerpt of the *PermissionSet* defined in the policy file declaring the WSS_Sandbox trust level.

```
<PermissionSet class="NamedPermissionSet" version="1"
        Name="SPSandBox">
    <IPermission class="AspNetHostingPermission"
            version="1" Level="Minimal" />
    <IPermission  class="SharePointPermission"
            version="1" ObjectModel="True" UnsafeSaveOnGet="True" />
    <IPermission  class="SecurityPermission"
            version="1" Flags="Execution" />
</PermissionSet>
```

The listing defines the following permissions:

- SharePointPermission.ObjectModel

- SharePointPermission.UnsafeSaveOnGet

- SecurityPermission.Execution

- *AspNetHostingPermissionLevel = Minimal*

The CAS policy applied to a sandboxed solution is defined in the wss_usercode.config file, which is available in the SharePoint14_Root\CONFIG folder. However, the SharePoint Server Object Model is not completely available. You have access only to a subset of the namespaces and types normally available.

Note If you need to do more with your sandboxed solutions, you can take advantage of an external full-trust proxy, which will be discussed beginning on page 650.

 More Information For further details about the namespaces and types available in a sandboxed solution, read the document, "Namespaces and Types in Sandboxed Solutions," which is available on MSDN OnLine at *http://msdn.microsoft.com/en-us/library/ee537860.aspx*.

A sandboxed solution by default can deploy the following features:

- Content Types/Fields
- Content Type Binding
- Custom actions
- Declarative workflows
- Features
- List Definitions
- List Instances
- Module/files
- Navigation
- Onet.xml
- Event Receivers (of type *SPItemEventReceiver*, *SPListEventReceiver*, *SPWebEventReceiver*)
- Web Parts (not Visual Web Parts)
- WebTemplate feature elements

Moreover, still by default, you cannot deploy the following features:

- Application Pages
- Custom Action Group
- Farm-scoped features
- HideCustomAction element
- Visual Web Parts
- Web Application-scoped features
- Workflows with code

You can find some custom project templates on the network that allow you to slightly change these default behaviors. For example, on Codeplex there is a Visual Web Part template that you can use to deploy Visual Web Parts through sandboxed solutions.

Solutions Monitoring

While a sandboxed solution runs, the SharePoint environment collects the following data:

- CPU execution time
- Memory consumption
- Database query time
- Abnormal termination
- Critical exceptions
- Unhandled exceptions
- Data marshaling size
- Percent processor time
- Process handle count
- Process thread count
- Database query count
- Process CPU cycles
- Unresponsive process count

Each data collected is translated into *resource points* through a conversion process based on *resource measures*, which calculates the number of resource points consumed by every package. A farm administrator can configure the maximum number of resource points that can be consumed daily by a Site Collection. If the Site Collection exceeds that limit, all the sandboxed solutions will be put in offline for the remainder of the day. Of course, you can configure or even disable the quota templates defined in the product.

In addition, each individual sandboxed solution has an *AbsoluteLimit* property that defines the maximum level of resource points that can be consumed serving a single request. If a sandboxed solution exceeds that limit during a single request, the worker process hosting the solution will be automatically restarted. There is also a *WorkerProcessExecutionTimeout* limit that can be exceeded by a single request. Similarly with the *AbsoluteLimit* property, if a sandboxed solution exceeds the *WorkerProcessExecutionTimeout* limit, a worker process recycle occurs. All these properties and limits can be configured and tuned by a farm administrator, by using Windows PowerShell.

Solutions Validation

One last interesting topic about sandboxed solutions is validation. You can develop and install solution validation classes to provide custom verification and validation processes. As you have already seen in the previous sections, when you activate a new solution from the solution gallery, the validation process is invoked. This process involves validating the solution first, and then each assembly deployed by the solution.

The validation process can implement any custom validation logic; if the validation process fails, you can raise an error message and redirect the user to a specific custom error page. In the section, "Implementing a Solution Validator," beginning on page 647, you will learn how to develop a solution validator.

Creating a Sandboxed Solution

To create a sandboxed solution, you need to start from a new project targeting SharePoint 2010. In the first step of the SharePoint Customization Wizard (Figure 23-4), select to deploy a sandboxed solution, which is the proposed default. Figure 23-5 shows the property grid of a SharePoint 2010 project, underlying the target deployment property.

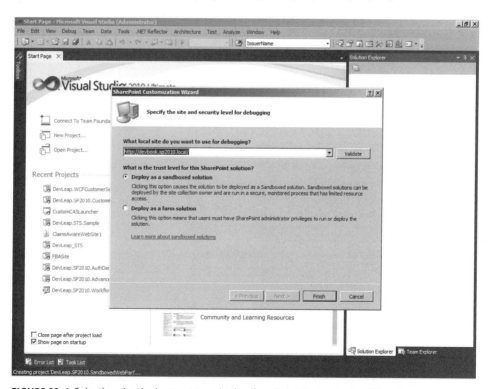

FIGURE 23-4 Selecting the deployment type in the SharePoint Customization Wizard.

Later, you will be able to change the target deployment choice by editing the project properties.

Once you have defined a sandboxed project, the development process is nearly the same as any other. However, you should be aware that you will not have access to all the classes and types available in SharePoint 2010, because the context is restricted.

For example if you try to write a line of code such as the following:

```
SPSecurity.RunWithElevatedPrivileges(...)
```

The IntelliSense of Visual Studio will not provide you help, because the *SPSecurity* class requires a higher level of trust. Of course, if you write custom code that uses forbidden types, your code will compile anyway. However, when you will try to execute it, you will get an exception of type *SPUserCodeSolutionExecutionFailedException*.

FIGURE 23-5 The property to select whether the current SharePoint 2010 project targets the Solutions Gallery.

Listing 23-8 presents a Web Part deployed through a sandboxed solution.

LISTING 23-8 A Web Part deployed by means of a sandboxed solution.

```
public class ListOfItems: WebPart {

    [WebBrowsable(true)]
    [Personalizable(PersonalizationScope.Shared)]
    [WebDescription("Title of the Source list")]
    [WebDisplayName("Source list")]
    [Category("Data Foundation")]
    public String SourceListTitle { get; set; }
```

```
    protected GridView grid;

    protected override void CreateChildControls() {
        if (!String.IsNullOrEmpty(this.SourceListTitle)) {
            SPWeb web = SPContext.Current.Web;
            SPList sourceList = web.Lists[this.SourceListTitle];

            this.grid = new GridView();
            this.Controls.Add(grid);

            List<String> listItemsTitles = new List<string>();

            foreach (SPListItem item in sourceList.Items) {
                listItemsTitles.Add(item.Title);
            }
            this.grid.DataSource = listItemsTitles;
            this.grid.DataBind();
        }
        else {
            this.Controls.Add(new LiteralControl("Please configure this Web Part"));
        }
    }
}
```

Press F5 in Visual Studio to automatically deploy your solution into the solution gallery of the target site, and you can now use the custom Web Part.

Implementing a Solution Validator

A solution validator is a class inheriting from type *SPSolutionValidator*, which is available in namespace *Microsoft.SharePoint.UserCode*. This class offers a couple of methods:

```
public virtual void ValidateAssembly(SPSolutionValidationProperties properties,
    SPSolutionFile assembly);
public virtual void ValidateSolution(SPSolutionValidationProperties properties);
```

The former must be overridden in order to validate a single assembly deployed by a solution. It receives an argument of type *SPSolutionValidationProperties*, which provides some information about the solution package, and an argument of type *SPSolutionFile*, which describes the assembly. The latter method validates an entire solution, occurs before execution of *ValidateAssembly*, and still receives an argument of type *SPSolutionValidationProperties*.

If you need to develop a custom solution validator, you should start from an Empty SharePoint Project template so that you can take advantage of the deployment capabilities of Microsoft Visual Studio 2010. To deploy a solution validator you need to select a farm-level solution and add a farm-level feature.

Listing 23-9 displays a sample solution validator.

LISTING 23-9 A sample solution validator.

```
[Guid("39C408AE-AE75-4FFC-BBC2-D420A0207981")]
public class DevLeapSolutionValidator : SPSolutionValidator {
    private const string validatorName = "DevLeap Solution Validator";

    public DevLeapSolutionValidator() { }

    public DevLeapSolutionValidator(SPUserCodeService userCodeService) :
        base(validatorName, userCodeService) {
        // This should be an hash code of the validator solution
        // For the sake of simplicity it has been used
        // the current year value
        this.Signature = 2011;
    }

    public override void ValidateAssembly(SPSolutionValidationProperties properties,
      SPSolutionFile assembly) {
        base.ValidateAssembly(properties, assembly);

        // Check if the assembly name contains DevLeap
        if (assembly.Location.Contains("DevLeap")) {
            // Set the Valid flag to false
            properties.Valid = false;
            // Set the error message
            properties.ValidationErrorMessage = "Invalid assembly file";
            // Redirect to a custom error page (application page)
            properties.ValidationErrorUrl = String.Format(
              "/_layouts/DevLeap.SP2010.SandboxValidator/InvalidAssembly.aspx? " +
              "package={0}&assembly={1}",
                properties.PackageFile.Location, assembly.Location);
        }
        else {
            // Set the Valid flag to true
            properties.Valid = true;
        }
    }

    public override void ValidateSolution(
      SPSolutionValidationProperties properties) {
        base.ValidateSolution(properties);

        // Check if the package file name contains DevLeap
        if (properties.PackageFile.Location.Contains("DevLeap")) {
            // Set the Valid flag to false
            properties.Valid = false;
            // Set the error message
            properties.ValidationErrorMessage = "Invalid solution package";
        }
```

```
        else {
            foreach (SPSolutionFile file in properties.Files) {
                // You could also check every single file of the solution
            }
        }

        // Set the Valid flag to true
        properties.Valid = true;
    }
}
```

The validator itself is a public class that you need to add to the current project. It inherits from the *SPSolutionValidator* base class. Every solution validator class needs to have a *Guid* attribute with a unique GUID value. In addition, you need to implement a public constructor that accepts a parameter of type *SPUserCodeService*. That constructor will rely on the base class constructor, passing the validator name and the argument of type *SPUserCodeService* received. Internally, the constructor will initialize the value for the *Signature* property of the current validator instance. For example, this property should be calculated as the hash code of the current version of the validator, and it should change when you change the validator. Lastly, Listing 23-9 shows the implementation of both the *ValidateSolution* and *ValidateAssembly* methods. Notice that both the methods return their result assigning a value of *true* or *false* to the *Valid* property of the argument of type *SPSolutionValidationProperties*. The default value for the *Valid* attribute is *false*.

A solution validator must be registered in the environment, and for this purpose, you can use a Windows PowerShell script or a custom feature with a feature receiver, both registering the solution validator by using the SharePoint Server Object Model. Listing 23-10 shows a feature receiver registering the sample validator illustrated in Listing 23-9.

LISTING 23-10 A feature receiver configuring a custom solution validator.

```
[Guid("19dfd704-461a-48ec-a7f4-0411354b56e6")]
public class SandboxValidatorFeatureEventReceiver : SPFeatureReceiver {
    public override void FeatureActivated(SPFeatureReceiverProperties properties) {
        SPUserCodeService userCodeService = SPUserCodeService.Local;
        if (userCodeService != null) {
            SPSolutionValidator validator =
                new DevLeapSolutionValidator(userCodeService);
            userCodeService.SolutionValidators.Add(validator);
        }
    }

    public override void FeatureDeactivating(
        SPFeatureReceiverProperties properties) {
        SPUserCodeService userCodeService = SPUserCodeService.Local;
```

```
        if (userCodeService != null) {
          SPSolutionValidator validator =
            new DevLeapSolutionValidator(userCodeService);
          userCodeService.SolutionValidators.Remove(validator.Id);
        }
      }
    }
```

Figure 23-6 depicts the output of a failed validation process. This output uses a custom application page included in the sample solution validator project that accompanies this chapter.

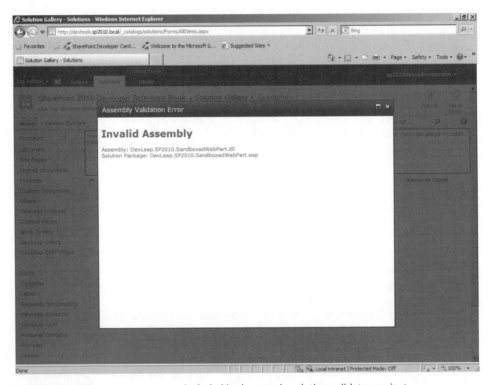

FIGURE 23-6 The custom error page included in the sample solution validator project.

Full-Trust Proxies

You have already seen that by default, a sandboxed solution can perform only a small set of operations, due to security policy restrictions. Suppose that you need to develop a custom Web Part that queries a SQL Server database to show a list of records. Listing 23-7 illustrates that with a sandboxed solution, you do not have a *SqlClientPermission*. Thus, you could think that a sandboxed solution isn't the right solution.

Fortunately, the architecture of sandboxed solutions provides the capability to utilize external full-trust proxies, deployed and authorized by farm administrators so that you can provide full-trust code execution capabilities to sandboxed solutions. Because the full-trust proxies can be installed by farm administrators only, you do not reduce the stability and security of your environment. Similarly, you have the capability to provide a set of rich utility libraries, available to all authorized sandboxed solutions and monitored by farm administrators.

Implementing a Full-Trust Proxy

To develop a custom full-trust proxy you need to create a new "Empty SharePoint Project" project configured for farm-level deployment. The assembly containing the proxy needs to be marked with the attribute *AllowPartiallyTrustedCallers* of .NET CAS, because it will be deployed in GAC and will be invoked by sandboxed solutions, which are partially trusted callers. This attribute can be inserted in the *AssemblyInfo.cs* source code file by using the following syntax:

```
[assembly:AllowPartiallyTrustedCallers]
```

The full-trust proxy must also be implemented as a public class, which inherits from the *SPProxyOperation* base abstract class available in the *Microsoft.SharePoint.UserCode* namespace. Listing 23-11 shows the definition of the *SPProxyOperation* class.

LISTING 23-11 The definition of the *SPProxyOperation* class.

```
public abstract class SPProxyOperation {
    protected SPProxyOperation();
    public abstract object Execute(SPProxyOperationArgs args);
}
```

Here, you can see an *Execute* abstract method, which must be overridden in order to implement the execution logic of the custom full-trust proxy. The *Execute* method returns a result of type *Object*, which allows you to manage any kind of result, and accepts an argument of type *SPProxyOperationArgs*, or any type inherited from *SPProxyOperationArgs*. If you need to provide some custom arguments to the method that you want to execute, you should implement a custom *SPProxyOperationArgs* class.

For example, if you have a custom sandboxed solution that needs to query an external database, you could implement the full-trust proxy as a class that queries a target database that accepts a custom argument representing the connection string of the target SQL Server. Listing 23-12 presents a sample implementation of a full-trust proxy, together with a custom *SPProxyOperationArgs* class.

LISTING 23-12 The custom implementation of a full-trust proxy.

```
[Serializable]
public class RetrieveNWindCustomersArgs : SPProxyOperationArgs {
    public String SqlConnectionString { get; set; }
}

public class RetrieveNWindCustomers : SPProxyOperation {
    public override object Execute(SPProxyOperationArgs args) {
        // Prepare a variable to host the result
        DataSet result = null;

        // Check if the args parameter is of custom type
        RetrieveNWindCustomersArgs typedArgs = args as
            RetrieveNWindCustomersArgs;
        if (args != null) {
            // In case args is of the right type
            using (SqlConnection cn =
              new SqlConnection(typedArgs.SqlConnectionString)) {
                using (SqlDataAdapter da =
                  new SqlDataAdapter("SELECT * FROM Customers", cn)) {
                    result = new DataSet();
                    da.Fill(result);
                }
            }
        }

        return result;
    }
}
```

The custom *SPProxyOperationArgs* class implementation is marked with the *Serializable* attribute and should contain only serializable members. In fact, the full-trust proxy and the sandboxed consumer will work in different processes and the SharePoint engine will serialize the argument while passing it from the consumer to the proxy.

The inner implementation of the *Execute* method is up to you. In the current example, the code simply queries the table *Customers* of the well-known Northwind database.

Registering the Full-Trust Proxy

After implementing the proxy, you need to define a feature with a feature receiver that will use some custom code for registering it in the farm. Listing 23-13 provides the code of the feature receiver that registers and un-registers the current sample proxy.

LISTING 23-13 The code of the feature receiver handling the registration of the sample proxy.

```
[Guid("5a1b6767-dc11-40e0-8785-0be2271b2bd1")]
public class FullTrustProxyFeatureEventReceiver : SPFeatureReceiver {
  public override void FeatureActivated(SPFeatureReceiverProperties properties) {
    // Retrieve e reference to the UserCodeService
    SPUserCodeService userCodeService = SPUserCodeService.Local;
    if (userCodeService != null) {
      // Define a variable to describe the proxy
      SPProxyOperationType proxyOperation =
        new SPProxyOperationType(
          this.GetType().Assembly.FullName,
          typeof(RetrieveNWindCustomers).FullName);

      // Add the proxy to the UserCodeService
      userCodeService.ProxyOperationTypes.Add(proxyOperation);

      // Save changes
      userCodeService.Update();
    }
  }

  public override void FeatureDeactivating(
    SPFeatureReceiverProperties properties) {
    // Retrieve e reference to the UserCodeService
    SPUserCodeService userCodeService = SPUserCodeService.Local;

    if (userCodeService != null) {
      // Define a variable to describe the proxy
      SPProxyOperationType proxyOperation =
        new SPProxyOperationType(
          this.GetType().Assembly.FullName,
          typeof(RetrieveNWindCustomers).FullName);

      // Remove the proxy to the UserCodeService




      userCodeService.ProxyOperationTypes.Remove(proxyOperation);

      // Save changes
      userCodeService.Update();
    }
  }
}
```

Listing 23-13 shows that there is a collection of *ProxyOperationTypes* offered by the *SPUserCodeService*, to which you can add instances of the *SPProxyOperationType* class. Once you have updated the contents of the collection, you need to invoke the *Update* method of the *SPUserCodeService*, as with many classes of the SharePoint Server Object Model, to persist changes to the back-end database.

Consuming the Full-Trust Proxy

To use the proxy from a sandboxed solution, you need to implement a classic sandboxed solution and write some implementation code that invokes the proxy by using the native SharePoint infrastructure. Listing 23-14 illustrates a custom Web Part that uses the proxy implemented in Listing 23-12.

LISTING 23-14 A Web Part that employs the full-trust proxy.

```
public class ShowNWindCustomers : WebPart {
  protected GridView gridCustomers;

  [WebBrowsable(true)]
  [Personalizable(true)]
  public String SqlConnectionString { get; set; }

  protected override void CreateChildControls() {
    // In case the Web Part is configured
    if (!String.IsNullOrEmpty(this.SqlConnectionString)) {
      // Prepare the custom argument
      RetrieveNWindCustomersArgs args =
        new RetrieveNWindCustomersArgs() {
          SqlConnectionString = this.SqlConnectionString,
        };

      // Invoke the proxy operation
      DataSet data = SPUtility.ExecuteRegisteredProxyOperation(
        typeof(RetrieveNWindCustomers).Assembly.FullName,
        typeof(RetrieveNWindCustomers).FullName,
        args) as DataSet;

      // In case there is data in the result
      if (data != null) {
        this.gridCustomers = new GridView();
        this.Controls.Add(this.gridCustomers);

        this.gridCustomers.DataSource = data;
        this.gridCustomers.DataBind();
      }
      else {
        this.Controls.Add(new LiteralControl(
          "Invalid result from remote proxy."));
      }
    }
    else {
      this.Controls.Add(new LiteralControl(
        "Please configure the SQL Connection String."));
    }
  }
}
```

The core of the implementation is the invocation of the *ExecuteRegisteredProxyOperation* method of the *SPUtility* class. The method accepts the full name of the assembly and the full name of the class implementing the full-trust proxy, plus the arguments for the target method. Listing 23-14 shows that the argument is an instance of the *RetrieveNWindCustomersArgs* class defined in Listing 23-12.

Sandboxed Solutions and Office 365

The new and upcoming Office 365 offering proposed by Microsoft includes a SharePoint 2010 Online edition with which you can use a SharePoint environment offered as a service in the cloud. To extend and customize a SharePoint 2010 Online environment, you can use either of the following techniques and tools:

- Configuration using the web browser

- Customization using Microsoft SharePoint Designer 2010

- Development of custom code deployed using sandboxed solutions

Figure 23-7 displays a schema of the development options available with SharePoint 2010 Online.

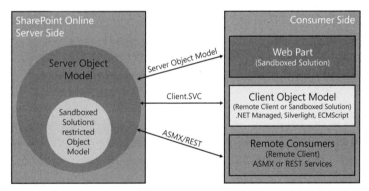

FIGURE 23-7 The schema of the development options available with SharePoint 2010 Online.

It's pretty clear that you need to have a solid knowledge of sandboxed solutions if you are to confidently face the future of SharePoint and of the cloud offering by Microsoft.

Summary

In this chapter, you learned what CAS is and how SharePoint takes advantage of it in securing its environment. In addition, you learned how to develop farm-level solutions that target the /bin folder of a web application, enforcing a custom security policy. Finally, you concentrated on sandboxed solutions, which should be the first choice when you're developing custom solutions. You saw the architecture of the sandboxed solutions, how to develop a sandboxed solution of your own, how to validate solutions, and how to develop full-trust proxies for sandboxed solutions.

PART VII
Enterprise Features

Chapter 24
Programming the Search Engine

This chapter begins the last section of the book, "Enterprise Features," which covers topics that generally target enterprise-level companies. Undoubtedly, the search engine is one of the main features of SharePoint since its early editions. In Microsoft SharePoint 2010 the search engine has been improved to satisfy one fundamental requirement expressed by customers and end users alike: everyone would like to search everything, everywhere, from a unique search center. If you think about your everyday life experience or about the common user experience when using a PC, you will probably agree that the main and most frequent task that users perform is searching. The success of the main Internet search engines confirms this.

In this chapter, you will learn how to utilize the native search engine of SharePoint 2010. All of the contents in this chapter will be illustrated from a developer's perspective. Thus, you will not see any kind of information about how to configure, deploy, and maintain a SharePoint search infrastructure. Instead, you will learn how to customize, extend and develop the search engine.

Search Engine Overview for Developers

The Search Engine of SharePoint 2010 is a service application based on a professional and scalable architecture, which relies on many server roles and services to provide you with a first-class enterprise-level solution.

When using Microsoft SharePoint Server 2010, the search engine can index the following content sources:

- Microsoft SharePoint sites
- File shares
- Internet websites
- Microsoft Exchange public folders
- External databases
- External Line of Business (LOB) systems

Figure 24-1 illustrates the architecture of the search engine.

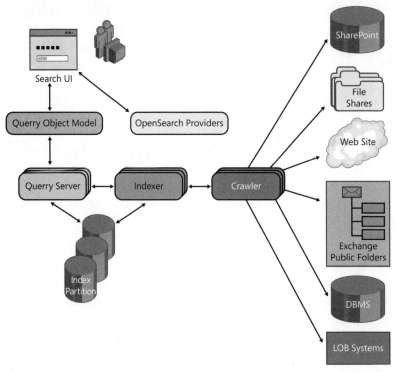

FIGURE 24-1 The architecture of SharePoint 2010 search engine.

To index these content sources, the search engine is based on the following server roles:

- **Crawler**   This is the service that collects data from the configured content sources. It leverages Connectors, which are custom extensions allowing reading contents from external sources. You can develop custom connectors, in case of need. You can also buy connectors from third parties.

- **Indexer**   This service extracts information from crawled items to improve efficiency of results. It organizes indexed information in Index Partitions for better performances.

- **Query Servers**   This service accepts and manages query requests from end users and returns results.

- **Search Center**   This is the standard search user interface provided by SharePoint.

When an end user searches content using the standard Search UI, depending on the user's rights and permissions the query is passed to a query server, which searches the index for a corresponding result. Before sending the results back to the end user, the engine is capable of invoking another filter, called a security trimmer, that can further filter the results. The query servers query an index database, which is populated by the index service while crawling content sources. Thus, the query does not execute in real-time against the content sources, but it is based on a back-end database that must be populated and maintained up to date via scheduled updates. This behavior improves performance and scalability, although it reduces update rapidity. When you need to index and query millions of items and terabytes of content, you have no choice but to rely on this kind of architecture. All of the main search engines on the Internet (Microsoft Bing, Google, Yahoo!, and so on) work in the same manner.

> **More Information** For further details about creating a custom security trimmer, read the document, "Writing a Custom Security Trimmer for SharePoint Server Search," which is available on MSDN Online at *http://msdn.microsoft.com/en-us/library/ee819930.aspx*.

Beginning with Microsoft SharePoint Server 2010, when end users query the search engine they receive results back from both the search query engine and from external locations. As you will see beginning on page 670 in the section, "Federation Framework," the external locations can provide search capabilities through various protocols, including the OpenSearch 1.0/1.1 protocol (*http://www.opensearch.org/*). The main search engines on the Internet implement the OpenSearch protocol. This allows you to, as stated in the introduction of this chapter, query everything, everywhere, from a unique search center—which is SharePoint!

> **Important** The OpenSearch support provided by SharePoint executes queries in real-time against the external providers. Although it is a great capability, you should consider that sometimes the results could be unavailable or slow to retrieve if there is network congestion or the external provider is overloaded. Fortunately, the Web Parts that handle querying federated providers by default work asynchronously with AJAX, and together, handle connectivity issues.

As a developer, you have the capability to extend the search engine mainly in the following areas:

- **Search UI** You can modify the rendering of search results, customizing the XSLT templates applied by default. You can also inherit and customize many of the native search Web Parts provided by SharePoint.

- **OpenSearch** You can develop OpenSearch providers of your own, making external contents searchable by SharePoint users.

- **Query Object Model and Federated Search Object Model** You can write custom code or applications that take advantage of these object models to query the search index and/or federated locations.

- **Query Web Service** You can write consumer applications that use a search Web Service (search.asmx), which allows querying the search Index via SOAP from remote sites.

- **Ranking** Similar to many enterprise-level search engines, SharePoint has a ranking model for prioritizing and ordering search results. You can write custom code to change the standard ranking model for search results. This is an advanced topic that will not be covered in this book.

- **Custom Content Sources** There are many extensibility areas for crawling external content sources. For example, you can develop custom connectors, protocol handlers, content filters, and security trimmers. This topic is worthy of an entire book by itself, so I will not cover it in this chapter.

In the following sections, you will delve into many of these extensibility areas.

Customizing and Extending the User Interface

The first and most frequent area of extensibility for the search engine is the user interface. First, if you do not already have one, you need to create a new website of type "Basic Search Center" or "Enterprise Search Center," that you will use to experiment with the examples and demonstrations illustrated in this section. In general, it is quite common to have a search site that will be used by your users as the entry point for every search they will do. A search center site solves exactly that need and has a home page providing the classic search box interface. Once you have invoked the search engine, the results—if any—will be provided in a dedicated result page. Figure 24-2 presents the typical output of the search result page.

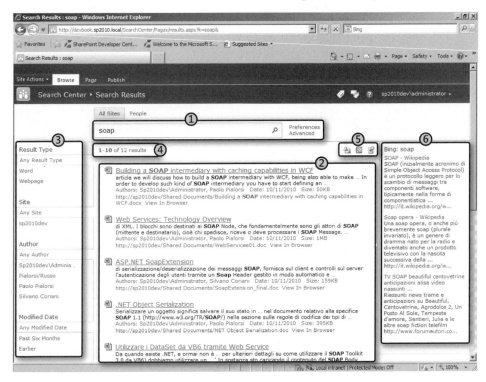

FIGURE 24-2 A screenshot of a typical search result page in a search center site.

In Figure 24-2, the main areas of interest are highlighted and numbered to correspond with the following descriptions:

1. **Search Box**   This is one of the fundamental Web Parts of the native environment. It renders the search box used by end users to search content. It can be customized to show search scopes and help users with query suggestions.

2. **Search Core Results**   Another fundamental Web Part used for rendering the results of a search. This will be discussed in detail later in this section.

3. **Refinement Panel**   A new feature of SharePoint 2010, with which end users can refine their searches, filtering results based on metadata of results. For example, you can use this panel to filter results based on content type, author, category, and so on. It is rendered using a Web Part.

4. **Search Statistics**   This is a Web Part that provides some statistical information about the results of the search query.

5. **Search Actions Links**   This is a Web Part that provides some useful links to subscribe alerts or feeds about the current search. It also provides a link to make the search available in the Windows Desktop Search.

6. **Federated Results**   This is a Web Part that renders results from an external federated location.

All of these sections and Web Parts can be customized at various levels. You can use these Web Parts in any site—for example, in Wiki Pages or in Web Part Pages— not just in Search Center sites. To use these Web Parts, you simply need to activate the Search Server Web Parts feature in the target site.

Customizing the Output via XSLT

If all you need to do is simply customize the output of the search pages, you can take advantage of the native capabilities of SharePoint. For example, if you would like to customize the output of the Search Core Results Web Part (item 2 in Figure 24-2), you should be aware that its output is based on an XSLT template. Thus, if you know a little bit about XSLT, you can easily customize the output from Microsoft SharePoint Designer 2010, for example, without writing a line of compiled code. By default, SharePoint 2010 renders results based on a default XSLT template, which can be defined in a centralized place through the SharePoint Central Administration. In fact, under the Search Service Application management page, you can define and manage the list of Federated Locations. There you can also find a default rendering template for search results of each available data location. The location defining the results of local searches is the Local Search Results location.

However, if you would like to customize nothing more than a single result page—perhaps because you are rendering an Internet publishing site and you want its search results to adhere to the public website layout—you can change the XSLT used by that single search result page. To do this, you need to edit the search result page and manage properties of the Search Core Results Web Part (SCRWP). Figure 24-3 illustrates the editor part of the SCRWP.

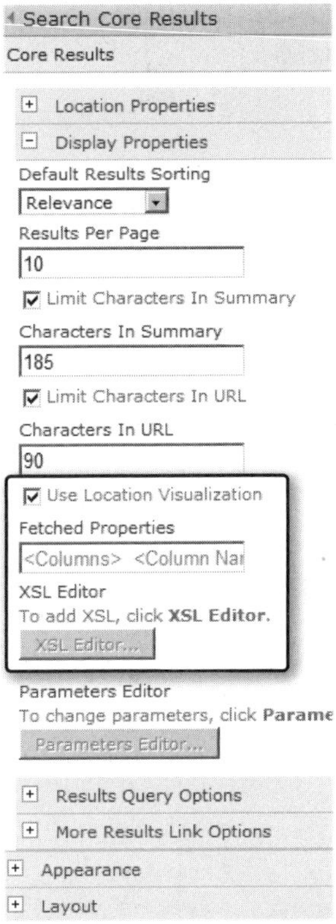

FIGURE 24-3 The editor part of the Search Core Results Web Part.

If you clear the Use Location Visualization check box, you will be able to provide a custom XSLT of your own by clicking the XSL Editor ... button. The XSLT transformation will receive an XML input such as that shown in Listing 24-1.

LISTING 24-1 The XML provided for input to the Search Core Results Web Part.

```
<All_Results>
  <Result>
    <workid>1</workid>
    <rank>222</rank>
    <title>Title of document or web page</title>
    <author>Author of document or web page</author>
    <size>1025</size>
    <sitename>http://www.sample.com</sitename>
    <url>http://www.sample.com/folder/document.aspx</url>
    <imageurl>/_layouts/images/aspx16.gif</imageurl>
    <description>This is the summary of the document or web page. The summary is
generated from the original document based on matches with query terms. In some cases,
the summary is a description provided by the author.</description>
    <write>December 26, 2004</write>
  </Result>
</All_Results>
```

To retrieve a sample of this source XML, you can simply provide an XSLT transformation that copies the source XML into the output, as shown in the following:

```
<?xml version="1.0" encoding="utf-8"?>
<xsl:stylesheet version="1.0" xmlns:xsl="http://www.w3.org/1999/XSL/Transform">
  <xsl:template match="/">
    <xmp><xsl:copy-of select="*"/></xmp>
  </xsl:template>
</xsl:stylesheet>
```

The XML contains a *Result* element for each item, together with a child element for each metadata/field property with a lowercase name. Thus, it is really simple to render the results using a custom XSLT. Listing 24-2 presents a sample XSLT transformation that changes the default rendering of the SCRWP.

LISTING 24-2 A custom XSLT for rendering search results in the Search Core Results Web Part.

```
<?xml version="1.0" encoding="utf-8"?>
<xsl:stylesheet version="1.0" xmlns:xsl="http://www.w3.org/1999/XSL/Transform"
    xmlns:msxsl="urn:schemas-microsoft-com:xslt" exclude-result-prefixes="msxsl">

  <xsl:output method="xml" indent="yes"/>
  <xsl:param name="Keyword" />
  <xsl:param name="IsDesignMode">True</xsl:param>
  <xsl:param name="ShowMessage" />
  <xsl:param name="ResultsNotFound" />

  <xsl:template match="/All_Results">
    <xsl:if test="$IsDesignMode = 'False'">
      <xsl:choose>
        <xsl:when test="$ShowMessage = 'True'">
          <div>
            <xsl:value-of select="$ResultsNotFound" />
            <xsl:text disable-output-escaping="yes"> </xsl:text>
            <strong>
              <xsl:value-of select="$Keyword" />
            </strong>
          </div>
        </xsl:when>
        <xsl:otherwise>
          <div>
            <xsl:for-each select="Result">
              <div>
                <xsl:text
                  disable-output-escaping="yes">  </xsl:text>
                <a href="{url}">
                  <img src="{imageurl}" border="0" />
                  <xsl:text
                    disable-output-escaping="yes">  </xsl:text>
                  <xsl:value-of select="title" />
                </a>
              </div>
```

```
          </xsl:for-each>
        </div>
      </xsl:otherwise>
    </xsl:choose>
  </xsl:if>
  <xsl:if test="$IsDesignMode = 'True'">
    <div>Design mode ...</div>
  </xsl:if>
</xsl:template>


</xsl:stylesheet>
```

As Listing 24-2 illustrates, there are some XSLT parameters passed from the SCRWP to
the rendering XSLT. The current example uses just a few of them (*Keyword*, *IsDesignMode*,
ShowMessage, *ResultsNotFound*). However, the SCRWP can offer you more than 50 parameters, which could help you during rendering. For a complete list of these parameters you
can read the standard XSLT configured by default. Figure 24-4 shows the output in the web
browser that results when you apply the XSLT defined in Listing 24-2.

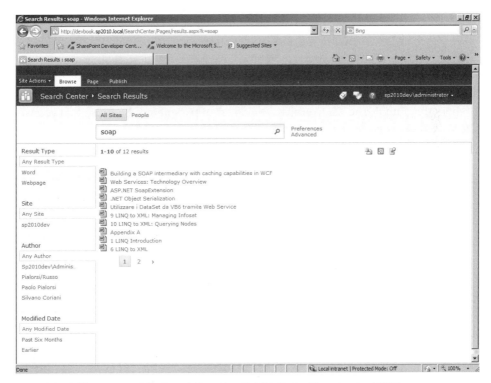

FIGURE 24-4 The output of the Search Core Results Web Part with customized XSLT.

If you would like to change the metadata columns returned in the search result, you can
change the content of the Fetched Properties property, as shown earlier in Figure 24-3. That

property simply enumerates the list of fetched properties using a *Column* element for each property. Listing 24-3 shows the default content of that property.

LISTING 24-3 The default XML content of the Fetched Properties property of the SCRWP.

```
<Columns>
  <Column Name="WorkId"/>
  <Column Name="Rank"/>
  <Column Name="Title"/>
  <!-- XML omitted for the sake of brevity  -->
</Columns>
```

You can add a *Column* element with the property *Name* of the metadata/field property that you would like to add to the results, and then you can render that property with a custom XSLT template. To add a custom column, you also need to define it in the search engine configuration, within the SharePoint Central Administration, in the Search Service Application administration page.

Developing Custom Web Parts

The search center rendering is based mainly on infrastructural Web Parts provided out of the box by SharePoint. However, sometime it might be useful to slightly change the default behavior of these native Web Parts. For example, think again about the Search Core Results Web Part. As you have already seen in the previous section, the Web Part uses an XSLT to render the output. The XSLT receives a wide list of parameters. Suppose that you would like to add some parameters to a custom XSLT of your own.

Starting with SharePoint 2010, it is really simple to accomplish this. In fact, in SharePoint 2010, many of the native Web Parts supporting the search capabilities have been made inheritable so that you can customize them with minimal effort.

> **Note** Prior to SharePoint 2010, the Web Parts that supported the search capabilities were marked as *sealed*. If you wanted to make change or customization, no matter how small, you needed to write a completely new Web Part from scratch.

Listing 24-4 demonstrates a custom Web Part, inheriting from the base SCRWP and overriding the method that generates the parameters passed to the XSLT, adding the current user name as a new parameter.

LISTING 24-4 A custom Web Part inherited from the Search Core Results Web Part.

```
public class CustomCoreResultsWebPart : CoreResultsWebPart {

  protected override void ModifyXsltArgumentList(
    Microsoft.SharePoint.WebPartPages.ArgumentClassWrapper argList) {

    // Invoke the base implementation
    base.ModifyXsltArgumentList(argList);

    // Add a parameter with the current user name
    String currentUserName = SPContext.Current.Web.CurrentUser.Name;
    argList.AddParameter("CurrentUserName", String.Empty, currentUserName);
  }
}
```

The base class to inherit from is the *CoreResultsWebPart*, which provides a lot of methods that you can override. However, the most useful methods are:

- *ConfigureDataSourceProperties*   Configures the properties of the datasource. For example you can override this method to change the search query or to force a fixed query.

- *CreateDataSource*   Creates the datasource for the SCRWP, which is a class of type CoreResultsDatasource or inherited from that type. Internally, *CreateDataSource* works with a *CoreResultsDatasourceView*, which represents a view on results data.

- *ModifyXsltArgumentList*   Used to customize arguments passed to the XSLT. Be careful while using this method, because officially it is reserved for internal use only.

- *SetVisualization*   Configures the source XSLT used to render the output.

In general, the amount of Web Parts from which you can inherit in the fields of search engine, number more than 50, and inspecting each one is beyond the scope of this book. Nevertheless, it is important to know that all of the Web Parts that render the search pages are coordinated by a unique *SharedQueryManager* object. This shared object executes the search query and returns results to the Web Parts of the search center. The main property of the *SharedQueryManager* is the *QueryManager* of type *Microsoft.Office.Server.Search.Query. QueryManager,* which represents the real query manager object.

A *QueryManager* is a class inheriting from *List<LocationList>*. By enumerating its content, you can inspect each search *Location* searched by the current page to retrieve the query sent by the end user, the query results, and some other useful information.

Listing 24-5 illustrates a code excerpt that uses the *SharedQueryManager*.

LISTING 24-5 A custom Web Part using the *SharedQueryManager*.

```
protected override void CreateChildControls() {
  base.CreateChildControls();

  // Get a reference to the current QueryManager
  QueryManager qm = SharedQueryManager.GetInstance(this.Page).QueryManager;

  // Get a reference to the first LocationList
  LocationList locationList = qm[0];

  // Get a reference to the first location
  Location location = locationList[0];

  // Retrieve an XPathNavigator on the results
  XPathNavigator locationNavigator = location.Result.CreateNavigator();
  XPathNodeIterator results = locationNavigator.Select("All_Results/Result");

  // For each Result element
  foreach (XPathNavigator result in results) {
    // Extract the title child node
    this.Controls.Add(new LiteralControl(String.Format("<div>{0}</div>",
      result.SelectSingleNode("title"))));
  }
}
```

The sample retrieves the first search *Location*, which represents the "Local Search Results," and retrieves each *Result* element from the XML representation of the corresponding search results. Even if you like to write a custom Web Part of your own, without inheriting from existing ones, you should rely on the *SharedQueryManager* class to coordinate the behavior of your code with the native infrastructure.

Federation Framework

One of the most brilliant features of the search engine of SharePoint 2010 is the federation framework, which adds to SharePoint the capability to define multiple search locations on which to search. This capability was actually added in the previous edition of SharePoint, within the Infrastructural Update, but now it's available by default in the SharePoint 2010 Server platform. Now, when a user searches contents in the SharePoint index, the search engine can simultaneously search other locations, as well, which can be defined from the Search Service Application administration page, within the SharePoint Central Administration. Each federated location defines a search location that can use one of the following target providers:

- **Search Index on this Server**   Searches in the index on the current server.

- **FAST Index**   Searches a FAST Search Server 2010 for SharePoint location.

- **OpenSearch 1.0/1.1** Searches another search engine that can receive a query by using a Representational Stateful Transfer (REST) URL and return results as structured XML (POX = Plain Old XML).

Figure 24-5 displays the Manage Federated Locations page.

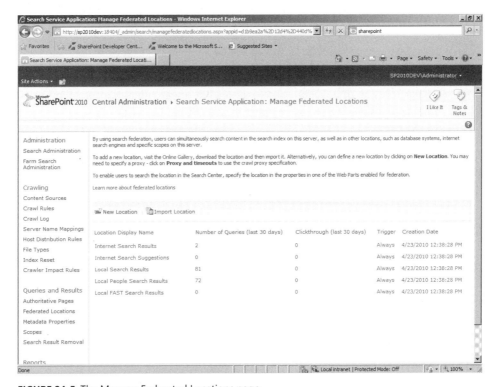

FIGURE 24-5 The Manage Federated Locations page.

To configure a custom location, you need to go to SharePoint Central Administration and open the Search Service Application administration page. There, you will find a Federated Locations menu item, under the Queries And Results menu group. You can define a new location either by filling out a definition form or importing a definition file with the extension .osdx (Open Search Definition XML), based on a specific XML schema. This section will concentrate on federating with an OpenSearch provider.

> **Important** Remember that when you query a federated location, the query is executed in real-time. However, when you query the search engine of SharePoint, you search an index, which has been populated by an indexer during content crawling. Thus, performances for retrieving results can be completely different.

When you press the New Location command, a long form appears, containing many configuration parameters. The most important are the following:

- **Location Name** A unique name that identifies the location. It cannot be changed after definition and is visible to administrators and developers only.

- **Display Name** The name that is displayed to end users if the location is enabled for displaying in the end users' interface (Web Parts).

- **Description** A brief description of the location.

- **Trigger** Defines when the location should be searched. For example, you can define a specific location that will be searched only if the search query inserted by an end user starts with a specified prefix or matches a particular pattern.

- **Location Type** Defines the type of location. Options are Search Index On This Server, FAST Index, and OpenSearch 1.0/1.1.

- **Query Template** Defines the query template to use for querying the target location. When using OpenSearch 1.0/1.1, this will be the URL of the search page. For example, if Microsoft Bing is the search engine, Query Template assumes a value of:

   http://www.bing.com/search?q={searchTerms}&format=rss

   where {*searchTerms*} represents a token that will be replaced with the query searched by the end users. If the location is of type Search Index On This Server, this property contains the search query to execute against the search server. Lastly, in case of a FAST Index provider, this field contains the search URL to provide to the FAST Index.

- **Display Information** Defines the default XSLT that is used for rendering the search results.

- **Restrictions and Credentials Information** Defines the credentials that are used to communicate with the external search location. You can choose one of the following authentication types:

   - Anonymous (default).

   - Basic Authentication based on configured username and password, or integrated with current user's credentials.

   - Digest Authentication based on configured username and password, or integrated with current user's credentials.

   - NTLM with current Application Pool identity.

❑ NTLM with configured username and password.

❑ NTLM integrated with current user's credentials.

❑ Forms Authentication based on configured username and password, or provided by each end user.

❑ Cookie Authentication retrieved from a manual authentication, or provided by each end user.

To be certain, the configuration is not trivial, but it is very complete and allows supporting a wide range of scenarios. Through this capability, you can federate the SharePoint search engine with all the main search engines available on the Internet (Microsoft Bing, Google, Yahoo!, and so forth) or with document management/data management applications that publish a query service accessible by URL.

An .osdx file defines almost the same configuration information, except is does so by using XML. This means you can configure all the most frequently used federation locations on a SharePoint environment. Then you can export all the federated locations as .osdx files, and you will be able to import them wherever you need.

Once you have defined a custom search location, either by using an .osdx file or manually, you will be able to configure it in the Search Center site. To do so, browse to the page that provides the search results, edit its contents, and add a new Web Part of type *Federated Results*, which is available under the Search group of Web Parts. After you add the Web Part, you can configure its properties.

Figure 24-6 depicts the editor part of the Federated Results Web Part. Note the property named *Location*. You can configure this to select the federated location that will be searched. You can also determine if the Web Part should use the default XSLT for rendering the results, or use a custom one that you provide. By default, a Federated Results Web Part works asynchronously to avoid making the user wait during query results retrieval, but you also have the option to switch to a synchronous query pattern.

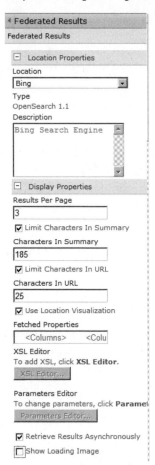

FIGURE 24-6 The editor part of the Federated Results Web Part.

Implementing a Custom Federation Provider

You learned in the previous section that a federated location of type *OpenSearch* can be used to query any kind of search service that is accessible via HTTP/HTTPS, using a parametric search URL and providing a structured XML response. Typically, the structured XML response is an RSS or Atom feed.

> **Important** To understand the current section and the proposed sample, you should already be familiar with Windows Communication Foundation and be capable of using it to develop Web-Centric services .

With Windows Communication Foundation (WCF), beginning with version 3.5 of .NET Framework, you can develop services that respond by using custom XML instead of classic SOAP messages. Furthermore, you can use WCF to define "Web-Centric" solutions. These are services that can talk with external systems, accepting HTTP requests (REST) and supporting generic XML input and output messages. These kinds of services are suitable for developing communication frameworks that target mainly AJAX or jQuery web solutions as well as for publishing custom RSS/Atom feeds.

However, you can also use such services to implement custom OpenSearch providers, searching any kind of data in the back-end. For example, you can define a custom WCF service that accepts REST requests and provides RSS/Atom answers, and queries a back-end database. You can define a federated location in SharePoint, making the custom WCF service available as a new federated location.

Listing 24-6 presents a WCF service contract and a WCF service implementing the described scenario.

LISTING 24-6 A WCF contract and service publishing an OpenSearch provider.

```
[ServiceKnownType(typeof(Rss20FeedFormatter))]
[ServiceKnownType(typeof(Atom10FeedFormatter))]
[ServiceContract(Namespace = "http://schemas.devleap.com/FeedService")]
public interface IDevLeapFeedService {
  [OperationContract]
  [WebGet(UriTemplate = "blog?q={searchTerm}&type={feedType}")]
  SyndicationFeedFormatter GetFeed(String searchTerm, String feedType);
}

[AspNetCompatibilityRequirements(
  RequirementsMode = AspNetCompatibilityRequirementsMode.Allowed)]
public class DevLeapFeedService : IDevLeapFeedService {
  public SyndicationFeedFormatter GetFeed(String searchTerm, String feedType) {
    // Prepare a SyndicationFeed to host the results
    SyndicationFeed feed = new SyndicationFeed("DevLeap Sample Feed",
      String.Format("All blog posts of {0}!", searchTerm),
      new Uri("http://blogs.devleap.com/Feed/"));

    // Define some generic information about the feed
    feed.Authors.Add(new SyndicationPerson("info@devleap.com"));
    feed.Categories.Add(new SyndicationCategory("Miscellanea"));
    feed.Description = new TextSyndicationContent("Sample feed for SP2010");

    // Populate the list of results
    List<SyndicationItem> items = new List<SyndicationItem>();

    // using random data
    items.AddRange(
      from i in Enumerable.Range(1, 30)
      let id = Guid.NewGuid().ToString()
```

```
        select new SyndicationItem(
          String.Format("Title {0}", i),
          new TextSyndicationContent("Text",
            TextSyndicationContentKind.Plaintext),
          new Uri("http://blogs.devleap.com/Feed/" + id),
          id, DateTimeOffset.Now));

    feed.Items = items;

    // Format the response as RSS or Atom
    if (feedType.ToLower() == "rss") {
      return new Rss20FeedFormatter(feed);
    }
    else if (feedType.ToLower() == "atom") {
      return new Atom10FeedFormatter(feed);
    }
    else {
      return null;
    }
  }
}
```

Listing 24-6 illustrates a classic WCF service contract, which is also marked with a couple of *ServiceKnownType* attributes that allow declaring that the service will provide both RSS and Atom answers. In addition, the *GetFeed* operation is marked with the *WebGet* attribute, which is specific for the web-centric approach of WCF. The *WebGet* instance applied to the *GetFeed* operation instructs WCF to accept requests with a URL pattern, such as the following:

```
/blog?q={searchTerm}&type={feedType}
```

The tokens *{searchTerm}* and *{feedType}* correspond to the arguments of the *GetFeed* operation. The service implementation is trivial and simply creates an instance of the *SyndicationFeed* class, which defines a generic feed. Then, it adds a fake list of items and returns the result formatted either with an *Rss20FeedFormatter* or an *Atom10FeedFormatter*, depending on the value of the *feedType* argument. Thus, if you invoke the service with a URL like the following:

```
http://server/FeedService/DevLeapFeedService.svc/blog?q=SharePoint&type=rss
```

the service will return a list of fictitious RSS items related to the query term "SharePoint."

From a configuration viewpoint, you need to publish the service through a web application with a *web.config*, configured such as the one shown in Listing 24-7.

LISTING 24-7 A sample web.config for publishing the OpenSearch provider service.

```xml
<?xml version="1.0"?>
<configuration>

  <system.serviceModel>
    <services>
      <service name="DevLeapFeedService">
        <endpoint address="" behaviorConfiguration="WebHttpBehavior"
          binding="webHttpBinding" contract="IDevLeapFeedService" />
      </service>
    </services>

    <behaviors>
      <endpointBehaviors>
        <behavior name="WebHttpBehavior">
          <webHttp/>
        </behavior>
      </endpointBehaviors>
    </behaviors>

  </system.serviceModel>

</configuration>
```

Figure 24-7 shows the result of a search which also displays the federated results coming out from the custom WCF service.

FIGURE 24-7 The Search Results page with federated results from the custom WCF service.

The only configuration parameters that deserve your attention in Listing 24-7 are the binding of type *webHttpBinding*, which is mandatory for web-centric services, and the custom end-point behavior that applies a *webHttp* behavior element to activate the web-centric support.

You can define an .osdx file describing the provider, or you can configure it manually. Regardless of the technique you use to configure the provider, you can include a Federated Results Web Part in the search results page, targeting the new provider you just defined.

Using the Search Engine by Code

Beginning with SharePoint 2010, you have two different sets of classes for playing with the search engine in server-side code:

- **Federated Search Object Model**   Use this object model to query multiple locations and merge all the results together.

- **Query Object Model**   Use this object model to query the index of SharePoint and FAST Search Server.

These classes are both contained in the same assemblies:

- Microsoft.SharePoint.dll

- Microsoft.Office.Server.dll

- Microsoft.Office.Server.Search.dll

By referencing these assemblies, which are all located in the SharePoint14_Root\ISAPI folder, you can query the search engine as well as any other federated location.

Federated Search Object Model

It's time to play with the new Federated Search Object Model. The main types you will use in this context are the *QueryManager* class, which you have already encountered in the previous sections, and the *SearchServiceApplicationProxy* class, which represents a reference to the service application proxy for the Search Service Application. Listing 24-8 gives you the definition of the *QueryManager* class.

> **More Information** For further details about what a service application proxy is, refer to Chapter 15, "Developing Service Applications,"

LISTING 24-8 The definition of the *QueryManager* class.

```
public sealed class QueryManager : List<LocationList> {

  public QueryManager();

  public string DefaultFASTSearchSort { get; set; }
  public int Timeout { get; set; }
  public bool TrimDuplicates { get; set; }
  public string UserQuery { get; set; }

  public XmlDocument GetResults(LocationList locationList);
  public bool IsTriggered(LocationList locationList);
  public void SendRequest(LocationList locationList, int count);
}
```

Table 24-1 provides a brief description of the main members of the *QueryManager* class.

TABLE 24-1 The Main Members of the *QueryManager* Class

Member Name	Description
Timeout	A property of type *Integer* that defines the query timeout in milliseconds.
TrimDuplicates	A property of type *Boolean* that allows removing duplicates from the results of search queries.
UserQuery	A property of type *String* that allows managing the query that will be sent to the configured federated search locations.
GetResults	A method to retrieve results of a search from all provided federated search locations. The result is structured XML which aggregates the results of each provided location.
IsTriggered	A method that returns a *Boolean* value, indicating whether any of the configured federated locations will be triggered by the currently configured query.
SendRequest	A method to send a search query to the provided federated locations.

Table 24-1 clearly shows that the list of federated locations is fundamental for querying and managing the Federated Search Object Model, because it is a required argument for every method. To access the list of configured federated locations, you will need to employee the search service application proxy. In fact, the *SearchServiceApplicationProxy* class offers a lot of methods for managing federated locations by code. Additionally, there is also a method for retrieving the full list of configured locations. Listing 24-9 browses all the locations available for a specific site collection.

LISTING 24-9 Browsing for all the configured federated search locations.

```
static void BrowseLocations(String siteUrl) {
  using (SPSite site = new SPSite(siteUrl)) {
    Int64 lastupdate;
    Boolean useCrawlProxy;
    // Retrieve a reference to the search service application proxy
    SearchServiceApplicationProxy searchServiceProxy =
      (SearchServiceApplicationProxy)
      SearchServiceApplicationProxy.GetProxy(SPServiceContext.GetContext(site));

    // Retrieve currently configured locations
    LocationConfiguration[] locationConfigurations =
      searchServiceProxy.GetLocationConfigurations(
        out lastupdate, out useCrawlProxy);

    // Browse locations
    foreach (LocationConfiguration lc in locationConfigurations) {
      Console.WriteLine("****************************************");
      Console.WriteLine("Location: {0}", lc.InternalName);
      Console.WriteLine("Type: {0}", lc.Type);
      Console.WriteLine("URL Template: {0}", lc.ConnectionUrlTemplate);
    }
  }
}
```

Here is an excerpt of the output produced by Listing 24-9:

```
****************************************
Location: InternetSearchResults
Type: OpenSearch
URL Template: http://search.live.com/results.aspx?q={searchTerms}&count={itemsPe
rPage}&first={startItem}&mkt={language}&format=rss&FORM=SHAREF
****************************************
Location: InternetSearchSuggestions
Type: OpenSearch
URL Template: http://search.live.com/QSOnly.aspx?q={searchTerms}&count={itemsPer
Page}&first={startItem}&mkt={language}&FORM=SHARES&format=rss
****************************************
Location: LocalSearchIndex
Type: LocalSharepoint
URL Template: {searchTerms}
...
```

If you need to query one or more of the available locations, you can invoke the *GetResults* method of the *QueryManager*, after you have configured a property named *UserQuery* for each target location or for the entire *QueryManager* instance. The *GetResults* method internally checks if there is at least one location capable of providing a result searching the currently configured *UserQuery* value and sends a request to search, using the *QueryManager. SendRequest* method.

The results provided by each location will be merged into a unique XML response. Listing 24-10 illustrates code searching a set of configured locations.

LISTING 24-10 Browsing for all the configured federated search locations.

```
static void SearchByFederation(String siteUrl, String searchTerms) {
  using (SPSite site = new SPSite(siteUrl)) {
    Int64 lastupdate;
    Boolean useCrawlProxy;
    // Retrieve a reference to the search service application proxy
    SearchServiceApplicationProxy searchServiceProxy =
      (SearchServiceApplicationProxy)
      SearchServiceApplicationProxy.GetProxy(SPServiceContext.GetContext(site));
    // Retrieve currently configured locations
    LocationConfiguration[] locationConfigurations =
      searchServiceProxy.GetLocationConfigurations(
        out lastupdate, out useCrawlProxy);

    LocationList locations = new LocationList();

    // Prepare locations for search
    foreach (LocationConfiguration lc in locationConfigurations) {
      locations.Add(new Location(lc.InternalName, searchServiceProxy));
    }

    // Create a QueryManager instance
    QueryManager manager = new QueryManager();
    manager.Add(locations);
    manager.UserQuery = searchTerms;

    // Search across all locations
    XmlDocument results = manager.GetResults(locations);
  }
}
```

The output XML will consist of some *channel* elements, provided by the locations of type *OpenSearch*, and *Result* elements, returned by locations of type *LocalSharepoint*.

Query Object Model

Another option available to you is using the legacy Query Object Model of SharePoint, which was available in earlier editions of the product. However, the Query Object Model allows querying only the SharePoint index; you cannot use it to query other federated locations. The main idea at the heart of the Query Object Model is to have a base abstract class, named

Query, which defines the abstract concept of a query. This class is then inherited to represent the various kinds of search queries supported by SharePoint, which are:

- **Keyword Query**   A query based on keywords, such as those written by the end user in the search box of a website.

- **Full Text SQL Query**   A query based on a specific SQL-like syntax, defined for querying the search engine index.

The former is implemented by the *KeywordQuery* class, while the latter is represented by the *FullTextSqlQuery* class. Listing 24-11 demonstrates a content search using the *KeywordQuery* class.

LISTING 24-11 Searching content by using the *KeywordQuery* class.

```
static void SearchByQueryObjectModelKeyword(String siteUrl, String searchTerms) {
  using (SPSite site = new SPSite(siteUrl)) {
    // Retrieve a reference to the search service application proxy
    SearchServiceApplicationProxy searchServiceProxy =
      (SearchServiceApplicationProxy)
      SearchServiceApplicationProxy.GetProxy(SPServiceContext.GetContext(site));
    KeywordQuery keywordQuery = new KeywordQuery(searchServiceProxy);

    // Define the query type
    keywordQuery.ResultTypes = ResultType.RelevantResults;
    keywordQuery.QueryText = searchTerms;

    // Execute the query
    ResultTableCollection result = keywordQuery.Execute();

    // Browse the results, if any
    if (result.Count > 0) {
      // Convert results into a DataTable
      ResultTable relevantResults = result[ResultType.RelevantResults];
      DataTable resultsDataTable = new DataTable();
      resultsDataTable.Load(relevantResults, LoadOption.OverwriteChanges);
      Console.WriteLine("Number of results: {0}", resultsDataTable.Rows.Count);

      foreach (DataRow row in resultsDataTable.Rows) {
        Console.WriteLine(row["Title"]);
      }
    }
  }
}
```

As the code sample illustrates, the *KeywordQuery* instance provides an *Execute* method, which internally executes the search query and returns a collection of *ResultTable* items. Each *ResultTable* instance represents a single set of results. The available sets of results are defined in the *ResultType* enumeration, and you should define which result types you expect from the search query configuring the *ResultTypes* property of the *KeywordQuery* object.

Listing 24-12 presents the same search, this time using the *FullTextSqlQuery* class.

LISTING 24-12 Searching content by using the *FullTextSqlQuery* class.

```
static void SearchByQueryObjectModelSQL(String siteUrl, String searchTerms) {
  using (SPSite site = new SPSite(siteUrl)) {
    // Retrieve a reference to the search service application proxy
    SearchServiceApplicationProxy searchServiceProxy =
      (SearchServiceApplicationProxy)
      SearchServiceApplicationProxy.GetProxy(SPServiceContext.GetContext(site));
    FullTextSqlQuery sqlQuery = new FullTextSqlQuery(searchServiceProxy);

    // Define the query type
    sqlQuery.ResultTypes = ResultType.RelevantResults;
    sqlQuery.QueryText = String.Format(
      "SELECT Title, Path FROM Scope() WHERE FREETEXT('{0}')", searchTerms);

    // Execute the query
    ResultTableCollection result = sqlQuery.Execute();

    // Browse the results, if any
    if (result.Count > 0) {
      // Convert results into a DataTable
      ResultTable relevantResults = result[ResultType.RelevantResults];
      DataTable resultsDataTable = new DataTable();
      resultsDataTable.Load(relevantResults, LoadOption.OverwriteChanges);
      Console.WriteLine("Number of results: {0}", resultsDataTable.Rows.Count);

      foreach (DataRow row in resultsDataTable.Rows) {
        Console.WriteLine(row["Title"]);
      }
    }
  }
}
```

This code sample is nearly the same as Listing 24-11. The only difference is the use of the *FullTextSqlQuery* class and the syntax used to define the SQL-like query assigned to the *QueryText* property.

> **More Information** For further details about the SharePoint Search SQL syntax, read the document, "SharePoint Search SQL Syntax Reference," which is available on MSDN Online at *http://msdn.microsoft.com/en-us/library/ee558869.aspx*.

Query Web Service

The last technique available to you for searching content through the search engine via code is the Query Web Service. This is an ASMX service, which is available only in SharePoint Server 2010, and not in SharePoint Foundation 2010. You can find it at the relative URL /_vti_bin/search.asmx of every SharePoint Server 2010. For more information about how to reference and use a Web Service published by SharePoint, refer to Chapter 5, "Client-Side Technologies." This section will focus only on the capabilities of the Query Web Service.

The first thing to note about the *search.asmx* service is that internally it works with the Query Object Model and not with the Federated Search Object Model. Therefore, using the *search. asmx* service, you can query only the SharePoint index and not federated locations. In addition, to execute a search query using this service you can utilize the *Query* or the *QueryEx* operations.

> **Note** There are some other operations available, which are provided mainly to better support the Microsoft Office client integration. You can use those operations, too; however, to simply query the index of SharePoint you can just rely only on *Query* and *QueryEx* operations.

Query queries the index and returns a generic structured XML response. *QueryEx* queries the index and returns a *DataSet* of ADO.NET, serialized as XML. Regardless of the type of the result you like to retrieve, the request for both the operations is an *XmlNode* representing an XML document with syntax such as that shown in Listing 24-13.

LISTING 24-13 An XML message to search content using the *search.asmx* service.

```xml
<?xml version="1.0" encoding="utf-8" ?>
<QueryPacket xmlns="urn:Microsoft.Search.Query">
  <Query>
    <SupportedFormats>
      <Format revision="1">urn:Microsoft.Search.Response.Document:Document</Format>
    </SupportedFormats>
    <Context>
      <QueryText language="en-US" type=""></QueryText>
    </Context>
  </Query>
</QueryPacket>
```

The XML represents a *QueryPacket* element, which contains a *Query* child element. The *Query* element defines the effective query to execute, within the element *Context/QueryText*, and the supported and accepted result types, within the *SupportedFormats* element. The *QueryText* element accepts a *type* attribute, which can assume a value of:

- **STRING**   To execute a keyword query.

- **MSSQLFT**   To execute a Full Text SQL query.

- **FQL**   To execute a query expressed with FAST Query Language. It applies only to FAST Search Server 2010 for SharePoint.

> **More Information** For a full reference about the schema of the *QueryPacket* message, read the document, "Microsoft.Search.Query Schema," which is available on MSDN Online at *http://msdn.microsoft.com/en-us/library/ms563775.aspx*.

Listing 24-14 shows you how to use an XML message to send to the *Query* to the search engine from a remote smart client, using a keyword query and searching for documents containing the keyword "SOAP".

LISTING 24-14 Using an XML message to search for documents containing the keyword "SOAP" via *search.asmx*.

```xml
<?xml version="1.0" encoding="utf-8" ?>
<QueryPacket xmlns="urn:Microsoft.Search.Query">
  <Query>
    <SupportedFormats>
      <Format revision="1">urn:Microsoft.Search.Response.Document:Document</Format>
    </SupportedFormats>
    <Context>
      <QueryText language="en-US" type="STRING">SOAP</QueryText>
    </Context>
  </Query>
</QueryPacket>
```

While in Listing 24-15, you can see an excerpt of code invoking the *search.asmx* service.

LISTING 24-15 Invoking the *search.asmx* service.

```csharp
QueryService search = new QueryService();
search.Credentials = System.Net.CredentialCache.DefaultCredentials;
search.Url = targetUrl.Text + "/_vti_bin/search.asmx";

XElement queryXml = XElement.Load(@"..\..\QueryPacket.xml");
XNamespace nsRequest = "urn:Microsoft.Search.Query";
XNode queryTextNode = queryXml.Descendants(
  nsRequest + "QueryText").FirstOrDefault();
```

```
if (queryTextNode != null) {
  XElement queryTextElement = queryTextNode as XElement;
  queryTextElement.SetValue(searchBox.Text);
  queryTextElement.Attribute("type").Value = "STRING";

  String xmlResultsText = search.Query(queryXml.ToString());
  XNamespace nsResponse = "urn:Microsoft.Search.Response";
  XNamespace nsDocument = "urn:Microsoft.Search.Response.Document";
  XElement xmlResults = XElement.Parse(xmlResultsText);

  results.DataContext =
        from r in xmlResults.Descendants(nsDocument + "Title")
        select r;
}
```

Listing 24-15 creates a web service proxy instance, configures the credentials, and loads a
pre-defined QueryPacket.XML file. Then, it configures the type of the query and the text
of the query in the XML request. Finally, it invokes the *Query* operation to retrieve an XML
response. The XML response will contain a *ResponsePacket* element, with a *Document* element for each item in the results, because the request specified to look for documents only.
Thus, the code uses a LINQ to XML query command (*Descendants*) to retrieve the *Title* element of each *Document*. Listing 24-16 presents the XML result of the *Query* operation.

LISTING 24-16 An excerpt of the XML result of the *Query* operation.

```
<ResponsePacket xmlns="urn:Microsoft.Search.Response">
  <Response>
    <Range>
      <StartAt>1</StartAt>
      <Count>10</Count>
      <TotalAvailable>12</TotalAvailable>
      <Results>
        <Document relevance="72660210" xmlns="urn:Microsoft.Search.Response.Document">
          <Title>Building a SOAP intermediary with caching capabilities in WCF</Title>
          <Action>
            <LinkUrl size="51617" fileExt="docx">http://sp2010rcdev/Articles and
Chapters/Building a SOAP intermediary with caching capabilities in WCF.docx</LinkUrl>
          </Action>
          <Description />
          <Date>2010-02-26T11:15:03</Date>
        </Document>
        <Document relevance="66470133" xmlns="urn:Microsoft.Search.Response.Document">
          <Title>9 LINQ to XML: Managing Infoset</Title>
          <Action>
            <LinkUrl size="499712" fileExt="doc">http://sp2010rcdev/Articles and
Chapters/CH09 - LINQ to XML - Managing Infoset.doc</LinkUrl>
          </Action>
          <Description />
          <Date>1998-02-10T13:00:00</Date>
        </Document>
```

```
       <!-- XML omitted for the sake of brevity -->

     </Results>
   </Range>
   <Status>SUCCESS</Status>
 </Response>
</ResponsePacket>
```

This querying technique is useful whenever you need to query a SharePoint index from an external smart client and you cannot use the Server Object Model.

Summary

In this chapter, you saw an overview, from a developer's perspective, of the architecture of the search engine of SharePoint. Then, you focused your attention on customizing and extending the user interface of the SharePoint search center and of the search Web Parts in general. You also saw what federated search is and how to define a custom federation provider based on OpenSearch 1.0/1.1. Lastly, you learned how to develop software solutions capable of searching content using the Federated Search Object Model, or the Query Object Model, or the Query Web Service from a remote smart client.

Chapter 25
Business Connectivity Services

The Business Connectivity Services is a fundamental application service of Microsoft SharePoint 2010. It provides capabilities to read and write data from external systems, such as Line of Business applications (LOB), web services, databases, or any other external source that offers a suitable connector. In this introductory chapter, you will be introduced to the architecture of the service and some useful case studies.

Overview of Business Connectivity Services

The Business Connectivity Services (BCS), formerly known as Business Data Catalog in Microsoft Office SharePoint Server 2007, allows accessing external data by using a CRUDQ (Create, Read, Update, Delete and Query) approach. It is a service application that ships natively with any edition of SharePoint 2010, including Microsoft SharePoint Foundation 2010. However, depending on the edition of SharePoint you install, there could be more or fewer features and capabilities. Figure 25-1 presents an architectural schema of BCS.

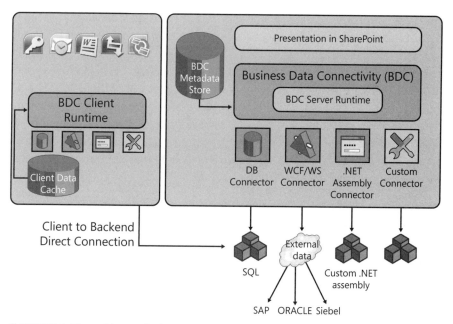

FIGURE 25-1 The architectural schema of the Business Connectivity Services in SharePoint 2010.

The service is based on a core engine, named Business Data Connectivity (BDC) that uses a BDC Server Runtime to connect with various data providers. The supported data providers are:

- **Database**   This can be any database based on Microsoft SQL Server, Oracle, OLE DB data providers, or ODBC data providers.

- **Web/WCF Services**   Any SOAP web service or any Windows Communication Foundation (WCF) service.

- **Custom .NET Assemblies**   You can define a custom Windows .NET assembly that will wrap any back-end data source.

- **Custom Connectors**   You can use or build custom connectors for reading and writing data from external data sources.

> **More Information** This chapter does not cover the development of a custom connector. If you are interested in this topic, read the document, "Creating Custom Business Connectivity Services Connectors Using SharePoint Server 2010," which is available on MSDN Online at *http://msdn.microsoft.com/en-us/library/ff953161.aspx.*

Regardless of the type of data provider that you use, the BDC Server Runtime will store configurations and shapes of data sources in a dedicated repository, which is called BDC Metadata Store and corresponds to a dedicated database file. SharePoint is a Presentation Layer for data managed using BCS, and every item that you read or write from an external data source is assigned an External Content Type (ECT) and can be consumed through an External Lists. There are also a bunch of Web Parts provided out of the box by SharePoint for rendering, filtering, and searching data that are available through BCS. In addition, an External List renders with an appearance and behavior that is almost the same of a standard SharePoint list of items. The capability to render external data in SharePoint as if it were internal data is a key feature of BCS; you can provide end users with a common experience for both internal and external data.

Also, if you have the SharePoint Server 2010 edition, you can consume BCS data (even offline) from client applications such as Microsoft Office 2010, using the BDC Client Runtime, which is a client-side engine that can be automatically installed by SharePoint on any PC client hosting Office 2010. The capability to work offline on the client side makes BCS very interesting for partially connected solutions such as smart clients and office business applications (OBA). For example, you can connect a Microsoft Outlook 2010 client to an External List, published through SharePoint and BCS, and take its data offline. This allows the user to work with the data, even when disconnected from the network. The offline data will be saved in a local storage of the client PC, within the current user profile folder. For security reasons, the data is also encrypted. If the user changes any of the items while offline, when she goes back on-line, the BDC Client Runtime will be able to synchronize the client-side data cache with the server-side online data.

> **Important** When working on a client, the BDC Client Runtime will connect directly to the data repository, without using SharePoint 2010 as an intermediary. Thus, if your repository is a database stored in a DBMS, the client will access the database directly; if the repository is accessed through a web/WCF service, the client will access the HTTP server directly. If you have any firewall between the client network and the server network, you will need to open the right TCP ports and protocols.

By default, the client accessibility and the offline capabilities are available only in Outlook 2010 and Microsoft SharePoint Workspace 2010. However, the BDC Client Runtime is provided together with an object model, which you can use from any .NET application. This means that you can write custom code in Microsoft Word 2010, Microsoft Excel 2010, and so on. You could also write some code in a custom .NET smart client of your own. An interesting aspect to note is that the offline data cache is unique on a per-user basis. Thus, offline data will be shared between multiple client applications, avoiding data duplication and concurrency conflicts within the same user's session.

To consume an external data source using BCS, you need to model the ECTs that you will use, together with a formal definition of the LOB system you are going to consume. This information can be defined with an XML file, built accordingly to a BCS-specific XML schema, or by using a tool like Microsoft SharePoint Designer 2010 or Microsoft Visual Studio 2010. Depending on the type of data provider you plan to use, either application could be useful. For example, SharePoint Designer 2010 is the ideal solution for modeling SQL Server–based solutions and web/WCF service–based solutions. Conversely, Visual Studio 2010 works very well with custom .NET assemblies and custom connectors. A generic XML editor is suitable for all the other situations.

Accessing a Database

It's time to begin consuming some data using BCS. As an example, consider a SQL Server database containing some hypothetical records of a CRM system. Figure 25-2 shows the schema of the target database that accompanies this chapter. Notice that there is a *Customers* table with a list of *Orders* that consists of *OrdersRows*, which is related to a table of *Products*.

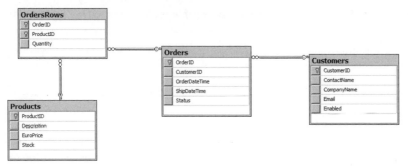

FIGURE 25-2 The schema of a sample CRM database that you will manage by using BCS.

As previously stated, the ideal tool for modeling a BCS connection to a DBMS is SharePoint Designer 2010. Start the application and open the target SharePoint site. Move to the External Content Types section in the quick launch bar on the left side of the UI, as shown in Figure 25-3.

FIGURE 25-3 The Site Objects quick launch menu of Microsoft SharePoint Designer 2010, shown with External Content Types highlighted.

To create a new ECT, on the Ribbon, under the New group, click External Content Type. A window appears (see Figure 25-4), in which you will set up a *CRMCustomer* entity corresponding to the records in the *Customers* table of the target DBMS.

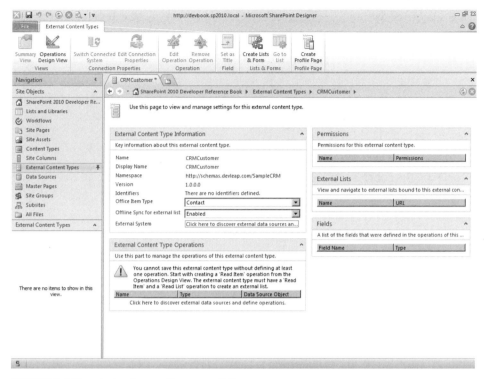

FIGURE 25-4 The window for creating a new ECT.

The following describes the information that you need to provide:

- **Name** The name of the ECT.

- **Display Name** The name that will be used for displaying the ECT.

- **Namespace** Describes a namespace, which can be any string, grouping ECTs of the same type or with a common data source.

- **Version** Provided solely for versioning purposes.

- **Identifiers** Defines (via a wizard) what you will see in the upcoming pages.

- **Office Item Type** Defines how the ECT will be presented in the office client UI. Possible values are: Generic List, Appointment, Contact, Task, and Post. For example, for a *Customers* table, each *Customer* row can be mapped to a Contact.

- **Offline Sync For External List** Enables or disables offline capabilities.

- **External System**   Links to the concrete definition of the external data source. This will be discussed shortly.

- **External Content Type Operations**   Allows browsing and managing operations available for the current ECT.

- **Permissions**   Used to manage access permissions for the current ECT.

- **External Lists**   Enumerates the external lists where the current ECT is used.

- **Fields**   Defines a list of the fields declared for the current ECT.

To define the concrete data source configuration, click the Click Here To Discover External Data Sources And Define Operations link adjacent to External System, or click the Operations Design View ribbon command.

A second page appears. Click the Add Connection button to define a new data connection, or you can also choose an existing data connection in the Data Source Explorer area. When you add a new connection, you must determine the type of data source to which you will connect. SharePoint Designer 2010 gives you the following three options:

- .NET Type

- SQL Server

- WCF Service

If you select SQL Server, a dialog appears, in which you need to provide the connection string. You also need to configure an authentication method, but this will not be covered in depth here because it is beyond the scope of this chapter. For the sake of simplicity, in the current example, simply use the default value Connect With User's Identity, which corresponds to a PassThrough connection that will use the identity of the user at runtime. If the web application is not configured to authenticate with Windows credentials, the NT Authority/Anonymous Logon account will be passed to the external system.

> **More Information**   For further details about BCS authentication and security infrastructure, read the document, "Business Connectivity Services security overview (SharePoint Server 2010)," which is available on TechNet Online at *http://technet.microsoft.com/en-us/library/ee661743.aspx*.

After defining the connection string, you are presented with the list of tables, views, and stored procedures that are available in the external database. Figure 25-5 illustrates the window, just after having completed the described steps.

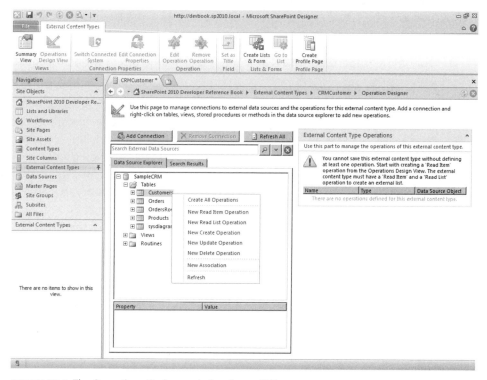

FIGURE 25-5 The Operations Designer window for an ECT.

Right-click an item (table, view, or routine) in the Data Source Explorer window. A contextual menu appears, from which you can add operations for managing data. Each operation corresponds to a method that will allow interaction with the data source. Using the SharePoint Designer 2010 interface, you can define the following operations:

- **Read Item**   Corresponds to the method for reading a single row/item.
- **Read List**   Corresponds to the method for reading a list of rows/items.
- **Create**   Creates a new row/item.
- **Update**   Updates an already existing row/item.
- **Delete**   Deletes an already existing row/item.

In addition, there is a Create All Operations command for creating all the operations in a single step, using a wizard. There is also a New Association command with which you can create a relationship between two ECTs in a master/detail fashion. This last topic is covered in the section "Associating Entities," beginning on page 719.

When you click the Create All Operations command, a wizard will guide you through three simple steps:

- **Operation Properties**   This is a summary of what the wizard will do for you.

- **Parameters Configuration**   Here, you can define all the fields of the ECT that you are creating. You must define an identifier field, but when using a SQL Server data source, SharePoint Designer 2010 can usually determine the identifier automatically, using the primary key of the table. If the primary key is composed with multiple columns, all of these columns will become required fields of the target ECT. If you choose to map the ECT to an Office type, you must satisfy some minimal requirements. For example, a contact of Office has to have a *LastName* property, and it is mandatory to map a field of the data source to that property. To do so, in the Properties section of the wizard, choose Office Property. From there, you can freely map all the fields that you like with their corresponding Office properties. You can also define a field that will be used in the data picker and columns of type External Data, while searching for items while in SharePoint.

- **Filter Parameters Configuration**   Use this step to define custom filters for selecting items. You can define various kinds of filters, such as Comparison Of Fields, Limitation Of Returned Rows, Paging, Timestamp Filtering, and Wildcard (*) Free Filtering.

Figure 25-6 depicts the main window for managing the ECT with all operations created and fields defined. Now, you are almost ready for consuming the list of ECTs. The only key points you should pay attention to are the following:

- You need to authorize users to consume the defined ECT.

- The identity that you will use to access the data source, depending on the authentication configuration you choose, will need to have access to the data source.

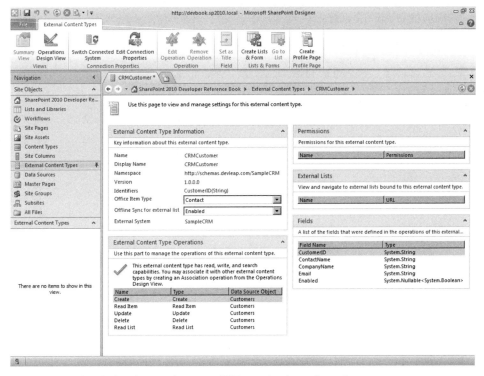

FIGURE 25-6 The window for creating a new ECT, completely configured.

Save the newly-defined ECT by pressing the Savebutton in the upper-left corner. Then, open the SharePoint Central Administration and browse to the management page of the Business Data Connectivity Services service application, as shown in Figure 25-7.

From this page, you can perform the following operations:

- Manage all the ECTs, the configured External Systems, or the BDC Models that you have defined in the farm.

- Import an external model defined in another farm or with an external tool.

- Set users and groups permissions for the entire metadata store or for a specific entity.

- Delete a previously defined ECT.

- Create, upgrade, or configure profile pages for an existing ECT. A profile page is a Web Part Page for managing the contents of a specific ECT.

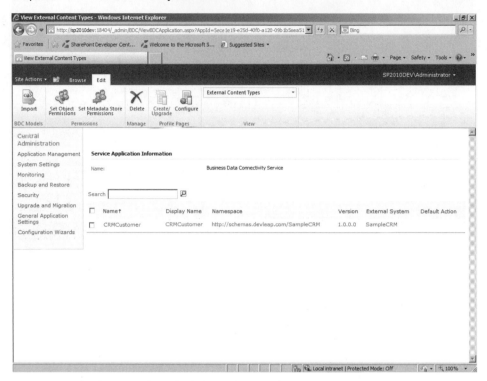

FIGURE 25-7 The SharePoint Central Administration page for managing Business Data Connectivity Services.

Select the *CRMCustomer* check box, and then on the Ribbon, click Set Object Permission or select Set Metadata Store Permissions. In the window that appears, you can define permissions for a specific user or group. The available permission mask allows you to define the following permissions:

- **Edit**   Specifies whether the user can edit the external systems, a single external system, a single ECT, or an operation.

- **Execute**   Allows the user to execute operations against an ECT.

- **Selectable In Clients**   Allows the user to create list of the target ECT.

- **Set Permissions**   The user can set permissions on the target item.

You can propagate permissions on descendant items to work with a permission inheritance model.

The minimum requirement for viewing and managing ECT data is to have both the Selectable In Clients and the Execute permissions applied.

 Important   Remember that at least one user or group must be assigned Set Permissions level to avoid creating non-manageable objects.

Now you are ready to create an external list for managing the *Customers* of the *SampleCRM* database. You can create the external list from SharePoint Designer 2010 or from the web browser. For this exercise, use the web browser. Browse to the target site where you want to make the list available and choose the menu item to create a new list instance. Choose an External List template and create it. You will be asked to provide the standard properties of a new list (name and quick launch behavior) and the name for the ECT. Select the target ECT, and you are done. Figure 25-8 illustrates the result. Notice that the user experience is exactly the same of browsing a native list of SharePoint.

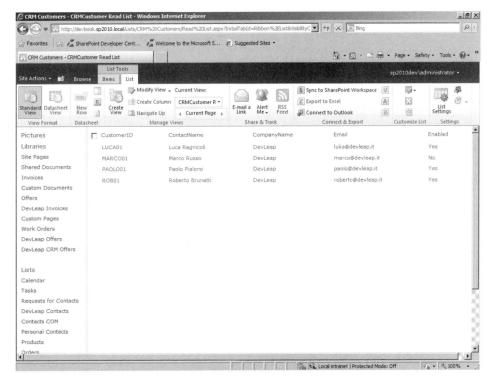

FIGURE 25-8 Browsing the *Customers* table through BCS in SharePoint 2010.

Note Depending on the authentication model you chose while creating the data source, you might receive an Access Denied By Business Data Connectivity message. If you do, check the trace log of SharePoint, which by default is in the SharePoint14_Root\LOGS folder, you should find an exception with a *High* level of severity, a value of Business Connectivity Services in the Area field, and an error message stating that BCS received an access denied exception while trying to access SQL Server. In this case, you should give the proper permissions, from a SQL Server perspective, to the user who is trying to access the SQL Server database. With the default authentication configuration (Connect with User's Identity) the database connection will be opened impersonating the user of the Application Pool, which by default in IIS7.x and SharePoint 2010 is NT AUTHORITY\IUSR.

BDC Model File

You can export the ECT model created in the previous section by using SharePoint Designer 2010 or via the management page of the Business Data Connectivity Services service application. If you try to export the *Customer* ECT definition, an XML file with extension .bdcm (Business Data Connectivity Model) will be generated that will look similar to Listing 25-1.

LISTING 25-1 The .bdcm file that defines the *Customer* ECT retrieved from the *SampleCRM* database.

```xml
<?xml version="1.0" encoding="utf-16" standalone="yes"?>
<Model xmlns:xsi="http://www.w3.org/2001/XMLSchema-instance"
xsi:schemaLocation="http://schemas.microsoft.com/windows/2007/BusinessDataCatalog
BDCMetadata.xsd" Name="CRMCustomer" xmlns="http://schemas.microsoft.com/windows/2007/
BusinessDataCatalog">
  <AccessControlList>
    <AccessControlEntry Principal="sp2010dev\administrator">
      <Right BdcRight="Execute" />
      <Right BdcRight="SetPermissions" />
      <Right BdcRight="SelectableInClients" />
    </AccessControlEntry>
  </AccessControlList>
  <LobSystems>
    <LobSystem Type="Database" Name="SampleCRM">
      <Properties>
        <Property Name="WildcardCharacter" Type="System.String">%</Property>
      </Properties>
      <AccessControlList>
        <!-- Code omitted for the sake of brevity -->
      </AccessControlList>
      <Proxy />
      <LobSystemInstances>
        <LobSystemInstance Name="SampleCRM">
          <Properties>
            <!-- Here are the database connection information -->
            <!-- Code omitted for the sake of brevity -->
          </Properties>
        </LobSystemInstance>
      </LobSystemInstances>
      <Entities>
        <Entity Namespace="http://schemas.devleap.com/SampleCRM" Version="1.1.0.0"
EstimatedInstanceCount="10000" Name="CRMCustomer" DefaultDisplayName="CRMCustomer">
          <Properties>
            <Property Name="OutlookItemType" Type="System.String">Contact</Property>
          </Properties>
          <AccessControlList>
            <!-- Code omitted for the sake of brevity -->
          </AccessControlList>
          <Identifiers>
            <Identifier TypeName="System.String" Name="CustomerID" />
          </Identifiers>
```

```xml
        <Methods>
          <Method Name="Create" DefaultDisplayName="CRMCustomer Create">
            <Properties>
              <Property Name="RdbCommandType" Type="System.Data.CommandType,
                System.Data, Version=2.0.0.0, Culture=neutral,
                PublicKeyToken=b77a5c561934e089">Text</Property>
              <Property Name="RdbCommandText" Type="System.String">INSERT INTO
[dbo].[Customers]([CustomerID] , [ContactName] , [CompanyName] , [Email] , [Enabled])
VALUES(@CustomerID , @ContactName , @CompanyName , @Email , @Enabled) SELECT
[CustomerID] FROM [dbo].[Customers] WHERE [CustomerID] = @CustomerID</Property>
              <Property Name="BackEndObjectType" Type="System.
String">SqlServerTable</Property>
              <Property Name="BackEndObject"
                Type="System.String">Customers</Property>
              <Property Name="Schema" Type="System.String">dbo</Property>
            </Properties>
            <AccessControlList>
              <!-- Code omitted for the sake of brevity -->
            </AccessControlList>
            <Parameters>
              <Parameter Direction="In" Name="@CustomerID">
                <TypeDescriptor TypeName="System.String" CreatorField="true"
IdentifierName="CustomerID" Name="CustomerID">
                  <Properties>
                    <Property Name="Size" Type="System.Int32">10</Property>
                  </Properties>
                  <Interpretation>
                    <NormalizeString FromLOB="NormalizeToNull"
ToLOB="NormalizeToEmptyString" />
                  </Interpretation>
                </TypeDescriptor>
              </Parameter>
              <!-- Code omitted for the sake of brevity -->
            </Parameters>
            <MethodInstances>
              <MethodInstance Type="Creator" ReturnParameterName="Create"
                ReturnTypeDescriptorPath="Create[0]" Default="true"
                Name="Create" DefaultDisplayName="CRMCustomer Create">
                <AccessControlList>
                  <!-- Code omitted for the sake of brevity -->
                </AccessControlList>
              </MethodInstance>
            </MethodInstances>
          </Method>
          <!-- Code omitted for the sake of brevity -->
        </Methods>
      </Entity>
    </Entities>
   </LobSystem>
  </LobSystems>
</Model>
```

The main element of a .bdcm file is the *Model* tag. This is the root element of the document, and it wraps an entire BDC model definition. *Model* has a dedicated *AccessControlList*, and it defines one or more *LobSystem* definitions. A *LobSystem* element defines from an abstract viewpoint an external data source. A concrete data source is represented by a *LobSystemInstance* element, instead. Each ECT in a *LobSystem* is described by an element *Entity*, which declares a new ECT, together with its *Identifiers* and *Methods*. A single model in general defines a set of entities. Meanwhile, the *Methods* are defined using single *Method* elements and are instantiated using elements of type *MethodInstance*. Each *MethodInstance* features a *Type* attribute, which defines the typology of method instance. Table 25-1 lists the available values for the *MethodInstance/@Type* attribute.

TABLE 25-1 The Available Values for the *MethodInstance/@Type* Attribute

Type	Description
AccessChecker	Checks the permissions for the calling security principal related to a collection of entities.
AssociationNavigator	Retrieves a list of associated (related) entities from a single entity.
Associator	Associates an entity instance with another.
BinarySecurityDescriptorAccessor	Retrieves a list of bytes defining the permissions for a set of security principals, related to a specific entity instance.
BulkAssociatedIdEnumerator	Retrieves IDs of entities associated with another.
BulkAssociationNavigator	Retrieves destination entities that are associated with multiple specified entities.
BulkIdEnumerator	Supports the search engine of SharePoint during incremental updates. *BulkIdEnumerator* returns some version information for entities whose IDs are provided to the method.
BulkSpecificFinder	Retrieves a set of entities given a set of IDs.
ChangedIdEnumerator	Supports the search engine of SharePoint during incremental updates. *ChangedIdEnumerator* returns IDs of entities that were modified since a specified date/time.
Creator	Creates a new instance of an entity.
DeletedIdEnumerator	Supports the search engine of SharePoint during incremental updates. *DeletedIdEnumerator* returns IDs of entities that were deleted since a specified date/time.
Deleter	Deletes an entity instance.
Disassociator	Removes an association between an entity instance and another one.
Finder	Retrieves a list of entity instances, based on a set of filtering conditions that can be declared within the *Method* definition.
GenericInvoker	Invokes a specific method or task in the target system.

Type	Description
IdEnumerator	Supports the search engine. *IdEnumerator* retrieves the field values for the identifier fields of a list of entities.
Scalar	Returns a single scalar value from the external system.
SpecificFinder	Retrieves a specific instance of an entity, based on its corresponding identifier.
StreamAccessor	Returns a single stream of bytes from a specific entity instance. *StreamAccessor* can be used to retrieve images, videos, attachments, and so on that are related to a specific entity instance.
Updater	Updates an entity instance.

When you define a BDC Model, regardless of the data provider you use in the back-end, you end up defining a file such as the one shown in Listing 25-1 and using methods like the ones illustrated here. SharePoint Designer 2010 and Visual Studio 2010 support just the most frequently used method instance types, while the others should be defined manually in the .bdcm file using an XML editor.

Offline Capabilities

If you have SharePoint Server 2010, you can experience the offline capabilities offered by BCS. Browse to and select an external list, such as the one you created in the previous section. To connect your list to Microsoft Outlook 2010 and make it available offline, on the Ribbon, click Connect To Outlook, (see Figure 25-9). This capability is available because you defined the ECT with an Office Contact behavior. A temporary window appears, displaying the message, "Preparing External List For Synchronization With Outlook."

FIGURE 25-9 The Ribbon bar of an External List with the Connect To Outlook command highlighted.

Next, an installer dialog window appears (Figure 25-10) that asks the end user for permission to install the BDC Client Runtime on the client side, (if it is not already installed) and to install the model schema for the entity that you are connecting with Outlook.

FIGURE 25-10 The pop-up dialog that appears when installing the client model and consuming the ECT.

In Figure 25-11 you can see the final output of the offline list in Outlook 2010.

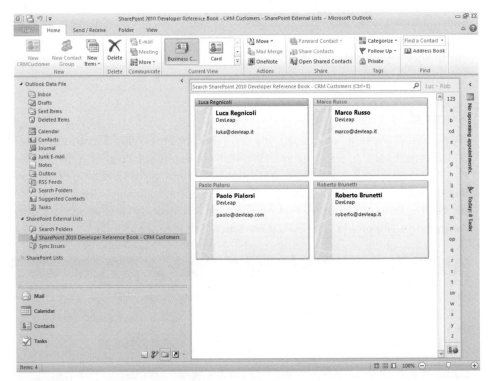

FIGURE 25-11 The list of contacts available in Outlook 2010 and corresponding to the list of *Customers*.

Now you can browse and edit data either from SharePoint 2010 within the web browser or using Outlook 2010, or still managing data directly on the database storage. Regardless of the interface you use for managing data, all your modifications will be sooner (online) or later (offline) synchronized with the back-end database.

As soon as you connect the list into the Microsoft Office client platform, it creates a folder under the local user's profile path (which, for example, should be C:\Users\[Your UserName]\ AppData\Local\Microsoft\BCS) where the offline data is stored. Notice that the folder is represented using a green color, because it is encrypted.

You can consume exactly the same data using Microsoft SharePoint Workspace 2010, which is a new component of the Office 2010 offering, created for the purpose of managing SharePoint data on the client side with offline editing capabilities.

Accessing a WCF/SOAP Service

Having the standard SharePoint 2010 user interface for accessing data stored in a DBMS with CRUDQ support is undoubtedly interesting and challenging. However, there are many companies that lock and secure their databases, preventing directly data access data from clients or even from servers, for security and privacy reasons. In these situations, there are articulated business solutions, built on top of the database, that provide access to data filtered by business rules and security policies. Quite often, the business rules are exposed or published through SOAP services, eventually implemented using WCF.

The Business Connectivity Services support connecting with SOAP Services over HTTP (Web Services) and optionally implemented with WCF can also make these kinds of applications available in SharePoint. A SOAP service can be consumed by BCS if it offers a minimum set of operations that are mandatory for the web/WCF Connector of BCS. For a minimal implementation that is capable of reading data with a read-only approach, you need to have a SOAP operation corresponding to a *Finder* method instance type, and another supporting the *SpecificFinder* type. From a SOAP perspective a *Finder* method is an operation that optionally accepts some filters and returns a collection of entities. While a *SpecificFinder* operation accepts an identifier and returns the corresponding entity. Specifically, every returned entity should have an identifying property, and the result of a *SpecificFinder* operation has to return an entity with at least the same properties as the result of the *Finder* operation. There cannot be a *Finder* method that returns more information than a *SpecificFinder* method. Listing 25-2 shows a WCF service contract satisfying these requirements.

LISTING 25-2 A WCF service contract satisfying the read-only requirements for WCF.

```
[ServiceContract(Namespace = "http://schemas.devleap.com/CustomersService")]
public interface ICustomersService {
    [OperationContract]
    Customer GetCustomerById(String customerID);

    [OperationContract]
    Customers ListAllCustomers();
}
```

```
[DataContract(Name = "Customer", Namespace = "http://schemas.devleap.com/Customers")]
public class Customer {
    [DataMember(Name = "CustomerID", Order = 1)]
    public String CustomerID { get; set; }

    [DataMember(Name = "ContactName", Order = 1)]
    public String ContactName { get; set; }

    [DataMember(Name = "CompanyName", Order = 1)]
    public String CompanyName { get; set; }

    [DataMember(Name = "Country", Order = 1)]
    public String Country { get; set; }
}

[CollectionDataContract(ItemName = "Customer", Name = "Customers", Namespace =
"http://schemas.devleap.com/Customers")]
public class Customers : List<Customer> {
    public Customers() : base() { }
    public Customers(IEnumerable<Customer> collection) : base(collection) { }
}
```

The sample contract uses a *Customer* entity and a *Customers* list of them. These types are
marked as serializable with the *DataContract* serialization engine used by WCF. The service
contract publishes only two operations: *GetCustomerById* and *ListAllCustomers*. The former
accepts the *customerID* (the identifier parameter) and returns a single *Customer* entity. The
latter, for the sake of simplicity, does not expect any argument and returns a list of *Customer*
instances.

If you would like to support a full CRUDQ scenario, you need to publish three more operations for the corresponding method types (*Creator*, *Updater*, *Deleter*). The *Creator* operation
should accept the entity to create as input and should return the identifier of the created
entity, or the whole created entity. The *Updater* operation should accept the entity and,
above all, its identifier. It is not required to return anything back to the caller, but it is not
forbidden. The *Deleter* operation should accept the identifier of the entity to delete. It is not
required to have a response. Listing 25-3 demonstrates an extended WCF contract, supporting the CRUDQ scenario.

LISTING 25-4 A WCF service contract satisfying the CRUDQ requirements for WCF.

```
[ServiceContract(Namespace = "http://schemas.devleap.com/CustomersService")]
public interface ICustomersService {
    [OperationContract]
    Customer GetCustomerById(String customerID);

    [OperationContract]
    Customers ListAllCustomers();
```

```
    [OperationContract]
    Customer AddCustomer(Customer item);

    [OperationContract]
    Customer UpdateCustomer(Customer item);

    [OperationContract]
    Boolean DeleteCustomer(Customer item);
}
```

The internal code of a service that implements such a contract is trivial and it will not be covered in this chapter. However, in the code samples that accompany this chapter, you will find a full sample implementation.

Once you have defined a service contract and a service implementation that adhere to the communication requirements, and you publish it through a dedicated endpoint, you can register a new ECT corresponding to the entity published by the service. The smarter tool for accomplishing this task is still SharePoint Designer 2010. The first part of the registration task is exactly the same as registering an external database. However, while adding a new connection for the external system behind the ECT, in the Data Source Explorer window, you need to select a new WCF Service data source type for the external data source. Figure 25-12 shows the modal dialog for configuring a data source of type WCF Service.

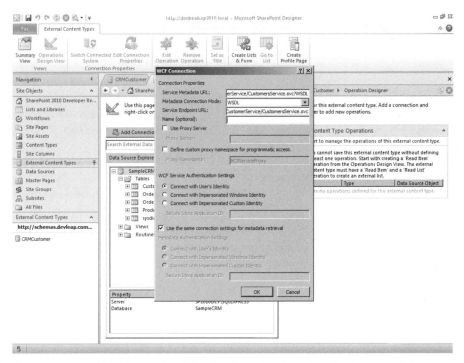

FIGURE 25-12 The WCF Connection dialog box for registering a WCF Service external data source.

The following list describes the configuration information:

- **Service Metadata URL**   The URL of the endpoint publishing the service's metadata.
- **Metadata Connection Mode**   The type of metadata published by the service. The available values are: WSDL, MetadataExchange (WS-MetadataExchange).
- **Service Endpoint URL**   The URL of the endpoint publishing the service.
- **Name**   An optional name for the service.
- **Use Proxy**   Specifies an HTTP proxy to use for contacting the service endpoint.
- **Define Custom Proxy Namespace For Programmatic Access**   Specifies a namespace for the auto-generated proxy code, in order to access the service proxy by custom code.
- **WCF Service Authentication Settings**   Specifies the authentication technique to use while communicating with the external service.
- **Metadata Authentication Settings**   You can optionally define a specific authentication mode for retrieving the service metadata.

After you register the external data source, you must define all the operations that you would like to support.

> **Note** While defining a WCF Service data source, if you provide a service or metadata address published by *localhost* you will receive the following error message: "The URL should not loop back to the local host." In fact, you cannot use a loopback URL (for instance, *localhost*) in a multi-server farm, because there wouldn't be guarantee of availability of the URL for every server of the farm. Therefore, you always need to publish services through qualified host names.

As with the SQL Server data source, you can add operations by right-clicking a SOAP operation in the Data Source Explorer window, which in the case of a WCF Service will show you all the available SOAP operations. Figure 25-13 displays the resulting window.

Notice in Figure 25-13 that the menu does not provide a command for configuring all the operations in one shot. This is because it cannot auto-generate them autonomously simply reading the service metadata, so you need to configure each individual operation, step by step. You should start by creating a *Finder* method, which is a Read List operation. Then, define a *SpecificFinder* method, which corresponds to a Read Item operation. Lastly, define the Create, Update, and Delete operations, in case they're needed. Each operation allows you to configure the input and output arguments via a wizard interface.

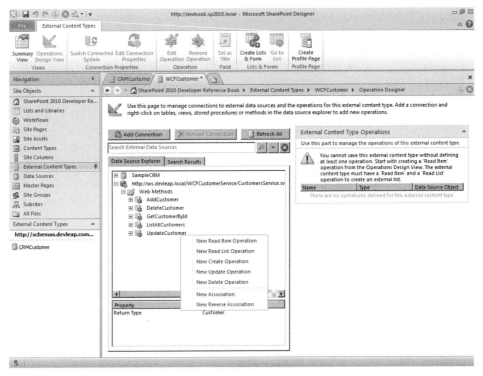

FIGURE 25-13 The Data Source Explorer window for the sample WCF Service data source.

During definition of the Read List operation, you need to define the entity identifier in the Return Parameter Configuration wizard step. You should also define a field to show in the entity picker. For the purposes of the current example, you should define the *CustomerID* property of each *Customer* entity as the identifier field, and the *ContactName* property as the field to show in picker. Figure 25-14 shows this wizard step.

Furthermore, when defining the Read Item operation, you have to map the identifier property to the corresponding argument of the *SpecificFinder* method in the Input Parameters Configuration wizard step. Then, in the Output Parameters Configuration step, you must define the entity identifier in the output message, and any property mapping to the corresponding Office property, if you defined the ECT as an Office Item Type.

The same considerations about the entity identifier are valid for the Create, Update, and Delete operations.

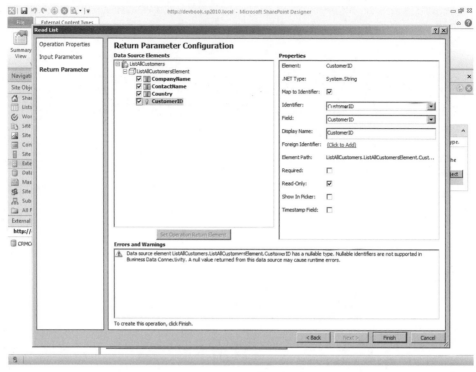

FIGURE 25-14 The Return Parameter Configuration wizard step that defines the Read List operation.

Once you have finished configuring the ECT, you need to save it, and then you can use it in external lists and in Office clients, too.

.NET Custom Model

A third opportunity you have while defining BCS solutions, is to develop a custom model in Visual Studio 2010. This capability is interesting whenever you need to consume a third-party data source, which is not directly accessible through a database connection or by using a web service. It's also useful when you need to aggregate data, eventually provided by non-homogeneous sources, using an intermediary proxy. A custom model is a .NET assembly, compiled in Visual Studio 2010 and built starting from a Visual Studio template project of type Business Data Connectivity Model. This project type is by necessity a full-trust, farm-level solution that deploys its assembly into the Global Assembly Cache (GAC). In fact, the custom model is accessible from any web application and can be shared across the farm. Inside the .NET assembly, you can write whatever code that you like, and you can use any kind of library, service, or data provider in order to read the target data source. From the BCS viewpoint, you define a .bdcm file within Visual Studio 2010, and you model a set of entities that will correspond to the ECT that you want to design. Visual Studio 2010 provides a specific Business Data Connectivity model designer and a BDC Explorer window to support model definition. Figure 25-15 illustrates the model designer, together with the BDC Explorer toolbox.

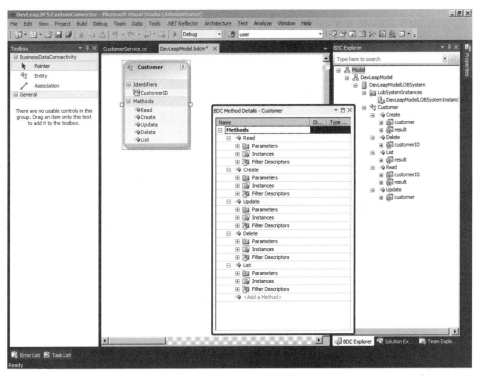

FIGURE 25-15   The BCS Model Designer available in Microsoft Visual Studio 2010.

The main goal of the model designer is to allow you to design entities and relationships (called associations in BCS) between entities. Each individual entity is made up of one or more identifier properties and some methods. The methods are defined and configured in terms of parameters, method instances, and filter descriptors using the BDC Method Details window. With the BDC Explorer, you can inspect the model by using the classic treeview approach. The result of modeling is a .bdcm file that you can manually import in SharePoint 2010 by using the Business Data Connectivity Services service application page in the SharePoint Central Administration, after you have deployed the corresponding assembly DLL into the GAC. Otherwise, you can take advantage of the automatic deployment provided by the Business Data Connectivity Model project template, which uses a feature receiver (defined in class *ImportModelReceiver* of namespace *Microsoft.Office.SharePoint. ClientExtensions.Deployment*) for importing the file into the Metadata Catalog of BCS.

It is interesting to know that when you design a model in the graphical designer, Visual Studio 2010 automatically creates a code file for each entity called *[Entity]Service.cs*, where *[Entity]* corresponds to the name of the entity handled by that class file. Within that file

Visual Studio 2010 will place static methods corresponding to the method instances declared in the designer. In addition, you can use the designer to define the method instances and parameters for each designed method as well as the data types of input, output, and return parameters.

To master the model design process, you should first define classes corresponding to all of the entities that you want to make available through the model. Then you should design the entities in the model designer and configure the methods that you want to make available. Remember that at the very least, you should define both a *Finder* and *SpecificFinder* methods. If you want to provide *Creator*, *Updater*, and *Deleter* methods, you can design them, too. In the accompanying code sample for this chapter, you will find a complete solution, which will be discussed in the next section.

Developing a Custom Model from Scratch

In this section, you will use a step-by-step approach to learn how to design a simple model that publishes a list of customers read from the *SampleCRM* database that you saw in the section, "Accessing a Database," on page 691. However, in this example you will read the customers using LINQ to SQL.

> **More Information** LINQ to SQL is a topic that will not be covered in this book. If you would like to understand how it works, read the book, *Programming Microsoft LINQ in .NET 4.0*, by Paolo Pialorsi and Marco Russo (Microsoft Press, 2010; ISBN: 978-0-7356-4057-3).

First, create a new SharePoint 2010 project of type Business Data Connectivity Model. prompted window appears with a pre-configured model designer, describing a *BdcModel1* model with a hypothetical *Entity1*, together with both an Entity1.cs and Entity1Service.cs classes. Remove the *Entity1* from the model as well as the related .CS files.

Add a LINQ to SQL model to the project and define a link to the table of *Customers* defined in the target *SampleCRM* SQL Server database. Configure the fields of the *Customer* type for supporting optimistic concurrency with no concurrency checks (*Update Check = Never*). This chapter will not cover details about how to manage these tasks, which are related to LINQ to SQL.

Next, rename the BCS model from *BdcModel1* to a more consistent name (the sample that accompanies this chapter uses a name of *DevLeapSampleCRM*). You should also rename accordingly the .BDCM file related to the current model. Add a new entity to the model, giving it a name of *Customer.* The designer will generate a CustomerService.cs file for you. Add a new identifier for the *Customer* entity, and add also a couple of methods named *ReadList* and *ReadItem.* To add an identifier property or a method, you can simply right-click the entity in the designer area and select the corresponding command menu.

Figure 25-16 depicts the project outline and the designer layout after you have completed the described tasks.

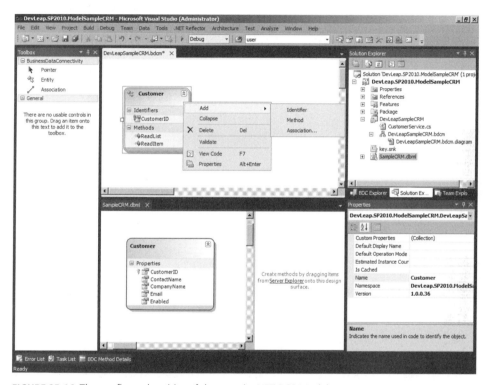

FIGURE 25-16 The configured entities of the sample .NET BCS Model..

Now you need to configure the two methods (Figure 25-17). The *ReadList* method will correspond to a *Finder* method, while the *ReadItem* method will be a *SpecificFinder.*

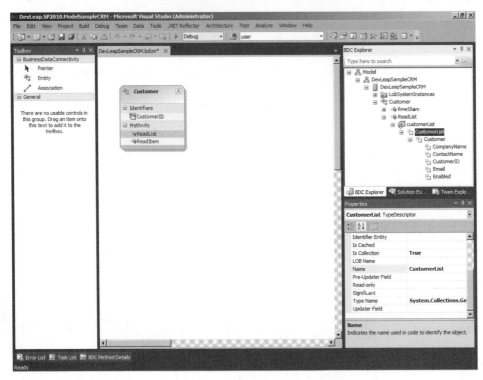

FIGURE 25-17 The BDC Explorer showing the configured *ReadList* method.

Start with the *ReadList* method. Select the method in the designer and show the BDC Method Details window, which by default appears in the bottom area of Visual Studio. If the window is not available, go to View | Other Windows to show it. To add a new method parameter, select the Parameters section and invoke the Create Parameter command by clicking the Add a Parameter item in the list of parameters. Give it a name in the property window of Visual Studio and choose a Direction of Return in the BDC Method Details window. Under the Type Descriptor column, select the Edit command and provide a value for the Name and the Type Name properties in the property grid. In the current example, you should use the name *customerList* for the parameter, *CustomerList* for the type descriptor, and a type value of *System. Collections.Generic.IEnumerable`1[DevLeap.SP2010.ModelSampleCRM.Customer, DevLeap. SP2010.ModelSampleCRM]* to the Type Name property of the type descriptor.

To define an *IEnumerable<T>* type, select the Is Enumerable check box in the editor for the Type Name property. In the context of the current example, the type *DevLeap.SP2010. ModelSampleCRM.Customer* represents a *Customer* entity of LINQ to SQL. Usually, it should be the type corresponding to the entity used by the BCS model. Also, verify that the property Is Collection has a value of *True*.

Next, right-click the *CustomerList* item in the BDC Explorer window, and then select Add Type Descriptor. Browse the types available in the current project, and then configure the type descriptor with a name of *Customer* and an underlying Type Name corresponding to the class published by LINQ to SQL. Then, configure each individual property of the *Customer* type by adding a type descriptor for each one, configuring its name and type according to what is defined in the LINQ to SQL model.

Now you are ready to add a new instance of the *ReadList* method, configuring that instance as a *Finder* method. Expand the Instances section under the *ReadList* method in the BDC Method Details window, and then click Add a Method Instance to invoke the Create Finder Instance command. Configure the method instance as illustrated in Figure 25-18.

FIGURE 25-18 The property grid showing the configuration
for the *ReadList* method instance.

Looking at the definition of *ReadList*, you can see a return parameter named *customersList* and type *CustomersList*, according to what has been configured in the BDC Explorer. You can also see a method instance of type *Finder*. The method instance is also marked as the default method.

Repeat the same steps for the *ReadItem* method. However, for this method you will have a parameter named *customerID* and a direction value of *In*. You will also have a parameter named *customer* with a direction value of *Return*. Because the single item returned by the *ReadItem* method will have exactly the same type descriptor of a single item returned by the *ReadList* method, you can copy and paste the type descriptor definition within the BDC Explorer. Finally, the method instance for the *Read* method will have a type of *SpecificFinder*.

Now you are ready to implement the model code. If you open the source code of the CustomerService.cs file, you can see that the designer defined the service code for you. Listing 25-2 shows this auto-generated code.

LISTING 25-2 The CustomerService.cs auto-generated file.

```csharp
public partial class CustomerService {
    public static Customer Read(string customerID) {
        throw new System.NotImplementedException();
    }

    public static IEnumerable<Customer> List() {
        throw new System.NotImplementedException();
    }
}
```

Replace the methods implementation with concrete code, and you will be ready to provide read-only data to BCS. Listing 25-3 shows you a concrete code implementation.

LISTING 25-4 The CustomerService.cs auto-generated file with concrete code implementation.

```csharp
public partial class CustomerService {
    private static SampleCRMDataContext GetDataContext() {
        SampleCRMDataContext dc = new SampleCRMDataContext("sqlConnectionString");
        return dc;
    }

    public static Customer Read(string customerID) {
        SampleCRMDataContext dc = GetDataContext();
        return (dc.Customers
            .FirstOrDefault(c => c.CustomerID == customerID));
    }

    public static IEnumerable<Customer> List() {
        SampleCRMDataContext dc = GetDataContext();
        return (from c in dc.Customers
                select c);
    }
}
```

Figure 25-19 presents the final outline of the project.

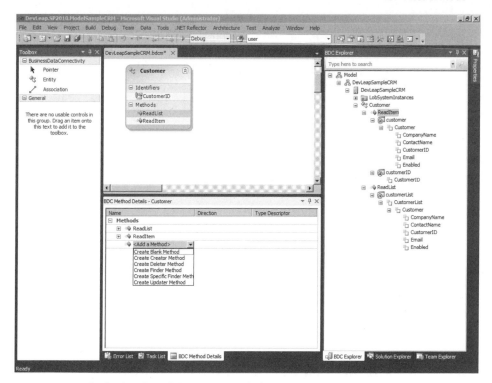

FIGURE 25-19 The final outline of the project, ready for providing read-only data to BCS.

You can add also the *Creator*, *Updater*, and *Deleter* methods. To do so, click the Add a Method command menu item illustrated in Figure 25-19 in the BDC Method Details window, The *Creator* method accepts a parameter of type *Customer* with a direction value of *In*, and it returns a result of type *Customer* with a direction value of *Return*. The *Updater* method accepts at least a parameter of type *Customer* with a direction value of *In*, but it will not return anything. The *Deleter* method accepts a parameter of type *customerID* with a direction value of *In*, but it too does not return anything.

After you finish designing your model, you can validate it by right-clicking the designer surface and selecting the Validate command. If your model is correctly defined, Visual Studio 2010 displays the message "Model validation completed with no errors" in the Output window.

In the previous pages you manually defined the methods. This was done for the sake of clarity and to make you aware of what is happening under the cover of a BCS Model designed in Visual Studio 2010. However, if you simply design your entities in the designer, define the identifier properties and the underlying type, and then select the Create ... Method command (illustrated in Figure 25-19), the designer will configure all the methods, parameters, and type descriptors for you, using a standard behavior. You only need to configure the structure of a single item; for the current example, this was the *Customer* type descriptor, which is returned by the *Finder* method instance, before adding all the other methods definitions. Then the designer will automatically copy the same type descriptor to all the methods.

Listing 25-5 presents the final implementation of the CustomerService.cs file.

LISTING 25-5 The CustomerService.cs file with concrete and complete code implementation.

```
public partial class CustomerService {
    private static SampleCRMDataContext GetDataContext() {
        SampleCRMDataContext dc = new SampleCRMDataContext("sqlConnectionString");
        return dc;
    }

    public static IEnumerable<Customer> ReadList() {
        SampleCRMDataContext dc = GetDataContext();
        return (from c in dc.Customers
                select c);
    }

    public static Customer ReadItem(string customerID) {
        SampleCRMDataContext dc = GetDataContext();

        return (dc.Customers
            .FirstOrDefault(c => c.CustomerID == customerID));
    }

    public static Customer Create(Customer newCustomer) {
        SampleCRMDataContext dc = GetDataContext();

        dc.Customers.InsertOnSubmit(newCustomer);
        dc.SubmitChanges();
        return (newCustomer);
    }

    public static void Update(Customer customer, string customerID) {
        SampleCRMDataContext dc = GetDataContext();

        dc.Customers.Attach(customer, true);
        dc.SubmitChanges();
    }

    public static void Delete(string customerID) {
        SampleCRMDataContext dc = GetDataContext();

        Customer customerToDelete = dc.Customers
            .FirstOrDefault(c => c.CustomerID == customerID);

        dc.Customers.DeleteOnSubmit(customerToDelete);
        dc.SubmitChanges();
    }
}
```

Associating Entities

Regardless of the type of data source provider you choose for designing your ECTs, it is important to know that you can define associations between entities of the same namespace/model. In fact, whenever you have entities with a relationship, you can design an association with which you can navigate through your data, moving across associations.

Depending on the tool that you use for designing your BCS models, you can define the following kind of associations:

- **One-to-many forward and/or reverse associations based on a foreign-key**   This models a classic 1-*n* relationship. An example of a one-to-many association is represented by a customer with his orders. It is based on a foreign-key and can be modeled within SharePoint Designer 2010.

- **Many-to-many associations**   These associations correspond to *n-n* relationships. An example of a many-to-many association is an association between a customer and his interest areas. In fact, a customer can have multiple interest areas, and every interest area can have multiple interested customers.

- **Self-referential associations**   These are associations that are self-referential for the same entity. An example could be a list of *Employees*, where each *Employee* is related to his manager, who is still an *Employee*.

- **Multiple related External Content Types**   These associations allow modeling between one entity and multiple entities. An example could be an association table with multiple identifying foreign-keys mapping to different tables, such as the description of a *Product* in a multi-language environment, where a description is identified by a *ProductID* and a *CultureCode*, respectively corresponding to the *Product* and *Culture* used to identify the *ProductDescription*.

As an example, consider the *SampleCRM* database and the *CRMCustomer* ECT defined in the section "Accessing a Database," on page 691. Add another ECT corresponding to the *Orders* table and call it *CRMOrder*. Each *Order* row is related to a specific *Customer* row, and the relationship is one-to-many, where the *CRMCustomer* is the source and the related *CRMOrder* instances are the destinations. From within SharePoint Designer 2010 you can select the Operations Design View of the destination ECT, and then click the Add Association menu item to create a new association.

> **Note** In SharePoint Designer 2010, you always need to create an association starting from the destination entity and not from the source entity.

When you undertake adding a new association, a wizard appears that asks you to select the source ECT and the related identifier (see Figure 25-20).

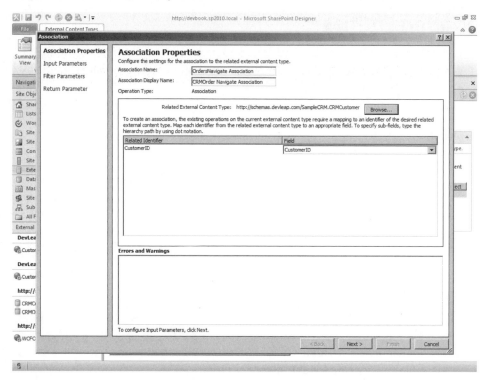

FIGURE 25-20 The first step of the wizard for creating an association between two ECT entities.

Then, you need to select the parameters to provide to the association. In fact, an association is a particular kind of *MethodInstance* definition, as are for example, the *Associator*, *AssociationNavigator*, *BulkAssociationNavigator* that you saw in Table 25-1. Thus, you have the capability to provide input parameters and filter parameters. The return type of the method is the related list of destinations.

You can use associations, for example, by using native Business Data Web Parts of SharePoint, creating pages that use the Business Data List and the Business Data Related List. These Web Parts are available only in the Enterprise edition of SharePoint Server 2010. Figure 25-21 demonstrates the output of these Web Parts when configured to render *CRMCustomer* and related *CRMOrder* instances.

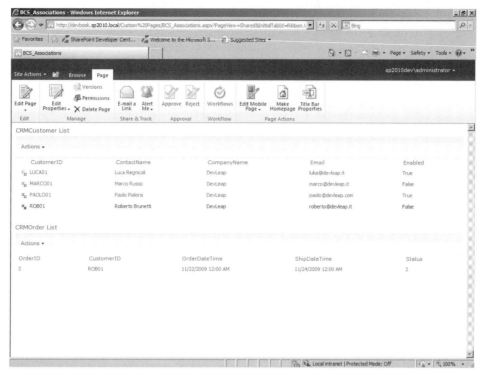

FIGURE 25-21 A Web Part Page showing the output of Business Data List and Business Data Related List when connected.

If you need to define an association different from a one-to-many, based on foreign-key, you can use a text editor for the .bdcm file or the Visual Studio 2010 BDC Model Designer.

Programming with BCS Object Model

The last topic of this chapter is about working with the Metadata Store and the ECTs by code, by using the BCS Object Model. In fact, as with many other service applications of SharePoint 2010, the BCS also provides a custom object model to manage the Metadata Store and the ECTs, in general. This section will not try to give you a full reference of the object model in only a few pages; rather, it will show you a couple of examples that are useful toward understanding the philosophy behind the scenes. Listing 25-6 shows a code excerpt that illustrates how to add a new instance of an ECT by code.

LISTING 25-6 Using the BCS Object Model to add a new instance of an ECT.

```
using (SPSite site = new SPSite("http://devbook.sp2010.local/")) {
    // Get a reference to the BDC Service Application Proxy
    SPServiceContext serviceContext = SPServiceContext.GetContext(site);
    BdcServiceApplicationProxy bdcProxy =
        (BdcServiceApplicationProxy)serviceContext.GetDefaultProxy(
            typeof(BdcServiceApplicationProxy));

    DatabaseBackedMetadataCatalog model =
        bdcProxy.GetDatabaseBackedMetadataCatalog();

    IEntity entity = model.GetEntity(
        "http://schemas.devleap.com/WCFCustomerService", "WCFCustomer");
    ILobSystem ls = entity.GetLobSystem();
    ILobSystemInstance lsi = ls.GetLobSystemInstances()[
        "http://ws.devleap.local/WCFCustomerService/CustomersService.svc?WSDL"];

    IView creatorView = entity.GetCreatorView("AddCustomer");
    IFieldValueDictionary customerFields = creatorView.GetDefaultValues();

    customerFields["CustomerID"] = "DM001";
    customerFields["CompanyName"] = "DevLeap";
    customerFields["ContactName"] = "Paolo Pialorsi";
    customerFields["Country"] = "Italy";

    Identity identifierValues = entity.Create(customerFields, lsi);
}
```

First, you need to get a reference to the service application proxy class, which for BCS is the *BdcServiceApplicationProxy* class. As you can see, you can retrieve a reference to the Metadata Store through a variable of type *DatabaseBackedMetadataCatalog*. Then, you can retrieve the entities as objects by implementing the *IEntity* interface of the *Microsoft. BusinessData.MetadataModel* namespace. Once you have an entity (for example, the definition of an ECT), you can retrieve an object of type *IView*, which represents a view for a specific operation. You can retrieve a reference to many of the methods available through the model. When you have a reference to a method that you wish to use, you can simply invoke it against a specific LOB System instance, which is a variable of type *ILobSystemInstance*, retrieved from the current entity's environment.

Listing 25-7 shows the code enumerating all the entities available through a BCS model.

LISTING 25-7 Using the BCS Object Model to retrieve a list of ECT instances.

```
using (SPSite site = new SPSite("http://devbook.sp2010.local/")) {
    // Get a reference to the BDC Service Application Proxy
    SPServiceContext serviceContext = SPServiceContext.GetContext(site);
    BdcServiceApplicationProxy bdcProxy =
        (BdcServiceApplicationProxy)serviceContext.GetDefaultProxy(
            typeof(BdcServiceApplicationProxy));

    DatabaseBackedMetadataCatalog model =
        bdcProxy.GetDatabaseBackedMetadataCatalog();

    IEntity entity = model.GetEntity(
        "http://schemas.devleap.com/WCFCustomerService", "WCFCustomer");
    ILobSystem ls = entity.GetLobSystem();
    ILobSystemInstance lsi = ls.GetLobSystemInstances()[
        "http://ws.devleap.local/WCFCustomerService/CustomersService.svc?WSDL"];

    // Enumerate all the customers
    IMethodInstance method = entity.GetMethodInstance(
        "ListAllCustomers", MethodInstanceType.Finder);
    IEntityInstanceEnumerator ieie = entity.FindFiltered(method.GetFilters(), lsi);
    IView view = entity.GetFinderView(method.Name);
    while (ieie.MoveNext()) {
        foreach (IField field in view.Fields) {
            if (ieie.Current[field] != null) {
                Console.WriteLine("{0}: {1}",
                    field.Name, ieie.Current[field].ToString());
            }
        }
    }
}
```

As you have just seen, you can invoke any method instance provided by any target data source provider. There are situations, such as workflow activities, custom scripts, Web Parts, and so on in which it is very useful to be able to interact with BCS models by code.

Summary

In this chapter, you saw a quick introduction of what BCS is and how it works on the server and client side. Then, you saw how to configure the three most popular kinds of data source providers: DBMS, WCF/SOAP Service, and the custom .NET Model. You also read a quick overview of the associations and of the BCS Object Model. You now have the basic elements to start playing with BCS in your real solutions.

Index

Symbols

$expand={Entity} keywords 173
$filter={predicate} keywords 173
$metadata keywords 173
$orderby={property} keywords 173
$skip=n keywords 173
$top=n keywords 173
.bdcm files 702
/code:<file> argument (SP-Metal.EXE) 108
.DOC or .DOCX documents, converting 417–422
/language:<language> argument (SPMetal. EXE) 108
/namespace:<namespace> (SPMetal.EXE) 108
.NET
  custom model for BCS solutions 710–718
.NET Framework
  LINQ providers in 102
  requirement to run SharePoint 14
  updating application from earlier version of 168
.NET object model
  about 55
.osdx file 673
/parameters:<file> argument (SPMetal. EXE) 107
/password:<password> argument (SPMetal. EXE) 107

/serialization:<type> argument (SPMetal. EXE) 108
/useremoteapi argument (SPMetal.EXE) 107
/user:<name> argument (SPMetal.EXE) 107
/web:<url> argument (SP-Metal.EXE) 107
.wsp package. *See* WSP (Windows SharePoint Services Solution Packages)
.xap files 220

A

Access
  integrating list content with 34
AccessChecker type 702
actions and conditions, custom
  about 555
  custom actions for Share-Point Designer 2010 557–563
  custom conditions for SharePoint Designer 2010 563
  dependency properties 555–557
ActivateOnDefault attribute 243
ActivationDependencies child element 245
ActivationProperties 395
Add a Comment 499
Add and Customize Pages permission 604
AddContentTypeField element 257

Add Event Receiver menu 262
AddFile 421
AddFolder 421
AddItem method 66, 160
Add Items permission 604
AdditionalPageHead Controlid 295
AddLibrary 421
Add method
  overloads in 93
  SPListCollection 84, 86
  SPUserCollection 98
  SPWebCollection 82
addNotification method 305
Add/Remove Personal Web Parts permission 605
Add Service Reference dialog box 174
addStatus method 305
Add Time to Date 499
AddUser method 71
AdjustHijriDays attribute 440
administrative pages 466–467
ADO.NET Data Services Update 171
AfterProperties 390
AfterUrl 390
AJAX (Asynchronous JavaScript and XML)
  supporting 215–220
AjaxCategoriesWeb-Part 218
alerting infrastructure
  using in lists 34
Alerts.asmx service 169
Alerts property 70

AllDayEvent_body field
   type 369
AllowBaseTypeRendering
   element 353
AllowClose property 190
AllowConnect
   property 190
AllowedContentTypes
   element 407
AllowEdit property 190
AllowHide property 190
AllowMinimize
   property 190
AllowsMultipleConnections
   property 214
AllowUnsafeUpdates
   property 79
 SPSite type 61
 SPWeb type 63
AllowZoneChange
   property 190
AllUsers property 63
AllUsersWebPart child
   element 303
AllWebs property
 SPSite type 61
AlternateCssUrl attri-
   bute 440
AlternateHeader attri-
   bute 440
AlterToDo value 580
AlwaysForceInstall
   attribute 243
Anonymous Access 606
Anonymous authentica-
   tion 589, 590
appendStatus method 305
ApplicationClassId
   property 462
application page
 templates 28
application pages,
   deploying 297–299
Application Programming
   Interfaces (APIs)

accessing data sources
   using 103
ApplicationResourceFiles
   child element 252
ApplicationVersion prop-
   erty 462
ApplyActivation
   activity 492
ApplyElementManifests 257
Apply Style Sheets permission 604
Apply Themes and Borders
   permission 604
Approve 68
Approve Items
   permission 604
architecture
 about SharePoint 13–18
arguments
 using SPMetal.EXE
   utility 107–108
ASMX Web Service client,
   ASP.NET 169–170
ASP.NET
 ASMX Web Service cli-
   ent 169–170
 control In Web Part 192–
   195
 integration 21
 LoadControl method
   of 195
 partially-trusted
   code 631–634
 SOAP services in 168–171
 upgrading Web Parts 234
 using 229
ASP.NET 3.5 SP1 14
AspNetHostingPermis-
   sion 630, 634
ASPX code 229, 230
ASPX page
 exploiting securing environment when de-
   veloping 79–80

Assemblies child ele-
   ment 252
Assign a Form to a
   Group 500
Assign a To-do Item 500
associating entities in BCS
   models 719–721
AssociationData 395, 519
Association form 537–544
AssociationNavigator
   type 702
AssociationUrl attri-
   bute 529
Associator type 702
Asynchronous JavaScript
   and XML (AJAX)
 supporting 215–220
asynchronous program-
   ming
 using 151
 with Web Parts 215,
   223–226
asynchronous values 398
AsyncPostBackTrigger 220
Attachments_body field
   type 369
Attachments property 67
attachments setting
 using in lists 36
Authentication.asmx ser-
   vice 169
authentication, claims-
   based
 types 592–594
 WS-Federation 607–611
authentication
   infrastructure
 about 589–590
 claims-based
   authentication 591–
   592
 classic mode
   authentication 590–
   591
 permission based authorizations 603–606

authentication
        methods 589
authentication types
    claims-based 592–594
    forms-based authentica-
        tion 589
    Windows authentica-
        tion 589, 592,
        594–596
authorizedType
        element 562
AutoActivateInCentralAd-
        min attribute 243

B

backward compatibility
    SharePoint Web Parts
        and 209
BaseConfigurationID
        attribute 440
BaseTemplateID
        attribute 440
BaseTemplateName
        attribute 440
BaseViewID attribute 336
Basic authentication 589,
        590
Basic Meeting Work-
        space 425
Basic Search Center 427
BCS (Business Connectivity
        Services)
    about 6, 23, 689–691
    accessing databases
        691–699
    accessing WCF/SOAP
        Service 705–710
    associating entities
        719–721
    BDC model files 700–703
    .NET custom model for
        BCS solutions
        710–718
    offline capabilities
        703–705

programming BCS Object
        Model 721–723
BCS Object Model, pro-
        gramming 721–723
BDC model files 700–703
BdcServiceApplicationProxy
        class 722
BeforeProperties 390
BeforeUrl 390
best practices
    enforcing security in web
        forms 78–80
    Server Object Model
        disposing resources
        73–76
    using LINQ to SharePoint
        on sites 113
BinarySecurityDescriptor
        Accessor type 702
Bin directory of hosting
        web application
    deployment 233
BindLookupList
        method 380
Bing
    Web Part querying 224–
        225
BingAsynchronousWeb-
        Part 225
Blank Meeting
        Workspace 426
Blank Site 425
Blog site 426
Boolean arguments
    systemUpdate 127
Boolean attributes
    ActivateOnDefault 243
    AlwaysForceInstall 243
    AutoActivateInCentralAd-
        min 243
    Hidden 244, 319
    ReadOnly 319
    Required 319
    RequireResources 244
    ShowInDisplayForm 319
    ShowInEditForm 319

    ShowInNewForm 319
Boolean properties
    AllowUnsafeUpdates 79
    Cancel 389
    DoesUserHavePermissions
        method 61, 66, 67
    IISAllowsAnonymous 62
    Impersonating 62
    IsDesignTime 72
    IsPopUI 72
    useUniquePermissions 83
    WriteLocked 62
Boolean values
    DesignerType Attri-
        bute 561
    MobileView 336
BreakRoleInheritance
        method
    SPListItem type 67
    SPList type 66
Browse Directories permis-
        sion 604
browsers
    opening documents pa-
        rameters for 46
    supporting ECMAS-
        cript 152
Browse User Information
        permission 605
BulkAssociatedIdEnumera-
        tor type 702
BulkAssociationNavigator
        type 702
BulkIdEnumerator type 702
BulkSpecificFinder
        type 702
BulletedList control 232
Business Connectivity
        Services (BCS)
    about 6, 23, 689–691
    accessing databases
        691–699
    accessing WCF/SOAP
        Service 705–710

Business Connectivity
　Services (BCS),
　continued
　associating entities 719–
　　722
　BDC model files 700–703
　offline capabilities 703–
　　705
　programming BCS Object
　　Model. 721–723
Business Data Connectivity
　Model project
　templates 27
Business Intelligence
　Center 426
Button child attribute 280,
　281
Button child elements 281
Button control 232

C

CalendarType attribute 440
callback function 312
CallExternalMethodActiv-
　ity 481, 575
CAML (Collaborative Appli-
　cation Markup Lan-
　guage) 66, 89–90
　about 106
　field rendering
　　using 365–367
　in Linq to SharePoint que-
　　ries 118, 120–121
　Query element and 337
　syntax to define
　　configuration
　　properties 377
CAMLRendering_body field
　type 369
CAMLRenderPattern 367
Cancel
　SPEventPropertiesBase
　　class 389
Canceled member 421
CancelJob member 421
Cancel member 421

Capture a version of the
　Document Set 499
CAS (Code Access Security)
　about 629–630
　partially-trusted ASP.NET
　　code 631–634
　SharePoint and 634–640
CatalogIconImageUrl prop-
　erty 190
Central Administration,
　SharePoint (SPCA)
　about 7–8, 15–16
　choosing templates when
　　creating Site Collec-
　　tions 17–18
Central Admin Site 426
ChangeConflictExcep-
　tion 127
ChangeConflicts
　property 127
ChangedIdEnumerator
　type 702
ChangeListItemConcur-
　rently procedure 88
Charitable Contributions
　Web Database 426
CheckBox child
　attribute 281
CheckBoxList control 232
CheckedOutByUser
　property 68
CheckForPermissions
　method, SPSite
　type 61
CheckIn 68
check-in documents 167
Check In Item 500
CheckInItemActivity
　activity 493
CheckIn method 95
CheckOut 68
check-out documents
　95–96, 167
Check Out Item 500
CheckOutItemActivity ac-
　tivity 493
CheckOut method 95

CheckOutType
　property 68, 95, 167
CheckPermissions
　SPListItem type 67
　SPList type 66
　SPWeb type 63
child elements
　ActivationDependen-
　　cies 245, 252
　AllUsersWebPart 303
　ApplicationResource-
　　Files 252
　Assemblies 252
　CheckBox 281
　CodeAccessSecurity 252
　ColorPicker 281
　ComboBox 281
　CommandUIExten-
　　sion 268
　ContextualGroup 281
　ContextualTabs 282
　Controls 282
　DropDown 282
　DwpFiles 252
　ElementFile 257
　ElementManifest 245, 257
　FeatureManifests 252
　FlyoutAnchor 282
　Gallery 282
　GalleryButton 282
　Group 282
　GroupTemplate 282
　InsertTable 282
　Label 282
　MaxSize 282
　Menu 282
　MenuSection 282
　MRUSplitButton 282
　Properties 245
　QAT 283
　Resources 252
　Ribbon 283
　RootFiles 253
　Scale 283
　Scaling 283
　SiteDefinitionManifests 252
　Spinner 283

SplitButton 283
Tab 283
TemplateFiles 253
TextBox 283
ToggleButton 283
UpgradeActions 245
UrlAction 268
Choice field type 318
ChooseDoclibItem
    value 561
ChooseListItem value 561
ChromeState property 190
ChromeType property 190
ClaimReleaseTask value 580
claims-based authentica-
    tion
  about 592–593
  types 592–594
  WS-Federation and 607–
    611
ClaimsIdentity instance 592
claims mapping 624–625
ClaimsPrincipal in-
    stance 592
classes
  ClientContext 139–140,
    143
  ClientValueObject 145,
    146–147
  ComponentModel.Activ-
    ity 555
  ConversionJob 421
  ConversionJobStatus 421
  CreateParameters 456
  CustomPropertyTool-
    Part 200
  CustomSecurityTokenSer-
    vice 615
  DataContext 177–178
  dcServiceApplication-
    Proxy 722
  DocumentSet 410
  File 166, 167
  FullTextSqlQuery 683
  KeywordQuery 682
  ListCreationInforma-
    tion 159

MenuItemTemplate
    class 277
PageAsyncTask 226
ProtocolServiceAccess-
    Rights 461–462
ProtocolServiceApplica-
    tion 458
ProtocolServiceApplica-
    tionProxy 470
ProtocolService
    Client 469–470, 473
ProtocolServiceData-
    base 456
ProtocolService
    Proxy 470–472
QueryManager 669, 679
RegExTextField 349
SPDatabase 456
SPDatabaseParam-
    eters 456
SPEventProperties-
    Base 389, 400
SPField 351, 381
SPFieldMulticolumn 357
SPIisWebServiceApplica-
    tion 459, 461
SPItemEvent
    Properties 389
SPListEvent
    Properties 391–392
SPListEventReceiver 391
SPProxyOperation 651
SPProxyOperation-
    Args 651–652
SPServiceContext 469
SPSolutionValidator 647
SPWebEventProper-
    ties 394
SPWebEventReceiver 393
SPWorkflowEvent
    Properties 395
SPWorkflowEvent
    Receiver 394
SPWorkflowManager
    577–578
SPWorkflowTask 578
WebPart 207–208

classic mode authentica-
    tion 590
Click event handler 226,
    232
ClientContext class
    139–140, 143
ClientContext.Load<T>
    method 142
Client Object Model
  about 22, 137–138, 138
  concurrency conflicts and
    handling exceptions
    in 161–163
  creating and updating list
    items 160
  creating lists 159
  data retrieval engine
    of 141
  deleting list items
    163–164
  differences between
    Managed and Silver-
    light 150–152
  document libraries
    check-in and check-out
      documents 167
    copying files 167–168
    creating 165
    downloading docu-
      ments 166–167
    moving files 167
    updating docu-
      ments 165
  ECMAScript 152–157
  Managed 139–147
    types and members
      available in 140
  paging queries of list
    items 164–165
  Silverlight 147–152
    creating Silverlight Ap-
      plications 148–151
ClientObjectQueryable
    Extension 143–144
ClientObject type 145–146
ClientOnClickNavigateUrl
    property 277

ClientOnClickPostBack-
Confirmation prop-
erty 277
ClientOnClickScript
property 277
ClientOnClickUsingPost-
BackEvent
property 277
ClientValueObject
class 145, 146–147
close method 310
CLR (Common Language
Runtime)
checking digital signa-
tures and 233
loading assemblies 234
Code Access Security (CAS)
about 629–630
partially-trusted ASP.NET
code 631–634
SharePoint and 634–640
CodeAccessSecurity child
element 252
Code activity 481
CodeBesideAssembly
attribute 529
CodeBesideClass
attribute 529
collaboration templates 9
Collaborative Application
Markup Language
(CAML) 66, 89–90
about 106
in Linq to SharePoint queries 118, 120–121
Collation attribute 440
Collect Data from a
User 500
ColorPicker child
attribute 281
Column element name 109
columns
in lists
configuring 41
defining 33
managing 37–39

site 46–47
ComboBox child
attribute 281
CommandAction attribute
substitution tokens using
CommandAction
attribute 287
commands
Document Ribbon 44
CommandUIDefinition
element 280, 281–
283, 286
CommandUIExtension
element 268, 280
commonModalDialogClose
method 310
commonModalDialogOpen
method 310
communication activities
for workflow
services 575–577
Communities category
about 5
CompensatableSequence
activity 482
CompensatableTransaction-
Scope activity 483
Compensate activity 481
CompleteTask activity 492
CompletionType 395
Composites category
about 6
Computed_body field
type 369
concurrency conflicts
87–88
in Client Object
Model 161–163
using LINQ to SharePoint
queries 126–130
ConditionedActivityGroup
activity 482
ConfigurationPermission 630
ConfigureDataSourceProp-
erties 669
connectable Web Parts 210

ConnectionConsumerAt-
tribute 214
ConnectionPointType
property 214
ConnectionProviderAttrib-
ute 211, 214
consumer Web Part
212–214
consuming full-trust
proxy 654–655
Contacts Web Data-
base 426
ContainsDefaultLists
attribute 440
content approval engine
using in lists 34
Content Databases
in web applications 15
content management 5
content pages,
deploying 301
ContentTypeBinding,
feature element 246
ContentType element
name 109
ContentTypeId property 67
content type project
templates 27, 28
Content Types 320–323
about 47
attributes available
for 326
creating 48–49
Document 328–329
element 322
hierarchical organization
of 48
IDs 323–326
in lists 33
schema 320–323
settings in lists 36
Workflow Task 547–549
XmlDocuments
element 327
ContentTypes property
feature element 246

SPListItem type 67
SPList type 66
SPWeb type 63
Context 519
ContextEvent 386
ContextPageInfo
    property 72
ContextualGroup child
    attribute 281
ContextualTabs child
    attribute 282
ContinueOnConflict
    values 126
contribute, definition of 32
ControlAssembly
    attribute 266, 276
ControlClass attribute 266,
    276
Control, feature
    element 246
ControlId values in Share-
    Point 295
Controls child attribute 282
ControlSrc attribute 266
ConversionJob class 421
ConversionJobStatus
    class 421
CopyFrom 67
copying files 96, 167–168
CopyItemActivity
    activity 493
Copy List Item 500
Copy method 67
CopyTo 67, 69
CorrelationToken
    property 533
Create 410
Create Alerts
    permission 604
CreateChildControls
    method 186, 213,
    360–361
Create Column, select-
    ing 37–39
CreateDataSource 669

Created by a specific per-
    son 498
Created in a specific date
    span 498
Create factory method
    SPSite type 57
Create Groups permis-
    sion 604
CreateItemActivity activ-
    ity 493
Create List Item 500
CreateListItem value 561
Create method 458
CreateParameters class 456
Create Subsites permis-
    sion 604
CreateTask activity 492
CreateTaskWithContent-
    Type activity 492
Creator attribute 243
Creator type 702
CRMCodeAvailable
    activity 575
CrossProjectLink_body field
    type 369
cross-site-scripting
    avoiding issues with
    78–80
    SafeGuard 236–237
CRUDQ scenario, support
    of 706
Currency field type 318
CurrentUserId 390
CustomAction
    about 265, 265–272
    element on Ribbon
    menu 280
    elements 265–272
    feature element 246
    supported attri-
    butes 266–268
CustomActionGroup
    about 265
    element 273, 273–274
    feature element 247
    supported attributes 273

custom actions
    CustomActionGroup
    element 273–274
    HideCustomAction
    element 275
    in SharePoint user
    interface 265
    locations for defining 272
    Server-Side Custom
    Actions 276–278
custom content, deploying
    application pages
    297–299
    content pages 301–304
    generic content 296–297
    images 295–297, 301
    Web Part Pages 299–301
CustomizedCssFiles
    attribute 440
CustomJSUrl attribute 440
CustomPropertyToolPart
    class 200
CustomSecurityTokenSer-
    vice class 615
CustomUpgradeAction tag
    configuring 257
Custom Views
    defining 339–342

D

data
    limiting return 42
    LINQ to SharePoint
    deleting existing items
    from lists using 125
    inserting new items into
    lists using 124–125
    managing 122–125
    querying 117–122
    managing with REST
    API 177–179
    querying for data with
    .NET and LINQ
    API 173–177
    sorting in lists 41
    storing offline 34

databases
  accessing with BCS
    data 691–699
  querying 103
  role of 17–18
  Service Application
    456–458
dataBindList method 158
DataContext class 118, 127,
  177–178
DataContext.GetList<T>
  method 111
DataContractSerializer
  engine 133
Data Provisioning
  about 22
  Contact Types 320–328
  List Definitions 329–342
datasheet settings
  in lists 37
data sources
  accessing different 103
DateTime_body field
  type 369
DateTime field type 318
Date value
  DesignerType
    Attribute 561
deactivating features 249
debug-enabled version of
  ECMAScript 152
Decision Meeting Work-
  space 426
Declare Record 500
DefaultDocuments
  element 407
DefaultResourceFile
  attribute 243
DefaultValueAttribute 199
Default values 398
DefaultView attribute 336
Delay activity 482
delegate controls 291–294
DeleteAllOnSubmit
  method 125

DeletedIdEnumerator
  type 702
Deleted values
  in EntityState
    property 123
Delete Item 500
DeleteItemActivity
  activity 493
Delete Items permission 604
Delete method
  SPFile type 69
  SPListItem type 67
  SPList type 66
  SPSite type 61
  SPWeb type 63
DeleteObject method 179
Deleter type 702
DeleteTask activity 492
Delete Versions permis-
  sion 604
deleting (recycling) existing
  items in lists
  using LINQ to Share-
    Point 125
DemandAccess
  method 460
dependency properties of
  custom actions and
  conditions 555–557
deploying
  application pages 297–
    299
  content pages 301–304
  generic content 296
  images 295, 301
  Service Application
    proxy 473–474
  Service Applications 467–
    469
  Web Part Pages 299–301
  workflow forms 553
  workflows 528–530
  workflow services 573–
    575

deploying to Web
  Part 233–237
DeploymentServerType as
  feature element
  attribute 252
Description as feature element attribute 252
Description attribute 243,
  266, 273, 441
  workflow feature ele-
    ment 529
Description method 71
Description property 190
design, definition of 32
DesignerType Attribute
  values for 561
developing Workflows
  about 23
Dialog Framework 309–
  314
dialog settings
  in lists 37
Digest authentication 589,
  590
digital signatures
  checking 233
direct method call 146
DisableAttachments attri-
  bute 332
Disassociator type 702
Discard Check Out
  Item 500
disconnected entities
  in data stored in Linq to
    SharePoint 132–134
DisplayFormToolbar
  location 272
display modes for Web
  Parts, chang-
  ing 204–205
DisplayName attri-
  bute 316–317, 336
DisplayName property 214
DisplayPattern field
  type 366
Dispose, calling 111–112

Dispose member name
  SPItemEventProperties
    class 390
  SPListEventProperties
    class 391
  SPWebEventProperties
    class 394
disposing resources 73–76
DnsPermission 630, 634
Do Calculation 499
Document Center 426
Document Content
  Types 328–329
DocumentConverter, fea-
  ture element 247
document ID 411–416
document libraries
  about 10–11
  check-in and check-out
    documents 95–96
  check-in documents 167
  check-out documents 167
  configuring to auto-
    matically receive
    emails 34
  copying and moving
    files 96
  copying files 167–168
  creating 42–46, 92–93,
    165
  downloading docu-
    ments 94–95,
    166–167
  managing versions of
    documents 97
  moving files 167
  updating docu-
    ments 165–169
  uploading docu-
    ments 93–94
Document Object Model
  (DOM)
  navigating XML data
    using 103

Document Ribbon
  commands 44
DocumentSet class 410
document sets
  about 401–403
  handling 410–412
  provisioning 403–411
document template
  parameters 46
Document Workspace 425
DoesUserHavePermissions
  SPListItem type 67
  SPList type 66
  SPSite type 61
downloading docu-
  ments 94–95,
  166–167
DropDown child attri-
  bute 282
DropDownList control 232
DropDownList in-
  stance 380
Dropdown value 561
DwpFiles child element 252

E

EAP, custom Web Parts and
  223
ECB (Edit Control Block)
  menu 268–270
ECMAScript Client Object
  Model 152–157
Edit Control Block [ECB]
  menu 268–270
EditControlBlock loca-
  tion 272
EditFormToolbar loca-
  tion 272
Edit Items permission 604
Editor Parts 200–204
EditorZone 200
EditPattern field type 366
Edit Personal User Informa-
  tion permission 605

ElementFile child ele-
  ment 257
ElementManifest child element 245, 257
element names, defin-
  ing XML parameter
  files 109–110
elements manifest files
  feature
  defining deployed Web
    Part 248
email event receivers
  395–396
Email value
  DesignerType Attri-
    bute 561
empty element tem-
  plates 28
empty SharePoint project
  templates 27
EnableMinorVersions attribute 332
EnableWorkflowModifica-
  tion activity 492, 547
EngineAssembly attri-
  bute 529
EngineClass attribute 529
Enterprise Search
  Center 427
enterprise templates 9
EntityList<T> class 125
EntityState property
  values 123–124
Enumerate Permissions
  permission 605
EnvironmentPermis-
  sion 630, 634
ErrorException 395
error handling code cau-
  tion when defin-
  ing 262
ErrorMessage 389
error messages
  Unhandled Exception 159

event deployment and
binding 397–399
EventDriven activity 482
event handlers
Click 226, 232
searchCommandAsyn-
chronously_Click 226
EventHandlingScope
activity 482
event loops, avoiding 396
event properties
ConnectionProvider
Attribute 214–215
SelectedIndex-
Changed 217
event receivers
about 23
email 395–396
item-level 386–390
list-level 391–393
project templates 27
types of 385–387
web-level 393–394
workflow 394–395,
565–566
EventReceivers property
SPList type 66
SPSite type 61
SPWeb type 64
event security 400
event synchronization
398–400
EventType 389
EventUserToken 389
Excel
files as data source 103
integrating list content
with 34
Excel Services
about 14
farm using 17
exception handling
in Client Object Mod-
el 161–163
exception messages
Unhandled Exception 161

ExcludeColumn element
name 109
ExcludeContentType ele-
ment name 110
ExcludeFromOfflineClient
attribute 441
ExcludeList element
name 109
ExcludeOtherColumns ele-
ment name 109
ExcludeOtherContentTypes
element name 110
ExcludeOtherLists element
name 109
ExecuteQuery method 140,
159, 161–162
Export 410
ExportMode property 190
extension elements sup-
ported by file pro-
visioning document
sets 407
Extract Substring from End
of String 500
Extract Substring from Index of String 500
Extract Substring from Start
of String 500
Extract Substring of String
from Index with
Length 500

F

FailOnFirstConflict
values 126
farm level, deploying solutions at 635
farm, SharePoint
about 14–16
creating 57–59
Service Applications
in 16–17
Farm values 242
FAST Index 670
FAST Search Center 427
FaultHandler activity 482

FBA (Forms-Based Authen-
tication) 141
about 589, 596
configuring with SQL
Membership Pro-
vider 597–603
Feature Activation
event 259
Feature Deactivating
event 259
Feature Designer 29
Feature element and
solution element
attributes 251–252
Feature elements
attributes supported
by 243
feature elements types
for 246–248
FeatureId
attribute 267, 391
Feature Installation
event 259
feature manifest
about 241–242
as list of element mani-
fest 246–248
deploying files for Web
Parts 245
Feature tag child ele-
ments 245
file structure 242–243
supporting multi-
language 246
FeatureManifests child
element 252
feature receivers
about 259–262
features
about 241
deactivating and unin-
stalling 249
deploying 248–254
upgrading 256–258
versioning number attri-
bute 257

Features property
  SPSite type 61
  SPWeb type 64
Feature Uninstalling
  event 259
FeatureUpgrading event
  about 259
  handling of 262–263
federated search object
  model 678–681
federation framework,
  search engine 670–
  676
federation provider,
  implementing cus-
  tom 674–678
FieldAdded event 391, 393
FieldDeleted event 391
FieldDeleting event 391
Field Elements 319
Field, feature element 247
Field member name 391
FieldName member
  name 391
FieldNames value
  DesignerType
  Attribute 561
FieldRenderingControl
  property 348, 357
FieldRenderingMobileCon-
  trol property 348
fields
  custom field types developing 349–350
  custom list 35–39
  E-Mail field type developing 349–354
  field editor about cus-
  tomizing 376–380
  field types about
  345–347
  mobile devices rendering
  on 369–373
  Multicolumn 354–357
  on Create Column
  page 38–39

properties persistence
  381–384
rendering control
  358–360
rendering mobile tem-
  plates 374–375
rendering patterns 366
rendering templates 361–
  365
rendering using
  CAML 365–367
rendering using
  XSLT 367–369
SPField class 347–349
XSLT Mode Values Tem-
  plates 369
Fields property
  SPList type 66
  SPWeb type 64
FieldType elements 353
Field Types 318
  Boolean 318
  Choice 318
  Currency 318
  DateTime 318
  Lookup and Lookup-
  Multi 318
  MultiChoice 318
  Note 318
  Number 318
  SPField 345
  SPFieldAttachments 345
  SPFieldBoolean 345
  SPFieldCalculated 345
  SPFieldChoice 345
  SPFieldComputed 345
  SPFieldCrossProjectLink
  345
  SPFieldCurrency 346
  SPFieldDateTime 346
  SPFieldFile 346
  SPFieldGuid 346
  SPFieldLookup 346
  SPFieldMultiChoice 346
  SPFieldMultiColumn 346
  SPFieldMultiLineText 346

SPFieldNumber 346
SPFieldPageSeparator
  346
SPFieldRecurrence 346
SPFieldText 346
SPFieldUrl 346
SPFieldUser 346
Text 318
URL 318
User and UserMulti 318
FieldUpdated event 391
FieldUpdating event 391
FieldValueType
  property 348
FieldXml member
  name 392
File class 166
file conversion ser-
  vices 417–422
FileCreationInformation
  type 166
FileIOPermission 630, 634
File property
  SPContext type 72
  SPList type 67
files
  copying 96, 167–168
  moving 96, 167–168
Files property
  SPWeb type 64
filters
  using in lists 41
Finder type 702
Find Interval Between
  Dates 500
Firefox
  support of ECMAS-
  cript 152
Float value 561
FlyoutAnchor child attri-
  bute 282
Folder property 67, 142
folders
  SPList type 66
  SPWeb type 64
  using in lists 33, 36, 42

Folders collection
    property 93
form digest control, us-
    ing 78–80
Forms-Based Authentica-
    tion (FBA) 141
    about 589, 596
    configuring with SQL
        Membership Pro-
        vider 597–603
forms, task
    about 547
forms, workflow
    deploying 553–554
    management
        about 535
        association 537–544
        initiation 544–546
        modification 547
        task 547–553
FormTemplates
    element 407
FormUrls element 407
full control, definition of 32
Full Text SQL Query 682
FullTextSqlQuery class 683
full-trust proxies 650–654
FullUrl member name
    SPWebEventProperties
        class 394

G

GAC (Global Assembly
    Cache)
    about 233
    as custom action 559
    deploying into 635
    implementing full trust
        proxies and 651
    Web Part deployment
        and 188
    workflows and 515
GalleryButton child attri-
    bute 282
Gallery child attribute 282
Garbage Collector 73

GenerateProtocolNumber
    method 459,
    469–470, 473
generic content, deploy-
    ing 295–297,
    296–297
GenericInvoker type 702
GetAssociationData
    method 542–544
GetByTitle method 147
GetCategoryProvider
    method 211
get_current method 154
GetCustomListTemplates
    method 61
GetCustomProperty
    method 351
GetCustomWebTemplates
    method 61
GetDocumentSet 410
GetEffectiveRightsForAcl
    method 61
GetFieldValueAsHtml
    method 348
GetFieldValueAsText
    method 348
GetFieldValueForEdit
    method 348
GetFieldValue method 348
GetFile method 64
GetItemById method 66,
    86–87
GetItemByIdSelectedFields
    method 87
GetItems method 66
GetOutputClaims
    method 614–615
GetRecycleBinItems
    SPSite type 61
    SPWeb type 64
GetRecycleBinStatistics 61
GetResults property
    type 679
GetScope method 614
GetSiteData method 64
GetTemplatesForItem
    value 580, 581

GetToDosForItem
    value 580
GetUserEffectivePermis-
    sions method 64
GetValidatedString
    method 348
GetWorkflowDataForItem
    value 580
GetWorkflowTaskData
    value 580
Global Assembly Cache
    (GAC) 188, 233, 559
    deploying into 635
    implementing full-trust
        proxies and 651
    workflows and 515
GlobalNavigation Contro-
    lid 295
graphical rendering
    style 42
Group by
    configuring lists using 41
Group child attribute 282
GroupId attribute 267
    HideCustomAction ele-
        ment 275
groups
    managing membership
        of 98–99
    managing permissions
        of 99
Groups
    child attribute 282
    method 64
    property 70
GroupTemplate child attri-
    bute 282
Group Work Site 426

H

HandleExternalEvent
    activity 482
handling exceptions 76–77
    in Client Object
        Model 161–163

handling FeatureUpgrading
events 262–263
hardware requirements of
SharePoint 13
HeaderPattern field
type 366
Health Analyzer, Share-
Point 8
"Hello World Web
Part" 184–187
Hidden
attribute 244
field attribute 319
property 66
HideActionId attribute
HideCustomAction
element 275
HideCustomAction
about 265
element 275
feature element 247
HistoryList 519
HistoryListId 519
HistoryListUrl 520
HTTP client
consume REST API
using 173
HyperlinkBaseUrl attribute
of Module element 300
Hyperlink value 561

I

IAjaxTriggerControlPro-
vider 219
iButtonControl 232
ICellConsumer inter-
face 215
ICellProvider interface 215
ICRMService interface 575
ICustomMapping inter-
face 135
Id attribute 244
HideCustomAction
element 275
workflow feature
element 529

Id CustomAction
element attribute 267
group attribute 273
identity management and
refresh
in Linq to SharePoint que-
ries 130–132
Identity Provider (IP)
about 608
registering 624–625
trusting 622–623
IdEnumerator type 703
IDisposable interface 73
ID property
ConnectionConsumerAt-
tribute 214
ConnectionProviderAt-
tribute 214
SPGroup type 71
SPListItem type 67
SPList type 66
SPSite type 62
SPUser type 70
SPWeb type 64
IDs, Content Type 323–326
IEnumerable<T>
method 125, 145
If any value equals
value 498
If current item field
equals 498
IfElse activity 482
IFilterConsumer inter-
face 215
IFilterProvider inter-
face 215
IgnoreIfAlreadyExists
attribute
supported by Module
element 301
IIS 7 integrated mode 21,
26
IISAllowsAnonymous
property 62
IListConsumer inter-
face 215

IListProvider interface 215
ILogger interface 77
ImageButton control 232
images, deploying 295–
297, 301
ImageUrlAltText attri-
bute 244
ImageUrl attribute 244,
267, 273
Impersonating property 62
Import member name 410
import reusable workflow
project
templates 27
import SharePoint solution
package
templates 27
IncludeHiddenColumns ele-
ment name 109
IncludeHiddenContent-
Types element
name 110
IncludeHiddenLists element
name 109
index, search engine
and 660
InitData function 157–158
InitializeWithField
method 380
InitializeWorkflow activ-
ity 492
InitiationData 395, 520
initiation form 544–546
init parameters 150
inline editing
using in lists 41
InsertAllOnSubmit
method 125
inserting new items into
lists
using LINQ to Share-
Point 124–125
InsertRequestForContact-
WebPart 193–194
InsertTable child attri-
bute 282

InstallPath property 462
InstanceId 395
InstantiationUrl attribute 529
Integer value 561
Internet Explorer
  support of ECMAScript 152
InvalidateList 391
InvalidateListItem 389
InvalidateWeb 389, 391, 394
InvokeWebService activity 482
InvokeWorkflow activity 482
IParametersInConsumer interface 215
IParametersInProvide interface 215
IParametersOutConsumer interface 215
IParametersOutProvider interface 215
IP (Identity Provider)
  about 608
  registering 624–625
  trusting 622–623
IRowConsumer interface 215
IRowProvider interface 215
ISAPI Filter Aspnet_isapi.dll 21
IsDesignTime property 72
IsolatedStorageFilePermission 630
IsolatedStoragePermission 634
IsPopUI property 72
IsPropertyAvailable method 147
IsSiteAdmin property 70
Issues Web Database 426
IsTriggered property type 679

Item 520
ItemAdded event 386, 387
ItemAdding event 386
ItemAttachmentAdded event 386
ItemAttachmentAdding event 386
ItemAttachmentDeleted event 386
ItemAttachmentDeleting event 386
ItemCheckedIn event 386
ItemCheckedOut event 386
ItemCheckingIn event 386
ItemCheckingOut event 386
ItemCount property 66
ItemDeleted event 386
ItemDeleting event 386
ItemFileConverted event 386
ItemFileMoved event 386
ItemFileMoving event 386
ItemId 520
ItemId property 72
item-level event receivers 386–390
item-level permissions in lists 36
Item property
  SPContext type 72
Items property
  SPList type 66
ItemUncheckedOut event 386
ItemUncheckingOut event 386
ItemUpdated event 386
ItemUpdating event 386
ItemUrl 520
IU (User Interface)
  extending search engine 662–669
IVersioningPersonalizable interface 235–236

J

JavaScript code block for URL attributes 271
JavaScript platform 152
JobId member name ConversionJob class 421
jQuery and ECMAScript application 155–158
JScript platform 152

K

KeepChanges value 128
KeepCurrentValues 128
Kerberos authentication 589, 590–591
Key Distribution Center (KDC) 591
KeywordQuery class 682
keywords
  for HTTP client 173

L

Label child attribute 282
Language Integrated Query. See LINQ (Language Integrated Query)
Length property 69
libraries
  creating document 42–46
  email-enabled 34
limited access, definition of 32
LinkButton control 232
LINQ (Language Integrated Query)
  about 101–107
  code structure of 104–106
  converting queries into requests 144
  modeling LINQ to SharePoint entries 107–117

calling Dispose 111–112
elements available for
    defining XML param-
    eter files 109–110
providing argu-
    ments 107–108
using LINQ to Share-
    Point 113
XML parameters
    for 108–109
querying for data with
    REST API 173–176
to SharePoint data
disconnected enti-
    ties 132
disconnected entities
    in 132–134
managing 122–125
querying 117–122
to SharePoint queries
deleting existing items
    from lists using 125
handling concurrency
    conflicts 126–130
identity management
    and refresh 130–132
inserting new items into
    lists using 124–125
using with SharePoint 21
ListAdded event 391
ListAdding event 391
List attribute
of Module element 300
ListBox control 232
ListControl instance 232
ListCreationInformation
    class 159
list definition project
    templates 27, 28
List Definitions
Custom Views defin-
    ing 339–342
List element 331–332
List schema file 329–330
ListTemplate definition
    file 342–343

MetaData element 332–
    340
ListDeleted event 391
ListDeleting event 391
Listen activity 482
ListId member
SPWorkflowActivation-
    Properties 520
ListId member name
SPItemEventProperties
    class 390
SPListEventProperties
    class 392
ListId property 72
ListID property 89
ListInstance, feature ele-
    ment 247
list instance template 28
ListItem 390
ListItemCollectionPosition
    property 91
ListItemCreationInforma-
    tion type 160
ListItemID property 89,
    390
ListItem property 72, 142
list items
creating 85–86
creating and
    updating 160
deleting 88–89
deleting using Client
    Owner Model 163–
    166
modifying 86–87
paging queries of 164–
    165
querying 89–91
list-level event receiv-
    ers 391–393
List member
SPWorkflowActivation-
    Properties 520
List member name
SPItemEventProperties
    class 142, 390

SPListEventProperties
    class 392
ListNames value
DesignerType Attri-
    bute 561
list of permissions, de-
    fined in SharePoint
    2010 604–605
List property
SPContext type 72
XML parameters file 109
lists
creating 32–33, 83–86
creating columns in 37–
    39
creating using Client Ob-
    ject Model 159
creating views for 39–42
deleting items from 125,
    179
features and capabilities
    of 33–34
inserting new items
    using LINQ to Share-
    Point 124–125
of items in websites
    10–11
Remove Workflows page
    for 532
templates 34–38
Lists.asmx service 169
List Settings command
    36–37
Lists property
SPWeb type 64
ListTemplate
definition file 342–343
feature element 247
ListTitle member name
SPItemEventProperties
    class 390
SPListEventProperties 392
ListView on Ribbon
    ment 280
LoadAfterUI argument 153
LoadControl method 195

Load method
of IVersioningPersonaliz-
able 236
LoadQuery<T>
method 144, 145
Load<T> method 140–141
Locale attribute 441
Localizable argument 153
Location attribute 267, 273
HideCustomAction
element 275
locations for custom
actions 272
Lock 69
LockedByUser property 69
logical architecture of
SharePoint 14–16
LoginName property 70
Log to History List 499
LogToHistoryListActiv-
ity 493
LogToOperations
method 77
Lookup 346
Lookup and LookupMulti
field type 318
Lookup_body field
type 369
Lookup Manager of a
User 500

M

Manage Alerts permis-
sion 605
Managed Client Object
Model 139–147
types and members avail-
able in 140
Manage Lists permis-
sion 604
management forms
about 535–537
association 537–544
initiation 544–546
modification 547

Manage Permissions per-
mission 604
Manage Personal Views
permission 605
Manage Web Site permis-
sion 604
MapFile element 257
MapFrom method 135
mapping claims 624–625
MapTo method 135
MaxSize child attribute 282
meetings templates 9
MemberChangeConflict
method 135
MemberConflicts prop-
erty 127
Menu child attribute 282
MenuItemTemplate
class 277
MenuSection child attri-
bute 282
metadata
for column contact
items 33–34
MetaData element 332–
340
MethodInstance types 702
Microsoft Access
integrating list content
with 34
Microsoft ASP.NET 3.5
SP1 14
Microsoft Excel
files as data source 103
integrating list content
with 34
Microsoft Internet Explorer
support of ECMAS-
cript 152
Microsoft .NET
support for services com-
pliant with OData
specification 173
Microsoft .NET Framework
3.5 14

Microsoft .NET Framework
4.0 14
Microsoft Office
integrating list content
with 34
Microsoft Office 365, sandboxed solutions
and 655
Microsoft SharePoint
about 3
architecture of 12–18
capabilities of 4–6
concepts used in 7–13
feature manifest
about 241–242
as list of element mani-
fest files 246–248
deploying files for Web
Parts 245
file structure 242–243
supporting multi-
language 246
feature receivers 259–262
features
about 241
deactivating and
uninstalling 249
deploying 248–254
for building custom web
solutions 20–24
upgrading 256–258
FeatureUpgrading events
handling of 262–263
list of permissions defined
in 604–605
main Controlid values in
SharePoint 295
native connectable inter-
faces 215
permissions available
in 630
requirements for run-
ning 13–17
Status Bar and Notifi-
cation Area fea-
tures 305–309

trusted identity providers 621–627
Web Parts 245
workflow architecture in 489–493
workflow custom activities 492–493
workflow targets and association 491–492
Microsoft SharePoint 2010
search engine of 670
Microsoft.SharePoint.ApplicationRuntime namespace 21
Microsoft.SharePoint.Client namespace 139
Microsoft SharePoint Designer 2010
about 24–25, 502–503
custom actions for 557
custom conditions for 563–565
integration with Visio 2010 510
using SharePoint Foundation with 18
workflows
about 495–497
actions 499–501
conditions 498–499
outline definition 503–506
structured of published 502
workflows, designing
about 502–503
settings 507–508
user experience 508–510
Microsoft SharePoint Foundation 2010
about 14, 18–19
sandboxed solutions in
about 639–640

architecture of 640–644
creating 645–647
monitoring 644
validating 645
Microsoft SharePoint Online 20
Microsoft SharePoint Server 2010
Enterprise 19–20
for Internet Sites 20
platform 14
SOAP services in 168–169
Standard edition 19
Microsoft.SharePoint.SiteSettings location 272
Microsoft.SharePoint.StandardMenu location 272
Microsoft Silverlight 220–223
scenarios of 222
Microsoft SQL Server Management Studio 17
Microsoft Visio 2010
Integration with Microsoft Designer 510–512
Microsoft Visio Studio 2010
correlation tokens 533
site workflows 534
workflow modeling
about 515
associating a target list 530–531
creating projects 515–519
deploying workflow 528–530
outlines 519–527
versioning workflow 531–533
Microsoft Visual Studio 2010
about 26–29

accessing initiation form 544
creating association form 538
creating feature event receivers 262
developer tools in 27–28
packaging with 254–256
SharePoint Server Explorer 28–29
Solution Explorer feature in 29
support for services compliant with OData specification 173–175
using SharePoint Foundation with 18
Visual Web Part template in 195–197
Microsoft Windows PowerShell 24
MobileCustomListField 374
MobileDefaultView attribute 336
mobile devices
field rendering mobile templates 374–375
rendering views on 42
supporting rendering fields 369–373
MobileView attribute 336
model extensions
in LINQ to SharePoint model 134–136
ModeratedList attribute 332
modification form 547
ModificationUrl attribute 529
Modified by a specific person 498
Modified in a specific date span 499

Modified View command 40–41

ModifyXsltArgumentList 669

Module
element 300, 301
feature element 247, 299–301
project templates 27

MoveTo 69

moving files 96, 167–168

MRUSplitButton child attribute 282

MultiChoice field type 318

Multipage Meeting Workspace 426

N

Name argument 153

Name attribute 441
of Module element 300
supported by Module element 301
workflow feature element 529

Name member name ConversionJob class 421

Name property
SPFile type 69
SPGroup type 71
SPUser type 70

native actions offered by SharePoint Designer 2010 499–500

Native Activities Offered by workflow foundation 481–483

native conditions offered by SharePoint designer 2010 498–499

native connectable interfaces
SharePoint 215

native Content Type 547–549

native site definitions 424–428

NavBarHome attribute supported by Module element 301

NewFormToolbar location 272

NewPattern field type 366

NewServerRelativeUrl 394

n feature element 247

Note_body field type 369

Note field type 318

NTLM authentication 589–591

Number 346

Number_body field type 369

Number field type 318

O

ObjectChangeConflict
class 127–128
method 135
property 127

OData specification 137, 173–177

Office
integrating list content with 34

Office 365, sandboxed solutions and 655

offline
client availability setting 37
storing data 34

offline capabilities, BCS 703–705

OnAdded method 348, 381

OnAddingToContentType method 348

OnDeletingFromContentType method 348

OnDeleting method 348, 381

OnPreRender method 213

OnTaskChanged activity 493

OnTaskCreated activity 493

OnTaskDeleted activity 493

OnUpdated method 381

OnWorkflowActivated activity 493

OnWorkflowItemChanged activity 493

OnWorkflowItemDeleted activity 493

OnWorkflowModified activity 493

OpenBinary 69

OpenBinaryDirect static method 167

OpenBinaryStream 69

Open Database Connectivity (ODBC)
querying data with 103

Open Data Protocol 137–138

Open Items permission 604

Open permission 605

OpenPopUpPage method 310

OpenSearch 1.0/1.1 671

OpenSite 389

OpenWeb 390

OpenWeb method 62, 63

Operator value 561

OriginatingUserToken event 389

Originator 520

OriginatorEmail 520

OriginatorUser 520

out of the box
list templates 34–35

out-of-the-box solutions
for designing Web Part code 195–197

Override Check Out permission 604

OverwriteCurrentValues 128

OWSTIMER.EXE 585

P

Package Designer 254–256
Package Explorer 254–256
PageAsyncTask class 226
Page_Load method 552
PagingInfo property 91
paging query results 164–165
Parallel activity 482
ParameterNames value 561
parameters in web parts, configurable 198–200
ParentWebId 394
ParseAndSetValue method 348
ParseControl method
  using 229
  using with (X)HTML code 232
ParserEnabled attribute 441
partially-trusted ASP.NET code 631–634
Path attribute
  of Module element 300
  supported by Module element 301
Pause for Duration 499
Pause until Date 499
permissions
  available in.NET and SharePoint 630
  DoesUserHavePermissions 66
  in lists 34, 36
PermissionSet elements 634
Permissions Levels 604–606
  Add and Customize Pages 604
  Add Items 604
  Add/Remove Personal Web Part 605

Apply Style Sheets 604
Apply Themes and Borders 604
Approve Items 604
Browse Directories 604
Browse User Information 605
Create Alerts 604
Create Groups 604
Create Subsites 604
Delete Items 604
Delete Versions 604
Edit Items 604
Edit Personal User Information 605
Enumerate Permissions 605
Manage Alerts 605
Manage Lists 604
Manage Permissions 604
Manage Personal Views 605
Manage Web Site 604
Open 605
Open Items 604
Override Check Out 604
Update Personal Web Parts 605
Use Client Integration Features 605
Use Remote Interfaces 605
Use Self-Service Site Creation 604
View Application Pages 604
View Items 604
View Pages 605
View Version 604
View Web Analytics Data 604
PersonalizableAttribute attribute 198
Personalization Site 427

Person is a valid SharePoint user 499
Person value 561
physical architecture of SharePoint 14–16
Policy activity 482
PortalName attribute 441
PortalUrl attribute 441
PostponedEvent 395
postsList control 232
PowerPoint Broadcast Site 426
PresenceEnabled attribute 441
PreviewDisplayPattern field type 366
PreviewEditPattern field type 366
PreviewNewPattern field type 366
PreviewValueTyped property 357
PrintingPermission 630, 634
PrivateList attribute 332
ProductVersion attribute 441
projects
  types of project templates 27–29
prompts SharePoint presents 11
Properties child element 245
PropertyBag, feature element 247
PropertyOrFieldNotInitializedException 143
PropertySchema element 354
ProtocolServiceAccessRights class 461–462
ProtocolServiceApplication class 458

ProtocolServiceApplication-
    Proxy class 470
ProtocolServiceClient
    class 469–470, 473
ProtocolServiceDatabase
    class 456
ProtocolServiceProxy
    class 470–472
provider Web Part 210,
    211, 214–215
Provision member
    name 410
published workflows, struc-
    ture of 502
PublishingConsole
    ControlId 295
Publishing Portal 427
Publishing Site 427
Publishing Site with Work-
    flow 427

Q

QAT child attribute 283
Query element 337
QueryFeatures method 257
querying
    contents of list of con-
        tacts 139–140,
        142–144
    for data with .NET and
        LINQ 173–177
    LINQ to SharePoint
        Data 117–122
    paging results 164–165
QueryManager class 669,
    679
Query Object Model 681–
    683
query template, targeting
    search locations 672
Query Web Service 684–
    687
QuickLaunchDataSource
    ControlId 295
QuickLaunchEnabled attri-
    bute 441

R

RadioButtonList con-
    trol 232
Rapid Application Develop-
    ment (RAD) tools 24
RawSid property 70
read, definition of 32
ReadList method 714
ReadLocked property 62
Read method 715
ReadOnly attribute 326
ReadOnly field attri-
    bute 319
ReadOnly property 62
ReceiveActivity activity 483
ReceiverAssembly attri-
    bute 244, 260, 263
ReceiverClass attri-
    bute 244, 260, 263
ReceiverData 389
Receivers, feature ele-
    ment 247
Records Center 426
Recurrence_body field
    type 369
Recycle 69
RecycleBin property
    SPListItem type 67
    SPSite type 62
    SPWeb type 64
recycling (deleting) existing
    items in lists
    using LINQ to Share-
        Point 125
RedirectUrl 389
ReflectionPermission 630
refresh and identity
    management
    in Linq to SharePoint
        queries 130
RefreshMode argu-
    ment 127
RefreshPage method 310
RegExTextField class 349
RegionalSettings
    property 72

registering full-trust
    proxy 652–653
Registering the Identity
    Provider 624–625
RegistrationId
    attribute 267
    type 268
RegistrationType 268
    attribute 267
RegistryPermission 630
RelativeWebUrl 390, 395
Relying Party (RP)
    about 608
    building 617–621
removeAllStatus
    method 305
removeNotification
    method 305
removeStatus method 305
RemoveUser method 71
Remove Workflows page
    for lists 532
Replicator activity 482
RequiredAdmin attri-
    bute 266, 273
Required field attri-
    bute 319
requirements for running
    SharePoint 13–14
RequireResources attri-
    bute 244
RequireSiteAdministrator
    attribute 267
ResetItem method 72
ResetWebServer as fea-
    ture element attri-
    bute 252
ResetWebServerMode-
    OnUpgrade as fea-
    ture element attri-
    bute 252
Resolve method 127–128
Resources child
    element 252
REST API
    about 171–172
    interface 137

managing data 177–179
querying for data 173–177
restrictions and credentials information, communicating with external search location 672
retrieveContacts method 154
return data
limiting 42
ribbon
Documents 43–44
Modified View command on 40–41
Ribbon child attribute 283
Ribbon commands
archiving multiple items 283–291
defining 279–283
RichText field attribute 319
Rights attribute 267
RollbackTask activity 493
RootFiles child element 253
RootFolder property 66, 93
RootWebOnly attribute 267
of Module element 300
RootWeb property 62
RP (Relying Party)
about 608
building 617–621
RSS feeds
capability of 34
RSSFeedViewerWebPart control 229
output browser of 229
source code of 227–228

S

Safari
support of ECMAScript 152
SafeControls 236–238, 278

SAML token-based Authentication 589
sandboxed environment executing ASP.net code in 631–634
sandboxed solution
about 254
sandboxed solutions
about 639–640
architecture of 640–644
creating 645–647
monitoring 644
Office 365 and 655
validating 645
SaveBinary 69
SaveBinaryDirect static method 166
SaveChanges method 178–179
scalability
about 223
Service Applications to support 17
scalable software solution 223
Scalar type 703
Scale child attribute 283
Scaling child attribute 283
Schema.xml List attributes 336
SchemaXml property 66
Scope attribute 244
ScriptBlock attribute 267
ScriptSrc attribute 267
Sealed attribute 326
Search.asmx service 169
searchCommandAsynchronously_Click event handler 226
search-driven applications
about 6
search engine
customizing and extending user interface 662–664

customizing output via XSLT code 664–667
developing custom Web Parts 668–669
Federated Search Object Model 678–683
federation framework and 670–677
overview for developers 659–662
Query Web Service 684–687
using by code 678–683
search settings
using with lists 36
SecurableObject property 142
security
checking digital signatures 233
enforcing in web forms 78
event 400
full-trust proxies 650–654
Web Parts SafeControls 236–238
security infrastructure
about 23
SecurityPermission 630, 634
Security Token Service 593–594
Security Token Service, building 611–617
Security Token Service (STS)
implementing with Windows Identity Foundation
about 608, 611
building Relying Party 617–621
building Security Token Service 611–617
trusting 622–623
SelectedIndexChanged event 217

SelectedValue control 232
selectItemCommand con-
    trol 232
SendActivity activity 483
Send an Email 499
Send Document Set to
    Repository 499
SendEmail activity 493
SendRequest property
    type 679
Send To menu
  customizing targets
    for 46
SendToOfficialFile 410
Sequence activity 482
Sequence attribute 267,
    273
sequential workflow project
    templates 27
server exceptions
  Unhandled Exception 161
Server Object Model
  about 21, 55
  best practices
    disposing resources
      73–77
    enforcing security in
      web forms 78–80
    handling excep-
      tions 76–77
    working with transac-
      tions 78
  concurrency conflicts
    87–88
  creating site collection
    80–81
  creating websites 82–83
  Document Libraries
    check-in and check-out
      documents 95
    creating 92–93
    downloading docu-
      ments 94–95
    managing versions of
      documents 97
    uploading docu-
      ments 93–94

groups
  managing membership
    of 98–99
  managing permissions
    of 99
  hierarchical organization
    of 56–57
list items
  creating 82–85
  deleting 88–89
  modifying 86–87
  querying 89–91
SPContext type 71
SPControl type 71
SPDocumentLibrary
  type 68
SPFarm type 57–59
SPFile type 68–69
SPGroup type 69, 71
SPListItem type 65, 67
SPList type 65–66
SPServer type 57
SPService type 57
SPSite type 59–62, 65–66
SPUser type 69
SPWebApplication
  type 57, 60
SPWeb type 60–65
users
  creating new 97–98
  managing permissions
    of 99
workflow 576–579
ServerRelativeUrl 394
server-side tools 21
service applications
  about 16–17
  administrative pages
    466–467
  architecture of 445–448
  consumer 473–474
  creating 449–450
  creating new data-
    base 458–465
  custom protocol 450–453
  databases 456–458
  deploying 467–469

developing code
  for 454–456
proxies 473–474
proxies for 469–472
service instances 465
situations involving 474
solution outline for 453–
  454
supporting scalability 17
Service Provider (SP) 608
Set Content Approval
  Status 499–500
Set Field in Current
  Item 500
SetState activity 493
setStatusPriColor
  method 305
Set Time Portion of Date/
  Time Field 499
Settings member name
  ConversionJob class 421
SetupPath attribute 336
  of Module element 300
SetVisualization 669
Set Workflow Status 499
Set Workflow Variable 499
Sever-Side Custom Ac-
  tions 276–278
SharedFields element 407
SharedQueryManager
  object 669
SharePoint
  about 3
  architecture of 12–18
  capabilities of 4–6
  CAS and 634, 634–640
  concepts used in 7–13
  deploying through Pack-
    age Designer and
    Package Explor-
    er 254–255
  editions of 18–20
  feature manifest
    about 241–242
    as list of element mani-
      fest files 246–248

deploying files for Web
    Parts 245
file structure 242–243
supporting multi-
    language 246
feature receivers 259–262
features
    about 241
    deactivating and
        uninstalling 249
    deploying 248–254
    for building custom web
        solutions 20–24
    upgrading 256–258
FeatureUpgrading events
    handling of 262–263
list of permissions defined
    in 604
main Controlid values
    in 295
permissions available
    in 630
requirements for run-
    ning 13–17
Status Bar and Notifi-
    cation Area fea-
    tures 305–309
technique to develop
    asynchronous Share-
    Point Web Parts 226
trusted identity providers
    621–627
versions prior to
    2010 226
Web Parts 245
workflow architecture
    in 489–493
workflow custom activi-
    ties 492–493
workflow targets and
    association 491–492
SharePoint 2010
    search engine of 670
    UI (User Interface)
        265–272

SharePoint Central Admin-
    istration interface
    configuring Anonymous
        Access from 606
    configuring FBA
        through 602
SharePoint Central Admin-
    istration (SPCA)
    about 7–8, 15–16
    choosing templates when
        creating Site Collec-
        tions 17–18
SharePoint Client Object
    Model. *See* Client
    Object Model
SharePoint:
    DelegateControl 291
SharePoint Designer 2010
    about 24
    custom actions for
        557–563
    custom conditions
        for 563–565
    integration with Visio
        2010 510
    using SharePoint Founda-
        tion with 18
    workflows
        about 495–497
        actions 499–501
        conditions 498–499
        outline definition
            503–506
        structure of published
            502
    workflows, designing
        about 502–503
        settings 507–508
        user experience
            508–510
SharePoint farm
    about 14, 31
    Service Applications
        in 16–17
SharePoint:FormDigest
    control 153

SharePoint Foundation
    2010
    about 14, 18–19
    sandboxed solutions in
        about 639–640
    architecture of
        640–644
    creating 645–647
    monitoring 644
    SOAP services in 168–169
SharePoint Health
    Analyzer 8
SharePoint Online 20
SharePointPermission 630,
    634
SharePointProductVersion
    as feature element
    attribute 252
SharePoint:ScriptLink con-
    trol 153
SharePoint Server 2010
    Enterprise edition 19–20
    for Internet Sites 20
    platform 14
    SOAP services in 168–169
    Standard edition 19
SharePoint Server
    Explorer 28–29
SharePoint Server
    Object Model. *See
    also* Server Object
    Model
SharePointServiceLocator
    type 77
SharePoint sites
    preconfigured levels
        of user group
        rights 31–32
SharePoint SiteSettings for
    locations for custom
    actions 274
SharePoint SOAP ser-
    vices 168–171
SharePoint web.config Files,
    configuring 600–601

SharePoint web forms
  enforcing security in 78–
    80
ShowInDisplayForm field
    attribute 319
ShowInEditForm field attri-
    bute 319
ShowInLists attribute 268
ShowInNewForm field at-
    tribute 319
ShowInReadOnlyContent-
    Types attribute 268
ShowInSealedContentTypes
    attribute 268
showModalDialog
    method 310
ShowPopupDialog
    method 310
showWaitScreenSize
    method 310
showWaitScreenWithNo-
    Close method 310
Sid property 70
Silverlight
  application browsers 221
  Client Object Model
    about 147–152
    creating Silverlight Ap-
      plications 148–150
    differences with Man-
      aged Client Object
      Model 150–151
  control
    choosing this type
      with 32–33
    creating Document Li-
      brary 42–43
  external applications
    and 220–223
  scenarios of 222
  Web Part 148, 220–223
SinglePerson value 561
Site Actions menu 50–51
Site Assets Library 46
Site Collection
  deploying .wsp package
    at 254

Site Collection Adminis-
    tration & Features
    page 250
Site Collection Administrator
    9
site collection, creating
    new 80–81
Site Collections
  about 8–9
  enabling users or roles to
    access 603
  in web applications 15
  websites stored in 50–51
site columns
  about 46–47
  defining 315–316
  Field Attributes of 319–
    320
  Field Types of 318
SiteData.asmx service 169
SiteDefinitionManifestschild
    element 252
site definition project
    templates 27
site definitions
  about 428–431
  native 424–428
  vs. web templates 444
  with Visual Studio
    431–438
SiteDeleted 393
SiteDeleting 393
SiteId 389, 520
Site member
    SPWorkflowActivation-
      Properties 520
site members user
    group 31
site owners user group 32
Site property 64, 72, 142
Sites.asmx service 169
Sites category
  about 5
site templates
  about 17, 423
SiteUrl 520
SiteUsers property 64

Site values 242
site visitors user group 31
site workflows 534
SmallSearchInputBox
    Controlid 295
SmtpPermission 630
SOAP services 168–171,
    579–581
SOAP/WCF Service, access-
    ing 705–710
Social Meeting Work-
    space 426
SocketPermission 630
Solution element
  child elements 252
Solution element as fea-
    ture element attri-
    butes 251–252
Solution Explorer 29
  configuring features 255
  for creating feature event
    receivers 262
SolutionId as feature ele-
    ment attribute 252
SolutionId attribute 244
Solution Package
  files installing 251
solutions
  deploying 248–254
  upgrading features 256–
    258
Solutions property 62
solution validator, imple-
    menting 647–650
sorting
  columns in lists 41
SPCheckinType 95
SPContentDatabase
    type 257
SPContext type 71–72
SPControl type 71
SP.Core.js files 152
SPDatabase class 456
SPDatabaseParameters
    class 456
SPDateTimeField type 360

SPDocumentLibrary
type 68
SpecificFinder type 703
SPEmailEventReceiver 398
SPEventPropertiesBase
class 389, 400
SPFarm type 261
creating 57–59
SPFeatureReceiver
classes 259–260
SPFeatureReceiverProp-
erties argument
type 261
SPField class 351, 381
Multicolum 357
SPField field types
Attachments 345
Boolean 345
Calculated 345
Choice 345
CrossProjectLink 345
Currency 346
DateTime 346
File 346
Guid 346
MultiChoice 346
MultiColumn 346
MultiLineText 346
PageSeparator 346
Recurrence 346
Text 346
Url 346
User 346
SPFile types 68–69
SPGroup type 69, 71
SPIisWebServiceApplication
class 459, 461
Spinner child attribute 283
SPItemEventProperties
class 389, 389–390
SPItemEventReceiver base
class 386
SP.js files 152
SPListCollection
method 84

SPListEventProperties
class 391–392
SPListEventReceiver 385
class 391
SPListItemCollection
method 86
SPListItem type 65, 67
SPListTemplateType enu-
meration 84
SPList type 65–66
SplitButton child attri-
bute 283
SPMetal.EXE utility
modeling LINQ to Share-
Point using 107–117
calling Dispose 111–112
elements available for
defining XML param-
eter files 109–110
providing argu-
ments 107–108
using LINQ to Share-
Point 113
XML parameters
for 108–110
SPPrincipal type 69–70, 99
SPProxyOperationArgs
class 651–652
SPProxyOperation
class 651
SPRequestModule 21
SP.Ribbon.js files 152
SPRoleAssignment type 70
SPRoleDefinition type 70
SP.Runtime.js files 152
SPServer type 58
SPServiceCollection 58
SPServiceContext class 469
SP (Service Provider) 608
SPService type 58–59
SPSite type 59–62, 65–66,
257, 261
SPSolutionValidationProp-
erties type 647
SPSolutionValidator
class 647

SPTextField type 360
SPTimer service, workflows
and 585
SP.UI.ModalDialog
classes 309–314
SP.UI.Notify Class meth-
ods 305
SPUrlZone enumeration 60
SPUserCodeService
parameter 649
SPUserCollection
method 98
SPUser instances 593
SPUserToken class 60
SPUser type 69–70
SPVirtualPathProvider 21
SPWebApplication type 58,
60, 257, 261
SPWebCollection
method 82
SPWebEventProperties
class 394
SPWebEventReceiver 385
class 393
SPWebPartManager 184
SPWebService type 257
SPWeb type 60–65, 261
SPWorkflowActivationProp-
erties type 519–520
SPWorkflowEventProperties
class 395
SPWorkflowEventRe-
ceiver 385
class 394
SPWorkflowManager
class 578–579
SPWorkflowTask class 578
SqlClientPermission 630,
634
SQL language
querying databases
with 103
SQL Membership Provider,
configuring FBA
with 597–603

SQL Server database, configuring 597–599

SQL Server permissions, configuring 601–602

Start Approval Process 500

Start Custom Task Process 500

Start Document Set Approval Process 500

Started member name ConversionJob class 421

Start Feedback Process 500

Start number name 421

StartWorkflow 581
  value 580

state machine workflow project
  templates 27, 28

StaticName attribute 316–317

Status 389

Status Bar and the Notification Area 305–309

StatusUrl attribute 529

Stop Workflow 499

StreamAccessor type 703

Stringbuilder value 561

string properties
  SchemaXml 66

structured of published work flows in SharePoint Designer 2010 502

STSADM.EXE command upgrading solution using 256

STSADM.EXE command line 637

STSADM.EXE command line tool
  deploying .wsp package 253–254
  illustration of 248

STS (Security Token Service)
  implementing with Windows Identity Foundation

about 608, 611

building Relying Party 617–621

building Security Token Service 611–617

trusting 622

SubmitChanges method 126

Subweb attribute 441

Survey value 562

Suspend activity 482

SVCUTIL.EXE tool 543

SynchronizationScope activity 482

synchronous
  programming in Web Part 225–226
  values 398

SyndicationEnabled attribute 441

SystemUpdate 67

systemUpdate argument 127

T

Tab child attribute 283

Tabs child attribute 283

Tabular View 41

target web applications, configuring 625–627

task forms 547–553

TaskList 520

TaskListContentTypeId attribute 529

TaskListId 520

TaskListUrl 520

Team Site 425

TemplateAlias 280

TemplateFiles child element 253

TemplateId 392

TemplateName 520

templates
  application page project 28

Business Data Connectivity Model project 27

content type project 27, 28

custom list 35–39

document 93

document parameter 46

empty element 28

empty SharePoint project 27

Event Receiver project 27

field rendering on mobile devices 374–375

functional groups of 9

import reusable workflow project 27

import SharePoint solution package 28

list definition project 27, 28

list instance 28

module project 27

names for creating web-site collections 81

names for creating web-sites 82–83

query, targeting search locations 672

sequential workflow project 27

site
  about 17–18, 423
  definitions 428–431
  definitions of native 424–428
  with Visual Studio 431–438

site definition project 27

site definitions vs. web 444

standard list 34–35

user control 28

Visual Web Part 195–196

web 439–443

Web Part project 27

TemplateType
  property 159

Terminate activity 482
TerminatedByUserId 395
TextArea value 562
Text_body field type 369
TextBox child attribute 283
TextBox value 562
Text field type 318
Threading
 ASP.NET and 223–224
Throw activity 482
Time24 attribute 441
Timeout property type 679
TimeZone attribute 441
Title as feature element at-
 tribute 252
Title attribute 244, 273,
 441
 workflow feature element
 529
Title CustomAction attri-
 bute 268
Title field contains key-
 words 499
TitleIconImageUrl property
 190
Title property
 SPFile type 69
 SPListItem type 67
 SPList type 66
 SPWeb 64
 Web Part 190
ToBe
 Deleted values 123
 Inserted values 123
 Recycled values 123
 Updated values 123
ToggleButton child attri-
 bute 283
tokens contained in UrlAc-
 tion element 271
TopNavigationDataSource
 Controlid 295
totaling rows 41
transactions
 working with 78

TransactionScope activ-
 ity 483
TreeViewAndDataSource
 Controlid 295
TreeView control 217
TreeViewEnabled attri-
 bute 441
TriggerControlID 218
TriggerEventName 218
TrimDuplicates property
 type 679
trusted identity providers
 configuring target web
 application 625–627
 IP/STS 622–623
 registering the Identity
 Provider and Map-
 ping Claims 624–625
trusted (partially) ASP.NET
 code in sandbox en-
 vironment 631–634
Type attribute
 for View element 336
 in ListTemplate ele-
 ment 342
 supported by Module ele-
 ment 301

U

UIPermission 630
UI (user interface)
 creating custom action
 using custom action
 element 265–272
 CustomActionGroup ele-
 ment 273–274
 delegate controls 291–
 294
 HideCustomAction ele-
 ment 275
 Ribbon Commands
 279–283
 Server-Side Custom
 Actions 276–278
 Status Bar and the Notification Area 305–309

UI (User Interface)
 about customizing 22
 Dialog Framework 309–
 314
 extending 265–272
 preconfigured rights
 31–32
 Ribbon commands,
 archiving multiple
 items 283–291
UIVersion attribute 244,
 268
UIVersionConfigurationEn-
 abled attribute 441
Unchanged values
 in EntityState proper-
 ty 123
Undeclare Record 500
UndoCheckOut 69
uninstalling features 249
UpdateAllTasks activity 493
UpdateItemActivity activ-
 ity 493
Update List Item 500
UpdateListItem value 562
Update method
 SPFile type 69
 SPGroup type 71
 SPListItem type 67
 SPList type 66
 SPUser type 70
 SPWeb type 64, 65
UpdateObject method 178
UpdateOverwriteVersion
 67
UpdatePanel 217
Update Personal Web Parts
 permission 605
Updater type 703
updateStatus method 305
UpdateTask activity 493
UpdateTaskFromControls
 method 552
updating
 .wsp package 256
Updating event 387

UpgradeActions
child element 245
element 258
upgradesolution command 257
upgrade using STSADM.
EXE command 256
upgrading
Web Parts 233
upgrading, solutions and
features 256–258
uploading documents 93–94
UrlAction child element 268, 271
Url attribute 336
of Module element 300
supported by Module element 301
URL_body field type 369
URL field type 318
Url property
SPFile type 69
SPListItem type 67
SPSite type 62
Use Client Integration Features permission 605
User and UserMulti field type 318
User_body field type 369
user control template 28
UserDisplayName 394
SPListEventProperties 390
SPListEventProperties class 392
Use Remote Interfaces permission 605
user interface. *See* UI (User Interface)
UserLoginName member name
SPItemEventProperties class 390
SPListEventProperties class 392

SPWebEventProperties class 394
UserQuery property type 679
users
creating new 97–98
managing permissions of 99
Users property
SPGroup type 71
SPWeb type 64
UserToken member name
ConversionJob class 421
UserToken property 70
Use Self-Service Site Creation permission 604
useUniquePermissions property 83

V

Verbs property 207
Verbs, Web Part 205–207
Version attribute 244
versioning
in LINQ to SharePoint model 134
managing document 97
of lists 34
workflow 531–533
VersioningEnabled attribute 332
versioning in Web Parts 233–237
Versionless 390
VersionRange element 258
Versions property
SPFile 69
SPList type 67
version upgrading 258
View Application Pages permission 604
View element
attributes of 336–337
viewers user group 31
View Items permission 604

view only, definition of 32
View Pages permission 605
views
creating in lists 33, 39–42
in Modified View command 40–41
Views
defining custom views 339–342
ViewToolbar location 272
View Versions permission 604
View Web Analytics Data permission 604
VirtualPath property 462
Visio 2010
Integration with Microsoft Designer 510–512
Visio Process Repository 427
Visio Studio 2010
correlation tokens 533
site workflows 534
workflow modeling
about 515
associating a target list 530–531
creating projects 515–519
deploying workflow 528–530
outlines 519–527
versioning workflow 531–533
VisualInsertRequestFor ContactWebPart 195–196
Visual Studio 2010
about 26–29
accessing initiation form 544
creating association form 538
creating feature event receivers 262

packaging with 254–256
project templates in 27–28
SharePoint Server Explorer feature in 28–29
site definitions with 431
Solution Explorer feature in 29
support for services compliant with OData specification 173
using SharePoint Foundation with 18
Visual Web Part template in 195–197
Visual Web Part 195–197
project templates 27

W

Wait for Field Change in Current Item 500
WCF/SOAP Service, accessing 705–710
WebAdding 393
web applications services about 15
WebApplication values 242
WebBrowsableObject property 201
web browsers 221
supporting ECMAScript 152
WebDeleted 393
WebDeleting 393
Web element name 109
web forms
enforcing security in 78–80
WebId member SPWorkflowActivation-Properties 520
WebId member name SPListEventProperties Class 392
SPWebEventProperties class 394

web-level event receivers 393–394
Web member
SPEventPropertiesBase class 390
SPListEventProperties class 392
SPWebEventProperties class 394
SPWorkflowActivation-Properties 520
WebMoved 393
WebMoving 393
WebPart class 207–208
WebPartManager control about 184
Web Part Page
merging into Web Part 226
Silverlight Web Part insurance in 220
upgrading Web Part on 234
WebPartPage 184
WebPartPermission 630, 634
Web Parts
about 183–184
asynchronous programming for 223–226
configurable parameters 198–200
connectible 209–215
creating custom classes 200–204
Cross-Site-Scripting Safe-Guard 236–237
custom Web Part Verbs 205–207
deploying pages 299–301
deploying to 233–237
deployment 188–192
developing search engine custom 668–669
features 12

handling display modes 204–205
"Hello World" 184–187
project type templates 27
SafeControls 236–238
standard classic 192–195
support of AJAX 215–220
upgrading 233
visual 195–198
XSLT rendering 226–232
Web Parts versioning 233
WebPartVerbCollection 205
Web Part Verbs 205–207
WebPartZoneID attribute 336
WebPermission 630, 634
Web property 72, 142
WebProvisioned 393
Webs.asmx service 169
Web Service Definition Language (WSDL) 169
WebServiceInput activity 483
WebServiceOutput activity 483
web service, workflow 579
websites
creating 82–83
defining data repository 50–51
list of items in 10–11
Site Collections and 8
template names for creating 81–83
WebTemplate
element, attributes supported by 440–441
feature element 247
web templates 439–443, 444
WebUrl member
SPWorkflowActivation-Properties 520
WebUrl member name
SPListEventProperties class 392

WebUrl member
    name, *continued*
  SPListEventReceiver
    class 390
  SPWorkflowEventProper-
    ties class 395
Web values 242
WelcomePageFields ele-
    ment 407
WelcomePageView element
    407
While activity 483
Windows Authentica-
    tion 589, 592,
    594–595
Windows Identity Founda-
    tion (WIF)
  about 607
  implementing an
    STS 611–621
  implementing in
    STS 611–621
WindowsIdentity in-
    stance 590
Windows PowerShell
  about 24
  deploying .wsp pack-
    age 253–254
  script syntax for installing
    and activating fea-
    tures using 249
WindowsPrincipal in-
    stance 590
Windows SharePoint
    Services Solution
    Packages. *See* WSP
    (Windows SharePoint
    Services Solution
    Packages)
Word Automation Services
    417–422
WorkflowActions, feature
    element 247
WorkflowAssociation, fea-
    ture element 247

WorkflowCompleted 394
workflow dependency
    property ("wdp"
) 557
workflow event receivers
    394–395
workflow feature element
  attributes of 529
Workflow, feature element
    247
workflow forms
  deploying 553–554
  management
    association 537
    initiation 544–546
    modification 547
  task forms 547–553
workflow foundation (WF).
    See also SharePoint
    Designer 2010
  architecture 479–483
  custom activities
    486–488
  definitions 484–486
  execution mode 489
  types 483–484
WorkflowId member
  SPWorkflowActivation-
    Properties 520
WorkflowManager prop-
    erty 62
Workflow member
  SPWorkflowActivation-
    Properties 520
workflow modeling
  about 515
  associating with target
    list 530–531
  creating projects 515–519
  deploying workflow 528–
    530
  outlines 519–522
  versioning workflow
    531–533
WorkflowPostponed 394

workflows
  custom actions and con-
    ditions
    about 555
  custom actions for
    SharePoint Designer
    2010 557
  custom conditions for
    SharePoint Designer
    2010 563–565
  dependency proper-
    ties 555–557
  developing
    about 23
  developing import usable
    workflow project
    templates 27
  developing sequential 27
  developing state ma-
    chine 28
  event receivers 565–566
  in lists 34
  management by code
    web service 579–585
    workflow Server Object
      Model 576–579
    Server Object Mod-
      el 576–579
    SPTimer service and 585
    web servers 579–585
  workflow services
    about 566–568
    communication activi-
      ties 575–576
    deploying 573–575
    implementing 568–572
    web 579–585
  workflows in SharePoint
    architecture of 489–493
  Workflows property 67
  WorkflowStarted 394
  WorkflowStarting 394
  WritableFieldNames
    value 562
  WriteLocked property 62

WSDL (Web Service Definition Language) 169
WS-Federation, and claims-based authentication 607–611
WSP (Windows SharePoint Services Solution Packages)
about 23
deploying STSADM.EXE command 253–254
files installing 251
manifest with security policy deployment 636, 638
solutions, sandboxed solutions
about 639–640
architecture of 640–644
creating 645–647
monitoring 644
validating 645

updating 256
WSS_Minimal vs. WSS_Medium Policy Levels 634

X

XAML user control code 149–150
XML data
navigating 103
XML definition file for custom fields 352–353
XmlDocuments element 327
XML parameters
for SPMetal.EXE 108–110
Xml property
SPList type 67
SPUser type 70
XPath/XQuery
navigating XML using 103
XSD.EXE tool 543

XSLT code
finding controls created by 232
output of transformation 230
rendering fields using 367–369
search engine output via 664–667
transforming RSSFeedViewerWebPart 229
XSLT Rendering in Web Parts 226–232
XSLT transformation
accepting native Web parts 227
output 230, 230–233
xsnScope element 329

Z

Zone 62, 390

About the Author

Paolo Pialorsi is a consultant, trainer, and author who specializes in developing distributed applications architectures and Microsoft SharePoint enterprise solutions. He is the author of *Programming Microsoft LINQ* and *Introducing Microsoft LINQ* (Microsoft Press), and has written three Italian-language books about XML and Web Services. Paolo is one of the content owners of the Italian edition of the Microsoft SharePoint Conference, and a popular speaker at industry conferences.

What do you think of this book?

We want to hear from you!

To participate in a brief online survey, please visit:

microsoft.com/learning/booksurvey

Tell us how well this book meets your needs—what works effectively, and what we can do better. Your feedback will help us continually improve our books and learning resources for you.

Thank you in advance for your input!

Stay in touch!

To subscribe to the *Microsoft Press® Book Connection Newsletter*—for news on upcoming books, events, and special offers—please visit:

microsoft.com/learning/books/newsletter